THE BENGHAZI

BETRAYAL

THE BENGHAZI BETRAYAL

THE TRUE, MINUTE-BY-MINUTE

ACCOUNT OF

VALOR AND ABANDONMENT

by

James "Mac" McCarty

Second Edition

Visit *www.TheBenghaziBetrayal.com*

ALSO BY THE AUTHOR

"The Vatican Conspiracies"
(A Novel)

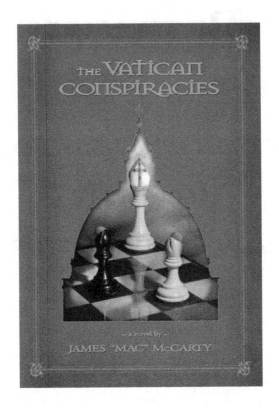

Visit *www.VaticanConspiracies.com*

Buy the Book at www.Amazon.com

ALSO BY THE AUTHOR:

Forthcoming:

*The Emperor Obama:
An American Betrayal*

*Book I – Foreign Policy, National
Security and Terrorism*

*Book II – Domestic, Environmental and
Immigration Policy*

Second Edition

Copyright © 2020 by James E. McCarty.

All rights reserved, including the right to reproduce this book or portions thereof in any form whatsoever.

ISBN 9781717850690

Visit *www.TheBenghaziBetrayal.com*

DEDICATION

To Glen Doherty, Sean Smith, Ambassador J. Christopher Stevens and Tyrone Woods, who gave their lives in Benghazi, Libya for a government that would abandon them; to their surviving comrades Mark Geist and Dave Ubben, who were wounded severely in the battle to save their fellow Americans left alone thousands of miles from home; and to the rest of the surviving Benghazi CIA and State Department security agents and members of "Team Tripoli," who all heroically risked their lives for their compatriots on that fateful, horrible night in North Africa.

MISSION COMPOUND & CIA ANNEX

State Department facility in Benghazi, Libya

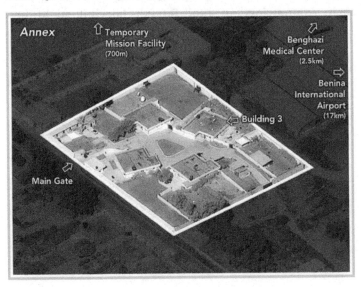

Central Intelligence Agency facility in Benghazi, Libya

Source: House Select Benghazi Committee Report, p. 4

THE TRUE ACCOUNT OF VALOR AND ABANDONMENT

Contents

ALSO BY THE AUTHOR	iv-v
DEDICATION	vii
MISSION COMPOUND & CIA ANNEX	viii
PREFACE	xiv
KEY CHARACTERS	xviii
INTRODUCTION	xxiii

PART I: REVOLUTIONARY LIBYA

1. "Mad Dog of the Middle East" — 2
2. The Bush-Qadhafi Deal — 5
3. The "Arab Spring" — 9
4. "Bloodbath": The Libyan Civil War — 16
5. "The Humanitarian Vulcans" — 19
6. Barack's "Grand Libyan Adventure" — 24
7. "We Came, We Saw, He Died!" — 30
8. Christopher Stevens Goes to Libya — 38
9. "Things Could Go Wrong" — 41

PART II: BEFORE THE ATTACKS

10. Benghazi: "The Most Dangerous City" — 47
11. The Benghazi "Special Mission Compound" — 49
12. The CIA Annex: "We're Walmart Security Guards" — 51
13. "How Thin Does the Ice Have to Get?" — 53
14. "Unpredictable, Volatile, and Violent" — 62
15. Tripwire: "You Were Waiting to Die" — 71
16. Security: "We Couldn't Keep What We Had" — 82
17. "We Needed More, Not Less" — 89
18. "The Taliban Is Inside the Building" — 101
19. "It Was the Best Bad Plan" — 110
20. Unlicensed: "Terminate the Contract" — 128

21. "Heightened Alert"   134
22. "It Was Worth the Risk"   136
23. "So Nice to Be Back in Benghazi"   147
24. "Expeditionary Diplomacy"   150
25. "Why Spy" in Benghazi?   154

PART III: DURING THE ATTACKS

26. A Protest in Cairo   159
27. "Assuming We Don't Die Tonight"   164
28. "F***! GUNFIRE!"   170
29. "Shelter & Wait"   176
30. "We're Gonna Do Something Fun Tonight!"   179
31. "Safe Haven"   183
32. "Greg, We Are Under Attack!"   185
33. "You're in My World Now"   190
34. "Washington, We Have a Problem"   191
35. *"Stand Down!* You Need to *Wait!"*   196
36. "F.E.S.T." or Famine   206
37. Rescue Posse: "Team Tripoli" Saddles Up   211
38. *"Fire!* The Ambassador Is Missing!"   214
39. "If You Don't Get Here Soon, We're All Going to Die!"   217
40. "You Guys Got to *Go!"*   225
41. "Like Being in a Brick Oven"   229
42. "Is Anything Coming?"   235
43. "Do Everything Possible"   237
44. A Predator Over Benghazi   242
45. "We're Comin' in Hot!"   245
46. The Defenders of the Alamo   251
47. Panetta's Council of War   255
48. "We Chose Not to Do It"   261
49. Ansar al-Sharia Claims Credit   282
50. Team Tripoli Departs   284
51. The First Attack on the CIA Annex   285
52. Secretary Clinton Calls Libya's President   288
53. Panetta's 7:00 P.M. Order   290

THE TRUE ACCOUNT OF VALOR AND ABANDONMENT

54. Ambassador Stevens Is Found 296
55. Secretary Clinton Calls Greg Hicks 298
56. Assault from Zombieland 301
57. "Spinning Up" 303
58. Team Tripoli Arrives in Benghazi 306
59. Navel-Gazing 309
60. "No One Stood Watch" 320
61. Ambassador Stevens Is Pronounced Dead 322
62. "Deploy Now . . . Maybe" 324
63. Inaction Items 329
64. Not So FAST 333
65. Expendable: Abandoning Benghazi for Tripoli 335
66. Over-Lawyered? 344
67. Standing Guard on the Rooftops 347
68. A Secret Order to "Not Deploy" to Benghazi? 349
69. "Operation Eagle Claw" 352
70. "Foggy Bottom" Speaks 356
71. Assassination Confirmed 359
72. The President Speaks with Secretary Clinton 361
73. "Bug Out" in Tripoli 363
74. Team Tripoli Leaves Benghazi Airport 365
75. F.E.S.T. Is "Off the Menu" 366
76. Where *Is* the President? 369
77. "Welcome to the Party, We're Having a Blast!" 380
78. "Mortars! MORTARS! *MORTARS!!*" 382
79. Ambush 393
80. "Bigger Balls Than the Military" 397
81. A White House in the Fog 407
82. Americans Evacuate the Annex 410
83. Forklifts & Nap Time 415
84. "I'm Going to Frigging Walk Out of This Town" 421
85. Libyan Flight Clearance Is Received 426

86. The Evacuation Out of Tripoli	427
87. Better Late Than Never?	428

PART IV: AFTER THE ATTACKS

88. Chaos in the Obama Kingdom	433
89. Spinning the "Benghazi Narrative"	438
90. "Fog of War"	446
91. Thorns in the Rose Garden	450
92. The "60 Minutes" Interview	455
93. The "Special Briefing" for Reporters	461
94. Massaging the Talking Points	463
95. "The Protest of All Ages"	476
96. "Terrorists? *What* Terrorists?"	486
97. "Sparked": The Video Did It	498
98. The Fallen Come Home	512
99. "It Was 9/11 Everywhere"	518
100. Coulda, Shoulda, Woulda, Souda	526
101. "They Stood & They Watched & Our People Died"	528
102. Looting the Mission Compound . . . Again	531
103. "Poisoned Chalice"	533
104. Hero Hicks Is Demoted	552
105. The FBI "Investigates"	556
106. "Not Optimal"	563
107. Politicizing Benghazi: Taking Candy from a Romney	566
108. "The Agency" to the Rescue	577
109. The ARB Report: "You Are on Your Own"	580
110. Speak No Evil	609
111. The Congressional Investigations	612
112. Team Obama Reacts to Congress	627
113. Unaccountable	630
114. Bringing the Terrorists "To Justice"	641

PART V: CONCLUSIONS

115. The Corrected "Benghazi Narrative"	658
116. Other Specific Conclusions	663

117. Unanswered Questions 678
118. "What Difference, At This Point, Does It Make?" 682
119. Final Thoughts 688

APPENDIX: KEY DELAYS ON THE NIGHT OF BENGHAZI 692

ACKNOWLEDGMENTS 703

ABOUT THE AUTHOR 705

Preface

I never planned to write about Benghazi. Not on the night it happened, and not during the weeks of confusion and excuses and justifications and deception that followed. Not during the 2012 presidential campaign and debates in which Benghazi became a major issue between incumbent President Obama and Republican challenger Mitt Romney. And not during the initial congressional investigations that inevitably ensued.

I was saddened and disappointed and frustrated by the whole affair. But probably like many Americans, I mostly attributed the tragic result in Benghazi to the galactic incompetence of the federal government. (As a former federal employee, I have learned over the years this almost always is a safe default position.)

Then, in early July 2016, I began to read what I consider the best congressional investigative product to come out of the crisis – the House Select Benghazi Committee's majority report. (I rely on this analysis heavily in this work.) As I read, I became depressed. As I read further, I was shocked. And as I waded deeper into the report I was *pissed*. I simply could not believe my government had been so grossly negligent, so feckless, so utterly incompetent, so deceptive, and so politically manipulative. Most of all, I could not believe my nation's leaders had so clearly abandoned and betrayed nearly three dozen Americans under terrorist attack in a distant, dangerous land where their government had sent them in the line of duty.

I resolved to channel my fury in a constructive way. I decided to write an historical summary and analysis of the entire Barack H. Obama presidency (which I considered a disaster). I would include a detailed chapter on the Benghazi fiasco. I planned to use it as a central exhibit demonstrating how Obama had failed his country as its leader for eight long years. However, as I climbed the mountains of available research, each night the draft chapter on Benghazi grew in length and complexity. Eventually, I realized the multifaceted Benghazi story was completely unwieldy for a single chapter in a book of the scope I had in mind. And so, at my computer screen very late one night in September 2016, I surprised myself by concluding, "Well, it looks like we have a separate book on Benghazi!"

Thus, this work was born. I decided to publish this book before my analysis of the full Obama administration (forthcoming soon in two

THE TRUE ACCOUNT OF VALOR AND ABANDONMENT

parts[1]), believing I could finish the former relatively quickly. Silly me; it was not to be. There simply was too much material on Benghazi to research, too many contradictions and inconsistencies and gaps to resolve, too much information and too many witnesses and documents withheld from public scrutiny for too long, and too damned much lying and misdirection going on. I decided to opt for thoroughness and accuracy, at the expense of speed.

Obviously, warehouses full of articles and books and reports already have been written about Benghazi. However, many of these have focused on one or two particular aspects of the tragedy, without connecting it to other pieces of the mosaic. For example, many writers concentrated principally on the security situation leading up to Benghazi. Some analyzed only the reasons the United States chose to be there.

Others assessed the actual "Battle of Benghazi" itself. (Among these last is the excellent book by Mitchell Zuckoff, *13 Hours: The Inside Account of What Really Happened in Benghazi*, written with the aid of the CIA security contractors who fought in Benghazi.[2] I commend *13 Hours* to my readers, and I have relied heavily upon it in my research. It since has been made into a superb motion picture of a similar title.[3])

Also, many pieces about Benghazi have focused principally upon the aftermath of the crisis, about the American government's (often pathetic) post facto explanations and excuses for what happened and why, and about the various investigations of those issues.

---

[1] *The Emperor Obama: An American Betrayal,* Book I – Foreign Policy, National Security and Terrorism; and *Id.,* Book II – Domestic, Environmental and Immigration Policy (both to be available at www.amazon.com).

[2] Mitchell Zuckoff with the Annex Security Team, *13 Hours: The Inside Account of What Really Happened in Benghazi* (Twelve, Hatchett Book Group, New York; 2014) ("Zuckoff, *13 Hours*"). See Stephen F. Hayes, Book Review, *13 Hours: The Inside Account of What Really Happened in Benghazi, The Wall Street Journal* online (Sept. 10, 2014) ("... *13 Hours* is a crisply written, gripping narrative of the events of the battle in Benghazi that adds considerable detail to the public record of what happened there.... What the five [CIA security contractor] survivors have to say is at once compelling and enthralling, infuriating and heartbreaking").

[3] *13 Hours: The Secret Soldiers of Benghazi* (Paramount Pictures, 2016). This movie's premier (a charitable event) is held in AT&T Stadium in Dallas, Texas on January 12, 2016. Some 30,000 people reportedly attend, including many military service members, in what one local media outlet calls "the largest ever world premier for a feature film ..." CBS DFW, "Thousands Attend '13 Hours' Premier at AT&T Stadium," CBS Local website (Jan. 13, 2016).

xv

Moreover, many authors of earlier efforts did not have available the Select Benghazi Committee's excellent work product. Similarly, they lacked access to the important disclosures various litigants have pried loose from a defiant Obama (and later Trump) administration through recent court actions. (The conservative watchdog organization "Judicial Watch" has been particularly successful in such worthy endeavors. Remarkably, some of these court cases continue as we go to press.)

I attempt here to weave together all of these various (sometimes competing and contradictory) strands of evidence and analysis. Where possible, I do so from the vantage points of the people involved. I endeavor to convey the true, minute-by-minute story of exactly what happened in that remote North African city on the terrible night of September 11-12, 2012, and the following deadly morning, and in the corridors of power in Washington, D.C. more than five thousand miles away. I also highlight the staggering heroism of a relative handful of Americans that night.

Finally, I try to convey the enormous mendacity of the highest officials in the United States government as they repeatedly lie to and mislead the American people (with a hefty assist from the mainstream media), in a blatant (but depressingly successful) effort to win reelection for President Barack Obama. And to salvage their own political careers in the process.

When I'm not writing, I make my living practicing law. I often must gather, organize, review, analyze and summarize mountains of evidence. I must eliminate the insignificant and irrelevant data; detect and highlight the inconsistencies, falsehoods and gaps in the evidence; ascertain when witnesses are evasive, shading the truth or outright lying; and summarize the relevant, complex evidence in writing in a logical and coherent fashion that clients, other non-lawyers, attorneys, regulators, judges and juries can grasp. Creating *The Benghazi Betrayal* sorely has tested each of these skills.

Next a few words concerning the book's structure. This work contains voluminous footnotes. I have endeavored always to cite the sources for my facts, as well as those supporting (and sometimes disputing) my conclusions and analysis. It is not my intention to bore or distract or confuse the reader with these citations. Also, I am mindful of the late federal Court of Appeals Judge Abner Mikva's admonition that "If God had intended us to use footnotes, he would have put our eyes in vertically instead of horizontally." However, my subject is highly controversial. Further, much of my evidence and conclusions are surprising – even shocking. Thus, I believe detailed substantiation is essential.

For most readers, however, my advice is simply to *ignore the footnotes*. (Unless, of course, you become especially interested in a particular fact or conclusion and are in the mood to explore it further. Otherwise, the author cannot be responsible for readers who fall into a footnote and can't get out.) The heart of this story is in the main text, not the footnotes. Nevertheless, for you intrepid footnote readers, I include citations to (and often quotes from) resources relevant to my facts, analysis, conclusions and opinions.

This book contains what I consider to be an important Appendix to assist the reader in weighing through the massive amount of material in this book. The Appendix "Key Delays on the Night of Benghazi" is a chart summarizing some of the most significant delays in our government's actions (and inactions) concerning the Benghazi tragedy. It is a timeline of selected key events that documents beyond question the incompetency and complete lack of urgency of the U.S. government in the middle of this national security crisis.

Also, to highlight many of the erroneous and false statements made by key players in the Benghazi affair, I have included on our website a collection of "Key Lies of Benghazi." There also is a summary list of "Key Quotations" on the website (at *www. TheBenghaziBetrayal.com*), all of which are included in this book. The website also includes an "Epilogue" summarizing what became of many of the key characters in subsequent years. Finally, our website contains a chart summarizing some of the close links between the Obama administration and the mainstream media.

This Second Edition adds information regarding the Benghazi tragedy concerning recent events, and from several books and other sources that were discovered by the author or published subsequent to the release of our First Edition.

I hope you enjoy this book. I would appreciate your feedback in the form of a review at *www.Amazon.com*. Thank you for buying and reading this work. ■

James "Mac" McCarty
Broomfield, Colorado USA
May 2020

Key Characters

(Ages are as of the Night of Benghazi)

THE WHITE HOUSE:

John O. Brennan (56). Assistant to the President for Homeland Security and Counterterrorism Adviser. Although he is one of the president's top counterterrorism advisors, Brennan appears to be largely "missing in action" on the Night of Benghazi.

Thomas E. Donilon (57). National Security Advisor. On the Night of Benghazi Donilon appears to defer to his deputy, Denis McDonough, to "lead" the U.S. government's pathetic response to the terror attacks.

Jacob "Jack" Lew (57). White House Chief of Staff. Although he is present in the White House on the Night of Benghazi, Lew does not appear to play any significant role in responding to the attacks.

Denis McDonough (42). Deputy National Security Advisor. To the extent anyone is coordinating the entire U.S. government's actions (and inactions) on the Night of Benghazi, it is Denis McDonough. However, he will be woefully ill-informed of the true facts on the ground in Libya.

Barack H. Obama (51). President of the United States and Commander in Chief. Although he ultimately is responsible for protecting the besieged Americans on the Night of Benghazi, he will never make it to the White House Situation Room. His whereabouts on this night largely remain a mystery to this day. He fails to call any Libyan leader to seek help. Obama never speaks with Secretary Panetta or General Dempsey again following their regularly-scheduled 5:00 p.m. meeting at the White House.

Ben Rhodes (35). Deputy National Security Advisor for Strategic Communications, National Security Council. Rhodes will be a principal architect of the "Benghazi Narrative," designed to help minimize the significance of the terror attacks in Benghazi in order to win a presidential election just weeks away.

THE TRUE ACCOUNT OF VALOR AND ABANDONMENT

THE U.S. DEPARTMENT OF DEFENSE:

Jeremy Bash. Chief of Staff to Secretary of Defense Leon Panetta. Bash will represent the Pentagon on the marathon, two-hour interagency meeting of "Deputies" that leisurely discusses the crisis while it is ongoing five thousand miles away.

General Martin E. Dempsey (59). Chairman of the Joint Chiefs of Staff. Along with Defense Secretary Panetta, he will brief President Obama on the attacks in the Oval Office at 5:00 p.m. on the Night of Benghazi. He then will work with Panetta to identify three different U.S. military forces that can deploy during the crisis. Like Panetta and General Ham, Dempsey fails to ensure the U.S. military acts with urgency and efficiency during the attacks and evacuations.

General Carter F. Ham (60). Commander, U.S. Africa Command ("AFRICOM"). Forces under his command will fail to meet all of their timetables on the Night of Benghazi, and never will enter Benghazi to rescue the three-dozen besieged Americans there. Most of his troops never will get closer to Libya than Sigonella Naval Air Station in Sicily. Ham will retire just weeks after Benghazi.

Leon E. Panetta (74). Secretary of Defense. After briefing President Obama, Panetta will preside over a "Council of War" from 6:00 to 7:00 p.m. on the Night of Benghazi. Following this conference, he will claim he orders three different military units to "Deploy Now" to respond to the crisis. None of the three units ever will make it to Benghazi. Only one unit makes it to Libya, but it arrives well after the Battle of Benghazi is over. Panetta will not remain at the Pentagon to "stand watch" to ensure his forces deploy quickly. He will never speak to the Secretary of State during the attacks and evacuations.

Vice Admiral James "Sandy" Winnefeld (56). Vice Chairman of the Joint Chiefs of Staff. On the Night of Benghazi, after participating in Secretary Panetta's 6:00 p.m. "Council of War" Winnefeld goes home to host a dinner party for foreign dignitaries while the Battle of Benghazi rages.

THE U.S. DEPARTMENT OF STATE:

Hillary R. Clinton (65). Secretary of State. Clinton later will claim she had no involvement in the decisions that denied additional security in Benghazi, and that in fact significantly reduced security assets there.

On the Night of Benghazi she will go home while her Ambassador, Chris Stevens, remains missing. She will not speak with Secretary of Defense Panetta a single time during the crisis.

Gregory N. Hicks. Deputy Chief of Mission, Tripoli, Libya. Hicks will take over as Chief of Mission in Tripoli following Ambassador Stevens' death. Hicks will supervise the evacuation of the U.S. Embassy on the Night of Benghazi, and will coordinate U.S. communications with the Americans besieged in Benghazi.

Patrick F. Kennedy (63). Under Secretary of State for Management. Kennedy made or approved many of the disastrous security decisions involving Libya generally, and Benghazi specifically. He will continue his mistakes on the Night of Benghazi, arguing the U.S. military should restrain itself in various ways, the "F.E.S.T." terrorism crisis-response team should not be deployed, and the Libyan government must approve any deployment of U.S. forces into that country.

Charlene Lamb. Deputy Assistant Secretary of State for Diplomatic Security. A subordinate of Patrick Kennedy's, she also made many unfortunate security-related decisions concerning the U.S. diplomatic outposts in Libya. She will be one of only four mid-level State Department employees suspended (with pay) for eight months for their actions concerning Benghazi.

Cheryl Mills (47). Chief of Staff and Counselor to Secretary of State Clinton. Mills will have extensive involvement in assembling, coordinating with, and overseeing the Benghazi "Accountability Review Board" charged with investigating the State Department's actions regarding the Benghazi tragedy.

Susan E. Rice (47). United States Ambassador to the United Nations. Although Rice had no involvement in any manner concerning Benghazi, she will be sent on five Sunday news shows to explain the crisis. Her appearances will be a disaster, and very likely cost her the nomination to succeed Hillary Clinton as Secretary of State.

Sean Patrick Smith (34). Information Management Specialist with the U.S. Foreign Service. In September 2012 he was temporarily assigned to the Special Mission Compound in Benghazi. Smith will be one of four Americans murdered by the terrorists on the Night of Benghazi.

THE TRUE ACCOUNT OF VALOR AND ABANDONMENT

J. Christopher "Chris" Stevens (52). U.S. Ambassador to Libya. Stevens will be assassinated by a terrorist mob on the Night of Benghazi after they set his residence on fire. He is the first U.S. ambassador assassinated in thirty-three years.

Mark I. Thompson. Deputy Coordinator for Operations, U.S. State Department, and head of the U.S. government's "Foreign Emergency Support Team" ("F.E.S.T."). U.S. officials will reject Thompson's recommendation to deploy F.E.S.T. to Libya on the Night of Benghazi.

Dave Ubben (about 31). A Diplomatic Security Agent with the State Department, one of five such security men stationed at the Mission Compound in Benghazi. He found the body of Sean Smith in the burned-out Mission Villa. Later, Ubben will be one of two Americans severely wounded during the terrorist attacks on the Night of Benghazi.

THE U.S. CENTRAL INTELLIGENCE AGENCY:

David H. Petraeus (59). Director of the Central Intelligence Agency. Little is known of Petraeus' involvement in responding to the terror attacks on the Night of Benghazi.

Michael J. Morell (54). Deputy Director of the CIA (2010-2013). After the attacks, Morell will become responsible for preparing the now-infamous CIA "Talking Points" intended to explain what happened in Benghazi.

Tripoli Chief of Station. The top CIA official in Libya. On the Night of Benghazi, he organized and deployed "Team Tripoli," an improvised group of CIA security contractors and two U.S. special operations soldiers. Team Tripoli will be the only U.S. help headed to Benghazi.

Benghazi CIA Annex Chief of Base. Known only as "Bob," he is the top CIA official in Benghazi. It is his last posting before retirement. On the Night of Benghazi, he reportedly tells five of his security contractors and their "Team Lead" they must wait before leaving the Annex to attempt to rescue the State Department personnel at the Mission Compound.

CIA Security Contractors:

Dave "D.B." or "Boone" Benton (38, a pseudonym). Private security contractor assigned to Benghazi.

Glen A. "Bub" Doherty (42). Private security contractor assigned to Tripoli. While a member of "Team Tripoli," he will be murdered in the dawn terrorist mortar attack on the CIA Annex on September 12, 2012.

Mark "Oz" Geist (46). Private security contractor assigned to Benghazi. He will be severely injured in the dawn terrorist mortar attack on the CIA Annex.

Kris "Tanto" Paronto (41). Private security contractor assigned to Benghazi.

Jack Silva (38, also a pseudonym). Private security contractor assigned to Benghazi.

John "Tig" Tiegen (36). Private security contractor assigned to Benghazi.

Tyrone S. "Rone" Woods (41). Private security contractor assigned to Benghazi. He will be murdered in the dawn terrorist mortar attack on the CIA Annex.

◆ ◆ ◆

Introduction

On the night of Tuesday, September 11, 2012 – the eleventh anniversary of 9/11 – a large group of Islamic terrorists attacks a United States diplomatic compound in Benghazi, Libya. Benghazi is a port city on the Mediterranean Sea, located on Libya's northeastern coast. At the time, Benghazi is among the most dangerous places on the planet. Very early the following morning, terrorists also assault a nearby covert Central Intelligence Agency base in Benghazi known as "the Annex."

When the battle is over, four Americans have been murdered by the terrorists, including the United States Ambassador to Libya, J. Christopher Stevens. Ambassador Stevens is the first American ambassador to be killed in the line of duty since 1979.[4] Two other Americans are wounded severely in their brave efforts to defend their compatriots.[5]

It forever will be remembered as the "Night of Benghazi."

These unprovoked terror attacks take place only 56 days before the presidential election in which President Barack Obama is seeking a second term against Republican candidate Mitt Romney. A number of the polls are tightening.[6] *The political timing of the Benghazi terror*

---

[4] "The Benghazi Attack of September 11, 2012," A Judicial Watch Special Investigative Report, Judicial Watch website (Jan. 22, 2013) ("Judicial Watch Benghazi Investigative Report"), p. 2; Hillary R. Clinton, *Hard Choices* (Simon & Schuster; 2014) ("Clinton, *Hard Choices*"), Chap. 17, p. 398; Zuckoff, *13 Hours*, Chap. 2, p. 47; and David D. Kirkpatrick and Steven Lee Myers, "Libya Attack Brings Challenges for U.S.," *The New York Times* online (Sept. 12, 2012) ("Kirkpatrick and Myers, Libya Attack Brings Challenges for U.S.").

[5] Some media reports will claim there are as many as seven Americans wounded at Benghazi. E.g., Guy Benson, "Bombshell: CIA Using 'Unprecedented' Polygraphing, 'Pure Intimidation' to Guard Benghazi Secrets," Townhall.com website (Aug. 2, 2013) (quoting report by CNN's Jake Tapper). The author has found no credible evidence supporting more than two Americans with anything more than minor injuries.

[6] E.g., "What They Told Us: Reviewing Last Week's Key Polls – Week Ending September 15, 2012," Rasmussen Reports (Sept. 15, 2012) ("The presidential election remains a neck-and-neck affair. . . . It's unclear how perceptions of the candidates will be impacted by the murder this week of the U.S. ambassador to Libya and attacks on U.S. embassies in Cairo and elsewhere in the Middle East. . . ."); Gallup Editors, "Romney 49%, Obama 48% in Gallup's Final Election Survey," Gallup Polling (Nov. 5, 2012) ("President Barack Obama and Republican challenger Mitt Romney are

attacks hardly could be worse for President Obama.[7] This fact likely explains many of the otherwise incomprehensible, conflicting, dawdling and even deplorable decisions and statements the Obama administration will make, and the actions it will take (and fail to take) during and after the attacks. All of this occurs in a pathetic attempt to minimize the adverse political fallout from Benghazi specifically, and from the Obama administration's failed policy in Libya generally.

This book attempts to take the reader step-by-step, minute-by-minute through the true facts of what really happened in the Benghazi tragedy. Along the way, it seeks to answer as many as possible of the nagging "Why" questions that still remain. However, even as Barack Obama's presidency ended, there still were far too many unresolved issues regarding the Benghazi debacle.

As the following exposition will demonstrate, the Benghazi fiasco ranks among the most disgraceful events of the entire eight years of the Obama administration. (The author discusses Obama's entire presidency in two separate forthcoming books.[8]) This work discusses many of the key events in this American tragedy: the deeply flawed

---

within one percentage point of each other in Gallup's final pre-election survey of likely voters, with Romney holding 49% of the vote, and Obama 48%. . . . Gallup's final allocated estimate of the race is 50% for Romney and 49% for Obama"); Press Release, "National: Romney Leads in Monmouth Poll," Monmouth University Poll (Oct. 22, 2012) ("The latest *Monmouth University Poll* of voters nationwide shows Mitt Romney holding on to a three point lead over Barack Obama in next month's presidential race. The GOP challenger continued to make gains in every issue area after the second debate"); "Transcript of Obama on '60 Minutes,'" Fox News online (Sept. 24, 2012) (". . . [S]ix weeks before the election, President Obama maintains a small lead in the polls"); James Rosen, "The Benghazi Transcripts: Top Defense Officials Briefed Obama on 'Attack,' Not Video or Protest," Fox News online (Jan. 14, 2014) ("Rosen, Top Defense Officials Briefed Obama on 'Attack,' Not Video or Protest") (". . . Obama's hotly contested bid for re-election was entering its final stretch . . ."); and Scott Wilson and Karen DeYoung, "Benghazi E-mails Show Clash Between State Department, CIA," *The Washington Post* online (May 10, 2013) ("Wilson and DeYoung, Benghazi E-mails Show Clash Between State Department, CIA") (referencing "a then-close presidential campaign").

[7] E.g., Susan Cornwell and Tabassum Zakaria, "U.S. Security at Benghazi Mission Called 'Weak,'" Reuters World News Online (Oct. 10, 2012) ("Cornwell and Zakaria, U.S. Security at Benghazi Mission Called 'Weak'") ("Republican charges that the United States was caught unprepared for the attack have put the administration of President Barack Obama, a Democrat, on the defensive ahead of the November 6 presidential election").

[8] See *The Emperor Obama: An American Betrayal, Book I – Foreign Policy, National Security and Terrorism*; and *Id., Book II – Domestic, Environmental and Immigration Policy* (both to be available at www.amazon.com).

THE TRUE ACCOUNT OF VALOR AND ABANDONMENT

decision to overthrow the Libyan dictator Qadhafi, and to do so without the constitutionally required congressional authorization; the horrible American misjudgments about security in Libya leading up to the attacks; the reckless decision to deploy American diplomats to the ultra-dangerous city of Benghazi; the betrayal of Americans who are sent there by failing to provide them adequate security before the assaults; the feckless derelictions of duty by the White House, National Security Council and Department of Defense during the battles; and the many deceptions, half-truths, mixed-messages, misdirection and cover-ups by Team Obama following the attacks.

The Benghazi scandal is political at every stage: irresponsible politics leading up to the attacks; disgraceful politics and timidity and abandonment during the attacks; and an appalling amount of naked politics (by all sides) following the disaster leading up to the presidential election of 2012. The malfeasance occurring in the Benghazi tragedy alone could support the impeachment of President Obama, his Secretary of Defense, or his Secretary of State – indeed, of all three. And yet, none of this transpires.

The Benghazi Riddle

Unraveling the enigma that is Benghazi has proven a daunting task. It is akin to assembling a giant, complex jigsaw puzzle containing many thousands of pieces. Mostly by design of Team Obama and their allies, some of the key puzzle pieces have been removed. Some merely have been hidden to be discovered later by truth-seekers;[9] other parts remain hidden to this day; still other pieces likely have been destroyed entirely.[10] Some sections have been modified intentionally so they no

---

[9] E.g., Judicial Watch: State Department Documents Show Its Security Contractor Operating Without a License in Benghazi on Day of Terrorist Attack (Discussing email from State Department Deputy Assistant Secretary dated October 17, 2012 and shared with Congress: ". . . [T]he fact that the dispute between BMG and XPAND meant the company was operating without a license is glossed over, any reference to the September 11, 2012, emergency Benghazi security situation is specifically omitted, and he [the email's author] describes Visintainer's response in July as 'invoking collaborative resolution to the said dispute'").

[10] E.g., Katie Pavlich, "Techies Instructed to Delete Hillary's Emails: This Looks Like Covering Up a Lot of Shady Sh*t," Townhall.com website (Sept. 13, 2013) (computer support firm uses "BleachBit" to "acid wash" Clinton's unauthorized private email server).

longer fit properly into the underlying puzzle.¹¹ And to add to the already considerable confusion, some con artists have fabricated counterfeit puzzle pieces.¹² Despite these challenges, this book seeks to assemble accurately as much of the Benghazi mosaic as possible.

Viewed another way, researching the Benghazi saga has been akin to entering the amusement park "funhouse" of one's youth. Standing in the middle of the house's Benghazi "Chamber of Mirrors," one is surrounded by Looking Glasses. Mirrors cover every wall, the floor and the ceiling. Some are concave, some convex, some flat, some darkened. Every reflected image seems distorted. Very quickly the researcher becomes disoriented by all the conflicting, contradictory, incomplete, overlapping pieces of evidence that assault the eyes. Determining what is real and what is warped and deformed feels nearly impossible. At times, one must close one's eyes and rest until the dizziness subsides and the search for truth can resume.

Investigations of Benghazi

Various groups and individuals later will attempt to make sense of the Benghazi crisis. These include U.S. governmental bodies, some within the American news media, and other private entities. This book examines many of these efforts.

The principal Executive Branch governmental inquiry of the Benghazi debacle is the State Department's "Accountability Review Board." We analyze this bungling and compromised effort in detail below (Chapter 109).

The U.S. Congress also will conduct numerous investigations of Benghazi. These attempts by congressional panels to investigate Benghazi are fractured and largely inept. (As discussed below, after an

---

[11] E.g., Leon Panetta with Jim Newton, *"Worthy Fights: A Memoir of Leadership in War and Peace"* (Penguin Books; 2014) ("Panetta, *Worthy Fights*") (emphasis added) ("One conspiracy theory held that the *CIA security team in Tripoli* had been ordered by their own chain of command to "stand down." That was not only false but directly the opposite of everyone's efforts in response to the president's orders, which was to move as quickly as possible to help"), Chap. 16, p. 430.

[12] See, e.g., "'60 Minutes' Apologizes for Benghazi Report," CBS This Morning (Nov. 8, 2013); and Erik Wemple, "The Disaster of the '60 Minutes' Benghazi Story," *The Washington Post* online (May 5, 2014) (Revealing hoax by "Dylan Davies," allegedly a contract security official for the State Department, who falsely claims to "60 Minutes" he is present on the ground at the Mission Compound on the Night of Benghazi attacks, while telling the FBI a different story).

incomprehensibly and unforgivably lengthy delay, in May 2014 the then Speaker of the U.S. House of Representatives, the massively incompetent and timid John Boehner (R-OH), *finally* establishes a select House Committee to investigate the Benghazi fiasco thoroughly ("Select Benghazi Committee" or "Select Committee"). For a year and one-half, Boehner inexplicably has prevented a Republican-sponsored bill creating such a committee from coming to a vote.[13] The Select Committee is comprised of twelve members, seven Republicans and five Democrats. Boehner wisely appoints former federal prosecutor Congressman Trey Gowdy (R-SC) as chairman.[14]

Much of the following factual material is based upon this Select Benghazi Committee's final majority report ("Benghazi Committee Report"). It is approved on July 8, 2016, but not formally published until December 7, 2016. (This is, after all, the federal government.[15]) This report summarizes the Select Committee's *two-year investigation.*[16]

This complete report is so long (almost 1,000 pages) most Americans never will even look at it. It often reads like it was written by a committee (which, of course, it was). Despite its detractors, through his separate research the author has become convinced this majority report is one of the most authoritative and accurate analyses available of the Benghazi Betrayal. Accordingly, the author relies upon and cites the Select Committee's report extensively throughout this work.

---

[13] Jed Babbin, "Whitewashing Benghazi," The American Spectator online (Feb. 25, 2014) ("Babbin, Whitewashing Benghazi").

[14] Benghazi Committee Report, p. II (Republicans: Chairman Trey Gowdy (R-SC); Rep. Susan Brooks (R-IN); Rep. Jim Jordan (R-OH); Rep. Mike Pompeo (R-KS); Rep. Martha Robey (R-AL); and Rep. Peter Roskam (R-IL). And Democrats: Ranking Minority Member Elisha E. Cummings (D-MD); Rep. Tammy Duckworth (D-IL); Rep. Linda Sanchez (D-CA); Rep. Adam Schiff (D-CA); and Rep. Adam Smith (D-WA)).

[15] The author hereby discloses he was an employee of this same federal government for twelve years.

[16] Final Report of the Select Committee on the Events Surrounding the 2012 Terrorist Attack in Benghazi, Together With Additional and Minority Views, House of Representatives (Dec. 7, 2016), U.S. Government Publishing Office website ("Benghazi Committee Report"). The Benghazi Committee Report also can be found at the Select Committee's website. In this book, the author cites the pagination of the official December 7, 2016 version, which differs from that in the report on the Select Committee's website.

Although several other books have been published about the Benghazi tragedy, most are written before the Benghazi Committee Report is available.[17] Also, some are written before the release of key Obama administration emails and other documents (many discussed below) that have been uncovered in subsequent litigation. And, of course, they are published before this book.

One important side-effect of the Select Benghazi Committee's inquiry is the revelation of the existence of a private, unlawful email server used by Hillary Clinton during her tenure as Secretary of State.[18] This will launch another scandal entirely separate from her culpable role in endangering her agency's employees in the Benghazi debacle.[19] It is possible this disclosure of her illicit, "homebrew" email server through the Select Committee's work – perhaps even more so than her Benghazi Betrayal – costs Hillary Clinton the White House in the surprising election of 2016.[20] Truly, it ranks among the great ironies of modern United States political history.

The Democratic minority on the Select Committee will issue a separate, 339-page report, frequently dissenting from the majority's conclusions. The author finds this minority report to be misleading, unpersuasive, inconsistent and highly political.[21] Accordingly, the

---

[17] E.g., Zuckoff, *13 Hours*; Burton & Katz, *Under Fire*; Aaron Klein, *The Real Benghazi Story* (WND Books, 2014); and David Brock and Ari Rabin-Havt, *The Benghazi Hoax* (Media Matters for America, 2013) ("Media Matters, *The Benghazi Hoax*").

[18] See, e.g., Michael S. Schmidt, "Hillary Clinton Used Personal Email Account at State Dept., Possibly Breaking Rules," *The New York Times* online (Mar. 2, 2015); and Mollie Hemingway, "5 Big Takeaways From the House Benghazi Report," The Federalist website (June 28, 2016) ("Hemingway, 5 Big Takeaways From the House Benghazi Report") (". . . The [Select Benghazi] committee did manage to uncover Secretary Clinton's breathtaking use of a private email account and server, something no previous investigative or oversight committee had known. . . ."). For a detailed analysis of the Hillary Clinton email server scandal, see the author's forthcoming book, *The Emperor Obama: An American Betrayal, Book I – Foreign Policy, National Security and Terrorism* (to be available at www.amazon.com).

[19] David M. Herszenhorn, "House Democrats Release Benghazi Report to Blunt Republican Inquiry," *The New York Times* online (June 27, 2016).

[20] E.g., Lolita C. Baldor, Josh Lederman and Matthew Lee (Associated Press), "Militant Accused in Benghazi Attack on His Way to US Jail," Fox News online (Oct. 31, 2017) (". . . It was the [House Select] Benghazi probe that revealed Clinton used a private email server for government work, prompting an FBI investigation that proved to be an albatross for her presidential campaign").

[21] E.g., Benghazi Committee Report, Minority Report ("Section II of our report documents the grave abuses that Select Committee Republicans engaged in during this

author accords this minority report little weight in his analysis of the Benghazi crisis.

The American news media also explores what happens in Benghazi, and the events leading up to and following it. Several media outlets (most notably Fox News and CNN) prepare documentaries on the tragedy. We discuss these in detail in this book. However, most of the American media does a remarkably poor job covering the Benghazi crisis.[22] This book discusses many examples of this problem, as well as a number of laudable exceptions.

Private, non-media entities also will investigate Benghazi. Among the most serious of these is that conducted by the conservative watchdog group "Judicial Watch."[23] Primarily by means of aggressive Freedom of Information Act ("FOIA") litigation, Judicial Watch has been instrumental in uncovering key documents previously withheld by the Obama (and later Trump) administrations.[24] (When the reader learns in these pages what was in some of these emails and other documents, it will become clear why Team Obama wants them to remain hidden.)

(One of the most delicious ironies of modern American political life is the elevation in 2018 of Mike Pompeo to become the U.S. Secretary

---

investigation. Republicans excluded Democrats from interviews, concealed exculpatory evidence, withheld interview transcripts, leaked inaccurate information, issued unilateral subpoenas, sent armed marshals to the home of a cooperative witness, and even conducted political fundraising by exploiting the deaths of four Americans"), p. 651.

[22] E.g., Review & Outlook, "The Missing Benghazi Email," *The Wall Street Journal* online (April 30, 2014) ("*Wall Street Journal* Opinion, The Missing Benghazi Email") ("Most of the media refuses to cover what happened in Benghazi in 2012 . . ."); and Sharyl Attkisson, *Stonewalled: My Fight for Truth Against the Forces of Obstruction, Intimidation, and Harassment in Obama's Washington* (HarperCollins, New York; 2014) ("Attkisson, *Stonewalled*") (". . . The [Obama] administration has deflected attention from its missteps by declaring the Benghazi story a scandal manufactured by Republicans for political purposes. Many in the media adopt the narrative and lose interest. The stories they do publish are often written as political reports without a thorough examination of what I consider key apolitical issues at heart"), Chap. 4, p. 171.

[23] See, e.g., Judicial Watch Benghazi Investigative Report.

[24] E.g., Press Release, "Judicial Watch: New Benghazi Email Shows DOD Offered State Department 'Forces That Could Move to Benghazi' Immediately – Specifics Blacked Out in New Document," Judicial Watch website (Dec. 8, 2015) ("Judicial Watch Release, New Benghazi Email Shows DOD Offered State Department 'Forces That Could Move to Benghazi' Immediately").

of State. As a member of the Select Benghazi Committee, Pompeo has done stellar work in identifying, documenting, and publicizing the Obama administration's concealment of evidence regarding the Benghazi saga.[25] Now, as we go to press, Pompeo has the power to order the complete disclosure of the State Department's participation in concealing State's improper conduct regarding Benghazi. He controls State's lawyers who are litigating to prevent the release of State records concerning Benghazi. After Secretary Pompeo has concluded the Trump administration's vital efforts to de-nuclearize the Korean Peninsula, he should focus like a laser on ordering the immediate disclosure of non-classified State documents relating to the Benghazi fiasco. It is time for the estimable Pompeo to end the stonewalling.)

To set the table for what happens on the Night of Benghazi, the reader first must understand what transpires before, during and shortly after the tumultuous Libyan revolution of 2011. Part I summarizes this vital subject. (Readers familiar with these background facts have the author's permission to skip Part I.) Parts II-IV then focus specifically on the Benghazi tragedy of September 2012 and its aftermath. Part V summarizes the author's conclusions. ∎

---

[25] See, e.g., Benghazi Committee Report, Additional Views of Reps. Jim Jordan and Mike Pompeo ("Additional Views of Reps. Jordan and Pompeo") ("Despite its claims, we saw no evidence that the administration held a sincere interest in helping the [Select] Committee find the truth about Benghazi. . . . So while the investigation uncovered new information, we nonetheless end the Committee's investigation without many of the facts, especially those involving the President and the White House, we were chartered to obtain"), p. 417; and *Id.* (". . . Yet, our confidence grew that there was more to be learned even as the administration stonewalled at virtually every turn. . . ."), p. 419.

Part I:

Revolutionary Libya

1

"Mad Dog of the Middle East"

For his entire adult life, Colonel Mu'ammar al-Qadhafi[26] is one evil son-of-a-bitch. From the moment he seizes power in Libya (at the ripe old age of 27) in a bloodless military coup in 1969, he is a complete tyrant. A nasty piece of work. (President Ronald Reagan calls Qadhafi "the Mad Dog of the Middle East."[27])

For the next 42 years, "Colonel" Qadhafi will rule Libya as a ruthless, megalomaniacal dictator. He tolerates absolutely no political opposition or independent press, and creates a massive security apparatus to keep his population in check. (Oddly, he never promotes himself to "General" or "Field Marshall," as most despots are fond of doing. He will die "Colonel Qadhafi.") Luckily for him, Qadhafi inherits the wealth that flows from the discovery of oil in Libya in the early 1950s. It will keep his inefficient, socialistic regime afloat for the next four decades.

(The mercurial Qadhafi also is among the flakiest leaders on the planet. His many reported eccentricities include: a fondness for flamenco dancing; surrounding himself with a "busty Ukrainian nurse" and a retinue of voluptuous female "security guards" in high heels; dressing in eccentric costumes and dark sunglasses (even indoors); when traveling staying in a luxurious Bedouin tent instead of hotels or embassies; delivering interminable (and unintelligible) speeches; and a fear of flying over bodies of water.[28])

During Qadhafi's reign in December 1979, a mob attacks the United States embassy in Libya and sets it ablaze. The U.S. shuts its embassy

---

[26] There are as many different spellings for the late Libyan dictator's name as the author had excuses for why he never got his homework done on time. The author has chosen to adopt a spelling frequently used by the U.S. State Department (among others).

[27] Zuckoff, *13 Hours*, Chap. 1, p. 12; and Burton & Katz, *Under Fire*, Prologue, p. 11.

[28] E.g., Tara Bahrampour, "U.S. Embassy in Tripoli Reopens," *The Washington Post* online (Sept. 22, 2011) ("Bahrampour, U.S. Embassy in Tripoli Reopens"); William J. Dobson, "Why Gaddafi Was the Quintessential 20th-Century Dictator," *The Washington Post* online (Oct. 21, 2011); Burton & Katz, *Under Fire*, Prologue, p. 11; and Attkisson, *Stonewalled*, Chap. 4, p. 181.

down in May 1980, after withdrawing all diplomatic and other government personnel from Libya. According to the U.S. State Department, "From 1980 until 2006, the U.S. did not have an open Embassy in Libya, although relations were not formally severed."[29]

Early in his reign, Qadhafi becomes involved in terrorism.[30] His brand of terrorism is secular, not Islamic-inspired. Indeed, throughout his reign Qadhafi will remain a staunch opponent of fundamentalist Islam, including al Qaeda in later years.[31] (This is among the reasons President Obama's decision to topple Qadhafi in 2011, discussed below, will prove questionable.) By the mid-1980s, he trains his terrorism sights on the United States. In April 1986, Qadhafi authorizes the bombing of a popular discotheque in West Berlin, Germany, which many American soldiers are known to frequent. Three people are killed, including two American soldiers; about 230 people are wounded, including 79 Americans. Many believe the disco bombing is a retaliation for the U.S. sinking of two Libyan patrol boats in March 1986 in the Gulf of Sirte, off the Libyan coast. (Much later in 2001, four persons will be convicted of the discotheque bombings, two with connections to the Libyan embassy in East Berlin.)[32]

In response to the disco bombing, ten days later President Reagan approves jet aircraft bombing attacks on targets in Tripoli and Benghazi, Libya. It is known as "Operation Eldorado Canyon." Targets include Qadhafi's residential compound in Tripoli, a Libyan naval academy, the Tripoli military airport and several army barracks. The attacks by 66 U.S. jets are believed to kill some 60 to 100 people. These include at least 15 civilians, among them reportedly Qadhafi's adopted baby child. (Many in the U.S. intelligence community dismiss this last alleged casualty as pure propaganda.) There are reports the real

---

[29] "A Guide to the United States' History of Recognition, Diplomatic and Consular Relations, by Country, Since 1776: Libya," Office of the Historian, Bureau of Public Affairs, State Dept. website; and Embassy of the United States, Tripoli, Libya official website.

[30] Bret Baier, "New Revelations on Attack in Benghazi," Fox News Channel (Oct. 28, 2012) ("Baier, New Revelations on Attack in Benghazi") (*Watch video there*; Go to 1:30-41).

[31] Burton & Katz, *Under Fire*, Prologue, pp. 11-12.

[32] Nathalie Malinarich, "Flashback: The Berlin Disco Bombing," BBC News online (Nov. 13, 2001); and Steven Erlanger, "4 Guilty in Fatal 1986 Disco Bombing Linked to Libya," *The New York Times* online (Nov. 14, 2001).

goal of the mission is to kill Qadhafi, but he survives without injury.[33] Some claim the American CIA will make further plans over the ensuing years to attempt to eliminate Qadhafi.

Qadhafi still hasn't learned his lesson. In December 1988, two Libyan agents plant a bomb on Pan Am Flight 103, which explodes over Lockerbie, Scotland. The blast kills all 259 souls on board, and eleven people on the ground. The victims include 189 Americans. By then, President Ronald Reagan is on his way out of office. His successor, George H.W. Bush, decides not to retaliate militarily. However, Bush pursues sanctions against Libya, which the United Nations finally imposes in 1992, as Bush exits the presidential stage.[34]

Eventually, two Libyan intelligence officers are arrested and tried for the Lockerbie bombing. One of the defendants, Abdel Basset Ali Al-Megrahi, is convicted; the other is acquitted. Qadhafi always will deny he has ordered the Lockerbie explosion. (This despite the fact his regime ultimately will pay nearly three billion dollars in compensation to the families of the bombing victims.)[35] Almost no one believes him. But Qadhafi does have a strong incentive to appease the West in order to obtain the lifting of the sanctions imposed on his regime.

Later, when the U.S. State Department begins announcing a public list of "State Sponsors of Terrorism," Libya finds itself a member of this dubious club.[36] Qadhafi's history does not inspire optimism for the future. ∎

---

[33] "On This Day, 1986: US Launches Air Strikes on Libya," BBC News online (April 15, 2005?); and Nathalie Malinarich, "Flashback: The Berlin Disco Bombing," BBC News online (Nov. 13, 2001).

[34] Sewell Chan, "2 Lockerbie Bombing Suspects, Libyans, Sought by U.S. and Scotland," *The New York Times* online (Oct. 15, 2015); Bill Gertz, *Treachery* (Crown Forum, New York; 2004) ("Gertz, *Treachery*"), Chap. 7, pp. 138 and 147-148; and Baier, New Revelations on Attack in Benghazi (*Watch video there*; Go to 1:30-41).

[35] "A Byte Out of History: Solving a Complex Case of International Terrorism," FBI website (Dec. 19, 2003); and Interview of Col. Mu'ammar Qadhafi with George Negus, Journeyman Pictures (Feb. 2010) (*Watch video there*; Go to 5:30 - 8:24).

[36] "State Sponsors of Terror Overview Report," Country Reports on Terrorism, Office of the Coordinator for Counterterrorism, State Dept. website (April 26, 2006).

2

The Bush - Qadhafi Deal

Move ahead some 15 years. After 9/11, President Bush the Younger invades Afghanistan in 2001 and topples the hideous Taliban regime.[37] Next, Bush invades Iraq in 2003 and overthrows its ruler, the psychotic Saddam Hussein.[38] In Libya, Colonel Mu'ammar al-Qadhafi grows concerned. Might *he* be next?[39] Ronald Reagan had sent a few dozen war planes to Libya; Bush 43 has sent entire invading *armies* into Afghanistan and Iraq!

At this time, Libya still is on the U.S. list of officially-designated state sponsors of terrorism. Qadhafi has active, but secret, nuclear, chemical and biological weapons programs going back at least as early as 1997.[40] He also has a ballistic missile development program.[41]

In his epiphany that follows, in March 2003 – the same month Bush invades Iraq – Qadhafi sends feelers to the United Kingdom. He proposes talks with Britain and the U.S. aimed at dismantling the Libyan nuclear and chemical arms programs. Despite Qadhafi's reputation, the U.S. and U.K. agree to discuss the issue with Qadhafi. A series of secret talks are conducted in London, then Tunisia, and later in Libya.[42] Later in the year and into 2004, the Colonel makes a deal with the United States: Qadhafi will surrender to the U.S. all of his stockpiles of, and ingredients for, weapons of mass destruction. This includes his centrifuge equipment and stockpiles of uranium hexaflouride (a gas that can produce highly-enriched uranium for use in

---

[37] "U.S. Relations With Afghanistan," Fact Sheet, Office of the Special Representative for Afghanistan and Pakistan, State Dept. website (Updated Jan. 3, 2017), and sources cited therein.

[38] CNN Library, "Operation Iraqi Freedom and Operation New Dawn Fast Facts," CNN online (Updated April 10, 2017).

[39] Gertz, *Treachery* ("No doubt the U.S. military action to oust Saddam Hussein was weighing heavily on Qadhafi's mind. As one Western diplomat put it, 'The Iraqi lesson was so bitter. And so clear'"), Chap. 7, p. 151.

[40] *Id.*, Chap. 7, pp. 138-143.

[41] *Id.*, Chap. 7, pp. 138, 143, 149-150, 152-153 and 157-160.

[42] *Id.*, Chap. 7, pp. 138-139.

nuclear bombs). Libya also will pledge not to support international terrorism "or other acts of violence targeting civilians."[43] In return, the U.S. will remove certain economic sanctions, begin the process of normalizing relations with Libya, and (implicitly) let Qadhafi remain in power and stay alive.[44] President George W. Bush agrees to Qadhafi's terms.

In December 2003, Libya announces publicly it is eliminating its weapons of mass destruction. Qadhafi further agrees to adhere to the "Missile Technology Control Regime," which restricts missiles to a range of 186 miles. Qadhafi also assents to abide by various other international arms control treaties designed to limit the proliferation of weapons of mass destruction, including those covering chemical and biological weapons.[45] The U.S., the United Kingdom and various relevant international agencies work to enforce this agreement.[46]

Qadhafi later will admit "Of course there was" a weapons of mass destruction program in Libya. But he denies he ends his arms program because of Bush's invasion of Iraq. He insists the "world has changed" and even before the Iraq war he has begun reviewing whether his program still is necessary.[47] (Yeah . . . Right.)

For his part, Qadhafi begins to cooperate with the West in combating terrorism.[48] Specifically, he works with the United Kingdom

---

[43] "State Sponsors of Terror Overview Report," Country Reports on Terrorism, Office of the Coordinator for Counterterrorism, State Dept. website (April 26, 2006); and Gertz, *Treachery*, Chap. 7, pp. 138, 143-145 and 151.

[44] "Country Reports on Terrorism," Office of the Coordinator for Counterterrorism, State Dept. website (April 27, 2005); Baier, New Revelations on Attack in Benghazi (*Watch video there*; Go to 1:40 - 2:24) (Frank Gaffney, president of The Center for Security Policy: "Mu'ammar Qadhafi's transformation from rogue eccentric, even bizarre terrorist sponsor, into one of America's most reliable allies is, I think, going to be seen by historians as one of the more bizarre twists of American diplomatic history"); and Interview of Professor Glenn Reynolds, Univ. of Tennessee Law School, with Tucker Carlson, "Tucker Carlson Tonight," Fox News Channel (Dec. 1, 2017).

[45] Gertz, *Treachery*, Chap. 7, p. 143.

[46] "Country Reports on Terrorism," Office of the Coordinator for Counterterrorism, State Dept. website (April 27, 2005).

[47] Interview of Col. Mu'ammar Qadhafi with George Negus, Journeyman Pictures (Feb. 2010) (*Watch video there*; Go to 4:09 - 5:29).

[48] E.g., Erin McLaughlin, "Libyan Rebels Push Toward Remaining Gadhafi Strongholds," ABC News online (Sept. 3, 2011) ("According to documents seen by the Associated Press, the CIA was one of a number of foreign intelligence services that worked with Libya's agencies in the war on terror. . . . The security documents show

"to curtail terrorism-related activities of the Libyan Islamic Fighting Group." (Qadhafi has a further reason to do so, as this group seeks his overthrow.) Libya also extradites some terror suspects to other nations, most notably to Egypt. Qadhafi also works with other countries to prevent Libya from being used as a safe haven for international terrorists. Finally, Libya promises to respond to information requests relating to the 1988 Lockerbie bombing of Pan Am flight 103.[49]

The United States and its western allies still do not trust Qadhafi completely. After all, once a terrorist, ... More concretely, in 2004 U.S. intelligence obtains reports suggesting Qadhafi may have joined in a plot to assassinate Crown Prince Abdullah, the head of Saudi Arabia's government.[50]

Despite the inevitable doubts about Qadhafi's truthfulness and reliability, pursuant to this 2003-2004 agreement the Bush administration takes a series of steps to eliminate many economic sanctions against Libya. Further, the U.S. resumes a direct diplomatic presence in Libya. In February 2004, it sends U.S. personnel to staff a "U.S. Interests Section" in Tripoli. In June 2004, this facility is upgraded to a "Liaison Office." At the end of May 2006, the U.S. and Qadhafi exchange "diplomatic notes," confirming America's Liaison Office in Tripoli has been upgraded further to Embassy status.[51] In December 2008, the U.S. embassy announces the arrival in Tripoli of

---

intimate links between the CIA and Gadhafi's ousted regime, including intelligence-sharing and handing over suspected terrorists to Libya for interrogation").

[49] "Country Reports on Terrorism," Office of the Coordinator for Counterterrorism, State Dept. website (April 27, 2005) (". . . Libya . . . took significant steps to cooperate in the global war on terrorism in 2004. . . ."); "State Sponsors of Terror Overview Report," Country Reports on Terrorism, Office of the Coordinator for Counterterrorism, State Dept. website (April 26, 2006) ("Libya . . . continued to take significant steps to cooperate in the global war on terror. . . . Libya continued to cooperate with the United States and the international community in the fight against terrorism. . . . Despite its increasing level of cooperation, Libya remained on the state sponsors of terrorism list and was subject to corresponding sanctions. . . .").

[50] Gertz, *Treachery*, Chap. 7, p. 146.

[51] Embassy of the United States, Tripoli, Libya official website; and "A Guide to the United States' History of Recognition, Diplomatic and Consular Relations, by Country, Since 1776: Libya," Office of the Historian, Bureau of Public Affairs, State Dept. website; and "Country Reports on Terrorism," Office of the Coordinator for Counterterrorism, State Dept. website (April 27, 2005).

Gene A. Cretz, the first U.S. Ambassador to Libya in 36 years.[52] In 2009, the U.S. will complete a state-of-the-art Embassy compound in Tripoli (begun under President Bush).[53]

The Bush administration is holding up its end of the bargain it has struck with Qadhafi. And for the next few years, the Libyan dictator largely behaves himself under the Bush-Qadhafi accord.[54] ∎

---

[52] "Embassy Renews Educational Partnership With Libya," *State Magazine*, Issue No. 536 (July/Aug. 2009) State Dept. website; and Bahrampour, U.S. Embassy in Tripoli Reopens.

[53] Scott Stewart, "The Benghazi Report and the Diplomatic Security Funding Cycle," Stratfor website (Dec. 27, 2012) ("Stewart, The Benghazi Report and the Diplomatic Security Funding Cycle"); and Scott Stewart, "Diplomatic Security in Light of Benghazi," Stratfor website (Sept. 27, 2012) ("Stewart, Diplomatic Security in Light of Benghazi").

[54] Andrew C. McCarthy, "Hillary Clinton's Benghazi Debacle: Arming Jihadists in Libya . . . And Syria," National Review online (Aug. 2, 2016) ("McCarthy, Hillary Clinton's Benghazi Debacle: Arming Jihadists in Libya . . . And Syria") ("The Obama administration, like the Bush administration, had touted Qaddafi as a key counterterrorism ally against rabidly anti-American jihadists in eastern Libya").

3

The "Arab Spring"

Fast forward to late 2010 and early 2011. Barack H. Obama has succeeded George W. Bush as President of the United States. North Africa and the Middle East begin to experience a string of democratic-sounding uprisings that become known as the "Arab Spring."

What happens in the nations affected by this movement sets the context for the coming U.S. intervention in Libya, as analyzed in detail below. Moreover, these events might explain (at least partially) why the U.S. is in Benghazi on that tragic night in September 2012. Accordingly, we discuss this Arab Spring development in some of these other countries briefly.

The revolts begin in Tunisia, Libya's neighbor to the west. Rebellions of various magnitudes will follow in Egypt, Yemen, Morocco, Bahrain, Libya and Syria. President Obama's administration decides to intervene in some of these countries (Libya, Egypt and, to a more limited extent, Syria and Bahrain), but not in others (Tunisia, Yemen and Morocco).

Tunisia: The "Jasmine Revolution"

The Arab Spring revolts commonly are described as beginning in Tunisia in December 2010.[55] There, the autocratic President Zine al-Abidine Ben Ali has been in office for 24 years. His is one of the most firmly controlled regimes in the Arab world. On December 17, an unemployed street vendor, Mohammed Bouazizi, becomes distraught when police confiscate his illegal produce stand. In defiance, Bouazizi, 26, sets himself ablaze in front of a government building. He will die

---

[55] One can argue the Arab Spring truly begins in Tehran, not in Tunisia. As President Obama himself remarks, it is in Iran during the so-called "Green Revolution" that peaceful protests first spring up in the Middle East. "Remarks by the President on the Middle East and North Africa," The White House, Obama White House Archives (May 19, 2011) ("... Let's remember that the first peaceful protests in the region were in the streets of Tehran, where the government brutalized women and men, and threw innocent people into jail...."). The Obama administration essentially ignores this uprising, making no effort to support the protestors.

two weeks later. Soon, several other unemployed Tunisian youths attempt suicide, at least one successfully.

Mass popular protests ensue, fueled by social media. The demonstrations principally target corruption, police brutality and unemployment. After 29 days of revolt, Ben Ali's regime is toppled. This surprising phenomenon becomes known to many as the "Jasmine Revolution." Ben Ali is forced into exile.[56] In October 2011 elections create a "Constituent Assembly," which drafts a new constitution.[57] The Obama administration applauds this revolt, but takes no concrete action in Tunisia to help overthrow Ben Ali.[58]

Tunisia itself is not central to our story. However, Bouazizi's self-immolation and the resulting Jasmine Revolution literally "ignites" the Arab Spring. Its flames soon will spread to Egypt and Libya, and affect dramatically what follows there.

The Overthrow of Egypt's Mubarak

On the other side of Libya to the east, long-festering turmoil in Egypt breaks into the open on January 25, 2011. It will become known as the "January 25 Revolution." For the thirty years since Anwar Sadat's assassination by Islamist extremists in 1981, Egyptian strongman Hosni Mubarak has ruled Egypt. Mubarak (now 83) is a virtual dictator. However, Mubarak has been a loyal U.S. ally and has honored the "separate peace" deal the U.S. under President Jimmy Carter struck with Egypt and Israel at Camp David in 1979.[59]

---

[56] "Remarks by the President on the Middle East and North Africa," The White House, Obama White House Archives (May 19, 2011); Mona Eltahawy, "Tunisia's Jasmine Revolution," *The Washington Post* online (Jan. 15, 2011); and BBC News, "Tunisia Country Profile," BBC News online (Updated Jan. 17, 2017).

[57] "U.S. Relations With Tunisia," State Dept. website (Updated Aug. 22, 2013).

[58] "Statement by the President on Events in Tunisia," The White House, Obama White House Archives (Jan. 14, 2011).

[59] "Milestones of American Diplomacy," Bureau of Resource Management FY 2003 Performance and Accountability Report, State Dept. website (Dec. 2003) ("1979: Israel-Egypt Peace Treaty (Camp David Accords) ended 30 years of conflict between the two countries and provided possible framework for comprehensive peace in the Middle East"); and Susan Rice, *Tough Love: My Story of the Things Worth Fighting For* (Simon & Schuster, New York; 2019) ("Rice, *Tough Love*"), Chap. 14, p. 278 ("... President Hosni Mubarak was deposed in Egypt, after three decades of both repressing his people and serving as a reliable regional partner of the U.S.").

THE TRUE ACCOUNT OF VALOR AND ABANDONMENT

Encouraged by the protests in Tunisia, various Egyptian youth groups have set January 25 to protest corruption and the increasing brutality of Mubarak's security services. The anti-government protestors stage marches, demonstrations, strikes, occupations of public places and non-violent acts of civil disobedience. Then, violent clashes result between the protestors and Mubarak's security forces. Unlike revolts elsewhere (including Libya), in Egypt protests especially are focused at a specific central location, Cairo's Tahrir Square. Night after night for 18 days, tens and later hundreds of thousands of anti-Mubarak demonstrators gather there under the ever-present eyes of international television cameras. This ubiquitous news coverage plays a key role in the eventual success of the January 25 Revolution.[60] The regime attempts to suppress the (mostly) peaceful revolt by beating and killing unarmed civilians, cutting of telephone and internet service, and arresting "scores of journalists and activists." These tactics backfire. They simply draw more protestors to Tahrir Square.[61]

Despite Mubarak's three decades of honoring the Israeli-Egyptian peace pact with the U.S., President Obama decides Mubarak must go.[62] Ultimately, on February 11 Mubarak resigns and turns the government over to a military council.[63] A few days later, on February 15, President Obama urges the world, ". . . [S]o far at least, we're seeing the right signals coming out of Egypt. . . . [L]et's look at Egypt's example as opposed to Iran's example [where the regime brutally put down protestors]. . . ."[64] The people of Libya (and elsewhere) will hear him. U.S. Secretary of State Hillary Clinton visits Egypt in March 2011 to

---

[60] Sudarsan Raghavan and Heba Mahfouz, "Egypt's Mubarak Freed from Detention Six Years After His Overthrow," *The Washington Post* online (Mar. 24, 2017).

[61] Leila Fadel, "With Peace, Egyptians Overthrow a Dictator," *The Washington Post* online (Feb. 11, 2011).

[62] E.g., "Remarks by the President on the Situation in Egypt," Obama White House Archives (Feb. 1, 2011) (". . . . After his speech tonight, I spoke directly to President Mubarak. He recognizes that the status quo is not sustainable and that a change must take place. . . . What is clear – and what I indicated tonight to President Mubarak – is my belief that an orderly transition must be meaningful, it must be peaceful, and it must begin now").

[63] Leila Fadel, "With Peace, Egyptians Overthrow a Dictator," *The Washington Post* online (Feb. 11, 2011).

[64] Press Conference by the President, The White House, Obama White House Archives (Feb. 15, 2011); and BBC News, "Egypt: Obama Sees 'Right Signals' from Military," BBC News online (Feb. 15, 2011).

lend further American support to Egypt's supposed journey toward democracy.

In presidential elections in June 2012 (the first in Egypt in 50 years), the Egyptian people narrowly choose the Muslim Brotherhood's candidate, Mohamed Morsi.[65] Such is the situation in Egypt on September 11, 2012. As summarized in Chapter 26 below, on this morning events in Cairo will erupt and spill over into the Obama administration's response to, and the news media's coverage of, the Night of Benghazi.[66]

Democratic Protests in Bahrain

Bahrain is an island nation in the Persian Gulf, situated between Saudi Arabia and Qatar. Critically, the U.S. has a vital interest in Bahrain because the American Navy's Fifth Fleet is based there. Pro-democracy demonstrations begin in Bahrain on February 14, 2011, as part of what Bahrainis call a "Day of Rage." They are inspired at least partly by the uprisings in Tunisia and Egypt. Oppressed Shiites (the majority) rally against the Bahraini government (controlled by the Sunni royal family). The ruling constitutional monarchy unleashes its military.[67] The police and army kill seven demonstrators. Later, Saudi Arabia and the United Arab Emirates send troops to Bahrain to help put down the protestors.[68]

---

[65] BBC News online, "Egypt Profile – Timeline," (Updated June 8, 2017); and BBC News, "Egypt Profile – Overview," BBC News online (Updated Nov. 6, 2015).

[66] Later, in July 2013, the Egyptian military (and much of the population) has had enough of the Muslim Brotherhood. A senior Egyptian officer, Field Marshal Abdel Fattah al-Sissi, leads a military coup and removes (and later jails and prosecutes) the now unpopular President Morsi. The military outlaws the Muslim Brotherhood in Egypt. In elections held in May 2014, al-Sissi is elected president. CIA World Factbook on Egypt (Updated Aug. 1, 2017). As this book goes to press, al-Sissi continues to govern.

[67] Robert M. Gates, *Duty: Memoirs of a Secretary at War* (Alfred A. Knopf, New York; 2014) ("Gates, *Duty*") (Crown Prince of Bahrain told Gates ". . . Arab rulers in the Gulf saw Bahrain as a proxy in the struggle with Iran and that the lesson they took from events in Tunisia and Egypt was that those governments had erred by showing weakness. . . ."), Chap. 13, p. 516.

[68] Gates, *Duty* (Saudi Arabia sends more than 1,000 troops), Chap. 13, p. 517; Ethan Bronner and Michael Slackman, "Saudi Troops Enter Bahrain to Help Put Down Unrest," *The New York Times* online (Mar. 14, 2011); BBC News, "Bahrain Country Profile," BBC News online (Updated Aug. 27, 2017); David Sirota, "Emails Show Clinton Foundation Donor Reached Out to Hillary Clinton Before Arms Export Boost,"

During these protests, President Obama's State Department (led by Hillary Clinton) effectively intervenes by approving substantially increased sales of significant military weapons to the kingdom. The Sunni monarchy uses these weapons to suppress the Shiite political uprisings.[69] (These U.S. weapons sales occur around the time the Bahraini government, its Crown Prince, and Bahrain Petroleum all make substantial donations (directly or indirectly) to the Clinton family's private "charitable" foundation.[70] Also, did we mention the U.S. Fifth Fleet is based in Bahrain?)

Thus, in sharp contrast to Egypt above and Libya (discussed below), in Bahrain Obama's government intervenes in favor of the ruling *government*, and against the democratic protestors seeking greater freedom.[71] As of this writing, the Bahraini royal family will survive the uprisings.

The Syrian Civil War

The conflict in Syria commences in March 2011. A group of students is arrested in the city of Dara'a for scrawling "Down with the regime" on building walls. Public outcries follow. Syrian President

---

International Business Times online (Aug. 22, 2016); and Michael Hastings, "Inside Obama's War Room," *Rolling Stone Magazine* online (Oct. 13, 2011) ("Hastings, Inside Obama's War Room") ("In Bahrain – home of the U.S. 5th Fleet – the administration looked the other way as the royal family allowed the military to violently crush peaceful street protests").

[69] David Sirota, "Emails Show Clinton Foundation Donor Reached Out to Hillary Clinton Before Arms Export Boost," *International Business Times* online (Aug. 22, 2016).

[70] Russ Read, "Bahrain's Prince Got Audience With Clinton After Donating $32 Million to Her Foundation," The Daily Caller online (Aug. 22, 2016) ("Newly released Department of State documents reveal that the Crown Prince of Bahrain was given an audience with then-Secretary of State Hillary Clinton after he donated $32 million to her foundation. . . . [Doug] Band and [Huma] Abedin's email exchanges show that Bahrain's Crown Prince Salman had to go through the Clinton Foundation in order to set up a meeting with Clinton after the former Secretary of State declined to meet after official requests were made" through the State Department); and Sarah Westwood, "Emails Show Bahrain Leader Sought Meeting With Clinton Through Foundation," *Washington Examiner* online (Aug. 22, 2016) ("The Kingdom of Bahrain has given up to $100,000 to the Clinton Foundation").

[71] Ethan Bronner and Michael Slackman, "Saudi Troops Enter Bahrain to Help Put Down Unrest," *The New York Times* online (Mar. 14, 2011) (". . . The United States – which has continued to back the monarchy – . . . has long been allied with Bahrain's royal family and has based the Navy's Fifth Fleet in Bahrain for many years").

Bashar al-Assad responds brutally. When nationwide public demonstrations ensue, Assad retaliates with even greater force. Soon, the country descends into an armed civil war. President Obama and other world leaders repeatedly call for Assad to step aside, to no avail.[72]

At least publicly, President Obama sends only non-lethal aid to the "moderate Syrian opposition."[73] He openly sends no lethal aid. However, as discussed in Chapter 25, there later will be reports his administration secretly is sending shoulder-fired missiles and other weapons to certain Syrian rebels.[74] Some of these reportedly are transmitted through Libya. According to some reports, they are purchased by the CIA there, and funneled through the CIA's operations in Benghazi.

President Assad (supported by his solid allies Russia and Iran) survives the near world-wide condemnation of his actions in savagely combatting the rebels. This includes his apparent repeated use of chemical weapons against them (thus ignoring President Obama's phony "red line" warning against employing such atrocities).[75] As a result of this civil war, hundreds of thousands of Syrians have perished. The conflict also has displaced millions of Syrians, both within their own country and to other nations whose destabilization is threatened as a result. (The U.S. under Obama will receive substantial numbers of these Syrian refugees.) But Assad will outlast Obama. And as this book

---

[72] E.g., "Remarks of the President to the White House Press Corps," The White House, Obama White House Archives (Aug. 20, 2011); (". . . I have indicated repeatedly that President al-Assad has lost legitimacy, that he needs to step down. . . . The international community has sent a clear message that rather than drag his country into civil war he should move in the direction of a political transition. . . ."); and Fact Sheet, "U.S. Relations with Syria," Bureau of Near Eastern Affairs, State Dept. website (Mar. 20, 2014).

[73] Fact Sheet, "U.S. Relations with Syria," Bureau of Near Eastern Affairs, State Dept. website (Mar. 20, 2014); and CBS/AP, "Obama: Chemical Weapons in Syria Are a "Red Line," CBS News online (Aug. 20, 2012) ("The U.S. has limited its aid so far to humanitarian relief and communications equipment while trying to help the opposition come up with a blueprint for a post-Assad future, which the U.S. says is only a question of time. . . .").

[74] E.g., Schwartz, A Spymaster Steps Out of the Shadows (". . . As the Syria conflict deepened and Obama drew criticism for his indecision, The [New York] Times reported that Brennan's C.I.A. undertook a billion-dollar covert campaign to arm and train rebels fighting against the Syrian leader, Bashar al-Assad. . . .").

[75] "Remarks of the President to the White House Press Corps," The White House, Obama White House Archives (Aug. 20, 2011); and CBS/AP, "Obama: Chemical Weapons in Syria Are a "Red Line," CBS News online (Aug. 20, 2012).

goes to press, Barack is gone, Bashar is still in power, and the Syrian civil war rages on.

The above context is important. But our real story lies in Libya. We turn next to analyze in detail how the Arab Spring plays out there, and how this will come to affect America, its diplomats, and its spies during the future crisis in Benghazi. ■

4

"Bloodbath": The Libyan Civil War

The uprising that will become the Libyan revolution starts on February 15, 2011. It is just four days after Mubarak's resignation in Egypt.[76] Many Libyans fed up by Qadhafi's unfair rule take heart from what they see happening next door in Tunisia. Protests begin in Benghazi in eastern Libya, the country's second largest city. They spread to other Libyan cities and towns.

What begins as nonviolent protests soon escalates into armed conflict. The armed resistance begins in Benghazi, but quickly spreads to other parts of the country. Within days, Qadhafi's security forces are battling armed rebels. At first, the rebels make significant gains in eastern Libya.[77]

The rebellion that seeks to oust Qadhafi is conducted by a number of rebel groups. Many of them coordinate their efforts under a "rebel leadership council" that becomes known as the "National Transitional Council" ("NTC").[78]

Like any tyrant worthy of the name, beginning in early March Qadhafi swiftly moves to put down the revolt with his usual brutality. There are reports his regime is firing on unarmed demonstrators.[79] The rebels make a series of rather spectacular claims (some of which later will prove to be false) regarding the scope of Qadhafi's alleged carnage.[80] (These charges are reminiscent of the Kuwaitis' improbable claims concerning alleged atrocities by Saddam Hussein's forces in

---

[76] Gates, *Duty*, Chap. 13, p. 510.

[77] *Id.*, Chap. 13, p. 510.

[78] Libya Country Profile, BBC News online (Updated Mar. 1, 2017) ("BBC, Libya Country Profile").

[79] Gates, *Duty*, Chap. 13, p. 510; and Rice, *Tough Love*, Chap. 14, p. 279.

[80] Hastings, Inside Obama's War Room ("It is still debatable whether Libyan civilians ever faced a genocidal threat [from Qadhafi]. But . . . the concerns about atrocities by Qaddafi seemed all too real at the time. . . .").

THE TRUE ACCOUNT OF VALOR AND ABANDONMENT

1990-1991 during their invasion of Kuwait in the prelude to Operation Desert Storm.[81]) The Libyan opposition grows.

So does the violence Qadhafi uses against the rebels. In addition to his own soldiers, the strongman relies on help from loyal tribal clans and mercenaries to attempt to put down the rebellion.[82] In contrast, many of the rebel opposition reportedly are disorganized teenagers, without training or combat experience.

Qadhafi tells the media the rebels of eastern Libya are terrorists. He appears on state-wide television and reportedly promises to "march in our millions" to "purify" Libya "inch by inch, house by house, home by home, corner by corner, person by person. Until the country is clean of the dirt and impurities."[83] He threatens to kill "the rats" in Benghazi.[84] It is extreme rhetoric like this that soon will make President Obama more amenable to the argument humanitarian concerns justify U.S. intervention.[85]

Just to avoid things getting boring, during the revolution Qadhafi reportedly releases some 16,000 criminals from Libyan jails and prisons. A year later as the Benghazi tragedy approaches, a majority of them will remain at large.[86]

Because of the revolt and Qadhafi's violent reaction, the United States soon evacuates its new embassy in Tripoli. Embassy operations in Tripoli are suspended on February 25, 2011.[87] The U.S. then imposes

---

[81] E.g., Douglas Walton, "Appeal to Pity: A Case Study of the *Argumentum Ad Misericordiam*" ("A fifteen year-old Kuwaiti girl named Nayirah had a pivotal effect on the U.S. decision to invade Kuwait by testifying to a senate committee (while crying) that Iraqi soldiers had pulled babies out of incubators in a hospital in Kuwait, and left them to die. Subsequent investigations revealed no basis for this claim, and that it was part of a public relations campaign, financed mainly by Kuwaitis, to get support for the invasion").

[82] Burton & Katz, *Under Fire*, Prologue, pp. 9-10; and Libyan Civil War Documentary, PressTV (*Watch video there*; Go to 11:43 - 12:24).

[83] Libyan Civil War Documentary, PressTV (Translation) (*Watch video there*; Go to 10:30-50 and 14:15-28).

[84] Gates, *Duty*, Chap. 13, p. 518.

[85] Hastings, Inside Obama's War Room; and Gates, *Duty*, Chap. 13, p. 518.

[86] "Security Incidents Since June 2011," by Regional Security Office, U.S. Embassy, Tripoli, Libya (Circa July 21, 2012) ("Libya Security Incidents Since June 2011"), p. 51.

[87] Benghazi Committee Report, p. 10; and Report of the Benghazi Accountability Review Board, State Dept. website (Dec. 19, 2012) ("Benghazi ARB Report"), p. 13.

various economic sanctions in response to Qadhafi's repression.[88] On March 16, the United States forces Libya to suspend its embassy operations in Washington, D.C.[89]

Unlike the revolt in neighboring Egypt, there are far fewer international media resources and facilities in eastern Libya. Thus, many in the outside world do not immediately have access to view the brutality of Qadhafi's response to the rebels. This situation will worsen when Qadhafi reportedly takes down the internet in Libya during the rebellion, making it difficult to post amateur video clips of the violence.[90]

By mid-March 2011, Libyan rebel forces already are close to disintegration. Qadhafi's army is nearing the rebel stronghold of Benghazi. Members of regional groups such as the Arab League, as well as the governments of France and Great Britain, demand action in Libya by NATO to stop a bloodbath by Qadhafi's forces.[91]

U.S. President Barack Obama has a momentous decision to make. ∎

---

[88] Executive Order No. 13566 by President Barack H. Obama, "Blocking Property and Prohibiting Certain Transactions Related to Libya," Treasury Dept. website (Feb. 25, 2011).

[89] "A Guide to the United States' History of Recognition, Diplomatic and Consular Relations, by Country, Since 1776: Libya," Office of the Historian, Bureau of Public Affairs, State Dept. website.

[90] Libyan Civil War Documentary, PressTV (*Watch video there*; Go to 12:25-59).

[91] Gates, *Duty*, Chap. 13, p. 517; Rice, *Tough Love*, Chap. 14, pp. 280-281; Edward Klein, *The Amateur* (Regnery Publishing, Inc.; 2012) ("Klein, *The Amateur*"), Chap. 19, pp. 218-219; and Karen Parrish, Press Release, "Gates Outlines U.S. Role as NATO Takes Libya Mission," DoD News, American Forces Press Service, Defense Dept. website (Mar. 31, 2011) ("Gates Outlines U.S. Role as NATO Takes Libya Mission").

5

"The Humanitarian Vulcans"

Beyond the economic sanctions, Barack Obama's foreign policy and national security officials are in sharp disagreement over whether and how to react to Qadhafi's cruel actions.[92]

According to former Defense Secretary Robert Gates and former U.S. Ambassador to the United Nations Susan Rice (and author and reporter Edward Klein), two highly-visible members of Obama's team favor U.S. intervention in Libya on humanitarian grounds. They are Samantha Power (Senior Director for Multilateral Affairs, National Security Council) and Rice herself. They are joined by Deputy NSC Advisor Ben Rhodes. Power will base her justification for military intervention in Libya on a proposed international law doctrine she has advocated previously called "Responsibility to Protect." Gates describes this as ". . . the responsibility of civilized governments to intervene – militarily, if necessary – to prevent the large-scale killing of innocent civilians by their own repressive governments. . . ."[93] Later, when the Libyan rebels begin to collapse, after her initial reluctance to intercede Secretary of State Hillary Clinton forcefully will join Power and Rice. (Edward Klein calls this trio the "Humanitarian Vulcans.") Clinton reportedly urges Obama to commence a bombing campaign against Qadhafi.[94]

---

[92] For a detailed story (from a sometimes dubious publication) of the internal Obama administration debate on Libya, see Hastings, Inside Obama's War Room.

[93] Gates, *Duty*, Chap. 13, pp. 511 and 518; Rice, *Tough Love* ("Libya was an urgent case, I believe, where the risks and costs of intervention to the U.S. were tolerable when weighed against the humanitarian benefits"), Chap. 14, pp. 281-282 and 293; Klein, *The Amateur*, Chap. 19, pp. 216-218; Mark Landler, "Rice to Replace Donilon in the Top National Security Post," *The New York Times* online (June 5, 2013) (". . . Ms. Rice is known for her outspoken views on human rights and other issues. She advocated the NATO-led military intervention in Libya . . ."); and interview of Professor Glenn Reynolds, Univ. of Tenn. Law School, with Tucker Carlson, "Tucker Carlson Tonight," Fox News Channel (Dec. 1, 2017).

[94] Gates, *Duty*, Chap. 13, p. 511; Klein, *The Amateur*, Chap. 19, pp. 213, 218-219 and 222; and Interview of Professor Glenn Reynolds, Univ. of Tennessee Law School, with Tucker Carlson, "Tucker Carlson Tonight," Fox News Channel (Dec. 1, 2017). See also Robert G. Kaufman, "What's a Reagan Internationalist to Do?" *The Wall Street*

(In supporting regime change in Libya, Hillary Clinton reportedly relies upon the advice of long-time Clinton family confidant Sidney Blumenthal. Clinton wants to hire Blumenthal at the State Department, but Blumenthal's reputation is so dodgy President Obama forbids it. However, Clinton quietly continues using Blumenthal as an outside, informal adviser. Oh, by the way, Blumenthal reportedly has business interests in Libya. Although he gives Clinton bad advice on removing Qadhafi, in fairness he reportedly later accurately warns her trouble is brewing in Benghazi. This time, she will ignore his advice.[95] Clinton is "0 for 2.")

Others in the administration counsel against starting a third war in the region. This group reportedly includes Vice President Joe Biden (who always and everywhere has opposed military intervention), National Security Advisor Tom Donilon and his deputy Denis McDonough, Defense Secretary Robert Gates, Joint Chiefs Chairman Admiral Mike Mullen, counterterrorism advisor John Brennan, and then White House Chief of Staff Bill Daley. Still others support a middle ground approach of simply providing arms to the rebels, but taking no further steps to intervene.[96]

Journal online (Sept. 14, 2016) ("As secretary of state, Mrs. Clinton bears heavy responsibility for the debacle in Libya. She was the administration's leading proponent for American intervention under the auspices of the United Nations, NATO, and the Arab League, bypassing the Congress. . . ."); Hemingway, 5 Big Takeaways From the House Benghazi Report (". . . Hillary Clinton's signature policy achievement was her push to invade Libya, so the political ramifications were serious for her as well. As her Deputy Chief of Staff and Director of Policy Jacob Sullivan characterized it in 2011, Clinton had 'leadership/ownership/ stewardship of this country's Libya policy from start to finish'. . . ."); and Editorial, "Military Support Offered in Benghazi – Why Would White House Say No?" Investor's Business Daily online (Dec. 10, 2015) (". . . It was Secretary of State Clinton's war, so she owns Libya and every disaster related to it"). See also Hastings, Inside Obama's War Room.

[95] Gregory Hicks, "What the Benghazi Attack Taught Me About Hillary Clinton," Fox News Opinion online (Sept. 11, 2016) ("Hicks, What the Benghazi Attack Taught Me About Hillary Clinton") (". . . Despite the fact that Sydney Blumenthal had alerted her to the increasing danger for Americans in Benghazi and Libya, Mrs. Clinton apparently never asked security professionals for an updated briefing on the situation in Libya. Either she could not correlate the increased tempo of attacks in Libya with the safety of our diplomats, demonstrating fatal incompetence, or she was grossly negligent").

[96] Gates, *Duty*, Chap. 13, pp. 511 and 518; *Id.* (". . . I was adamantly opposed to intervening in Libya . . . I was blunt and stubborn, but I wasn't insubordinate") Chap. 13, p. 512; Rice, *Tough Love*, Chap. 14, p. 281; Klein, *The Amateur*, Chap. 19, pp. 213 and 219; and Hastings, Inside Obama's War Room.

THE TRUE ACCOUNT OF VALOR AND ABANDONMENT

It is important to understand in March 2011 *Libya poses no threat to any of America's vital strategic interests.*[97] Qadhafi has ceased developing weapons of mass destruction and ballistic missiles. In fact, he reportedly has turned all components for them over to the United States. As far as the U.S. can tell, he has stopped supporting terrorism. (However, as noted, there was a troubling report back in 2004 Qadhafi may have conspired with others to assassinate Crown Prince Abdullah, the leader of the Saudi Arabian government.[98])

Qadhafi is exporting oil to Europe and the West, and is not threatening to stop these sales. Unlike Bahrain (home to the U.S. Fifth Fleet), the U.S. has no military bases in Libya. Qadhafi's small navy is not committing or threatening piracy or other hostile acts in the Mediterranean Sea, nor even in the Gulf of Sidra off the Libyan coast.

Moreover, unlike Syria, Libya has no close alliances with any of America's key adversaries, such as Iran, Russia, China and North Korea. (Qadhafi previously has purchased copious amounts of equipment from all of these nations for his weapons of mass destruction programs.[99] However, these likely are purely commercial transactions born of expediency, and not rooted in any solid geopolitical alliances.)

(Qadhafi is such a danger to Western Civilization that at parties he and his family host in 2007 through 2010 he reportedly pays $1 million each to celebrities such as Beyonce, Mariah Carey and Nellie Fertado

---

[97] Gates, *Duty* ("I believed that what was happening in Libya was not a vital national interest of the United States. . . ."), Chap. 13, p. 511; Interview of Defense Secretary Robert Gates with Jake Tapper, "This Week," ABC News (Mar. 28, 2011) (Question by Jake Tapper: "Do you think Libya posed an actual or imminent threat to the United States?" Secretary Gates: "No, no. It was not a vital national interest for the United States, but it was an interest . . .") (*Watch video there*; Go to 0:04-53); Hastings, Inside Obama's War Room (Defense Secretary Gates "offered a last-ditch case against [U.S.] intervention, arguing that Libya had little strategic value. . . ."); Ryan Lizza, "The Consequentialist: How the Arab Spring Remade Obama's Foreign Policy," *The New Yorker* Magazine online (May 2, 2011) ("Lizza, The Consequentialist") (Brent Scowcroft, former National Security Advisor to Presidents Gerald Ford and George H.W. Bush, to Lizza: ". . . Of all the countries in the region there [apparently the Middle East and North Africa], our real interests in Libya are minimal"); and Klein, *The Amateur* ("In Libya, Obama plunged the United States into a long and costly military campaign that had little strategic value and less public support"), Chap. 19, p. 213.

[98] Gertz, *Treachery*, Chap. 7, p. 146.

[99] *Id.*, Chap. 7, pp. 139-160.

to sing.[100] Conservative author, columnist and radio talk show guest host Mark Steyn jokes if Qadhafi instead had given this money to the Clinton Family Foundation or to Bill Clinton to give a speech on diarrhea in Africa, he still would be alive today.[101])

Some in the Obama administration theorize if Qadhafi continues killing his own people, some of them may flee to other countries (particularly Egypt) and destabilize those nations.[102] The supreme irony will be "destabilization" comes only when the Obama administration helps to overthrow the existing leaders in Libya and Egypt during the euphoric early weeks of the "Arab Spring"! Team Obama will cause the very thing they say they are trying to prevent.

The reality in 2011 is that, geopolitically speaking, Libya is a "nothing-burger." Hence, the only case for attacking and removing Qadhafi is humanitarian: he is a bastard to his people, some of them have revolted, and many of them are dying at the hands of Qadhafi's vicious army and security forces.[103] When Obama eventually unleashes

---

[100] Scott Shane, "WikiLeaks Cables Detail Qaddafi Family's Exploits," *The New York Times* online (Feb. 22, 2011); and Wolf Blitzer, "The Situation Room," CNN (possibly April 12, 2011).

[101] Guest Host Mark Steyn on "The Rush Limbaugh Show" (Sept. 16, 2016).

[102] E.g., Gates Outlines U.S. Role as NATO Takes Libya Mission (summarizing congressional testimony of Defense Secretary Robert Gates: "The secretary said Libya's possible destabilizing effect in the Middle East represents a strong national interest for the United States. . . . Gadhafi's use of force against the Libyan people created the prospect of significant civilian casualties and hundreds of thousands of refugees fleeing to Egypt, Gates said, potentially destabilizing that country in the midst of its own difficult transition." Secretary Gates: "It continues to be in our national interest to prevent Gadhafi from visiting further depredations on his own people, destabilizing his neighbors, and setting back the progress the people of the Middle East have made in recent weeks").

[103] Remarks of President Obama Brasilia Address on Libyan Civil War (Mar. 19, 2011), Obama White House Archives ("Obama Brasilia Remarks on Libya") (". . . [W]e cannot stand idly by when a tyrant tells his people that there will be no mercy, and his forces step up their assaults on cities like Benghazi and Misurata, where innocent men and women face brutality and death at the hands of their own government"); Gates Outlines U.S. Role as NATO Takes Libya Mission (quoting congressional testimony of Defense Secretary Robert Gates: "In the case of Libya, our government, our allies, and our partners in the region, watched with alarm as the regime of Moammar Gadhafi responded to legitimate protests with brutal suppression and a military campaign against his own people"); United Nations Security Council Resolution No. 1970 (2011), Adopted by the Security Council at Its 6491st Meeting, United Nations website (Feb. 26, 2011); and United Nations Security Council Resolution No. 1973 (2011), Adopted by the Security Council at Its 6498th Meeting, United Nations website (Mar. 17, 2011).

THE TRUE ACCOUNT OF VALOR AND ABANDONMENT

the "Dogs of War" in Libya, he will insist he is "acting in the interests of the United States *and the world.*" Despite this, the American people do not appear to be hankering for a war in Libya.[104]

In his memoir *Duty*, Defense Secretary Gates writes:
> I reminded my colleagues that when you start a war, you never know how it will go. The advocates of military action expected a short, easy fight. How many times in history had that naïve assumption proven wrong? In meetings, I would ask, "Can I just finish the two wars we're already in before you go looking for new ones?"[105]

Sadly, Gates also will explain:
> ...I had tried to raise all the issues for which the administration was being criticized – an open-ended conflict, an ill-defined mission, Qaddafi's fate, and what came after him – but the president *"had not been interested* in getting into any of that."[106]

(*Not interested?*)

Predictably, many of the same Democrats and analysts who think in hindsight it was a horrible mistake for George W. Bush to remove Saddam Hussein in Iraq now believe it is a swell idea for Barack Obama to topple Qadhafi in Libya.[107] Soon they will get their wish. ■

---

[104] Obama Brasilia Remarks on Libya (emphasis added); and Chris Stirewalt, "Five Target Audiences for Obama's War Speech," Fox News online (Mar. 28, 2011) ("Whether it is a result of Obama's low profile in defending the war or just general war fatigue among the American people, Gallup found initial public support for the conflict was lower than any U.S. military intervention of the past 20 years. Since the U.S. entered the war, Obama has also seen his own job approval rating dip").

[105] Gates, *Duty*, Chap. 13, pp. 511-512.

[106] *Id.* (emphasis added), Chap. 13, p. 521.

[107] See, e.g., Chris Stirewalt, "Five Target Audiences for Obama's War Speech," Fox News online (Mar. 28, 2011) ("... Obama can be comforted to know that he has the backing of his party's leaders on the Libyan war. ... In Libya, Obama has engaged in a preemptive strike on a foreign country that posed no immediate threat to the U.S. and done so without the blessing of Congress – all things that liberals and Obama accused George W. Bush of doing in Iraq").

6

Barack's "Grand Libyan Adventure"

By mid-March 2011, various world leaders are calling for Qadhafi to go. But in typical fashion, President Obama dithers.[108] (However, in comparison with some of his other decisions, such as whether to authorize a military "surge" in Afghanistan and what to do about the Syrian civil war, his Libyan decision seems downright decisive.) Ultimately, in what he describes as a "close call," a reluctant Obama sides with Secretary of State Hillary Clinton and against his Defense Secretary, Robert Gates.[109] Obama executes an "about face" on U.S. policy towards Qadhafi.[110] Obama, too, says Qadhafi has "lost legitimacy" and it is time for him to leave.[111]

President Obama has decided to authorize the Pentagon to use American military force to prevent Qadhafi from killing those revolting against him – but not "significant" military force. However, Obama splits the baby in half. He determines to endorse a NATO air war

---

[108] Hastings, Inside Obama's War Room (". . . [O]nce those [Arab Spring] governments actually began to fall, the Obama administration was slow to distance itself from the oil-rich autocrats the U.S. had supported for decades"); and Lizza, The Consequentialist (". . . Obama's instinct was to try to have it both ways. . . . Obama's ultimate position, it seemed, was to talk like an idealist while acting like a realist. . . . The days leading up to Obama's decision [to intervene militarily in Libya] were perplexing to outsiders. . . . Obama seemed to stay hidden that week. . . .").

[109] Gates, *Duty* (In a private side conversation with Gates after the key decision meeting, ". . . [T]he president said the Libyan military operation had been a 51-49 call for him"), Chap. 13, p. 518; and Lizza, The Consequentialist (". . . In Libya, he [Obama] overruled Gates and his military advisers and pushed our allies to adopt a broad and risky intervention. . . .").

[110] McCarthy, Hillary Clinton's Benghazi Debacle: Arming Jihadists in Libya . . . And Syria (". . . Secretary Clinton led the policy shift in which our government changed sides in Libya – shifting support to the Muslim Brotherhood and its allies, just as Mrs. Clinton had urged shifting U.S. support to the Muslim Brotherhood in Egypt. In Libya, this included arming 'rebels,' who naturally included a heavy concentration of jihadists").

[111] "Remarks by the President in Address to the Nation on Libya," National Defense University, Washington, D.C., Obama White House Archives (Mar. 28, 2011) (". . . [T]here is no question that Libya – and the world – would be better off with Qaddafi out of power. . . ."); and Baier, New Revelations on Attack in Benghazi (*Watch video there*; Go to 2:35-45).

against Qadhafi, but only if it is done under the auspices of the United Nations ("U.N.").[112] (*Pssst! Barry! What about Congress? Aren't they supposed to have a say in this type of activity?*) It is a classic example of Barack Obama's strong preference for action by international bodies, instead of acts pursued in the name of American sovereignty.[113]

(Defense Secretary Gates later discloses he considers resigning over Obama's Libya decision. But he does not. When a president orders his Defense Secretary to wage an obviously unconstitutional war, it is the Secretary's duty to refuse and to resign in protest. In his memoir, Gates attempts to justify his decision by claiming he is planning to leave office soon anyway.[114] Sorry, that is a pitifully inadequate excuse.)

The U.N. Security Council obliges Obama. Earlier on February 26, 2011, the Security Council already had passed Security Resolution No. 1970. Resolution 1970 imposes an immediate arms embargo against Libya, an asset freeze against Qadhafi and his family, and a travel ban against the Qadhafi family and specified other Libyans.[115]

Robert Gates writes:

> The situation in Libya forced everyone's hand. Qaddafi's forces began to have some military success and pushed east. By March 14, there was real danger they could soon move on

---

[112] Obama Brasilia Remarks on Libya (emphasis added) ("Today *I authorized* the Armed Forces of the United States to begin a *limited military action* in Libya in support of an international effort to protect Libyan civilians. That action has now begun"); and Gates, *Duty* (". . . [I]t was clear that the president was not going to act alone or without international sanction. He wanted any military operations to be under NATO auspices"), Chap. 13, p. 515.

[113] Obama Brasilia Remarks on Libya (emphasis added) ("So we must be clear: Actions have consequences, and *the writ of the international community must be enforced*. That is the cause of this coalition [to intervene in the Libyan civil war] . . . I'm also proud that we are acting as part of a coalition that includes close allies and partners who are prepared to meet their responsibility to protect the people of Libya and uphold *the mandate of the international community*"). See also Charles Krauthammer, "Barack Obama's Stillborn Legacy: At Home and Abroad, the President's Agenda Is In Tatters," New York Daily News online (Oct. 6, 2016) ("The President's vision was to move away from a world where stability and the 'the success of liberty' (JFK, inaugural address) were anchored by American power and move toward a world ruled by universal norms, mutual obligation, international law and multilateral institutions. No more . . . unilateralism . . .").

[114] Gates, *Duty*, Chap. 13, p. 521.

[115] United Nations Security Council Resolution No. 1970 (2011), Adopted by the Security Council at Its 6491st Meeting, United Nations website (Feb. 26, 2011); NATO "Statement on Libya," NATO website (April 14, 2011); and NATO "Statement on Libya," NATO website (June 8, 2011).

Benghazi, and few doubted that the city's capture would lead to a bloodbath. . . .[116]

In her memoir, *Tough Love*, Ambassador Rice quotes from remarks she delivered to the U.N. Security Council in mid-March, 2011, in attempting to gain support for broad military action against Qadhafi. She bluntly tells the Council:

> . . . We will not support a simple no-fly zone, which will do nothing to stop the forces massing on the ground heading for Benghazi. With the *robust mandate* we seek, *we will take out Libyan air defenses, their heavy weapons – like tanks, artillery, and aircraft – and halt advancing columns of soldiers*. This would need to be an *unfettered mandate* to protect civilians, and I don't want any ambiguity about what we intend to do with it. This will be an *air war* to save innocent lives. The U.S. is prepared to join *militarily* with like-minded countries in a coalition to enforce the resolution to save innocents. . . .[117]

An "air war." It doesn't get much clearer than that.

On March 17, 2011, the Security Council passes Resolution 1973. This authorizes "all necessary measures" – thereby including military action – to protect Libyan civilians and civilian populated areas under attack or threat of attack. Resolution 1973 also calls for a "No-Fly Zone." It expands both the asset freeze and travel ban previously imposed by Resolution 1970. Finally, 1973 expressly forbids any "foreign occupation force" in Libya, effectively barring the use of ground troops.[118] This will help President Obama avoid what he considers a major foreign policy blunder by George W. Bush in Iraq.

---

[116] Gates, *Duty*, Chap. 13, p. 517.

[117] Rice, *Tough Love* (emphasis added), Chap. 14, p. 283.

[118] United Nations Security Council Resolution No. 1973 (2011), Adopted by the Security Council at Its 6498th Meeting, United Nations website (Mar. 17, 2011), pp. 3-4, ¶¶4-12; "Checklist of Resolutions Adopted by the Security Council from August 1, 2010 to July 31, 2011," United Nations website, pp. 390-398 and 408; NATO Fact Sheet, "Operation Unified Protector: Protection of Civilians and Civilian-Populated Areas," NATO website (June 2011) ("NATO June 2011 Fact Sheet"); and Gates Outlines U.S. Role as NATO Takes Libya Mission ("There will be no American boots on the ground in Libya," quoting congressional testimony of Defense Secretary Robert Gates).

THE TRUE ACCOUNT OF VALOR AND ABANDONMENT

The United States votes for this resolution, thereby officially waging war on Qadhafi. This U.N. resolution will form the basis for NATO's subsequent intervention in Libya.[119]

Nominally, the Security Council merely has voted to act to protect civilians. In reality, the Council's action will prove a death sentence for Mu'ammar Gadhafi. *The New Yorker's* Ryan Lizza describes the vote as "... the first time in its sixty-six years that the United Nations authorized military action to preempt an 'imminent massacre.'"[120]

This war may be "official," but is it *constitutional?* President Obama is acting under the auspices of a resolution adopted by the United Nations Security Council. But he fails to ask the United States Congress for authorization to use military force in Libya in this act of war, as required by the inconvenient U.S. Constitution.[121] The Constitution does not authorize the U.N. Security Council to empower a U.S. president to employ military force. Obama claims to have consulted Democrat and Republican leaders in Congress,[122] but under the Constitution that's not enough. (Details, details.)

Indeed, just a few years earlier in December 2007, then-candidate Barack Obama himself previously had taken a different position:

> The President does not have the power under the Constitution to unilaterally authorize a military attack in a situation that

---

[119] "Checklist of Resolutions Adopted by the Security Council from August 1, 2010 to July 31, 2011," United Nations website, p. 395; and Jim Garamone, Press Release, "NATO Assumes Command of Libya Operations," DoD News, American Forces Press Service, Defense Dept. website (Mar. 31, 2011) ("The operations [of NATO in Libya] are taking place under the auspices of the United Nations Security Council Resolution 1973. . . . Alliance officials stressed that the alliance will adhere strictly to the mission delineated by the U.N. resolution"); and NATO "Statement on Libya," NATO website (June 8, 2011).

[120] Lizza, The Consequentialist.

[121] See, e.g., Victor Davis Hanson, "The Next President Unbound," Townhall.com website (Sept. 28, 2016) ("If a President [Hillary] Clinton decides to strike North Korea, would she really need congressional authorization, considering Obama's unauthorized Libyan bombing mission?"); and Hastings, Inside Obama's War Room ("In his effort to forge a new, more multilateral model for intervention, . . . the White House had done little to line up the one U.S. body that is actually vested with the constitutional authority to authorize a war: Congress").

[122] Terence P. Jeffrey, "FLASHBACK – Obama: 'I Authorized' Intervention in Libyan Civil War Because 'Writ of International Community Must [Be] Enforced,'" CNSNews.com (Oct. 21, 2012), citing Louis Fisher, former constitutional scholar at the Library of Congress; and Obama Brasilia Remarks on Libya.

does not involve stopping an actual or imminent threat to the nation.[123]

In addition to the Constitution, on Libya the Obama administration also ignores the War Powers Act. This statute requires a president to obtain congressional approval within 90 days for any military action.[124] The Obama White House claims this act does not apply because, well, Barack's Grand Libyan Adventure really isn't military action at all! Supposedly, this is because "U.S. operations do not involve sustained fighting or active exchanges of fire with hostile forces, nor do they involve U.S. ground troops."[125] (Really?) However, at least Obama does "notify" Congress before the bombs fall.[126]

Obama has decided this Libyan engagement does not constitute "hostilities" as defined in the War Powers Act. Thus, he believes he can continue his Libyan Adventure indefinitely, without any congressional authorization. This is despite the fact the Justice Department and the Defense Department's General Counsel advise him the War Powers Act *does* apply. (Obama instead relies upon the contrary legal advice of his White House counsel and the State Department's legal adviser.)[127]

(Let's just take a step back and analyze Obama's constitutional and statutory arguments for a few moments. Someone is about to beat the living crap out of the Qadhafi regime that runs Libya. At an absolute minimum, that "someone" appears to be NATO and some of its member nations. The U.S. is (by far) the most powerful nation in NATO, and (by far) its biggest financial contributor. America is planning to lend considerable help to NATO in this military endeavor, even if we are not ourselves doing much of the "heavy lifting." Isn't the

---

[123] Gates, *Duty*, Chap. 13, p. 520; and Charlie Savage, "Barack Obama's Q&A," *The Boston Globe* online (Dec. 20, 2007), cited in Interview of Defense Secretary Robert Gates with Jake Tapper, "This Week," ABC News (Mar. 28, 2011) (*Watch video there*; Go to 1:49 - 2:12).

[124] Title 50, United States Code, Sections 1541-1548.

[125] Charlie Savage and Mark Landler, "White House Defends Continuing U.S. Role in Libya Operation," *The New York Times* online (June 15, 2011); and McCarthy, Hillary Clinton's Benghazi Debacle: Arming Jihadists in Libya . . . And Syria (". . . [T]he Obama administration . . . preposterously maintained that bombing another country's government was not really 'war' anyway . . ."). See also Obama Brasilia Remarks on Libya (". . . [W]e will not deploy any U.S. troops on the ground"). See also Obama Brasilia Remarks on Libya (emphasis added) ("Today *I authorized* the Armed Forces of the United States to begin a *limited military action* in Libya . . .").

[126] Gates, *Duty*, Chap. 13, p. 519.

[127] *Id.*, Chap. 13, p. 520.

THE TRUE ACCOUNT OF VALOR AND ABANDONMENT

U.S. at a minimum, well, agreeing or "conspiring" with NATO and the U.N. Security Council and Great Britain and France and others to wage war against Libya? Isn't the U.S. "aiding and abetting" NATO's war against Libya? And isn't that the same as joining a war against Libya?)

Some resolutions authorizing the war in Libya are introduced in Congress. They do not become law. In June 2011, the feeble, now Republican-controlled House of Representatives adopts a toothless resolution whining about the Obama's actions.[128] It is purely symbolic.

By whatever name, and with nary a peep from Congress, the people of the United States of America are now at war with the nation of Libya. And Barack Obama has thrown George Bush's earlier understanding with Mu'ammar Qadhafi into the trash can of history.[129] In so doing, Obama has raised a cosmic question: Why should any foreign leader (say, the head of North Korea) ever again trust an agreement to disarm reached with an American president?[130] ∎

---

[128] E.g., Press Release, "Kerry, McCain Introduce Libya Resolution," Senate Foreign Relations Committee website (June 21, 2011); and "H.Res. 292 – Declaring that the President Shall Not Deploy, Establish, or Maintain the Presence of Units and members of the United States Armed Forces on the Ground in Libya, and for Other Purposes," House of Representatives website (June 3, 2011); and "Speaker Boehner Unveils Resolution on Libya," House of Representatives website (June 2, 2011). See also "Speaker Boehner Floor Statement on Libya Resolution," House of Representatives website (June 24, 2011).

[129] Interview of Professor Glenn Reynolds, Univ. of Tennessee Law School, with Tucker Carlson, "Tucker Carlson Tonight," Fox News Channel (Dec. 1, 2017) ("We didn't keep that promise [Bush 43 made to Qadhafi]").

[130] Interview of Rep. Ron DeSantis (R-FL) with Mark Levin, "Life, Liberty & Levin," Fox News Channel (June 10, 2018) (emphasis in original) ("One of the problems that we are going to face is . . . Qadhafi was worried that having a nuclear program made his regime *less* stable because they saw that the United States was serious about weapons of mass destruction, so that he gave up his program. Obama comes in six, seven years later and he helps take the guy out, so that sends a signal to people like Kim Jung Un, 'Well, gee, why would I want to do a deal with the United States if they're going to end up just pulling the rug out from under me later? That's why Trump has said, 'Look, we will do protection.' Because I think Obama's policy there really did damage to our de-nuclearization efforts. Not just with North Korea, but with other countries"); and Interview of Professor Glenn Reynolds, Univ. of Tennessee Law School, with Tucker Carlson, "Tucker Carlson Tonight," Fox News Channel (Dec. 1, 2017) (Tucker Carlson's question: ". . . But I wonder what effect it has on the countries in the region and around the world. I mean, next time we go to a leader or strongman somewhere and say 'Look, disarm and we'll reward you,' why would anybody ever follow those instructions again?"; Answer by Prof. Reynolds: "Oh, we're ruined for a generation with this. I mean, right now we'd like Kim Jong Un [leader of North Korea] to give up his nukes, and he probably wouldn't anyway, but we certainly can't make him any promises he'd believe because who *would?*") (emphasis in original response).

29

7

"We Came, We Saw, He Died!"

NATO's mission in Libya begins on March 18, 2011. It is called "Operation Unified Protector."
Not all NATO members are enthusiastic about Barack's Grand Libyan Adventure. Despite this, all 28 NATO members eventually vote to support this military mission. However, only half will provide "some kind of contribution." According to Robert Gates, "only eight actually provided aircraft for the strike mission."[131]

On March 19, President Obama officially authorizes the Pentagon to conduct war against Libya.[132] The air campaign against Qadhafi begins this same day. According to Defense Secretary Gates, this air campaign is supposed to be a "highly coordinated operation." (However, desiring "a little extra publicity," French President Sarkozy sends his planes in "several hours" before the agreed kick-off time!)[133]

Nominally, this U.S. air war is commanded by U.S. Africa Command. However, AFRICOM has few personnel, and never was intended to carry out major combat missions such as this air campaign against Libya. According to U.S. Air Force Major Jason Greenleaf:

> Instead, AFRICOM had to rely heavily on European Command's personnel, facilities, and expertise to execute the mission successfully. . . . AFRICOM struggled to put together a last-minute air campaign.[134]

NATO's campaign has several military objectives: To assault Qadhafi's military, thus ending attacks and threat of attacks against civilians; to force withdrawal of all regime forces to their bases; to enforce a "No-Fly Zone"; to promote the arms embargo by precluding

---

[131] Gates, *Duty*, Chap. 13, p. 522.

[132] Obama Brasilia Remarks on Libya.

[133] Gates, *Duty*, Chap. 13, p. 518.

[134] Maj. Jason R. Greenleaf, USAF, "The Air War in Libya," Air & Space Power Journal (March-April 2013) ("Greenleaf, 'The Air War in Libya'").

THE TRUE ACCOUNT OF VALOR AND ABANDONMENT

shipments of arms by air and sea; and to assist immediate humanitarian aid in reaching Libyan civilians.[135]

Another objective – removing Qadhafi from power – is less explicit, but obvious.[136] And like NATO, Barack Obama denies regime change is an American military goal in Libya, although manifestly it is.[137]

The arms embargo phase of Operation Unified Protector begins quickly. By March 23, NATO aircraft and warships are patrolling the approaches to Libyan territorial waters. Their goal is to reduce the supply of mercenaries, arms and ammunition into Libya. (By the end of May, this operation will involve nearly twenty submarines and other warships.) These NATO ships also clear mines planted in harbors by pro-Qadhafi forces, aiding delivery of humanitarian aid by sea. They are supported by NATO fighter jets and maritime patrol aircraft.[138]

The first wave of U.S. attacks (including submarine-launched cruise missiles) destroys the Libyan air defense system.[139] Also, the "No-Fly Zone" quickly closes Libyan airspace to all non-NATO flights except humanitarian ones. This effectively grounds Qadhafi's air force, precluding it from further attacks against civilians (including rebels).[140]

---

[135] "In Berlin, NATO Allies and Partners Show Unity and Resolve on All Fronts," NATO website (April 14, 2011; Updated Aug. 2, 2016). See also NATO "Statement on Libya," NATO website (April 14, 2011); NATO "Statement on Libya," NATO website (June 8, 2011); and "NATO and Partners Will Stay the Course on Libya," NATO website (June 8, 2011).

[136] NATO "Statement on Libya," NATO website (April 14, 2011) ("Qadhafi and his regime have lost all legitimacy through their comprehensive and repeated refusal to abide by UNSC Resolutions 1970 and 1973"); and NATO "Statement on Libya," NATO website (June 8, 2011) ("Time is working against Qadhafi who has clearly lost all legitimacy and therefore needs to step down. There is no future for a regime that has systematically threatened and attacked its own population. . . .").

[137] "Remarks by the President in Address to the Nation on Libya," National Defense University, Washington, D.C., Obama White House Archives (Mar. 28, 2011) (". . . [T]here is no question that Libya – and the world – would be better off with Qaddafi out of power. I, along with many other world leaders, have embraced that goal, and will actively pursue it through non-military means. But broadening our military mission to include regime change would be a mistake"). See also Gates Outlines U.S. Role as NATO Takes Libya Mission (summarizing congressional testimony of Defense Secretary: "Gates stressed that coalition military operations in Libya are not aimed at ending the regime of Moammar Gadhafi"); and Gates, *Duty*, Chap. 13, p. 520.

[138] NATO June 2011 Fact Sheet.

[139] Greenleaf, "The Air War in Libya," pp. 42 and 45-46.

[140] *Id.*

America calls its own (limited) piece of this NATO mission "Operation Odyssey Dawn." For the U.S., Odyssey Dawn begins on March 19, when the first NATO airstrikes occur. This operation is a U.S. Africa Command task force providing "operational and tactical command and control of U.S. military forces" supporting the anti-Qadhafi coalition.[141] According to the Pentagon, "During the first phase of Operation Odyssey Dawn, U.S. forces provided the bulk of military assets and firepower, logistical support and overall command and control. . . .").[142] According to Robert Gates, the U.S. initially commits 19 ships and 18,000 troops to the Libyan operation.[143]

Despite its imposing "Operation Odyssey Dawn" moniker, this U.S. lead in Libya is a short-term affair. Ever since NATO's founding, the United States has been its lynchpin. Despite this, President Obama determines the U.S. itself will not contribute substantial airpower to the NATO campaign.[144] Defense Secretary Gates tells Congress at the end of March that, as NATO picks up the baton, U.S. forces will "significantly ramp down" the American commitment to Operation Unified Protector.[145] Indeed, the Defense Secretary downplays the entire U.S. military campaign to such an extent he describes it blithely as a "limited kinetic operation."[146] (Not so limited if you are Mu'ammar Qadhafi or one of his pilots.[147] And seriously, have you ever heard a war called this before?)

---

[141] "Operation Odyssey Dawn," Defense Dept. website (caption in photograph).

[142] Gates Outlines U.S. Role as NATO Takes Libya Mission (summarizing congressional testimony of Defense Secretary Robert Gates).

[143] Gates, *Duty*, Chap. 13, p. 521.

[144] E.g., Obama Brasilia Remarks on Libya (emphasis added) (". . . [T]he United States will contribute our unique capabilities at the front end of the mission to protect Libyan civilians, and enable the enforcement of a no-fly zone that will be *led by our international partners*. . . .").

[145] Gates Outlines U.S. Role as NATO Takes Libya Mission. See also Gates, *Duty*, Chap. 13, p. 520.

[146] "Gates Defends Libya Action Minus Congressional OK," Fox News online (June 19, 2011) ("Gates Defends Libya Action Minus Congressional OK"). See also Hastings, Inside Obama's War Room.

[147] Gates Defends Libya Action Minus Congressional OK (Secretary of Defense Robert Gates: ". . . [F]rom our standpoint at the Pentagon, we're involved in a limited kinetic operation. If I'm in [Libyan dictator Muammar al-Qaddafi's] palace, I suspect I think I'm at war").

THE TRUE ACCOUNT OF VALOR AND ABANDONMENT

In what will become a famous but unfortunate phrase, one anonymous Obama aide describes America's approach in Libya as "Leading from Behind." (As Libya later will continue to unravel, some say it is more like "Bleeding from Behind.") Team Obama prefers to call it "Burden Sharing," and rejects the "Leading from Behind" label.[148] Regardless, the unflattering "Leading from Behind" moniker sticks. For some, it becomes a metaphor for the Obama administration's entire foreign policy.[149]

By March 31, NATO assumes command of the entire military air campaign against Qadhafi. NATO takes this "hand off" from U.S. Africa Command.[150] The U.S. moves to the "back seat" in Libya.

From now on, instead of the U.S., aircraft and pilots of France, the United Kingdom, Italy and (to a lesser extent) Spain will do the heavy lifting in the skies above Libya. Canada also participates. Two non-NATO Muslim nations also will join in the coalition, Qatar and the United Arab Emirates.[151] Eventually, fourteen nations will take part in the coalition with NATO.[152]

(America's NATO allies may lead the fighting, but President Obama later brags he takes the lead in "organizing" the fight. In a

---

[148] Baier, New Revelations on Attack in Benghazi (*Watch video there*; Go to 2:45 - 3:20); and Hastings, Inside Obama's War Room (quoting Anne-Marie Slaughter, former head of Policy Planning at the State Department: "It isn't leading from behind. . . . We created the conditions for others to step up. That exemplifies Obama's leadership at its best. The world is not going to get there without us – and we did it in a way where we're not stuck, or bearing all the costs").

[149] E.g., Lizza, The Consequentialist (". . . Obama may be moving toward something resembling a doctrine. One of his advisers described the President's actions in Libya as 'leading from behind.' . . . [I]t does accurately describe the balance that Obama now seems to be finding. . . ."); and Victor Davis Hanson, "Trump Seeks Middle Ground in Foreign-Policy Balancing Act," Townhall.com website (April 19, 2018) ("We know that tough talk alone does not necessarily convince North Korea, China and Iran to abandon their past strategies of aggression, which were often honed during the Obama administration's 'lead from behind' recessionals").

[150] Jim Garamone, Press Release, "NATO Assumes Command of Libya Operations," DoD News, American Forces Press Service, Defense Dept. website (Mar. 31, 2011); and "Ministers Determined to Pursue Operation in Libya As Long As Threats Persist," NATO website (Oct. 6, 2011); and Greenleaf, "The Air War in Libya," p. 30.

[151] Jim Garamone, Press Release, "NATO Assumes Command of Libya Operations," DoD News, American Forces Press Service, Defense Dept. website (Mar. 31, 2011).

[152] "Operation Odyssey Dawn," Defense Dept. website; and Greenleaf, "The Air War in Libya" (". . . [O]nly six European countries delivered any offensive capability. . . ." They are France, the U.K., Italy, Spain, Sweden and Denmark), pp. 37-38.

presidential debate in October 2012, Obama claims he and America "took leadership in organizing an international coalition" that "liberates" Libya.¹⁵³)

In its air campaign over Libya, NATO will employ jet fighter aircraft, surveillance and reconnaissance aircraft, air-to-air refueling tankers, armed drones (unmanned) and attack helicopters.¹⁵⁴ Over the next weeks, NATO pilots strike numerous targets in Libya. These include: surface-to-air missile systems; surface-to-surface missile launchers; multiple rocket launchers; radar and anti-aircraft sites; artillery tanks and armored personnel carriers; "technicals" and other heavy military equipment vehicles; military storage facilities; and command and control facilities in Tripoli.¹⁵⁵

As part of its now restricted role, the U.S. military operates missile-armed drones in Libya during NATO's campaign against Qadhafi's troops.¹⁵⁶ In addition, U.S. submarines and destroyers in the Mediterranean fire cruise missiles against Qadhafi's forces.¹⁵⁷ (But the U.S. is not engaged in "military action.") The U.S. provides overhead surveillance data and other intelligence to NATO pilots and the rebels. The U.S. also undertakes aerial refueling and "search and rescue" for NATO warplanes.¹⁵⁸ One official explains the U.S. is using "satellites,

---

¹⁵³ Transcript of Presidential Debate Between President Barack Obama and Former Governor Mitt Romney (Oct. 22, 2012), CBS News website (". . . [I]t's important to step back and think about what happened in Libya. Keep in mind that I and Americans took leadership in organizing an international coalition that made sure that we were able to, without putting troops on the ground at the cost of less than what we spent in two weeks in Iraq, liberate a country that had been under the yoke of dictatorship for 40 years. Got rid of a despot who had killed Americans . . .").

¹⁵⁴ NATO June 2011 Fact Sheet.

¹⁵⁵ NATO June 2011 Fact Sheet; and "Operation Odyssey Dawn," Defense Dept. website (caption in photograph).

¹⁵⁶ Benghazi Committee Report, p. 63.

¹⁵⁷ "Operation Odyssey Dawn," Defense Dept. website; and Hastings, Inside Obama's War Room.

¹⁵⁸ Gates Outlines U.S. Role as NATO Takes Libya Mission ("The U.S. focus as the operation continues will be electronic attack, aerial refueling, lift, search and rescue, and intelligence, surveillance and reconnaissance support . . . ," summarizing congressional testimony of Defense Secretary Robert Gates); and Gates Defends Libya Action Minus Congressional OK.

drones, manned aircraft and signal intercepts of ground communications for the NATO mission . . ."[159]

In April, the NATO war gets personal for the autocrat Qadhafi. NATO airstrikes kill one of his sons (Saif al-Arab) and three of his grandchildren. Perhaps in retaliation, in early May a mob of Qadhafi security forces and pro-Qadhafi supporters heavily damages the now-abandoned, state-of-the-art U.S. Embassy in Tripoli that was completed only two years earlier. The facility is rendered unusable.[160]

By the end of May, NATO and its partners have conducted more than 9,000 air sorties over Libya. Over 3,400 of these are "strike" sorties.[161] Eventually, NATO pilots will fly 26,500 sorties, which include "hundreds" of drone strikes and bombing missions.[162] American pilots flew about 25 percent of these sorties, and the U.S. supplied a full half of the aircraft used by the alliance. The U.S. also flew 80 percent of the air-refueling and "intelligence, surveillance, and reconnaissance" missions.[163] (U.S. military action? What military action?)

At one point, Qadhafi's forces shoot down an American aircraft. The pilot survives. He is saved by local Libyans, including a man who later will aid America again on the Night of Benghazi.[164] (Troops on the ground? No, I don't see any.)

On June 8, NATO and its eight operational partners of Operation Unified Protector agree to extend NATO's mission in Libya for another 90 days, until the end of September.[165]

---

[159] Thomas Erdbrink and Liz Sly, "Libyan War Becomes Manhunt for Gaddafi," *The Washington Post* online (Aug. 24, 2011).

[160] Stewart, The Benghazi Report and the Diplomatic Security Funding Cycle; Stewart, Diplomatic Security in Light of Benghazi; Bahrampour, U.S. Embassy in Tripoli Reopens; and Simon Denyer, "New Reports Emerge on Ransacking of U.S. Embassy in Tripoli," *The Washington Post* online (Aug. 31, 2011).

[161] NATO June 2011 Fact Sheet.

[162] Greenleaf, "The Air War in Libya," p. 38; and Hastings, Inside Obama's War Room (over 22,000 sorties).

[163] Greenleaf, "The Air War in Libya," p. 38.

[164] Jennifer Griffin, "EXCLUSIVE: CIA Operators Were Denied Request for Help During Benghazi Attack, Sources Say," Fox News online (Oct. 26, 2012) ("Griffin, CIA Operators Were Denied Request for Help During Benghazi Attack"). Like many news outlets at this time, many of Fox News' claimed "facts" in this report turn out to be incorrect.

[165] "NATO and Partners Will Stay the Course on Libya," NATO website (June 8, 2011); and NATO "Statement on Libya," NATO website (June 8, 2011).

On July 15, the U.S. officially recognizes the Transitional National Council, an umbrella organization of rebel groups, as the legitimate Libyan government.[166] (So long, Colonel Mu'ammar!) The TNC, based in Benghazi, now has preeminence among all Libyan rebel groups.[167]

By late August, the end is near. Tripoli falls on August 24th, and Qadhafi flees the city.[168] (He likely has escaped through a network of secret tunnels leading from his Tripoli compound.[169]) Soon after, his wife and three of his children reportedly leave Libya, crossing the border into Algeria.[170] The rebels' manhunt for Qadhafi is on.[171]

The U.S. State Department reopens its Embassy in Tripoli on September 22, but in a temporary facility (the U.S. ambassador's former residence).[172] In mid-October, Secretary of State Hillary Clinton meets in Tripoli with the new Libyan Prime Minister, Mahmoud Jibril (a former rebel leader). The stated purposes of her trip are to congratulate the Libyans on jettisoning Qadhafi, to help with the transition to "democracy" (supposedly including unifying the rebels), and to forge a stronger partnership with the new Libyan government.[173] Clinton promises Jibril the international coalition that helped defeat Qadhafi will continue to protect Libyan civilians.[174] (If only they could protect American civilians in Libya.) Around this same time, Hillary

---

[166] "A Guide to the United States' History of Recognition, Diplomatic and Consular Relations, by Country, Since 1776: Libya," Office of the Historian, Bureau of Public Affairs, State Dept. website.

[167] Benghazi ARB Report, p. 14.

[168] Thomas Erdbrink and Liz Sly, "Libyan War Becomes Manhunt for Gaddafi," *The Washington Post* online (Aug. 24, 2011); and Hastings, Inside Obama's War Room.

[169] Erin McLaughlin, "Libyan Rebels Push Toward Remaining Gadhafi Strongholds," ABC News online (Sept. 3, 2011).

[170] Leila Fadel, "Gaddafi's Wife, Three of His Children Apparently Flee to Algeria," *The Washington Post* online (Aug. 29, 2011).

[171] Thomas Erdbrink and Liz Sly, "Libyan War Becomes Manhunt for Gaddafi," *The Washington Post* online (Aug. 24, 2011).

[172] "A Guide to the United States' History of Recognition, Diplomatic and Consular Relations, by Country, Since 1776: Libya," Office of the Historian, Bureau of Public Affairs, State Dept. website; and Bahrampour, U.S. Embassy in Tripoli Reopens.

[173] Martha Raddatz, "Hillary Clinton Visits Libya to Meet Rebel Leaders," ABC News online (Oct. 18, 2011).

[174] Jessica Rettig, "Qadhafi's Death Won't Mean End for U.S. Role in Libya," U.S. News & World Report online (Oct. 20, 2011).

THE TRUE ACCOUNT OF VALOR AND ABANDONMENT

Clinton will pose for a regal, flattering November 2011 *Time* magazine cover trumpeting an article praising her use of "Smart Power."[175]

(In fact, Clinton's "end zone dances" will prove tragically premature. They are painfully reminiscent of President Bush's May 2003 "Mission Accomplished" moment aboard the aircraft carrier USS Abraham Lincoln during the Iraq war.[176])

Also by mid-October, TNC fighters are tightening their grip around the Libyan coastal city of Sirte. It is the last stronghold of Qadhafi and his supporters. On October 20, a large convoy of vehicles containing Qadhafi and some of his loyalists attempts to make a run for it from Sirte, where the dictator has been hiding. NATO aircraft attack the fast-moving convoy, killing a son of Qadhafi and other supporters. The convoy scatters. Survivors, including Qadhafi himself, flee on foot. Qadhafi is swiftly captured by rebels. Soon afterwards, he is shot dead. There are reports his body is sodomized by some of the rebels.[177]

In a videotaped remark to a CBS News reporter when informed of reports of Qadhafi's death, Secretary of State Hillary Clinton laughingly gloats: "We came, we saw, he died."[178] (How uplifting.)

The Libyan revolution is over. The violence and chaos are not. ∎

---

[175] Massimo Calabresi, "Hillary Clinton & the Rise of Smart Power," *Time* Magazine online (Nov. 7, 2011).

[176] Jarrett Murphy, Associated Press, "Text of Bush Speech," CBS News online (May 1, 2003) (Under a huge banner proclaiming "Mission Accomplished," President George W. Bush declares: ". . . Major combat operations in Iraq have ended. In the Battle of Iraq, the United States and our allies have prevailed. And now our coalition is engaged in securing and reconstructing that country. . . .") (*Watch video there*; Go to 1:02-14).

[177] "Muammar Gaddafi: How He Died," BBC News Africa online (Oct. 31, 2011); Baier, New Revelations on Attack in Benghazi (*Watch video there*; Go to 4:52 - 5:00); and Jessica Rettig, "Qadhafi's Death Won't Mean End for U.S. Role in Libya," U.S. News & World Report online (Oct. 20, 2011).

[178] "Clinton on Qaddafi: We Came, We Saw, He Died," CBS News online (Oct. 20, 2011) (*Watch video there*); and Interview of Professor Glenn Reynolds, Univ. of Tennessee Law School, with Tucker Carlson, "Tucker Carlson Tonight," Fox News Channel (Dec. 1, 2017).

8

Christopher Stevens Goes to Libya

By March 2011, the Obama administration appoints State Department career diplomat J. Christopher Stevens as the U.S. "Special Representative" to the Transitional National Council, the rebel umbrella group.[179]

Stevens, then 50, previously has served in Egypt, Syria, Israel (in Jerusalem) and Saudi Arabia. From 2007 to 2009, Stevens serves as Deputy Chief of Mission (number two diplomat) in Libya. He is fluent in Arabic. Stevens seems the perfect choice as the U.S. envoy to the TNC. In April, Secretary of State Clinton sends Stevens to Libya while the Libyan revolution still rages. Qadhafi controls Tripoli, but the rebels hold Benghazi.[180]

Stevens arrives in Benghazi on a Greek cargo ship, the *Aegean Pearl*, on April 5th. He is carrying $60,000 in cash. He and his twelve-person team set up temporary "offices" in the Tibesty Hotel. (Eight or ten of his party are called "Diplomatic Security Agents."[181] However, it is a virtual certainty some of them are with the CIA.) Stevens will continue to serve as Special Representative to the TNC for the next six months.[182]

Stevens' assignment as Special Representative involves communicating with the rebels to learn more about them to determine

---

[179] "A Guide to the United States' History of Recognition, Diplomatic and Consular Relations, by Country, Since 1776: Libya," Office of the Historian, Bureau of Public Affairs, State Dept. website.

[180] Remarks of Secretary of State Hillary Clinton on the Deaths of American Personnel in Benghazi, Libya, State Department Treaty Room, Washington, D.C., State Dept. Archives website (Sept. 12, 2012); and Baier, New Revelations on Attack in Benghazi (*Watch video there*; Go to 3:20-30).

[181] Benghazi Committee Report (Eight DSAs), p. 264; and Benghazi ARB Report (Ten DSAs), p. 13.

[182] Benghazi Committee Report, p. 10; Benghazi ARB Report, p. 13; Baier, New Revelations on Attack in Benghazi (*Watch video there*; Go to 3:20-35); and Erin Burnett, "Benghazi Timeline: 'We Are Under Attack,'" CNN (Circa Aug. 7, 2013) ("Burnett, Benghazi Timeline: 'We Are Under Attack'") (Interview of Chris Stevens' father, Jan Stevens, with Erin Burnett) (*Watch video there*; Go to 0:35-57).

THE TRUE ACCOUNT OF VALOR AND ABANDONMENT

whether the U.S. government should support them. While in Libya, Stevens reportedly also meets and coordinates with *al-Qaeda-linked* rebel groups, including the Libyan Islamic Fighting Group![183] (The enemy of my enemy is my friend?) Later, once the Obama administration determines to endorse the rebels, Stevens' job expands to comprise funneling U.S. aid to these rebels, including weapons.[184]

(According to an American arms dealer, Marc Turi, in 2011 the U.S. decides to funnel deadly conventional weapons to the anti-Qadhafi rebels. *The Washington Times* reports these weapons include automatic rifles, machine guns, explosives and anti-tank rockets.[185] Because of United Nations sanctions, it apparently is against U.S. law to provide such weapons directly to the Libyan rebels. Instead, the U.S. allegedly uses Turi to sell weapons to the nations of Qatar and the United Arab Emirates (U.A.E.), which in turn will transfer some or all of them to the Libyan rebels. Later, the State Department apparently decides to cut Turi out of the picture and handle the operation itself. In 2014 the U.S. Justice Department will bring federal charges against Turi. The arms dealer later will claim some of these weapons were diverted from Libya to Syria. However, the U.S. will drop its criminal suit against Turi when the presiding judge orders Justice to turn over classified U.S. documents about Libya to the defense.[186]

(More than three years after Benghazi, the Select Committee will send President Obama the following question in connection with its investigation: "14. Did you authorize a covert action or covert

---

[183] McCarthy, Hillary Clinton's Benghazi Debacle: Arming Jihadists in Libya . . . And Syria.

[184] Stewart, Diplomatic Security in Light of Benghazi; McCarthy, Hillary Clinton's Benghazi Debacle: Arming Jihadists in Libya . . . And Syria; and Schwartz, A Spymaster Steps Out of the Shadows (". . . As the Syria conflict deepened and Obama drew criticism for his indecision, The [New York] Times reported that Brennan's C.I.A. undertook a billion-dollar covert campaign to arm and train rebels fighting against the Syrian leader, Bashar al-Assad. . . .").

[185] Rowan Scarborough, "Charges Dropped in Libya Weapons Scheme," *The Washington Times* online (Oct. 5, 2016).

[186] "Special Report" with Bret Baier, Fox News Channel (Oct. 11, 2016); Rowan Scarborough, "Charges Dropped in Libya Weapons Scheme," *The Washington Times* online (Oct. 5, 2016); and Kenneth P. Vogel and Josh Gerstein, "Obama DOJ Drops Charges Against Alleged Broker of Libyan Weapons," POLITICO website (Oct. 4, 2016; Updated Oct. 5, 2016).

operation to provide lethal assistance to Libyan rebels?" Obama will decline to answer.[187])

On June 1, a car bomb explodes in the parking lot of Stevens' Benghazi hotel. The intent is to take down the hotel. The Americans wisely decide to look for a safer residence.[188]

As the civil war rages on, by August 2011 Stevens and his team have located and rented a large villa on the west side of Benghazi in the Western Fwayhat neighborhood. It will become known as the "Special Mission Compound" (discussed in detail in Chapters 11 and 19). Stevens and his team will live there for several months as the revolution plays out.[189]

While he is in Libya, Stevens sees Qadhafi fall, the U.S. Embassy in Tripoli reopen, and the tyrant killed.[190] Stevens leaves Benghazi in November 2011, and returns to the U.S. While there, Stevens is nominated and confirmed as the new U.S. Ambassador to Libya. (He replaces the departing Ambassador Gene Cretz.[191]) Ambassador Stevens is sworn in on May 14, 2012. Later this same month he returns to Libya to represent the U.S. to the new Libyan government. The U.S. continues to use the Mission Compound in Benghazi.[192] ∎

---

[187] Benghazi Committee Report, Appendix C, pp. 467-469.

[188] Baier, New Revelations on Attack in Benghazi (*Watch video there*; Go to 3:35-42); and Prepared Testimony of Under Secretary of State Patrick Kennedy Before House Oversight Committee (Oct. 10, 2012) ("Kennedy House Oversight Prepared Testimony"), p. 3.

[189] Benghazi Committee Report, p. 10; Baier, New Revelations on Attack in Benghazi (*Watch video there*; Go to 3:36-52); and Zuckoff, *13 Hours*, Chap. 1, p. 8.

[190] Benghazi Committee Report, p. 10; and Baier, New Revelations on Attack in Benghazi (*Watch video there*; Go to 3:36-52).

[191] Press Release, "President Obama Announces More Key Administration Posts," The White House, Office of the Press Secretary, Obama White House Archives (April 11, 2012).

[192] Benghazi Committee Report, p. 10.

9

"Things Could Go Wrong"

In the months following Qadhafi's overthrow and death, Libya literally comes unraveled.[193] The National Transitional Council has taken over the task of running Libya. It will last less than a year.

According to Michael Hastings of *Rolling Stone*, before and during the Libyan civil war President Obama and his administration actually do attempt to consider the all-important question: after Qadhafi, "What's Next?"[194] (However, merely discussing the likely future results does not equate with a good plan to deal with them.[195]) To the

---

[193] E.g., Bahrampour, U.S. Embassy in Tripoli Reopens (". . . [F]issures have begun to show among the victors, with tension rising between regional factions, and between secularists and Islamists"); and AP, "Red Cross Says Attack on Libya Office Wounds 1," Fox News online (June 12, 2012) ("AP, Red Cross Says Attack on Libya Office Wounds 1") ("The attacks [by militants in Libyan cities of Benghazi and Misrata] were reminders of how chaotic, insecure and fragmented Libya remains eight months after an armed rebellion toppled longtime dictator Moammar Gadhafi. The transitional leadership based in the capital of Tripoli has failed to impose its authority on much of the oil-rich North African nation. Instability has increased as cities, towns, regions, militias and tribes all act on their own, setting up independent and often conflicting power centers").

[194] E.g., Hastings, Inside Obama's War Room. One must view Rolling Stone's articles with some caution. Compare Sabrina Rubin Ederly, "A Rape on Campus: A Brutal Assault and Struggle for Justice at UVA," Rolling Stone online (Nov. 19, 2014); with Ravi Somaiya, "Rolling Stone Article on Rape at University of Virginia Failed All Basics, Report Says," *The New York Times* online (April 5, 2015); and Ben Sisario, Hawes Spencer and Sydney Ember, "Rolling Stone Loses Defamation Case Over Rape Story," *The New York Times* online (Nov. 4, 2016).

[195] E.g., Hastings, Inside Obama's War Room ("'It's good Qaddafi didn't fall right away,' one U.N. official involved in post-intervention planning confided to an insider. 'There was no plan ready'"). Compare *Id.* (Senior Obama administration official: "The big lesson from Iraq, to state the obvious, wasn't so much whether we could defeat Saddam. . . . It was the day after, the year after, the decade after. It was about whether we could secure the peace"). Compare News Transcript of Remarks by Secretary Panetta Aboard the USS John C. Stennis, Bremerton, Wash., Defense Dept. website (Aug. 22, 2012) (emphasis added) (". . . [A]s a result of that [NATO] operation we brought Gadhafi down and *gave Libya back to the Libyan people*"). Compare Interview of Professor Glenn Reynolds, Univ. of Tennessee Law School, with Tucker Carlson, "Tucker Carlson Tonight," Fox News Channel (Dec. 1, 2017) (". . . There wasn't much of a plan on what to do next . . .").

extent it is true Team Obama considers in advance the fallout if Qadhafi is removed, they come up with all the wrong predictions and answers. Obama and Hillary Clinton fail (as political leaders usually do) to prepare an accurate forecast of "what happens next," and how to cope with it.[196] In reality, what is next in Libya is anarchy, instability, death, terrorism, weapons proliferation and chaos.

The BBC reports Qadhafi's toppling results in a "power vacuum" in which the NTC "struggled to impose order on the many armed militia that had become active in the months leading up to the ouster of [Gadhafi]."[197] Weapons, illegal immigrants and foreign fighters flow throughout Libya.[198] Libya will become a major source of supply for

---

[196] Gates, *Duty* ("... I agreed with several members [of Congress] that 'we should not overestimate our ability to influence' what would happen after Qaddafi fell...."), Chap. 13, p. 521; Rice, *Tough Love* ("... We underestimated the difficulty of establishing a unified, stable government in a country where there had never been actual institutions, only the writ and whim of one man...."), Chap. 14, p. 292; Hastings, Inside Obama's War Room (A senior Obama administration official: "Qaddafi is going to fall eventually.... The question is: What demons are waiting that we don't yet know about?"); and Editorial, "Military Support Offered in Benghazi – Why Would White House Say No?" Investor's Business Daily online (Dec. 10, 2015) ("... It was Secretary of State Clinton's war, so she owns Libya and every disaster related to it").

[197] BBC, Libya Country Profile ("The toppling of long-term leader Muammar Gaddafi in 2011 led to a power vacuum and instability, with no authority in full control"); Hassan Morajea, "Militia Holding Bomber's Relatives Emerged in Libya's Chaos," *The Wall Street Journal* online (May 25, 2017) ("... [D]ozens of armed Libyan militias ... have surfaced following the 2011 collapse of Moammar Gadhafi's government. The resulting power vacuum gave rise to groups that took the place of traditional security forces, and operate with few checks on their power"); and Burton & Katz, *Under Fire* ("... The ancient town [of Benghazi] was simmering with passions and preclusions of peace and in the power vacuum of a civil war had become a nerve center for the North African jihad...."), Chap. 6, p. 72.

[198] E.g., Benghazi ARB Report (citing "the ready availability of weapons in eastern Libya"), p. 38; AP, Red Cross Says Attack on Libya Office Wounds 1 ("There are also concerns about the proliferation of thousands of weapons, including rockets, machine guns and rocket-propelled grenades in Libya in the aftermath of the civil war last year"); Bahrampour, U.S. Embassy in Tripoli Reopens ("There are thousands of unaccounted for weapons in Libya, many of which were seized by rebel forces as they stormed Gaddafi government bases"); Jake Tapper via "Good Morning America," "Security Team Commander Says Ambassador Stevens Wanted His Team to Stay in Libya Past August," ABC News online (Oct. 8, 2012) ("Tapper, Security Team Commander Says Ambassador Stevens Wanted His Team to Stay in Libya Past August") (As of February 2012 "... There continues to be large numbers of weapons throughout Tripoli, with gunfire heard throughout the city on a daily basis"); Yasmine Ryan, "Libya Says US Consulate Attack 'Pre-Planned,'" Al Jazeera online (Sept. 14, 2012) ("One of the biggest factors contributing to the ongoing instability in Libya is the

THE TRUE ACCOUNT OF VALOR AND ABANDONMENT

ISIS fighters in both Syria and Iraq. Within eleven months of Qadhafi's death, tragedy will be next for Americans in Benghazi.

Journalist Sharyl Attkisson reports that in 2011 al Qaeda is known to be in Libya's capital, Tripoli. There, al Qaeda reportedly seeks to locate and acquire some of the thousands of missing man-carried portable missiles ("MANPADS") the rebels have looted from Libyan military bases after Qadhafi's fall. When the U.S. Embassy in Tripoli reopens on September 22, 2011, then U.S. Ambassador Gene Cretz presciently asserts, ". . . I think there is a genuine cause to be concerned that things could go wrong."[199]

In late 2011 and throughout 2012, Libya continues to deteriorate. By fall 2012, the new Libyan government is so weak and unstable it still relies upon "armed militants to keep the peace."[200] Obama and his national security team have made a complete "pig's ear" out of Libya.[201]

---

proliferation of arms left over from the 2011 conflict that toppled Muammar Gaddafi, combined with a central government severely weakened by tribal rivalries"); and Benghazi Committee Report (Redacted) (Testimony of unidentified CIA official: ". . . There [was] . . . a lot of evidence of foreign fighters coming in from outside the country"), p. 20.

[199] Sharyl Attkisson, "8 Major Warnings Before Benghazi Terrorist Attacks," Sharyl Attkisson website (Oct. 22, 2015) ("Attkisson, 8 Major Warnings Before Benghazi"); Attkisson, *Stonewalled*, Chap. 4, p. 181; and Bahrampour, U.S. Embassy in Tripoli Reopens.

[200] "CIA Saw Possible Terror Ties Day After Libya Hit: AP," CBS News online (Oct. 19, 2012) ("CBS News, CIA Saw Possible Terror Ties Day After Libya Hit: AP"). See also Rice, *Tough Love* (". . . After some months, the interim Libyan government proved to be divided and ineffectual. The international effort to support the new government faltered for lack of strong leadership from the U.N., Europe, or the U.S. . . ."), Chap. 14, p. 292; Stewart, Diplomatic Security in Light of Benghazi (". . . The Libyan central government has very little authority outside of Tripoli, the capital, and heavily armed tribal and regional militias control many parts of the country. . . ."); Prepared Testimony of Lt. Col. Andrew Wood before House Oversight Committee, House Oversight Committee website (Oct. 10, 2012) ("Wood House Oversight Prepared Testimony") (". . . . Libyans struggled with a Transitional government that hesitated to make decisions and was forced to rely upon local or tribal militias with varying degrees to [sic of] loyalty. . . ."), p. 2; and "CNN Finds, Returns Journal Belonging to Late U.S. Ambassador," CNN online (Sept. 23, 2012) ("CNN Finds, Returns Journal Belonging to Late U.S. Ambassador") (". . . [A]t this point in time . . . the Libyan government in and of itself acknowledges, very openly, that it is incapable of controlling these various groups [of militias]. . . .") (*Watch video there*; Go to 4:44 - 7:19).

[201] See, e.g., Robert G. Kaufman, "What's a Reagan Internationalist to Do?" *The Wall Street Journal* online (Sept. 14, 2016) (". . . Libya has become a breeding ground of

43

In September 2015, Obama will admit to the United Nations, "... Even as we helped the Libyan people bring an end to the reign of a tyrant, our coalition could have and should have done more to fill a vacuum left behind."[202] In 2016 he will claim, "I have said on several occasions that we did the right thing in preventing what could have been a massacre, a blood bath in Libya. And we did so as part of an international coalition and under U.N. mandate."[203] (So if the U.N. is involved, it cannot be a cluster you-know-what?)

Obama never totally admits his Grand Libyan Adventure is a mistake. Instead, he blames the Libya "mess" on the lack of follow-up by Europeans. In a highly-publicized interview with *The Atlantic* in March 2016, Obama will accuse then British Prime Minister David Cameron of becoming "distracted by a range of other things" after the Libyan campaign. Obama tells *The Atlantic* he had expected Europeans "being invested in a follow up" in light of their geographic proximity to Libya.[204]

Also in his *Atlantic* interview, Obama privately will refer to Libya as a "shitshow."[205] (Hard to dispute.) Trying to clean up after Obama's

---

Islamist terrorism because America's mission was ill-defined and its withdrawal premature"); and Thomas Sowell, "Hillary 2.0 and Benghazi: Same Song, Different Verse Two Decades Later," The Stream website (Oct. 27, 2015) ("Sowell, Hillary 2.0 and Benghazi") ("Having intervened in Libya to help overthrow the government of Muammar Qaddafi, who was no threat to America's interests in the Middle East, the Obama administration was confronted with the fact that Qaddafi's ouster simply threw the country into such chaos that Islamic terrorists were now able to operate freely in Libya").

[202] Remarks by President Barack Obama Before United Nations General Assembly, Obama White House Archives (Sept. 28, 2015). See also Allie Malloy and Catherine Treyz, "Obama Admits Worst Mistake of His Presidency," CNN online (Updated April 11, 2016) ("Malloy and Treyz, Obama Admits Worst Mistake of His Presidency").

[203] Remarks by President Obama and Prime Minister Lee of Singapore in Joint Press Conference, East Room, The White House, Obama White House Archives (Aug. 2, 2016).

[204] Excerpts from Jeffrey Goldberg, "'The Obama Doctrine': *The Atlantic's* Exclusive Report on the U.S. President's Hardest Foreign Policy Decisions," *The Atlantic* online (Mar. 10, 2016) ("Goldberg, The Obama Doctrine"); and Malloy and Treyz, Obama Admits Worst Mistake of His Presidency.

[205] Goldberg, The Obama Doctrine, quoted in Malloy and Treyz, Obama Admits Worst Mistake of His Presidency. See also Rice, *Tough Love* ("Libya remains a state without an effective government, and an exporter of refugees and instability. . . . [W]hat we left behind [in Libya] is . . . a fractured state without an effective central government,

all-too-candid *Atlantic* remarks, one National Security Council spokesperson explains Obama continues to believe "all of us – including the United States – could have done more in the aftermath of the Libyan intervention."[206]

In a rare on-air acknowledgement of imperfection, in an April 2016 interview Obama admits in Libya he and his team have failed to plan adequately for the post-Qadhafi period. He is asked what is the worst mistake of his presidency. He responds, "Probably failing to plan for *the day after* what I think was the right thing to do in intervening in Libya."[207]

In her memoir, Susan Rice concludes:

> ... [W]hile we and our European partners won the war, we failed to try hard enough and early enough to win the peace. Whether it could have been won at all is a real question; but not having given it our best shot, we will never know.[208]

These failures will contribute significantly to the coming tragedy of Benghazi, to which we now turn. ■

---

continued factional fighting, a lingering terrorist threat, and a source of insecurity in the region...."), Chap. 14, p. 293.

[206] Malloy and Treyz, Obama Admits Worst Mistake of His Presidency (quoting Ned Price, National Security Council Spokesman).

[207] "Exclusive: President Barack Obama on 'Fox News Sunday,'" Fox News online (April 10, 2016) (emphasis added). See also Remarks by President Obama and Prime Minister Lee of Singapore in Joint Press Conference, East Room, Obama White House Archives (Aug. 2, 2016) (emphasis added) ("... I think that all of us, collectively, were not sufficiently attentive to what had to happen *the day after, and the day after, and the day after that*, in order to ensure that there were strong structures in place to assure basic security and peace inside of Libya").

[208] Rice, *Tough Love*, Chap. 14, pp. 293-294.

PART II:

BEFORE THE ATTACKS

10

Benghazi: "The Most Dangerous City"

Benghazi, Libya in September 2012 is a very hazardous place.[209] Authors Fred Burton and Samuel Katz describe it as "the most dangerous city in North Africa."[210] (And that's a tough neighborhood, indeed.)

It is just eleven months after the United States assists in overthrowing Libya's oppressive dictator of 42 years, Mu'ammar Qadhafi (discussed above in Chapters 5-9). As noted in Part I, post-Qadhafi Libya is violent and unstable.[211] The country's post-revolution transitional government is extremely feeble and unsteady.

During the revolt, various well-armed (but largely untrained) local militias and extremist groups have formed in Benghazi and elsewhere in eastern Libya. Almost all militias are Muslims. Some of these groups despise America. Qadhafi supporters in particular are angered by the U.S. role in removing their leader's regime. By September there still is no true central government authority functioning in Benghazi, or anywhere else in the eastern part of the country.[212]

Benghazi has changed since Stevens left ten months ago. "A growing [Islamist] extremist movement had taken hold within the city limits. . . ."[213] It is known publicly Ansar al-Sharia openly operates a

---

[209] National Review Editors, What We Do Know About the Benghazi Attack Demands a Reckoning ("Why did the State Department and CIA have compounds in Benghazi, one of the most dangerous places in the world, particularly for Americans?").

[210] Burton & Katz, *Under Fire*, Chap. 9, p. 93.

[211] E.g., Baier, New Revelations on Attack in Benghazi (*Watch video there*; Go to 7:40 - 8:11); and Attkisson, *Stonewalled* (Post Qadhafi, ". . . Libya was suffering under an unstable and deteriorating security situation. Terrorists and antigovernment forces had found a firm foothold among the disorganization and chaos. There was potential danger around every corner"), Chap. 4, p. 179.

[212] "CIA Saw Possible Terror Ties Day After Libya Hit: AP," CBS News online (Oct. 19, 2012) ("CBS News, CIA Saw Possible Terror Ties Day After Libya Hit: AP"); Stewart, Diplomatic Security in Light of Benghazi (". . . The Libyan central government has very little authority outside of Tripoli, the capital, and heavily armed tribal and regional militias control many parts of the country. . . ."); Benghazi Committee Report, pp. 20-21; and BBC, Libya Country Profile.

[213] Benghazi Committee Report, p. 19.

"headquarters" in Benghazi. (After the tragedy, furious residents will storm this facility and seize it to protest the attacks on Americans.)[214] An unidentified CIA official later explains the situation to the Select Committee:

> The level of armed conflict and fighting between the various groups increased. The level of assassinations, attacks on foreign entities increased. ... There [was] ... a lot of evidence of foreign fighters coming in from outside the country.
>
> Specifically in June of 2012, right before the elections, the Islamist militia had an overt show of force, where they had a military parade roll in from eastern Libya to downtown Benghazi. ... I guess it was a message to the Libyan electorate that we are here and have a presence and we want to establish Islamic State inside Libya and we want sharia to be the law of the country. So there was ... a lot of attempts to intimidate the populace in Libya by these extremist groups.[215]

The February 17 Martyrs Brigade that later will be enlisted to "protect" the American facilities in Benghazi reportedly also participates in this pro-Sharia parade.[216] It is an ominous harbinger. ∎

---

[214] Suliman Ali Zway and Kareem Fahim, "Angry Libyans Target Militias, Forcing Fight," *The New York Times* online (Sept. 21, 2012) ("'We want justice for Chris,' read one sign among the estimated 30,000 Libyans, including families, who marched into Benghazi's main square on Friday to protest in front of the chief encampment of Ansar al-Shariah").

[215] Benghazi Committee Report (Redacted), p. 20. See also Suliman Ali Zway and Kareem Fahim, "Angry Libyans Target Militias, Forcing Fight," *The New York Times* online (Sept. 21, 2012) ("... Months ago, members of Ansar al-Shariah brandishing weapons paraded through Benghazi and called for an Islamic state"); and Attkisson, *Stonewalled*, Chap. 4, pp. 183-184.

[216] Burton & Katz, *Under Fire*, Prologue, p. 13.

11

The Benghazi
"Special Mission Compound"

As discussed above, in Benghazi, Libya in September 2012 the United States maintains a temporary diplomatic station. The U.S. State Department calls this facility the "Special Mission Compound."[217] The State Department first begins using this facility in mid-2011.[218] It is a large, beautiful walled villa complex the U.S. rents and has converted into a makeshift diplomatic outpost.[219] (The key word here is "makeshift.")

The Mission Compound is located on the west side of Benghazi. (See the Diagram at the beginning of this book.) The large compound is "more than 300 yards long and nearly 100 yards wide." It is surrounded by a concrete wall. (After renting the Mission, the State Department has raised the height of this wall to twelve feet, and added barbed wire and concertina razor wire on top.[220])

There are two large steel gates in the compound wall: the Main Gate (often known as "Charlie 1" or "C 1"), and Back Gate ("Charlie 3" or "C-3").[221] The Main Gate includes a separate, secure "pedestrian gate" used by individuals without vehicles.[222] However, the Senate Select Intelligence Committee later will find these "entry gates and doors"

---

[217] "Briefing by Senior Administration Officials to Update Recent Events in Libya," Via Teleconference, Office of the Spokesperson, State Dept. website (Sept. 12, 2012) ("September 12 Special Briefing").

[218] Prepared Testimony of Deputy Assistant Secretary of State Charlene Lamb Before House Oversight Committee, Oversight Committee website (Oct. 10, 2012) ("Lamb Oversight Committee Prepared Testimony"), p. 2.

[219] Baier, New Revelations on Attack in Benghazi (*Watch video there*; Go to 3:43-53).

[220] Lamb Oversight Committee Prepared Testimony, p. 2; "Report of the U.S. Senate Select Committee on Intelligence, Review of the Terrorist Attacks on the U.S. Facilities in Benghazi, Libya, September 11-12, 2012," Congress.gov website (Jan. 15, 2014) ("Sen. Intelligence Committee Benghazi Report") (Redacted), p. 17; and Baier, New Revelations on Attack in Benghazi (*Watch video there*; Go to 5:16-28).

[221] Benghazi Committee Report, p. 4.

[222] "Benghazi Timeline: How the Attack Unfolded," CBS News online (May 13, 2013) ("CBS Benghazi Timeline").

were "unhardened." There is a guard booth next to the Main Gate, which contains monitors for video cameras.²²³

The Mission is monitored by several such video cameras. (Additional surveillance cameras are present but still in their crates, because State has yet to send a technical team to install them. Also, the camera monitor in the guard booth next to the Main Gate is inoperable and in need of repair on September 11, 2012.²²⁴)

The main (and largest) building on the compound – known as "the Villa" or "Building C" – is located near the compound's center. The Villa is divided into two areas. The "public section" includes meeting space and common areas. The second "residential section" includes a living room, dining area, kitchen, several bedrooms and – most important – a large "safe haven" area.²²⁵

Nearby and directly across from the Villa is "Building B." It is the main residence for the State Department Diplomatic Security Agents ("DSAs").²²⁶ The DSAs' job is to protect State Department personnel both within the Mission Compound, and when their work takes them outside the facility. Building B also houses a "cantina" or dining area where Mission staff eat. Directly across a small patio from Building B is the Mission's "Tactical Operations Center" (or "TOC"). The TOC contains offices for the DSA security staff, with phones and security monitors. It is here the DSAs monitor the Mission's video cameras.

Near the Main Gate is a smaller, fourth building used as an on-site barracks for the "February 17 Martyrs Brigade" – local armed Libyans hired by State to help with security (discussed further below).²²⁷

Such is the stage where the "Battle of Benghazi" soon will commence. ∎

---

²²³ Sen. Intelligence Committee Benghazi Report (Redacted), pp. 17 and 19.

²²⁴ Kirkpatrick and Myers, Libya Attack Brings Challenges for U.S.; Sen. Intelligence Committee Benghazi Report, p. 19; and Hearing Before Committee on Oversight and Government Reform, House of Representatives (May 8, 2013) ("House Oversight Committee Hearings") (Remarks of Rep. James Lankford (R-OK)), p. 109.

²²⁵ Lamb Oversight Committee Prepared Testimony, p. 2.

²²⁶ Lamb Oversight Committee Prepared Testimony, p. 2; and CBS Benghazi Timeline.

²²⁷ Baier, New Revelations on Attack in Benghazi (*Watch video there*; Go to 4:06-33); Lamb Oversight Committee Prepared Testimony, p. 2; CBS Benghazi Timeline; and Benghazi Committee Report, p. 32.

12

The CIA Annex: "We're Walmart Security Guards"

In Benghazi in September 2012, the American Central Intelligence Agency operates a secret facility it calls "the Annex." It is located about one-half mile (as the crow flies) from the Mission Compound. The Annex will become a major part of the Benghazi tragedy.

The covert Annex reportedly is staffed by fewer than two dozen or so personnel who reside and work here. (Predictably, the precise number is classified. CNN reports there are 21 personnel at the Annex.[228]) These include the CIA's Chief of Base (publicly known only as "Bob"), his Deputy Chief of Base, a senior security official, and various men and women case officers, analysts, "specialists" and translators. Some have military experience; most do not.[229] This Benghazi Annex station reportedly is "Bob's" last posting before retirement.[230]

Among the CIA staff at the Annex are six civilian contract security agents. They are all ex-military. They are part of the CIA's "Global Response Staff" ("GRS"). GRS is created following the original 9/11 attacks in 2001. GRS contractors protect CIA personnel in numerous countries worldwide. They are not CIA employees, but rather independent contractors. Each of them essentially runs their own small "contractor business" under a written agreement with the U.S. government. They do not get to pick their assignment locations. A typical GRS rotation period is 60-75 days on a job, with some as long as 90 days. These can be extended (as they will be in Benghazi) for extenuating circumstances (such as an ambassador's short-notice visit

---

[228] "Exclusive: Dozens of CIA Operatives on the Ground During Benghazi Attack," The Lead Blog with Jake Tapper, CNN online (Aug. 1, 2013).

[229] Zuckoff, *13 Hours*, Chap. 2, p. 29; and Goldman and Miller, Former CIA Chief in Benghazi Challenges the Story Line of the New Movie *'13 Hours.'*

[230] Interview of John "Tig" Tiegen and Others with Megyn Kelly, "The Kelly File," Fox News Channel (Jan. 4, 2016) (*Watch video there*; Go to 8:06-30). See also Zuckoff, *13 Hours*, Chap. 1, p. 24.

to Benghazi). Until Benghazi, even the existence of the GRS largely is unknown to most people.

The GRS men's job in Benghazi is to safeguard the 15 or so case officers and other CIA personnel who operate out of the Annex. Essentially, these GRS agents are bodyguards. They accompany the CIA officers whenever the latter must leave the Annex.

The GRS agents assigned to the Annex in September 2012 all have extensive military training. They are supervised by a "Team Lead," who reportedly still works for the CIA.[231] The author therefore is unable (and unwilling) to identify him.

The six Benghazi GRS operators under the Team Lead are: two former Navy SEALs, Jack Silva (a pseudonym, age 38) and Tyrone "Rone" Woods (41); three former Marines, Dave "D.B." or "Boon" Benton (also a pseudonym, 38), Mark "Oz" Geist (46), and John "Tig" Tiegen (36); and former Army Ranger Kris "Tanto" Paronto (41).[232]

(As detailed below, these Benghazi GRS security contractors will play a pivotal role in the upcoming Battle of Benghazi. These six men are the subject of Mitchell Zuckoff's excellent book, *13 Hours*[233] (on which the five surviving contractors collaborated). They also are fêted as "The Secret Soldiers of Benghazi" in the superb 2016 Paramount movie of the same title.[234])

According to one of the GRS operators, in Benghazi the CIA's case officers "... don't want us there, until something bad happens." Kris "Tanto" Paronto views "Bob" as the worst of the CIA personnel here. Tanto later explains, "As far as he's concerned, we're Walmart security guards."[235] ■

---

[231] Goldman and Miller, Former CIA Chief in Benghazi Challenges the Story Line of the New Movie *'13 Hours.'*

[232] Zuckoff, *13 Hours*, Cast of Characters, pp. xiii-xv.

[233] Zuckoff, *13 Hours*.

[234] *13 Hours: The Secret Soldiers of Benghazi* (Paramount, 2016).

[235] Zuckoff, *13 Hours*, Chap. 2, p. 36.

13

"How Thin Does the Ice Have to Get?"

Under the Vienna Convention on Diplomatic Relations (which took effect in 1964), it is the responsibility of the "host country" to secure diplomatic facilities of "guest nations" within the host's borders.[236] This does not always happen. For example, in late 2019 when Iranian-backed militias stormed the U.S. Embassy in Baghdad and set fires, the Iraqi government failed to deploy its military forces to protect the American facility. Similarly, in 2012 the Libyan government's weakness and instability, and the chaos throughout the country, make such protection a very "iffy" proposition in Tripoli and Benghazi.

This point is made vividly in a memorandum prepared in February 2012 by Joan Polaschik, then U.S. Deputy Chief of Mission (number two diplomat) in Libya. According to ABC News, a draft version of the memorandum first notes a general "increase in violent crime, including homicides, carjackings, and armed robberies." The document then states:

> ... [It] is likely that the Libyan government will not make any significant progress in demobilizing the revolutionary militias or establishing any credible national security structures until after the election for the constitutional assembly and formation of a new government ... Until these militias are off the streets and a strong national police force is established, we will not have a reliable, host government partner that is capable of responding to the Embassy's security needs. *It is likely that we will need to maintain a heightened security posture for the foreseeable future.*[237]

Security in Libya will only get worse after this memorandum is penned.[238] At this time, Eric Nordstrom is the senior Regional Security Officer ("RSO") for Libya. Nordstrom later will tell congressional

---

[236] Stewart, Diplomatic Security in Light of Benghazi.

[237] Tapper, Security Team Commander Says Ambassador Stevens Wanted His Team to Stay in Libya Past August (emphasis added).

[238] Tapper, Security Team Commander Says Ambassador Stevens Wanted His Team to Stay in Libya Past August (*Watch video* there; Go to 0:48-58).

investigators *the Government of Libya "was overwhelmed and could not guarantee our protection."*[239] (One can argue this statement makes the case it is too dangerous to have *any* State personnel there.)

Indeed, five months later in a July 9 cable to the State Department, recently-installed Ambassador Chris Stevens refers to the "... lack of host nation security support..." and the "... absence of an appropriate host nation security presence..."[240] Weeks later in an August 2 cable to State, Stevens writes, "... [H]ost nation security support is lacking and cannot be depended on to provide a safe and secure environment for the diplomatic mission of outreach performed by FSO [Foreign Service Officer] and other USG [U.S. Government] personnel on the ground [here no doubt referencing the CIA's personnel]."[241]

State Department Responsibility for Security

Host nation obligations aside, within the U.S. State Department it is the responsibility of the Bureau of Diplomatic Security to protect American diplomats and their facilities abroad. According to the State Department in 2013:

> The Bureau of Diplomatic Security (DS), the law enforcement and security arm of the U.S. Department of State, provides a secure environment for the conduct of American diplomacy. To advance American interests and

---

[239] "House Probes Security Leading Up to Libya Attack" (emphasis added), CBS News online (Oct. 18, 2012) ("CBS News, House Probes Security Leading Up to Libya Attack"); and CBS News, U.S. Memo Warned of High Risk of Libya Violence.

[240] Unclassified but Redacted Cable, "TRIPOLI – Request for Extension of TDY Security Personnel," by Ambassador Stevens, American Embassy Tripoli (July 9, 2012), available at House Oversight Committee website ("Stevens July 9 Security Extension Cable to State"), p. 2.

[241] Unclassified but Redacted Cable, "Request to Add LES Ambassador Protective Detail Bodyguard Positions in US Embassy Tripoli," by Ambassador Stevens, American Embassy Tripoli (Aug. 2, 2012), available at House Oversight Committee website ("Stevens August 2 Bodyguard Request Cable to State"), p. 1; Sundby, Ambassador Warned Libya Was "Volatile and Violent"; and Peter Ferrara, Opinion, "Benghazi: Obama's Actions Amount to a Shameful Dereliction of Duty," Forbes online (Oct. 25, 2012) ("Ferrara, Benghazi: Obama's Actions Amount to a Shameful Dereliction of Duty"). See also Additional Views of Reps. Jim Jordan and Mike Pompeo ("... After Qaddafi, the U.S. knew that we could not count on host nation security in a country where militias held significant power...."), p. 416.

foreign policy, DS protects people, property, and information at 275 State Department missions worldwide. . . .[242]

The U.S. State Department assigns a "threat level" rating to each of these overseas diplomatic posts. There are four ratings: Critical, High, Medium and Low. In September 2012, only fourteen of the 275 posts are rated either High or Critical. Benghazi and Tripoli both are among the fourteen.[243]

Senior RSO Nordstrom ". . . arrived in Tripoli on September 21, 2011, with Ambassador Cretz, in the midst of the Libyan Civil War."[244] In this role, Nordstrom advises U.S. Ambassador to Libya Cretz on security and law enforcement matters.[245] Within months Nordstrom is becoming frustrated by the security situation in Libya. At a meeting in February 2012 to discuss staffing resources, the realization dawns on Nordstrom he will never receive the security resources he needs in Libya. Nordstrom later testifies to the House Oversight Committee, "It was abundantly clear we were not going to get resources until the aftermath of an incident." He continues, "And the question that we would ask is . . . how thin does the ice have to get before someone falls through?"[246]

Significantly, one of the key officials at State headquarters in Washington to whom Nordstrom is reporting during this period is Charlene R. Lamb. Lamb is Deputy Assistant Secretary ("DAS") for International Programs, within State's Bureau of Diplomatic Security.[247] DSA Lamb is one of the most significant players in what

---

[242] "Diplomatic Security, 2012 Year in Review," U.S. Department of State, Bureau of Diplomatic Security, State Dept. website (June 2013).

[243] House Oversight Committee Hearings (May 8, 2013) (Remarks of Rep. John Mica (R-FL)), p. 110.

[244] Prepared Statement of Eric Allan Nordstrom, Regional Security Officer, Tripoli, Libya, before House Oversight Committee (Oct. 10, 2012), p. 3.

[245] House Oversight Committee Hearings (May 8, 2013) (Introductory Remarks of Chairman Darrell Issa (R-CA)), p. 7.

[246] Nordstrom Oversight Committee Testimony (Oct. 10, 2012), pp. 105-106; Jake Tapper, "Security Officer on State Department Blocking Requests: 'For Me the Taliban Is Inside the Building,'" ABC News online (Oct. 10, 2012) ("Tapper, Security Officer: 'For Me the Taliban Is Inside the Building'"); and Cornwell and Zakaria, U.S. Security at Benghazi Mission Called "Weak." See also Wood House Oversight Prepared Testimony ("The RSO struggled to obtain additional personnel there [in Benghazi] but was never able to attain the numbers he felt comfortable with"), p. 3.

[247] Lamb Oversight Committee Prepared Testimony, p. 1.

will become the Benghazi tragedy. As we shall discover below, this Bureau and Lamb will make or recommend (or at least participate in) many of the critical security-related decisions affecting State's Benghazi outpost. (As also discussed below, Lamb (but not Nordstrom) will be among four mid-level managers later "disciplined" for her poor performance in the Benghazi tragedy.)

Despite the significant dangers to U.S. diplomats in lawless Libya, and the U.S.'s earlier pivotal role in helping the rebels win the revolution there, the U.S. now elects to observe most of the diplomatic niceties in dealing with the new Libyan "government." For example, U.S. diplomats at the Tripoli Embassy feel they must wait for the Libya Ministry of Interior to grant approval to use armed guards in general,[248] and specifically to issue firearms permits to U.S. security guards in Libya![249] State also will fret to ensure a local security firm it has hired in Libya has the proper Libyan government security license.[250]

---

[248] Unclassified but Redacted Cable, "Request for DS TDY and FTE Support" by Ambassador Gene Cretz, American Embassy Tripoli (Mar. 28, 2012) (Referencing "our two departing MSD teams"), p. 1 ("Cretz March 28 Increased Security Personnel Cable to State"), available at House Oversight Committee website (". . . [C]omplete elimination of our USDH TDY security presence is contingent upon post receiving host government permission to arm our LES [locally engaged security?] bodyguard force"), p. 2; Stevens July 9 Security Extension Cable to State (". . . Given the GoL's [Government of Libya's] traditional sensitivities regarding armed security personnel, Post does not recommend deployment of either an armed LGF [local guard force] or CPT [close protection team] element without notification to and licensing from the GoL"), p. 2.

[249] Cretz March 28 Increased Security Personnel Cable to State (Complaining of "complications regarding GOL [Government of Libya] firearms permits," noting "Currently the LGF [Local Guard Force] contractor [in Benghazi, likely the 17 February Brigade] is able to obtain only short-term (48-72 hr) firearms permits for specific VIP visits"), p. 2; Stevens July 9 Security Extension Cable to State (Complaining of ". . . GoL delays in issuing firearms permits for our LES [locally engaged security?] close protection/bodyguard unit"; and noting some trained close protection team members ". . . could be fully deployed once firearms permits have been received from the Ministry of Interior. Permits for the first 11 LES close protection team members took more than 2 months and required Ambassadorial intervention with the Ministry of Interior"), p. 2. This problem is especially ironic and frustrating, given at this time even children freely can purchase heavy weapons and ammunition without permits at open-air markets on the streets of Tripoli, Benghazi and other Libyan cities. See, e.g., Burton & Katz, *Under Fire* (". . . [I]n post-civil-war Benghazi an AK-47 and a truckload of 7.62 mm ammo were as easy to come by as a Starbucks coffee in midtown Manhattan"), Chap. 7, p. 81.

[250] See Judicial Watch: State Department Documents Show Its Security Contractor Operating Without a License in Benghazi on Day of Terrorist Attack.

THE TRUE ACCOUNT OF VALOR AND ABANDONMENT

(Moreover, as discussed below (in Chapters 59, 63 and 85), when the stuff later hits the fan on the Night of Benghazi, the U.S. State Department will insist the Libyan government must grant advance clearance to any U.S. military rescue flights sent into Libya. In other words, State is pretending Libya has a "real" government because, well, the Obama administration ensures this by helping to overthrow Qadhafi's hateful regime. Doesn't it?)

However, despite Eric Nordstrom's justified concerns, the State Department's security situation in Libya at this time is not completely bleak. Present in Libya are three State Department "Mobile Security Deployment" ("MSD") teams.[251] Each MSD unit is a six-man security team. Many MSD unit members are ex-Green Berets or former Navy SEALs.[252] Unfortunately, as explained below, when the security situation in Libya worsens, the State Department will reduce these MSD assets significantly there.

Defense Department's Role in Diplomatic Security

The Department of Defense also aids the State Department in protecting U.S. diplomatic facilities abroad. In this regard, however, the U.S. military repeatedly has warned the State Department it will be very difficult for Defense to protect or rescue State personnel in North Africa in particular. Vice Chairman of the Joint Chiefs of Staff, Vice Admiral James Winnefeld, later testifies to the Select Benghazi Committee:

> ... North Africa [is] ... a big place. We've constantly reminded State while I was the Vice Chairman and also ... National Security Council staff, gently, politely, that if you're counting on reactive forces from DOD to pull your fat out of the fire, basically, when there's an event going on, you're kidding yourselves. It's just too hard to get there. Usually, an event is over fairly quickly, and even in the best alert posture we can be in, it's going to be *a couple of hours, two or three hours*, before we can be someplace. [In the Benghazi saga, it

---

[251] Alex Sundby, "Ambassador Warned Libya Was 'Volatile and Violent,'" CBS News online (Oct. 19, 2012) ("Sundby, Ambassador Warned Libya Was 'Volatile and Violent'"); Wood House Oversight Prepared Testimony, p. 3; and CBS Benghazi Timeline.

[252] CBS Benghazi Timeline; and Baier, New Revelations on Attack in Benghazi (*Watch video there*; Go to 10:17-39). See also Attkisson, *Stonewalled*, Chap. 4, p. 176.

will prove to be more than *23 hours* before organized U.S. military help arrives in *Tripoli*; it never arrives in Benghazi.]

So what you should really be counting on is using these forces to either preemptively reinforce . . . or preemptively evacuate an area, like an embassy. Don't count on us to drop in in the middle of the night and stop a situation that's going on.

Now that won't prevent us from trying, certainly. If there's an event in a place . . . like a Benghazi and *if* we're postured in order to get there, *we'll certainly try, we'll always try*, but I've made it very clear to them – and they understand this – that *they need to be very careful in their risk assessments*. And it's a lot easier to reinforce and get out early than it is to save something that's under fire. . . . So we've tried to make it very, very clear to [the State Department], try, please, please, to *do good risk assessment and evacuate or reinforce so that we don't have to rescue you in the middle of a firefight*.[253]

(We consider in detail below whether the State Department performs a "good risk assessment," and whether DoD does "certainly try" to rescue Americans during the Battle of Benghazi.)

DoD "Site Security Teams"

According to authors Burton and Katz, in 2011 it becomes obvious the State Department's diplomatic security personnel are understaffed in dealing with all the unrest and violence erupting during the "Arab Spring" (discussed above in Chapters 3 and 4). To address some of these security challenges, the Department of Defense creates some twenty "Site Security Teams" ("SSTs"). These will function world-wide in some of the most dangerous spots on the globe. (They become known as the "traveling circus.") Some operate regionally, while others – as in Libya – conduct their mission within a single country.[254]

With the State Department's concurrence, the Defense Department deploys an SST to Libya. The Libya SST reports to Special Operations Command Africa ("SOCAFRICA").[255] SOCAFRICA is a sub-unit of

---

[253] Benghazi Committee Report (emphasis added), p. 69.

[254] Burton & Katz, *Under Fire*, Chap. 7, p. 78.

[255] Wood House Oversight Prepared Testimony, p. 1.

the United States Special Operations Command, and serves directly under the operational control of U.S. Africa Command ("AFRICOM").[256] *AFRICOM has U.S. military command responsibility for the entire African continent, except Egypt.*[257]

Beginning on February 12, 2012, this Libya SST is commanded by Lieutenant Colonel Andrew Wood. He is a respected 24-year special forces veteran, and a member of the Utah National Guard.[258] According to Wood, the Libya SST provides security, medical and communications support "for every facet of security that concerned the Embassy" in Tripoli.[259]

The Libya SST is based in Tripoli, but *moves around Libya as needed.*[260] It consists of a 16-member security team, whose members all are active-duty U.S. special operations soldiers with extensive military background. (Like State's MSD security teams, the SST includes a number of SEAL, Delta Force and Green Beret personnel.) On the ground in Libya, this SST is answerable directly to the Regional

---

[256] Wood House Oversight Prepared Testimony, p. 1; and United States Special Operations Command website.

[257] Benghazi Committee Report, p. 57.

[258] Wood House Oversight Prepared Testimony, p. 1; and Baier, New Revelations on Attack in Benghazi (*Watch video there*; Go to 3:53 - 4:05 and 6:26-52). Lt. Col. Wood voluntarily comes forward to identify himself to congressional investigators as a fact witness after learning of the tragedy on the Night of Benghazi. Wood House Oversight Prepared Testimony (". . . I feel duty bound to come forward in order to inform and provide a portion of ground truth information. I feel a sense of honor for those individuals who have died in the service of their country. . . ."), p. 1.

[259] Wood House Oversight Prepared Testimony, p. 1. See also Sen. Intelligence Committee Benghazi Report (Redacted), p. 20; and Tapper, Security Team Commander Says Ambassador Stevens Wanted His Team to Stay in Libya Past August (quoting draft Embassy document describing SST's functions in Tripoli as including: augmenting security escort work; protecting the Embassy; training local guards; serving as a Quick Reaction Force; and providing "vital medical, communications, explosive ordnance disposal (EOD), as well as, command and control enablers that are critical to post's security efforts").

[260] Wood House Oversight Prepared Testimony (emphasis added) (". . . The SST supported security for movements of diplomatic officers in and around Tripoli *and other parts of Libya* as their work required. . . ."), p. 1; and Sen. Intelligence Committee Benghazi Report (Redacted), p. 20.

Security Officer (then Eric Nordstrom) and ultimately to the Chief of Mission in Libya (i.e., the U.S. ambassador to Libya).[261]

SST Commander Wood later will testify, "The SST loaned considerable support to the Department of State's security posture in this uncertain and volatile environment."[262] Wood explains the SST is "closely integrated" with regular State diplomatic security agents working directly for the Libya Regional Security Officer (Nordstrom), as well as with the MSD units. Wood describes the working relationship among these three security teams as "great." Through Wood, the SST and the Libya RSO exchange intelligence. Wood explains he sends daily "situation reports" to his SOCAFRICA chain of command, and copies the Libya RSO on these. He also conducts thrice-weekly video teleconferences with SOCAFRICA. RSO Nordstrom reciprocates, and exchanges information on security and threats with Wood and his unit.[263]

In February 2012, the U.S. Embassy in Tripoli requests the SST mission in Libya be extended for another four-month tour of duty. The SST team's deployment is due to expire on or around April 5. Then Ambassador Cretz, his Deputy Chief of Mission Joan Polaschik, and RSO Nordstrom all support the SST's extension.

ABC News claims it obtains a draft copy of an Embassy memorandum requesting the extension. It reportedly is written by Deputy Chief of Mission Polaschik, and is circulated to various State personnel and the SST team. The draft memorandum states, "Quite simply, we cannot maintain our existing levels of Embassy operations, much less implement necessary staffing increases, without a continued SST presence."[264] Polaschik's document wisely concludes, "... A loss of SST now would severely and negatively impact our ability to achieve the Department's policy and management objectives at this

---

[261] Wood House Oversight Prepared Testimony, p. 1; Baier, New Revelations on Attack in Benghazi (*Watch video there*; Go to 6:26-52); Burton & Katz, *Under Fire*, Chap. 7, p. 78; and CBS Benghazi Timeline.

[262] Wood House Oversight Prepared Testimony, p. 1.

[263] *Id.*, p. 2.

[264] Tapper, Security Team Commander Says Ambassador Stevens Wanted His Team to Stay in Libya Past August (*Watch video there*; Go to 0:14-49).

THE TRUE ACCOUNT OF VALOR AND ABANDONMENT

critical time in Libya's transition."[265] The request to extend the SST for four months is granted.[266]

Critically, this Libya SST is funded by the Department of Defense, not the State Department.[267]

The new Libyan government, the U.S. State Department, and the American military all have joined hands to protect U.S. diplomats in Libya. What could possibly go wrong? ■

---

[265] Tapper, Security Team Commander Says Ambassador Stevens Wanted His Team to Stay in Libya Past August.

[266] Wood House Oversight Prepared Testimony, pp. 2-3; and Tapper, Security Team Commander Says Ambassador Stevens Wanted His Team to Stay in Libya Past August (*Watch video there*; Go to 0:48-52).

[267] Sen. Intelligence Committee Benghazi Report (Redacted) (". . . The SST . . . was provided by the DoD at no expense to the Department of State . . ."), p. 20; Attkisson, Benghazi Accountability Review Board Comes Under Renewed Criticism (State Department witnesses told the House Oversight Committee ". . . [I]t was [Under Secretary of State Patrick] Kennedy's decision to send home the 16-man military security team the Defense Department had offered to provide at no cost to the State Department . . ."); and Senate Foreign Relations Committee Hearing, C-SPAN online (Dec. 20, 2012) (Remarks and questions by Sen. Bob Corker (R-TN)) (*Watch video there*; Go to 5:14 – 6:48).

14

"Unpredictable, Volatile, and Violent"

According to Libya SST Commander Lieutenant Colonel Andrew Wood (who is on the ground at the time), in Spring 2012 the Libyan security situation begins to shift. Militant attacks become more "targeted." Moreover, the targets increasingly are *western*.[268]

Others in the U.S. government also detect these worsening security circumstances in Libya. The intelligence community ("IC"), Defense Department, and State Department officials themselves all warn of this growing concern.

On March 28, 2012, the U.S. Ambassador to Libya, Gene Cretz, and his Regional Security Officer, Eric Nordstrom, send a cable to their superiors at the State Department. As discussed below, the principal purpose of the cable is to request additional security personnel. In the process, the cable comments on the current Libyan security posture. Cretz and Nordstrom observe:

> ...[T]he security environment in Tripoli remains uncertain and unstable. Although there has been a marked decrease in the number of militia checkpoints around Tripoli, the Transitional National Council (TNC) has not yet succeeded in demobilizing the multiple militias or bringing them into a centralized command and control structure. This uncertain environment is likely to continue through the entire transition cycle, which ... is expected to last at least one year beyond the June 2012 election for the constituent assembly....[269]

A January 2014 report on the Benghazi tragedy by the Senate Select Intelligence Committee later will conclude:

---

[268] Wood House Oversight Prepared Testimony ("... Targeted attacks against westerners were on the increase...."), p. 3; Baier, New Revelations on Attack in Benghazi (Interview with Lt. Col. Andrew Wood) (*Watch video there*; Go to 7:12-46); Tapper, Security Team Commander Says Ambassador Stevens Wanted His Team to Stay in Libya Past August ("... [A]fter it [the U.S. Embassy in Tripoli's February 2012 request to extend the SST's tour of duty in Libya] was made, security in Libya devolved even more when it came to the targeting of Americans") (*Watch video there*; Go to 0:48-58); and Babbin, Whitewashing Benghazi.

[269] Cretz March 28 Increased Security Personnel Cable to State, pp. 1-2.

THE TRUE ACCOUNT OF VALOR AND ABANDONMENT

FINDING #1: In the months before the attacks on September 11, 2012, the IC provided ample strategic warning that the security situation in eastern Libya was deteriorating and that U.S. facilities and personnel were at risk in Benghazi.[270]

The Senate panel's report continues:

> The IC produced hundreds of analytic reports in the months preceding the September 11-12, 2012, attacks, providing strategic warning that militias and terrorist and affiliated groups had the capability and intent to strike U.S. and Western facilities and personnel in Libya. ...[271]

The author has found numerous factual errors and other flaws in the Senate Intelligence panel's Benghazi report. (This intelligence committee's report is issued in the very final days of Democrat control over the Senate and its committees.) However, on this issue of IC advance security warnings this committee's findings are amply supported. A few examples will demonstrate this.

To her credit, State's Charlene Lamb also is paying attention to this deteriorating security situation in Benghazi. (Recall she is the Deputy Assistant Secretary of State for Diplomatic Security.) According to the Republican staff of the House Foreign Affairs Committee, on June 11, 2012, Lamb engages in an email exchange on this topic of Benghazi risks with her superiors at State. Lamb writes:

> ... This is very concerning when you start putting the events together: The recent big demonstration that was openly anti-American, the attack on our compound, and now this UK motorcade attack. *If the tide is turning and they are now looking for Americans and Westerners to attack that is a game changer. We are not staffed or resourced adequately to protect our people in that type of environment.* We are a soft target against the resources available to the bad guys there. Not to mention there is no continuity because we do everything there [in Benghazi] with [temporary duty] personnel. ...[272]

---

[270] Sen. Intelligence Committee Benghazi Report, p. 9.

[271] *Id.*, p. 9.

[272] Email from Dep. Assistant Secretary for Diplomatic Security C. Lamb to Principal Dep. Assistant Secretary for Diplomatic Security S. Bultrowicz, with carbon copies to Assistant Secretary of State for Diplomatic Security E. Boswell and Dep. Assistant Secretary of State for Countermeasures Gentry Smith, Re: British Motorcade Attacked in Benghazi, June 11, 2012 (emphasis added), quoted in Majority Staff Report, House

Lamb sends this incendiary email to her boss, Scott Bultrowicz, Principal Deputy Assistant Secretary of State for Diplomatic Security. Copies are sent to Assistant Secretary of State for Diplomatic Security, Eric Boswell, and Gentry Smith, Deputy Assistant Secretary of State for Countermeasures.[273] (The author has found no indication Patrick Kennedy receives this email.) It should set on fire the hair of these three recipients. But apparently, it has no such effect. These recipients immediately should convey this alarming message to their agency's highest officials. Whether they do so is unknown.

On June 12, 2012, the Defense Intelligence Agency ("DIA") issues a report entitled "Libya: Terrorists Now Targeting U.S. and Western Interests." According to the Senate Intelligence Committee, the DIA's document states:

> *We expect more anti-U.S. terrorist attacks in eastern Libya* [redacted], due to the terrorists' greater presence there. . . . This will include terrorists conducting more ambush and IED [improvised explosive device] attacks as well as more threats against [redacted].[274]

Again according to the Senate Intelligence panel, six days later on June 18, the Pentagon Joint Staff's daily intelligence report addresses terrorism in Libya. One of the report's unclassified slides is headed, "Terrorism: Conditions Ripe for More Attacks, Terrorist Safe Haven in Libya." This slide continues:

> . . . [Redacted] support will increase Libyan terrorist capability in the permissive post-revolution security environment. Attacks will also increase in number and lethality as terrorists connect with AQ [al Qaeda] associates in Libya. *Areas of eastern Libya will likely become a safe haven by the end of 2012* [redacted].[275]

Foreign Affairs Committee, "Benghazi: Where Is the State Department Accountability?" House Foreign Affairs Committee website (Sept. 19, 2013) ("House Foreign Affairs Benghazi Majority Staff Report"), p. 8.

[273] House Foreign Affairs Benghazi Majority Staff Report, p. 23.

[274] Sen. Intelligence Committee Benghazi Report (Redacted; emphasis added), pp. 9-10; and Terence P. Jeffrey, "Stevens Cabled Washington: CIA Says AQ [Al Qaeda] Training Camps Within Benghazi," cnsnews.com (Jan. 15, 2014) ("Jeffrey, Stevens Cabled Washington: CIA Says Al Qaeda Training Camps Within Benghazi").

[275] Sen. Intelligence Committee Benghazi Report (Redacted; emphasis added), p. 10. See also Jeffrey, Stevens Cabled Washington: CIA Says Al Qaeda Training Camps Within Benghazi; Babbin, Whitewashing Benghazi; McCarthy, Hillary Clinton's Benghazi Debacle: Arming Jihadists in Libya . . . And Syria (After Qadhafi fell,

THE TRUE ACCOUNT OF VALOR AND ABANDONMENT

Also in mid-2012, recently-named U.S. Ambassador Chris Stevens sends a series of cables to State Department headquarters summarizing the mounting security threats in Libya. For example, in a June 25 cable from Stevens to State, he observes according to local contacts "Islamic extremism" appears to be increasing in eastern Libya (which includes Benghazi). It is entitled, "Libya's fragile security deteriorates as tribal rivalries, power plays and extremism intensify." The cable explains al Qaeda's flag "has been spotted several times flying over *government* buildings and training facilities."[276] Stevens also writes to State that Libyan extremists are "targeting international organizations and foreign interests."[277]

(An explanation of the significance of "cables" within the State Department may be helpful. At State, a cable is an "official" record transmitted through the agency's so-called "front channel." A mere email or telephone call or text message, while it may discuss important matters, is not "official." Hence, cables are used when the sender wishes a matter to become part of State's official records.[278] Conversely, avoiding using cables is a means by which the State bureaucracy can avert a subject becoming "official." Stevens' use of cables to transmit his security concerns over Libya therefore is highly significant.)

On July 1 the State Department increases the "danger pay" allowance in Libya from 25 percent to 30 percent of base pay.[279] (As

---

"... Libya then became a safe haven for terrorists who turned on the American and Western forces that had cleared the path for them"); and National Review Editors, What We Do Know About the Benghazi Attack Demands a Reckoning ("In reality, the terror threat still remained grave, especially in a post-Qaddafi Libya that had collapsed into chaos and provided a refuge for terrorists, including groups tied to al-Qaeda and ISIS").

[276] Sundby, Ambassador Warned Libya Was "Volatile and Violent"; Attkisson, 8 Major Warnings Before Benghazi; Baier, New Revelations on Attack in Benghazi (*Watch video there*; Go to 9:24-47); and Ferrara, Benghazi: Obama's Actions Amount to a Shameful Dereliction of Duty.

[277] Baier, New Revelations on Attack in Benghazi (*Watch video there*; Go to 9:24-47).

[278] "Benghazi: Exposing Failure and Recognizing Courage," Hearing Before the Committee on Oversight and Government Reform, House of Representatives, Testimony of Eric A. Nordstrom (May 8, 2013) ("WITNESS LAST NAME Oversight Committee Testimony") (Response to questions of Rep. Cynthia Lummis (R-WY)), p. 84.

[279] Stevens July 9 Security Extension Cable to State, p. 2; and CBS News, U.S. Memo Warned of High Risk of Libya Violence.

events will demonstrate, it is still not high enough. Also, as Oversight Committee Chairman Darrell Issa (R-CA) later will query, why in the world does State increase hazardous duty pay in Libya while at the same time reducing security assets there (as discussed in detail below in Chapter 17)?[280])

Sometime in July 2012, Chris Stevens meets with the Libyan Minister of the Interior. During this sit-down, Stevens reportedly requests increases in "static security." According to later testimony of Eric Nordstrom, also during this session the Interior Ministry officials highlight "growing extremism in the east, particularly in Benghazi and Derna and Sirte."[281]

In response to these growing threats, around this time Ambassador Stevens, an avid runner, begins to curtail his morning jogs near the Embassy in Tripoli. This follows the posting by extremists of his jogging routine on a website. He no longer runs alone.[282] Indeed, on "several occasions" the SST leader Lt. Col. Wood runs with him. The SST is "heavily involved" in Stevens' personal security detail while he runs.[283]

On July 6, the U.S. Central Intelligence Agency prepares its own report on security in Libya. It is entitled, "Libya: Al-Qa'ida Establishing Sanctuary." Again based on the Senate Select Intelligence panel's report, this CIA document asserts, "Al-Qa'ida-affiliated groups and associates are exploiting the permissive security environment in Libya to enhance their capabilities and expand their operational reach." The CIA report adds that al Qaeda-affiliated terrorist groups already have conducted training, constructed communications networks, and

---

[280] House Oversight Committee Hearings (Oct. 10, 2012) (Remarks of Chairman Darrell Issa (R-CA)) (". . . [Y]ou don't reduce security at the same time as you are increasing hazardous duty pay. It doesn't make sense. . . ."), p. 106.

[281] Nordstrom Oversight Committee Testimony (May 8, 2013) (Response to questions of Rep. Tony Cardenas (D-CA)), p. 76.

[282] Wood House Oversight Prepared Testimony (". . . In June the Ambassador received a threat on Facebook with a public announcement that he liked to run around the Embassy compound in Tripoli"), p. 2; Burnett, Benghazi Timeline: "We Are Under Attack" (*Watch video there*; Go to 2:53 - 3:05); and Burton & Katz, *Under Fire*, Chap. 7, p. 79.

[283] Wood House Oversight Prepared Testimony, p. 2.

"facilitated extremist travel across North Africa from *their safe haven in parts of eastern Libya.*"[284]

On July 9, another cable from Ambassador Stevens and RSO Nordstrom to the State Department warns of continuing security problems in Libya. It states:

> ...Overall security conditions continue to be unpredictable, with large numbers of armed groups and individuals not under control of the central government, and frequent clashes in Tripoli *and other major population centers*. National parliamentary elections have been delayed from 6/19 to 7/7, with post expecting an increased likelihood of election related political violence during and after the election period.[285]

This cable references "an increase in violence against foreign targets" and "Libya's fragile security environment." In this July 9 cable the Ambassador asserts, "... *SST's deployment has been critical* to our ability to navigate the transition to a more locally-based security team" while continuing to support a "high volume of VIP visits" and other security efforts.[286]

Regarding State's Benghazi outpost in particular, the July 9 cable states:

> ...Post anticipates supporting operations in Benghazi with at least one permanently assigned RSO employee from Tripoli, however, would request continued TDY [temporary duty assignment] support to fill a minimum of 3 security positions in Benghazi.[287]

Sometime on or shortly after July 21, 2012, the Regional Security Office of the American Embassy in Tripoli issues a document summarizing "Security Incidents Since June 2011."[288] Eric Nordstrom writes this report just days before his posting in Libya ends. It is a two-column, *51-page bombshell*. (By CBS News's count, it contains some 230 security incidents![289]) The document details an extensive

---

[284] Sen. Intelligence Committee Benghazi Report (Redacted; emphasis added), pp. 10-11; and Jeffrey, Stevens Cabled Washington: CIA Says Al Qaeda Training Camps Within Benghazi.

[285] Stevens July 9 Security Extension Cable to State (emphasis added), p. 1.

[286] *Id.* (emphasis added), p. 2.

[287] *Id.*, p. 2.

[288] Libya Security Incidents Since June 2011.

[289] CBS News, House Probes Security Leading Up to Libya Attack (Regional Security Officer Eric Nordstrom provided House Oversight Committee "with a list of 230

series of such episodes throughout Libya, most of which have occurred in Tripoli and Benghazi. These include successful and attempted assassinations, murders, car and other bombings, firefights, hand grenade attacks, kidnappings, car-jackings, arsons, beatings and incidents of torture.

Nordstrom's report concludes:

The risk of U.S. Mission personnel, private U.S. citizens, and businesspersons encountering an isolating event as a result of militia or political violence is HIGH. The Government of Libya does not yet have the ability to effectively respond to and manage the rising criminal and militia related violence, which could result in an isolating event. . . . Local officials remain concerned with the chaos and radicalization that could result from protracted civil conflict in Libya. Neighboring countries fear extremist groups who could take advantage of the political violence and chaos should Libya become a failed state.[290]

(As discussed below, DAS Charlene Lamb has ordered RSO Nordstrom *not* to recommend extending the mission of Defense's SST military security team. Is this report Nordstrom's revenge for being silenced by DAS Lamb on the issue of renewing the SST?)

Meanwhile, that SST team is scheduled to leave Libya by the end of August 2012. At this time, Lt. Col. Wood later testifies, "Fighting between militias was still common . . . Some militias appeared to be degenerating into organizations resembling free lance criminal operations. . . ."[291]

Eric Nordstrom's migraine-filled posting to Libya ends on July 26, 2012. He later testifies to the House Oversight Committee that after this point he never again is asked by "leadership or management" at State's Diplomatic Security Bureau for his thoughts or suggestions regarding

---

security incidents between Sept. 2011 and July 2012"); CBS News, "U.S. Memo Warned of High Risk of Libya Violence," CBS News online (Oct. 18, 2012) ("CBS News, U.S. Memo Warned of High Risk of Libya Violence"); Baier, New Revelations on Attack in Benghazi (*Watch video there*; Go to 9:15-23); and Nordstrom Oversight Committee Testimony (May 8, 2013) (Response to questions of Rep. Jim Jordan (R-OH)) (confirming there are more than 200 security incidents in Libya in 13 months prior to Benghazi attack), p. 102.

[290] Libya Security Incidents Since June 2011 (emphasis added), p. 51.

[291] Wood House Oversight Prepared Testimony, pp. 2-3.

security in Libya!²⁹² (Why take advantage of current, hard-earned, hands-on expertise on such a trivial issue? Perhaps high State officials cannot forgive Nordstrom for his incendiary "farewell" report.)

Five days after Nordstrom departs, on July 31 Gregory Hicks arrives at the Tripoli Embassy as the new Deputy Chief of Mission – Ambassador Stevens' second-in-command. It doesn't take Hicks long to ascertain Embassy security is woefully inadequate. The astute Hicks grows very concerned about the Embassy's vulnerability. He learns Americans on the ground there fear they are "exposed." Hicks later confirms to the House Oversight panel he even requests training in firearms for the *diplomats* there!²⁹³

At later House Oversight Committee hearings, Congressman (later Senator) James Lankford (R-OK) expresses views consistent with those of Hicks:

> We know that the Tripoli facility was even at a greater risk than Benghazi. There were even more vulnerabilities in Tripoli than there were in Benghazi, both in physical security around the facility and in actual staffing, the people there, the gun toters, . . . the door kickers and such, people that would actually be there to be able to provide that security. The minimum level was not provided.²⁹⁴

In an August 2 cable (in which he requests additional security, discussed below), Ambassador Stevens warns:

> The security condition in Libya remains unpredictable, volatile, and violent. . . . [V]iolent security incidents continue to take place due to the lack of a coherent national Libyan security force and the strength of local militias and large numbers of armed groups.²⁹⁵

On August 8, just over a week after Hicks arrives, Ambassador Stevens sends yet another official warning cable to State. In it, he explains "*a series of violent incidents* has dominated the political

---

[292] Nordstrom Oversight Committee Testimony (May 8, 2013), p. 15; and *Id.* (Response to questions of Rep. Cynthia Lummis (R-WY)), p. 83.

[293] Hicks Oversight Committee Testimony (May 8, 2013) (Response to questions of Rep. James Lankford (R-OK))("It's true"), p. 109.

[294] House Oversight Committee Hearings (May 8, 2013) (Remarks of Rep. James Lankford (R-OK)), p. 109.

[295] Stevens August 2 Bodyguard Request Cable to State, p. 1.

landscape." He adds, "What we have seen are not random crimes of opportunity, but rather *targeted and discriminate attacks*."[296]

On August 19, the Pentagon's Joint Staff produces another relevant slide as part of its daily intelligence report. It is entitled, "Libya: Terrorists to Increase Strength During Next Six Months." This slide asserts:

> There are no near-term prospects for a reversal in *the trend towards a terrorist safe haven in Libya*, and *areas of eastern Libya will likely become a broader safe haven by the end of 2012. The conditions in Libya will allow terrorists to increase attacks against Western and Libyan interests in the country*, as well as attempt attacks in the region and possibly Europe in the next six months.[297]

Then, on September 5 – only five days before Chris Stevens arrives in Benghazi – U.S. Africa Command prepares a "Theater Analysis Report" addressing terrorism in Libya. It is entitled, "Libya: Extremism in Libya Past, Present, and Future." AFRICOM's report states:

> Disarray in Libya's security services, and a likely focus by authorities on pursuit of Qadhafi loyalists is likely allowing jihadists in Libya freedom to recruit, train, and facilitate the movement of fighters and weapons. *The threat to Western and U.S. interests and individuals remains high, particularly in northeast-Libya*.[298]

(Is anyone at the State Department even *reading* any of these intelligence community reports and diplomatic cables from their ambassador in Libya?) ∎

---

[296] Attkisson, Before Death, Amb. Stevens Warned of "Violent Libya Landscape" (emphasis added); and Attkisson, *Stonewalled*, Chap. 4, p. 186; Babbin, Whitewashing Benghazi (emphasis added); CBS Benghazi Timeline (emphasis added); and Baier, New Revelations on Attack in Benghazi (emphasis added) (*Watch video there*; Go to 11:08-30).

[297] Sen. Intelligence Committee Benghazi Report (Redacted; emphasis added), p. 11.

[298] *Id.* (Redacted; emphasis added), p. 11.

15

Tripwire: "You Were Waiting to Die"

The above warnings regarding security concerns in Libya in general are alarming by themselves. However, for some time prior to September 11, 2012, U.S. national security agencies and other government officials have been warning the rest of the U.S. government – and the State Department in particular – of the dangers of operating *in Benghazi itself.*

Some nine months prior to the terrorist attacks in Benghazi (and two months after Qadhafi's overthrow), the State Department sends a security officer to Benghazi to assess the threat level there. In a later interview with the Select Benghazi Committee, that officer describes his subsequent follow-up report to his superior at the State Department:

> I told him that *this was a suicide mission*; that there was *a very good chance that everybody here was going to die*; that there was absolutely no ability here to prevent an attack whatever. . . . He said, "Everybody back here in D.C. knows that people are going to die in Benghazi and nobody is going to care until somebody does die."[299]

Events in Benghazi certainly seem to bear him out. As described in Part I above, the situation in Libya is chaotic and dangerous following the Libyan revolution, during which the U.S. and NATO help overthrow the Libyan dictator, Qadhafi. This chaos is particularly acute in eastern Libya, including Benghazi.[300]

---

[299] The Editors, "What We Do Know About the Benghazi Attack Demands a Reckoning," National Review online (June 28, 2016) ("National Review Editors, What We Do Know About the Benghazi Attack Demands a Reckoning") (emphasis added). See also CNN Report, "Why Didn't the U.S. Military Respond in Time in Benghazi?" CNN (Aug. 6, 2013) ("CNN Report, Why Didn't the U.S. Military Respond in Time in Benghazi?") (House Oversight Committee member Rep. Jason Chaffetz (R-UT): "How come that didn't rise to the level where somebody said, 'You know, we just can't operate in this environment.' It was a deathtrap") (*Watch video there*; Go to 3:59 - 4:06).

[300] Charlie Savage and Adam Goldman, "At Trial, a Focus on the Facts, Not the Politics, of Benghazi," *The New York Times* online (Oct. 1, 2017) ("Savage and Goldman, At Trial, a Focus on the Facts, Not the Politics, of Benghazi") ("The attacks [in Benghazi] crystallized Libya's descent into chaos after the 2011 Arab Spring

Among the numerous militias now operating in Benghazi and other parts of eastern Libya is Ansar al-Sharia. This group's goal is to spread Islamic sharia law throughout Libya through "jihad" (holy war).[301] As discussed below, it later will be revealed this militia is among the terrorist groups that participate in the Benghazi attacks. In November 2012, CBS lists this militia as among the "likely culprits" in Benghazi, describing it as "the Islamic extremist militia Ansar al Sharia, which was based in eastern Libya and *enjoyed huge power in Benghazi before the attack.*"[302] (Maybe CBS should have told the State Department about them.)

Intrepid investigative reporter Sharyl Attkisson asserts the evacuation plan for the U.S. Mission in Benghazi states:

... [T]he majority of Loyalist insurgents tasked with carrying out this plan [Operation Papa Noel, a terrorist plot targeting foreign diplomatic missions and oil fields in Libya] are still active and free in Benghazi. ... Islamic terrorist elements do exist in this area of the country, and have been reported by open sources to be *gaining operational capability.*[303]

Again according to Attkisson, in an online posting in 2012, al Qaeda reportedly warns of "its intent to attack the Red Cross, the British, and then the Americans in Benghazi. The goals are accomplished in order."[304] (The nasty old Red Cross reportedly is targeted because it is

---

uprising, which, with help from NATO air power, had toppled the country's longtime dictator, Col. Muammar el-Qaddafi").

[301] Stephen F. Hayes, "The Benghazi Talking Points," *The Weekly Standard* online (May 13, 2013) ("Hayes, The Benghazi Talking Points").

[302] CBS News, "Sources: Office of the DNI Cut 'al Qaeda' Reference from Benghazi Talking Points, and CIA, FBI Signed Off," CBS News online (Nov. 20, 2012) (emphasis added).

[303] Attkisson, 8 Major Warnings Before Benghazi (emphasis added); and Attkisson, *Stonewalled*, Chap. 4, pp. 178-179.

[304] Attkisson, 8 Major Warnings Before Benghazi; and Eric Schmitt and Mark Landler, "Focus Was on Tripoli in Requests for Security in Libya," *The New York Times* online (Oct. 12, 2012) ("Schmitt and Landler, Focus Was on Tripoli in Requests for Security in Libya") (Lt. Col. Andrew Wood: "We were the last thing on their target list to remove from Benghazi"). See also Attkisson, *Stonewalled* ("... [I]n an online posting, al-Qaeda had stated its intent to attack the Red Cross, the British, and then the Americans in Benghazi. With the first two promises fulfilled, the attack on Benghazi was the last outstanding threat. It seemed just a matter of time"), Chap. 4, p. 180.

"one of the strongholds of Christian missionary activity."[305] What horrible people!)

On April 6, 2012, a small "IED" is hurled over the wall of the U.S. Benghazi Mission Compound, but causes no injuries.[306] On April 10 an explosive device is hurled at a convoy driving in Benghazi, whose passengers include the United Nations' Special Envoy to Libya, Ian Martin. He survives.[307] On May 22, the building of the Benghazi chapter of the International Committee of the Red Cross ("ICRC") is struck by rocket-propelled grenades.[308] Six days later, the "Omar Abdurrahman" group (possibly Libyan jihadists[309]) claims credit for the ICRC attack, and *threatens the U.S.* on social media sites.[310] On June 6, a bomb explodes at the Mission Compound itself! It tears a 9x12-foot hole near the facility's Main Gate. The Omar Abdurrahman group again claims responsibility.[311]

Five days later on June 11 in Benghazi, a rocket-propelled grenade strikes a convoy that includes the British Ambassador to Libya, Dominic Asquith. The attack injures two of his security detail.[312] Lt. Col. Wood, commander of the American SST in Libya, happens to be in Benghazi at this time. Wood assists U.S. diplomatic security agents from the Mission in providing "medical and security assistance for wounded UK security personnel."[313] Afterwards, Wood conducts a

---

[305] AP, Red Cross Says Attack on Libya Office Wounds 1.

[306] Sen. Intelligence Committee Benghazi Report, p. 13.

[307] *Id.* (Redacted), pp. 12-13 & n. 51; Attkisson, 8 Major Warnings Before Benghazi; Babbin, Whitewashing Benghazi; and CBS Benghazi Timeline.

[308] Sen. Intelligence Committee Benghazi Report (Redacted), pp. 12-13 & n. 51; Attkisson, 8 Major Warnings Before Benghazi; and CBS Benghazi Timeline.

[309] See AP, Red Cross Says Attack on Libya Office Wounds 1.

[310] Sen. Intelligence Committee Benghazi Report (Redacted), p. 12 n. 51.

[311] Benghazi Committee Report, p. 323; Sen. Intelligence Committee Benghazi Report (Redacted), pp. 12-13 & n. 51; Attkisson, 8 Major Warnings Before Benghazi; CBS Benghazi Timeline; and Baier, New Revelations on Attack in Benghazi (*Watch video there*; Go to 8:27-34). *View photograph* at "Political Violence Against Americans," U.S. Dept. of State, Bureau of Diplomatic Security (July 2013), State Dept. website, p. 7.

[312] Sen. Intelligence Committee Benghazi Report (Redacted), pp. 12-13 & n. 51; AP, Red Cross Says Attack on Libya Office Wounds 1; and Burton & Katz, *Under Fire*, Prologue, pp. 5-7 and 13.

[313] Wood House Oversight Prepared Testimony, p. 2; and Attkisson, *Stonewalled*, Chap. 4, p. 184.

post-attack investigation. He concludes the ambush "definitely" is an assassination attempt by people who "knew what they were doing."[314] This assassination effort leads the U.K. to withdraw from the city the next day.[315]

Someone in the Pentagon is watching all this. On June 12, the Defense Intelligence Agency issues a report entitled, "Libya: Terrorists Now Targeting U.S. and Western Interests." This report cautions about growing ties between al Qaeda and local Libyan terrorists in the *area around Benghazi*.[316]

On June 18, gunmen attack the Tunisian consulate in Benghazi and burn its flag.[317] On July 29, "a number of IEDs" are found and defused on the property of Benghazi's Tibesti Hotel (which is frequented by western diplomats and business persons).[318] The former Libyan Military Intelligence building in Benghazi is bombed on August 1.[319] On August 5, after an ICRC building in Misratah (400 kilometers west of Benghazi across the Gulf of Sidra) is struck by RPGs (for the second time), the Red Cross withdraws its representatives from both Benghazi and Misratah.[320] According to CNN, during this period the United Nations also closes its office in Benghazi.[321] (However, other key sources do not mention this last event.[322])

---

[314] Attkisson, 8 Major Warnings Before Benghazi; Wood House Oversight Prepared Testimony, p. 2; Babbin, Whitewashing Benghazi; CBS Benghazi Timeline; and Baier, New Revelations on Attack in Benghazi (*Watch video there*; Go to 8:34 - 9:15).

[315] Sen. Intelligence Committee Benghazi Report (Redacted), p. 12 n. 51; Babbin, Whitewashing Benghazi; Hicks Oversight Committee Testimony (May 8, 2013) (Response to questions of Rep. Connolly (D-VA)), p. 55; Attkisson, *Stonewalled*, Chap. 4, p. 184; and Burton & Katz, *Under Fire*, Prologue, pp. 8 and 13-14.

[316] Sen. Intelligence Committee Benghazi Report (Redacted), pp. 9-10; and Babbin, Whitewashing Benghazi.

[317] Sen. Intelligence Committee Benghazi Report (Redacted), p. 13 n. 51.

[318] *Id.* (Redacted), pp. 13-14 n. 51.

[319] *Id.* (Redacted), p. 14.

[320] *Id.* (Redacted), p. 13 n. 51; and Burton & Katz, *Under Fire*, Prologue, p. 14.

[321] CNN Report, Why Didn't the U.S. Military Respond in Time in Benghazi? (*Watch video there*; Go to 3:35-42).

[322] E.g., Benghazi Committee Report, p. 134 (noting only IED attack on motorcade of United Nations Envoy); and Sen. Intelligence Committee Benghazi Report (Redacted), pp. 12-14.

THE TRUE ACCOUNT OF VALOR AND ABANDONMENT

Given all these security problems, one State Department official responsible for ensuring the U.S. can respond to terrorism threats, Mark Thompson, later testifies: "all the indicators" are the Benghazi facility likely would be considered a "possible or even likely target of a terrorist incident."[323] (We will learn much more about Mark Thompson later.)

The Senate Intelligence Committee later will conclude, ". . . [I]ntelligence reports made clear that extremist groups in eastern Libya, including Ansar al-Sharia, were not only running training camps there, but also plotting and carrying out attacks against U.S. and Western interests in the months prior to the attacks in Benghazi."[324] "Between March and August of 2012, western targets are attacked at least 20 times in Benghazi by terrorists using increasingly powerful and sophisticated weapons, including rocket-propelled grenades and improvised explosive devices."[325]

The pattern is now clear. Terrorists repeatedly are attacking foreign government facilities and personnel in Benghazi itself, and increasingly

---

[323] Thompson Oversight Committee Testimony (May 8, 2013) (Response to questions of Rep. Patrick Meehan (R-PA)), p. 74.

[324] Sen. Intelligence Committee Benghazi Report (Redacted), p. 24.

[325] Babbin, Whitewashing Benghazi. See also Sen. Intelligence Committee Benghazi Report (Redacted) ("As the Accountability Review Board [discussed below] found, there were at least 20 security incidents involving the Temporary Mission Facility, international organizations, non-governmental organizations, and third-country nationals and diplomats in the Benghazi area in the months leading up to the September 11, 2012, attacks"), p. 12; Kirkpatrick and Myers, Libya Attack Brings Challenges for U.S. ("Benghazi, awash in guns, has recently witnessed a string of assassinations as well as attacks on international missions, including a bomb said to be planted by another Islamist group that exploded near the United States mission there as recently as June [2012]"); Eric Schmitt, "Fact Checking the House Benghazi Committee's Findings," *The New York Times* online (June 28, 2016) ("The Obama administration received intelligence reports that Islamist extremist groups were operating training camps in the mountains near Benghazi. By June, the city had experienced a string of assassinations, as well as attacks on the Red Cross and on a British envoy's motorcade. Mr. Stevens emailed his superiors in Washington in August, alerting them to 'a security vacuum' in the city"); CBS News, U.S. Memo Warned of High Risk of Libya Violence ("In Benghazi, violent episodes appeared to be on the rise starting in June 2012 . . ."); and Tapper, Security Team Commander Says Ambassador Stevens Wanted His Team to Stay in Libya Past August (summarizing Western targets being hit in Benghazi).

the targets are *western* governments and organizations.³²⁶ (Without doubt, it is time for the United States to "get the hell out of Dodge."³²⁷)

In the midst of these attacks, on August 15 an "Emergency Action Committee" ("EAC") meeting takes place at the Mission Compound in Benghazi in the "cantina" within Building B. It is convened by the Principal Officer at the Mission (then a diplomat named Eric Gaudiosi³²⁸). The EAC is an interagency panel that convenes when an embassy or other diplomatic facility, such as the Benghazi Mission, is confronting major security threats.³²⁹ The specific purpose of this sit-down is "to evaluate [the Special Mission] Post's tripwires in light of the *deteriorating security situation in Benghazi*."³³⁰ (As detailed below, by this time some MSD teams and the SST have already left or are on their way out of Libya.³³¹)

---

³²⁶ E.g., Wood House Oversight Prepared Testimony (". . . Targeted attacks against westerners were on the increase. . . ."), p. 3; and Interview of Rep. Trey Gowdy (R-SC) on "America's Newsroom," Fox News online (Circa Oct. 3, 2012) (". . . It's a pattern that is impossible to ignore, isn't it? It's an increasing series of escalations of violence. And apparently this administration was the only group in the world that was not aware that this area was dangerous. . . .") (*Watch video there*; Go to 1:00-17).

³²⁷ CNN Report, Why Didn't the U.S. Military Respond in Time in Benghazi? (House Oversight Committee member Rep. Jason Chaffetz (R-UT): "How come that didn't rise to the level where somebody said, 'You know, we just can't operate in this environment.' It was a deathtrap") (*Watch video there*; Go to 3:59 - 4:06); McCarthy, Hillary Clinton's Benghazi Debacle: Arming Jihadists in Libya . . . And Syria (". . . [W]e have never gotten to the bottom of why the State Department, under Mrs. Clinton's direction, had an installation in Benghazi, one of the world's most dangerous places for Americans"); and House Oversight Committee Hearings (May 8, 2013) (Remarks of Rep. Patrick Meehan (R-PA)) (". . . I am struggling to find out how we had a United States Ambassador in a marginally safe American compound in an increasingly hostile area on an iconic day like September 11th with limited security. . . ."), pp. 72-73.

³²⁸ Hicks Oversight Committee Testimony (May 8, 2013) (Response to questions of Rep. Carolyn Maloney (D-NY)), p. 87.

³²⁹ Sen. Intelligence Committee Benghazi Report (EAC is convened "in response to emergencies or security matters"), p. 15.

³³⁰ Sen. Intelligence Committee Benghazi Report (Redacted; emphasis added), p. 15.

³³¹ Cretz March 28 Increased Security Personnel Cable to State (referencing "our two departing MSD teams"), p. 1; Baier, New Revelations on Attack in Benghazi (*Watch video there*; Go to 9:48 - 10:46); CBS Benghazi Timeline; Ferrara, Benghazi: Obama's Actions Amount to a Shameful Dereliction of Duty; Burnett, Benghazi Timeline: "We Are Under Attack" (*Watch video there*; Go to 4:14-28); Hicks Oversight Committee Testimony (May 8, 2013) (Response to questions of Rep. Turner (R-OH)), pp. 51-52; and Cornwell and Zakaria, U.S. Security at Benghazi Mission Called "Weak."

THE TRUE ACCOUNT OF VALOR AND ABANDONMENT

At this EAC conference, an unidentified CIA officer reportedly asserts to the group Benghazi now is home to approximately ten Islamist militias and training camps, some of which are affiliated with al Qaeda.[332] State's Principal Officer observes the security situation in Benghazi is "trending negatively," and *"this daily pattern of violence would be the 'new normal' for the foreseeable future."*[333] The Principal Officer and a CIA officer "expressed concerns with the lack of host nation security" to support the Mission facility.[334] Also during this meeting "The Regional Security Officer [now John Martinec] 'expressed concerns with the ability to defend Post *in the event of a coordinated attack* due to limited manpower, security measures, weapons capabilities, host nation support, and the overall size of the [Mission] compound.'"[335] (No kidding; is anyone sensing a pattern here?)

According to the Senate Intelligence Committee, the next day, August 16, Ambassador Stevens sends a "Secret" cable (again, an official communication) to State Department headquarters. It summarizes the above takeaways from this EAC meeting. In this cable, Stevens raises "additional concerns about the deteriorating security situation *in Benghazi*" in light of the points made at the EAC meeting.[336] According to Fox News, this classified cable expressly includes RSO Martinec's warning at the EAC conference the Mission cannot defend against a "coordinated attack."[337] In this cable, Stevens

---

[332] Sen. Intelligence Committee Benghazi Report, p. 15; and Catherine Herridge, "Exclusive: Classified Cable Warned Consulate Couldn't Withstand 'Coordinated Attack,'" Fox News online (Oct. 31, 2012) ("Herridge, Classified Cable Warned Consulate Couldn't Withstand Coordinated Attack").

[333] Sen. Intelligence Committee Benghazi Report (emphasis added), p. 15.

[334] *Id.*, p. 15; and Burton & Katz, *Under Fire*, Chap. 6, p. 63.

[335] Sen. Intelligence Committee Benghazi Report (Redacted; emphasis added), p. 16; Burton & Katz, *Under Fire*, Chap. 6, p. 63; Babbin, Whitewashing Benghazi; and Herridge, Classified Cable Warned Consulate Couldn't Withstand Coordinated Attack.

[336] Sen. Intelligence Committee Benghazi Report (Redacted; emphasis added), pp. 15-16. Compare Burton & Katz, *Under Fire*, Chap. 6, p. 63 (asserting "Secret" cable is sent by RSO in Tripoli, not by Amb. Stevens).

[337] Herridge, Classified Cable Warned Consulate Couldn't Withstand Coordinated Attack (*Watch video* there; Go to 0:01 - 1:24); and Catherine Herridge, Pamela K. Browne and Cyd Upson, "Clinton State Department Silenced Them on Benghazi Security Lapses, Contractors Say," Fox News online (Sept. 12, 2017) ("Herridge et al, Clinton State Department Silenced Them on Benghazi Security Lapses, Contractors Say") (*Watch video* there).

also conveys the intent of the Mission in Benghazi to submit requests for additional security to Embassy Tripoli.[338]

Following this EAC session and Stevens' follow-up cable, little changes. The Senate intelligence panel "... found no evidence that significant actions were taken by the State Department between August 15 ... and September 11, 2012, to increase security at the Mission facility in response to the concerns raised in that [EAC] meeting."[339] However, this Senate committee asserts it also finds no evidence any subsequent requests by the Benghazi post "for additional physical security upgrades and staffing needs" are forwarded by the Tripoli Embassy to the State Department headquarters before the September 11 attacks.[340]

(It is possible Ambassador Stevens is still awaiting a reply to earlier cables he has sent on July 9 and August 2 pleading for more security in Libya (discussed below). Or perhaps he wants to see the situation in Benghazi for himself before making yet another request for more security there?)

According to CBS News, on August 27 – just 15 days before Ambassador Stevens will arrive in Benghazi – the State Department reportedly issues a travel warning for Libya. The statement cites the threats of car bombings and assassinations in Tripoli *and Benghazi*.[341] (Is the State Department even reading its own travel warnings?)

Such is the extremely dangerous security situation in Benghazi into which Secretary of State Hillary Clinton sends Ambassador Chris Stevens and his administrative assistant Sean Smith, protected by only five State Department security guards, in September 2012. (Instead of getting *out* of Dodge, Clinton's State Department sends diplomats *into* Dodge.)

As will be seen in greater detail later, one of Clinton's key lieutenants making security decisions during this period is her department's Under Secretary for Management, Patrick F. Kennedy. (He has been a foreign service employee since 1973.[342])

---

[338] Herridge, Classified Cable Warned Consulate Couldn't Withstand Coordinated Attack.

[339] Sen. Intelligence Committee Benghazi Report (Redacted), p. 16.

[340] *Id.* (Redacted), p. 19.

[341] Attkisson, *Stonewalled*, Chap. 4, p. 187; and CBS Benghazi Timeline.

[342] State Dept. website.

THE TRUE ACCOUNT OF VALOR AND ABANDONMENT

This Under Secretary position is one of the most important (if least known) of State Department offices. And in this role, Kennedy will be at the center of the entire Benghazi debacle. The State Department's website describes his Under Secretary duties as follows:

> The Under Secretary is responsible for providing the operational platform and facilities that the United States needs to carry out its foreign policy mission. Responsible for the people, resources, budget, facilities, technology, financial operations, consular affairs, logistics, contracting, and security for Department of State operations, and is the Secretary's principal advisor on management issues.[343]

In carrying out these key functions, it cannot be argued Kennedy is uninformed of the U.S. security posture in Libya. Gregory Hicks later will testify Kennedy must approve who comes to Tripoli and Benghazi, and who doesn't. Embassy Tripoli is required to send a *daily* report to Kennedy's office listing everyone who is in Libya![344]

Indeed, Kennedy later admits under oath he personally knows there are "very real dangers" in Benghazi. His House Oversight Committee testimony is replete with references to such threats.[345] Despite all these attacks and intelligence reports and warning cables and concerns and alerts, and the intelligence communities' and Ambassador Stevens' many warnings, Kennedy later will tell Congress:

> We had no actionable intelligence ... about this threat in Benghazi.... And therefore ... I never went to the Secretary of State and told her it was time to leave Benghazi.[346]

---

[343] *Id.*

[344] Hicks Oversight Committee Testimony (May 8, 2013) (Response to questions of Rep. John Duncan, Jr. (R-TN)), pp. 55-56; and Additional Views of Senators Chambliss, Burr, Risch, Coats, Rubio, and Coburn, Sen. Intelligence Committee Benghazi Report ("Additional Views of Senators Chambliss, Burr, et al.") ("... DCM [Deputy Chief of Mission] Hicks also told the Committee that Mr. Kennedy approved every person who went to Libya and received a daily report on the number of personnel, their names, and their status...."), p. 10.

[345] Kennedy House Oversight Prepared Testimony (emphasis added) ("Why is it necessary for representatives of the United States to be in Benghazi despite the *very real dangers* there?"; "There was *no doubt* that it [Benghazi] was dangerous"; "The transitional authorities *struggled to provide basic security* [in Benghazi]. Extremists sought to exploit any opening to advance their own agenda"; "... Ambassador Stevens stayed in Benghazi during those difficult days"; and "*dangerous places* like Benghazi"), pp. 2-4.

[346] Attkisson, *Stonewalled*, Chap. 4, p. 185; Attkisson, 8 Major Warnings Before Benghazi; and CBS News, U.S. Memo Warned of High Risk of Libya Violence (State

(No "actionable intelligence"? How about an extremely lengthy series of very *recent, actual terrorist attacks* on western governments and organizations *in Benghazi?*[347])

Similarly, Clinton herself later testifies, "Senator, I want to make clear that no one in the State Department, the intelligence community, any other agency, ever recommended that we close Benghazi."[348] (Why *not?* Why did *you* appoint or keep such *idiots* like Kennedy and Lamb as managers at your agency to oversee security at your diplomatic posts? Or do Clinton's managers realize her political future requires Libya and Benghazi be portrayed as a foreign policy success?[349])

It is important to note then Deputy Chief of Mission in Libya, Gregory Hicks, also believes the State Department should have remained in Benghazi. He later tells the House Oversight Committee it "absolutely" is a wise decision for the U.S. to stay in Benghazi after the British have closed their post and departed. Hicks testifies:

> We needed to stay there [Benghazi] as a symbolic gesture to a people that we saved from Qadhafi during the revolution. As we know, Qadhafi's forces were on the doorstep of Benghazi right before the NATO bombing commenced. And ... Chris went there as a symbolic gesture to support the dream of the people of Benghazi to have a democracy. ... And he also understood from the Secretary herself that Benghazi was important to us and that we needed to make it to be a permanent constituent post.[350]

However, Kennedy's and Clinton's testimony regarding maintaining the Special Mission in Benghazi does not appear to tell the whole story.

Dept. has continued to cite threat assessment conducted by the Director of National Intelligence which stated that there was, "no actionable intelligence that an attack on our post in Benghazi was planned or imminent").

[347] Attkisson, *Stonewalled* ("'One wonders what it would have taken to trigger alarm bells at [State Department] headquarters"), Chap. 4, p. 185.

[348] Clinton Senate Armed Services Committee Testimony (Jan. 23, 2013); and CNN Report, Why Didn't the U.S. Military Respond in Time to Benghazi? (*Watch Video there*; Go to 4:12-28).

[349] Hemingway, 5 Big Takeaways From the House Benghazi Report, quoting from Additional Views of Reps. Jordan and Pompeo: "Secretary Clinton pushed for the U.S. to intervene in Libya, which at the time represented one of her signature achievements. To leave Benghazi would have been viewed as her failure and prompted unwelcome scrutiny of her choices...."), p. 420.

[350] Hicks Oversight Committee Testimony (May 8, 2013) (Response to questions of Rep. Carolyn Maloney (D-NY)), p. 105.

THE TRUE ACCOUNT OF VALOR AND ABANDONMENT

According to the House Oversight Committee, a Diplomatic Security "desk officer" for Libya, Brian Papanu, describes to the committee's investigators a meeting he has on July 2, 2012 with Under Secretary for Management Kennedy. During this meeting, the question arises whether the State Department intends to keep the Benghazi Mission open beyond December 2012. Papanu reportedly explains that Kennedy replies "He had to check with S." Asked what "S" meant, Papanu tells the investigators, "That would be Secretary of State."[351]

If Papanu is telling the truth (and the author knows of no reason to doubt him), Secretary Clinton almost certainly discusses Benghazi security issues and the possibility of withdrawing from this city with Kennedy before the September 11 attacks. This is directly contrary to her later sworn testimony to Congress. (Someone is lying to Congress.)

Former CIA Director General Michael Hayden concludes, "What they had decided to do with the security posture was inconsistent with the threat assessment that was readily available."[352] A CNN reporter asks Hayden whether the U.S. flag should have been flying over Benghazi on September 11, 2012 – by some accounts the only major western flag remaining. Hayden believes the then current strategic intelligence is sufficient to have merited the closing of the U.S. outpost in Benghazi. Asked whether the U.S. flag still should have been flying there, Hayden replies:

> I don't think so. There was plenty of warning [to justify leaving Benghazi]. It's kind of what we call strategic warning – that you knew things bad could happen. Tactical warning – "It's going to happen tonight at 7:00 o'clock" – not so much. If you were waiting for tactical warning sitting out there in the consulate [sic] in Benghazi, you weren't waiting for intelligence . . . You were waiting to die.[353] ∎

---

[351] "Benghazi Attacks: Investigative Update Interim Report on the Accountability Review Board," House Oversight Committee website (Sept. 16, 2013) ("House Oversight Interim Report on Benghazi ARB"), p. 65; and Sharyl Attkisson, "Benghazi Accountability Review Board Comes Under Renewed Criticism," CBS News online (Sept. 19, 2013) ("Attkisson, Benghazi Accountability Review Board Comes Under Renewed Criticism").

[352] CNN Reports, Why Didn't the U.S. Military Respond in Time in Benghazi? (Interview of General Michael Hayden (Ret.) with John King) (*Watch video there*; Go to 3:18-25).

[353] *Id.* (*Watch video there*; Go to 4:31-57).

16

Security: "We Couldn't Keep What We Had"

While all the intelligence agency warnings discussed above are being issued, American diplomats on the ground in Libya can see for themselves how dangerous the situation in Tripoli and Benghazi and elsewhere is becoming. They repeatedly will beg for help. Their pleas will be in vain.

From September 21, 2011 through July 26, 2012, Eric Nordstrom is the head security officer at the U.S. Embassy in Tripoli, Libya.[354] During this period as "Regional Security Officer" ("RSO") he will make multiple requests to the State Department for enhanced security in Libya. As noted above, State already has approved an extension of the SST unit's mission in Libya for four months until August.[355]

There is a great deal of confusion among congressional investigators, the media, State Department employees, and Team Obama regarding these many requests for enhanced security. We will attempt to sort it out here.

The February 2012 Request for More Security

As early as mid-February 2012, U.S. diplomats in Libya know they need more security assets. Then U.S. Ambassador to Libya Gene Cretz and his Deputy Chief of Mission Joan Polaschik fly from Libya to Washington to request additional security personnel. They meet with Charlene Lamb, and separately with Patrick Kennedy and other senior State officials.[356]

The March 28 Request for More Security

As a follow-up to Cretz and Polaschik's February visit to Washington, on March 28, 2012, Eric Nordstrom prepares an official

---

[354] CBS News, U.S. Memo Warned of High Risk of Libya Violence.

[355] Wood House Oversight Prepared Testimony, p. 3.

[356] Additional Views of Senators Chambliss, Burr, et al., p. 9.

cable (approved by Cretz and Polaschik) to State Department headquarters. This cable requests an increased level of State Department security assets in Libya. The request is based upon the "vast increase" in the U.S. diplomatic and related programs in the country, as well as the reduction in the MSD assets that is occurring.[357]

The Nordstrom/Cretz security request of March 28 is very detailed, and obviously has been carefully thought out. It recommends very specific staffing levels and personnel categories, and explains why each staffer is needed. The cable seeks full-time staffing positions in Tripoli for one RSO, one Deputy RSO, and four Assistant RSOs. The cable also expressly contemplates "continued operations in Benghazi" through calendar year 2012. Concerning Benghazi, the March 28 request seeks *five* TDY ("temporary duty assignment") Diplomatic Security agents at this post, on 45-60-day rotations.[358]

On April 19, 2012, by cable the State Department officially denies Embassy Tripoli's request for five additional DSAs for Benghazi. This denial occurs less than two weeks after the initial IED attack on the Benghazi Mission Compound noted above.[359]

Recommendations to Extend the SST

At this time, DoD's SST is the U.S. diplomats' principal security asset in Libya. Its commander, Lieutenant Colonel Wood, strongly recommends to the State Department that SST's deployment in Libya be extended past August 2012.[360] (Wood's pleas will go unheeded in Washington.[361])

Lt. Col. Wood is not alone. He later tells ABC News the Embassy staff's "first choice was for us to stay. That would have been the choice of the embassy people in Tripoli."[362] (Indeed, why would any rational

---

[357] Cretz March 28 Increased Security Personnel Cable to State, pp. 2-3.

[358] *Id.* pp. 1-3.

[359] Benghazi Committee Report, p. 320; and Nordstrom Oversight Committee Testimony (May 8, 2013) (Response to questions of Rep. James Lankford (R-OK)), p. 108.

[360] Baier, New Revelations on Attack in Benghazi (*Watch video there*; Go to 7:06-10 and 9:47 - 10:47).

[361] *Id.* (*Watch video there*; Go to 7:06-10 and 9:47 - 10:47).

[362] Tapper, Security Team Commander Says Ambassador Stevens Wanted His Team to Stay in Libya Past August.

person expect anything different?) Wood tells CBS News Stevens and his Tripoli staff fight hard to keep security forces in Libya. Wood explains, "It was quite a degree of frustration on their part. They were – I guess you could say – clenched-fist over the whole issue."[363] Wood testifies to Congress, "We were fighting a losing battle. We couldn't even keep what we had. . . ."[364]

However, on this SST issue Embassy Tripoli faces a major obstacle. Eric Nordstrom, the State Department's soon-to-be-departed RSO for Libya, later testifies he is *ordered* by Deputy Assistant Secretary Charlene Lamb at State headquarters *not* to seek renewal of this SST![365] Nordstrom will claim he interprets this directive as meaning ". . . there was going to be too much political cost" to extend the SST's stay in Libya.[366] (Remember, the Pentagon pays for the SST, not the State Department.)

The evidence is confusing regarding whether Ambassador Stevens himself actually requests another extension of the SST's tour of duty in Libya beyond August. The Senate Committee on Intelligence claims Stevens twice refuses a personal offer from General Carter Ham, head of Africa Command, to extend the SST's deployment in Libya.[367] However, Lt. Col. Wood tells ABC News Stevens strongly supports another extension of the SST in Libya.[368] What is the truth?

---

[363] Attkisson, Before Death, Amb. Stevens Warned of "Violent Libya Landscape."

[364] Wood Oversight Committee Testimony (Oct. 10, 2012) (Response to questions of Rep. Jim Jordan (R-OH)), p. 106; and Tapper, Security Officer: "For Me the Taliban Is Inside the Building." See also Attkisson, *Stonewalled* ("It was becoming clear to everyone on the ground [in Libya] that as things grew more dangerous, they were going to have to do more with less"), Chap. 4, p. 180.

[365] Nordstrom Oversight Committee Testimony (Oct. 10, 2012) (Response to questions of Rep. Dennis Ross (R-FL)), pp. 91-92; and Tapper, Security Officer: "For Me the Taliban Is Inside the Building" (Earlier Nordstrom had said he was "specifically told" that "You can't request an SST extension. How I interpreted that was there was going to be too much political cost").

[366] Tapper, Security Officer: "For Me the Taliban Is Inside the Building."

[367] Sen. Intelligence Committee Benghazi Report (Redacted), pp. 20-21.

[368] Tapper, Security Officer: "For Me the Taliban Is Inside the Building" (Lt. Col. Wood, SST commander, "sent home in August – against his wishes and, he says, the wishes of the late Ambassador Chris Stevens . . ."); and Tapper, Security Team Commander Says Ambassador Stevens Wanted His Team to Stay in Libya Past August ("U.S. Ambassador to Libya Chris Stevens wanted a Security Support Team, made up of 16 special operations soldiers, to stay with him in Libya after their deployment was scheduled to end in August, the commander of that security team told ABC News") (*Watch video* there; Go to 0:22-30 and 0:58 - 1:10).

THE TRUE ACCOUNT OF VALOR AND ABANDONMENT

(Does Chris Stevens receive an order similar to Nordstrom's not to seek another SST extension? What sense would it make for the agency to muzzle Nordstrom, yet allow his superior to request the very same assistance? No sense, of course. Also, the ambassador is no fool. It is obvious from his multiple cables during this period he knows how dangerous Libya has become. Would he really endanger himself and his entire Libya diplomatic team by declining an offer of significant security assistance with no adverse impact on his budget? The author concludes he would not – *unless* his superiors at State *order* him to do so.

(On this issue, the author accords considerable weight to the perspective of Lt. Col. Wood. As SST commander in Libya, he has a seat on the Libya "Country Team" comprised of top U.S. government managers in country. He later testifies he is "closely involved with the operational planning and support to the RSO's security objectives." Wood meets "regularly" and has "frequent conversations" with Ambassadors Cretz and (later) Stevens, as well as with other members of the Country Team. When RSO Nordstrom rotates out of Libya at the end of July, until Wood's own departure two weeks later, he becomes the most senior member of the Country Team next to Ambassador Stevens. Wood is very well "plugged in" to the security situation in Libya.[369] Accordingly, the author concludes Stevens desires a continuation of SST's mission, but cannot officially say so.)

The July 9 Request for More Security

Because RSO Nordstrom (and likely Stevens) is directed by superiors not to ask for an SST extension, the U.S. diplomats in Tripoli must get creative. On July 9, Stevens and Nordstrom send another cable to State requesting an extension of 13 security agent positions in Benghazi (but not explicitly the SST).[370]

More specifically, Ambassador Stevens and Nordstrom's July cable asks for continuing assistance of a "minimum of 13" temporary duty security personnel in Libya. The cable explains these assets are

---

[369] Wood House Oversight Prepared Testimony, pp. 1-2.

[370] Stevens July 9 Security Extension Cable to State. See also Schmitt and Landler, Focus Was on Tripoli in Requests for Security in Libya ("In a stream of diplomatic cables, embassy security officers warned their superiors at the State Department of a worsening threat from Islamic extremists, and requested that the teams of military personnel and State Department security guards who were already on duty be kept in service").

"required to maintain current transportation security and incident response capability while we transition to a locally based security support structure." Poignantly, this extension is requested for another 60 days – through "mid-September 2012." The cable suggests these 13 agents could be from a combination of State's MSD unit members, trained State Department Diplomatic Security personnel, and DoD SST team members.[371] (Note this request appears to be a clever "back door" means of requesting an extension of at least some SST members, without explicitly saying it would like the entire team to remain.)

Like Nordstrom's earlier March 28 cable, this request is not expressly denied, but the higher-ups at State in "Foggy Bottom" (as the State Department's Washington headquarters is known) simply do not respond officially.[372] According to Nordstrom's later testimony, it is "relatively unheard of" in the State Department not to reply to such official cables.[373] However, Gregory Hicks later will claim Stevens' July 9 request *is denied* – by Under Secretary Patrick Kennedy.[374] Explicit denial or not, the recommendation clearly is not granted.

(As Gregory Hicks subsequently explains, this refusal to permit the additional bodyguards will prove very significant. If they had been authorized, Hicks asserts "they would have traveled to Benghazi with the ambassador, and the Sept. 11 attack might have been thwarted."[375])

---

[371] Stevens July 9 Security Extension Cable to State, pp. 1-2; Sundby, Ambassador Warned Libya Was "Volatile and Violent"; and CBS Benghazi Timeline. See also Hicks, What the Benghazi Attack Taught Me About Hillary Clinton.

[372] Nordstrom Oversight Committee Testimony (Oct. 10, 2012) (Response to questions of Rep. Dennis Ross (R-FL)), pp. 91-92; Nordstrom Oversight Committee Testimony (May 8, 2013) (Response to questions of Rep. Rob Woodall (R-GA)) ("I largely got a nonresponse. The responses that I did get were you don't have specific targeting, you don't have specific threats against you. The long and short of it is you are not dealing with suicide bombers, incoming artillery, and vehicle bombs like they are in Iraq and Afghanistan, so basically stop complaining"), p. 86; Sen. Intelligence Committee Benghazi Report (State Department did not fulfill Amb. Stevens' July 9 request for 13 additional security personnel, and "State Department headquarters never responded to the request with a cable"), p. 15; Babbin, Whitewashing Benghazi; and CBS News, House Probes Security Leading Up to Libya Attack.

[373] Nordstrom Oversight Committee Testimony (May 8, 2013) (Response to questions of Rep. Rob Woodall (R-GA)), p. 86.

[374] Hicks, What the Benghazi Attack Taught Me About Hillary Clinton.

[375] *Id.* See also Nordstrom Oversight Committee Testimony (May 8, 2013) (Response to questions of Rep. Tony Cardenas (D CA)) ("... And what we were looking at is that you were going to have a downsizing of personnel in Tripoli. So anytime the Ambassador would have traveled, that would have impacted security in both locations

The August 2 Request for More Security

August 2012 arrives in Libya. Eric Nordstrom now has left the country. Embassy Tripoli has lost on the issue of maintaining the SST unit. Yet Christopher Stevens knows he and Gregory Hicks and the other Americans remaining in Libya still need greater protection.

As noted above, in an August 2, 2012 cable, Ambassador Stevens cautions, "The security condition in *Libya* remains unpredictable, volatile, and violent." Because of the poor security support provided by the Libyan government, in this cable Ambassador Stevens calls for an additional 11 "protective detail bodyguard positions" at the U.S. Embassy in Tripoli. In this request, the diplomat explains the additional guards "will fill the vacuum of security personnel currently at Post on TDY [temporary duty] status who will be leaving within the next month and will not be replaced."[376] (Stevens makes clear in his cable this refers to State's planned withdrawal of the SST and of the third and final MSD team, as well as some DSAs.[377]) Stevens estimates the cost of this proposal at just over $335,000 annually.[378]

By the night Christopher Stevens and Sean Smith are murdered on September 11, 2012, not a single one of these requests for enhanced security has been approved by their superiors at Foggy Bottom.

In this August - September 2012 timeframe, the U.S. State Department confronts only three possible, rational strategies concerning its facility in Benghazi: (1) Close the Mission and leave Benghazi entirely;[379] (2) Close the Mission and use only local Libyans

---

because you would have been splitting up resources, which is what I think ultimately happened"), p. 76.

[376] Stevens August 2 Bodyguard Request Cable to State, p. 1; Sundby, Ambassador Warned Libya Was "Volatile and Violent"; Sharyl Attkisson, "Before Death, Amb. Stevens Warned of "Violent" Libya Landscape," CBS News online (Oct. 20, 2012) ("Attkisson, Before Death, Amb. Stevens Warned of 'Violent Libya Landscape'"); CBS Benghazi Timeline; and Ferrara, Benghazi: Obama's Actions Amount to a Shameful Dereliction of Duty.

[377] Stevens August 2 Bodyguard Request Cable to State, p. 1. See also Wood House Oversight Prepared Testimony, p. 3.

[378] Stevens August 2 Bodyguard Request Cable to State, p. 2.

[379] See Sen. Intelligence Committee Benghazi Report ("RECOMMENDATION: Where adequate security is not available, the Department of State should be prepared to evacuate or close diplomatic facilities under the highest threat, as it has in recent years in Sana'a, Yemen, and Damascus, Syria"), p. 26; and "On-the-Record Briefing by

or undercover personnel in this city;[380] or (3) Maintain the Mission (or a safer, alternative facility, possibly co-locating with the CIA Annex) and beef up security there dramatically. Instead, as explained next, State will adopt a fourth, entirely irrational option: it reduces security significantly in Libya and keeps diplomats openly in the Benghazi Mission Compound. Calamity will result. ∎

Under Secretary Kennedy," Special Briefing, State Dept. Archives website (Oct. 10, 2012) ("Kennedy October 10 Briefing") ("We live with risk, but . . . we look for ways to mitigate that risk . . . and then we come up with a strategy. If we cannot mitigate that risk, we withdraw. We withdrew from Tripoli. We withdrew from Damascus") (*Watch video there*; Go to 6:59 - 8:52).

[380] See Stewart, The Benghazi Report and the Diplomatic Security Funding Cycle (". . . Is a permanent U.S. presence even required in a place like Benghazi, or can the missions in such locations be accomplished by a combination of visiting diplomats, covert operatives and local employees?").

17

"We Needed More, Not Less"

As noted above, the intelligence agencies, the military, and the diplomats and security personnel on the ground in Libya all support additional security there. Terrorist attacks against western government facilities and foreign organizations are increasing at an alarming pace. So naturally the Obama State Department does the exact *opposite*: it actually *reduces* security assets in Libya in the months leading up to the Benghazi attacks![381] It does so despite all the violent terror attacks in eastern Libya summarized above (Chapters 14-15).

In an interview with CBS News correspondent Sharyl Attkisson, Lt. Col. Wood tells her that for the environment on the ground he and other U.S. Embassy senior staff in Tripoli "felt we needed more, not less" security assets in Libya. According to Wood, instead they were told "to do with less. For what reasons, I don't know."[382]

Withdrawal of the MSD Teams

Shortly after Lt. Col. Wood assumes command of the Libya SST in February 2012, the State Department removes one of the three Mobile Security Deployment teams from Libya. State does so over Ambassador Cretz's objection.[383] Soon after Cretz departs from Libya in mid-May,[384] State withdraws a second MSD squad.[385] Wood claims

---

[381] Attkisson, 8 Major Warnings Before Benghazi; and Ferrara, Benghazi: Obama's Actions Amount to a Shameful Dereliction of Duty (emphasis in original) ("As the anniversary of 9/11 approached, the Obama Administration should have known that more security was necessary to protect diplomatic missions in the increasingly hostile country, especially on that sensitive date. But they did just the opposite, *reducing* security. . . .").

[382] CBS News, U.S. Memo Warned of High Risk of Libya Violence (*Watch video* there; Go to 0:32 - 1:59).

[383] Attkisson, *Stonewalled*, Chap. 4, pp. 181-182.

[384] Gene Allan Cretz Biography, Office of the Historian, State Dept. website.

Ambassador Stevens and RSO Nordstrom fight this decision.[386] Wood later testifies that by July the third and final MSD team "was restricted from performing security work and limited to only training local guard force members in July." The RSOs and Ambassadors Cretz and later Stevens reportedly will seek to replace these departing MSD assets with "regular diplomatic security personnel."[387] Despite Embassy Tripoli's pleas, the last of the MSD teams is withdrawn by the State Department from Libya by the end of August 2012.[388]

Withdrawal of DC-3 Aircraft

While Lt. Col. Wood is commanding the SST in Libya, U.S. personnel have been utilizing a DC-3 fixed-wing, propeller aircraft in that country. The DC-3 has been "reengineered to play a security and support role." This aircraft is used for "resupply trips" in the Mediterranean region. It also allows U.S. personnel to travel between Tripoli and Benghazi at will (about a one-hour flight). Significantly, this DC-3 can transport various types of equipment – *including weapons not allowed on commercial flights*. However, on May 3, 2012, Ambassador Stevens is advised that Undersecretary of State Patrick Kennedy has "determined that support for Embassy Tripoli using the DC-3 will be terminated immediately." Lt. Col. Wood tells investigative reporter Sharyl Attkisson, "For security personnel, that was a great asset." When the aircraft is withdrawn, "It was a loss again. It was 'okay, now how are we going to compensate for this?' Again, sub-optimizing to do the same thing you were trying with less resources."[389]

---

[385] Cretz March 28 Increased Security Personnel Cable to State (Referencing "second MSD team currently deployed until mid-May" and recommended to be replaced by proposed Diplomatic Security Agents), p. 2.

[386] Attkisson, *Stonewalled*, Chap. 4, p. 183.

[387] Wood House Oversight Prepared Testimony, p. 3.

[388] *Id.*, p. 3; Babbin, Whitewashing Benghazi; CBS Benghazi Timeline; and Baier, New Revelations on Attack in Benghazi (*Watch video there*; Go to 10:17-46).

[389] Attkisson, *Stonewalled*, Chap. 4, p. 184-185.

Withdrawal of the SST Force

According to CBS News, witnesses tell the House Oversight Committee investigators it is Under Secretary Patrick Kennedy's decision to send the SST team home from Libya – despite the Defense Department's reported offer to continue providing this team at no cost to the State Department![390] (Are we sensing a pattern concerning Kennedy's decision-making?)

The Senate Intelligence Committee's report summarizes the State Department's plans during this period for the SST in Libya as follows:

> State Department headquarters made the decision not to request an extension of the SST's mission in August 2012, approximately one month prior to the attacks, because State believed that many of the duties of the SST could be accomplished by local security forces, DS agents, or other State Department capabilities. As a result, DoD changed the mission of its DoD personnel in Libya from protection of the U.S. Embassy to [redacted] training with the Libyan security forces. [Redacted][391]

As a result, most of the Defense Department's SST team is scheduled to leave Libya in early August 2012. The Senate panel further asserts Deputy Chief of Mission Gregory Hicks tells them the DoD wants the "nature" of the SST team changed "as much as State wanted it changed."[392]

In the Tripoli Embassy, Ambassador Stevens is struggling to cope with this decision by State to remove the SST. As noted above, on July 9, 2012, Stevens sends a cable to the State Department. It advises conditions in Libya do not meet "prior benchmarks" for "a complete drawdown of TDY security personnel." These benchmarks had been established by Embassy Tripoli, the State Department and AFRICOM.[393]

Stevens' July 9 cable summarizes the State Department's then-current plans to reduce U.S. diplomatic security in Libya. Stevens notes

---

[390] Attkisson, Benghazi Accountability Review Board Comes Under Renewed Criticism; Attkisson, *Stonewalled*, Chap. 4, p. 221; and Sen. Intelligence Committee Benghazi Report (Redacted), p. 20.

[391] Sen. Intelligence Committee Benghazi Report (Redacted; footnote omitted), p. 20.

[392] *Id.* (Redacted), p. 20.

[393] Stevens July 9 Security Extension Cable to State, p. 1; Sundby, Ambassador Warned Libya Was "Volatile and Violent"; and CBS Benghazi Timeline.

as of July 9 there are 34 security personnel in country. These include 16 SST soldiers, 11 MSD members, and seven other State diplomatic security personnel (including the RSO, Eric Nordstrom). On July 13 this number will be reduced to 27 personnel. By August 5 (when the SST will depart), the Libya Post will decline to ten individuals performing security – 4 MSD trainers and six diplomatic security agents. By August 13, the security total will fall further to only seven agents (including the four MSD members who principally do only training of local Libyans).[394] This security trajectory is alarming by any measure.

Stevens' July 9 cable summarizes the extensive efforts of State's Embassy in Tripoli to "transition from emergency to normalized security operations," and to "transition to a more locally-based security team . . ." On this latter issue, Stevens discusses the numerous challenges his Post is experiencing in hiring and training effective local Libyan security guards. Stevens also explains that, despite his own team's many efforts, the Government of Libya "remains extremely limited in its ability to sustain a security support presence at USG compounds . . ."[395]

On August 1, Secretary of Defense Panetta signs an order officially transferring the SST from the authority of the Chief of Mission (Ambassador Stevens) to General Carter Ham, head of AFRICOM. This same order changes the SST's status from a security team to a "training team." On August 6, two members of Lt. Col. Wood's team are caught in a violent attempted carjacking in Tripoli, resulting in a firefight. Reportedly because of this incident, General Ham decides to transfer all but four of the team out of Libya, effective mid-August.[396] (If Libya is so damned important to U.S. interests, wouldn't a rational military commander transfer more soldiers *into* Libya in the face of these threats? As explained below, it is these remaining four special ops personnel who later will be prohibited from going to Benghazi on a rescue mission.)

Insanely, despite Ambassador Stevens' and Eric Nordstrom's repeated requests for enhanced security, during August Colonel

---

[394] Stevens July 9 Security Extension Cable to State, p. 2.

[395] *Id.*, p. 2.

[396] Hicks Oversight Committee Testimony (May 8, 2013) (Response to questions of Rep. Michael R. Turner (R-OH)), pp. 51-52.

Wood's SST force is withdrawn from Libya.[397] Wood's last day as SST commander is August 14.[398]

As noted above, at about the same time the SST is withdrawn from Libya, State transfers out the last remaining MSD security unit.[399] Only regular diplomatic security agents, a handful of U.S. military personnel, and local Libyan guards now remain in Libya.

Within weeks of the Benghazi attacks, ABC News interviews a "senior State Department official" who "asked not to be identified because of the ongoing internal investigation [by the Accountability Review Board, discussed below in Chapter 109]." This anonymous official misleadingly tells ABC News the U.S. Libyan Embassy's Regional Security Officer *"never specifically requested* that the SST's tour be extended past August . . ."[400] There is an excellent reason for this. As discussed earlier, Libya RSO Eric Nordstrom later testifies his State Department superior *Charlene Lamb has ordered him not to request the extension of the SST unit!* (He continues to request more security in general terms, without specific reference to the SST.)[401]

The same anonymous State official tells ABC News when the SST unit is transferred out there is "no net loss of security personnel." Nordstrom supposedly "asked for a number of U.S. shooters because of the pending SST redeployment and he was at that number."[402] ABC News further reports this same State leaker claims the SST was based in Tripoli and would have been there that night, not in Benghazi (a subject we discuss in detail below).[403]

---

[397] Wood House Oversight Prepared Testimony, p. 2; Stevens August 2 Bodyguard Request Cable to State (SST's security mission ends August 3), p. 2; Baier, New Revelations on Attack in Benghazi (*Watch video there*; Go to 9:48 - 10:46); CBS Benghazi Timeline; Ferrara, Benghazi: Obama's Actions Amount to a Shameful Dereliction of Duty; and Burnett, Benghazi Timeline: "We Are Under Attack" (*Watch video there*; Go to 4:14-28).

[398] Wood House Oversight Prepared Testimony, p. 1.

[399] *Id.*, p. 3.

[400] Tapper, Security Team Commander Says Ambassador Stevens Wanted His Team to Stay in Libya Past August (emphasis added) (*Watch video there*; Go to 1:20-32).

[401] Nordstrom Oversight Committee Testimony (Oct. 10, 2012) (Response to questions of Rep. Dennis Ross (R-FL)), pp. 91-92.

[402] Tapper, Security Team Commander Says Ambassador Stevens Wanted His Team to Stay in Libya Past August.

[403] *Id.* (*Watch video there*; Go to 1:38-50). Although the ABC article mistakenly says the SST would have been in *Benghazi*, Tapper's on-air report clearly states the State

Nordstrom testifies he never receives a satisfactory explanation from State regarding why the SST's tour is not extended. He explains:
> As I testified before, ... what I perceived that it was some sort of – explained to me that *it would be somehow embarrassing or politically difficult for State Department to continue to rely on DOD*, and that there was an element of that. That was never fully verbalized. But *that was certainly the feeling that I got going away from those conversations* [apparently with Charlene Lamb].[404]

In sharp contrast to State's worries, Lt. Col. Wood testifies his superior officer AFRICOM head General Carter Ham is "fully supportive" of extending the SST mission in Libya for as long as the State Department feels it is needed. Wood claims the SST resources "absolutely" are available for Libya.[405] Indeed, as stated earlier, according to the Senate Intelligence panel General Ham twice *personally* offers Ambassador Stevens an extension of the SST's tour of duty in Libya "in the weeks before the terrorist attacks." However, the panel claims Stevens declines both offers.[406]

Could SST Have Helped in Benghazi?

In her testimony after the event, Charlene Lamb will explain Lt. Col. Wood's team was based in Tripoli, and spent most of its time there. Therefore, Lamb claims, "It [the Libya SST] would not have made any difference in Benghazi."[407]

Under Secretary Patrick Kennedy repeats this same narrative. In a press briefing on October 10, he will claim the SST was based in

---

Department official claims the SST would have been in *Tripoli* on the Night of Benghazi.

[404] Nordstrom Oversight Committee Testimony (May 8, 2013) (Response to questions of Rep. Rob Woodall (R-GA)) (emphasis added), p. 85. See also *Id.* (Response to questions of Rep. Doug Collins (R-GA)), pp. 90-91; and Stevens August 2 Bodyguard Request Cable to State (MSD team to depart on August 30, 2012), p. 2.

[405] Wood Oversight Committee Testimony (Oct. 10, 2012) (Response to questions of Rep. Dennis Ross (R-FL)), p. 92; and Attkisson, *Stonewalled* (Question: "So there was no pressure from the military to pull your [SST] team out?" Lt. Col. Wood: "No, none whatsoever"), Chap. 4, p. 186.

[406] Sen. Intelligence Committee Benghazi Report (Redacted), pp. 20-21.

[407] Lamb House Oversight Committee Testimony (Oct. 10, 2012), pp. 56-57; and CBS News, House Probes Security Leading Up to Libya Attack.

THE TRUE ACCOUNT OF VALOR AND ABANDONMENT

Tripoli and "provided security to Tripoli, *not Benghazi*."[408] Kennedy grudgingly does admit, "On a *small number of occasions, a couple of SST members* would travel to Benghazi *for very specific reasons*, but they were not part of the *long-term* security presence in Benghazi."[409] (Kennedy's assertion is a lie. The SST *does* provide security in Benghazi. Wouldn't protecting a U.S. Ambassador on the 9/11 anniversary be the ultimate "very specific reason" to go to Benghazi? And Chris Stevens and the others did not need "long-term security" there; they needed only a few days' worth.) In December 2012, high-level officials again will try this silly "But the SST was stationed in Tripoli" excuse before the Senate Foreign Relations Committee.[410]

One "senior administration official" tells *The New York Times*, "This was not a SWAT team with a DC-3 on alert to jet them off to other cities in Libya to respond to security issues."[411] (So the SST members could not have flown on the same commercial jet Ambassador Stevens flew to Benghazi in September 2012? They could not, as discussed below, have flown the next day on the chartered plane used by "Team Tripoli"? It is more deception.)

The Democrat-controlled Senate Intelligence Committee also admits the SST "traveled to Benghazi two or three times..." on security-related missions.[412] This panel concludes, "...The SST provided the Ambassador with various security capabilities and, although not located in Benghazi, provided a greater pool of security resources in Libya from which the State Department could draw."[413] (It is an embarrassment State officials such as Lamb and Kennedy and the

---

[408] Kennedy October 10 Briefing (emphasis added) (*Watch video there*; Go to 1:10-54).

[409] *Id.* (emphasis added).

[410] Testimony of Deputy Secretary of State for Management & Resources Thomas Nides Before Senate Foreign Relations Committee Hearing, C-SPAN online (Dec. 20, 2012) (See also remarks and questions by Sen. Bob Corker (R-TN)) (*Watch video there*; Go to 5:14 – 6:48).

[411] Schmitt and Landler, Focus Was on Tripoli in Requests for Security in Libya.

[412] Sen. Intelligence Committee Benghazi Report (Redacted) ("... SST personnel were based in and spent most of their time in Tripoli, but traveled to Benghazi two or three times in order to: augment the lack of DS agents there, do a security assessment of the Mission Facility in Benghazi, train local guard forces, deliver excess defense equipment, and improve the security of the Temporary Mission Facility...."), p. 20, citing committee interviews.

[413] *Id.* (Redacted), p. 20.

unnamed "senior administration official" even would attempt to deny this obvious fact.)

SST commander Wood's later testimony will prove Lamb and Kennedy to be liars. "On two occasions I sent SST members to Benghazi *to support and bolster security* at that location."[414] Wood also will explain to ABC News the SST plans to accompany Ambassador Stevens *"for protection"* on a June 2012 trip to Benghazi, but the trip is canceled.[415] Indeed, Wood says he himself "traveled to Benghazi on two occasions." Once Wood went with the Libya RSO "to evaluate the security situation there" in Benghazi. On the second occasion, Wood conducted some (unspecified) work for the Defense Attaché's office.[416] Authors Burton and Katz also write that while Tripoli was its primary focus, "The SST split its time between the embassy in Tripoli and the Special Mission Compound in Benghazi."[417]

(Wood's and the Senate committee's contrary statements aside, on their face Lambs' and Kennedy's assertions are *appalling*. They have airplanes in Tripoli. It is 400 miles – a one-hour flight – from Tripoli to Benghazi.[418] As discussed below, the seven brave men who comprise "Team Tripoli" will be able to charter an aircraft and get to Benghazi nearly four hours before the final mortar attack. Why couldn't Wood's military team have done so were it still in Tripoli? Indeed, why couldn't they have used the very aircraft chartered for Team Tripoli? And perhaps been joined by some or all members of Team Tripoli, had there been space in the plane?

(Lamb should be fired for her misleading, mendacious testimony under oath *alone*. But, of course, she is not.)

---

[414] Wood House Oversight Prepared Testimony, pp. 1-2. See also Attkisson, *Stonewalled* ("The truth is that Wood and his team members *did* travel to Benghazi for their official duties") (emphasis in original), Chap. 4, p. 188.

[415] Tapper, Security Team Commander Says Ambassador Stevens Wanted His Team to Stay in Libya Past August (emphasis added) ("Stevens didn't typically travel to Benghazi during Wood's rotation in Libya, Wood said, though the ambassador made some attempts to travel there in June and Wood said that the Security Support Team was planning on accompanying him *for protection* during that planned trip. Ultimately, plans fell through and Stevens' schedule kept him in Tripoli") (*Watch video there*; Go to 1:50-58); and Attkisson, *Stonewalled*, Chap. 4, p. 188.

[416] Wood House Oversight Prepared Testimony, p. 2.

[417] Burton & Katz, *Under Fire*, Chap. 7, pp. 78-79.

[418] Benghazi Committee Report, p. 7.

THE TRUE ACCOUNT OF VALOR AND ABANDONMENT

Under Secretary Kennedy further dismisses the idea the SST team could make a difference – apparently even had they been in Benghazi. He testifies to the House Oversight Committee:

...[I]n the end, this is an inherently risky operation. We cannot withdraw always to fortresses. . . .[419] But an attack of that kind of lethality, *we are never going to have enough guns*. We are a diplomatic service. . . . [W]e are not an armed camp ready to fight it out as the U.S. military does if there was an attack on a U.S. military facility in Afghanistan . . .[420]

(Why is it then, as explained below, the very first call the Mission DSAs will make during the initial attack is to the nearby CIA Annex to plead for shooters with guns? Perhaps Kennedy should ask the surviving Americans whether they would have liked to have those additional 16 SST guns on this Night of Benghazi.[421] Sadly, Kennedy cannot ask Chris Stevens and Sean Smith.)

Moreover, four special operations soldiers remain stationed in Tripoli. They earlier had been part of Woods' SST team, and *"had previously augmented security at the Benghazi Mission compound*, but they were no longer able to do so."[422] According to the Select Committee, they "were no longer able to do so" because Under Secretary Kennedy has "terminated the SST's responsibilities for the Embassy's security in August of 2012. As a result, the SST was no longer able to travel with Stevens or augment security in Benghazi."[423] (In other words, in the colorful Air Force pilot jargon, Patrick Kennedy totally "screws the pooch." *Again*. But on the night of September 11 *this is a life-and-death emergency!* Technicalities and niceties should

---

[419] Kennedy House Oversight Testimony (Oct. 10, 2012) (Response to questions of Rep. Danny K. Davis (D-IL)), p. 83; Cornwell and Zakaria, U.S. Security at Benghazi Mission Called "Weak"; and Schmitt and Landler, Focus Was on Tripoli in Requests for Security in Libya. See also Kennedy October 10 Briefing (". . . [T]he lethality of an armed massed attack by dozens of individuals is something greater than we've ever seen in Libya over the last period that we've been there") (*Watch video there*; Go to 9:41 - 10:58).

[420] Kennedy House Oversight Testimony (Oct. 10, 2012) (Response to questions of Rep. Christopher S. Murphy (D-CN)), p. 85.

[421] See House Oversight Committee Hearings (May 8, 2013) (Remarks of Chairman Darrell Issa (R-CA)) (". . . I'm afraid the deafness at least [at] Under Secretary Kennedy's level is not in any way curable by technology known to amplify sound"), p. 111.

[422] Benghazi Committee Report (emphasis added), p. 15.

[423] *Id.* (footnote omitted), p. 15.

go out the window. Kennedy or no Kennedy, whatever the limits of the SST's responsibilities on paper, these remaining four special operators should be ordered *immediately* to deploy to Benghazi! Instead, as discussed below, they will be ordered effectively to "stand down" and stay in Tripoli.)

Lt. Col. Wood also disagrees with the notion expressed by Lamb and Kennedy and others the SST could not have made a difference in Benghazi. In October 2012, he tells Fox News, ". . . [T]he more guns you have in a firefight, the better chance you have of winning."[424] Wood adds the high caliber of the SST's soldiers is such "they could make a difference in any firefight."[425] Wood also testifies the SST group makes a difference every day they are in Libya merely by virtue of their "deterrent effect."[426] (To this point, consider the potential discouragement if word had spread among the militants in Benghazi the SST team is camped inside the Mission Compound's walls on the Night of Benghazi.)

(Earlier, less than four weeks after the attack, ABC News claims Lt. Col. Wood tells them he is not claiming the SST would have made a difference in the result in Benghazi. "That's way speculative; I don't even know the facts of what happened that night," ABC quotes Woods as saying.[427] However, the author notes the possibility Wood knows more facts by the time he speaks with Fox News that same month and expresses a different opinion.)

The Impact of Reduced Security Forces

The effect of these SST and MSD withdrawals is to reduce significantly the security assets at the Embassy in Tripoli. At this time, Chris Stevens' Deputy Chief of Mission is Gregory Hicks, who has arrived in Tripoli only recently on July 31.[428] At this time, Hicks later explains, there are approximately "55 diplomatic personnel" in the

---

[424] Baier, New Revelations on Attack in Benghazi (*Watch video there*; Go to 13:10-15).

[425] *Id.* (*Watch video there*; Go to 6:52 - 7:06).

[426] Wood Oversight Committee Testimony (Oct. 10, 2012) (Response to questions of Rep. Dennis Ross (R-FL)), p. 92.

[427] Tapper, Security Team Commander Says Ambassador Stevens Wanted His Team to Stay in Libya Past August.

[428] Prepared Statement of Gregory Hicks, House Oversight Committee Hearings (May 8, 2013), p. 11; and House Oversight Committee website.

Tripoli Embassy and an "annex" (to which Embassy staff will evacuate on the Night of Benghazi). (Apparently, 28 of these are at the Tripoli Embassy residence, and the remainder already are at the annex.)[429] As Stevens' top deputy in Libya, Hicks later describes the effect of this reduction in Tripoli on the Benghazi security situation as follows:

. . . Mrs. Clinton sent our people in Benghazi into harm's way. And she then delegated her responsibility – her legal obligation to protect our oversees Americans – to others. And those people then reduced our security complement in Tripoli from 34 [1.5 security officers per diplomat] to six [one security officer per 4.5 diplomats]. So that when Chris Stevens went to Benghazi he could only take two security agents with him, instead of the dozen or more that he should have had with him. . . . [S]he delegated the decision to divide our people in Benghazi into two separate facilities. The law says that decision can't be delegated. . . .[430]

The Select Benghazi Committee similarly concludes:

Losing 28 security agents reduced not only the security resources available to the Embassy [in Tripoli], but also those available to the Benghazi Mission compound. With limited security agents in Tripoli, there were no surplus security agents to send to augment security in Benghazi – without leaving the Embassy in Tripoli at severe risk.[431]

Hicks also claims, ". . . [T]he truth is that she [Hillary Clinton] and her delegated authorities took our security away. . . . There were no military forces standing by to come and rescue us if something happened."[432] (Didn't that prove all too true?)

---

[429] Hicks Oversight Committee Testimony (May 8, 2013), p. 27.

[430] Interview of Gregory Hicks with Martha MacCallum, "America's Newsroom," Fox News Channel (Sept. 15, 2016) (*Watch video there*; Go to 2:44 - 3:29). See also Benghazi Committee Report, p. 16 (". . . [D]uring August 2012, the total number of State Department security agents assigned to the Embassy in Tripoli dropped from 34 individuals to six"); Interview of Gregory Hicks with Megyn Kelly, "The Kelly File," Fox News Channel (Sept. 13, 2016) (*Watch video there*; Go to 1:06 - 2:20); and Hicks, What the Benghazi Attack Taught Me About Hillary Clinton.

[431] Benghazi Committee Report, p. 16. See also Hicks, What the Benghazi Attack Taught Me About Hillary Clinton.

[432] Interview of Gregory Hicks with Megyn Kelly, "The Kelly File," Fox News Channel (Sept. 13, 2016) (*Watch video there*; Go to 3:00-19). See Hicks Oversight Committee Testimony (May 8, 2013) (Question by Rep. Jason Chaffetz (R-UT): "Mr. Hicks, is it fair to say that the people on the ground trying to make the security decisions, that they were not able to get the resources, they weren't able to fortify the

State Denies Security Personnel Are Reduced

Despite these obvious truths, the State Department apparently is in complete denial. Again according to ABC News, subsequently on October 8, 2012 – two days before the initial House Oversight public hearings will occur – the State Department issues a preemptive public statement. Fearing what is coming, this document no doubt is intended to take some wind out of the Oversight Committee's sails. The statement reportedly asserts:

> The SST was enlisted to support the re-opening of Embassy Tripoli, to help ensure we had the security necessary as our diplomatic presence grew. *They were based in Tripoli and operated almost exclusively there.* When their rotation in Libya ended, Diplomatic Security Special Agents were deployed and maintained a constant level of security capability. So *their departure had no impact whatsoever on the total number of fully trained American security personnel in Libya generally, or in Benghazi specifically.*[433]

Despite all of these security asset reductions, an unnamed spokesperson for the State Department will repeat this same nonsense to CBS News.[434] It is a complete lie. There clearly are fewer security personnel in Libya as a result of these cuts in the SST and MSD. As Hicks explains, had these withdrawn assets stayed Ambassador Stevens could take many more than just two protective agents with him to Benghazi. Further, during the battle Team Tripoli would have had access to many additional "shooters" to accompany them to Benghazi, or (if space was lacking) to go on the chartered plane in their stead.

(Who is this mystery State spokesperson? Quite possibly Alice N. Wonderland.) ■

---

facility, they didn't have the personnel that they requested? . . ."; Answer: "Yes, it's fair to say"), p. 101.

[433] Quoted in Tapper, Security Team Commander Says Ambassador Stevens Wanted His Team to Stay in Libya Past August (emphasis added). The author relies on ABC News for this text because he was unable to locate this State Department pronouncement on the agency's website.

[434] CBS News, U.S. Memo Warned of High Risk of Libya Violence ("[A]ny withdrawal of security personnel prior to the Benghazi attack had 'no impact whatsoever on the total number of fully trained American security personnel *in Libya overall* or in Benghazi specifically'").

18

"The Taliban Is Inside the Building"

It seems almost inconceivable supposedly responsible government officials not only deny repeated petitions for increased security under these hazardous conditions, but in fact *withdraw* security assets. *Why* do they do it?

State Department Procedures

It is useful to start by reviewing the traditional, longstanding procedures within the State Department for reviewing requests for additional security overseas. According to a report by the majority (Republican) staff of the House Foreign Affairs Committee (which cites a "former senior political appointee" at State), the process works like this: A security request from a diplomatic post "simultaneously" is routed through both the Bureau of Diplomatic Security (run during the relevant period by Eric Boswell), and the "the relevant regional bureau." In the case of Benghazi, this would be the Bureau of Near Eastern Affairs (headed on an acting basis by Beth Jones). Each Bureau's Assistant Secretary (Boswell and Jones) reviews the security request, and makes a recommendation to the Under Secretary for Management (Patrick Kennedy). "The Under Secretary for Management then is responsible for approving or rejecting security requests in consultation with the Deputy Secretary for Management and Resources" (Thomas Nides).[435]

According to a House Oversight Committee report on Benghazi, Beth Jones testified "... [B]efore the Benghazi attack, any disagreements between her Bureau [Near Eastern Affairs] and the Diplomatic Security Bureau would be *adjudicated by Pat Kennedy*."[436]

---

[435] House Foreign Affairs Benghazi Majority Staff Report, p. 11.

[436] House Oversight Interim Report on Benghazi ARB (emphasis added), pp. 64-65.

The State "Official" Security Perspective

A Select Benghazi Committee member, Representative Lynn Westmoreland (R-GA), has proposed an answer to why this process yielded such a horrible outcome in Benghazi. Despite the known risks to American diplomats, Westmoreland feels, ". . . [T]he appearance of no boots on the ground was more important to the administration."[437] (If he is correct, this is *sickening*.)

Former U.S. Ambassador to the United Nations, John Bolton, has a similar theory regarding why the SST team is withdrawn and the MSD assets are reduced and eventually removed:

> I think that what was motivating the State Department was that if we had security that would have truly been appropriate, it would have been an admission that conditions on the ground in Libya were not safe. And that would have violated the worldview that . . . this had been an administration success.[438]

(Of course, Bolton later would become President Trump's third National Security Advisor.)

Subsequent congressional inquiries also provide important insights into the decision-making calculus of the Obama administration's top security managers during this period – particularly those in the State Department.

At later House Oversight hearings following the debacle, Eric Nordstrom, Regional Security Officer for Libya through July 2012, testifies his requests for additional security assets are blocked by a State Department policy to "normalize operations and reduce security resources."[439] (In the author's words, the administration cannot let the world – and especially the U.S. electorate – know what a "shitshow" Libya is becoming, as we've noted above President Obama amazingly

---

[437] Statement of Rep. Lynn Westmoreland (R-GA) on Release of Benghazi Committee Report, The Select Committee on Benghazi website (July 8, 2016). See also Catherine Herridge Report, "Special Report," Fox News Channel (Nov. 18, 2016) (Select Committee member Mike Pompeo (R-KS) chastises Hillary Clinton and her State Department team for ignoring the rising terror threat in Libya because it did not fit the Obama administration's "political narrative") (*Watch video there*; Go to 1:15-23).

[438] Baier, New Revelations on Attack in Benghazi (*Watch video there*; Go to 10:42 - 11:09).

[439] CBS News, House Probes Security Leading Up to Libya Attack.

conceded.[440]) Under further questioning, Nordstrom clarifies he mainly has attempted to avoid *reductions* in security in Libya, rather than seeking a substantial *increase* in security resources.[441]

Nordstrom reportedly tells Oversight staff investigators that Charlene Lamb, State's Deputy Assistant Secretary for Diplomatic Security, seeks to keep the number of security personnel in Benghazi "artificially low." Nordstrom further advises investigators Lamb feels the Benghazi Mission does not require any diplomatic security agents because there is a "safe haven" in the Mission residence in case of any emergency.[442] (Then why, as explained below, will Chris Stevens and Sean Smith – just two men – have *five* DSAs in Benghazi, when only four DSAs (plus four special forces soldiers who are part of a "training mission") will be left behind at the Tripoli residential compound to protect some 28 diplomatic personnel?[443] And are we to believe an American diplomat in Benghazi can function effectively by hiding in the Villa residence, never leaving the grounds of the Mission Compound, so as to remain near the safe haven? In October 2012, Hillary Clinton herself states, "Our people can't live in bunkers and do their jobs."[444])

In further testimony Nordstrom subsequently will describe the State Department's decision-making process as "strange." While he is in Libya, Nordstrom claims it is unclear whether Charlene Lamb is making security-related decisions herself, or whether they are being "kicked up to a higher level." He thinks "largely DAS Lamb" is making these decisions. However, Nordstrom claims Lamb is dealing directly with Under Secretary for Management Patrick Kennedy. This is despite the fact Kennedy is two levels above her on the organization chart![445] While Kennedy is within his authority to do so, this effectively cuts out of the State security loop two levels of managers between Kennedy and Lamb. (These are Eric Boswell and his deputy, Scott Bultrowicz. Both nonetheless later will be "disciplined" – placed on paid leave for eight

---

[440] Goldberg, The Obama Doctrine, quoted in Malloy and Treyz, Obama Admits Worst Mistake of His Presidency.

[441] CBS News, House Probes Security Leading Up to Libya Attack.

[442] *Id.*

[443] Hicks Oversight Committee Testimony (May 8, 2013), p. 27.

[444] Schmitt and Landler, Focus Was on Tripoli in Requests for Security in Libya.

[445] For a partial State Department Organization Chart as of May 2012, see House Foreign Affairs Benghazi Majority Staff Report, p. 6.

months – for their roles in Benghazi.) Nordstrom testifies, "... [C]ertainly I felt that anything that DAS Lamb was deciding certainly had been run by Under Secretary Kennedy."[446] (As we are seeing regarding Benghazi, it appears all roads lead to Patrick Kennedy's desk.[447])

Eric Nordstrom testifies about the implications of putting such requests for enhanced security in an official cable, as he and Ambassador Stevens do repeatedly. Nordstrom explains:

> If I sent something by email or informally discussed it by telephone, it is still valuable, but unless it is on that cable it is not official. My experience in the past was that as soon as we put those recommendations [regarding security], just as Greg [Hicks] just alluded to, as soon as we put that onto an official cable, somehow we were seen as embarrassing the Department of State because we are requiring them to live up to their end of the bargain.[448]

---

[446] Nordstrom Oversight Committee Testimony (May 8, 2013) (Response to questions of Rep. Rob Woodall (R-GA)), p. 85.

[447] E.g., Hicks Oversight Committee Testimony (May 8, 2013) (Response to questions of Rep. John Duncan, Jr. (R-TN)) ("... I think that in our system of government the decision-making authority is at the level of presidentially appointed, Senate confirmed individuals. It's at the level of Assistant Secretary or higher. Now the reporting coming out of Embassy Tripoli on conditions there, particularly the fact that we had to provide a daily report of who was in country to Under Secretary Kennedy and the fact that he made the decision as to who came to Tripoli and Benghazi or who didn't, that budgets came to his table and that security threat environment reports also came to his table would suggest that there was some responsibility there"), pp. 55-56; and *Id.* (Response to questions of Rep. Tim Walberg (R-MI)) ("Again, ... given the decision-making that Under Secretary Pat Kennedy was making with respect to Embassy Tripoli and Consulate Benghazi operations, he has to bear some responsibility"), p. 63; and Sen. Intelligence Committee Benghazi Report (Redacted) ("... [S]ome senior Foreign Service officers and DS agents who met with the [later-created Independent Panel on Best Practices] identified the Under Secretary for Management (M) as the senior security official in the Department responsible for final decision making regarding critical security requirements," although this role was "not identified by Congress in the Diplomatic Security Act of 1986"), pp. 16-17.

[448] Nordstrom Oversight Committee Testimony (May 8, 2013) (Response to questions of Rep. Cynthia Lummis (R-WY)), p. 84, referencing Hicks Oversight Committee Testimony (May 8, 2013) (Response to questions of Rep. Cynthia Lummis (R-WY) (Post Benghazi attacks, when Hicks and new Libya Regional Security Officer John Martinec cabled list of needed security improvements in order for Embassy to remain in Tripoli, "... I learned later that that cable was not well received by Washington leadership"), p. 84.

Nordstrom describes his feelings towards the State Department's denial of his repeated requests for more security. He testifies that after he asks the State Department for twelve security agents, in a phone conversation discussing this request a State manager named "Jim" – who works for Charlene Lamb – replies, "You are asking for the sun, the moon and the stars." In response to Nordstrom's perplexity "Jim" further explains, "Well, you know, this is a political game. You have to not make us look bad here, that we're not being responsive."[449] Nordstrom claims he responds:

> Jim, you know what makes [sic] most frustrating about this assignment? It's not the hardships, it's not the gunfire, it's not the threats. It's dealing and fighting against the people, programs and personnel who are supposed to be supporting me. . . For me, the Taliban is on the inside of the building.[450]

"The building" is State's Washington, D.C. headquarters at Foggy Bottom.

After this exchange, Nordstrom sends an email to his superior in Libya, Deputy Chief of Mission Polaschik. He writes:

> I doubt we will ever get [Diplomatic Security] to admit in writing what I was told [in] reference [to] Benghazi that DI/ [International Programs] was *directed by Deputy Assistant Secretary Lamb to cap the agents in Benghazi at 3*, and force post to hire local drivers. This is apparently a verbal policy only but one which DS/IP [Bureau of Near Eastern Affairs] doesn't plan to violate. *I hope that nobody is injured as a result of an incident in Benghazi, since it would be particularly embarrassing to both DS and DAS [Lamb] if it was a result of some sort of game they are playing.*[451]

At what CBS News describes as a "hastily scrambled" press event later the same day of Nordstrom's testimony (October 10, 2012), Under Secretary for Management Patrick Kennedy is asked to respond to

---

[449] Additional Views of Senators Chambliss, Burr, et al., p. 9; and Attkisson, *Stonewalled*, Chap. 4, p. 183.

[450] Nordstrom Oversight Committee Testimony (Oct. 10, 2012) (Response to questions of Rep. Jim Jordan (R-OH)), p. 106; Tapper, Security Officer: "For Me the Taliban Is Inside the Building"; Attkisson, *Stonewalled*, Chap. 4, p. 183; and CBS News, House Probes Security Leading Up to Libya Attack (*Watch video there*; Go to 0:00-27).

[451] Additional Views of Senators Chambliss, Burr, et al. (emphasis added), p. 9, citing SSCI Transcript, Member and Staff Interview of Eric Nordstrom (June 27, 2013), pp. 24-25.

Nordstrom's provocative assertion about "the Taliban." Kennedy can manage only, ". . . I was simply surprised to hear language like that used."[452] (Wow, such a powerful rebuttal.)

Nordstrom also is asked by congressional investigators why, if he knows Charlene Lamb is going to continue saying "no" to his security requests, he continues asking her. Nordstrom explains he does so:

> . . . [B]ecause it was the right thing to do. And it was the resources that were needed. And if people also on the other side felt that that was the right thing to do, to say no to that, they could at least have the courtesy to put that in the official record [i.e., to deny it by official cable].[453]

Hillary Clinton's Role in Libya Security

Contrary to Hillary Clinton's subsequent claims, Eric Nordstrom testifies before Congress he expects Secretary Clinton "absolutely" would have read, or been briefed on, his March 28 request for enhanced security in Libya.[454] (Recall Clinton's pivotal role in shoving Qadhafi off his throne. Given this and her desire for future political office, it seems inconceivable Secretary Clinton is not following security developments in Libya closely from her current perch at State.[455])

Eric Nordstrom's opinions notwithstanding, in her book *Hard Choices*, Clinton later will claim, "day-to-day questions about security *rarely* rose to the top levels of the Department, and, as a result, there was inadequate leadership in regard to matters of security."[456]

---

[452] Kennedy October 10 Briefing (*Watch video there*; Go to 4:18 - 5:28).

[453] Nordstrom Oversight Committee Testimony (May 8, 2013) (Response to questions of Rep. Rob Woodall (R-GA)), p. 85.

[454] Nordstrom Oversight Committee Testimony (May 8, 2013) (Response to questions of Rep. Doug Collins (R-GA)), p. 90; and Guy Benson, "The Damning Dozen: Twelve Revelations from the Benghazi Hearings," Townhall.com website (May 9, 2013) ("Benson, The Damning Dozen: Twelve Revelations from the Benghazi Hearings").

[455] Additional Views of Reps. Jordan and Pompeo (emphasis added) (". . . The American people expect that when the government sends our representatives into such dangerous places they receive adequate protection. *Secretary Clinton paid special attention to Libya. She sent Ambassador Stevens there.* Yet, in August 2012, she missed the last, clear chance to protect her people"), p. 416.

[456] Clinton, *Hard Choices*, Chap. 17, p. 408 (emphasis added). See also *Id.* ("Security matters are handled by officials responsible for security. It's rare that such a cable would come to the Secretary of State's desk. . . . The professionals charged with security should be the ones making security decisions"), p. 409.

THE TRUE ACCOUNT OF VALOR AND ABANDONMENT

Clinton's statement is half true. (This is way above average for her.) There clearly is inadequate leadership on security issues in her agency. However, then Under Secretary of State Patrick Kennedy is part of the "top levels" of the State Department. (His position requires Senate confirmation.[457]) However, even under the alternative assumption such security requests to State officials do rarely rise to high-level management, doesn't this speak volumes about the inadequacy of the State Department's leadership? If diplomats in *one* very dangerous country alone make scores of requests for enhanced security, who would design a system in which such a serious problem is not raised to the highest levels?)

Regarding Clinton's involvement in security issues, Eric Nordstrom also testifies Clinton *must* have been involved in the various requests initially to deploy, and then to extend twice, the tour of duty of the SST force in Libya. Because the SST team is a Defense Department asset, Nordstrom explains its assignment to another agency must be requested by an agency head – Secretary Clinton herself.[458]

In her book about her State Department tenure, Clinton explains every one of the two million communications sent each year is addressed to the Secretary of State. In practice, "only a fraction are actually meant for the Secretary's eyes."[459] (Even if this practice is reality, it sounds like Clinton's people are awful at assessing what "fraction" of those millions of messages the agency head needs to see.)

The Select Benghazi Committee Democrat minority report defends Hillary Clinton on the Benghazi security issue. A heading in its report concludes, "Secretary Clinton Never Personally Denied Security Requests."[460] (So because Clinton is detached and disengaged and disinterested, she is not responsible? Why the hell doesn't her immediate staff get her into this Libya security loop, and damned quickly?)

---

[457] "Senior Officials," State Dept. website.

[458] Nordstrom Oversight Committee Testimony (May 8, 2013) (Response to questions of Rep. Doug Collins (R-GA)), p. 90.

[459] Clinton, *Hard Choices*, Chap. 17, p. 408.

[460] "Honoring Courage, Improving Security, and Fighting the Exploitation of a Tragedy," Report of the Democratic Members of the House Select Committee on Benghazi (June 2016), p. 780; and Associated Press, "House Republicans Fault US Military Response to Benghazi," Fox News online (June 28, 2016) ("Fox News, House Republicans Fault US Military Response to Benghazi").

Clinton's approach to diplomatic security issues is directly contrary to the recommendations of the Accountability Review Board investigating the bombing of two U.S. embassies in East Africa in 1998. That ARB recommended, "The Secretary of State should *personally* review the security situation of embassy chanceries and other official premises, closing those which are highly vulnerable and threatened but for which adequate security enhancements cannot be provided..."[461]

Clinton's "Sergeant Schultz Defense" ("I see *nothing!* I hear *nothing!* I know *nothing!*)[462] seems inconsistent with another of Hillary Clinton's assertions in her memoir:

> As Secretary of State, I was accountable for the safety of almost seventy thousand people at the Department and USAID [U.S. Agency for International Development, a State entity created to combat world poverty and promote democratic societies] and our more than 270 posts around the world. When something went wrong, as it did in Benghazi, it was my responsibility.[463]

(Apparently not so much.)

The White House Role in Libya Security

The Obama White House repeatedly attempts to distance itself from security decisions in Libya. Vice President Joe Biden will claim in October 2012 the White House is not informed about additional requests for security in Libya. He asserts, "We weren't told they wanted more security *again*. We did not know they wanted more

---

[461] Dept. of State Report of the Accountability Review Boards, Bombings of the US Embassies in Nairobi, Kenya and Dar es Salaam, Tanzania on August 7, 1998 (Jan. 8, 1999), Executive Overview, State Dept. Archives website (emphasis added); and Benghazi Committee Report, Appendix K, p. 619. See also House Foreign Affairs Benghazi Majority Staff Report ("... Especially given the United States' deep involvement in Libya, it appears that Secretary Clinton did not meet the expectations set by the 1998 ARB"), p. 11.

[462] For readers too young to remember, the "Sergeant Schultz" allusion refers to a clownish character in the ancient situation comedy TV series, "Hogan's Heroes" of the author's youth. Schultz was a bumbling Luftwaffe prison guard who repeatedly averted his eyes from the anti-Nazi activities and misdeeds of his captive prisoners-of-war.

[463] Clinton, *Hard Choices*, Chap. 17, p. 406.

security *again*."⁴⁶⁴ (This use of the word "again" is interesting, possibly suggesting the White House is aware of *previous* requests for additional security.)

White House spokesperson Jay Carney also declares security decisions relating to diplomatic posts are made at the State Department, not the White House.⁴⁶⁵ (But isn't the White House still responsible for the State Department's decisions?⁴⁶⁶ Or does "The Buck" no longer stop at the president's desk?⁴⁶⁷) ∎

---

⁴⁶⁴ Transcript of Vice Presidential Debate Between Vice President Joe Biden and Rep. Paul Ryan (R-WI), *The New York Times* online (Oct. 11, 2012) (emphasis added); and Schmitt and Landler, Focus Was on Tripoli in Requests for Security in Libya (emphasis added).

⁴⁶⁵ Schmitt and Landler, Focus Was on Tripoli in Requests for Security in Libya.

⁴⁶⁶ ABC News Transcript of Second 2012 Presidential Debate Moderated by Candy Crowley of CNN's "State of the Union" (Oct. 16, 2012), ABC News online (". . . [W]hen I say that we are going to find out exactly what happened, everybody will be held accountable. And I am ultimately responsible for what's taking place there because these are my folks, and I'm the one who has to greet those coffins when they come home. . . .").

⁴⁶⁷ Famous sign on U.S. President (1945-1953) Harry S. Truman's Oval Office desk: "The Buck Stops Here." David McCullough, "Truman" (Simon & Schuster, New York; 1992), Chap. 11, p. 467 "The Buck Stops Here."

19

"It Was the Best Bad Plan"

As explained previously, in September 2012 Charlene Lamb is a State Department official in charge of safety and security for all State Department diplomatic facilities worldwide, including Benghazi. As noted, Lamb is a Deputy Assistant Secretary within the agency's Bureau of Diplomatic Security.

The Benghazi Mission Compound in September 2012 is designated by the U.S. government as a "critical" or "high threat" facility. (Indeed, so is the U.S. Embassy in Tripoli.)[468]

Physical Security Improvements to the Mission

According to Charlene Lamb, when the State Department acquires the lease to the Mission Compound in Benghazi in 2011 it makes a number of "security upgrades." (The Benghazi Accountability Review Board Report (discussed in detail in Chapter 109) will assert these are made in 2012.[469]) As noted above, these include extending the height of the perimeter wall to twelve feet, and adding concertina razor wire and barbed wire on top. State also adds large concrete blocks outside the Mission's exterior to "provide anti-ram protection." Inside each of the exterior steel gates, State has installed "steel drop bars" to help control vehicle traffic. Equipment to detect explosives is added inside the outer wall. Security grills are installed on windows accessible from the ground, including those in the Villa's "safe haven." Some of these are "escape windows" containing "emergency releases." Wooden doors are hardened with steel, and locks are reinforced. Additional security lighting is added. An "Imminent Danger Notification System" is added. Finally, guard booths and sandbag emplacements are constructed "to

---

[468] Nordstrom Oversight Committee Testimony (May 8, 2013) (Response to questions of Rep. James Lankford (R-OK)), p. 40.

[469] Benghazi ARB Report, Finding 2, p. 5.

create defensive positions *inside* the compound."[470] (Does it sound like they are expecting trouble? And note these sandbags are positioned to defend against a foe who already has breached the exterior of the Mission Compound!)

Prior Security Incidents at the Mission

There are good reasons for these security improvements. The Special Mission itself has been the target of several fairly recent security incidents. On March 8, 2012, several large explosions occur within 400 meters of the U.S. Mission Compound facility in Benghazi. There are no injuries, and no damage to the Mission.[471]

On March 22, seven militia members armed with AK-47s begin kicking at the Mission's Back Gate, demanding access to the compound and firing their weapons into the air. These would-be intruders belong to the Libyan Ministry of Defense. They later apologize to Mission personnel.[472]

On April 6, *former security guards at the Mission Compound* throw an improvised explosive device over the compound's fence! Again, there are no injuries. And as noted above, on June 6, a bomb explodes at the Mission, tearing a large hole in the outer wall near the facility's Main Gate. Yet again, no one is hurt.[473] But this luck can't last forever.

---

[470] Lamb Oversight Committee Prepared Testimony (emphasis added), pp. 2-3; Sen. Intelligence Committee Benghazi Report (Redacted), p. 17; and Benghazi ARB Report, Finding 2, pp. 5 and 33.

[471] Libya Security Incidents Since June 2011, p. 24.

[472] *Id.*, p. 25.

[473] CNN Report, Why Didn't the U.S. Military Respond in Time in Benghazi? (*Watch video there*; Go to 3:35-51); Baier, New Revelations on Attack in Benghazi (*Watch video there*; Go to 8:20-34); Press Release, "Senators McCain, Graham and Ayotte Release Statement on Benghazi Attack," Senator John McCain website (May 22, 2013) ("Statement of Senators McCain, Graham and Ayotte"); Attkisson, 8 Major Warnings Before Benghazi; Baier, New Revelations on Attack in Benghazi (*Watch video there*; Go to 8:27-34); and Kirkpatrick and Myers, Libya Attack Brings Challenges for U.S. ("Benghazi, awash in guns, has recently witnessed a string of assassinations as well as attacks on international missions, including a bomb said to be planted by another Islamist group that exploded near the United States mission there as recently as June [2012]").

The Mission as a "Temporary" Facility

The Benghazi Mission Compound is designated a "temporary" State Department outpost.[474] After the embassy bombing in Beirut, Lebanon, decades earlier, the U.S. government created minimum security standards for U.S. diplomatic facilities abroad. (These often are referred to as the "Inman standards," after Admiral Bobby Inman. He chaired the 1984 Advisory Panel on Overseas Security that first recommended such standards following the 1983 embassy and Marine barracks bombings in Lebanon.[475]) The Mission Compound in Benghazi does *not* meet these standards.[476] On September 11, 2012, it also does not meet the standards for the minimum number of security personnel at such facilities.[477]

The Mission is not merely a residence for U.S. diplomats in Benghazi. It also functions as a full-time office facility. As such, the Mission normally also would have to meet the office facility standards under the "Secure Embassy Construction and Counterterrorism Act of 1999" ("SECCA").[478]

It is Under Secretary of State for Management Patrick Kennedy who officially has designated the Benghazi Special Mission a "temporary" post.[479] This has the effect of exempting it from these established

---

[474] September 12 Special Briefing ("The facility we are working in [in Benghazi] is an interim one").

[475] Benghazi ARB Report, Key Recommendations, p. 11 n. 2; Stewart, Diplomatic Security in Light of Benghazi; Burton & Katz, *Under Fire*, Chap. 2, pp. 28-29; and Hemingway, 5 Big Takeaways From the House Benghazi Report.

[476] Stevens July 9 Security Extension Cable to State (". . . Despite field expedient physical security upgrades to improve both the temporary Embassy and Villas [Mission] compound, neither compound meets OSPB [Overseas Security Policy Board] standards. . . ."), p. 2; and Nordstrom Oversight Committee Testimony (May 8, 2013) (Response to questions of Rep. James Lankford (R-OK)), pp. 39-40.

[477] Baier, New Revelations on Attack in Benghazi (*Watch video there*; Go to 5:48 - 6:09).

[478] Benghazi ARB Report, Finding 2, pp. 30-31; see also *Id.* ("The insufficient Special Mission compound security platform was at variance with the appropriate Overseas Security Policy Board (OSPB) standards with respect to perimeter, interior security, and safe areas"), p. 33.

[479] E.g., Nordstrom Oversight Committee Testimony (May 8, 2013) (Response to questions of Rep. Stephen Lynch (D-MA)) (". . . I think that what still remains unseen is who made that decision to go ahead and assume that this is going to be a temporary facility. At one point . . . I was told by the colleagues in OBO [presumably Bureau of Overseas Buildings and Operations] and DS [Diplomatic Security] that the

minimum Inman standards and SECCA standards for U.S. diplomatic outposts abroad.[480] Yet according to State Department security official Eric Nordstrom, only the Secretary of State can waive these security standards.[481] (Editors of the conservative *National Review* suspect Kennedy's "temporary" designation is done for the very purpose of avoiding the Inman standards.[482])

Regarding this "temporary" status of the Mission, Select Benghazi Committee members Mike Pompeo (R-KS) and Jim Jordan (R-OH) report, "We also learned it was an improvised designation not used at any of the State Department's other 275 facilities around the world."[483]

At subsequent House Oversight Committee hearings, State Department witnesses tell the panel Under Secretary of State Kennedy's decision to maintain the Mission Compound as a temporary

---

recommendations that we wanted to make, the upgrades both in Tripoli and Benghazi would not be made.... And they said, and I quote, 'it's my understanding the M, Under Secretary for Management, agreed to the current compounds being set up and occupied condition [sic] as is....'"), p. 50.

[480] Baier, New Revelations on Attack in Benghazi (*Watch video there*; Go to 5:48 - 6:08); House Oversight Interim Report on Benghazi ARB, pp. 35-38; Briefing on the Accountability Review Board Report by Deputy Secretary William J. Burns, Chairman Thomas Pickering and Vice Chairman Admiral Michael Mullen, State Dept. Archives website, (Dec. 19, 2012) ("Benghazi ARB Report Briefing for the Media") (ARB Vice-Chairman Michael Mullen: "... The buildings at Special Mission Benghazi did not meet Department standards for office buildings in high-threat areas, and in a sense, fell through the cracks bureaucratically by being categorized as temporary residential facilities...."); Burton & Katz, *Under Fire*, Chap. 4, pp. 45-46; and Attkisson, Benghazi Accountability Review Board Comes Under Renewed Criticism. See also Stewart, Diplomatic Security in Light of Benghazi ("... Working and living in an environment such as Benghazi where there are heavily armed Islamist militias is dangerous, but there are simply some things that cannot be done without personnel on the ground. Someone somewhere made the decision that the benefits of having U.S. personnel in Benghazi outweighed the risk of housing them in a building that did not meet security standards, and a waiver was granted for the Benghazi facility. The presence of a U.S. ambassador at a post with a security waiver located in such a volatile environment is another issue...").

[481] Nordstrom Oversight Committee Testimony (May 8, 2013) (Response to questions of Rep. James Lankford (R-OK)), p. 40.

[482] National Review Editors, What We Do Know About the Benghazi Attack Demands a Reckoning ("... [T]he Benghazi 'facility' – not a consulate, much less an embassy – appears to have been designated 'temporary' precisely to rationalize skirting the stringent security provisions the State Department requires for permanent outposts").

[483] Additional Views of Reps. Jim Jordan and Mike Pompeo, p. 440; and Hemingway, 5 Big Takeaways From the House Benghazi Report.

facility hinders State officials' ability to assign security agents there. These witnesses assert because Benghazi is not a "permanent" mission, "they had to rely mainly on temporary assignments to address security needs instead of assigning dedicated agents through the normal process." These temporary duty assignments depend upon an ever-revolving group of individual *volunteers*, who must persuade their supervisors to release them for high-risk, short-term duty in Benghazi. (Put bluntly, these TDY volunteers are the "step children" of State's diplomatic security service.) Diplomatic Security officials later testify they have raised their concerns over this problem with "more senior State Department officials" in the months preceding the attacks.[484]

On July 2, 2012, Under Secretary Kennedy meets with some of his subordinates to discuss various diplomatic facility subjects – including security issues. In preparing for this meeting, Ambassador Eric Boswell, Assistant Secretary for Diplomatic Security, directs his subordinate Charlene Lamb to ensure a diplomatic security representative at this conference with Kennedy emphasizes the Bureau of Diplomatic Security's concerns regarding the personnel and security challenges in Benghazi. (As discussed below, both Boswell and Lamb later will be suspended with pay for eight months for their roles in the Benghazi fiasco.) In an email to Lamb days before on June 29 Boswell writes:

> Re the Benghazi item, DS [Diplomatic Security] should express its concern over the resource drain that the endless TDYs in Benghazi in [sic is] inflicting on us, and also *concern that the overall security situation in Libya, Tripoli included, is deteriorating. We can't keep up these TDYs*

---

[484] House Oversight Interim Report on Benghazi ARB, pp. 34-35; Benghazi ARB Report, Finding 2 ("The short-term transitory nature of Special Mission Benghazi's staffing, with talented and committed, but inexperienced, American personnel often on temporary assignments of 40 days or less, resulted in diminished institutional knowledge, continuity, and mission capacity"), p. 4; Benghazi ARB Report Briefing for the Media; and Stewart, The Benghazi Report and the Diplomatic Security Funding Cycle ("At the very least, the State Department will need to review its policy of designating a facility as a 'special mission' – Benghazi was designated as such – to exempt it from meeting established physical security standards. . . . [I]f it is deemed necessary to keep a permanent presence in a place like Benghazi, then security standards need to be followed, especially when a facility is in place for several months. Temporary facilities with substandard security cannot be allowed to persist for months and years").

indefinitely. And having said that, if we are required to keep going in Benghazi we must salute and do it.[485]

Why No Marines at the Mission?

DSAs aside, the Benghazi Mission Compound has no Marine security contingent, as it likely would had it been an American Embassy.[486] In her memoir, Hillary Clinton explains Marines are assigned to "only a little over half" of all U.S. diplomatic posts around the globe. She states where they are stationed, their function is "protection and, if necessary, the destruction of classified materials and equipment." Clinton then claims, ". . . [B]ecause there was no classified processing at the diplomatic compound in Benghazi, there were no Marines posted there."[487] Shortly after Benghazi, a State Department spokesperson provides a similar explanation for the absence of Marines in Benghazi. She also will assert Marine security guards at diplomatic posts "are not bodyguards per se."[488]

Was this restricted role of Marines true in September 2012? The current State Department website clearly explains another of the Marine's responsibilities at diplomatic posts is "to *protect U.S. citizens* and property," including *responding to "facility intrusion attempts."*[489]

---

[485] House Oversight Interim Report on Benghazi ARB (emphasis added), p. 35, citing Email from Eric J. Boswell to Charlene R. Lamb Re "FWD: AGENDA for NEA-SCA EX Meeting with US Kennedy – 7/2/12" (June 29, 2012).

[486] Prepared Statement on the Attacks on the US Facilities in Benghazi, Libya Before Senate Armed Services Committee by Secretary of Defense Leon Panetta, Defense Dept. Archives website (Feb. 7, 2013) ("Panetta Senate Armed Services Prepared Testimony"); Daily Press Briefing by State Department Spokesperson Victoria Nuland, State Dept. Archives website (Oct. 12, 2012); Bret Baier, "13 Hours at Benghazi: The Inside Story," Fox News Channel (Sept. 5, 2014) ("Baier, 13 Hours at Benghazi: The Inside Story") (*Watch video there*; Go to 4:30-41); and Clinton, *Hard Choices*, Chap. 17, p. 393.

[487] Clinton, *Hard Choices*, Chap. 17, pp. 393-394.

[488] Daily Press Briefing by State Department Spokesperson Victoria Nuland, State Dept. Archives website (Oct. 12, 2012) (Marine security guards ". . . are primarily assigned to protect classified information, classified equipment, in those posts that are classified. . . .").

[489] "U.S. Marine Security Guards: Safeguarding American Missions Around the World," State Dept. website (emphasis added) (". . . The primary mission of MSGs [U.S. Marine Security Guards] is *to protect U.S. citizens* and property as well as to prevent the compromise of classified U.S. government information under a range of circumstances, including hostile assaults. They respond immediately to crises large and

Obviously, the Marines' role today is broader than mere protection of classified information and equipment. However, according to the Senate Intelligence Committee's subsequent report on Benghazi, the State Department simply reiterates to the panel this "no classified information" excuse for the absence of any Marines.[490] It appears the committee accepts this rationale without analysis.[491]

(The author suspects the truth is Foggy Bottom wants to avoid at all costs the presence of any Marines in order to steer clear of implying Benghazi is too dangerous a place for diplomats to be.)

Hiring Local Libyan Guards

The February 17 Martyrs Brigade

During this period the State Department desires to transition to using more local Libyans to provide security.[492] In addition to the handful of its own DSAs in Benghazi, State has contracted with a local militia group, the "February 17 Martyrs Brigade" ("17 February Brigade" or "17 February"), to provide additional interior armed security to the Mission Compound. According to the Benghazi Accountability Review Board (discussed in detail in Chapter 109), 17 February actually "is an umbrella organization, made up of many different militias with differing ideologies, some of which are extremist in nature."[493] It appears the Libyan government effectively has foisted these 17 February forces upon the State Department. The top U.S. security official in Libya, Eric Nordstrom, later testifies this militia

---

small, including demonstrations, bomb threats, fires, nuclear/biological/chemical threats, and facility intrusion attempts. . . .").

[490] Sen. Intelligence Committee Benghazi Report (". . . According to the State Department, the Mission facility did not store classified information, and therefore no Marine contingent was present"), p. 39.

[491] *Id.* (Concurring in State Department proposal "to expand the Marine Security Guard Program to increase protection at high-risk facilities beyond solely the protection of classified information"), p. 40.

[492] E.g., Stevens July 9 Security Extension Cable to State (". . . SST's deployment has *been critical* to our ability to navigate the transition to a more locally-based security team"), pp. 1-2; and Tapper, Security Team Commander Says Ambassador Stevens Wanted His Team to Stay in Libya Past August ("The State Department pushed the American diplomats to develop plans to transition its security staffing to one that incorporated more locally based assets . . .") (*Watch video there*; Go to 1:20-39).

[493] Benghazi ARB Report, p. 39.

"absolutely" has ties with Islamic extremists.[494] (Query: Why should the most powerful nation on the globe allow a pitifully weak, provisional government we had just saved from destruction by Qadhafi to "foist" *anything* on us?)

Following Benghazi, State Department spokesperson Marie Harf will go to great lengths trying to differentiate between the "17 February Militia" – with which the U.S. works in Benghazi – and the "17 February Martyrs Brigade" – which Harf insists the U.S. does not work with.[495] (The author finds Harf's attempted "explanation" to be impenetrable. It also appears inconsistent with Regional Security Officer Eric Nordstrom's July 2012 report on violence in Libya, which uses the two terms interchangeably.)

On site at the Mission is "a rotating set of three to four armed [17 February] guards who lived on compound to operate as a quick reaction force to respond to any security incidents against the Mission."[496] However, one DSA subsequently tells the Select Committee, ". . . really what we counted on them to do was make a phone call to the 17th February Martyrs Brigade so that we could receive backup in case something happened."[497] (Great, a phone call; how comforting.)

Under this "plan," that call first will go to a group of about twenty 17 February Brigade members located at a "base" or barracks about two kilometers (about one and one-quarter miles) from the Mission Compound. This militia body has "heavy weapons" and "heavy vehicles." This off-site "unit" of the 17 February Brigade has trained to respond to an incident at the Mission in the past (and in fact has done

---

[494] Nordstrom Oversight Committee Testimony (May 8, 2013) (Response to questions of Rep. Blake Farenthold (R-TX)) (The 17 February Brigade ". . . was the unit . . . that was provided to us by the Libyan Government. . . . That was the unit that the Libyan Government had initially designated for VIP protection. It is very difficult to extract ourselves from that"), pp. 80-81.

[495] Daily Press Briefing by State Department Deputy Spokesperson Marie Harf, State Dept. Archives website (Sept. 10, 2014).

[496] Benghazi Committee Report, p. 28. See also Lamb Oversight Committee Prepared Testimony, p. 3 (On September 11, 2012, there are three members of the Libyan 17th February Brigade on the Compound).

[497] Benghazi Committee Report, p. 28. See also Michael Birnbaum, "Sensitive Documents Left Behind With Little Security at U.S. Diplomatic Post in Libya," *The Washington Post* online (Oct. 3, 2012) ("Birnbaum, Sensitive Documents Left Behind With Little Security at U.S. Diplomatic Post in Libya").

so). They "were expected to respond to any event that necessitated them in the future."[498]

(These 17 February militia members generally do not wear snappy uniforms or even insignia identifying who they are. Many wear plain civilian attire. As a result, in the chaos to come on the Night of Benghazi, it will be almost impossible for Americans in Benghazi to tell friend from foe among the armed Libyans on the streets – or even on the Mission Compound grounds.)

The Blue Mountain Guard Force

The State Department also has contracted with another entity, The Blue Mountain Group ("BMG"), to enhance security at the Mission Compound. This company's "Blue Mountain Guard Force" ("Blue Mountain") is an *unarmed* force. Its primary responsibility is surveillance at the entrance gates, as well as of the compound's interior. Blue Mountain's staff is charged with screening people and vehicles before they are allowed to enter the Mission Compound.[499] Their personnel reportedly are paid minimum wage, and have poor training.[500]

(State's agreement actually is with a 50-50 partnership between BMG and a Libyan firm, XPAND Corporation. XPAND actually holds the license from the Libyan government to provide security services in Libya. BMG provides the local guards and trains them.[501])

The Blue Mountain Group is a company based in Hereford, Wales, in the United Kingdom, not in Libya. According to Fox News, a competitor of BMG's, Torres Advanced Enterprise Solutions ("Torres AES"), claims Benghazi possibly is the first diplomatic security contract BMG ever receives from the U.S. government! Torres AES asserts Benghazi is the very first "high threat" contract

---

[498] Benghazi Committee Report, pp. 28-29. See also Benghazi ARB Report, p. 35.

[499] Benghazi Committee Report, pp. 27-28.

[500] Burton & Katz, *Under Fire*, Chap. 5, pp. 55-56.

[501] Catherine Herridge, "State Department Stayed Out of Contractors' Dispute Over Consulate Security, Letters Show," Fox News online (Oct. 3, 2012) ("Herridge, State Department Stayed Out of Contractors' Dispute Over Consulate Security"); and "Judicial Watch: State Department Documents Show Its Security Contractor Operating Without a License in Benghazi on Day of Terrorist Attack," Judicial Watch website (Dec. 11, 2014) ("Judicial Watch: 'State Department Documents Show Its Security Contractor Operating Without a License in Benghazi on Day of Terrorist Attack'").

THE TRUE ACCOUNT OF VALOR AND ABANDONMENT

BMG has handled anywhere in the world.[502] The conservative watchdog group Judicial Watch also claims BMG had no U.S. government security experience.[503] (Indeed, at the time we go to press BMG's website contains only a few sentences discussing its security consulting and "close protection" services. The site lists none of its representative clients for those services. The site devotes most of its space to detailing the security-related training courses and equipment it offers for sale. The author can find no mention of providing protection for diplomatic or other government facilities.[504])

In contrast, Torres AES reportedly has won guard services contracts in Iraq, Pakistan and Jordan.[505] Fox News claims BMG did not immediately respond to Fox's questions regarding these allegations of Torres AES.[506] (In subsequent chapters we discuss even more incendiary charges by Torres AES regarding Benghazi.)

---

[502] Catherine Herridge Exclusive Report, "Tucker Carlson Tonight," Fox News Channel (Sept. 12, 2017). See also Judicial Watch: State Department Documents Show Its Security Contractor Operating Without a License in Benghazi on Day of Terrorist Attack ("It's unclear from the documents [the State Department later is forced to disclose in FOIA litigation] why the Benghazi contract was instead awarded to BMG [Blue Mountain Group], which apparently previously had never provided security for a U.S. government agency"); Herridge et al., Clinton State Department Silenced Them on Benghazi Security Lapses, Contractors Say (Quoting Torres AES official Brad Owens: "Blue Mountain U.K. is a teeny, tiny little security company registered in Wales that had never had a diplomatic security contract, had never done any high threat contracts anywhere else in the world that we've been able to find, much less in high threat areas for the U.S. government. They had a few guys on the ground") (*Watch video* there); and Anna Giaritelli, "Security Officers Who Survived Benghazi Say Clinton's Team Silenced Them: Report," *Washington Examiner* online (Sept. 13, 2017) (same). The *Washington Examiner's* headline and story incorrectly assert Torres AES security personnel were in Benghazi in September 2012 and survived the terrorist attacks. In fact, even if Torres AES's story is true, that company had not yet begun providing security at the Mission Compound by September 11, 2012.

[503] Judicial Watch: State Department Documents Show Its Security Contractor Operating Without a License in Benghazi on Day of Terrorist Attack ("It's unclear from the documents [released by the State Department pursuant to court order] why the Benghazi contract was instead awarded to BMG, which apparently had never previously provided security for a U.S. government agency").

[504] See Blue Mountain Group website.

[505] Judicial Watch: State Department Documents Show Its Security Contractor Operating Without a License in Benghazi on Day of Terrorist Attack.

[506] Catherine Herridge Exclusive Report, "Tucker Carlson Tonight," Fox News Channel (Sept. 12, 2017).

(Shortly after the Benghazi attacks, on September 18 State Department spokesperson Victoria Nuland emphatically will deny State has employed any private security firm at the Mission Compound. The agency retracts this erroneous claim shortly afterward.[507])

According to Judicial Watch, there previously have been problems with the Blue Mountain Guards at the Mission. Several of these guards reportedly walk off the job out of concerns for their safety. (Those are the smart ones.) Further, a BMG commander apparently is dismissed following an "altercation" with a member of the 17 February brigade.[508]

Former Regional Security Officer for Libya Eric Nordstrom later is questioned about the reliability of these local Libyan security personnel. Nordstrom testifies to the House Oversight Committee he has no confidence in these guards, and is concerned in particular about their "training deficiencies." He claims he alerts officials in Washington, D.C. to these problems. Nordstrom explains he seeks to have some counterintelligence vetting of these local guards, but is turned down. Officials in Washington want the U.S. Libya post to pay for any such vetting, but the latter lacks the funds. Nordstrom asserts regarding these local guards, "I think . . . it was the best bad plan. It was the only thing we had."[509]

Local Libyans' View of Security at the Mission

Local Benghazians, too, are concerned about security threats at the Benghazi Mission. According to two Republican investigators in Congress, in the weeks prior to the Benghazi tragedy some of the unarmed Libyan Blue Mountain security guards receive warnings from their family members. They allegedly are advised to quit their jobs at

---

[507] E.g., Judicial Watch: State Department Documents Show Its Security Contractor Operating Without a License in Benghazi on Day of Terrorist Attack (". . . State Department spokesperson Victoria Nuland emphatically denied on September 18, 2012, that State had hired any private firm to provide security at the American mission in Benghazi. The department later retracted that claim").

[508] Judicial Watch: State Department Documents Show Its Security Contractor Operating Without a License in Benghazi on Day of Terrorist Attack.

[509] Nordstrom Oversight Committee Testimony (May 8, 2013) (Response to questions of Rep. Patrick Meehan (R-PA)), p. 73; and *Id.* (Response to questions of Rep. Blake Farenthold (R-TX)), pp. 80-81.

the Mission Compound due to "rumors in the community of an impending attack."[510]

According to *The New York Times*, a Libyan politician, Fathi Baja, claims to have breakfasted with Ambassador Stevens before he is murdered. Baja tells the *Times* security at the Mission Compound is "sorely inadequate for an American ambassador in such a tumultuous environment." The *Times* further quotes Baja as stating, "This country is still in transition, and everybody knows the extremists are out there."[511]

The same *Times* article also quotes the Deputy Interior Minister of Libya, Wanis al-Sharif. According to this piece, al-Sharif "faulted the Americans at the mission for failing to heed what he [al-Sharif] said was the Libyan government's advice to pull its personnel or beef up its security, especially in light of the recent violence in the city and *the likelihood that the video would provoke protests.*"[512] (Here al-Sharif is referring to an anti-Muslim video entitled *Innocence of Muslims* (the "Video," discussed in detail below), soon to become infamous worldwide.)

Finally, according to The Associated Press (as cited by CBS News), ". . . [T]he location of U.S. diplomat enclaves is an open secret for the locals [in Libya]."[513]

Mission Security as September 11 Approaches

Despite all these warnings and attacks and requests for more security, the Benghazi Mission Compound in August-September 2012

---

[510] Birnbaum, Sensitive Documents Left Behind With Little Security at U.S. Diplomatic Post in Libya, citing Letter from Darrell Issa, Chairman, House Committee on Oversight and Government Reform, and Jason Chaffetz, Chairman, House Subcommittee on National Security, Homeland Defense, and Foreign Operations, to Secretary of State Hillary Rodham Clinton, Oversight Committee website (Oct. 2, 2012); and Herridge, State Department Stayed Out of Contractors' Dispute Over Consulate Security.

[511] Kirkpatrick and Myers, Libya Attack Brings Challenges for U.S. See also Stewart, The Benghazi Report and the Diplomatic Security Funding Cycle (". . . Is a permanent U.S. presence even required in a place like Benghazi, or can the missions in such locations be accomplished by a combination of visiting diplomats, covert operatives and local employees?").

[512] Kirkpatrick and Myers, Libya Attack Brings Challenges for U.S. (emphasis added).

[513] CBS News, CIA Saw Possible Terror Ties Day After Libya Hit: AP.

has very minimal human security assets.⁵¹⁴ There are only three assigned Diplomatic Security Agents at the compound.⁵¹⁵ (Ordinarily, there are supposed to be five DSAs here. However, the Special Mission Compound reportedly enjoys its full complement of five DSAs for *only 23 days* over the period from January 1 through September 9, 2012!)⁵¹⁶

None of these three DSAs now at the Mission ever has served at a "high risk" post before.⁵¹⁷ According to authors Burton and Katz, all have less than ten years experience as a DSA agent, and most have fewer than five years.⁵¹⁸ However, Gregory Hicks later tells the Select Committee all of them are "brand new to the service and on temporary duty assignment."⁵¹⁹ Benghazi is a sufficiently dangerous posting the DSAs are not permitted to bring their spouses or children with them.⁵²⁰ (As noted below, Stevens will bring two more DSAs with him from Tripoli to Benghazi.)

Again according to Burton and Katz, the DSAs have a mixture of backgrounds. They include former Marines, an Iraqi war veteran, former police officers, and "academics." "Some were battle trained and had seen war."⁵²¹ Those among the five DSAs who had not previously

---

⁵¹⁴ "Dispute Over Nature of Libya Attack Continues; Witness Tells CBS There Was No Protest," CBS News online (Oct. 18 [sic 19?], 2012) ("CBS News, Dispute Over Nature of Libya Attack Continues") (Senator Susan Collins (R-ME): "I'm just stunned and appalled that there wasn't better security for all of the American personnel at that consulate [sic] given the high threat environment").

⁵¹⁵ Benghazi Committee Report, p. 13.

⁵¹⁶ House Oversight Interim Report on Benghazi ARB (incorrectly citing end of date range as September 2013), p. 33, citing Benghazi ARB Report (issued in December 2012), p. 31. But compare Sen. Intelligence Committee Benghazi Report (Redacted) (". . . [T]he Mission facility met the minimum personnel requirements for Diplomatic Security agents as accepted by the U.S. Embassy in Tripoli at the time of the August 15 EAC meeting (specifically, the three Diplomatic Security Agents were assigned to guard the Mission compound) . . ."), p. 16.

⁵¹⁷ Benghazi Committee Report, p. 13; and Lamb Oversight Committee Prepared Testimony, p. 3.

⁵¹⁸ Burton & Katz, *Under Fire*, Chap. 6, p. 68.

⁵¹⁹ Benghazi Committee Report, p. 16.

⁵²⁰ Burton & Katz, *Under Fire* (". . . Benghazi was a hardship post – no spouses or children permitted. It was a spartan post inside the hell of a raging inferno. . . ."), Chap. 6, p. 62.

⁵²¹ *Id.*, Chap. 6, p. 68.

been stationed outside the U.S. did not even receive "overseas RSO training" before being posted in Benghazi![522]

As Burton and Katz explain, in Benghazi "Who lives and dies depends a great deal on training, teamwork, and fate. The agents at the compound knew that they were on their own."[523]

Well, not *completely* on their own. One of the Global Response Staff security contractors stationed at the nearby CIA Annex is ex-Army Ranger Kris "Tanto" Paronto. Two years after the tragedy, he tells Fox News that prior to the Night of Benghazi he issues blunt warnings to the DSA agents at the Mission. Paronto claims he tells them, "You know, if you guys get attacked, you guys are going to die. You know that, right?" Paronto says he then promises the DSAs if they ever need assistance, they should call the GRS agents and the latter will come help.[524] The Senate Intelligence panel later concludes although there was no formal written agreement, "there was a common understanding that each group would come to the other's aid if attacked..."[525] It is a pledge the GRS men soon will honor on the Night of Benghazi.

Tanto Paronto is not the only American in Libya concerned about danger in Benghazi. According to the Select Benghazi Committee, Ambassador Stevens cancels a planned trip to Benghazi, scheduled for early August 2012, "because of security."[526] This cancellation apparently does not impact Secretary Clinton's view (or that of her senior staff) of the security situation in Benghazi generally, or at the

---

[522] *Id.*, Chap. 6, p. 68.

[523] *Id.*, Chap. 6, p. 72.

[524] Baier, 13 Hours at Benghazi: The Inside Story (*Watch video there*; Go to 4:40-50); Hicks, What the Benghazi Attack Taught Me About Hillary Clinton ("U.S. personnel assigned to Benghazi tried to overcome this severe disadvantage [of having two separate facilities] through an agreement that the security personnel from each facility would rush to the other facility's aid in the event it was attacked"); and Clinton, *Hard Choices* ("... [T]here was an understanding between security officials in both agencies that in an emergency, a CIA rapid-response team would deploy to the State Department compound to provide extra protection"), Chap. 17, p. 389.

[525] Sen. Intelligence Committee Benghazi Report, p. 27. See also Clinton, *Hard Choices* ("... [T]here was an understanding between security officials in both agencies [CIA and State] that in an emergency, a CIA rapid-response team would deploy to the State Department [Mission] compound to provide extra protection...."), Chap. 17, p. 389.

[526] Benghazi Committee Report, pp. 11.

Mission Compound specifically.[527] (Query: why is it too dangerous for Stevens to travel to Benghazi in August, but not too dangerous just weeks later on the anniversary of 9/11?)

On or about August 22, Embassy Tripoli "fully informs" State Department officials in Washington that Ambassador Stevens will be traveling to Benghazi in September. According to Gregory Hicks, *no one at State in Washington raises any concerns about Stevens going there*.[528] (This is despite the fact that, as discussed in the following chapter, at this exact time State is becoming aware its security contract for Benghazi with the Blue Mountain Group is imploding.)

About two weeks later on September 8 – just two days before a U.S. ambassador will arrive – the 17 February Brigade militia informs the DSAs the militia no longer will provide off-compound security in Benghazi! At a meeting on September 9, "leading militia officials" inform America's top diplomat then in Benghazi (presumably then acting Principal Officer, David McFarland) the militias "could no longer guarantee the safety of *the compound*." The Select Committee concludes, "The meeting underscored that the militias in Benghazi controlled what little security environment existed there. Not having off-compound support from a militia would significantly threaten Stevens' safety."[529]

According to *The Washington Post*, on this same day, September 9, a member of the Mission's security personnel reportedly drafts a memorandum to the 17 February Martyrs Brigade. Ominously, it discusses the possibility of an attack on the Mission Compound in early September. The unsigned memorandum states, "In the event of an attack on the U.S. Mission, QRF [quick reaction force] will request

---

[527] Additional Views of Reps. Jordan and Pompeo (". . . The American people expect that when the government sends our representatives into such dangerous places they receive adequate protection. Secretary Clinton paid special attention to Libya. She sent Ambassador Stevens there. Yet, in August 2012, she missed the last, clear chance to protect her people"), p. 416.

[528] Hicks Oversight Committee Testimony (May 8, 2013) (Response to questions of Rep. Doug Collins (R-GA)), p. 90. See also Attkisson, *Stonewalled* (". . . Hicks says that Stevens's daily plans were routinely circulated within the State Department. Specifically, his planned travel to Benghazi was shared with headquarters via email several weeks in advance of the visit and in regular staffing reports during the trip. Headquarters 'knew Chris was going to Benghazi for five days during a gap between principal officers until Benghazi's new principal officer arrived,' Hicks tells me with certainty"), Chap. 4, p. 191.

[529] Benghazi Committee Report (emphasis added), pp. 13 and 15.

additional support from the 17th February Martyrs Brigade." The *Post* further reports, "The memorandum tells the militia security force to summon more guards from its nearby base if the mission is attacked, suggesting that the Americans there were concerned that the regular guard force would be inadequate in an emergency." (No kidding.) The *Post* will find this document in the Mission ruble following the September 11 attacks![530]

It is at this point on September 9 *at the very latest* the State Department should cancel Ambassador Stevens' trip, and withdraw the remaining U.S. diplomatic staff from Benghazi.[531] Tragically, the agency does neither.

The Senate Intelligence Committee later will conclude, "... [T]he Mission facility had a much weaker security posture than the Annex, with a significant disparity in the quality and quantity of equipment and security upgrades."[532] This panel then issues one of its formal findings on this subject:

> FINDING #2: The State Department should have increased its security posture more significantly in Benghazi based on the deteriorating security situation on the ground and IC [Intelligence Community] threat reporting on the prior attacks against Westerners in Benghazi – including two incidents at the Temporary Mission Facility on April 6 and June 6, 2012.[533]

---

[530] Birnbaum, Sensitive Documents Left Behind With Little Security at U.S. Diplomatic Post in Libya.

[531] Kennedy October 10 Briefing ("We live with risk, but... we look for ways to mitigate that risk... and then we come up with a strategy. If we cannot mitigate that risk, we withdraw. We withdrew from Tripoli. We withdrew from Damascus") (*Watch video there*; Go to 6:59 - 8:52; Sen. Intelligence Committee Benghazi Report (Given available intelligence and the fact many "tripwires" had been crossed "... [T]he Committee believes the State Department should have recognized the need to increase security to a level commensurate with the threat, or suspend operations in Benghazi"), p. 26; and Stewart, The Benghazi Report and the Diplomatic Security Funding Cycle ("... Is a permanent U.S. presence even required in a place like Benghazi, or can the missions in such locations be accomplished by a combination of visiting diplomats, covert operatives and local employees?").

[532] Sen. Intelligence Committee Benghazi Report (Redacted), p. 19.

[533] *Id.* (Redacted), pp. 11-12.

Conclusions Regarding the Mission's Security

In sum, including local Libyan guards, *theoretically* there are more than thirty *armed* personnel available to defend the Mission Compound during Ambassador Stevens' visit.[534] These include the five DSAs at the Mission, six Central Intelligence Agency contract security agents assigned to the nearby CIA Annex, the three (sometimes four) armed 17 February Brigade guards on duty at the Mission, and the twenty or so offsite 17 February members two kilometers away.

In the real world, as the reader will see, when the proverbial stuff hits the proverbial fan on September 11, only about *fourteen* security guards are available to raise their firearms and shoot at the bad guys at the Mission. Of these, the five DSAs (and perhaps one or more of the 17 February guards) prove unwilling to do so at the Mission.

One State Department official later will discuss with House Oversight Committee investigators his concerns regarding security at the Mission Compound. William Roebuck is Office Director for the Maghreb Office. According to CBS News, Roebuck tells investigators he is sufficiently concerned about the insufficient number of Diplomatic Security Agents in Benghazi he considers "forcing the issue" by urging the Mission Compound be shut down. Roebuck is quoted as telling the committee, ". . . people out there were not able to do their work, they weren't able to move, they weren't able to do the contact work that they wanted to do."[535]

Despite all of these security shortcomings at the Mission Compound, the State Department's Diplomatic Security chief, Charlene Lamb, later will deny the obvious. In October 2012 she testifies before the House Oversight Committee, "We had the correct number of [security] assets in Benghazi at the time of 9/11 for what had been agreed upon."[536] (Agreed upon between whom? Her and Patrick Kennedy? Certainly not agreed upon with Ambassador Stevens or Gregory Hicks or Eric Nordstrom or John Martinec or Lt. Col. Andrew Wood.[537])

---

[534] Benghazi Committee Report, pp. 28-29.

[535] Attkisson, Benghazi Accountability Review Board Comes Under Renewed Criticism.

[536] Lamb House Oversight Committee Testimony, p. 53; and Cornwell and Zakaria, U.S. Security at Benghazi Mission Called "Weak."

[537] E.g., Wood House Oversight Prepared Testimony ("The security in Benghazi was a struggle and remained a struggle throughout my time there [February to August 2012].

THE TRUE ACCOUNT OF VALOR AND ABANDONMENT

Even the Democrats' minority report on the Select Benghazi Committee (written by political protectors of President Obama and Hillary Clinton) concludes the State Department has provided "woefully inadequate" security in Benghazi.[538] (Unless you are Charlene Lamb, it is difficult to conclude otherwise.) ■

The situation remained uncertain and reports from some Libyans indicated it was getting worse. Diplomatic security remained weak. . . ."), p. 3.

[538] "Honoring Courage, Improving Security, and Fighting the Exploitation of a Tragedy," Report of the Democratic Members of the House Select Committee on Benghazi (June 2016) (The State Department's "Security measures in Benghazi were woefully inadequate as a result of decisions made by officials in the Bureau of Diplomatic Security . . ."), p. 754.

20

Unlicensed: "Terminate the Contract"

According to one private security firm, by late August 2012 some managers at the State Department are having serious misgivings about their Blue Mountain security firm at the Benghazi Mission Compound. As noted above, Torres Advanced Enterprise Solutions ("Torres AES") provides diplomatic security services to U.S. diplomatic embassies and consulates around the globe.[539] As this book is written, Torres AES serves clients in numerous African countries, including Egypt and Sudan (but not Libya).[540]

Rewind to early 2012. Torres AES is an unsuccessful bidder for the approximately $783,000 security contract at the Benghazi Mission. Blue Mountain Group ("BMG") wins that contract over Torres AES and at least one other bidder.[541] (BMG apparently submitted a slightly lower bid.[542]) At the State Department this contract award is managed by one Jan Visintainer. The *Washington Examiner* (whose article about the subject of this chapter contains some serious factual errors) describes Jan Visintainer as "a senior State official who was close to Clinton."[543] (Thus far, the author has been unable to verify this supposed close nexus with Secretary Clinton.)

Now fast-forward to late August 2017. Torres now will claim to Fox News that five years earlier, by August 31, 2012, the State Department contacts Torres AES *about two weeks before the Benghazi*

---

[539] See Torres Advanced Enterprise Solutions website.

[540] *Id.*

[541] Judicial Watch: State Department Documents Show Its Security Contractor Operating Without a License in Benghazi on Day of Terrorist Attack.

[542] "Local Guard Force – U.S. Mission to Benghazi, Solicitation No. S-AQMMA-12-R-0121, Prepared for U.S. Department of State by Torres Advanced Enterprise Solutions (Jan. 23, 2012), cited in Catherine Herridge Exclusive Report, "Tucker Carlson Tonight," Fox News Channel (Sept. 12, 2017); and Herridge et al., Clinton State Department Silenced Them on Benghazi Security Lapses, Contractors Say (*Watch video there*).

[543] Anna Giaritelli, "Security Officers Who Survived Benghazi Say Clinton's Team Silenced Them: Report," *Washington Examiner* online (Sept. 13, 2017).

tragedy in early September 2012. State allegedly asks if Torres AES will take over the security contract for the Mission Compound "as soon as possible"! Torres AES officials say it agrees to do so, but it will take two to three weeks or so to implement.[544] *If* this is true, it is astounding the State Department does not immediately direct Chris Stevens to postpone his visit to Benghazi until Torres AES can assume responsibility and replace Blue Mountain there. (This may only take a week or so.)

Torres AES's officials suggest the State Department wants to pull Blue Mountain's Benghazi contract because of *State's* concerns over security performance. However, things appear to be a bit more complicated. It may be it is a company called "XPAND Corporation," Blue Mountain's 50-50 Libyan partner, rather than State itself that is developing cold feet regarding Blue Mountain's security abilities and performance.

As early as June 6, 2012, Blue Mountain alerts State's Visintainer of problems developing between Blue Mountain and its Libyan partner, XPAND.[545] Fox News reports that in October 2012, an unidentified "source" tells Fox of two State Department meetings, one held in June and a second in July 2012, in which Blue Mountain's security performance is discussed. This source, which Fox says claims to have knowledge of these meetings, tells Fox the Blue Mountain Group's Libyan partner (which Fox calls "Blue Mountain Libya") feels the security provided by it's U.K. partner is "substandard and the situation was unworkable."[546] Fox reports the Libyan partner attempts to bring in a third party – an unidentified "American contractor" – to improve

---

[544] Catherine Herridge Report, "Happening Now," Fox News online (Sept. 13, 2017); Catherine Herridge Exclusive Report, "Tucker Carlson Tonight," Fox News Channel (Sept. 12, 2017); and Herridge et al., Clinton State Department Silenced Them on Benghazi Security Lapses, Contractors Say (*Watch video* there). See also Anna Giaritelli, "Security Officers Who Survived Benghazi Say Clinton's Team Silenced Them: Report," *Washington Examiner* online (Sept. 13, 2017). As noted above, the *Washington Examiner's* headline and story incorrectly assert Torres AES security personnel were in Benghazi in September 2012 and survived the terrorist attacks. Even if Torres AES's story is true, that company had not yet begun providing security at the Mission Compound by September 11, 2012, and the author believes while its personnel might have been in Benghazi, they were not at the Mission (or the CIA Annex) on the Night of Benghazi.

[545] Judicial Watch: State Department Documents Show Its Security Contractor Operating Without a License in Benghazi on Day of Terrorist Attack.

[546] Herridge, State Department Stayed Out of Contractors' Dispute Over Consulate Security.

security. Fox claims the State Department declines to become involved in this effort.[547]

Specifically, again according to Fox News, despite these security concerns within the State Department, on July 10, 2012 State's Visintainer writes to the Libyan partner, "The U.S. government is not required to mediate any disagreements between the two parties of the Blue Mountain Libya partnership." Visintainer advises the partners "to resolve their differences and successfully complete this contract."[548] She reportedly adds that to date "contract performance is satisfactory."[549] This is still further evidence State is on notice of (yet disregards) security problems at its Benghazi outpost.[550]

But the parties don't fix it themselves. Instead, on August 20 Blue Mountain and XPAND formally agree to dissolve their partnership. But it is XPAND that holds the security license from the Libyan government to operate there. This means Blue Mountain Group now is unlicensed in Libya!

On September 9, 2012, a lawyer for XPAND reportedly writes Visintainer at State seeking to bar Blue Mountain from using XPAND's license in Libya, including at the Benghazi Mission. Documents regarding this incident finally are pried out of a resistant State Department in late 2014 by Freedom of Information Act ("FOIA") litigation brought by the conservative watchdog group "Judicial Watch."[551] (According to the Judicial Watch documents, the day after the tragedy in Benghazi XPAND's legal counsel writes Ms. Visintainer again, essentially saying "never mind," it's okay for Blue Mountain to use our Libya license for a while.[552] Great, thanks a

---

[547] *Id.*

[548] Judicial Watch: State Department Documents Show Its Security Contractor Operating Without a License in Benghazi on Day of Terrorist Attack.

[549] Herridge, State Department Stayed Out of Contractors' Dispute Over Consulate Security.

[550] *Id.* ("Letters obtained exclusively by Fox News appear to show the State Department refused to get involved when the company tasked with protecting the U.S. Consulate [sic] in Benghazi, Libya, raised security concerns, the latest indication that warning signs may have been ignored in the lead-up to last month's terror attack").

[551] Complaint in *Judicial Watch, Inc. v. U.S. Department of State* (No. 13-CV-00243), U.S. District Court for the District of Columbia, Judicial Watch Document Archive (Feb. 25, 2013); and Judicial Watch: State Department Documents Show Its Security Contractor Operating Without a License in Benghazi on Day of Terrorist Attack.

[552] Judicial Watch: State Department Documents Show Its Security Contractor Operating Without a License in Benghazi on Day of Terrorist Attack.

lot. All the Americans are now gone from Benghazi – and four are dead.)

(By the way, responses to FOIA requests to the State Department are handled by the agency's "Bureau of Administration."[553] This bureau in turn reports to the Under Secretary for Management.[554] During all time periods relevant to the Benghazi tragedy, that Under Secretary is – wait for it – our old friend Patrick Kennedy. That's correct. The same individual who ultimately controlled the process that denied numerous FOIA requests for documents pertaining to the Benghazi debacle[555] is the same man who made so many of the horrific, miscalculated decisions denying requests for more security to U.S. diplomats in Benghazi and Tripoli! Small wonder State's records concerning Benghazi had to be pried out of the agency with a judicial crowbar in litigation.)

While it creates a technical legal problem for the State Department and Blue Mountain, by itself this loss of licensure does not necessarily pose any actual security concerns on the ground in Benghazi. However, there is more to the story. Apparently, it is the Blue Mountain Group in the U.K. – not XPAND in Libya – that in fact *trains and manages* the Blue Mountain guards at the Mission Compound.[556] One State official reportedly describes this as an "emergency situation." On the very morning of September 11, 2012, an unnamed BMG official promises to call Visintainer soon about this mess. This same day, State security official David Sparrowgrove writes to Visintainer and others, "The dissolution of the partnership leaves BMG without a security license to operate in Libya and the Libyan partner [XPAND] has no capacity to manage the guards or the contract. As a result, we feel the best course of action is to terminate the contract in short order."[557]

---

[553] State Dept. website, Bureau of Administration webpage.

[554] State Dept. website, Under Secretary for Management webpage.

[555] Perhaps Patrick Kennedy should have read a presidential memorandum regarding public information requests. Issued in the first days of the new Obama administration, the memorandum reportedly asserts, ". . . [I]n the face of doubt, openness prevails." Such requests should be responded to "promptly and in a spirit of cooperation." Schwartz, A Spymaster Steps Out of the Shadows.

[556] Daily Press Briefing by Marie Harf, Deputy Spokesperson, State Dept. Archives website (Dec. 12, 2013); and Judicial Watch: State Department Documents Show Its Security Contractor Operating Without a License in Benghazi on Day of Terrorist Attack.

[557] Judicial Watch: State Department Documents Show Its Security Contractor Operating Without a License in Benghazi on Day of Terrorist Attack.

This lack of any management capability over the local Blue Mountain Guards *does* have possible security implications for the Americans at the Benghazi Mission. On the Night of Benghazi and possibly during the preceding days or even weeks leading up to the attacks, the Blue Mountain Guards may be unsupervised by their own employer, with only the Mission's DSAs overseeing them.

These circumstances suggest XPAND must want out of its partnership with Blue Mountain Group very badly. After all, are there so many other profitable business relationships in chaotic post-revolutionary Benghazi? Why, just four months or so after winning the State contract, does XPAND bail during the very time period (June through August 2012) when security in Benghazi literally is going to hell in a hand basket? Does XPAND see disaster looming ahead? (Apparently, the State Department does not – until it is too late.)

All of this raises a burning question: Does the State Department even *tell* Ambassador Stevens it is experiencing problems with the BMG security firm in Benghazi? Insofar as the author can ascertain, Stevens' Deputy, Gregory Hicks, later will not mention Torres AES or Blue Mountain's dispute with XPAND in his lengthy testimony and interviews on multiple occasions before Congress and its investigative staff. Surely Stevens would have told his right-hand deputy Hicks this vital information had Stevens known of it. And certainly the astute and honorable and precise Mr. Hicks would have mentioned it to congressional investigators. Yet the author has found no evidence Hicks ever does. There is one overpowering inference to be drawn from this: *State may not have shared this troublesome news about BMG with Stevens or Hicks!* (If true, this would be gross negligence.)

Torres AES's astonishing 2017 claims must be taken with a hefty grain of salt. First, Torres AES officials wait five years before coming forward with their story. Second, when they do go to the media it is after losing not only the original security contract at the Mission Compound, but also 18 of the last 20 U.S. State Department contracts on which they have bid! However, owner Jerry Torres defends his firm's tardy whistle-blowing. He claims to Fox News that, at the time of the Benghazi disaster, he is concerned with the livelihood of his firm's approximately 8,000 employees.[558] Nevertheless, it is possible "sour grapes" may be a factor (perhaps even a decisive one) in Torres AES's 2017 allegations.

---

[558] Catherine Herridge Exclusive Report, "Tucker Carlson Tonight," Fox News Channel (Sept. 12, 2017); and Herridge et al., Clinton State Department Silenced Them on Benghazi Security Lapses, Contractors Say (*Watch video there*).

Still, Judicial Watch has documented how the State Department goes to considerable lengths to hide from Congress and the public this entire security license incident involving Blue Mountain and XPAND.[559]

As we shall discuss later in Chapter 110, Torres AES will claim to Fox News (again belatedly in 2017) the State Department is guilty of other serious misconduct after the Benghazi tragedy concerning State's security contracting involving Benghazi. (In a nutshell, Torres AES claims Visintainer instructs them not to discuss Benghazi with the government or the media.) Fox News claims neither Visintainer nor Blue Mountain would respond to Fox's inquiries about Torres AES's blockbuster 2017 allegations.[560]

(By the way, the author's attempt to find information regarding Ms. Visintainer on the State Department's website (including in its archives) yielded but one result, a mention of her name at the above-mentioned press briefing in December 2013. Has Ms. Visintainer since joined the federal witness protection program? In any event, the elusive Jan Visintainer will not be among the four State Department employees who later are disciplined for their role in the Benghazi debacle. See Chapter 113.) ∎

---

[559] E.g., Judicial Watch: State Department Documents Show Its Security Contractor Operating Without a License in Benghazi on Day of Terrorist Attack (Discussing email from State Department Deputy Assistant Secretary dated October 17, 2012 and shared with Congress: "... [T]he fact that the dispute between BMG and XPAND meant the company was operating without a license is glossed over, any reference to the September 11, 2012, emergency Benghazi security situation is specifically omitted, and he [the email's author] describes Visintainer's response in July as 'invoking collaborative resolution to the said dispute'").

[560] Catherine Herridge Report, "Happening Now," Fox News online (Sept. 13, 2017).

21

"Heightened Alert"

It is now the eve of the eleventh anniversary of 9/11. In preparation, on September 10, 2012, the day Christopher Stevens will arrive in Benghazi, President Obama holds a conference call with numerous "key national security principals." The ostensible purpose is to put the entire nation on heightened security alert. The true purpose turns out to be primarily public relations.

Participants in this call include Defense Secretary Leon Panetta, Joint Chiefs Chairman General Martin Dempsey, Secretary of State Hillary Clinton, CIA Director David Petraeus, National Intelligence Director James Clapper, Matt Olsen of the National Counterterrorism Center, and John Brennan as the president's advisor on counterterrorism. The purpose of the call is to discuss the protection of U.S. persons and facilities abroad. According to a readout of the call, the American military is instructed by Obama to "do everything possible to protect the American people, both at home and abroad."[561] However, the U.S. government reportedly has received no intelligence concerning specific threats for the 9/11 date.[562]

Defense Secretary Leon Panetta states they are "already tracking an inflammatory anti-Muslim video that was circulating on the Internet and inciting anger across the Middle East against the United States –

---

[561] Panetta, *Worthy Fights*, Chap. 16, pp. 426-427; and "Readout of the President's Meeting with Senior Administration Officials on Our Preparedness and Security Posture on the Eleventh Anniversary of September 11th," Obama White House Archives (Sept. 10, 2012); and Benghazi Committee Report (quoting same), p. 19.

[562] Panetta Senate Armed Services Prepared Testimony; Sen. Intelligence Committee Benghazi Report (Redacted) ("To date, the Committee has not identified any intelligence or other information received prior to September 11, 2012, by the IC or State Department indicating specific terrorist planning to attack the U.S. facilities in Benghazi on September 11, 2012"), p. 23; Panetta, *Worthy Fights* ("Our assessment to the president [on September 10, 2012] was unanimous: Although there were persistently general threats against U.S. interests and facilities, we saw no specific intelligence or warning about an attack on or around the 9/11 anniversary"), Chap. 16, p. 427; Clinton, *Hard Choices* (". . . [T]he intelligence community, as they've testified since, relayed no actionable intelligence about specific threats against any U.S. diplomatic post across the Middle East and North Africa"), p. 386. See also Benghazi Committee Report (Testimony of Vice Admiral Leidig of AFRICOM), p. 57; and Benghazi ARB Report, Finding 4, p. 38.

THE TRUE ACCOUNT OF VALOR AND ABANDONMENT

even though the U.S. government had nothing to do with it." (This Video is *Innocence of Muslims*, by Egyptian-American filmmaker Mark Basseley Youssef, aka Nakoula Basseley Nakoula.[563]) Panetta adds they are bracing for possible "demonstrations in Cairo and elsewhere across the region."[564] *Despite this concern over the Video, Panetta mobilizes no military assets to prepare to deploy to Cairo or Libya or anywhere else in North Africa.*

Based on this September 10 security conference call, Defense supposedly places its forces on "higher alert because of the potential for what could happen."[565] But at least in northern Africa, southern Europe and the Mediterranean – including in Spain, Italy, Croatia, Crete and Libya – this "higher alert" appears to be all theater. There is no actual modification in the posture of any U.S. military assets there. Indeed, the commander of AFRICOM, General Carter Ham, later will tell the House Armed Services Committee, ". . . [N]either he or anyone working for him was consulted as part of the [Obama Counterterrorism Advisor John] Brennan 9/11 planning process" in 2012![566]

As the Select Committee concludes, ". . . the call for a 'heightened alert' did not cause any actual adjustments in its [DoD's] posture for assets that could respond to a crisis in North Africa." No military training exercises or inspections are interrupted. "No fighter jets or tankers were placed on a 'heightened alert' status" at, or re-positioned to, U.S. bases in Sigonella, Sicily or Aviano, Italy or Souda Bay, Crete or Rota, Spain (all discussed below).[567] (Some "heightened" alert.) ■

---

[563] E.g., Randy Kreider, "'*Innocence of Muslims*' Film maker Ordered Back to Prison," ABC News online (Nov. 8, 2012). This article explains Youssef also has used the aliases "Nakoula Basseley Nakoula" and "Sam Bacile" (both spelled in various ways).

[564] Benghazi Committee Report (emphasis added), p. 19. See also Panetta, *Worthy Fights*, Chap. 16, p. 427.

[565] Benghazi Committee Report, p. 19, quoting Panetta, *Worthy Fights*, p. 225. The author is unable to locate this quotation in Mr. Panetta's book, and suspects the Select Committee intended to cite only Panetta's testimony to the panel.

[566] "Readout of House Armed Services Committee, Subcommittee on Oversight and Investigations Classified Briefing on Benghazi," House Armed Services Committee website (June 26, 2013).

[567] Benghazi Committee Report, p. 19.

22

"It Was Worth the Risk"

The Obama administration never explains adequately to the American people exactly what Ambassador Stevens and his staff (much less the CIA agents one-half mile away at the Annex) even are *doing* in perilous Benghazi on September 11, 2012. *Why* is his five-day visit planned to such a wickedly dangerous place? Why *do* U.S. personnel remain when almost every other western nation and international entity has abandoned Benghazi?[568]

As we have discussed above, there are at least eight reasons why Christopher Stevens should not be going to Benghazi today: (1) Benghazi is "the most dangerous city" in North Africa; (2) Tomorrow is the anniversary of 9/11; (3) Human security assets at the Mission Compound are ludicrously inadequate, and the two security men Stevens is taking can make little difference; (4) The physical security structure at the Mission also is substandard; (5) The State Department just days before has decided to terminate the contract of the Blue Mountain force that helps guard the Mission, but the new contractor (Torres AES) needs more time to take over (see Chapter 20); (6) On September 8, the 17 February militia has advised Mission staff it can no longer provide security outside the Mission compound; (7) On September 9, militia officials inform America's top diplomat then in Benghazi the militias can no longer guarantee the safety of the compound itself; and (8) Rumors of a protest in Cairo and other signs of Middle East unrest over the anti-Islam Video are swirling around the region (if not within Libya itself). As Ambassador Stevens boards his

---

[568] McCarthy, Hillary Clinton's Benghazi Debacle: Arming Jihadists in Libya . . . And Syria ("What mission was so important the United States kept personnel in the jihadist hellhole of Benghazi in 2012? . . . [W]e have never gotten to the bottom of why the State Department, under Mrs. Clinton's direction, had an installation in Benghazi, one of the world's most dangerous places for Americans"); and National Review Editors, What We Do Know About the Benghazi Attack Demands a Reckoning ("Again, as [congressmen] Jordan and Pompeo observe, the [Select Benghazi] committee never got an answer to the obvious question: 'What was so important in Benghazi that it meant risking the lives of Americans in what many apparently considered a suicide mission?'").

commercial flight, the U.S. State Department knows all these facts. Yet its people make no effort to stop Stevens from going.

In light of these risk factors, if Stevens' trip is not canceled entirely why is it not at least postponed?[569] However, according to the DSAs who protect him, Stevens is "determined" and "adamant" to go to Benghazi in September 2012.[570]

We consider next some justifications for Stevens' perilous journey that conceivably might justify such an enormous risk to a U.S. ambassador. Note that whether the State Department should maintain an outpost in Benghazi is a separate issue from whether Ambassador Stevens himself personally needs to be present in Benghazi.

The Diplomatic Case for a Benghazi Mission

Some argue there is no diplomatic purpose for maintaining the Mission Compound in Benghazi in the first place.[571] Recall that the U.S. closes its Embassy in Tripoli in February 2011. During the period from April 2011 (when Chris Stevens arrives) through September 2011 (when the U.S. Embassy reopens), Benghazi is State's *only* diplomatic post in Libya. However, after the U.S. reopens its Embassy in Tripoli, why is a Benghazi diplomatic outpost still necessary?

Indeed, there are some documents indicating the State Department at one time plans to close its Benghazi Mission at the end of 2012. The Senate Intelligence panel suggests this may account for the reluctance of some in Washington to expend much money on additional security for a post slated to be discontinued.[572]

This issue comes to a head within the agency in December 2011. Jeffrey Feltman, head of State's Near Eastern Division, sends an internal memorandum discussing reasons for remaining in Benghazi to Under Secretary for Management, Patrick Kennedy. Feltman's "Sensitive But Unclassified" memorandum states, in part:

---

[569] Benghazi Committee Report, p. 19; Panetta, *Worthy Fights*, Chap. 16, p. 427; and Kirkpatrick and Myers, Libya Attack Brings Challenges for U.S.

[570] Benghazi Committee Report, pp. 11-12.

[571] E.g., McCarthy, Hillary Clinton's Benghazi Debacle: Arming Jihadists in Libya . . . And Syria ("There was no defensible security arrangement or diplomatic need for the State Department facility in Benghazi (U.S. diplomatic functions were handled in Tripoli)").

[572] Sen. Intelligence Committee Benghazi Report (Redacted), p. 17 & n. 68.

A continued presence in Benghazi will emphasize U.S. interest in the eastern part of Libya. Many Libyans have said the U.S. presence in Benghazi has a salutary, calming effect on easterners who are fearful that the new focus on Tripoli could once again lead to their neglect and exclusion from reconstruction and wealth distribution and *strongly favor a permanent U.S. presence in the form of a full consulate.* They feel the United States will help ensure they are dealt with fairly. . . .[573]

As recommended by Feltman in his memo, Kennedy approves "a continued U.S. presence in Benghazi through the end of calendar year 2012. . . ." As Feltman further recommends, Kennedy authorizes a "combined footprint of 35 U.S. government personnel in Benghazi," including eight State Department and two temporary duty positions.[574] This total figure of 35 personnel no doubt includes the CIA's personnel at its Benghazi Annex. (Feltman will leave the State Department before the Benghazi tragedy to take a position at the United Nations.[575] Good move.)

Some outside State also argue there are advantages to having a diplomatic office in Benghazi even after reopening Embassy Tripoli. Analyst Scott Stewart of security consultant Stratfor presents this case:

One reality of Libya after the revolution is that . . . the country is very divided and the central government has little authority outside of Tripoli. There has also been a long history of an east-west divide in Libya, with Tripoli and Benghazi as the opposing centers of power. Because of this, it makes a great deal of sense for the United States to want to open an office in Benghazi to take the pulse of eastern Libya. The United States also intervened on behalf of the rebels, who were originally based in Benghazi, and U.S. diplomats, led by Stevens, established an office there in early April 2011 to coordinate U.S. aid for the rebels . . .

Benghazi and Darnah also have long been hotbeds of jihadism in Libya, so having an office in eastern Libya is a

---

[573] Action Memo for Under Secretary Kennedy Re "Future Operations in Benghazi, Libya" (Dec. 27, 2011) (emphasis added), House Oversight Committee website; and Burton & Katz, *Under Fire*, Chap. 6, pp. 66-67.

[574] Action Memo for Under Secretary Kennedy Re "Future Operations in Benghazi, Libya" (Dec. 27, 2011), House Oversight Committee website.

[575] Babbin, Whitewashing Benghazi.

logical step in support of efforts to monitor these groups. Additionally, with the vast quantities of weapons that were looted from arms depots in the Benghazi area, including large numbers of shoulder-launched surface-to-air missiles, Benghazi is a good place to base efforts to monitor the flow of such weapons or even to stage programs to recover and destroy them.[576]

(Or perhaps to send them to Syrian rebels fighting Bashar al-Assad?)

The Mission Compound in Benghazi usually is headed by a foreign service employee called the "Principal Officer." Because of the perpetual staffing rotations of temporary personnel, for two weeks beginning in early September until about September 15th, there will be no Principal Officer at the Mission. Ambassador Stevens directs David McFarland, Chief Political Officer at the Embassy in Tripoli, to serve as "Acting" in that role for the first ten days of the month.[577] Stevens himself plans to cover as Acting Principal Officer during the second week until the new Principal Officer arrives around mid-September.

Stevens can send any one of a number of individuals from the U.S. Embassy in Tripoli to serve in that temporary capacity (as he has done for the days prior to September 10). He could send his Deputy Chief of Mission, Greg Hicks. Why must Stevens *himself* go to Benghazi?

President Obama later tells the United Nations Stevens returns to Benghazi "to review plans to establish a new cultural center and modernize a hospital."[578] (A *New York Times* article on September 12 also cites the "cultural center" purpose.[579]) Are these goals worth risking numerous American lives? And who makes the decision to do so, Obama or Clinton? Or the State Department's Patrick Kennedy, Under Secretary for Management? Or someone at the CIA?

---

[576] Stewart, Diplomatic Security in Light of Benghazi.

[577] Hicks Oversight Committee Testimony (May 8, 2013), p. 25.

[578] Remarks by the President Barack H. Obama to the U.N. General Assembly, United Nations Headquarters, New York, Obama White House Archives (Sept. 25, 2012).

[579] Kirkpatrick and Myers, Libya Attack Brings Challenges for U.S. (Ambassador Stevens "... was visiting the city Tuesday from the United States Embassy Compound in Tripoli to attend the planned opening of an American cultural center ...").

Kennedy later claims, "it was worth the risk" to be in Benghazi as the "new Libya" is being born.[580] He testifies to the House Oversight Committee that Ambassador Stevens:

> ... understood that the new Libya was being born in Benghazi and that it was critical that the United States have an active presence there. ... He knew his mission was vital to U.S. interests and values, and was an investment that would pay off in a strong partnership with a free Libya.[581]

Kennedy asserts, "... The United States is better off because Chris Stevens went to Benghazi."[582] He then predicts the partnership with Libya "is going to last us decades."[583] (How much of this risk do *Kennedy* and *his* family assume?)

Three months after the tragedy, Secretary Clinton will argue to Congress it is important to "support the emerging democracies of the region, including Libya." This is the best way to "advance our interests and values," and to "provide the region a path away from extremism." She asserts this is why Chris Stevens is in Benghazi. "He knew that a new Libya was being born there, and that America had to be a part of it – to support reformers, counter extremism, and stem the dangerous flow of weapons."[584]

(On the ground in Africa the "new Libya" pretty much *sucks*.)

The Mission as "Cover" for the CIA

We should not overlook another possibility. Is the entire Mission Compound staff just a ruse to provide diplomatic "cover" to the CIA

---

[580] Kennedy October 10 Briefing ("... On the basis of the information we had at that point, it was worth the risk. ...") (*Watch video* there; Go to 9:41 - 10:58); and CBS News, House Probes Security Leading Up to Libya Attack.

[581] Kennedy House Oversight Prepared Testimony, p. 3. See also Kennedy October 10 Briefing ("A word of why ... we're in Benghazi. ... [A] new Libya was being born. ... [I]t's birth took place in Benghazi. It was still one of the major two regions in that country. And what needed to happen is we had to be represented both in the capital, but we also had to be represented in Benghazi ... where so much was going on. We had to be there if we were going to participate in the new Libya, if we were going to build the partnership that is going to last us decades") (*Watch video* there; Go to 3:34 - 4:14).

[582] Kennedy House Oversight Prepared Testimony, p. 3.

[583] Kennedy October 10 Briefing.

[584] Letter from Secretary of State Hillary Rodham Clinton to Chairman John F. Kerry, Senate Committee on Foreign Relations, State Dept. Archives website (Dec. 18, 2012), pp. 6-7.

for whatever is going on at the Annex in Benghazi (discussed in Chapter 25)?[585] As explained below, in the prosecution of one of only two individuals ever arrested for the Benghazi attacks, prosecutors reportedly claim the defendant "told others he believed the American diplomatic presence in Benghazi was cover for a U.S. intelligence-gathering facility and vowed to 'do something about this facility.'"[586]

John Bolton, former U.S. Ambassador to the U.N. and National Security Advisor to President Trump, finds this explanation unlikely. He believes this theory only would make sense if the two facilities are co-located, not in two different places about one-half mile apart.[587]

Another security analyst discusses a related explanation with CNN. Geoff Porter, president of North Africa Risk Consulting, suggests one possible reason why security staffing at the Mission Compound is so lacking. Porter believes the CIA may want the U.S. to keep a low security profile overall in Benghazi to protect the CIA's work in collecting information and perhaps weapons.[588] (In any event, whether they are just a "front" for the CIA, or whether their mission is

---

[585] McCarthy, Hillary Clinton's Benghazi Debacle: Arming Jihadists in Libya . . . And Syria (Regarding the Special Mission Compound in Benghazi, "Was its real purpose to give diplomatic cover to covert intelligence operations (such as those at the nearby CIA compound)? If so, did those operations include aiding and abetting the arming of the Syrian rebels? . . . Were U.S. personnel stationed as sitting ducks in Benghazi in order to help supply weapons to Syria, where it was inevitable they would fall into the hands of America's enemies? Perhaps we'll soon find out").

[586] Spencer S. Hsu, "U.S. Will Not Seek Death Penalty for Accused Ringleader in Benghazi Attacks," *The Washington Post* online (May 10, 2016) ("Hsu, U.S. Will Not Seek Death Penalty for Accused Ringleader in Benghazi Attacks"). See also Spencer S. Hsu, "Baring Grievous Wounds, Dry Humor, U.S. Agent Lays Out Key Evidence at Benghazi Trial," *The Washington Post* online (Oct. 5, 2017) ("Hsu, Baring Grievous Wounds, Dry Humor, U.S. Agent Lays Out Key Evidence at Benghazi Trial") ("In an indictment after Abu Khattala's [sic] June 2014 capture in Libya . . . and in opening statements . . . Justice Department prosecutors told jurors that Abu Khattala [sic] thought the diplomatic mission was cover for an illegal U.S. intelligence facility in Benghazi, allegedly asking at a meeting in a mosque a year before the attacks, 'How can we allow spying among us?'").

[587] Interview of Former U.S. Ambassador to the United Nations John Bolton with Jonathan Hunt, "On the Hunt," Fox News Channel (Circa May 2013) (*Watch video there*; Go to 2:40 - 3:03).

[588] Burnett, Benghazi Timeline: "We Are Under Attack" (*Watch video there*; Go to 3:45 - 4:03).

substantive but subordinate to the CIA's efforts, as a matter of simple decency the diplomats at the Mission still deserve adequate security.[589])

Consider Porter's "collecting weapons" theory. According to a report by CNN in 2013, Chris Stevens is sent to Benghazi to assist the CIA in collecting weapons that have been raided by militants from Qadhafi's armories and stockpiles. (NATO's failure to secure these weapons is a major shortcoming of its Libyan campaign.[590] However, the U.N. Security Council's prohibition of "boots on the ground" likely renders this result inevitable.) As noted above, in September 2012 dangerous weapons literally flow throughout Libya, including Benghazi.[591] In CNN's report, Geoff Porter explains his theory: "... [O]ne of the things that the U.S. was interested in doing – and in particular the CIA – was collecting weapons." CNN's report claims it is this mission that brings Stevens to Benghazi.[592]

---

[589] E.g., Interview of Donald Rumsfeld with Matt Lauer, The Today Show (May 14, 2013) (*Watch video there*; Go to 1:20-36) ("... [T]he first problem was if you're going to put people at risk, you have to try to protect them. And the British took their people out, 'cuz they knew they were at risk. And the Americans were left in, and they weren't provided the kind of security that they needed. Obviously, because they're dead").

[590] McCarthy, Hillary Clinton's Benghazi Debacle: Arming Jihadists in Libya... And Syria ("... Besides arming jihadists, the [Obama] administration took no meaningful steps to make sure that Qaddafi's military arsenals did not fall into terrorist hands. . . .").

[591] E.g., AP, Red Cross Says Attack on Libya Office Wounds 1 ("There are also concerns about the proliferation of thousands of weapons, including rockets, machine guns and rocket-propelled grenades in Libya in the aftermath of the civil war last year"); Stewart, Diplomatic Security in Light of Benghazi ("... [W]ith the vast quantities of weapons that were looted from arms depots in the Benghazi area, including large numbers of shoulder-launched surface-to-air missiles, Benghazi is a good place to base efforts to monitor the flow of such weapons or even to stage programs to recover and destroy them"); Lama Hasan, Matthew McGarry and Jean-Nicholas Fievet, "Looters Steal Gadhafi's Weapons, Including Surface-to-Air Missiles," ABC News online (Sept. 8, 2011) ("Defeated in battle, Moammar Gadhafi's army left behind armories brimming with weapons, and the rebels have helped themselves. It's not just guns that have been plundered. Almost every outpost captured by opposition forces has yielded weapons, everything from AK-47 assault rifles to grenades to surface-to-air missiles (SAMs). And the rebels tell ABC News that they don't have enough resources to safeguard them all . . ."); and Burton & Katz, *Under Fire*, Chap. 7, p. 81 ("... [I]n post-civil-war Benghazi an AK-47 and a truckload of 7.62 mm ammo were as easy to come by as a Starbucks coffee in midtown Manhattan").

[592] Burnett, Benghazi Timeline: "We Are Under Attack" (*Watch video there*; Go to 1:18-38).

(As discussed in Chapter 25, others believe the CIA in Benghazi is doing far more than merely collecting or destroying weapons. They believe the CIA is gathering and funneling these weapons (likely via Turkey) to rebels in Syria who are waging civil war against Bashar al-Assad's regime there. Former federal prosecutor and conservative *National Review* columnist Andrew McCarthy concludes, "I believe that one significant mission [of the Americans in Benghazi] was the coordination of weapons transfers from Libya to Syrian jihadists."[593])

Opening a Permanent Consulate

Gregory Hicks and the Select Benghazi Committee suggest a different reason for Stevens to be in Benghazi at this time. According to that panel's majority report, Hillary Clinton is planning to make a diplomatic visit to Libya in October 2012.[594] (In earlier 2013 testimony before the House Oversight Committee, Gregory Hicks will assert this Clinton visit is planned for Tripoli in December 2012, after the presidential election.[595]) During this visit, Ambassador Stevens purportedly is anxious to present Clinton with a "deliverable." According to the Select Committee majority, Stevens' "deliverable" is to be Clinton personally announcing and presiding over the transition from the unofficial Mission Compound into the establishment of a different, "permanent" U.S. Consulate in Benghazi.[596] Hicks testifies to the Oversight Committee that Stevens tells Hicks that, in his "exit interview" with Secretary Clinton after he is sworn in as ambassador, she instructs Stevens "we need to make Benghazi a permanent post." Stevens reportedly promises Clinton he will make it happen.[597]

---

[593] McCarthy, Hillary Clinton's Benghazi Debacle: Arming Jihadists in Libya . . . And Syria. See also Eric Schmitt, "C.I.A. Said to Aid in Steering Arms to Syrian Opposition," *The New York Times* online (June 21, 2012) ("A small number of C.I.A. officers are operating secretly in southern Turkey, helping allies decide which Syrian opposition fighters across the border will receive arms to fight the Syrian government, according to American officials and Arab intelligence officers").

[594] Benghazi Committee Report, pp. 12-13.

[595] Hicks Oversight Committee Testimony (May 8, 2013) (Response to questions of Rep. Thomas Massie (R-KY)), p. 89.

[596] *Id.* (Response to questions of Rep. Thomas Massie (R-KY) and Chairman Darrell Issa (R-CA)), p. 89.

[597] *Id.* (Response to questions of Rep. Doug Collins (R-GA)), p. 90; and Toensing, Administration Relying on Shoddy Benghazi Report to Absolve Itself of Blame (Note: Toensing is legal counsel for Gregory Hicks).

Money to accomplish this goal is available. However, *it must be transferred from another State Department account by September 30, 2012* (the end of the federal government's fiscal year). Otherwise, it will be lost.[598] As Gregory Hicks later testifies, "... Timing for this decision was important. Chris needed to report before September 30th, ... on the physical and the political and security environment in Benghazi to support an action memo to convert Benghazi from a temporary facility to a permanent facility...."[599] (Are Stevens and three other Americans ultimately sacrificed on a budget altar to achieve this time-sensitive fiscal goal? No doubt this planned conversion to a permanent consulate in Benghazi would have been spun by President Obama and Clinton during the election campaign as "proof" the administration's toppling of Qadhafi has been a worthwhile success.[600])

According to Hicks, the instructions to accomplish this goal came from "the executive office of the Bureau of Near Eastern Affairs."[601] In mid-September 2012, this bureau is headed by Acting Assistant Secretary Beth Jones.[602] (She is one of many senior State officials who will *not* be sanctioned over Benghazi.[603])

---

[598] Benghazi Committee Report ("The hope was to establish a permanent consulate in Benghazi for the Secretary to present to the Libyan government during her trip"), pp. 11-13; Hicks Oversight Committee Testimony (May 8, 2013) (Response to questions of Rep. James Lankford (R-OK)) ("We had funds available that could be transferred from a fund set aside for Iraq and could be dedicated to this purpose [converting the Benghazi outpost to a permanent facility]. They had to be obligated by September 30th"), p. 41; and Toensing, Administration Relying on Shoddy Benghazi Report to Absolve Itself of Blame (Note: Toensing is legal counsel for Gregory Hicks).

[599] Hicks Oversight Committee Testimony (May 8, 2013) (Response to questions of Rep. James Lankford (R-OK)), p. 40.

[600] See Hemingway, 5 Big Takeaways From the House Benghazi Report, quoting from Additional Views of Reps Jordan and Pompeo ("Secretary Clinton pushed for the U.S. to intervene in Libya, which at the time represented one of her signature achievements. To leave Benghazi would have been viewed as her failure and prompted unwelcome scrutiny of her choices"), p. 420.

[601] Hicks Oversight Committee Testimony (May 8, 2013) (Response to questions of Rep. James Lankford (R-OK)), p. 41.

[602] *Id.* (Response to questions of Rep. Trey Gowdy (R-SC)), p. 33; and Benghazi Committee Report, pp. 82 and 90.

[603] Guy Benson, "Report: Yes, Hillary's Benghazi 'Investigation' Was a Whitewash, Townhall.com website (Sept. 16, 2013) ("Benson, 'Yes, Hillary's Benghazi "Investigation" Was a Whitewash.'"

Gregory Hicks' rationale for Stevens' September 2012 trip to Benghazi is consistent with the Select Benghazi Committee's conclusion. Hicks, then a 21-year career diplomat, explains this part of Stevens' mission to the Select Committee, including why it must be done by Ambassador Stevens himself:

... [W]hen we have a visit by a major political figure, like the Secretary of State, like the President, ... we try to make that visit important publicly. And so we generally will create a list of what we call deliverables, items of importance to the bilateral relationship. So we hoped for the Secretary to announce the opening of a permanent consulate in Benghazi during her visit[.]

[Question: Was ... there anything related to making Benghazi a permanent post that was part of the purpose of Ambassador Stevens going to Benghazi in September?]

Oh, absolutely. ... [W]e had begun the process of developing a political rationale for having a permanent post in Benghazi. I sent in that rationale at the end of August to the executive director of the NEA [Near Eastern Affairs] bureau. We had begun a process of identifying locations and drawing plans for such a post.

...

And we understood that the situation in eastern Libya was unstable and ... Chris Stevens wanted to make sure that what we were doing ... was the right course of action. And he personally, because he had the contacts in the region, because he had their trust. He was the only person that we felt could go to Benghazi and get a clear picture of the political situation there and the security situation there as well.[604]

Consolidating Benghazi Facilities

Gregory Hicks states one additional aspect of this plan to establish a permanent consulate in Benghazi includes consolidating the Mission

---

[604] Benghazi Committee Report, pp. 12-13. See also Hicks Oversight Committee Testimony (May 8, 2013) (Response to questions of Rep. James Lankford (R-OK)) ("According to Chris, Secretary Clinton wanted Benghazi converted into a permanent constituent post"), p. 40; and *Id.* (Response to questions of Rep. Tony Cardenas (D-CA)) ("... He [Stevens] went there to do his job. He felt that he had a political imperative to go to Benghazi and represent the United States there in order to move the project forward to make the Benghazi consulate a permanent constituent post"), p. 76.

Compound and CIA Annex into a single facility. Hicks asserts federal law requires all U.S. government personnel at a foreign diplomatic post be located at a single site. Only the Secretary of State (with the concurrence of the agency head whose staff will be located elsewhere) can waive this rule. Hillary Clinton never does so with respect to Benghazi. Hicks claims this waiver obligation cannot be delegated, but Clinton does exactly that.[605] (She wants her fingerprints on *nothing*.)

The Senate Intelligence Committee also concludes, "There were plans to co-locate the Mission facility and the Annex starting in 2013, but no changes were made before the September 11, 2012 attacks." The former Annex Chief of Base reportedly tells this intelligence panel he and Ambassador Stevens have discussed this subject, and CIA officers have surveyed different possible locations. He asserts, ". . . [T]here was absolutely a plan to do that."[606]

Moreover, Hicks also testifies to the House Oversight Committee, "In addition, Chris wanted to make a symbolic gesture to the people of Benghazi that the United States stood behind their dream of establishing a new democracy."[607]

Later, Hicks will elaborate to Fox News on Stevens' mission: "Chris Stevens had some very serious work to do. One of his primary missions in Benghazi was to correct the mistake of . . . having two facilities, to combine our personnel into one permanent consulate. And Hillary Clinton asked him to do that." Hicks also confirms Clinton has planned a trip to Libya in October 2012, "where we hoped she would be able to announce that consolidation of facilities." Hicks adds, "So Chris Stevens was doing his job in Benghazi, and he knew the risks, yes, but that's the definition of courage: to understand the risks, to understand that you have a job to do, and then you go and do it anyway."[608] ■

---

[605] Hicks, What the Benghazi Attack Taught Me About Hillary Clinton ("Notably, one of the primary goals of Ambassador Stevens' fatal visit was to begin consolidating our Benghazi personnel into one facility, which would have concentrated our security posture in Benghazi's volatile and violent environment").

[606] Sen. Intelligence Committee Benghazi Report, p. 26.

[607] Hicks Oversight Committee Testimony (May 8, 2013) (Response to questions of Rep. James Lankford (R-OK)), p. 40.

[608] Interview of Gregory Hicks with Martha MacCallum, "America's Newsroom," Fox News Channel (Sept. 15, 2016) (*Watch video there*; Go to 3:51 - 5:00).

23

"So Nice to Be Back in Benghazi"

Ambassador Chris Stevens finally arrives back in Benghazi by commercial flight on September 10, 2012.[609] Two Diplomatic Security Agents accompany him from Tripoli. (Both reportedly are "rookie" DSAs.[610]) There are now only five State Department security personnel at the Mission Compound in the most dangerous city in North Africa.[611]

"Senior" State Department officials later will assert Stevens is *"traveling* with five diplomatic security agents, two more than his regular contingent of three, in light of the increased threat environment."[612] (Why couldn't Stevens also take at least a few Marines with him from Tripoli to Benghazi, as he does the two DSA agents? Alternatively, if Lt. Col. Wood's SST unit's deployment had been extended in Tripoli, Stevens could have taken some (or all) of them with him.)

Only four DSAs remain behind at the U.S. Embassy in Tripoli. They must protect about 28 "diplomatic personnel" there.[613] In contrast, five DSAs are needed to protect two "diplomatic personnel" in Benghazi. This speaks volumes about the greater level of risk in Benghazi.

As noted, a handful of local militia members provide further security at the compound (who largely will prove to be ineffectual). The looming anniversary of September 11 obviously heightens further what is already a risky environment in Benghazi.

---

[609] Benghazi Committee Report, pp. 12 and 15.

[610] Attkisson, *Stonewalled*. Chap. 4, p. 187.

[611] Lamb Oversight Committee Prepared Testimony, p. 3; CBS News, House Probes Security Leading Up to Libya Attack; and Benghazi Committee Report, pp. 13 and 15-16.

[612] Josh Rogin, "State Department: No Video Protest at the Benghazi Consulate [sic]," ForeignPolicy.com (Oct. 9, 2012) (emphasis added).

[613] Benghazi Committee Report, pp. 15-16.

In planning sessions for Stevens' Benghazi trip, newly-arrived Regional Security Officer John Martinec expresses "serious concerns" about Stevens' security on the trip. In response to Martinec's apprehension, Stevens modifies his travel plans in at least three ways. First, the visit will be conducted in a low-profile manner. It will not be announced in advance, and Stevens' meetings will not be scheduled until just before he departs Tripoli. Second, Stevens shortens his trip. Instead of departing on September 8 (as originally planned), he will arrive in Benghazi on the 10th. And third, the one public event Stevens plans will occur at the very end of his trip, just prior to his departure back to Tripoli.[614]

During his Benghazi visit Stevens wisely has determined to schedule as many meetings as possible inside the Mission Compound.[615] Indeed, Stevens says he wishes to "avoid the RPG reception that the UK Amb[assador] got...."[616]

After arriving in Benghazi, Stevens takes a security briefing at the CIA Annex. Its Chief of Base "Bob" later claims, "We did try to convey [to Stevens] the seriousness of the terrorism environment in eastern Libya."[617] "Due to the worsening security environment in Benghazi," the five Mission DSAs request support from the Annex's six GRS agents to help secure Stevens' off-compound movements while in Benghazi. The CIA's GRS men agree to do so, reaffirming Tanto Paronto's earlier promise to back up the Mission security team.[618]

(Interestingly, as private contractors the GRS operators purchase their own private medical and life insurance. If they are injured or killed while protecting Stevens, it is not at all clear their insurance even will cover such activities as protecting a State Department ambassador,

---

[614] Hicks Oversight Committee Testimony (May 8, 2013) (Response to questions of Rep. Tony Cardenas (D-CA)), p. 76.

[615] Benghazi Committee Report, p. 17.

[616] *Id.*, p. 17.

[617] Adam Goldman and Greg Miller, "Former CIA Chief in Benghazi Challenges the Story Line of the New Movie *'13 Hours,'*" *The Washington Post* online (Jan. 15, 2016) ("Goldman and Miller, Former CIA Chief in Benghazi Challenges the Story Line of the New Movie *'13 Hours'*").

[618] Benghazi Committee Report, p. 17.

THE TRUE ACCOUNT OF VALOR AND ABANDONMENT

which is beyond the scope of their stated CIA contractual obligations![619] Yet none of them hesitates to volunteer.)

Despite these dangers, during his brief time there Stevens writes in his diary, "It is so nice to be back in Benghazi."[620]

On this day of his arrival Stevens also participates in the opening of a cultural center – one of the publicly-announced purposes of his trip.[621] By the evening of September 10, the ambassador's presence in Benghazi has become a matter of public and media knowledge. Stevens meets this evening – outside the Mission Compound – with the Benghazi Local Council. To the consternation of Stevens' DSAs and the GRS men, the event is attended by local media![622] If they didn't know Stevens was here before, the bad guys know it now.

Chris Stevens' mother, Mary Commanday, tells CBS News just weeks after the attacks her son never expressed concern for his personal safety in Libya. She says he trusts his bodyguards to protect him.[623]

Patricia Smith, mother of Sean Smith, tells a contrasting story. Her son is one of four Americans who will perish in Benghazi. She relates that on the night of September 10, while Stevens meets with the Local Council in Benghazi, her son tells her he believes he is going to die.[624] ∎

---

[619] *13 Hours: The Secret Soldiers of Benghazi*, Extra Features DVD, "Uncovering Benghazi's Secret Soldiers" (Paramount, 2016).

[620] Zuckoff, *13 Hours*, Chap. 4, p. 83.

[621] Burnett, Benghazi Timeline: "We Are Under Attack" (*Watch video there*; Go to 1:32-37).

[622] Benghazi Committee Report, p. 18.

[623] Interview of Mary Commanday with Ben Tracy, "Mother of Slain Ambassador Speaks Out," "CBS This Morning," CBS News online (Oct. 18, 2012) (*Watch video there*; Go to 0:50 - 1:10).

[624] E.g., Interview of Patricia Smith with Graham Ledger, "The Daily Ledger," One America News Network (July 7, 2016) (*Watch video there*; Go to 5:00-21). See also Hicks Oversight Committee Testimony (May 8, 2013) (Response to questions of Rep. Jason Chaffetz (R-UT)) ("When I was there, I was very frustrated by the situation, at times even frightened by the threat scenario that we were looking at relative to the resources we had to try to mitigate that threat scenario"), p. 102.

24

"Expeditionary Diplomacy"

In her memoir, Hillary Clinton suggests that as a world leader, the U.S. essentially has an obligation to maintain its diplomats everywhere on the globe, no matter how dangerous. (So we should be in North Korea? In Syria? In Iran? In Somalia? *Really?*)
She writes:
> The United States has a vital role to play as a global leader, ... and when America is absent, *especially from unstable environments*, there are consequences. That's why I sent Chris Stevens to Libya in the first place; it's also why he wanted to be there. It was our responsibility ... to make sure that the men and women on the front lines always have the resources they need and to do everything we can to reduce the risks they face. America could not and would not retreat.[625]

During subsequent congressional hearings on Benghazi (discussed below), several State Department officials give a name to this philosophy: "expeditionary diplomacy." These State witnesses describe in differing ways the agency's recent and expanding policy of engaging in such heightened-risk diplomacy. This approach involves "operating diplomatic outposts in unstable environments which, in the past, the State Department believed were too dangerous to host diplomats."[626]

---

[625] Clinton, *Hard Choices* (emphasis added), Chap. 17, p. 411.

[626] Benghazi ARB Report, Introduction ("The Benghazi attacks took place against a backdrop of significantly increased demands on U.S. diplomats to be present in the world's most dangerous places to advance American interests and connect with populations beyond capitals, and beyond host governments' reach," such that State's "Bureau of Diplomatic Security (DS) is being stretched to the limit as never before"; citing "... the need for the U.S. government to be present in places where stability and security are often most profoundly lacking and host government support is sometimes minimal to non-existent"), p. 2. See Letter from Thomas P. Gibbons, Acting Assistant Secretary for Legislative Affairs, State Department, to The Honorable Darrell E. Issa, Chairman, Committee on Oversight and Government Reform, House of Representatives (Aug. 23, 2013), SCRIBD website ("Gibbons Aug. 23, 2013 Letter to Chairman Issa"), p. 3. See "Diplomatic Security, 2012 Year in Review," U.S. Department of State, Bureau of Diplomatic Security (June 2013), State Dept. website ("American diplomacy must continue in spite of these dangers [threats to the safety of American diplomatic personnel at their posts]...."), p. 2.

Under Secretary of State Patrick Kennedy endorses this concept in testimony before the House Oversight Committee:

> ... Ambassador Stevens understood that the State Department must operate in many places where the U.S. military cannot or does not, where there are no other boots on the ground, where there are serious threats to our security. ... He knew his mission was vital to U.S. interests and values, and was an investment that would pay off in a strong partnership with a free Libya. ... *Diplomacy, by its very nature, often must be practiced in dangerous places.* We send people to more than 275 diplomatic posts ... We do this because we have learned again and again that when America is absent – especially from the dangerous places – there are consequences: extremism takes root, our interests suffer, and our national security is threatened. ... *We must continue deploying our diplomats and development professionals to dangerous places like Benghazi. There is no other alternative.* As the Secretary said, "We will not retreat. We will keep leading, and *we will stay engaged <u>everywhere</u> in the world*, including in those hard places where America's interests and security are at stake. ..."[627]

(Fine. Send your diplomats to dangerous places when essential. But there *is* an alternative: *provide them security commensurate with the damned risk!* And actually, after the September 11, 2012 tragedy, your department *did* retreat from Benghazi. And, like Damascus, you haven't gone back.[628])

Several State Department officials later testify they questioned the wisdom of the agency's policy of expanding expeditionary diplomacy

---

[627] Kennedy House Oversight Prepared Testimony (emphasis added), pp. 3-4. See also Kennedy October 10 Briefing (emphasis added) ("... The State Department goes into inherently dangerous places all the time. That's our mission. We have to operate forward. We're there when the military is not there, we're there when others are not there. *It is our job to advance the U.S. national security everywhere.* ... We come up with a mitigation strategy to reduce the level of risk. But we're never going to end that risk") (*Watch video there*; Go to 6:59 - 8:52); and Daily Press Briefing by Deputy Spokesperson Marie Harf, State Dept. Archives website (Sept. 19, 2013) ("... [W]e operate in very dangerous places. This is our job. Our job is to go out there, all around the world, even when it's hard, even when it's dangerous, and do the tough work of diplomacy. ...").

[628] Kennedy October 10 Briefing ("... If we cannot mitigate that risk, we withdraw. We withdrew from Tripoli. We withdrew from Damascus") (*Watch video there*; Go to 8:42-52).

because it is too dangerous.[629] (No kidding. What about *balancing* the potential diplomatic rewards versus the known and predictable security risks?[630] There are some places on earth that are just too damned dangerous to send American civilians. In September 2012, Benghazi is one of them.[631] Later, in February 2013, President Obama reportedly admits this. Investigative reporter Sharyl Attkisson claims Obama tells a group of senators, "We screwed up. Chris shouldn't have been there."[632])

Previous Accountability Review Boards investigating the 1998 terrorist bombings of two U.S. embassies in Africa (known as the "Crowe Commission" after their chairman, Admiral William Crowe) take issue with this expeditionary diplomacy approach. As noted above, their combined ARB Report recommends closing diplomatic outposts that are *"highly vulnerable and threatened,"* if adequate security cannot be provided.[633] (Sounds like good advice. Too bad the State Department under Hillary Clinton does not follow it.[634] Amid

---

[629] Attkisson, Benghazi Accountability Review Board Comes Under Renewed Criticism.

[630] Benghazi ARB Report, Introduction (". . . Risk mitigation involves two imperatives – engagement and security – which require wise leadership, good intelligence and evaluation, proper defense and strong preparedness and, at times, downsizing, indirect access and even withdrawal. There is no one paradigm. . . ."), p. 3; and Opening Statement of Chairman John Kerry (D-MA), "Benghazi: Lessons Learned Opening Statement by Chairman John Kerry," Senate Foreign Relations Committee website (Dec. 20, 2012) (emphasis added) (". . . We have an expeditionary diplomatic corps, and they do face very real risks every day day in and day out. . . . We do not want to concertina wire America off from the world. Our challenge is to strike a *balance* between the necessity of the mission, available resources and tolerance for risk").

[631] Babbin, Whitewashing Benghazi (". . . Having wrongly decided that America had a national security interest in helping France topple Gaddafi, Obama's mistake was compounded by the decision to put American diplomats in a city that was known to be a safe haven for terrorists"); and Nordstrom House Oversight Committee Testimony (May 8, 2013) ("During the process, I had somebody ask me as part of the ARB why had I not requested . . . 50-caliber machine guns, for the consulate in Benghazi. I was awestruck. I said, if we are to the point where we have to have machine gun nests at a diplomatic institution, isn't the larger question, what are we doing? Why do we have staff there?"), pp. 64-65.

[632] Attkisson, *Stonewalled*, Chap. 4, p. 191.

[633] Dept. of State Report of the Accountability Review Boards, Bombings of the US Embassies in Nairobi, Kenya and Dar es Salaam, Tanzania on August 7, 1998 (Jan. 8, 1999), Executive Overview, State Dept. Archives website (emphasis added).

[634] House Oversight Committee Hearings (May 8, 2013) (Remarks of Rep. James Lankford (R-OK)) (". . . In 1998, this same thing occurred and we have not learned the

intensifying terrorist threats, within eleven months after Benghazi new Secretary of State John Kerry will close "nearly two dozen" diplomatic posts.[635] ∎

---

lesson. . . . [W]e did not do the most basic minimum security that was required by the State Department's standards set after the bombings in Nairobi, Kenya and in Tanzania. We did not do the basics. We did not provide the level of security. . . ."), p. 109; and Hemingway, 5 Big Takeaways From the House Benghazi Report (". . . Clinton, who was in charge of American policy in Libya, chose not to remove Americans from Benghazi or beef up security").

[635] House Foreign Affairs Benghazi Majority Staff Report, p. 18.

25

"Why Spy" in Benghazi?

We discussed previously the reasons why State Department personnel are in Benghazi. There remains the question why the *CIA* also is here at its Annex – and in far greater numbers than State. Whatever the truth about Stevens and the diplomats at the Mission Compound, these CIA personnel at the Annex sure by God are not working on a new "cultural center," or modernizing a hospital, or working on establishing a permanent diplomatic consulate. *Why are they here?*

Whatever the CIA is doing, secrecy naturally plays an important role.[636] According to a CIA cable, at least as of June 2012 the CIA believes its Annex in Benghazi largely still is a secret facility.[637] Indeed, it is so secret that on the Night of Benghazi the U.S. military's Africa Command and its Commander, General Carter Ham, other top military officials, and many civilian U.S. government decision-makers, are unaware of the existence of the Benghazi Annex![638] (It is difficult to plan to protect Americans at a facility you do not even know exists.[639]

---

[636] Sen. Intelligence Committee Benghazi Report (Intelligence Community and State Department personnel should ". . . generally be co-located overseas except where the IC [Intelligence Community] determines that, for operational reasons, co-location is not helpful in meeting mission objectives or that it poses a security risk. . . ."), p. 38; and Aaron Klein, "Secret Purpose of Benghazi Annex Still Secret," WorldNetDaily website (Jan. 27, 2014) ("Klein, Secret Purpose of Benghazi Annex Still Secret").

[637] Sen. Intelligence Committee Benghazi Report (June 12, 2012 CIA cable from Benghazi: ". . . [A]s a direct result of a concerted effort to build and maintain a low profile we believe that the locals for the most part do not know we are here and housed/officed in a separate stand alone facility from our [United States Government] USG counterparts"), p. 38. But compare *Id.* ("Although officially under cover, the Annex was known by some in Benghazi as an American facility. . . ."), p. 7. See also Klein, Secret Purpose of Benghazi Annex Still Secret.

[638] Sen. Intelligence Committee Benghazi Report (". . . [T]he Committee received conflicting information on the extent of the awareness within DoD of the Benghazi Annex. According to U.S. AFRICOM, neither the command nor its Commander were aware of an annex in Benghazi, Libya. . . ."), pp. 27-28; Klein, Secret Purpose of Benghazi Annex Still Secret; and Benghazi Committee Report, p. 92.

THE TRUE ACCOUNT OF VALOR AND ABANDONMENT

This lack of knowledge likely contributes to the extensive confusion, delay and indecisiveness that characterize the federal government's decisions and actions on this Night of Benghazi.) However, some Defense Department personnel reportedly *are* aware of the Annex's presence.[640] But some of these people reportedly and mistakenly believe this Annex is at the same location as State's Special Mission Compound.

The precise number of CIA staff at the Annex remains classified. According to one of its sources, CNN reports there are 21 Americans working at the Annex on the Night of Benghazi.[641] This is three times the number of Americans at the Mission Compound.

Some later speculate the U.S. facilities in Benghazi may be so poorly protected to avoid drawing "undue attention to a top secret operation." As Townhall's Guy Benson correctly observes, "But if that's the case, they were taking a massive risk – and the risk had deadly consequence."[642] Could it really be the case the CIA asks the State Department to expose its diplomats and security agents to protect secret CIA activities?

As noted above in Chapter 22, a 2013 CNN report asserts the CIA is engaged in "collecting weapons" in Benghazi, and Stevens travels there to assist in this effort.[643] Fox News also will report the CIA Annex is tracking and repurchasing missing weapons. These weapons include 20,000 "MANPADS," shoulder-held missiles capable of destroying commercial aircraft.[644] According to a report by then Regional Security

---

[639] Additional Views of Senators Chambliss, Burr, et al. (". . . We are puzzled as to how the military leadership expected to effectively respond and rescue Americans in the event of an emergency when it did not even know of the existence of one of the U.S. facilities. . . ."), p. 12.

[640] *Id.* (". . . [I]t is the Committee's understanding that other DoD personnel [besides AFRICOM] were aware of the Benghazi Annex"), p. 28; and Klein, Secret Purpose of Benghazi Annex Still Secret.

[641] Guy Benson, "Bombshell: CIA Using 'Unprecedented' Polygraphing, 'Pure Intimidation' to Guard Benghazi Secrets," Townhall.com website (Aug. 2, 2013) (quoting report by CNN's Jake Tapper).

[642] E.g., Guy Benson, "Bombshell: CIA Using 'Unprecedented' Polygraphing, 'Pure Intimidation' to Guard Benghazi Secrets," Townhall.com website (Aug. 2, 2013).

[643] Burnett, Benghazi Timeline: "We Are Under Attack" (*Watch video there*; Go to 1:18-38).

[644] Griffin, CIA Operators Were Denied Request for Help During Benghazi Attack. Like most early reports, this Fox News article gets a number of the details regarding Benghazi wrong. See also Bahrampour, U.S. Embassy in Tripoli Reopens (U.S.

Officer for Libya, Eric Nordstrom, the Libyan government has attempted such a weapons buy-back program, with little success.[645]

The Washington Post reports "CIA operations in the area [of Benghazi] included disarming militias, including ones affiliated with Islamist extremist groups, several months after the U.S. military role in toppling Libyan leader Moammar Gaddafi."[646] However, most of the Annex CIA staff are "non-shooters," such as case officers, analysts and interpreters. And most of the "shooters" at the Annex are serving as bodyguards for the "non-shooters." Exactly *how* are the CIA case officers disarming militias? Perhaps Fox News is correct, and the CIA is buying the weapons from militants. (This is the plot adopted in the movie *13 Hours*.) If so, it seems probable the militias will part with only *some* of their weapons in exchange for cash from the Americans. (Also, it is best not to think too much about what the Libyans will do with the money they make from any such arms sales to the CIA.)

If these reports of buying Libyan arms are true, the CIA personnel in Benghazi do not appear to be storing any of these collected weapons at the Annex. As discussed below, one of the risks of Annex GRS security guards going to the Mission Compound to attempt a rescue is these men will take with them virtually every heavy weapon at the Annex.[647]

Others speculate the staff at the secret CIA Annex covertly is coordinating the shipment of the former Libyan military stockpile of weapons to rebels in Syria, possibly through Turkey.[648] Some reports claim the weapons are going to *al Qaeda-linked* rebels.[649] (Do the

---

Ambassador to Libya Gene Cretz: "It's clear that we're worried"; U.S. and other countries reported working with Transitional National Council (TNC) to track down and secure arms, "perhaps in the form of buybacks" according to *The Washington Post*).

[645] Libya Security Incidents Since June 2011, p. 51.

[646] Wilson and DeYoung, Benghazi E-mails Show Clash Between State Department, CIA.

[647] Benghazi Committee Report, pp. 48-49.

[648] E.g., Damien McElroy, "CIA 'Running Arms Smuggling Team in Benghazi When Consulate Was Attacked,'" *The Telegraph* online (Aug. 2, 2013) (Citing CNN, "The television network said that a CIA team was working in an annex near the consulate on a project to supply missiles from Libyan armouries to Syrian rebels").

[649] E.g., McCarthy, Hillary Clinton's Benghazi Debacle: Arming Jihadists in Libya . . . And Syria ("What mission was so important the United States kept personnel in the jihadist hellhole of Benghazi in 2012? . . . I believe that one significant mission was the coordination of weapons transfers from Libya to Syrian jihadists").

terrorists on the Night of Benghazi get hold of any of these weapons flowing through the CIA Annex? But as noted, only the GRS bodyguards at the Annex apparently have any heavy weapons.)

Nearly a year after Benghazi, CNN's Jake Tapper reports on his blog the CIA's Annex facility serves "to supply missiles from Libyan armouries to Syrian rebels."[650] Asked about this scenario, Hillary Clinton later will testify to the Senate, "I don't know. I don't have any information on that."[651]

According to writers for the former *The Weekly Standard*, "... [T]he CIA was using the Benghazi annex to track extremists, including al Qaeda operatives, in eastern Libya." Significantly for events to come, that same article claims the terrorists in Libya also are "hunting the CIA"![652]

What *are* the CIA personnel really doing in Benghazi in September 2012 at their covert Annex facility? We still don't know for certain. ∎

---

[650] "Exclusive: Dozens of CIA Operatives on the Ground During Benghazi Attack," The Lead Blog with Jake Tapper, CNN online (Aug. 1, 2013) ("Speculation on Capitol Hill has included the possibility the U.S. agencies operating in Benghazi were secretly helping to move surface-to-air missiles out of Libya, through Turkey, and into the hands of Syrian rebels").

[651] Clinton Senate Foreign Relations Committee Testimony (Dec. 20, 2012) (Response to questions from Sen. Rand Paul (R-KY)).

[652] Stephen Hayes and Thomas Joscelyn, "The Benghazi Report," *The Weekly Standard* online (Dec. 15, 2014) ("Hayes and Joscelyn, The Benghazi Report"). See also Kenneth R. Timmerman, "The Shadowy Iranian Spy Chief Who Helped Plan Benghazi," *New York Post* online (June 20, 2014) ("The CIA Annex in Benghazi housed an NSA [National Security Agency] listening post that secretly monitored communications of jihadi groups").

PART III:

DURING THE ATTACKS

26

A Protest in Cairo

Days prior to September 11, 2012, several agencies of the U.S. government begin to monitor a planned protest at the U.S. Embassy in Cairo (about 600 miles to the east of Benghazi[653]). It is scheduled for September 11. (The Cairo Embassy has been the target of another demonstration earlier in January 2012, in which protestors burnt an American flag outside the Embassy.[654])

One reason prompting the planned Cairo protest is an anti-Islamic Video made in America, and whose trailer in Arabic recently has been posted on YouTube.[655] On September 10, the U.S. Department of Homeland Security issues an intelligence report warning the Cairo Embassy might be targeted as a response to this film, and as a platform to call for release of the "Blind Sheik." (The latter, Muslim cleric Sheik Omaar Abdel-Rahman, is then serving a life sentence in the U.S. for his role in planning several terrorist bombings that authorities ultimately disrupt. Several Abdel-Rahman followers perpetrate the 1993 bombing of the World Trade Center in New York City. That blast kills six and injures more than 1,000.[656] Abdel-Rahman has since died in a U.S. prison.[657])

Most of the U.S. Embassy's employees in Cairo have been instructed not to come to work on September 11. According to *The New York Times*, at approximately 6:00 a.m. the U.S. Embassy in Cairo issues the following statement on its website designed to ameliorate tensions among Muslims regarding the problematic Video:

---

[653] Benghazi Committee Report, p. 21.

[654] "Diplomatic Security, 2012 Year in Review," U.S. Department of State, Bureau of Diplomatic Security (June 2013), State Dept. website, p. 4.

[655] Burnett, Benghazi Timeline: "We Are Under Attack" (*Watch video there*; Go to 0:16-29). For an interview with the Video's maker by CNN's Jake Tapper, *watch at* https://www.youtube.com/watch?v=xitCdlo9IlQ.

[656] Benghazi Committee Report, p. 21; and "1993 World Trade Center Bombing Fast Facts," CNN Library, CNN online (Updated Feb. 21, 2017).

[657] "Omar Ahmad Rahman, 'Blind Sheik' Suspected in World Trade Center Bombing, Dead at 78," CBS News online (Updated Feb. 18, 2017).

The Embassy of the United States in Cairo condemns the continuing efforts by misguided individuals to hurt the religious feelings of Muslims – as we condemn efforts to offend believers of all religions. Today, the 11th anniversary of the September 11, 2001, terrorist attacks on the United States, Americans are honoring our patriots and those who serve our nation as the fitting response to the enemies of democracy. Respect for religious beliefs is a cornerstone of American democracy. We firmly reject the actions by those who abuse *the universal right of free speech* to hurt the religious beliefs of others.[658]

(Really? Since when is free speech a "universal right?" Someone should break this surprising news to the North Koreans, Chinese, Russians, Syrians, Iranians, Venezuelans and Cubans, to name just a few.)

The campaign of Republican presidential candidate Mitt Romney and others swiftly criticize the Embassy's statement as an inappropriate apology for anti-Islamic actions by some Americans.[659] According to "POLITICO," the Obama administration soon disavows the Cairo Embassy's initial statement. "'The statement by Embassy Cairo was not cleared by Washington and does not reflect the views of the United States government,' an administration official told POLITICO."[660] (After the Benghazi attacks, the U.S. news media will spend days focusing upon Romney's seemingly opportunistic criticisms of Embassy Cairo's statement, while paying less attention to the attacks themselves.[661])

At mid-day in Cairo on September 11, a crowd begins to gather at the U.S. Embassy. By two or so hours later, there reportedly are about

---

[658] "What They Said, Before and After the Attack in Libya," *The New York Times* online (Sept. 12, 2012) (*"New York Times,* What They Said, Before and After the Attack in Libya") (emphasis added). See also CBS Benghazi Timeline.

[659] *New York Times,* What They Said, Before and After the Attack in Libya.

[660] Byron Tau, "Obama Administration Disavows Cairo 'Apology,'" POLITICO44 Blog, POLITICO website (Sept. 11, 2012) ("The Obama administration is disavowing a statement from its own Cairo embassy that seemed to apologize for anti-Muslim activity in the United States"); and *New York Times,* What They Said, Before and After the Attack in Libya.

[661] Interview of Charles Krauthammer with Sean Hannity, "Hannity," Fox News Channel (Oct. 22, 2012) (*Watch video there*; Go to 1:42 – 2:46).

THE TRUE ACCOUNT OF VALOR AND ABANDONMENT

2,000 protestors assembled outside the Embassy. Some allegedly come armed with spray paint, but no weapons are observed or used.[662]

During this day in Washington, D.C., Defense Secretary Panetta, Secretary of State Clinton, and National Security Advisor Thomas Donilon meet at the White House to discuss "the developing situation in Cairo."[663] (Somehow, they never manage to arrange such a meeting on the Night of Benghazi.) However, following this conference no changes will be made in the U.S. security posture in North Africa.

In her memoir *Hard Choices*, Hillary Clinton subsequently will claim at this time she is not aware Chris Stevens even is in Benghazi! She writes, "*We* learned *later* that as events unfolded in Cairo, in neighboring Libya Ambassador Chris Stevens was visiting the country's second largest city, Benghazi."[664] As explained above, Embassy Tripoli has alerted the State Department as early as August 22 Stevens will be going to Benghazi in September.[665]

According to *The New York Times*, at around 6:00 p.m. (as many Cairo residents leave their workplaces), the crowd outside the Embassy begins to swell. Protestors spray paint graffiti on the Embassy perimeter wall. The *Times* reports that at about 6:30 p.m. "a small group of protestors" uses a ladder to scale the Embassy wall. A few demonstrators climb over that wall, tear up the U.S. flag, and replace it with what the Benghazi Select Committee describes as "a black militant Islamic flag." The *Times* asserts it will take five hours for Egyptian security officers to disperse all of the intruders peacefully from the Embassy compound.[666]

The New York Times further reports that also about 6:30 p.m. (as protesters are climbing over its outer wall), the American Embassy sends a Twitter message stating its condemnation earlier this morning "still stands. As does our condemnation of unjustified breach of the

---

[662] Benghazi Committee Report, pp. 21-22.

[663] Clinton, *Hard Choices*, Chap. 17, pp. 387-388.

[664] *Id.* (emphasis added), Chap. 17, p. 388.

[665] Hicks Oversight Committee Testimony (May 8, 2013) (Response to questions of Rep. Doug Collins (R-GA)), p. 90.

[666] Kirkpatrick and Myers, Libya Attack Brings Challenges for U.S.; Benghazi Committee Report, pp. 22-23; Baier, New Revelations on Attack in Benghazi (*Watch video there*; Go to 12:17-34). *See photograph* at "Diplomatic Security, 2012 Year in Review," U.S. Department of State, Bureau of Diplomatic Security (June 2013), State Dept. website, p. 25.

Embassy."⁶⁶⁷ The initial statement later is taken down from the Cairo Embassy's website, and the later Twitter message also is deleted.⁶⁶⁸

The demonstrations at the Cairo Embassy and elsewhere in the city will continue for days. No Americans are injured.⁶⁶⁹

The Select Benghazi Committee concludes, "Despite the size of the crowd of demonstrators in Cairo and the length of the demonstration, the protest in Cairo prompted no change in force laydown for the forces that might respond to unrest in North Africa." Like the president's security conference call of the previous day and the 9/11 anniversary date, the Cairo demonstration does not induce "any change in the U.S. military posture or asset readiness in the region."⁶⁷⁰

According to Deputy Chief of Mission in Libya Greg Hicks, the anti-Muslim film protest in Cairo is a "nonevent" in Libya.⁶⁷¹ Like Hicks and other U.S. personnel in Tripoli, the DSAs at the Benghazi Mission monitor social media. They can find no indication a comparable protest over the film trailer is planned in Benghazi.⁶⁷² Hicks also later testifies the Special Mission Compound has a protocol

---

⁶⁶⁷ *New York Times*, What They Said, Before and After the Attack in Libya.

⁶⁶⁸ See Cairo Embassy website ("404 Error – Page Note Found. We are sorry but the page you are looking for does not exist").

⁶⁶⁹ "Diplomatic Security, 2012 Year in Review," U.S. Department of State, Bureau of Diplomatic Security (June 2013), State Dept. website, p. 25.

⁶⁷⁰ Benghazi Committee Report, p. 23. See also *Id.* (The "anti-Muslim video . . . prompted no change in force posture or readiness even after protests erupted in Cairo . . ."), p. 131; and Attkisson, *Stonewalled* (citing sources who "say the CIF should have been staged hours *before* the Benghazi attacks . . . up to eight hours earlier when a giant mob of attackers descended upon the U.S. Embassy in Egypt . . . . That should've put all the wheels in motion . . . [T]he Egyptian attack should've been the wake-up call that put every possible resource on full alert, spinning up and positioning in case of trouble anywhere else in the region. But that didn't happen."), Chap. 4, p. 160.

⁶⁷¹ *Id.*, pp. 23-25; Hicks Oversight Committee Testimony (May 8, 2013) (Response to questions of Rep. Patrick McHenry (R-NC)) ("The YouTube video was a non-event in Libya"), p. 59; *Id.* (Response to questions of Rep. Gerald Connolly, (D-VA)) (". . . Our assessment in the embassy was that the video was not an instigator of anything that was going on in Libya . . . [W]e saw no demonstrations related to the video anywhere in Libya. The only event that transpired was the attack on our consulate on the night of September 11th"), p. 69; and Benjamin Bell, "Gregory Hicks: Hearing of Death of Christopher Stevens 'Saddest Moment' in My Career," ABC News online (Sept. 8, 2013) (Interview of Gregory Hicks with George Stephanopoulos) ("ABC News, Hicks Sept. 2013 Interview With Stephanopoulos") (*Watch video there*; Go to 3:33-47).

⁶⁷² Benghazi Committee Report, p. 25.

to be followed in the event of a protest. It never is activated on September 11.[673]

Although nothing is happening in Tripoli, Hicks texts Chris Stevens in Benghazi to alert him of the Cairo protest. He tells Stevens a mob has stormed the U.S. Embassy there, and is trying to tear down the U.S. flag. Stevens has not heard of it before receiving this text. He thanks his deputy for the news.[674]

Hicks and all five DSAs in Benghazi later testify to the Select Committee no protest ever occurs at the Mission prior to the terrorist attacks.[675] Accordingly, the DSA agents see "no reason to change their security posture" at the Mission on September 11.[676] It will prove a serious mistake. ∎

---

[673] Hicks Oversight Committee Testimony (May 8, 2013) (Response to questions of Rep. Patrick McHenry (R-NC)) (". . . The protocol of course was for us to evacuate immediately from the consulate and move to the annex"), p. 59.

[674] Hicks Oversight Committee Testimony (May 8, 2013), p. 24; and Benghazi Committee Report, p. 24.

[675] Benghazi Committee Report, pp. 26-27 (Gregory Hicks' testimony: "You know, for there to have been a demonstration on Chris Stevens' front door and him not to have reported it is unbelievable. And secondly, if he had reported it, he would have been out the back door within minutes of any demonstration appearing anywhere near that facility. And there was a back gate to the facility, and, you know, it worked"); and Additional Views of Reps. Jordan and Pompeo, pp. 426-427.

[676] Benghazi Committee Report, p. 25.

27

"Assuming We Don't Die Tonight"

When the sun rises over North Africa around 6:21 a.m. on September 11, 2012, CNN reports America's is the only major western flag still flying in Benghazi.[677] But not for long. After all, there are few (if any) other western targets left to assault.[678]

(The Senate intelligence panel and others will take issue with this CNN conclusion, insisting some other western countries and organizations still maintain a "diplomatic presence" in Benghazi.[679] Whether some or all of these involve anything more than renting a few hotel rooms is difficult to ascertain.)

On this day, there are seven State Department personnel residing at the Mission Compound in Benghazi. In addition to Ambassador Stevens, there are five Diplomatic Security Agents and Sean Smith, an Information Management Officer. Smith's job is to "run the administrative component of the Mission."[680] Among other duties, Smith is responsible for encrypting and sending the ambassador's cables to Tripoli, Washington, and elsewhere.

---

[677] CNN Report, Why Didn't the U.S. Military Respond in Time in Benghazi? (Interview of General Michael Hayden (Ret.) with John King) (*Watch video there*; Go to 4:31-36).

[678] Letter from Darrell Issa, Chairman, House Committee on Oversight and Government Reform, and Jason Chaffetz, Chairman, House Subcommittee on National Security, Homeland Defense, and Foreign Operations, to Secretary of State Hillary Rodham Clinton, Oversight Committee website (Oct. 2, 2012) (". . . Once the ICRC [International Committee of the Red Cross] pulled out, the US Consulate [sic] was the last Western flag flying in Benghazi, making it an ideal target for militants").

[679] Sen. Intelligence Committee Benghazi Report ("Although some countries and international organizations had reduced their presence in Benghazi, the United States maintained a diplomatic presence there similar to the UN, the European Union, and other Western countries such as Italy, France, Turkey, and Malta"), p. 26. See also Burton & Katz, *Under Fire*, Prologue, p. 16.

[680] Benghazi Committee Report, p. 25. See also Sen. Intelligence Committee Benghazi Report, p. 4.

THE TRUE ACCOUNT OF VALOR AND ABANDONMENT

The five DSAs are Alec Henderson, the senior agent on site, David Ubben, Scott Wickland, and two others identified only as "Zack" and "Reynaldo."[681]

As noted, there are no Marines or other U.S. military service members stationed here. (Joint Chiefs Chairman General Martin Dempsey later will testify the U.S. military has not provided any additional support to the Benghazi Mission prior to the September 11 attacks because they never receive a request to do so.[682])

Today, a number of video cameras are operating (the evidence is conflicting on how many). Video recordings are being made in the Mission's TOC of events occurring on the Mission grounds.[683] However, as previously mentioned, a camera monitor used by the Libyan guards near the Main Gate is broken. Some new video equipment remains in boxes; the State Department has not yet sent technicians to install them at the Mission.[684]

Except for the two DSAs who have accompanied Stevens from Tripoli to Benghazi, no additional security is in place at the Special Mission Compound in Benghazi on this September 11th anniversary. Inexplicably, it almost is viewed as just another day. (The duty rotation of several GRS agents at the nearby CIA Annex has been extended a few days to help protect Ambassador Stevens during his visit. But they remain stationed at the Annex, not the Mission.) However, because of the significance of the date, Stevens has decided to spend the entire day working within the Mission Compound.[685] It will not be enough to save him.

Very early on his last morning alive, Ambassador Chris Stevens sends a prescient email to his counterpart, the United Kingdom Ambassador to Libya: "I'm in Benghazi this week, lurking about with my eyes ever-peeled for RPG's [rocket-propelled grenades] hurtling towards my motorcade!"[686]

---

[681] Kennedy October 10 Briefing.

[682] Testimony Before Senate Armed Services Committee by General Martin Dempsey (Feb. 7, 2013); and Statement of Senators McCain, Graham and Ayotte.

[683] Benghazi Committee Report, pp. 35, 142, 213 and 311; and Zuckoff, *13 Hours*, Chap. 4, p. 84.

[684] Sen. Intelligence Committee Benghazi Report (Redacted), p. 19; and ARB Report, p. 35.

[685] Benghazi Committee Report, p. 20; and ARB Report, p. 34.

[686] Benghazi Committee Report, p. 9.

Meanwhile, also early this morning one of the DSAs at the Mission is advised a man in a local police uniform appears to be conducting surveillance of the compound. This involves taking photographs with his smart phone. The senior DSA duly reports this to his supervisors and others. These include Ambassador Stevens, the staffs of both the Mission and the Annex, and the head security officer at the Embassy in Tripoli.[687] Patricia Smith later says on this day – Sean's last – her son tells her the 17 February personnel are taking pictures of the compound, and he is afraid and "really scared."[688]

(The Select Committee reports as many as three different sources attempt to warn the U.S. government about a potential Benghazi attack before the fact. However, the committee's majority report is so redacted on this issue it is not possible for the author to make much sense of these alleged warnings.[689] The Senate Intelligence Committee's unclassified portion of its Benghazi report (also heavily redacted) discusses one of these alleged warnings. According to this report, a former "official" of the rebel Transitional National Council receives advance information of an "imminent attack" against the Mission facility. This TNC individual reportedly attempts to pass along this warning to the Libyan Intelligence Service, but his two contacts there are out of the country at this time. The CIA allegedly is unable to corroborate this TNC official's claim. In any event, this warning apparently does not reach the U.S. intelligence community until after the tragedy.[690])

On this Tuesday, Ambassador Stevens sends his final cable to the State Department. This includes a weekly report of Benghazi security incidents. He declares there are "Growing problems with security. . . ." in Benghazi. Stevens also notes local residents are showing "growing frustration with police and security forces (who were too weak to keep the country secure)."[691]

---

[687] *Id.*, pp. 20-21.

[688] Interview of Patricia Smith with Trish Regan, Fox Business News (Mar. 10, 2016) (*Watch video there*; Go to 2:44 - 3:24).

[689] Benghazi Committee Report (Redacted), pp. 30-31.

[690] Sen. Intelligence Committee Benghazi Report (Redacted), p. 23.

[691] Baier, New Revelations on Attack in Benghazi (*Watch video there*; Go to 12:34 - 13:01); Attkisson, Before Death, Amb. Stevens Warned of "Violent Libya Landscape"; Herridge, Classified Cable Warned Consulate Couldn't Withstand Coordinated Attack; and CBS Benghazi Timeline.

THE TRUE ACCOUNT OF VALOR AND ABANDONMENT

Back in the United States, at 11:18 a.m. Washington, D.C. time (5:18 p.m. Benghazi time), at the Pentagon in Arlington, Virginia, a ceremony observing the anniversary of 9/11 is underway. Attending are President Obama, First Lady Michelle Obama, Defense Secretary Leon Panetta, and Joint Chiefs Chair Martin Dempsey.[692] They are completely unaware of what a horrible rest of the day awaits them.

In a painful bit of irony, on this very September 11 before Benghazi goes to hell in a hand basket, President Obama issues a declaration under the National Emergencies Act. It extends the state of national emergency first declared by President George W. Bush after the 9/11 attacks. In his declaration President Obama says, "... I have determined that it is necessary to continue the national emergency declared with respect to persons who commit, threaten to commit, or support terrorism, and maintain in force the comprehensive sanctions to respond to this threat."[693]

As noted in the previous chapter, sometime in the early evening (probably shortly after 6:30 p.m. local time), Gregory Hicks in Tripoli texts Ambassador Stevens in Benghazi to advise him of the protests at the U.S. Embassy in Cairo. Hicks later explains that, until this Cairo demonstration, it has been a routine day at the U.S. Tripoli Embassy.[694]

By early afternoon in the U.S., news of the surveillance of the Benghazi Mission Compound earlier this day has reached official Washington. By about 1:00 p.m., the White House Situation Room begins receiving emails advising the Benghazi Mission is under "hostile surveillance."[695] No action is taken to heighten the Mission's security status.

Sometime this evening, Sean Smith reportedly has been chatting with a friend online. The friend says they will be in touch again soon. Smith presciently replies, "... [A]ssuming we don't die tonight. We saw one of our 'police' that guard the Compound taking pictures."[696]

---

[692] Megan Slack, "Marking the Eleventh Anniversary of 9/11," White House website (Sept. 11, 2012).

[693] "Message – Continuation of the National Emergency with Respect to Persons Who Commit, Threaten to Commit, or Support Terrorism," The White House, Obama White House Archives (Sept. 11, 2012).

[694] Hicks Oversight Committee Testimony (May 8, 2013), p. 24; and Benghazi Committee Report, p. 24.

[695] Ferrara, Benghazi: Obama's Actions Amount to a Shameful Dereliction of Duty, citing documents released by House Oversight Committee.

[696] Zuckoff, *13 Hours*, Chap 4, pp. 81-82.

At approximately 7:39 p.m. Benghazi time (1:39 p.m. Washington, D.C. time), Ambassador Stevens conducts his final visitor of the day to the compound's Main Gate. The guest is the Turkish Consul General, Ali Sait Akin. (Have they been coordinating the transfer of Libyan weapons to the rebels in Syria via Turkey, as some surmise is occurring?[697]) The affable Stevens then spends a few moments chatting with his Libyan guards in fluent Arabic. As he returns to the Villa with his two DSA guards, all is quiet.[698]

At 8:27 p.m., "four British security team members" leave the Mission Compound.[699] (These are British security agents who probably are in Benghazi only for the day. Pursuant to a pre-existing informal arrangement, they are dropping off an armored vehicle and various weapons the U.S. has agreed to store for the British when they need to come back to Benghazi periodically for very brief visits. As noted above, because of the security dangers the Brits otherwise have abandoned any permanent presence in Benghazi.[700]) No other visitors remain on the Mission grounds.

The most senior DSA, Alec Henderson, is in the Tactical Operations Center, doing paperwork. He has just completed his final security foot patrol of the compound, together with one of the local 17 February Brigade guards. All remains quiet. Three other DSAs are relaxing around the pool area behind the Villa, reportedly smoking cigars and playing cards. According to Burton and Katz, "Aces were high."[701] The fifth DSA is watching a video in the Villa's common area.[702]

---

[697] See McCarthy, Hillary Clinton's Benghazi Debacle: Arming Jihadists in Libya . . . And Syria ("It is incontestable that the Obama administration has worked closely with the Islamist government of Turkey in efforts to arm and train 'rebels' in Syria").

[698] Benghazi Committee Report, p. 25; Baier, New Revelations on Attack in Benghazi (*Watch video there*; Go to 14:03-20); Zuckoff, *13 Hours*, Chap 4, p. 81; Burnett, Benghazi Timeline: "We Are Under Attack" (*Watch video there*; Go to 1:38-46); and Josh Rogin, "State Department: No Video Protest at the Benghazi Consulate [sic]," ForeignPolicy.com (Oct. 9, 2012) (Quoting "senior" State Department official: "Everything is calm at 8:30 p.m., there is nothing unusual. There had been nothing unusual during the day outside").

[699] Benghazi Committee Report, pp. 25-26.

[700] Burton & Katz, *Under Fire*, Chap. 9, p. 94; and Zuckoff, *13 Hours*, Chap 4, p. 81.

[701] Burton & Katz, *Under Fire*, Chap. 9, pp. 95-97.

[702] Benghazi ARB Report, Timeline of the Attacks, p. 20; and Zuckoff, *13 Hours*, Chap. 9, p. 204.

THE TRUE ACCOUNT OF VALOR AND ABANDONMENT

(It is the anniversary of 9/11. They are in an extremely hostile city. A U.S. Ambassador is on site. This morning a policeman is seen taking photographs of the Compound. There has been a violent anti-American protest in Cairo this afternoon. Why aren't these security men patrolling the Mission Compound perimeter in full combat gear?)

Five unarmed Blue Mountain guards are present in the compound tonight. Two are assigned to the main entrance. These Blue Mountain guards are on duty, despite the fact their supervising entity now is unlicensed in Libya (as explained above in Chapter 20).

Three of four assigned armed 17 February Brigade guards also are on station in the compound this night. (The fourth is absent, with no replacement.) The three who are present are in the vicinity of the compound's Main Gate, near their barracks.[703]

By around 9:00 p.m., Ambassador Stevens retires to his bedroom in the Villa.[704] Shortly after 9:30 p.m., Stevens possibly still is writing in his diary. He summarizes the day's meetings. His final journal entry is heartbreakingly poignant: "Never ending security threats...."[705] Meanwhile, Sean Smith reportedly is online in his bedroom in the Villa, probably chatting on the web or playing one of his beloved internet video games with an opponent in another country.[706]

Neither man can know they both are about to die.

The Mission has requested a police vehicle be stationed at the front and back entrances all day and night during Stevens' visit. These vehicles are present on September 10, but are not here during most of September 11. One police pickup truck arrives outside the compound's Main Gate at 9:02 p.m. tonight. Two men are inside. This vehicle departs rapidly at 9:42 p.m., as the first attackers can be seen moving toward the Mission Compound. The police do not bother notifying anyone inside the compound, including the Blue Mountain or 17 February Brigade guards. They just *skedaddle*.[707]

Are these men in the police vehicle part of the oncoming mob? Or merely running from it? ■

---

[703] Benghazi Committee Report, p. 29; and Sen. Intelligence Committee Benghazi Report, p. 4.

[704] Baier, 13 Hours at Benghazi: The Inside Story (*Watch video there*; Go to 6:10-25).

[705] Benghazi Committee Report, p. 21; and Zuckoff, *13 Hours*, Chap. 4, p. 83.

[706] Zuckoff, *13 Hours*, Chap. 4, pp. 81-82 and 85.

[707] Benghazi Committee Report, pp. 29-31; Sen. Intelligence Committee Benghazi Report, p. 39; and Zuckoff, *13 Hours*, Chap. 4, pp. 83-84.

28

*"F***! GUNFIRE!"*

On this Night of Benghazi, there are now three Americans inside the main Villa building: Ambassador Stevens, Sean Smith and DSA Scott Wickland.[708] Wickland has principal responsibility for Stevens' and Smith's safety tonight.[709] Wickland is watching a movie.[710]

The other four DSAs are elsewhere on the compound grounds. As noted above, one agent is in the Tactical Operations Center[711] and the other three are outside the Villa relaxing near the swimming pool area.[712] Sadly, despite the treacherous locale, the 9/11 anniversary, and the earlier reports of protests in Cairo, these DSAs reportedly follow their standard procedure inside the compound and *are armed only with their pistols!*[713] Also, recall the Mission itself has been attacked twice in recent months (in April and June) – when no U.S. Ambassador even was present. Moreover, earlier today hostile surveillance of the compound has been observed.

The initial terrorist attack on the Mission Compound begins about 9:42 p.m., Benghazi time (3:42 p.m. Washington time).[714] The three DSAs outside the Villa building hear screaming, yelling, taunts and chanting in Arabic from outside the Mission's walls. The noises sound

---

[708] Kirkpatrick and Myers, Libya Attack Brings Challenges for U.S.; and September 12 Special Briefing.

[709] Hicks Oversight Committee Testimony (May 8, 2013), p. 24; and Kirkpatrick and Myers, Libya Attack Brings Challenges for U.S.

[710] Zuckoff, *13 Hours*, Chap. 9, p. 204.

[711] Additional Views of Reps. Jordan and Pompeo, p. 426.

[712] Benghazi Committee Report, p. 137.

[713] Benghazi ARB Report, Timeline of the Attacks (The DSAs "... were each armed with their standard issue sidearm pistol; their "kits," generally consisting of body armor, radio and M4 rifle, were in their bedroom/sleeping areas, in accord with Special Mission practice"), p. 20; and Zuckoff, *13 Hours*, Chap. 4, p. 82.

[714] Benghazi Committee Report, pp. 31 and 36, and Select Benghazi Timeline, p. 559.

close by. Then they hear gunfire and – ***BOOM!*** – a loud explosion near the Main Gate.[715] The DSAs around the pool think, *"What the . . . ?"*

In his bedroom inside the Villa, Sean Smith can hear the chants and other noises. He reportedly transmits to his gaming friend, "F***. GUNFIRE."[716] It will be his last message.

Inside the TOC, senior DSA Alec Henderson also hears noises outside, including shots and an explosion. He goes to the room's window to get a better listen. (He is unable to see out, as the window is blocked by bookcases on the inside and sandbags outside.)[717]

Suddenly, dozens of heavily-armed, chanting extremists breach the front "C1" pedestrian gate and storm into the compound. Some are shooting their AK-47s into the air. Most wear typical North African civilian clothes, although some have camouflage pants. A few of the mob have covered their faces with scarves. Charlene Lamb later testifies, "Dozens of attackers then launched a *full-scale assault* that was unprecedented in its size and intensity." Under Secretary of State Patrick Kennedy will describe the assault in similar terms. During this attack on the Mission, the militants will use small arms, AK-47s and other automatic weapons, grenades, rocket-propelled grenades ("RPGs"), and arson.[718]

(It is not known how the attackers are able to penetrate the pedestrian gate. It is possible one of the 17 February Brigade guards intentionally opens it in sympathy with the militants. Or has one of the Blue Mountain guards done so? Or perhaps (as in the past) the poorly-

---

[715] Benghazi Committee Report, p. 31; Burnett, Benghazi Timeline: "We Are Under Attack" (*Watch video there*; Go to 1:47 - 2:02); and Zuckoff, *13 Hours*, Chap. 9, p. 204.

[716] Zuckoff, *13 Hours*, Chap. 4, p. 85.

[717] Benghazi Committee Report, p. 142; and Zuckoff, *13 Hours*, Chap. 4, pp. 82 and 85-86.

[718] Baier, 13 Hours at Benghazi: The Inside Story (*Watch video there*; Go to 6:26-38); Zuckoff, *13 Hours*, Chap. 4, p. 84; Burnett, Benghazi Timeline: "We Are Under Attack" (*Watch video there*; Go to 1:47 - 2:13); Sen. Intelligence Committee Benghazi Report, p. 3; Kennedy House Oversight Prepared Testimony, p. 4; Lamb Oversight Committee Prepared Testimony (emphasis added), p. 4; Kennedy October 10 Briefing (". . . [T]he lethality of an armed massed attack by dozens of individuals is something greater than we've ever seen in Libya over the last period that we've been there"); and Benghazi ARB Report, Introduction, p. 1.

trained Blue Mountain men are negligent?[719] Or is one of the DSAs careless? We likely never will know.)

(Throughout this Night of Benghazi and afterwards, estimates of the attackers' numbers will vary widely. These range from senior DSA Alec Henderson's first assessment of "16 to 20 armed men,"[720] an initial State Department Alert of "approximately twenty,"[721] to a federal Indictment's reference to "about twenty armed men,"[722] to the Accountability Review Board's and Charlene Lamb's and Patrick Kennedy's "dozens,"[723] to author Zuckoff's "several dozen" swelling to "more than sixty,"[724] to sixty[725] or seventy,[726] to as many as 120,[727] and even "dozens if not hundreds."[728] Based on the evidence reviewed, the author believes the truth probably is in the range of seventy to eighty attackers, although this number could well be higher.)

---

[719] Benghazi ARB Report, Finding 3 ("They had left the gate unlatched before"), p. 35, cited in Zuckoff, *13 Hours*, Chap. 4, p. 84.

[720] Benghazi Committee Report, p. 142.

[721] CBS Benghazi Timeline. See also Hicks Oversight Committee Testimony (May 8, 2013) (DSA Alec Henderson's estimate of "at least twenty" armed hostile attackers), p. 25.

[722] Indictment, *United States v. Khatallah*, No. 1:14-cr-00212 (Oct. 14, 2014) ("Khatallah Superseding Indictment"), ¶20(c), p. 7; and Eyder Peralta, "Benghazi Suspect, Ahmed Abu Khattala [sic], Is Indicted on 17 New Charges," National Public Radio online (Oct. 14, 2014).

[723] CBS News, House Probes Security Leading Up to Libya Attack; Kennedy House Oversight Prepared Testimony (The assault in Benghazi is "an unprecedented attack by dozens of heavily armed men . . .") p. 4; Kennedy October 10 Briefing (". . . an armed massed attack by dozens of individuals. . . "); and Benghazi ARB Report ("dozens of armed attackers"), Finding 3, pp. 6 and 34. See also "Background Briefing on Libya" with Senior State Department Officials, State Dept. Archives website (Oct. 9, 2012) (". . . [T]here are dozens of armed men on the compound").

[724] Zuckoff, *13 Hours*, Chap. 4, p. 84.

[725] Sen. Intelligence Committee Benghazi Report (". . . at least 60 different attackers . . ."), p. 3; Hicks Oversight Committee Testimony (May 8, 2013), p. 26; and Babbin, Whitewashing Benghazi ("About 60 armed terrorists . . .").

[726] Benghazi Committee Report (DSA Scott Wickland's estimate), p. 34.

[727] Burnett, Benghazi Timeline: "We Are Under Attack" (*Watch video there*; Go to 2:20-28).

[728] Telephone Interview of Unnamed U.S. Serviceman "John" from Iowa with Sean Hannity, Sean Hannity Radio Show (Possibly May 7 or Nov. 26, 2013) ("Hannity Radio Interview with Unnamed U.S. Serviceman").

THE TRUE ACCOUNT OF VALOR AND ABANDONMENT

Alec Henderson returns from the TOC window to his desk. On a video monitor, he now can see the "dozens" of armed men flowing through the front pedestrian gate. He activates the Mission Compound's "Imminent Danger Notification System." A recorded voice begins to blare repeatedly throughout the compound, *"Duck and cover! Get away from the windows!"* Henderson then interrupts this recording, shouting his own emergency announcement over the compound's public address system: *"Attention on Compound, attention on Compound. This is not a drill! Repeat, this is not a drill!"* Then the "Duck and cover" warnings resume.[729]

The Mission Compound's perimeter is breached immediately, giving the DSAs almost no time to react.[730] Because they do not have their heavy weapons and the rest of their "battle kit," the DSAs must scramble to get them. (These kits include M-4 assault rifles and other weapons, ammunition, helmet, body armor and radios.) DSA Wickland races to his bedroom in the Villa. Dave Ubben runs from the area outside the Villa to his bedroom in the TOC building to grab his weapons and gear. Alec Henderson's weapons and kit apparently are in the Villa, but he remains in the TOC to coordinate the Mission's defense. The two remaining Tripoli DSAs must collect their M-4 weapons and battle kit from their temporary bedrooms in Building B.[731]

Critically, this need to secure their heavy weapons and combat equipment quickly fragments the defenders into three different locations: Wickland in the Villa, Ubben locked in the TOC with Henderson, and two other DSAs in Building B. Only Wickland is with the DSAs' assigned charges, Ambassador Stevens and Sean Smith. Because of the rapidity of the assault and the DSAs' need to arm themselves, from the outset the defenders physically are divided and out of position.[732]

(On the 9/11 anniversary in the most perilous city in North Africa after violent protests in Cairo earlier this day, why aren't the DSAs fully armed and in a better posture to defend their protectees in the

---

[729] Zuckoff, *13 Hours*, Chap. 4, p. 86; Benghazi Committee Report, p. 31; Sen. Intelligence Committee Benghazi Report (Redacted), pp. 3-4; Lamb Oversight Committee Prepared Testimony, p. 5; and CBS Benghazi Timeline.

[730] Benghazi ARB Report, pp. 34-35.

[731] Zuckoff, *13 Hours*, Chap. 4, pp. 82-83 and 87; Benghazi Committee Report, p. 33; and Sen. Intelligence Committee Benghazi Report, p. 5. See also Attkisson, *Stonewalled*, Chap. 4, p. 187.

[732] Zuckoff, *13 Hours*, Chap. 4, pp. 90-91.

Villa? According to Sharyl Attkisson, Lt. Col. Wood is confounded by this. He tells her, "*We* slept with our rifles. You never separated yourself from your weapon."[733])

Meanwhile, two of the five unarmed Blue Mountain guards flee through the Main Gate.[734] One or more of the three armed 17 February Brigade guards briefly engages the attackers with gunfire. It will be the only fire Libyan guards direct against the assailants during this first-wave attack.[735] In all, two (possibly three) of the Libyan security personnel are shot by the attackers, and two are beaten.[736] The attackers quickly corner the 17 February Brigade members inside the latter's barracks and set it ablaze with diesel fuel they have found stored on the premises. They also set fire to several Mission vehicles nearby.[737] (Amazingly, none of these 17 February or Blue Mountain guards will die this night.[738])

While some of the 17 February Brigade members at the Mission battle the attackers, others elsewhere may have been more sympathetic to the militants. Gregory Hicks later testifies to Congress he believes "Certainly elements of that militia were complicit in the attacks. The attackers had to make a long approach march through multiple checkpoints that were manned by February 17 militia."[739]

---

[733] Attkisson, *Stonewalled* (emphasis in original), Chap. 4, p. 187.

[734] Benghazi Committee Report, p. 32. See Clinton, *Hard Choices* (". . .[T]he Department had contracted with members of a local militia vetted by the CIA to be present at the [Mission] compound at all times, and also contracted unarmed local security guards to man the entry points. As became evident during the attacks, there were fatal weaknesses in their abilities and willingness to fulfill their security duties against fellow Libyans when they were most needed"), Chap. 17, p. 409.

[735] Benghazi Committee Report, p. 32.

[736] Lamb Oversight Committee Prepared Testimony (two guards wounded), p. 4; "Significant Attacks Against U.S. Diplomatic Facilities and Personnel 2006-2015," U.S. Department of State, Bureau of Diplomatic Security, State Dept. website (three Libyan contract guards wounded), p. 25; Benghazi ARB Report, p. 1 (three Libyan contract guards injured); and Benghazi Committee Report (One DSA agent: ". . . [A]t least one, if not two, of the local guards were shot . . . in the process. . . ."), p. 32.

[737] Benghazi Committee Report, p. 32; Sen. Intelligence Committee Benghazi Report, p. 3; Zuckoff, *13 Hours*, Chap. 4, p. 85; CBS Benghazi Timeline; Burnett, Benghazi Timeline: "We Are Under Attack" (*Watch video there*; Go to 2:02-10); and Baier, New Revelations on Attack in Benghazi (*Watch video there*; Go to 15:00-12).

[738] Benghazi Committee Report, p. 32.

[739] Hicks Oversight Committee Testimony (May 8, 2013) (Response to questions of Rep. Blake Farenthold (R-TX)), pp. 80-81.

Although the Mission occupants do not know it now, according to the Select Committee "the attackers were a mix of local extremist groups, including the Benghazi-based Ansar al-Sharia, al-Qaida in the Lands of the Islamic Maghreb, and the Muhammad Jamal Network out of Egypt." Members of three other extremist groups also participate, including al Qaeda in Iraq and al Qaeda in the Arabian Peninsula.[740]

(As discussed below in Chapter 114, an individual named Ahmed Abu Khatallah later is seized in Libya and prosecuted in U.S. court for his role in this assault. His prosecutors will claim Abu Khatallah is a leader of the attackers. They will assert the government's evidence at Khatallah's trial shows "Khatallah directed his group to carry out the violence, striking first at the U.S. Special Mission in Benghazi." According to *The Washington Post's* summary of court filings, prosecutors will allege during this initial attack Khatallah is "coordinating the efforts of his conspirators and turning away emergency responders..."[741] In his defense, Khatallah will claim he merely is directing traffic to keep passersby safe.)

A *New York Times* article published the following day quotes one alleged eyewitness: "They [the attackers] expected that there would be more American commandos in there [the Mission Compound]. They went in with guns blazing, with R.P.G.'s." This witness reportedly is Mohamed Ali, who is said to be a relative of the landlord who rents the Mission to the United States. Ali claims to have watched the battle.[742]

Much of this initial attack is captured by the Mission's functioning security cameras.[743] The recordings made of these video feeds clearly show a number of the militants are carrying heavy weapons.[744] (This fact, and the initial explosion heard by all, are at odds with the later Team Obama narrative that this attack grows out of a spontaneous protest, discussed in detail below.) ∎

---

[740] Benghazi Committee Report, pp. 33-34.

[741] Press Release, United States Attorney's Office, District of Columbia, "Ahmed Abu Khatallah Found Guilty of Terrorism Charges in September 2012 Attack in Benghazi, Libya," Justice Dept. website (Nov. 28, 2017) ("DOJ Press Release, 'Abu Khatallah Found Guilty of Terrorism Charges'"); and Hsu, U.S. Will Not Seek Death Penalty for Accused Ringleader in Benghazi Attacks.

[742] Kirkpatrick and Myers, Libya Attack Brings Challenges for U.S.

[743] E.g., Sen. Intelligence Committee Benghazi Report, p. 3.

[744] See, e.g., "Seeking Information on Benghazi Attacks," FBI website; and "Video: Seeking Information in Benghazi Attacks" (apparently in Arabic), FBI website.

29

"Shelter & Wait"

The DSAs at the Mission Compound immediately begin to implement the facility's "Emergency Action Plan." This entails "shelter in place, contact your support elements, and wait for their arrival."[745]

(Wow, what a helluva plan. "Shelter in place." Perhaps they should have added, "Pray your rosary." This "plan" screams out they *know* their security at the Mission Compound is inadequate.)

At once, senior DSA Alec Henderson in the Mission TOC contacts the GRS security team at the Annex to alert the CIA of the attack. He requests immediate assistance. (One GRS operator at the Annex, Kris "Tanto" Paronto, puts the time of this alert at 9:32 p.m. However, this is inconsistent with all other accounts placing the initial attack at about 9:42 p.m. The author has found Paronto's numerous descriptions of this Night of Benghazi to be consistent and accurate in virtually every other respect, and concludes Tanto's watch must have been running slow.)[746]

DSA Henderson later will testify before the Select Committee that throughout this Night of Benghazi he will update officials in Washington every 15 to 30 minutes. As two of the committee's Republican members conclude, this gives "the State Department virtually a front row seat to the attack."[747] In addition, the State Department's top diplomatic security official, Charlene Lamb, also will be monitoring the situation in Benghazi in real time. Four weeks after the attacks, Lamb testifies to Congress, ". . . I was in our Diplomatic Security Command Center ["DSCC"] monitoring multiple open lines with our agents for much of the attack."[748]

---

[745] Benghazi Committee Report, pp. 31-32.

[746] *Id.*, pp. 32, 36-37 and 44-45; Sen. Intelligence Committee Benghazi Report, p. 4; Zuckoff, *13 Hours*, Chap. 4, p. 91; Greg Miller, "CIA Rushed to Save Diplomats as Libya Attack Was Underway," *The Washington Post* online (Nov. 1, 2012) ("Miller, CIA Rushed to Save Diplomats as Libya Attack Was Underway"); Baier, 13 Hours at Benghazi: The Inside Story (*Watch video there*; Go to 5:31-42); and Burnett, Benghazi Timeline: "We Are Under Attack" (*Watch video there*; Go to 2:28-35).

[747] Additional Views of Reps. Jordan and Pompeo, p. 426.

[748] Lamb Oversight Committee Prepared Testimony, p. 4.

Meanwhile, one of the DSAs from Tripoli sprints from the Villa pool area to the TOC, erroneously believing Ambassador Stevens is there. Alec Henderson informs him Stevens is in the Villa. (On this 9/11 anniversary, why do any of these DSAs not even know where their principal protectee is at every minute?) The Tripoli DSA then hurries across the brick patio outside and into Building B to retrieve his M-4 weapon and tactical gear from his bedroom. There, he meets his fellow Tripoli DSA, who also is "jocking up" for combat.[749]

The two men decide to head back toward the Villa to help protect Ambassador Stevens. (Good thought.) On the way there, they encounter "a very large hostile force of 7 to 10 attackers" who wield AK-47s and RPGs. The two DSAs later testify they do not want to "inflame" an "already bad situation." Accordingly, they make the tactical decision not to shoot at the attackers. Instead, they retreat back into Building B.[750] (It's a bit hard to imagine how the situation can get much more "inflamed" by confronting the attackers – who likely are poorly trained, and may retreat at the first sign of hostile gunfire. In any event, the DSAs' job is to shoot the assailants. This they fail to do.[751] Had the departed SST special ops unit been camped on the Mission grounds, can one even *imagine* them not shooting at the bad guys?)

Whatever their justifications, none of the DSAs will claim to have shot once at the attackers during this first wave attack.[752] (Nevertheless, Secretary of State Hillary Clinton later will award each of the five DSAs the State Department's "Heroism Award."[753])

Once back in Building B, one of these DSAs contacts the Embassy in Tripoli, while the other calls the State Department's DSCC in Washington, D.C. It is 9:49 p.m. in Benghazi (3:49 p.m. in Washington). The two DSAs then barricade themselves in a back room of Building B, together with one of the local Libyan guards who has

---

[749] *Id.*, p. 5; Sen. Intelligence Committee Benghazi Report, p. 5; Zuckoff, *13 Hours*, Chap. 4, p 89; and CBS Benghazi Timeline.

[750] Benghazi Committee Report, p. 33; Sen. Intelligence Committee Benghazi Report, p. 5; and Zuckoff, *13 Hours*, Chap. 4, pp. 89-90.

[751] Sen. Intelligence Committee Benghazi Report ("The DS agents did not fire a single shot that night during the attack on the Temporary Mission Facility, according to testimony before the Committee"), p. 6.

[752] Benghazi Committee Report, p. 32; Sen. Intelligence Committee Benghazi Report (Redacted), p. 6; Attkisson, *Stonewalled*, Chap. 4, p. 187; and Babbin, Whitewashing Benghazi.

[753] Clinton, *Hard Choices*, Chap. 17, p. 415.

fled here. Some of the militants break through the main door of Building B. However, they are unable to breach the fortified doors of the back room where the three men have taken refuge.[754]

By now DSA Dave Ubben has collected his weapons and battle gear from his bedroom in the TOC building, and has joined Alec Henderson in the TOC. The two DSAs begin to call various "security elements" to request assistance. As they do so, they watch on the TOC's security monitors in anger and frustration as the attack unfolds. One of the DSAs sets up an open radio link to the CIA Annex, which permits continuous communication between the two outposts. The DSA asks Annex staff to notify the Libyan 17 February Brigade of the attack and request immediate assistance at the Mission. The DSAs also contact the Libyan Ministry of Foreign Affairs and appeal for help. Next, the DSAs call the lead State Department security officer in Tripoli. One DSA in the Mission TOC keeps Tripoli on a speakerphone virtually the entire time of the attack. Then they, too, call the DSCC in Washington.[755]

Throughout the course of this battle, the assailants will attempt to break into the Mission's Tactical Operations Center multiple times. Each time they are unsuccessful. This is due at least in part to improvements State has made to fortify this structure.[756]

Whether in the TOC, Building B, the Villa, the Libyan guards' barracks, or at the swimming pool, no one within the diplomatic Mission Compound believes they are witnessing a "demonstration" or "protest." They are being *attacked!*[757] ∎

---

[754] Burnett, Benghazi Timeline: "We Are Under Attack" (*Watch video there*; Go to 2:28-39); and Benghazi Committee Report, pp. 33, 36 and 143.

[755] Benghazi Committee Report, pp. 32-33 and 37; Sen. Intelligence Committee Benghazi Report, p. 4; and Zuckoff, *13 Hours*, Chap. 4, p. 90.

[756] Lamb Oversight Committee Prepared Testimony, p. 6; and Hicks Oversight Committee Testimony (May 8, 2013), p. 25.

[757] Zuckoff, *13 Hours* (". . . The attackers didn't wear insignia, and none of the Americans saw where they'd assembled or knew exactly when they'd arrived outside the gate. One thing was certain: They displayed a common desire to terrorize Americans at the Special Mission Compound. Or worse"), Chap. 4, p. 84.

30

"We're Gonna Do Something Fun Tonight!"

Meanwhile, at the nearby CIA Annex its personnel are preparing to wrap up another day. Five of the GRS contract security contractors are on-site. A sixth, Mark "Oz" Geist, is still away, safeguarding a CIA case officer who is attending a dinner meeting elsewhere in Benghazi.[758] Rone Woods, Tig Tiegen, and Tanto Paronto are not even supposed to be in Benghazi tonight; their rotations have been extended because of Ambassador Stevens' arrival.[759]

Jack Silva is in his bedroom on his laptop. His roommate, Tig Tiegen, is there too, preparing for bed. Tanto Paronto and D.B. Benton have drawn this "on call" duty shift. They are relaxing, viewing a movie (*Wrath of the Titans*). (It's uncertain what Tyrone Woods is doing.)[760] As with the DSA agents at the Mission, it is surprising their Team Lead or the Chief of Base ("Bob") does not put these GRS men on higher alert on this 9/11 anniversary (especially in light of the violent protests in Cairo).

Senior DSA Alec Henderson's first frantic call to the Annex is answered by the GRS Team Lead. When he hangs up, the Team Lead immediately announces over his two-way radio, "All GRS meet in the CP!" This "Command Post" is Building C's "Sensitive Compartmentalized Information Facility" or "SCIF." When no one replies after about 20 seconds, the Team Lead repeats with greater urgency, *"We need GRS in the room. NOW!"*[761]

The GRS agents instantly know from the tone of their Team Lead's voice something unusual is happening. As they turn off the movie,

---

[758] Baier, 13 Hours at Benghazi: The Inside Story (*Watch video there*; Go to 13:12-41); and Zuckoff, *13 Hours*, Chap. 4, p. 90.

[759] *13 Hours: The Secret Soldiers of Benghazi*, Extra Features DVD, "Uncovering Benghazi's Secret Soldiers" (Paramount, 2016).

[760] Zuckoff, *13 Hours*, Chap. 4, pp. 90-92.

[761] *Id.*, Chap. 4, p. 91.

Tanto Paronto reportedly tells D.B. Benton, "Shit, something's really happening. We're gonna get to do something fun tonight."[762]

CIA staffers standing outside in the Annex courtyard can hear gunfire and some explosions from the direction of the Mission outpost.[763] According to *The Washington Post*, "Bob [the Annex Chief of Base] said he first heard gunfire about 9:42 p.m. and *suspected immediately that the diplomatic compound was under attack*."[764])

As the GRS men hustle toward Building C's Command Post, on the way they learn from their Team Lead of the attack on the Mission Compound. Now outside, Tanto Paronto hears distant, amplified chants of *Allahu Akbar! Allahu Akbar!* ("God is great!").[765] "Immediately" the agents return to their quarters to finish dressing and begin collecting their combat equipment to respond.[766] They claim they are "jocked up" *within five minutes* or so of learning the Mission Compound is under assault.[767] This means they are loaded with automatic weapons, sidearms and knives; wearing their body armor, "chest rigs" with ammunition, and helmets; and carrying their night-vision gear and full canteens. They also have medical kits (containing such essentials as sterile gauze dressings, clotting agents and tourniquets). Finally, they each grab their personalized "go bag." These hold varying combinations of items, including additional ammo, flashlights and batteries, a GPS device, a compass, and (in some cases) diplomatic passports.[768]

"Team Annex" is ready for a fight.

---

[762] *Id.*, Chap. 4, p. 91.

[763] Benghazi Committee Report, p. 39; Baier, New Revelations on Attack in Benghazi (*Watch video there*; Go to 15:26-38); Zuckoff, *13 Hours*, Chap. 4, p. 92; and Baier, 13 Hours at Benghazi: The Inside Story (*Watch video there*; Go to 6:00-10).

[764] Goldman and Miller, Former CIA Chief in Benghazi Challenges the Story Line of the New Movie '13 Hours.'

[765] Zuckoff, *13 Hours*, Chap. 4, pp. 92-93.

[766] Miller, CIA Rushed to Save Diplomats as Libya Attack Was Underway.

[767] Benghazi Committee Report, pp. 37-38 and 45-46; Zuckoff, *13 Hours*, Chap. 4, pp. 94-95; "Top CIA Officer in Benghazi Delayed Response to Terrorist Attack, US Security Team Members Claim," Fox News Channel (Sept. 6, 2014) ("Fox News, Top CIA Officer in Benghazi Delayed Response to Terrorist Attack") (GRS Kris "Tanto" Paronto: "Five minutes, we're ready. It was thumbs up, thumbs up, we're ready to go"); and Baier, 13 Hours at Benghazi: The Inside Story (*Watch video there*; Go to 6:41-52).

[768] Zuckoff, *13 Hours*, Chap. 4, p. 93.

(In contrast, the Annex Chief of Base later tells the Select Committee it takes the GRS operators about 15 minutes to get ready.[769] The Deputy Chief of Base splits the difference and estimates the preparation time at approximately 10 minutes.[770] Whatever the precise time, the GRS agents have moved swiftly – unlike many government officials will in Washington and elsewhere this night. The distant sounds and sights of gunfire and explosives tell the GRS agents this is a true emergency.)

Later, the State Department official in charge of diplomatic security (joined by other government officials) misleadingly will describe the six GRS contractors as part of the Mission Compound's formal security detail! In her *prepared written* testimony Charlene Lamb will state, "In addition, stationed nearby at the embassy [sic] annex was a well-trained U.S. quick reaction security team."[771] In other words, Lamb hopes to make the State Department's pathetic diplomatic security assets in Benghazi look stronger by retroactively converting the half-dozen CIA contract bodyguards *protecting CIA Annex personnel at another location* into an official auxiliary "quick reaction security team" supposedly assigned to protect the Mission and Ambassador Stevens!

(At a State briefing the previous day, another, unidentified "Senior State Department Official" uses the same ruse, calling the GRS agents a "quick reaction security team."[772] At this briefing State also misleading asserts:

> Because ... unfortunately *we* couldn't fit everything on one compound, *we* had two – the principle [sic] compound *and the annex. We* had ... *our* security professionals divided between the two compounds.[773]

Again, State here falsely is claiming the GRS team as its own. This State official obviously also is attempting to obscure the fact the annex belongs to the CIA, not State. This briefing no doubt is held to defuse

---

[769] Benghazi Committee Report, p. 40.

[770] *Id.*, p. 48.

[771] Lamb Oversight Committee Prepared Testimony, p. 3.

[772] "Background Briefing on Libya" with Senior State Department Officials, State Dept. Archives website (Oct. 9, 2012) ("... [T]here is an additional security force at another U.S. compound two kilometers away [from the Mission Compound]. It serves as a rapid reaction force, a quick reaction security team ...").

[773] "Background Briefing on Libya" with Senior State Department Officials, State Dept. Archives website (Oct. 9, 2012) (emphasis added).

the impact of the Oversight hearing the next day. Should "cover your ass" be hyphenated?)

Even the Democrat-controlled Senate Intelligence Committee formally will find the Mission personnel "relied on the security officers at the CIA Annex *as a last resort* for security in the event of an attack."[774]

In her position as the State Department's Deputy Assistant Secretary of State for Diplomatic Security, Lamb likely has as much or more knowledge of State's physical diplomatic facilities throughout the world as any other single individual. (She will testify, "I'm responsible for the safety and security of more than 275 diplomatic facilities."[775]) Yet in her prepared testimony – written in advance, not spoken spontaneously under pressure at a hearing – she refers to the CIA Annex as the "embassy annex." This clearly describes the Annex as a State Department facility, because only State operates U.S. embassies. In fact, Lamb knows damned well it is a CIA facility, and knows Team Annex members are CIA contract bodyguards protecting CIA staff, not a "quick reaction security team" stationed there at the Annex to protect the Mission Compound and its personnel. *Lamb is lying to the Oversight Committee.*

In fact, these CIA GRS contractors have *no* employment or contractual or legal responsibility to protect the State Department's personnel at the Mission. (Indeed, as noted above their own private health and life insurance might not even cover them while attempting a rescue mission of State Department staff at the Mission, which is well beyond the scope of their contractual project duties to protect CIA personnel.[776]) They have pledged to do so out of nobility and valor. (Oh yeah, and patriotism.) ∎

---

[774] Sen. Intelligence Committee Benghazi Report (emphasis added), p. 27.

[775] Lamb Oversight Committee Prepared Testimony, p. 1.

[776] *13 Hours: The Secret Soldiers of Benghazi*, Extra Features DVD, "Uncovering Benghazi's Secret Soldiers" (Paramount, 2016).

31

"Safe Haven"

Tonight it is the job of Department of State security officer Scott Wickland personally to protect Ambassador Chris Stevens and Sean Smith. He will fail.

When DSA Wickland first hears the attackers' chants and gunshots, he goes swiftly to his bedroom in the Villa and grabs his helmet, vest and weapons. Wickland then guides the ambassador and communications specialist Sean Smith, who is donning his own vest and helmet, into the Villa's "safe haven" area.[777] The safe haven is protected by a metal, barred door the attackers will not be able to breach. Within the haven, bars also are placed on the windows. (It literally resembles a large, rather well-appointed jail cell.)[778] Wickland secures all three of the locks to the haven's heavy door. Then, with his loaded A-4 automatic rifle at the ready, he positions himself near the haven's entrance to guard Stevens and Smith from the mob.[779]

(Lt. Colonel Andrew Wood later explains this safe haven is designed merely to delay any aggressor temporarily until other help can arrive at the Mission Compound. The haven's occupants must rely on help from outside eventually reaching the Villa.[780])

---

[777] Lamb Oversight Committee Prepared Testimony, p. 5; Benghazi Committee Report, p. 33; Sen. Intelligence Committee Benghazi Report, p. 5; Burnett, Benghazi Timeline: "We Are Under Attack" (*Watch video there*; Go to 2:12-20); and CBS Benghazi Timeline. For a time, Fox News erroneously asserts it "reportedly" is DSA Dave Ubben who is guarding Ambassador Stevens and Sean Smith in the Villa on the Night of Benghazi. E.g., Baier, New Revelations on Attack in Benghazi (*Watch video there*; Go to 16:42 - 18:15 and 23:53 - 24:03). (Ubben will be one of the two Americans who later is severely wounded in the final terrorist attack at the CIA Annex.) Despite this and other errors in this report, the author believes Fox News' coverage is among the best media reporting on the Benghazi debacle.

[778] Baier, New Revelations on Attack in Benghazi (*Watch video there*; Go to 5:28-48).

[779] Benghazi Committee Report, p. 33; and Baier, 13 Hours at Benghazi: The Inside Story (*Watch video there*; Go to 7:22-43).

[780] Baier, New Revelations on Attack in Benghazi (*Watch video there*; Go to 17:48-59).

From inside the safe haven, DSA Wickland can hear the attackers banging on the Villa's outer doors. During this time, Wickland is on the radio attempting to relay these ongoing developments. (To whom he addresses his message is unspecified in the Select Committee's report, but it very likely is a DSA on duty in the Mission's TOC.) Wickland later testifies that over his radio he requests immediate assistance. He receives no response.

At approximately 10:00 p.m. (4:00 p.m. Washington time), the two DSAs then in the TOC report to DSCC in Washington that Ambassador Stevens and Sean Smith are located in the Villa's safe haven.[781]

BOOM! Suddenly, the Villa's doors are "blown open"! From his perch inside the haven, Wickland reports ". . . about 70 individuals . . . rushed into the building, all of them carrying AK-47s, grenades, RPGs, ..."[782] Fear grips the three Americans trapped in the safe haven. ∎

---

[781] Benghazi Committee Report, p. 34.

[782] *Id.*, p. 34.

32

"Greg, We Are Under Attack!"

From inside the Villa (probably from within the safe haven), on his own cell phone Ambassador Stevens quickly calls his Deputy in Tripoli, Gregory Hicks. He does not reach Hicks. Stevens tries again using a cell phone borrowed from his bodyguard, DSA Wickland. Again Stevens does not connect with his deputy.

Four hundred miles away at 9:45 p.m., three minutes into the attack, John Martinec, the Tripoli Embassy's senior Regional Security Officer, runs to Hicks' residence and notifies him of the crisis. "Greg, Greg, the Consulate's under attack!" Hicks, who has been watching television, immediately checks his phone and sees he has two missed calls. One is from Ambassador Stevens' phone. The other is from an unknown number (which will prove to be DSA Wickland's line).[783]

Hicks immediately calls back the number he doesn't recognize. Chris Stevens answers. The ambassador warns, "Greg, we are under attack!" Then the line goes dead. It is a bad night for cell phone service in Tripoli. Hicks tries both lines, but is unable to reach Stevens again.[784] Hicks is the last person outside the safe haven ever to speak with Stevens.[785]

Hicks later testifies that in his brief call Stevens says not one word about a demonstration outside the Mission Compound, which Stevens surely would have mentioned to Hicks had it happened.[786] (However, their final conversation is so brief this conclusion appears somewhat

---

[783] Hicks Oversight Committee Testimony (May 8, 2013), p. 24; Benghazi Committee Report, pp. 9 and 53; and ABC News, Hicks Sept. 2013 Interview With Stephanopoulos (*Watch video there*; Go to 1:16-45).

[784] Hicks Oversight Committee Testimony (May 8, 2013), p. 24; *Id.* (Response to questions of Rep. Trey Gowdy (R-SC)), p. 32; Benghazi Committee Report, pp. 9 and 53; Burnett, Benghazi Timeline: "We Are Under Attack" (*Watch video there*; Go to 2:40-50); ABC News, Hicks Sept. 2013 Interview With Stephanopoulos (*Watch video there*; Go to 1:42 - 2:00); and Clinton, *Hard Choices,* Chap. 17, p. 390.

[785] Hicks, What the Benghazi Attack Taught Me About Hillary Clinton.

[786] Hicks Oversight Committee Testimony (May 8, 2013) (Response to questions of Rep. Trey Gowdy (R-SC)), p. 32.

speculative, unless Hicks is referring to a time period earlier in the day when he communicates with Stevens about the Cairo protest.)

During these attempts to connect with the ambassador, Hicks already has begun walking swiftly toward the Tripoli Embassy's Tactical Operations Center (the "TOC," its command center). After being disconnected, Hicks quickens his pace further. Once in the TOC, he alerts the group there of his short call with Stevens. Embassy Tripoli springs into action. The staff quickly notify other relevant Embassy workers of the attack.[787]

In the Tripoli TOC, John Martinec already is on the phone with Alec Henderson, the senior DSA at the Benghazi Mission, to get an update. When the RSO finishes speaking with Henderson, Martinec advises Hicks that Henderson says the compound has been breached, and there are at least twenty armed hostile attackers there.[788]

Meanwhile, U.S. personnel in Tripoli call the Diplomatic Security Command Center in Washington, D.C.[789] Charlene Lamb, the State Department's top diplomatic security official later testifies, "From that point on, I could follow what was happening in almost real-time."[790] This apparently takes place over a "listen-only, audio-only feed."[791] (As discussed below, despite this near real-time communication channel, the State Department later will invoke the "fog of war" excuse for inaction, delay and mistakes.[792])

Greg Hicks then calls the Station Chief at the CIA Annex in Tripoli (the CIA's most senior officer in Libya). The CIA Chief already knows of the attack and tells Hicks the CIA Annex in *Benghazi* is mobilizing a response team to provide reinforcements to the Mission and help repel

---

[787] *Id.*, p. 24.

[788] Hicks Oversight Committee Testimony (May 8, 2013), p. 25.

[789] Benghazi Committee Report, p. 32.

[790] Lamb Oversight Committee Prepared Testimony, p. 5.

[791] CBS Benghazi Timeline.

[792] Clinton, *Hard Choices* ("The events of that September occurred in what is often called the 'fog of war,' with information hard to come by, and conflicting or incomplete reports making it difficult to tell what was actually happening on the ground, especially from thousands of miles away in Washington. To a frustrating degree, that fog persisted so long, in part because of continuing turmoil in Libya"), Chap. 17, p. 385. See House Oversight Committee Hearings (May 8, 2013) (Remarks of Rep. Kerry Bentivolio (R-MI)) (". . . The fog of battle is easily blamed when mistakes are made at the highest level. . . ."), p. 93.

the attack there.⁷⁹³ Possibly during this same call, Hicks and the Station Chief also discuss attempting to mobilize a rescue team from *Tripoli*. The two officials agree to proceed with using a chartered plane to take reinforcements from Tripoli to Benghazi.⁷⁹⁴ (Hicks and the Tripoli Station Chief are two of the very few U.S. officials who get it right this night – they understand their fellow Americans are waging an urgent, life-and-death struggle in Benghazi!)

"Within minutes" of learning of the crisis, U.S. personnel in Tripoli take two decisive steps in reaction to the Benghazi assault. First, they submit a request that an "intelligence, surveillance, and reconnaissance" drone now at a classified location (Darnah, Libya⁷⁹⁵) be repositioned to Benghazi "to provide tactical awareness of the situation on the ground." And second, the Chief of Station begins to organize a rescue team (about which he already has conferred with Greg Hicks) to respond swiftly to the Benghazi attacks.⁷⁹⁶ This group will become known as "Team Tripoli" (discussed below). Remarkably, as will be seen *Team Tripoli will be the only U.S. help actually headed to Benghazi this terrible night.*⁷⁹⁷

At approximately 10:00 p.m., Tripoli and Benghazi time (4:00 p.m. Washington time), Greg Hicks calls the State Department Operations Center in Washington. He alerts them of the Benghazi attacks, and the Tripoli Embassy's response.⁷⁹⁸

In an interview with congressional investigators Hicks later explains, "I was in communication with Washington all night long. I was reporting all night long what was happening to Washington by telephone."⁷⁹⁹ Hicks asserts he was reporting back to the State

---

⁷⁹³ Hicks Oversight Committee Testimony (May 8, 2013), p. 25.

⁷⁹⁴ *Id.*, p. 25.

⁷⁹⁵ Sen. Intelligence Committee Benghazi Report, p. 29.

⁷⁹⁶ Benghazi Committee Report, pp. 53-54 and 109; and Miller, CIA Rushed to Save Diplomats as Libya Attack Was Underway.

⁷⁹⁷ Benghazi Committee Report (Regarding Team Tripoli, ". . . they represent the only military 'asset' to reach Benghazi during the attacks"), p. 113.

⁷⁹⁸ Hicks Oversight Committee Testimony (May 8, 2013), p. 25; and ABC News, Hicks Sept. 2013 Interview With Stephanopoulos (*Watch video there*; Go to 3:11-33).

⁷⁹⁹ Sharyl Attkisson, "Diplomat: U.S. Special Forces Told 'You Can't Go' to Benghazi During Attacks," CBS News online (May 6, 2013) ("Attkisson, 'Diplomat: U.S. Special Forces Told "You Can't Go" to Benghazi During Attacks'"). See also Hicks Oversight Committee Testimony (May 8, 2013) (Hicks: "During the night I'm in touch

Department's Ops Center in Washington "every fifteen to twenty minutes."[800] (Fog of war?)

Hicks then urgently calls the chiefs of staff of both the Libyan president and prime minister to plead for immediate assistance from the Libyan government. He makes a similar emergency call to the head of American affairs at Libya's Ministry of Foreign Affairs.[801] The calls will be in vain.

While Hicks makes his frantic calls, the Tripoli Embassy's Defense Attaché, Lieutenant Colonel Keith Phillips, also leaps into action. He immediately calls the Libyan Ministry of Defense and the Chief of Staff of the Libyan Armed Forces to request assistance in Benghazi. Phillips also notifies the Joint Chiefs of Staff in D.C. and U.S. Africa Command of the attack.[802] (AFRICOM is headquartered in Stuttgart, Germany, rather than anywhere near Africa.) Hicks later asserts, "[T]he Defense Attaché worked assiduously all night long to try to get the Libyan military to respond in some way."[803] Phillips' endeavors largely will prove unsuccessful. Like Hicks, throughout this Night of Benghazi Lt. Col. Phillips will report on emerging events up his chain of command, to AFRICOM and from thence to the Joint Chiefs' staff at the Pentagon.[804]

Also stationed at the Tripoli Embassy is a "SOCAFRICA" lead officer. He is Lieutenant Colonel S. E. Gibson. On this night, Lt. Col. Gibson is communicating with his superiors at SOCAFRICA (also in Stuttgart).[805] (As detailed below, Gibson and three of his men later will be ordered by SOCAFRICA *not* to go to Benghazi to help the Americans under siege there.)

---

with Washington, keeping them posted of what's happening in Tripoli and to the best of my knowledge what I'm being told in Benghazi"), p. 27.

[800] ABC News, Hicks Sept. 2013 Interview With Stephanopoulos (*Watch video there*; Go to 4:21-31).

[801] Hicks Oversight Committee Testimony (May 8, 2013), p. 25.

[802] *Id.*, p. 25; and Attkisson, Diplomat: U.S. Special Forces Told "You Can't Go" to Benghazi During Attacks.

[803] Attkisson, Diplomat: U.S. Special Forces Told "You Can't Go" to Benghazi During Attacks.

[804] Hicks Oversight Committee Testimony (May 8, 2013), p. 25.

[805] Attkisson, Diplomat: U.S. Special Forces Told "You Can't Go" to Benghazi During Attacks.

THE TRUE ACCOUNT OF VALOR AND ABANDONMENT

Tonight, David McFarland is the Political Section Chief at the U.S. Embassy in Tripoli. Fortunately for him, he has just returned from a rotation in Benghazi. He served there as Acting Principal Officer for the first ten days of September. Once alerted of the attack, McFarland begins to phone the contacts he developed while in Benghazi to request help at the local level. McFarland also is in communication with an unidentified State department employee in Benghazi (presumably someone inside the Mission).[806]

When he finishes his initial frustrating round of calls with the Libyan officials, Greg Hicks telephones the State Department Operations Center again. He updates the staff there on the inconclusive results of his urgent contacts thus far. According to Hicks, throughout this Night of Benghazi he serves as principal coordinator among the U.S. Embassy in Tripoli, State's Ops Center in Washington, Libyan government officials, and the CIA's Chief of Station in Tripoli.[807] ■

---

[806] Hicks Oversight Committee Testimony (May 8, 2013), pp. 25 and 28.
[807] *Id.*, p. 25.

33

"You're in My World Now"

As noted above, on the Night of Benghazi GRS Oz Geist is protecting a CIA case officer who is attending a dinner meeting on CIA business in the city. While Rone Woods and his fellow Team Annex members are "jocking up," Rone calls Geist on the latter's cell phone. He tells Oz of the attack on the Mission Compound. He advises Oz to return with his protectee to the Annex immediately. Rone warns Oz to steer clear of the Mission area.[808]

When Geist tells his case officer she must return with him ASAP to the Annex, she is not amused. She isn't finished talking with her dinner companions. But Oz is forceful. He informs her she is in Geist's world now, she needs to be quiet and let Geist do what he needs to do. He wins the discussion.

Oz drives them at high speed back to the Annex, using an indirect route to avoid any militant roadblocks or ambushes.[809] ∎

---

[808] Baier, 13 Hours at Benghazi: The Inside Story (*Watch video there*; Go to 13:13-42); and Zuckoff, *13 Hours*, Chap. 5, p. 112.

[809] Baier, 13 Hours at Benghazi: The Inside Story (*Watch video there*; Go to 13:13-42); and Zuckoff, *13 Hours*, Chap. 5, pp. 112-113.

34

"Washington, We Have a Problem"

As the terrorists spread throughout the Mission Compound grounds in Benghazi, notice of the attack unfolds more slowly throughout Washington, D.C.

The State Department

According to the Select Committee, records of the State Department's Diplomatic Security Command Center (DSCC) show it first "receives notification" of the Benghazi disaster at 3:49 p.m. – seven minutes into the initial attack.[810] This is in the middle of the normal business day in Washington.

At State headquarters, Charlene Lamb is working in her office when she receives a phone call advising her the Libya RSO (John Martinec) is on the phone, and the Benghazi Mission Compound is under attack. (She can't recall whether this call came from the DSCC, or from the desk officer.) Lamb quickly alerts her boss, Scott Bultrowicz (Deputy Assistant Secretary for Diplomatic Security). The two immediately head for the DSCC. On their way there, Lamb phones a "liaison officer" who works for her. This officer has employees who work in the CIA Benghazi Annex. Lamb asks this officer to join them in the DSCC.[811]

Once they arrive there, Lamb testifies they begin to "identify security assets who could help them with the situation that was unfolding." She explains by this she means "Assets that were at the Annex facility" – in other words, the CIA's GRS contractors.[812] Lamb and her team also call AFRICOM and European Command "to see if they had any assets in theater that were nearby that could possibly be drawn on for additional support." (Lots of luck with that.) Lamb testifies that during this period she and Bultrowicz are discussing these

---

[810] Benghazi Committee Report, p. 57 n. 212.

[811] *Id.*, pp. 144-145.

[812] *Id.*, p. 145.

assets and options by phone with the latter's boss, Eric Boswell, and with Under Secretary Patrick Kennedy.[813]

Lamb later will explain that her (unidentified) "liaison" "had constant contact with the Annex. We had almost full-time connection to the DS agents that were on the ground . . ." Lamb later claims information received by the DSCC from the DSAs in Benghazi was relayed to Patrick Kennedy.[814]

Lamb and Bultrowicz may be in the DSCC, but Kennedy is not. (Is he embarrassed Benghazi has blown up in his face? He should be.) Instead, except for the marathon 7:30 Meeting teleconference, he remains in his office, monitoring emails, making and receiving telephone calls, "or coordinating activities as were required. . . ." From time to time during the crisis he goes to Secretary Clinton's office to update her on developments as he learns them from DSCC.[815]

Sixteen minutes after State is first notified, at 4:05 p.m. in Washington (10:05 p.m. Benghazi time), the State Department Operations Center issues an "Ops Alert" email. This is 23 minutes after the initial assault begins. This Alert notifies numerous senior State Department officials, the White House Situation Room, the office of the Director of National Intelligence, the FBI and others the Benghazi Mission Compound is under assault.[816] The Alert states:

> U.S. Diplomatic Mission in Benghazi Under Attack: The Regional Security Officer reports the diplomatic mission is under attack. Embassy Tripoli reports approximately *20 armed people fired shots; explosions* have been heard as well. Ambassador Stevens, who is currently in Benghazi, and four COM [Chief of Mission/Embassy] personnel are in the compound safe haven. The 17th of February militia is providing security support.[817]

---

[813] *Id.*, pp. 144-145.

[814] *Id.*, p. 145.

[815] *Id.*, pp. 145-146.

[816] Benghazi Committee Report, p. 34; CBS Benghazi Timeline; and Hayes, The Benghazi Talking Points.

[817] Sensitive But Unclassified State Department Ops Alert Email to Numerous Parties Re "U.S. Diplomatic Mission in Benghazi Under Attack" (Sept. 11, 2012; 4:05 p.m.) (emphasis added), Judicial Watch Document Archive (Posted Feb. 25, 2015); Benghazi Committee Report, p. 146; Sharyl Attkisson, "Emails Detail Unfolding Benghazi Attack," CBS News online (Oct. 24, 2012); Jake Tapper and John Parkinson, "White House Responds to Release of Real-Time Emails About Benghazi Attack," ABC News

(Query: Does this sound like State is describing a "spontaneous protest," as the Obama administration shortly will assert? The DSA agents on the ground this night later all will testify they report nothing tonight to State about a protest, and nothing about a Video.[818]) The Alert's number of individuals in the safe haven will prove erroneous. Shockingly, despite some news reports to the contrary, it appears the Pentagon's National Military Command Center is not even on the distribution list for this Ops Alert![819]

Secretary of State Hillary Clinton reportedly learns of the Benghazi assaults at around 4:00 p.m. Washington time, when Steve Mull, the Department's Executive Secretary, races to her office with the news.[820] At the latest, this occurs at (or shortly after) 4:05 p.m., when State's Ops Alert is disseminated. In her memoir Clinton writes she immediately calls National Security Advisor Tom Donilon. She also calls CIA Director David Petraeus, whose agency she knows operates the Annex in Benghazi with what she claims is a "heavy security force." (However, Clinton neglects to relate any details of either conversation.[821] Moreover, according to two Select Committee members, this call with Petraeus does not occur until 5:38 p.m., nearly two hours into the crisis. It will be their only conversation on this Night of Benghazi! They do not even speak after the CIA Annex comes under attack, at 6:34 p.m. Washington time.[822])

The White House

About the time the Ops Alert is triggered, White House officials learn of the attacks. At the time, the president is visiting wounded

---

online (Oct. 24, 2012) ("Tapper and Parkinson, White House Responds to Release of Real-Time Emails About Benghazi Attack"); and CBS Benghazi Timeline.

[818] Benghazi Committee Report, p. 145.

[819] Sensitive But Unclassified State Department Ops Alert Email to Numerous Parties Re "U.S. Diplomatic Mission in Benghazi Under Attack" (Sept. 11, 2012; 4:05 p.m.), Judicial Watch Document Archive (Posted Feb. 25, 2015); and Benghazi Committee Report, pp. 56-57.

[820] CBS Benghazi Timeline; and Clinton, *Hard Choices*, Chap. 17, p. 391.

[821] Clinton, *Hard Choices*, Chap. 17, p. 392.

[822] Additional Views of Reps. Jordan and Pompeo, pp. 444-445.

warriors at Walter Reed Medical Center when he likely is first told of the crisis at about 4:05 p.m.[823]

The Pentagon

Within the Defense Department's colossal structure, the first entity to receive notification of the Benghazi assault apparently is United States Africa Command.[824] According to the Select Committee, AFRICOM receives notice at 10:15 p.m. Stuttgart (and Benghazi) time, just over 30 minutes into the attack. (Why it doesn't immediately alert the Pentagon's National Military Command Center ("NMCC"), the Pentagon's operations center, is unknown.) Initially, AFRICOM appears to have very sketchy intelligence regarding what is occurring on the ground in Benghazi. Soon thereafter, AFRICOM learns Ambassador Stevens has gone missing.[825]

(General Ham, head of AFRICOM, later recalls receiving first word of the attack some 20 minutes or so earlier.[826] The author relies on the time adopted by the Select Committee.)

According to the Select Committee, news of the Benghazi attack does not reach the Pentagon's NMCC until *4:32 p.m. – an astonishing 50 minutes after the assault begins, and 27 minutes after State's first "Ops Alert" issues!* Members of the Joint Staff and the Secretary of Defense's staff are then notified.[827] In his memoir, Secretary Panetta intimates he learns of the attack sometime before approximately 4:30 p.m.,[828] although this likely happens a few minutes later.

---

[823] Geraldo Rivera and Craig Rivera, "Where Was President Obama During Benghazi Terror Attack?" Geraldo At Large, Fox News Channel (June 9, 2013) ("Rivera and Rivera, Where Was President Obama During Benghazi Terror Attack?") (*Watch video there*; Go to 2:18-30).

[824] For more information about AFRICOM, see its website at www.Africom.mil/.

[825] Benghazi Committee Report, p. 56; and *Id.*, Appendix G, Defense Dept. Timeline, p. 573.

[826] Rosen, Top Defense Officials Briefed Obama on "Attack" Not Video or Protest.

[827] Benghazi Committee Report, pp. 56-57, and Select Benghazi Timeline, p. 559.

[828] Panetta, *Worthy Fights*, Chap. 16, p. 427 ("On September 11, as I was heading out of my office with General Dempsey for my weekly meeting with the president at the White House, I received the first reports of violence at our diplomatic compound in Benghazi . . . I arrived at the White House between 4:30 and 4:45 p.m., and Dempsey and I presented what little information we had to the president as soon as we entered the Oval Office. . . ."). See also CBS Benghazi Timeline.

THE TRUE ACCOUNT OF VALOR AND ABANDONMENT

The staff of the Director of Operations of the Joint Chiefs of Staff contacts AFRICOM to seek additional information regarding the situation on the ground in Benghazi.[829] (Lots of luck with that. AFRICOM knows very few "facts," and some of these are misinformation.)

The CIA

It is more difficult to ascertain when the Central Intelligence Agency first learns of the Benghazi attacks. Presumably, the CIA case officers at the Benghazi CIA Annex alert the agency's headquarters in Langley, Virginia promptly while their GRS bodyguards are jocking up to head to the Mission. Remarkably, the Annex Chief of Base (known only as "Bob") later will tell *The Washington Post* he only speaks with CIA headquarters in a single phone call on this Night of Benghazi! "Bob" reportedly asserts it lasts a mere two minutes before Bob claims "I just cut it short."[830] (Yet another of many inexplicable events on this terrible night.) ■

---

[829] Benghazi Committee Report, p. 57.

[830] Goldman and Miller, Former CIA Chief in Benghazi Challenges the Story Line of the New Movie '13 Hours.'

35

"*Stand Down!* You Need to *Wait!*"

One of the most contentious issues in the saga of Benghazi is whether Team Annex is delayed in leaving the Annex to assist the Americans at the Mission. Some members of Team Annex maintain they *are* delayed; the CIA Chief of Base at the Annex insists they are *not*. This chapter examines who (if anyone) is telling the truth.

Back at the CIA Annex in Benghazi, it is now nearing 10:00 p.m. As the militants are abandoning their attempts to breach the Villa's safe haven, the armed GRS security contractors have loaded their weapons, ammo, first aid kits and other gear into two armored CIA vehicles. At least some of these men are sitting in these vehicles, ready to go, double- and triple-checking their weapons and gear. Over the past twelve minutes or so they have been seeking permission from their superiors to move out to the Mission Compound to attempt to rescue the besieged Americans there. Repeatedly, these supervisors – "Bob" the Chief of Base, his Deputy Chief of Base, and the GRS operators' Team Lead – all have ordered the men to "wait" before going to the diplomatic outpost.[831] The Chief of Base tells the GRS agents he is trying to get them some "technicals" (trucks armed with heavy machine guns), which the Team Lead has requested.[832]

---

[831] Benghazi Committee Report, pp. 38-47 ("GRS 4" operator (believed to be Kris "Tanto" Paronto): ". . . I looked at [the Chief of Base] and the team leader and said, hey, we're ready to go. [The Chief of Base] looked at the team leader, and he said tell these guys they need to wait. The team leader looks at me and says you guys need to wait"), p. 43; Baier, 13 Hours at Benghazi: The Inside Story (*Watch video there*; Go to 6:45-52); and Griffin, CIA Operators Were Denied Request for Help During Benghazi Attack (". . . When he [Tyrone Woods] and others heard the shots fired, they informed their higher ups at the annex to tell them what they were hearing and requested permission to go to the consulate and help out. They were told to 'stand down,' according to sources familiar with the exchange. Soon after, they again were told to 'stand down'").

[832] Benghazi Committee Report, pp. 38-41; and Fox News, Top CIA Officer in Benghazi Delayed Response to Terrorist Attack ("In a statement to Fox News, a senior intelligence official did allow that the security team was delayed from responding while the CIA's top officer in Benghazi tried to rally local support").

THE TRUE ACCOUNT OF VALOR AND ABANDONMENT

Is a "Stand Down" Order Issued?

It remains hotly disputed whether there is any formal "stand down" order from the Chief of Base. He later will deny issuing one.[833] The CIA also rejects the claim.[834] However, one unnamed GRS operator later testifies before the Select Committee there *is* a definite "stand down" command.[835] And at least two GRS agents ("Tanto" Paronto and "Tig" Tiegen) later tell interviewers they are told to wait.[836] They repeat their claim in the *13 Hours* book on which they collaborated with author Mitchell Zuckoff.[837] On Fox News Paronto insists:

> It happened on the ground – all I can talk about is what happened on the ground that night. . . . To us. To myself, twice – and to Tig, once. It happened that night. It happened. We were told to wait, stand – and stand down. We were delayed three times.[838]

Despite these assertions by men who are here on the ground at the Annex this night, a Senate Select Intelligence Committee Report issued in January 2014 astonishingly concludes:

---

[833] Benghazi Committee Report (". . . I did not issue a stand-down order"); and Goldman and Miller, Former CIA Chief in Benghazi Challenges the Story Line of the New Movie '13 Hours' ("Bob": "There never was a stand-down order. . . . At no time did I ever second-guess that the team would depart"), p. 41.

[834] Juju Chang, "*'Secret Soldiers of Benghazi'* Discusses Real-Life Events Behind '*13 Hours,*'" ABC News (Jan. 16, 2016) ("Chang, *'Secret Soldiers of Benghazi'* Discusses Real-Life Events Behind '*13 Hours'*") (*Watch video there*; Go to 3:56 - 4:02) (quoting CIA as calling movie's claims "shameful" and a "distortion of the events," and denying any "stand down" order), showing clip of *13 Hours: The Secret Soldiers of Benghazi.*

[835] Benghazi Committee Report, pp. 46-47 (Testimony of "GRS 1," believed to be John "Tig" Tiegen"); and *Id.* (One GRS to another: ". . . [H]e's [Chief of Base] telling us to stand down"), p. 44. See also Interview of John "Tig" Tiegen and Others with Megyn Kelly, "The Kelly File," Fox News Channel (Jan. 4, 2016) (*Watch video there*; Go to 7:38-50).

[836] Fox News, Top CIA Officer in Benghazi Delayed Response to Terrorist Attack; Interview of Kris "Tanto" Paronto with Sean Hannity, "Sean Hannity Radio Show" (April 5, 2017) (Paronto: GRS operators were told to wait three times, then disregarded their orders and went to the Mission Compound anyway); and Hayes and Joscelyn, The Benghazi Report.

[837] Zuckoff, *13 Hours*, Chaps. 4-5, pp. 94-111.

[838] Fox News, Top CIA Officer in Benghazi Delayed Response to Terrorist Attack; and Baier, 13 Hours at Benghazi: The Inside Story (*Watch video there*; Go to 8:38-53).

THE BENGHAZI BETRAYAL

. . . The Committee explored claims that there was a "stand down" order given to the security team at the Annex. Although some members of the security team expressed frustration that they were unable to respond more quickly to the Mission compound, the Committee found *no evidence of intentional delay or obstruction* by the Chief of Base or any other party.[839]

(*What? No evidence?* The author notes this Senate report is adopted in the waning days of Democrat control of the U.S. Senate and its committees. GRS agent Tanto Paronto says of the Senate committee's conclusion, "I don't know where they got that. . . . That's just silly. . . ."[840])

Weighing the preponderance of the evidence, it seems reasonably clear to the author the Chief of Base and Team Lead *do* tell the GRS operators to "wait" multiple times before the agents leave for the Mission Compound.[841] (It appears equally clear the inappropriately-named Senate Intelligence Committee is full of crap on this issue.)

Author Zuckoff (and his GRS collaborators), as noted, and the makers of the movie *13 Hours* both include a "stand down" scene in their stories.[842] Of course, this obviously is an attempt (successful) to heighten their narratives' dramatic appeal. It is not evidence. However, Kris Paronto describes the *13 Hours* movie as "very accurate."[843]

---

[839] Sen. Intelligence Committee Benghazi Report (Redacted; emphasis added; footnotes omitted), p. 5.

[840] Interview of Kris "Tanto" Paronto and Other GRS Agents with Megyn Kelly, "The Kelly File," Fox News Channel (Jan. 4, 2016) (*Watch video there*; Go to 13:10-46).

[841] Benghazi Committee Report, p. 41 (Chief of Base: "I may have said wait because we were trying to get this technical truck that the team lead wanted. But it wasn't 10 minutes, or 5 minutes. It was a short period of time. . . . The team lead was always cleared to go"); *Id.* (Q: "Team leader told you to wait?" A: "Yes"), p. 43; and Goldman and Miller, Former CIA Chief in Benghazi Challenges the Story Line of the New Movie *'13 Hours'* (Mitchell Zuckoff: "I think the evidence is extremely strong that the [GRS] guys' account is far more credible" than that of the CIA Chief of Base). See also Baier, New Revelations on Attack in Benghazi (*Watch video there*; Go to 20:07-28).

[842] See Zuckoff, *13 Hours*, Chaps. 4-5, pp. 94-111; and Chang, *"Secret Soldiers of Benghazi"* Discusses Real-Life Events Behind *"13 Hours"* (*Watch video there*; Go to 3:26-52), showing clip of *13 Hours: The Secret Soldiers of Benghazi*.

[843] Interview of Kris "Tanto" Paronto with Sean Hannity, "Sean Hannity Radio Show" (April 5, 2017).

Zuckoff later claims he makes "multiple requests" to the CIA to speak with "Bob," but is denied each time.[844]

Note none of this even would be an issue if the CIA and State Department facilities are co-located in the same facility, as Greg Hicks claims federal law requires.[845] The DSA and GRS agents already would be in one outpost, together with the Ambassador, Sean Smith, and the CIA personnel.

(It may be useful to examine the parties' motives to distort the truth. The Chief of Base, his deputy, and his GRS Team Lead naturally do not wish to be blamed for delaying a rescue mission in a life-and-death situation. And they certainly do not want to be held responsible for contributing to Chris Stevens' and Sean Smith's deaths. On the other hand, it is difficult to see what the Team Annex members stand to gain by lying. Each of them consistently has told the same story. Under either scenario, they still are heroes. The only reason to lie apparent to the author is to promote their possible personal vindictiveness against the Chief of Base. As noted above, according to the GRS members "Bob" is not their biggest fan. However, this seems a thin reed to support such an elaborate, coordinated and lengthy effort to deceive. But whoever is telling the truth, it seems *someone* commits perjury before the Select Committee.)

Back at the Annex, during this chaotic period the Chief of Base constantly is on his cell phone "calling partner militia organizations for assistance."[846] He later testifies he has called the police, 17 February Brigade, other militias, and Libyan intelligence, among others.[847] Now the Team Lead also begins making phone calls seeking to generate help.[848]

The personnel at the Annex are using a shared radio frequency with the Mission Compound staff. During this delay, by this radio the diplomatic security team members under attack at the Mission repeatedly beg the Annex group for assistance. As 10:00 p.m. comes and goes at the Annex, the security contractors are getting increasingly

---

[844] Goldman and Miller, Former CIA Chief in Benghazi Challenges the Story Line of the New Movie *'13 Hours.'*

[845] Hicks, What the Benghazi Attack Taught Me About Hillary Clinton.

[846] Benghazi Committee Report, pp. 38-40; and Sen. Intelligence Committee Benghazi Report (Redacted), p. 4.

[847] Benghazi Committee Report, pp. 38-40.

[848] *Id.*, pp. 42-43 and 46.

anxious and frustrated to leave for the Mission.[849] The GRS operators radio to the personnel at the Mission that the former have been told to wait.[850] The Mission security guards respond with increasing desperation:

> It was, GRS, where are you? Consulate's been overrun. Where are you? *Where are you?* Get your asses over here. We need your help. *Where are you?*[851]

According to Team Annex, chief DSA Alec Henderson pleads by radio to the Annex, *"If you guys don't get here, we're all going to f***ing die!"*[852]

Meanwhile, the CIA's Chief of Base continues working the phones at the Annex, trying to secure assistance (including gun trucks or technicals) for the Annex security team from "Libyan partner organizations," including local militias.[853] (Doesn't this perceived urgent need to beg third parties for heavy weapons establish that security in Benghazi was woefully inadequate before the attacks?) Ultimately, the Chief of Base is unsuccessful in obtaining any help from the CIA's Libyan "partners."[854] "Bob" later tells *The Washington Post* the militias that he and his deputy contact are "evasive." "Bob" claims one militia offers to shelter the U.S. personnel at a militia compound, and others "didn't necessarily want to help us, and some just didn't know what to do."[855]

---

[849] E.g., *Id.* ("Meanwhile, the Annex team members became anxious to depart"; Security contractor to Team Lead: "Hey, look, you know, we got to get going. We got to go. We got to go"), pp. 38-44.

[850] *Id.*, p. 43.

[851] *Id.*, p. 44. See also Fox News, Top CIA Officer in Benghazi Delayed Response to Terrorist Attack (GRS agent Kris "Tanto" Paronto: "We're starting to get calls from the State Department guys saying, 'Hey, we're taking fire, we need you guys here, we need help").

[852] Benghazi Committee Report, p. 9; Interview of Kris "Tanto" Paronto and Others with Megyn Kelly, "The Kelly File," Fox News Channel (Jan. 4, 2016) (*Watch video there*; Go to 9:34-46); and Zuckoff, *13 Hours*, Prologue, p. 4, and Chap. 5, p. 110.

[853] Benghazi Committee Report ("... Chief is like, hey. Yeah, I know. I'm just trying – like, hang on. I'm trying to make some – we're trying to get the technicals. We're trying to ... get you guys some weapons"), pp. 38-41; and Goldman and Miller, Former CIA Chief in Benghazi Challenges the Story Line of the New Movie *'13 Hours.'*

[854] Benghazi Committee Report, pp. 40 and 42.

[855] Goldman and Miller, Former CIA Chief in Benghazi Challenges the Story Line of the New Movie *'13 Hours.'*

Who, if anyone, orders the Chief of Base to give the "stand down" orders to the contractors? As noted, the Chief of Base adamantly denies he ever gives a "stand down" order. He claims he approves the GRS operators going, and is merely trying to secure additional resources for them. The Deputy Chief of Base supports his boss's story. This deputy later testifies the Chief of Base responds "Absolutely" when the Team Lead tells the chief "We got to go get those guys."[856] (More discrepancies.)

The CIA Chief of Base admits there was "a very short delay" when he "may have said wait" while he seeks these resources.[857] Is this his own decision? (If so, should the Chief of Base be sanctioned for a reckless decision? Or is he justified in attempting to cover the fact the CIA has vital secret operations being conducted out of the Annex, whose secrecy "Bob" wishes to maintain? And if so, what *are* those secret operations? Are they worth endangering the life of a U.S. ambassador and six other American government personnel?)

After more tense minutes of waiting, GRS agent John "Tig" Tiegen exits his vehicle and approaches the Chief of Base ("COB"), the latter's deputy and the Team Lead. Tiegen later testifies the following conversation ensues:

GRS: . . . Hey, . . . we've got to get over there. We're losing the initiative.

COB: Stand down, you need to wait. You need to come up with a plan.

GRS: No, it's too late to come up with a plan. We need to get over in the area, get eyes on, and then we can come up with a plan.[858]

Tig later confirms, "'Stand down, you need to wait.' That was from the chief of base . . . He used those exact words"[859]

---

[856] Benghazi Committee Report, p. 48.

[857] *Id.* (Chief of Base: ". . . I never had any doubt about the GRS people going to the State Department compound. I had great concerns and great worry about it but I did not, I did not tell anybody to stand down"), p. 41.

[858] *Id.*, pp. 46-47.

[859] Interview of John "Tig" Tiegen and Others with Megyn Kelly, "The Kelly File," Fox News Channel (Jan. 4, 2016) (*Watch video there*; Go to 7:38-50). See also Fox News, Top CIA Officer in Benghazi Delayed Response to Terrorist Attack (GRS agent John "Tig" Tiegen: "It had probably been 15 minutes I think, and . . . I just said, 'Hey, you know, we gotta – we need to get over there, we're losing the initiative. . . .' And Bob just looks straight at me and said, 'Stand down, you need to wait'"); and

His point made, an angry Tig returns to his vehicle. As the GRS agents sit anxiously in those vehicles, the terrorists are continuing to light the Mission's Villa and other buildings on fire. As Zuckoff describes the scene at the Annex, "From their idling vehicles, the [GRS] operators could vaguely see the orange flames rising from the Compound. With their doors flung open, they could hear chanting in the distance."[860]

Disputing the Chief of Base's version, one GRS operator later testifies, "But to me, no matter what, when he said stand down, or wait, or don't go, whatever, . . . I believe if we didn't leave on our own, we would have never left."[861] In a later newspaper interview the Chief of Base counters this assertion. ". . . [T]here never was any question that there was going to be a rescue mission. . . ."[862] (Yet another disputed version of events among many on this Night of Benghazi.)

While the aggravated GRS men are cooling their heels, a CIA civilian translator (a "non-shooter" with no military training) has been "recruited" to go with Team Annex in case they need to coordinate the Mission defense with friendly Benghazi militias.[863] Although he is not weapons-qualified, the interpreter doesn't hesitate to join Team Annex. Tanto Paronto hands him a loaded pistol. The man rushes inside a building to grab his helmet and armor, and swiftly returns.[864] (He is one intrepid man; he must be frightened out of his mind, but he goes.)

Team Annex Defies Orders

According to the surviving GRS operators (and the movie *13 Hours*), Tyrone Woods gathers Team Annex near the vehicles and tells them, "It's up to you. None of you have to go. But we are the only help they have."[865] Tanto Paronto later will insist this incident *did*

Baier, 13 Hours at Benghazi: The Inside Story (*Watch video there*; Go to 6:59 - 7:13). See also John Tiegen's website at https://www.johntiegen.com/.

[860] Zuckoff, *13 Hours*, Chap. 4, p. 101.

[861] Benghazi Committee Report, p. 47.

[862] Goldman and Miller, Former CIA Chief in Benghazi Challenges the Story Line of the New Movie *'13 Hours.'*

[863] Benghazi Committee Report, pp. 37-38.

[864] Zuckoff, *13 Hours*, Chap. 4, pp. 99-101.

[865] Interview of Kris "Tanto" Paronto and Other GRS Agents with Megyn Kelly, "The Kelly File," Fox News Channel (Jan. 4, 2016) (*Watch video there*; Go to 9:18-36); and

THE TRUE ACCOUNT OF VALOR AND ABANDONMENT

happen. All of the GRS agents elect to go.[866] (Even if this dramatic moment had not actually happened, something very like it must have occurred within the minds of the GRS men. Because in fact, they all know they do *not* have to go, but they all *do* go.)

Eventually, the five Annex security team contractors have had enough. They decide to disobey their "wait" orders.[867] One GRS operator testifies, "And so we can hear the State Department's cries for help on the radio, and we just reached a point where we decided to leave on our own."[868] Ultimately, their Team Lead joins them and reportedly tells the Chief of Base, "Hey, Chief, look we're going."[869]

Then, at about 10:03 to 10:05 p.m. – approximately 21 to 23 minutes after the first calls for help from the Mission Compound – the GRS security contractors and their Team Lead commandeer the two armored CIA vehicles and (along with their frightened translator) drive out the Annex's gate to aid their fellow Americans under attack at the nearby diplomatic outpost.[870] Before leaving the Annex compound, Tanto Paronto asks the CIA leaders who remain behind to get a drone and a Spectre gunship.[871] But for the bravery of these seven men, several more American lives might have been lost this night.[872]

Chang, "Secret Soldiers of Benghazi" Discusses Real-Life Events Behind *"13 Hours"* (*Watch video there*; Go to 3:08-27), showing clip of *13 Hours: The Secret Soldiers of Benghazi*.

[866] Megyn Kelly, "The Kelly File," Fox News Channel (Jan. 4, 2016) (*Watch video there;* Go to 3:15-24 and 9:18-36).

[867] Zuckoff, *13 Hours,* Chap. 5, pp. 110-111.

[868] Benghazi Committee Report, p. 42; and Baier, 13 Hours at Benghazi: The Inside Story (*Watch video there*; Go to 7:14-21).

[869] Benghazi Committee Report, p. 39.

[870] *Id.* ("At some point, though, the wait was too long, and we decided, you know, we couldn't wait any longer and we left...."), pp. 39, 42 and 47; and Sen. Intelligence Committee Benghazi Report (Redacted), p. 4. Compare Fox News, Top CIA Officer in Benghazi Delayed Response to Terrorist Attack ("After a delay of nearly 30 minutes, the security team headed to the besieged consulate without orders. They asked their CIA superiors to call for armed air support, which never came"); and Baier, 13 Hours at Benghazi: The Inside Story (Kris "Tanto" Paronto: Delay was "close to 25 minutes") (*Watch video there*; Go to 7:48-57).

[871] Baier, 13 Hours at Benghazi: The Inside Story (*Watch video there*; Go to 8:53 - 9:07).

[872] See Zuckoff's *"13 Hours"* for a riveting account of this rescue mission. As noted above, this book has since been made into a superb motion picture released by Paramount in early 2016 entitled *"13 Hours: The Secret Soldiers of Benghazi."*

The Risks of Team Annex's Departure

Team Annex's action does involve considerable risk. First, the Deputy Chief of Base is concerned Team Annex might meet elements of the "friendly" 17 February Brigade at the Mission Compound. The two allied groups could begin attacking each other in confusion.[873]

Second, there is also danger for the CIA personnel left behind. The GRS rescue team is taking all of the Annex's available shooters and "every piece of heavy automatic weapons, and every really solid defensive weaponry capability. . . ."[874] (This arguably contradicts the claims of some, discussed in Chapter 25, the CIA is collecting Libyan weapons at the Annex.) As noted, another GRS operator, "Oz" Geist, is away from the Annex, providing security for a CIA case agent who has a dinner meeting elsewhere in Benghazi.[875] If they encounter trouble, who will rescue *them*? The GRS team's departure effectively leaves the Annex defenseless until the rescue posse returns (if it ever does).[876]

Finally, the rescue risks exposing the CIA's secret facility and its operations in Benghazi. If a bunch of CIA security guards get involved in a firefight with a large gang of well-armed militants in Benghazi, the Annex's covert "cover" is virtually certain to be "blown."[877]

Could Team Annex Have Saved Stevens and Smith?

One of several nagging questions that endures from this Night of Benghazi is whether, had "Bob" not delayed them, Team Annex could have reached the Mission Compound in time to save Chris Stevens,

---

[873] Benghazi Committee Report (One GRS agent: ". . . [W]hen we rolled in [to the Mission Compound], we didn't know who we were going to be meeting"), pp. 47-49.

[874] *Id.*, pp. 48-49.

[875] Baier, 13 Hours at Benghazi: The Inside Story (*Watch video there*; Go to 13:12-41); Zuckoff, *13 Hours*, Chap. 4, p. 90; and Benghazi Committee Report, pp. 48-49.

[876] Benghazi Committee Report, pp. 48-49; and Goldman and Miller, Former CIA Chief in Benghazi Challenges the Story Line of the New Movie '13 Hours.'

[877] Zuckoff, *13 Hours* (". . . If the [GRS] operators' Quick Reaction Force remained at the Annex, the CIA wouldn't be forced to reveal or explain its presence in Benghazi. On the other hand, if American clandestine operators and contract security employees went into combat against radical Islamists, the battle would be guaranteed to attract global attention and massive scrutiny. Especially on September 11. . . ."), Chap. 5, p. 110.

Sean Smith or both. The answer is unknowable. Some members of Team Annex believe they *could* have saved the diplomats. In a subsequent Fox News interview Tanto Paronto asserts, "Yes, to me without the delay they would still be alive, my gut is yes." "Tig" Tiegen concurs. Tig adds, "I strongly believe if we'd have left immediately, they'd still be alive today."[878] In a separate ABC News interview, Tig says of the delay, "It cost the lives of Sean Smith and Ambassador Stevens."[879]

(The author believes this is unlikely. When they actually do leave the Annex, it will take the GRS team some 35 minutes to fight their way to the Mission Compound. Hence, even had they left the Annex at about 9:47 p.m., the earliest point they say they were all "jocked up" and ready to leave, they likely would not have arrived at the Mission until around 10:22. This is more than 20 minutes after the terrorists begin to set Ambassador Steven's Villa ablaze. Hence, the Team Annex members would have encountered the same toxic smoke Scott Wickland and the other DSA agents battled. And even had they found the two men, it is entirely possible they already would have succumbed to the smoke.

(However, it is critical to note the CIA Chief of Base knows nothing of these subsequent time periods and events when he issues his orders to wait. He cannot know whether his order is endangering further any of the seven Americans at the Mission. Out of prudence, he should assume it *is*.)

Conclusion Regarding Team Annex

The bottom line is the courageous members of Team Annex *do* load their six-shooters and ride to the rescue of their comrades at the Mission Compound. Any delay from the CIA Chief of Base or his deputy can only exacerbate an already daunting challenge. But it cannot diminish the heroism of Team Annex. ∎

---

[878] Fox News, Top CIA Officer in Benghazi Delayed Response to Terrorist Attack; and Baier, 13 Hours at Benghazi: The Inside Story (*Watch video there*; Go to 36:24-44). See also Interview of John "Tig" Tiegen and Other GRS Agents with Megyn Kelly, "The Kelly File," Fox News Channel (Possibly Jan. 4, 2016) (*Watch video there*; Go to 12:57 - 13:10).

[879] Chang, "Secret Soldiers of Benghazi" Discusses Real-Life Events Behind "*13 Hours*" (*Watch video there*; Go to 3:52-55), showing clip of *13 Hours: The Secret Soldiers of Benghazi*.

36

"F.E.S.T." or Famine

As Team Annex in Benghazi begins moving toward the Mission, a crusty former Marine at the State Department is in his office studying his computer screen intently.[880] **He is reading his agency's just-released 4:05 p.m. "Ops Alert."**

His concern grows with each word; his brow furrows more deeply. As he reads, he likely experiences a mixture of regret and excitement. He is sad his fellow Americans are in peril, but hopeful he and his colleagues may be able to help them.

The man is Mark Thompson. He is State's Deputy Coordinator for Operations of the Bureau of Counterterrorism. Thompson is among the U.S. government's leading counterterrorism experts. Basically, his job is to advise State's senior leadership on "operational terrorism matters," and to ensure the U.S. can respond rapidly to global terrorism crises. He is in direct charge of a key federal terror crisis response resource that stands at the ready on this Night of Benghazi.[881]

More specifically, along with his other duties Thompson heads the federal government's "Foreign Emergency Support Team" ("F.E.S.T."). (This is not to be confused with the "FAST" Marine platoons discussed below.) "The FEST is the U.S. government's only interagency, on-call, *short-notice* team poised to respond to *terrorist* incidents *worldwide*."[882] F.E.S.T. is part of State's Counterterrorism Bureau.[883] F.E.S.T. is the only part of this bureau charged with

---

[880] Thompson Oversight Committee Testimony (May 8, 2013) (Response to questions of Rep. Thomas Massie (R-KY)), p. 88.

[881] House Oversight Committee Hearings (May 8, 2013) (Introductory Remarks of Chairman Darrell Issa (R-CA)), p. 6.

[882] Benghazi Committee Report (emphasis added), p. 64, quoting State Dept. website ("State Department F.E.S.T. Webpage"); and House Oversight Committee Hearings (May 8, 2013) (Introductory Remarks of Chairman Darrell Issa (R-CA)), p. 6.

[883] State Department F.E.S.T. Webpage; and Thompson Oversight Committee Testimony (May 8, 2013) (Response to questions of Rep. Jason Chaffetz (R-UT)), pp. 36-39.

responding to a terrorism crisis.[884] Among other incidents, F.E.S.T. has "been deployed in response to a hostage-taking crisis and abductions of Americans," and is expert in hostage negotiations.[885]

When it comes to counterterrorism, Mark Thompson is the real deal. He is a former Marine veteran of 20 years. After being commissioned in 1977, as a Marine infantry officer Thompson leads platoons and companies of "Amphibious Ready Groups" in northern Europe, the Middle East and Africa. For four years, Thompson serves in the Western Pacific. In 1996 while still a Marine, Thompson is assigned to the State Department's Counterterrorism Office. When he retires from the Corps in 1998, State asks Thompson to stay on in a civilian counterterrorism position. He agrees to do so.[886]

While at State, Thompson has participated in – and in many cases led – F.E.S.T. hostage rescues and other missions around the world. Thompson's operations include (among others):

- 1997: State Department's lead officer in the return of Aimal (aka Amal) Kasi from Pakistan to the U.S. after a four-year international manhunt to stand trial for murdering two CIA employees;
- 1998: Operations officer in the State-led F.E.S.T. response to the bombings of U.S. embassies in Kenya and Tanzania (over 300 individuals murdered, including 12 Americans);
- 2000: Deployed with F.E.S.T. to Aden, Yemen in response to the terror bombing of the USS Cole (killing 17 U.S. sailors);
- 2001: Led F.E.S.T. unit to Latin America and achieved the safe recovery of hostages;
- 2002: Led F.E.S.T. to Asia, again securing the safe recovery of American hostages;
- 2004: Helped establish an "Office of Hostage Affairs" in wartime Baghdad, Iraq, which subsequently helped free U.S. and allied hostages;

---

[884] Thompson Oversight Committee Testimony (May 8, 2013) (Response to questions of Rep. Jason Chaffetz (R-UT)), p. 39.

[885] Benghazi Committee Report, p. 65; State Department F.E.S.T. Webpage; and Attkisson, *Stonewalled*, Chap. 4, p. 167.

[886] Prepared Statement of Mark I. Thompson, House Oversight Committee (May 8, 2013) ("Thompson Oversight Committee Prepared Testimony").

- 2006: Led a team to West Africa, obtaining release of American and other hostages; and
- 2009: Led F.E.S.T. team on a mission too classified to discuss at a House public hearing.[887]

Clearly, if you are in the U.S. government and you have a potential hostage situation, Mark Thompson is one of your first calls. In any rational world, Thompson will be a key part of the government's decision-making team on this Night of Benghazi. Instead, he virtually is shut out of this entire process. In subsequent testimony, Thompson will assert, ". . . I indicated that the portion of the [State Department] Counterterrorism Bureau that responds to crises, i.e., my part of the office, was pushed out of that discussion [concerning how to respond to and characterize the Benghazi attack]. . . ."[888]

Thompson's interagency F.E.S.T. team includes some 35 professionals from multiple federal agencies. These include State (including its Diplomatic Security Bureau), Defense (all branches), the FBI and other intelligence agencies, and still other agencies "as circumstances warrant."[889] Thompson's F.E.S.T. unit is loaded with counterterrorism professionals.[890]

The F.E.S.T. team itself is not comprised of "SWAT-type" personnel – the operators who are the actual "door kickers." Rather, F.E.S.T. members are the "facilitators" who "bring the operation and *coordinate* all aspects of a response" to a terrorist incident. In other words, F.E.S.T. *organizes, synchronizes and supports* the actions of the operators who kick in the doors with automatic weapons in hand.[891]

---

[887] Thompson Oversight Committee Prepared Testimony; House Oversight Committee Hearings (May 8, 2013) (Opening Remarks of Chairman Darrell E. Issa (R-CA)), p. 6; State Department F.E.S.T. Webpage; and "About CIA" Timeline, CIA website.

[888] Thompson Oversight Committee Testimony (May 8, 2013) (Response to questions of Rep. Eleanor Holmes Norton (D-D.C.)), p. 38. See also Toensing, Administration Relying on Shoddy Benghazi Report to Absolve Itself of Blame (". . . [Thompson] was excluded from all decisions, communications, and meetings on September 11 and 12, 2012. Why? . . ."; Note: Toensing is legal counsel for Gregory Hicks).

[889] State Department F.E.S.T. Webpage; Thompson Oversight Committee Prepared Testimony; and Thompson Oversight Committee Testimony (May 8, 2013) (Response to questions of Rep. Kerry Bentivolio (R-MI)), pp. 93-94.

[890] Thompson Oversight Committee Testimony (May 8, 2013) (Response to questions of Rep. Thomas Massie (R-KY)), p. 88.

[891] Thompson Oversight Committee Testimony (May 8, 2013) (Response to questions of Rep. Kerry Bentivolio (R-MI)), p. 94.

THE TRUE ACCOUNT OF VALOR AND ABANDONMENT

(However, one gets the impression Thompson himself could do some pretty serious "door-kicking" if the need arose.)

According to Thompson, at least twice yearly F.E.S.T. practices a "complete deployment to an overseas location to work with our interagency partners."[892] F.E.S.T. has its own dedicated aircraft. Critically, once a decision is made to deploy, "... the FEST is capable of launching *within four hours*."[893] (As will be seen, this would beat the response time of all three military forces ultimately launched on this night.)

There is some disparity in the evidence regarding who actually has authority to deploy F.E.S.T. The Select Benghazi Committee report states, "... FEST deploys overseas at the request of the Chief of Mission or the State Department, and can augment both U.S. and host nation capabilities with specialized crisis response expertise."[894] (If this is correct, Hillary Clinton herself can launch a F.E.S.T. team.) This is consistent with State's website.[895] However, the Select Committee further states (somewhat inconsistently), "Typically, the State Department requests deployment of the FEST in conjunction with the Joint Staff."[896] Mark Thompson himself later testifies State does not make the deploy decision. He explains, "... The National Security Council Deputies Committee authorizes the deployment...."[897] Because Thompson heads the F.E.S.T., the author assumes he is the reliable authority on this issue of who actually directs his team to deploy. Regrettably, this issue will prove purely academic to the Americans under siege in Benghazi.

On this September 11, after quickly reading and more slowly re-reading State's Ops Alert, Thompson's first call is to his counter-terrorism contacts at the National Security Council to learn more

---

[892] *Id.* (Response to questions of Rep. Thomas Massie (R-KY)), p. 88.

[893] Benghazi Committee Report (emphasis added), p. 65; Thompson Oversight Committee Testimony (May 8, 2013) (Response to questions of Rep. Jason Chaffetz (R-UT)), p. 36; and *Id.* (Response to questions of Rep. Tim Walberg (R-MI)) ("... That process [for deploying F.E.S.T.] ... is not one that is bureaucratic. It's one that can go from a cold start to wheels-up ... within hours"), p. 62.

[894] Benghazi Committee Report, pp. 64-65.

[895] State Department F.E.S.T. webpage at www.state.gov/j/ct/programs/fest/.

[896] Benghazi Committee Report, p. 65.

[897] Thompson Oversight Committee Testimony (May 8, 2013) (Response to questions of Rep. Mark Meadows (R-NC)), p. 92.

intelligence.[898] Thompson then begins to contact his F.E.S.T. unit members to advise them to be ready to launch on a moment's notice.[899] He is confident his team will be deploying to Libya this evening. According to Thompson's later testimony, the FBI members of F.E.S.T. endorse a F.E.S.T. mission in response to the Benghazi crisis. So do the Department of Defense members of the F.E.S.T. team.[900]

However, when Thompson contacts the office of Patrick Kennedy regarding the possibility of deploying F.E.S.T. to Libya, things get sticky. That office indicates to Thompson this might not be the right time to utilize F.E.S.T.[901]

F.E.S.T. sounds like the perfect asset to dispatch in this foreign crisis likely involving terrorists. This is even truer when, a short while later, State learns its ambassador is missing in Benghazi.[902] Yet, as explained below, inexplicably F.E.S.T. never will launch on this Night of Benghazi. ■

---

[898] *Id.* (Response to questions of Rep. Thomas Massie (R-KY)), p. 88.

[899] Attkisson, *Stonewalled* (citing unnamed Obama administration source, ". . . FEST team members 'instinctively started packing' as soon as they heard of the Benghazi attacks . . ."), Chap. 4, p. 168.

[900] *Id.* (Response to questions of Rep. Mark Meadows (R-NC)), p. 92.

[901] *Id.* (Response to questions of Rep. Thomas Massie (R-KY)), p. 88.

[902] *Id.* (Response to questions of Rep. Thomas Massie (R-KY)) (Asked when it would be appropriate to deploy F.E.S.T. if not on this Night of Benghazi: "There is no answer to that, sir"), p. 88; and Attkisson, *Stonewalled*, Chap. 4, pp. 166-167 and 222.

37

Rescue Posse: "Team Tripoli" Saddles Up

The Team Annex and F.E.S.T. members are not the only patriots hoping to aid the besieged Americans at the Mission Compound. Help eventually arrives from fellow Americans outside Benghazi. But it is not sent from the White House or the Pentagon or AFRICOM or CIA headquarters or State at Foggy Bottom. It comes from a handful of CIA contract security staff and military personnel in the Libyan capital of Tripoli.

There, while the GRS men in Benghazi are arguing with their CIA Chief of Base, and Mark Thompson is alerting his F.E.S.T. members in Washington, the CIA Chief of Station in Tripoli quickly assembles his own response team. It will be dubbed "Team Tripoli." It consists of the CIA's top GRS team leader in Libya, three other GRS agents, and a CIA linguist.[903]

Team Tripoli also includes two special operations servicemen.[904] The Defense Secretary and Joint Chiefs of Staff in Washington do not even know these two U.S. military personnel in the rescue party are stationed in Tripoli![905] (Their exact mission in Tripoli is somewhat murky; a redacted Senate Intelligence Committee report describes them as working for a "separate special operations task force."[906] A DoD press release issued in May 2013 states, "Special operations personnel . . . were in Libya in general support of embassy security and to aid the movement of embassy personnel."[907])

---

[903] Zuckoff, *13 Hours*, Chap. 9, p. 197; and Spencer S. Hsu, "CIA Officers Detail Part of Bloody Benghazi Attack at Terrorism Trial," *The Washington Post* online (Oct. 11, 2017) ("HSU, CIA Officers Detail Part of Bloody Benghazi Attack at Terrorism Trial").

[904] Jim Garamone, "DOD Cooperates with Congress on Benghazi Probes," Defense Dept. website (May 8, 2013) ("Pentagon Press Release, 'DOD Cooperates with Congress on Benghazi Probes'").

[905] Benghazi Committee Report (". . . The Secretary and the Joint Staff did not know those personnel were in Tripoli, much less were they considered as one of the potential assets to respond to the events in Benghazi. . . ."), p. 113.

[906] Sen. Intelligence Committee Benghazi Report (Redacted), p. 29.

[907] Pentagon Press Release, "DOD Cooperates with Congress on Benghazi Probes."

Team Tripoli is an improvised band that never has trained together as a unit. In less than an hour the rescue squad is assembled, and an aircraft has been arranged for the 450 mile trip to Benghazi.[908] (This contrasts starkly to the inaction and lack of exigency tonight that typifies the military commands supposedly activated by the U.S. government in Washington.)

Sending four of the five remaining Tripoli GRS security operators to Benghazi will leave the CIA staff in Tripoli highly vulnerable. Nevertheless, with the full support of Ambassador Steven's deputy, Gregory Hicks, the Tripoli Chief of Station makes the gutsy decision to attempt the operation.

One of the GRS contractors on Team Tripoli is former U.S. Navy SEAL Glen A. "Bub" Doherty. Doherty knows three of the GRS men stationed in Benghazi: Rone Woods, Jack Silva and Tanto Paronto. "Bub" looks forward to reuniting with them, although the circumstances certainly could be better.[909]

The diplomats at the U.S. Embassy in Tripoli, as well as the military personnel at AFRICOM, all support Team Tripoli's mission. However, it appears neither group plays any role in planning the operation or deploying the reaction team. According to the Select Committee, the CIA's Chief of Station in Tripoli (who as usual for security reasons has not been identified by name) is almost solely responsible for orchestrating this courageous endeavor.[910] (He deserves a medal, if he hasn't been awarded one already.)

Team Tripoli, "jocked up" with weapons and ammo and combat gear, arrives at Tripoli's Mitiga airport sometime between about 11:30 p.m. and 12:00 midnight, Benghazi time.

Near miraculously and with commendable foresight, just this very morning a CIA member of what will become Team Tripoli has negotiated an agreement to charter an aircraft if and as it might be needed in the future. Tonight shortly after learning of the attacks, the Tripoli CIA staff calls the airplane's owner. Reportedly for $30,000 in

---

[908] Benghazi Committee Report, pp. 54-55; and Pentagon Press Release, "DOD Cooperates with Congress on Benghazi Probes" (". . . [T]wo service members did go from Tripoli to Benghazi that evening. These personnel were members of a quick reaction force quickly put together").

[909] Zuckoff, *13 Hours*, Chap. 11, p. 245.

[910] Benghazi Committee Report, pp. 54 and 109.

THE TRUE ACCOUNT OF VALOR AND ABANDONMENT

U.S. dollars cash,[911] he agrees to take the response team to Benghazi promptly. (Because the plane is privately owned, it will be allowed to fly at night. This is in contrast to the Libyan military's C-130 aircraft, which is restricted to daylight flights.[912])

As they will do with Team Annex, Obama officials will tell the media after the fact this Team Tripoli all along is part of the pre-existing security forces available in Libya! Apparently reflecting comments by an unnamed State Department employee, CBS News reports "There was a *Quick Reaction Force on standby* in Tripoli to deploy *if needed*."[913]

(This is an obvious falsehood.[914] Team Tripoli is an improvised band of last-minute volunteers, not a pre-existing "Quick Reaction Force" on standby.[915] Team Tripoli does not even exist until the resourceful CIA Station Chief in Tripoli learns of the attacks in Benghazi, and immediately determines he must cobble together a rescue mission without delay. CBS News apparently needs a new source at State.) ■

---

[911] Hsu, CIA Officers Detail Part of Bloody Benghazi Attack at Terrorism Trial (Criminal trial testimony of two disguised CIA agents).

[912] Benghazi Committee Report, p. 55.

[913] CBS News, U.S. Memo Warned of High Risk of Libya Violence (emphasis added).

[914] For a pro-administration private entity's attempt to give Team Obama credit for Team Tripoli, see Media Matters, *The Benghazi Hoax* (emphasis added) (". . . Recall that in stark contrast to the claims that no help had been *sent by the Obama administration* to aid Americans in Benghazi, a seven-man security team *was scrambled* from the Libyan capital of Tripoli immediately after it became clear the diplomatic facility had come under attack. . . ."), Chap. XIII, p. 74.

[915] E.g., Pentagon Press Release, "DOD Cooperates with Congress on Benghazi Probes" (". . . [T]wo service members did go from Tripoli to Benghazi that evening. These personnel were members of a quick reaction force quickly put together").

38

"Fire! The Ambassador Is Missing!"

Back in the Benghazi Villa, at about 10:00 p.m. disaster strikes. The terrorists have been unable to breach the safe haven's fortified door. Even their attempts to shoot it open fail. Some of the attackers set fire to the Villa, including the area outside the safe haven. They use diesel oil apparently stored on the Mission's premises. The entire Villa quickly begins to fill with flames and heavy, noxious smoke.[916]

Watching security cameras in the Mission Compound's TOC, DSAs Henderson and Ubben realize to their horror the Villa is on fire. They "could see flames starting to lick out of the windows and black smoke started to pour out of the windows...." The two men understand the three Americans in the Villa are in "very big trouble." Within minutes of the fire starting, the DSAs in the TOC lose contact with the ambassador, and urgently report this fact to the lead security agent in Tripoli.[917]

In the meantime, from his safe haven perch, DSA Scott Wickland sees the attackers slowly have started to "kind of trickle out" of the Villa. For a moment his hopes surge. He observes the lights dim. Then Wickland realizes what he is seeing is not an electrical failure but *smoke!* Inside the safe haven, the Americans' fear now escalates to *terror*. They understand the militants are trying either to burn them alive or force them out of their refuge!

The panic of the men in the safe haven is immediate. *We have no fire masks!* As the Senate Intelligence Committee later will conclude, *"Benghazi [Mission Compound] was also severely under-resourced*

---

[916] Benghazi Committee Report, pp. 34-35; Sen. Intelligence Committee Benghazi Report, p. 5; Lamb Oversight Committee Prepared Testimony, p. 5; Zuckoff, *13 Hours* ("The attackers' intent was evident: They meant to use the Americans' own fuel to smoke them out or roast them alive"), Chap. 5, pp. 103-104; Baier, New Revelations on Attack in Benghazi (*Watch video there*; Go to 18:04 - 19:32); Baier, 13 Hours at Benghazi: The Inside Story (*Watch video there*; Go to 7:42-48); and Burnett, Benghazi Timeline: "We Are Under Attack" (*Watch video there*; Go to 4:29-50).

[917] Benghazi Committee Report, pp. 34-35.

with regard to weapons, ammunition, [non-lethal deterrents] and *fire safety equipment, including escape masks.*"[918]

Wickland later testifies he immediately tells Stevens and Smith they are going to have to move into the safe haven's bathroom. He begins crawling in that direction, yelling to Stevens and Smith, *"Follow me!"* From the bathroom (where the window is barred) he hopes to take his two protectees into a nearby bedroom with an emergency escape window that can be opened from the inside. Wickland later explains that when he arrives in the bathroom, acrid smoke is pouring in. He realizes Stevens and Smith have not followed him there. Because of the now-thick black smoke, Wickland and his charges have become separated. Due to this smoke, Wickland cannot see the two men; nor do they respond when the DSA calls out to them.[919]

Meanwhile, in another room Chris Stevens and Sean Smith are gasping for air. They are hugging the floor, praying the smoke and heat will rise to the ceiling. But their effort is futile. *They can't breathe! There is no oxygen!* Each gulp they inhale is more noxious than the last. Within moments, they begin to grow light-headed and nauseous. They become disoriented. Do they become unconscious before fully realizing their fate? One can only pray it is so.

Wickland later testifies due to the flames and toxic smoke, he becomes weak, and overcome by smoke and heat. (According to Gregory Hicks, a State Department medical officer later explains to him petroleum-based fires emit large quantities of highly dangerous cyanide gas.[920]) Wickland leaves the bathroom and crawls to his bedroom. There, he eventually escapes through the window. After catching his breath outside, Wickland goes back through the bedroom window into the safe haven multiple times. On each occasion, he is unable to locate either missing man in the dense diesel smoke.

---

[918] Sen. Intelligence Committee Benghazi Report (Redacted; emphasis added), p. 17. See also Benghazi ARB Report, p. 36 ("The Board also determined that the lack of fire safety equipment severely impacted the Ambassador's and Sean Smith's ability to escape the deadly smoke conditions").

[919] Benghazi Committee Report, p. 35; Sen. Intelligence Committee Benghazi Report, p. 5; Baier, 13 Hours at Benghazi: The Inside Story (*Watch video there*; Go to 9:29-58); and Baier, New Revelations on Attack in Benghazi (*Watch video there*; Go to 19:32 - 20:00).

[920] Hicks Oversight Committee Testimony (May 8, 2013), p. 26.

Eventually, Wickland realizes he will not survive another trip inside the Villa. The heat and choking smoke are just too overwhelming.[921]

Now outside again, Wickland unsteadily climbs a ladder to the Villa's roof. He pulls the ladder up behind him onto the roof. Once there, he begins to take gunfire from the militants. Wickland later says he understands at this point that down in the safe haven both Stevens and Smith probably have perished. At 10:14 p.m. (4:14 p.m. Washington time), Wickland radios to DSAs Henderson and Ubben in the Mission TOC that Stevens and Smith are "missing and unaccounted for."[922] It is horrific news. ∎

---

[921] Sen. Intelligence Committee Benghazi Report, p. 5; Zuckoff, *13 Hours*, Chap. 5, pp. 113-115; Hicks Oversight Committee Testimony (May 8, 2013), pp. 25-26; and Kennedy October 10 Briefing.

[922] Benghazi Committee Report, pp. 35-36 and 141; Sen. Intelligence Committee Benghazi Report, p. 5; Lamb Oversight Committee Prepared Testimony, p. 5; Baier, 13 Hours at Benghazi: The Inside Story (*Watch video there*; Go to 9:59 - 10:15); Zuckoff, *13 Hours*, Chap. 5, p. 115; and CBS Benghazi Timeline.

39

"If You Don't Get Here Soon, We're All Going to Die!"

As they leave the Annex, Rone Woods is driving the BMW, with Tanto Paronto at the wheel of the following Mercedes vehicle. Fearing such hazards as ambush, snipers and roadside explosives, all seven men in the armored SUVs constantly watch out for militants or unusual activity.[923] With all the armed Libyans on the streets, it will be virtually impossible for the GRS men to be completely certain who are friendlies, and who are the bad guys!

The GRS Team Lead's initial plan is to drive to one of the nearby militia or army facilities located on the way to the Mission, and secure some "technicals." Team Annex hopes to drive in those technicals the rest of the way to the Mission.[924]

The two vehicles at first take several side roads on a "back route" to avoid busy streets where the attackers at the Mission might see them coming.[925] Shortly after Team Annex departs the CIA facility, the distraught voice of an unidentified DSA from the Mission comes over their radios. "We need help. They're lighting the building on fire. . . filling with smoke."[926]

Roadblock!

A short while later the GRS team's SUVs approach a dark intersection. They encounter a militia roadblock comprised of "at least a couple vehicles" blocking "the most direct route" on the main road leading to the Mission's Front Gate. A number of armed Arab men are standing near these vehicles. Ominously, some are wearing black ski masks. Are they part of the force assaulting the Mission? Team Annex

---

[923] Zuckoff, *13 Hours*, Chap. 5, pp. 117-118.
[924] Benghazi Committee Report, p. 50.
[925] Zuckoff, *13 Hours*, Chap. 5, p. 117.
[926] *Id.*, Chap. 5, pp. 118-119.

fervently hopes these Arabs are with the 17 February militia.[927] They have no good option but to press on.

As they pull up to the blocked intersection and slow down, Team Annex hears one last, desperate radio call from the DSA agents: "You need to hurry up. The buildings are on fire! If you don't get here soon, we're all going to die!"[928]

Rone and Tanto park their vehicles. When the men at the roadblock do not raise their weapons, the armed GRS members slowly and cautiously exit their vehicles, weapons in hand. The Annex Team Lead and the CIA interpreter slowly approach the Arab men on foot. Weapons readied but lowered, the alert GRS agents watch intently from next to their SUVs.[929]

Suddenly, the men at the intersection begin receiving "ineffective, sporadic fire" from elsewhere. At first, it is difficult to tell the source of the gunshots. Then it becomes apparent the shots likely are coming from the direction of the Mission, which is still about 400 yards away. One militiaman at the roadblock drops to the ground and fires his machine gun towards the direction of the incoming fire. The firing stops.[930]

The interpreter and Team Lead learn to their great relief the Arabs at the intersection are indeed 17 February. The "commander" of these militiamen explains they were trying to approach the Mission Compound by this road, but retreated upon receiving fire. The commander agrees to help Team Annex attempt to retake control of the Mission grounds.[931]

Team Annex Splits Up

D.B. Benton and Tanto Paronto are becoming frustrated with this delay. They think, *We need to get moving!* Ever the Marine sniper, D.B. says, "Hey Tanto, let's get high." By this he means finding an elevated location on top of one of the surrounding buildings.[932] They may be

---

[927] Benghazi Committee Report, p. 49; and Zuckoff, *13 Hours*, Chap. 5, pp. 118-119.

[928] Baier, 13 Hours at Benghazi: The Inside Story (*Watch video there*; Go to 9:21-29); and Zuckoff, *13 Hours*, Chap. 5, pp. 119-120.

[929] *Id.*, Chap. 5, pp. 118-119.

[930] *Id.*, Chap. 5, pp. 120-122.

[931] *Id.*, Chap. 5, pp. 121-122; and Benghazi Committee Report, p. 50.

[932] Zuckoff, *13 Hours*, Chap. 5, p. 122.

THE TRUE ACCOUNT OF VALOR AND ABANDONMENT

able to pick off some militants who have been shooting at them and the 17 February militia at the intersection. With luck, they also hope to get a "bird's-eye view" of the Mission grounds to assist Team Annex's arrival there. (This is important because, with the DSA men at the Mission separated and barricaded inside three different buildings, and a surveillance drone not yet on site above Benghazi (see Chapter 44), the GRS operators effectively are "blind" as they approach the Mission.[933])

Tanto approaches his Team Lead, who is standing with the 17 February commander. Tanto gets approval to split into two groups. They will take separate routes on foot, and meet again at the Mission.[934] Paronto then tells Rone of his plan, and advises he will maintain radio contact. He promises to let Rone know "when I think it's clear to go down that road" leading to the Mission's Front Gate. Tanto grabs more ammo and his "go bag" from their vehicle. He instructs two nearby young militiamen holding AK-47s to come with him and D.B. They obey. Tanto and D.B., with the two young militiamen following, head to climb a nearby eight-foot wall separating them from a multi-floor building that may furnish a usable sniper perch. The four men head over the wall.[935]

Moving to the Mission Compound

Meanwhile, at the roadblock location where they have taken fire, the remainder of Team Annex decides to move on foot down the gravel road toward the Mission. Rone Woods, Jack Silva and Tig Tiegen begin walking through the intersection toward the street leading to the Mission. Rone now can see some of the attackers outside the Mission Compound. There are "eight or nine Arab men," some of whom begin shooting in his direction. Some of these attackers now are firing at Team Annex and the 17 February militiamen from behind concrete "Jersey barriers" placed in front of the Mission's Front Gate.[936]

A full-scale firefight is underway. Both sides begin firing automatic weapons, rocket-propelled grenades and grenade launchers, lighting the night on fire. One of the 17 February group begins firing heavy rounds from their "Technical" at the intersection. Then Tig launches three,

---

[933] *Id.*, Chap. 5, p. 111 and Chap. 6, p. 147.

[934] Benghazi Committee Report, p. 50.

[935] Zuckoff, *13 Hours*, Chap. 5, p. 123.

[936] *Id.*, Chap. 6, p. 132. See also Benghazi Committee Report, pp. 49-50.

high-explosive cartridges from the grenade launcher he has brought from the Annex. ***BOOM!!!*** The huge explosions in front of the Main Gate have the desired therapeutic effect: the incoming gunfire ceases, and the attackers clear the area.[937] The militants have messed with the wrong dudes.

The lull gives Team Annex the opportunity to move out for the Mission. Before departing, Tig grabs more weapons and ammo from the vehicle he has arrived in. Then he joins Rone and Jack. The 17 February militiamen show no inclination to join them. Rone radios Tanto to advise the latter the three GRS men are moving to the Mission down the front road. Tanto (who has not yet reached a high perch) radios back that, with the lull in fire, Rone's GRS team should be good to approach the Front Gate. Meanwhile, Tig is radioing the Annex Chief of Base to update him on Team Annex's status.[938]

Weapons poised, watching in every direction for would-be assailants, the three men proceed deliberately up the road in a combat crouch. With every step, they expect someone to engage them. Their minds carry two thoughts: save lives inside the Mission, but first *survive* in order to get there. They hug buildings, duck in and out of doorways and behind walls, and weave through several construction sites. Hearing voices behind them, they look back worriedly. Instead of danger, they see three of the 17 February militiamen from the intersection. They have followed Team Annex after all. They are on the other side of the road, mimicking the tactics of the GRS men they are trailing.[939] The GRS agents feel relief. *If 17 February was going to kill us, they would have done it at the intersection, where they had more men and bigger weapons.*

Jack and Tig now approach a large mound of dirt. They decide it could be a valuable sniper position and vantage point from which to observe the inside of the compound. After expending considerable energy climbing it with their heavy weaponry and combat gear, they realize it isn't high enough to do them any good. *Damn it!* They slide back down, cursing all the way.[940] Dirt from the hill clings to their sweat-soaked skin, making the warm evening even more uncomfortable.

---

[937] Zuckoff, *13 Hours*, Chap. 6, pp. 132-134. See also Benghazi Committee Report, pp. 49-50.

[938] Zuckoff, *13 Hours*, Chap. 6, p. 134.

[939] *Id.*, Chap. 6, pp. 136-137.

[940] *Id.*, Chap. 6, p. 137.

THE TRUE ACCOUNT OF VALOR AND ABANDONMENT

Finally, the GRS team and 17 February men reach the Mission Main Gate. Both the main vehicle gate and the adjacent pedestrian gate are propped wide open. Rone arrives first. He radios D.B. and Tanto, advising them the team at the front gate is ready to move inside. The three 17 February militia arrive next. Then Jack joins the group at the Jersey barrier in front of the Main Gate. Tig lags a few seconds behind, struggling to secure his ammo drum, whose clip has become loosened by his slide down the dirt mound. While he adjusts it, Tig radios the Annex advising their part of the GRS team is moving onto the Mission grounds from the front.[941]

Just then, at about 10:40 p.m., Rone rises quickly and sprints in a combat crouch through the open Main Gate, his automatic weapon ready for action. Seeing Rone move, Jack's SEAL training instantly kicks in: *No one goes in alone!* Jack races in, covering Rone's back.[942]

Before Tig can enter the gate behind Jack, he begins taking fire from someone at an intersection to the east. He drops to his belly behind a barrier to avoid the gunfire. Tig radios, "Hey base, I'm taking fire, but I'm not hit!" One of the 17 February fighters rises from about ten feet to the left of Tig. He unloads his entire AK-47 magazine – on full automatic – in the direction of the shooter. Then the 17 February ally gets back down to reload. Tig rises and prepares to fire his own machine gun at the attacker, but the incoming shooting has ceased. Their assailant is no longer an imminent threat.[943]

Suddenly an unarmed man is coming towards Tig with his hands raised. The man, seeming to have a death wish, is shouting repeatedly "Friendly! 17 February!" Tig doesn't have time to deal with this idiot, who doesn't seem dangerous. He motions for the 17 February fighter to his left to keep an eye on the uninvited new guest. Then Tig gets up and races into the Mission with his machine gun to join his buddies Jack and Rone. The Team Lead and interpreter "Henry" will follow just minutes later. (They have driven from the intersection to the Mission in their Mercedes SUV. "Henry" prudently will remain inside this vehicle for most of this rescue effort.[944])

---

[941] *Id.*, Chap. 6, pp. 137-139.

[942] *Id.*, Chap. 6, pp. 139-140.

[943] *Id.*, Chap. 6, p. 140.

[944] Zuckoff, *13 Hours*, Chap. 6, pp. 140-141 and Chap. 7, pp. 158 and 167; Benghazi Committee Report, p. 51; and Miller, CIA Rushed to Save Diplomats as Libya Attack Was Underway.

Tanto and D.B. Move to the Mission's Rear

While their three comrades are moving down the main road toward the Mission, D.B., Tanto and their two militiamen have climbed over the high cement wall near the intersection where Team Annex parked their vehicles. Their immediate objective is a tallish building they hope to climb as an observation post. First, to avoid an ambush they clear an adjacent cinder-block structure under construction. It is empty.[945]

As they reach the taller building D.B. and Tanto decide it is too far from the Mission to be of much help. Instead, they move on toward the diplomatic facility, lot by lot, covering each other. With each step, they prepare for hostile fire.[946]

Most of the structures they pass are single-story ones, useless for observation posts. Up the block, however, is a multi-story building under construction. They advance toward it. Once there, Tanto and D.B. make their way to the top, clearing each stairway and floor as they ascend. Now on the top floor, their hopes sink for two reasons. First, from here they can see clearly the awful flames engulfing the Mission buildings. Second, a row of trees obstructs their view of the Mission's grounds. "This is worthless," D.B. says. They descend quickly, having consumed precious time.[947]

The four men resume moving toward the Mission. They hopscotch through fields, and over and around walls. Their plan has morphed into finding the Mission's Back Gate and entering the facility there. As they proceed, Tig comes over the radio advising, "We're moving onto the Compound." Tanto replies they aren't at the Mission yet, but are on the way.[948]

As D.B. and Tanto are climbing one wall near the Mission, it collapses under Tanto, injuring his leg and arm. Nothing is broken. Bleeding, he picks himself up from the ground. He says, "I'm fine. We gotta go." They accelerate their pace, knowing they are behind the progress of the rest of the team.[949]

---

[945] Zuckoff, *13 Hours*, Chap. 6, pp. 141-142.

[946] *Id.*, Chap. 6, pp. 141-143.

[947] *Id.*, Chap. 6, pp. 142-143.

[948] *Id.*, Chap. 6, pp. 143-144.

[949] *Id.*, Chap. 6, pp. 144-145.

When they are about 50 yards from the Mission's Back Gate, they arrive at a grocery store. Outside, people are standing around watching the fires inside the Mission. Tanto instructs the two 17 February men to keep an eye on the crowd while he and D.B. move to the gate. The GRS operators encounter a 17 February commander, who is speaking into a phone in Arabic. Tanto and D.B. have no idea how this commander got here. They ask him whether the people at the grocery store are part of 17 February, or otherwise are friendly. The man replies in English, "No, they aren't."[950]

Tanto replies, "So, make sure they don't shoot at us. If they do, kill them."[951]

The commander nods. D.B. and Tanto progress to the Mission's Back Gate. But Tanto doesn't like it. He has a bad feeling about this 17 February man. Tanto is concerned the commander is warning the attackers D.B. and Tanto are coming in the back way. *Crap, what a night!*[952]

Now outside the Back Gate, Tanto and D.B. pause briefly, crouching behind concrete Jersey barriers. They decide to wait briefly to see if any of the attackers flee through the compound's rear entry as they are flushed from the front of the Mission by the rest of Team Annex. After "several minutes" no one comes out. Tanto radios Tig, "We're starting to come in. Don't shoot at us." Tig replies with a "Roger that."[953]

They attempt opening the Back Gate, but it's locked. Tanto quickly returns to the militia commander outside the grocery store. First he asks the commander to get a truck so they can ram the gate open. Then Tanto suggests they commandeer one of the vehicles driving by on a nearby street to use as a battering ram. The commander declines both requests.[954]

Although tired from climbing walls on the way here, a frustrated D.B. thinks, *"Screw it!"* Unable to see another entry, he climbs the Back Gate and drops into the compound. Instead of opening the gate promptly for Tanto and the two militia, D.B. first clears a nearby guard

---

[950] *Id.*, Chap. 6, p. 145.

[951] *Id.*, Chap. 6, p. 145.

[952] *Id.*, Chap. 6, p. 146.

[953] *Id.*, Chap. 7, p. 160.

[954] *Id.*, Chap. 7, pp. 161-162.

shack. Then he heads toward the center of the compound to connect up with Rone and Tig.

Now it's Tanto's turn to be frustrated. A "couple dozen" militia have joined their 17 February commander outside the Back Gate. Tanto is tired of waiting for D.B. to open the damned gate, and uneasy about being separated from his GRS buddies. (Not to mention being surrounded by 17 February militia he does not know or trust.) He heaves himself up and over the Back Gate. He opens it for the militiamen. Tanto instructs the commander to close and lock it when all of them are inside. The commander responds, "OK. Yes sir!" But, for whatever reason, he will not. This error (or is it intentional?) soon will allow militants to reenter the compound easily.[955]

Although it is more than an hour into the attack, all of Team Annex are now inside the Mission grounds. They have fulfilled their commitment to their State comrades. ■

---

[955] *Id.*, Chap. 7, pp. 159-163; and Baier, 13 Hours at Benghazi: The Inside Story (*Watch video there*; Go to 11:09-28).

40

"You Guys Got to Go!"

Shortly after Team Annex leaves for the Mission Compound, Oz Geist and the case officer he is protecting arrive back at the Annex. Oz now is the only GRS operator here. He has far more military experience than any of the CIA personnel present. This includes the Chief of Base, his deputy, and the two "site security" officers at the Annex. Oz wants to go join his comrades at the Mission Compound, but knows this is unwise.[956] Instead, he decides he must take command of the defense of the Annex until the other GRS agents return (if they ever do).

After exiting his vehicle, Oz watches various CIA staffers mill about the Annex courtyard, aimless and confused. *This is going to be like herding cats,* he tells himself.[957]

The Annex is a walled compound covering over two acres. (See the Diagram at the front of this book.) It is comprised of four large, one-story buildings, and several smaller ones. Schematically, picture a nearly square perimeter surrounded by a high concrete wall. Near the middle of the south wall (at "6:00 o'clock") is Building A. Building B is in the middle of the east wall (at 3:00 o'clock). Building C is close to, and near the center of, the facility's north wall (near 12:00 o'clock). (Building C contains the Tactical Operations Center and the Sensitive Compartmented Information Facility or "SCIF.") Building D is just north of the west perimeter (above 9:00 o'clock). At the center is a "small triangular courtyard."[958]

Fortunately, "in response to the ... deteriorating security situation and IC [intelligence community] threat reporting," the CIA Annex (unlike the Mission) recently has upgraded its security posture. Following the June 11 RPG attacks on the U.K. Ambassador's convoy in Benghazi, the CIA has conducted a security audit of its Annex. According to the Senate Intelligence panel, the "CIA quickly

---

[956] Zuckoff, *13 Hours*, Chap. 6, pp. 126-127.

[957] *Id.,* Chap. 6, p. 126.

[958] *Id.,* Chap. 2, pp. 29 and 31.

implemented additional security measures due to the threat of continued attacks against Western personnel in Benghazi." (Its public report redacts the specific improvements.) The committee concludes, "... [T]he physical security of the Annex was much more robust than that of the Mission facility . . ."[959]

Oz finds the Chief of Base, and gets a quick update of the situation at the Annex and with Team Annex. His mind begins to formulate a plan of defense.[960] Prior GRS planning sessions had assumed multiple GRS agents would be present to defend the Annex in case of trouble. Oz will have to improvise.

Oz identifies only six people at the Annex who can be classified as "shooters." These are Oz himself, the Annex chief of security, a CIA case officer with combat experience in Afghanistan, and three contract Libyan guards. Oz issues orders to prepare to defend against a possible attack. Despite his subordinate position as a mere rotating contractor, no one questions his dominant presence and confident manner. Everyone knows they are witnessing a true leader in action.[961]

First, Oz orders all non-shooters to congregate inside Building C. The personnel in this structure will be the highest defensive priority. Oz must know where every protectee is at any moment. If an attack occurs, he can't waste precious assets rounding up stragglers. He decrees only one person at a time may leave Building C, and then only if "absolutely necessary." Oz stations an armed Annex support staffer at Building C's door to enforce his directive. In this, he is backed up by the CIA Chief of Base. The only exception is for personnel who must make official cell phone calls; they are permitted outside to seek decent reception, provided they remain very near.[962]

Next, Oz races to his bedroom in Building B. He quickly dons his body armor, helmet and night-vision goggles. He gathers up his assault rifle, his "go bag" (containing extra magazines), and some tourniquets and other medical supplies. Just in case, he scoops up still more extra

---

[959] Sen. Intelligence Committee Benghazi Report (Redacted; emphasis added), pp. 17-18. See also *Id.* ("In sum, the Mission facility had a much weaker security posture than the Annex, with a significant disparity in the quality and quantity of equipment and security upgrades"), p. 19.

[960] Zuckoff, *13 Hours*, Chap. 6, pp. 126-127.

[961] Baier, 13 Hours at Benghazi: The Inside Story (*Watch video there*; Go to 13:41 - 14:03).

[962] Zuckoff, *13 Hours*, Chap. 6, pp. 127-128 and 130.

magazines and crams them into his pockets. The last thing he needs is to run out of ammo if a firefight arises. Then he hurries back outside.[963]

Once outdoors, Oz spots the Afghanistan combat veteran carrying his own assault rifle. Oz orders him up the ladder to Building C's flat rooftop. The GRS team earlier had decided upon this roof as their main defensive position. Oz follows the CIA man up the ladder to assess their situation for himself.[964]

Atop Building C's roof is a cinder-block parapet along the perimeter, about three feet high, which affords some cover. The GRS men previously have positioned large, sealed metal cans on the roof. These contain thousands of rounds of ammo for assault rifles and machine guns, as well as grenades.[965]

From his rooftop perch, Oz looks to the northwest. There, in the direction of the Mission, he sees tracer rounds blazing across the dark sky. Using his night-vision gear, Oz then surveys the area nearby the Annex. He particularly focuses on an area the GRS men call "Zombieland," to the north and east of the Annex. (They name it Zombieland because it resembles "the set of a movie about the undead.") Thankfully, Oz sees nothing unusual. He instructs the Afghan vet to continue standing sentry atop the roof, and to report to Oz immediately by radio if he sees or hears anything out of the ordinary. Oz descends the ladder and resumes his command duties.[966]

Once back on the ground, Oz finds the Annex Security Leader. Geist directs him to cover the Annex front gate area.[967]

Next, Oz turns his attention to fortifying the Annex perimeter. Months before, the GRS agents constructed several elevated steel platforms at various locations near the outer wall. The GRS team grandly refers to these ugly structures as their "towers." They are designed as shooting positions, and are high enough to allow the GRS men or other defenders to shoot over the walls in case of attack. Each platform is large enough for two men. Oz orders each of the three Libyan contract guards to mount a different tower: one by the front gate, a second to the rear of Building C, and the third at the southeast corner. If push comes to shove, Oz hopes these Libyans will be brave

---

[963] *Id.*, Chap. 6, p. 128.

[964] *Id.*, Chap. 6, p. 129.

[965] *Id.*, Chap. 6, p. 129.

[966] *Id.*, Chap. 2, p. 32 and Chap. 6, p. 129.

[967] *Id.*, Chap. 6, p. 130.

enough to stand and fight. At a minimum, he prays they at least will warn him if trouble approaches.[968] Oz's five available shooters are now in position.

Oz walks the interior of the Annex courtyard. On his radio, he hears the traffic between his GRS comrades, who still are moving toward the Mission, and the DSAs awaiting them. Things don't sound good. Oz heads back toward Building C.

When he arrives there, Oz learns the supervisor of their three Libyan contract guards has arrived at the Annex front gate and is requesting entry. The Annex staff know the man, so Oz allows him to enter. The man informs Oz he has come to urge the CIA Chief of Base to evacuate the facility promptly. The Libyan tells Oz, "You guys got to go. It's not safe for you here." (*No kidding.*) Oz takes the man to see the chief, then returns to making his rounds of their defensive positions.[969]

Oz doesn't stay to hear the conversation. He already knows the result. His brave compatriots on Team Annex are attempting under fire to rescue a U.S. ambassador and six other Americans trapped in a blazing villa, under siege by well-armed militants. *If* any of them make it out alive, they will need a sanctuary. The Annex must be their "Alamo"; they have nowhere else to go in this hellhole of Benghazi. Oz knows he and the CIA personnel are staying put.[970] ■

---

[968] *Id.*, Chap. 6, p. 130.

[969] *Id.*, Chap. 6, p. 130.

[970] *Id.*, Chap. 6, pp. 130-131.

THE TRUE ACCOUNT OF VALOR AND ABANDONMENT

41

"Like Being in a Brick Oven"

While the GRS rescue team is en route, some of the Diplomatic Security Agents come out of shelter and attempt to clear the Mission Compound. From what DSAs Henderson and Ubben can see on their security monitors inside the TOC, most (possibly all) of the attackers apparently have melted away for the time being.

First, a heavily-armed Dave Ubben exits the TOC and moves to clear nearby Building B (the DSA residence and "Cantina"). Ubben radios the two DSAs trapped there he is on his way. When Ubben arrives, the barricaded DSAs in the back room remove the barriers that have prevented the militants from reaching them and the Blue Mountain guard who is with them.[971]

During this time, DSA Henderson remains in the TOC. He continues updating the Annex, Embassy Tripoli, and State officials in Washington regarding their status at the Mission. He informs them Scott Wickland is suffering from severe smoke inhalation on the Villa's rooftop, Stevens and Smith remain missing, fires are engulfing much of the Mission, and attackers have been "roaming" the compound.[972]

Meanwhile, the two Tripoli DSAs and Dave Ubben instruct the Blue Mountain guard to remain hidden in the Cantina. Outside there is an undamaged armored vehicle, which the attackers failed to burn (probably having run out of diesel fuel). The three DSAs use this vehicle to drive the short distance to the main Villa where Stevens and Smith reside. It is still on fire. The DSAs leave their vehicle and set up a "small perimeter," and call for Scott Wickland to come down from the roof. Wickland descends the ladder. He is "vomiting from severe smoke inhalation and on the brink of unconsciousness."[973] But he is alive. It looks like he will survive.

Next, the other three DSAs begin searching inside the Villa for Stevens and Smith. Two of the men provide a "defense perimeter" while a third goes inside to look for the missing diplomats. The three

---

[971] Zuckoff, *13 Hours*, Chap. 5, p. 124.

[972] Benghazi Committee Report, p. 141; and Zuckoff, *13 Hours*, Chap. 5, pp. 123-124.

[973] Zuckoff, *13 Hours*, Chap. 5, p. 125.

DSAs rotate entering the smoking structure. They crawl on the floor, but still cannot avoid the same heavy, toxic smoke that earlier had defeated DSA Wickland. They retrieve gas masks and use them, but they are ineffective. The DSA men make multiple heroic attempts to locate Stevens and Smith inside the Villa, but are unsuccessful in the overwhelming heat and thick smoke.[974]

During the second search attempt at about 10:40 p.m., members of the Team Annex rescue posse begin to reach the Mission.[975] The DSAs inside the Mission have been alerted by radio the GRS men are outside heading into the compound. Three of Team Annex's members – Tig Tiegen, Rone Woods and Jack Silva – having cleared the main road and Main Gate, enter the compound from the front.[976] Two minutes later, the GRS Team Lead and the CIA linguist "Henry" enter the Mission, also through the Main Gate.[977]

(At about this point, back in Washington President Obama's helicopter is lifting off from Walter Reed Medical Center to return to the White House. The president will touch down on the South Lawn at about 4:50 p.m.[978])

Around this same time, some "friendlies" affiliated with the 17 February Brigade begin to arrive at the Mission.[979] (This is roughly an hour after the attacks begin. Better late than never.) They will continue to trickle onto the grounds for the next half-hour or so.[980]

As was the case outside the Mission, inside the compound Team Annex members will continue to have difficulty telling friend from foe. They all dress alike. And none are wearing any insignia identifying

---

[974] Benghazi Committee Report, pp. 50-51; Sen. Intelligence Committee Benghazi Report, pp. 5-6; Lamb Oversight Committee Prepared Testimony, p. 6; Kennedy October 10 Briefing; and Zuckoff, *13 Hours*, Chap. 5, p. 125.

[975] The Senate Select Intelligence Committee places this arrival time at 10:10 p.m., but this clearly is erroneous. Sen. Intelligence Committee Benghazi Report (Redacted), p. 5.

[976] Benghazi Committee Report, p. 51; and Baier, 13 Hours at Benghazi: The Inside Story (*Watch video there*; Go to 10:16-28).

[977] Benghazi Committee Report, p. 51; and Miller, CIA Rushed to Save Diplomats as Libya Attack Was Underway.

[978] Rivera and Rivera, Where Was President Obama During Benghazi Terror Attack? (*Watch video there*; Go to 2:27-35).

[979] Benghazi Committee Report, p. 51.

[980] Zuckoff, *13 Hours*, Chap. 7, pp. 165-166.

them as belonging to the 17 February Brigade. As the American security personnel like to quip: "What's the difference between how Libyans look when they're coming to help you versus when they're coming to kill you? Not much."[981]

Once inside the Main Gate Rone, followed by Jack, runs to the still-burning Villa building. There they meet up with two DSA agents who are searching for Stevens and Smith. One of the DSAs is Scott Wickland, who has recovered sufficiently to rejoin the rescue mission. Wickland is covered in soot and feels as bad as he looks. The other DSA is Dave Ubben. (The two DSAs from Tripoli currently are elsewhere.) Ubben tells the GRS men, "There's still guys in the building." Standing just outside the Villa door, the men can feel the heat emanating from inside the structure.[982]

Jack and Rone take over the search from the exhausted DSAs. Initially they enter the Villa through the same window on the Villa's patio the DSAs have been using. Time after time, they enter the smoke-filled structure to look for the missing men. Between each trip they return to the window for gulps of fresher air. Eventually, they become light-headed. Rone and Jack begin to rotate, going in one at a time. Still they cannot reach the far areas of the safe haven. Each time they are defeated by the intense smoke, vapors and heat. (Jack worries his contact lenses actually might melt in his eyes. Even through their heavy boots their feet are burning up.) Then the two GRS agents try entering through the front door, and then a rear door. Each time the result is the same: failure.[983]

While Jack and Rone are inside the Villa looking for Smith and Stevens, Tig Tiegen arrives in front of the Villa. Seeing no one but assuming his comrades must be inside, Tig takes up a defensive position at sandbags placed in front of the structure.[984]

According to author Zuckoff, as they search inside Jack thinks to himself, *There's no way in hell they possibly could be alive. There's no way to survive this for more than a few minutes.*[985]

The militants are still absent for the present. During this period, the Annex Team Lead and his men "repeatedly" tell the weary DSAs to

---

[981] *Id.*, Chap. 7, pp. 165-166.

[982] *Id.*, Chap. 7, pp. 150-151.

[983] Zuckoff, *13 Hours*, Chap. 7, pp. 152-154.

[984] *Id.*, Chap. 7, pp. 154-155.

[985] *Id.*, Chap. 7, p. 154.

leave the Mission Compound and go to the Annex. The DSAs refuse to go without Stevens and Smith.[986]

In the midst of this search for the two diplomats, at 4:54 p.m. back in Washington, the State Department's Operations Center issues another "Ops Alert" that will prove only partially correct. (It is sent to the same recipients as the prior Ops Alert.) It states:

> Embassy Tripoli reports the firing at the U.S. Diplomatic Mission in Benghazi has stopped and the compound has been cleared. A response team is on site attempting to locate COM [Chief of Mission] personnel.[987]

Yet again, for whatever reasons the Obama administration refuses to release this Ops Alert voluntarily. Instead, it must be obtained by Judicial Watch through an FOIA lawsuit.

Meanwhile, back in Benghazi some of the 17 February militia have joined the search inside the Villa for the ambassador and Sean Smith. The DSAs also have re-joined the effort. One DSA (identified by the Select Committee only as "DSA 4" but believed by the author to be Dave Ubben[988]) finds the body of Sean Smith inside a hallway in the Villa. Smith is unresponsive. Ubben and one of the Tripoli DSAs drag Smith's body to a window, and hand him to Jack Silva, who is now waiting outside. Smith has no pulse and is not breathing.[989]

As the DSA agents watch anxiously, using his SEAL training Jack examines Smith for bleeding or signs of trauma. He finds none. Jack can feel the limp man's body is cold. Jack tries unsuccessfully to detect breathing and a pulse. Jack tells Dave Ubben, "No, he's gone." Tears well in Ubben's eyes.[990]

At 11:01 p.m. (5:01 p.m. in Washington, D.C.), Sean Smith, husband and father of two, is reported killed in action. He is only

---

[986] Benghazi Committee Report, p. 52.

[987] Sensitive But Unclassified State Department Ops Alert Email to Numerous Parties Re "Update 1: U.S. Diplomatic Mission in Benghazi" (Sept. 11, 2012; 4:54 p.m.), Judicial Watch Document Archive (Posted Feb. 25, 2015); and CBS Benghazi Timeline.

[988] Hsu, Baring Grievous Wounds, Dry Humor, U.S. Agent Lays Out Key Evidence at Benghazi Trial (Describing testimony at criminal trial of Abu Khatallah: "... Ubben described recovering the body of Smith from the burning Villa...").

[989] Benghazi Committee Report, p. 53; Hicks Oversight Committee Testimony (May 8, 2013), p. 26; Zuckoff, *13 Hours*, Chap. 7, pp. 155-156; and Baier, 13 Hours at Benghazi: The Inside Story (*Watch video there*; Go to 10:38-45).

[990] Zuckoff, *13 Hours*, Chap. 7, pp. 156-157.

THE TRUE ACCOUNT OF VALOR AND ABANDONMENT

34 years old.[991] Smith's tragic prophecy to his mother has proven accurate.

(Late this evening (probably after midnight), Patricia Smith in San Diego will receive a horrific telephone call from an unknown government official advising her son tragically has died in Benghazi. She does not even know this is where Sean has been stationed.[992])

While Jack is examining Sean Smith, Rone Woods and Tig Tiegen meet up outside the Villa. They join the DSAs and 17 February men in searching inside for Ambassador Stevens, focusing once more on the safe haven area. The thick, toxic smoke again disorients the searchers, and they experience oxygen deprivation. With zero visibility, the searchers yell out for the missing man, and feel their way along the floors and walls.[993]

Once, Rone becomes disoriented. "I'm lost! I can't find my way out!" he yells. Tig re-directs him to safety. Rone will tell Tig, "Hey dude, thanks. You just saved my life. I thought I was gonna die in there." Tig replies, "Hopefully we'll all get out of this alive."[994] As the fates will have it, the valiant Rone in fact has only hours to live.

Now outside as they try to regain their breath, Tig and Rone hear the radio call from D.B. Benton and Tanto Paronto, advising they are about to enter the Mission grounds through the Back Gate. They leave the other searchers and go to provide cover for Tanto and D.B. Soon, the four GRS men link up toward the back of the grounds near where the Mission's orchard groves stand.[995]

The GRS team has expended great time and effort searching for the missing diplomats, but they haven't cleared all the Mission Compound. They still don't know to where all the attackers have disappeared. Now, D.B., Tanto and Tig join forces with some of the 17 February fighters

---

[991] Benghazi Committee Report, p. 53; Zuckoff, *13 Hours*, Chap. 7, p. 157; and Lamb Oversight Committee Prepared Testimony, p. 6.

[992] Interview of Patricia Smith with Trish Regan, Fox Business News (Mar. 10, 2016) (*Watch video there*; Go to 5:09-45).

[993] Benghazi Committee Report, pp. 51-53.

[994] Baier, 13 Hours at Benghazi: The Inside Story (*Watch video there*; Go to 10:29 - 11:09); and Zuckoff, *13 Hours*, Chap. 7, pp. 158-160. See also Interview of Mark "Oz" Geist and Other GRS Agents with Megyn Kelly, "The Kelly File," Fox News Channel (Jan. 4, 2016) (Geist: "He [John Tiegen] saved Tyrone's life by going in the building and finding him when he [Woods] was lost . . .") (*Watch video there*; Go to 13:46-54).

[995] Zuckoff, *13 Hours*, Chap. 7, pp. 159-163.

to check the orchard area for bad guys. Seeing none, they move toward the Mission's buildings.[996]

Meanwhile, Rone advances to the adjacent TOC and Cantina buildings. He soon is joined by Tanto, Tig and D.B. They split up briefly. Rone and D.B. go to clear the Cantina, which is empty. Tig and Tanto move to the TOC. There, they finally convince a suspicious Alec Henderson they are "friendlies," and the senior DSA unbars and exits the fortified structure. (Henderson has been concerned the militants who tried to break into the TOC earlier may have returned.) Tig sets up his machine gun in a defensive position outside the buildings, while Rone, D.B. and Tanto clear the rest of the TOC building. Then Henderson goes back inside to destroy classified and "other sensitive materials." D.B. and Tanto help him.[997]

The Mission grounds and buildings are all empty. *Where the hell have all the bad guys gone?*

Rone returns to the smoldering Villa. There, he once again attempts to help Jack Silva, the Team Lead, and the 17 February militiamen look for Chris Stevens. Although the DSA and GRS agents and the February 17 men search "multiple times" in the overpowering smoke, they still cannot find the ambassador.[998] GRS operator Tig Tiegen later describes the scene of their search: ". . . The smoke was still down there and you could still only see about maybe two feet in front of your face. It was just so thick and so hot. It was just like being in a brick oven. . . . It was extreme heat. . . . It was pretty intense."[999] ■

---

[996] *Id.*, Chap. 7, pp. 163-164.

[997] *Id.*, Chap. 7, pp. 164-167.

[998] Sen. Intelligence Committee Benghazi Report, p. 7; Zuckoff, *13 Hours*, Chap. 7, pp. 166-167; and Miller, CIA Rushed to Save Diplomats as Libya Attack Was Underway.

[999] Interview of John "Tig" Tiegen and Other GRS Agents with Megyn Kelly, "The Kelly File," Fox News Channel (Jan. 4, 2016) (*Watch video there*; Go to 12:00-57).

42

"Is Anything Coming?"

Gregory Hicks and the U.S. Defense Attaché in Libya have been making numerous urgent telephone calls to various entities in Libya, Germany and the U.S. seeking immediate assistance. It is now about 10:45 to 11:00 p.m. in Tripoli.

While 400 miles away in Benghazi the CIA and Diplomatic Security agents search for the two missing diplomats in the Villa, Hicks and Lt. Col. Keith Phillips finally find a moment to confer with each other. Phillips has been communicating about the crisis with AFRICOM in Stuttgart, and with the Joint Staff at the Pentagon.

Hicks asks Lt. Col. Phillips, "[I]s anything coming? Will they be sending us any help? Is there something out there?"[1000]

Phillips' response is devastating. He advises Hicks the nearest jet fighter planes that might help are at Aviano Air Base in northern Italy. It will take two to three hours to get them "on site." (In an earlier interview with congressional investigators, Hicks recalled Lt. Col. Phillips had said two to three hours to get jets "airborne."[1001]) Worse yet, there are no tanker planes close enough to support any air mission from Aviano![1002]

Later this night before the final, early-morning attack on the CIA Benghazi Annex, Hicks claims he asks Phillips again:

> .... [I]s there anything coming, is there anything out there to help our people from ... big military? And the answer, again, was the same as before. ... The answer was, it's too far

---

[1000] Hicks Oversight Committee Testimony (May 8, 2013), p. 26; and Zuckoff, *13 Hours*, Chap. 6, pp. 147-148.

[1001] Attkisson, Diplomat: U.S. Special Forces Told "You Can't Go" to Benghazi During Attacks.

[1002] Hicks Oversight Committee Testimony (May 8, 2013), p. 26; Zuckoff, *13 Hours*, Chap. 6, pp. 147-148; and Attkisson, Diplomat: U.S. Special Forces Told "You Can't Go" to Benghazi During Attacks.

away, there are no tankers, there is nothing, there is nothing that could respond.[1003]

Each time they speak, Hicks thanks Phillips for the grim update. As he ends these conversations he must have a sinking feeling in the pit of his stomach. Hicks knows Chris Stevens, Team Tripoli, and Hicks' other colleagues in Benghazi are on their own. ∎

[1003] Attkisson, Diplomat: U.S. Special Forces Told "You Can't Go" to Benghazi During Attacks.

43

"Do Everything Possible"

General Carter Ham, Head of Africa Command, is not at AFRICOM's headquarters in Stuttgart, Germany but happens to be working at the Pentagon on September 11, 2012. He later recalls that within 15 minutes after the attack in Benghazi begins, he learns of it by telephone from his AFRICOM Command Center.[1004] (The Select Committee will conclude AFRICOM first learns of the attack some 18 minutes later, at about 4:15 p.m., Washington time.[1005] In this book, the author relies on the Select Committee's conclusion.)

General Ham later testifies he immediately requests an urgent meeting with General Martin E. Dempsey, Chairman of the Joint Chiefs of Staff, and begins heading toward Dempsey's office. Once there, he reportedly briefs Dempsey on the attack in Benghazi.[1006] The two officers then quickly walk upstairs and together brief Defense Secretary Panetta. According to CBS News, Panetta and Dempsey learn of the attacks at about 4:30 p.m.[1007]

General Ham reportedly later will testify that when he briefs Dempsey and Panetta, there is no discussion of any protest or anti-Islamic Video. The entire context of these briefings is that there has been an "attack" on a U.S. facility in Benghazi. Pressed further, General Ham testifies "the nature of the conversation[s]" he has with Dempsey and Panetta is "this was a terrorist attack."[1008]

"Just minutes" after meeting with Ham, Secretary Panetta and Dempsey depart the Pentagon to meet with President Obama.[1009]

[1004] Rosen, Top Defense Officials Briefed Obama on "Attack" Not Video or Protest.

[1005] Benghazi Committee Report, p. 56.

[1006] Rosen, Top Defense Officials Briefed Obama on "Attack" Not Video or Protest.

[1007] CBS Benghazi Timeline.

[1008] Rosen, Top Defense Officials Briefed Obama on "Attack" Not Video or Protest (Quoting testimony of Gen. Ham: "Well, and with General Dempsey and Secretary Panetta, that is the nature of the conversation we had, yes, sir").

[1009] Panetta, *Worthy Fights*, Chap. 16, p. 427.

(Unless they are going to the White House Situation Room, they never should leave the Pentagon tonight. Instead, they should go swiftly to the National Military Command Center ("NMCC"), call the White House from there, and brief the president by phone instead of in person. They waste precious time during an emergency traveling to the White House and back.)

Panetta and Dempsey arrive at the White House by about 4:45 p.m.,[1010] just minutes after the Team Annex GRS agents in Benghazi begin to reach the Mission Compound.[1011] Panetta later testifies before Congress he and Dempsey confer at 5:00 p.m. with the president and National Security Advisor Thomas E. Donilon about the Benghazi attacks at their previously-scheduled weekly meeting.[1012] (According to Fox News, Vice President Biden also attends this gathering.[1013])

As will become clear later, it is significant neither Secretary Hillary Clinton nor anyone else from the State Department, nor anyone from the CIA, are present at this meeting to receive any orders the president might issue. Despite State's absence, this agency later surprisingly will control much of the key decision-making on this Night of Benghazi – even directly affecting how the U.S. military proceeds.

At the time of this briefing, Panetta and Dempsey know little more about the attack than a U.S. diplomatic building is on fire and Ambassador Stevens and another person are missing.[1014] (Just as this meeting convenes, as noted above in Chapter 41, a DSA agent is discovering the lifeless body of Sean Smith in the charred rubble of the Mission's Villa.[1015]) The president and his team no doubt discuss

---

[1010] *Id.*, Chap. 16, p. 427.

[1011] Benghazi Committee Report, pp. 36 and 51.

[1012] *Id.*, Select Benghazi Timeline, p. 559; Baier, New Revelations on Attack in Benghazi (*Watch video there*; Go to 26:16-22); Burnett, Benghazi Timeline: "We Are Under Attack" (*Watch video there*; Go to 5:26-49); and Zuckoff, *13 Hours*, Chap. 6, p. 146.

[1013] Baier, New Revelations on Attack in Benghazi (*Watch video there*; Go to 26:16-22).

[1014] Benghazi Committee Report, p. 69; Panetta, *Worthy Fights* ("We told him [President Obama] that some kind of attack had taken place that threatened our ambassador and compound in Benghazi, but we also cautioned that these were very preliminary reports"), Chap. 16, p. 427; and Rosen, Top Defense Officials Briefed Obama on "Attack" Not Video or Protest.

[1015] Benghazi Committee Report, pp. 52-53.

THE TRUE ACCOUNT OF VALOR AND ABANDONMENT

various possible military responses to the attack. President Obama later will sidestep a Fox News interviewer's question about whether Panetta tells Obama at this briefing the attacks involve terrorism.[1016]

(Because General Ham has not discussed any demonstration or Video with General Dempsey or Secretary Panetta, it seems unlikely these two men raise such topics at their 5:00 p.m. meeting with the president. Of course, it remains possible someone at this Oval Office briefing raises the "protest possibility," given the violent demonstration in Cairo just hours before.)

According to the Select Committee's summary of Panetta's testimony, "The President made clear that we ought to use all of the resources at our disposal to try to make sure we did *everything possible* to try to save lives *there* [in Benghazi]."[1017] In his memoir, Panetta later writes, "The president directed us to *do everything we could* to help our embattled embassy [sic] staff."[1018] (Then why don't Panetta and his department proceed to *do* that?) Despite Panetta's reference to "embassy staff," he clearly means the U.S. staff in Benghazi because only they are "embattled." At an absolute minimum, Panetta must intend to include the Benghazi Mission personnel.

Panetta later will testify to a Senate committee President Obama leaves operational details (including what military assets are available to assist the Americans under attack) "up to us." It will prove to be Barack Obama's last communication tonight with anyone in the U.S. military![1019]

According to Secretary Panetta, at this meeting President Obama never asks Panetta and General Dempsey how long it will take to get

---

[1016] Interview of President Barack Obama with Bill O'Reilly, Fox News Channel (Feb. 2, 2014) (*Watch video there*; Go to 0:00 - 2:01).

[1017] Benghazi Committee Report (emphasis added), pp. 69-70 and 86. See also Panetta Senate Armed Services Prepared Testimony (". . . General Dempsey and I met with President Obama and he ordered all available DOD assets to respond to the attack in Libya and to protect U.S. personnel and interests in the region. . . ."); and Senate Armed Services Testimony of Secretary of Defense Leon Panetta and General Martin Dempsey (Feb. 7, 2013) ("Panetta and Dempsey Armed Services Committee Testimony") (Response to questions of Sen. Kelly Ayotte (R-NH)).

[1018] Panetta, *Worthy Fights* (emphasis added), Chap. 16, pp. 427-428.

[1019] Defense Secretary Leon Panetta Senate Armed Services Committee Testimony (Feb. 7, 2013) (Response to questions of Sen. Kelly Ayotte (R-NH)); and Daniel Halper, "Panetta: Obama Absent Night of Benghazi," *The Weekly Standard* online (Feb. 7, 2013) (*Watch video there*; Go to 0:00-27 and 1:37-57).

military support to the Americans under attack in Benghazi.[1020] (One might have thought this a relevant question for a Commander in Chief to pose.)

At this relatively short briefing, the participants also reportedly spend some of their time discussing the situation in Cairo, where rather violent demonstrations have occurred earlier today at the U.S. Embassy (see Chapter 26).[1021]

The meeting with Obama ends around 5:30 p.m.[1022] Incredibly, *neither Panetta nor Dempsey ever will communicate directly with the president again this night!*[1023] (They should all be together in the Situation Room. At a minimum, for the rest of this night they should be burning up the phone lines between the Oval Office and the Pentagon's NMCC.) Further, Panetta subsequently admits in testimony he personally never communicates again with *anyone at the White House* on this Night of Benghazi![1024] (This is dereliction of duty.)

Moreover, according to two Select Benghazi Committee members, *Panetta and Secretary of State Hillary Clinton never once speak to each other during the entire 13 Hours of the Benghazi attacks and evacuation!*[1025] (How is this even *possible?*) And, as discussed below, Clinton will speak to the president but once – nearly six hours after the initial attack.[1026] Clinton also will speak with CIA Director Petraeus

---

[1020] Panetta and Dempsey Senate Armed Services Committee Testimony (Feb. 7, 2013) (Response to questions of Sen. Kelly Ayotte (R-NH)).

[1021] Daniel Halper, "Panetta: Obama Absent Night of Benghazi," *The Weekly Standard* online (Feb. 7, 2013).

[1022] Benghazi Committee Report, pp. 69-70; Additional Views of Reps. Jordan and Pompeo, p. 444; and Rivera and Rivera, Where Was President Obama During Benghazi Terror Attack? (meeting lasts 30 minutes) (*Watch video there*; Go to 3:15-45).

[1023] Panetta and Dempsey Senate Armed Services Committee Testimony (Feb. 7, 2013) (Response to questions of Sen. Kelly Ayotte (R-NH)); Benghazi Committee Report, p. 70; Additional Views of Reps. Jordan and Pompeo, p. 444; Statement of Senators McCain, Graham and Ayotte; Zuckoff, *13 Hours*, Chap. 6, p. 146; and Rivera and Rivera, Where Was President Obama During Benghazi Terror Attack? (*Watch video there*; Go to 3:15-45).

[1024] Panetta Armed Services Committee Testimony (Feb. 7, 2013) (Response to questions of Sen. Kelly Ayotte (R-NH)).

[1025] Additional Views of Reps. Jordan and Pompeo, pp. 444-445. See also James Nye, "Panetta: President Obama Was Absent Night of Benghazi Attack and Did Not Check In Once During the Night of the Deadly Terror Assault," Daily Mail online (Feb. 8, 2013).

[1026] Additional Views of Reps. Jordan and Pompeo, p. 444.

only once, at 5:38 p.m.[1027] (This is before the CIA Annex comes under attack.)

On this Night of Benghazi, in the middle of a national security crisis, there is an inexplicable, deplorable lack of communication among the highest leaders of the American government.

(Immediately after the 5:00 p.m. meeting with Obama, on their way back to the Pentagon Panetta and Dempsey should phone their staffs and issue orders to have all feasible rescue assets get ready urgently to deploy to Benghazi on an emergency basis. They also should order their staffs, if necessary, to find transport planes that can get to any areas where those assets are located ASAP, and get them in the air and on their way as soon as humanly possible. This would save vital time later. Failure to do so would be negligence. Yet there is no record of any such orders coming from Secretary Panetta until almost an hour and one-half later, at 7:00 p.m. (discussed below in Chapter 53). Sadly, this will be among the earliest of many examples of a complete lack of urgency by the U.S. military on this tragic night.) ∎

[1027] *Id.*, pp. 444-445.

44

A Predator Over Benghazi

Minutes after Sean Smith is pronounced dead, and while Leon Panetta and General Martin Dempsey are briefing the president, the first unmanned, *unarmed* drone arrives over the Mission Compound. (It also is known as a "remote piloted aircraft" or "RPA.") It is about 11:10 p.m. Benghazi time (5:10 p.m. Washington time).[1028] (This drone reportedly has been flying a mission elsewhere over eastern Libya.[1029])

From this point on, this drone begins transmitting live, real-time video of events on the ground in Benghazi to "multiple agencies."[1030] These reportedly include the White House, the Pentagon, the State Department and the CIA.[1031] (Fog of war?) Unnamed Defense Department officials reportedly tell CBS News "other reconnaissance aircraft" also is sent to Benghazi,[1032] but the author is unable to confirm this. The drone's video images are being recorded.[1033]

[1028] Benghazi Committee Report, p. 71, and Select Benghazi Timeline, p. 559; CBS Benghazi Timeline; Miller, CIA Rushed to Save Diplomats as Libya Attack Was Underway; and Clinton, *Hard Choices* (drone arrived over Benghazi approximately 90 minutes after attack commenced), Chap. 17, p. 394. Compare Prepared Statement of General Martin Dempsey, Chairman, Joint Chiefs of Staff, before Senate Armed Services Committee (Feb. 7, 2013) (drone "arrived on the scene approximately an hour later" after it is diverted to Benghazi "within minutes" of learning of the attacks), p. 4.

[1029] Sen. Intelligence Committee Benghazi Report, p. 6; and Clinton, *Hard Choices*, Chap. 17, p. 394.

[1030] Interview of Unnamed U.S. Serviceman with Sean Hannity.

[1031] Griffin, CIA Operators Were Denied Request for Help During Benghazi Attack (". . . Both [drones] were capable of sending real time visuals back to U.S. officials in Washington, D.C. Any U.S. official or agency with the proper clearance, including the White House Situation Room, State Department, CIA, Pentagon and others, could call up that video in real time on their computers").

[1032] Sundby, Ambassador Warned Libya Was "Volatile and Violent." See also Sharyl Attkisson, "Could U.S. Military Have Helped During Libya Attack?" CBS News online (Oct. 20, 2012) ("Attkisson, Could U.S. Military Have Helped During Libya Attack?") (emphasis added) ("CBS News has been told that, hours after the attack began, an unmanned Predator drone was sent over the U.S. mission in Benghazi, and that the

Months later, apparently around May 2013, an unidentified U.S. serviceman will call into the radio program of conservative talk show host Sean Hannity. The latter interviews the caller (who identifies himself only as "John from Iowa") at some length. (The author cannot verify the veracity of this anonymous caller's assertions, but believes they have the ring of truth and are worth repeating here. *The Huffington Post* later will report "John" in fact is the drone cameraman he claims to be, and still is on active duty with the Air Force.[1034]) The serviceman claims to be the "Central Operator" who controls remotely the infrared video camera of the Predator drone for the first ninety minutes of its flight over Benghazi on September 11, 2012. (He then is relieved by another Central Operator.) A different serviceman reportedly is piloting the drone.[1035] The alleged Central Operator claims to have been in contact with various individuals in the U.S. government while observing the video feed from this drone over Benghazi, but he declines to identify these persons.[1036]

According to this claimed camera operator, when their RPA arrives above the Mission the drone's operators observe the compound's buildings are still ablaze. Indeed, the fires from the Villa and other buildings tend to "wash out" the video feed somewhat when they train their drone's cameras on the blazing structures.[1037]

The fires notwithstanding, the drone's cameras reportedly capture "dozens if not hundreds" of individuals surrounding the Mission facility.[1038] The imagery from the drone's cameras reportedly is sufficiently precise to allow its operators to confirm the attackers have large weapons (such as AK-47s, rifles and RPGs). The drone operators cannot see objects as small as pistols, unless they are fired. In that case, the drone's infrared cameras can distinguish muzzle flashes of even small caliber sidearms.[1039]

---

drone and *other reconnaissance aircraft* apparently observed the final hours of the protracted battle").

[1033] Hannity Radio Interview of Unnamed U.S. Serviceman.

[1034] Amanda Terkel, "Benghazi Committee Finally Interviews the Mysterious 'John From Iowa,'" *The Huffington Post* online (June 9, 2016; Updated June 10, 2016).

[1035] Hannity Radio Interview of Unnamed U.S. Serviceman.

[1036] *Id.*

[1037] *Id.*

[1038] *Id.*

[1039] *Id.*

(Three years later, the Benghazi Select Committee wants to interview this drone camera operator. In February 2016, the committee asks the Defense Department to identify the anonymous drone cameraman. In April 2016, the Pentagon falsely tells the panel it is unable to identify the man! However, in May 2016, the Pentagon finally gives the committee what it purports is a complete roster of drone operators on duty on the Night of Benghazi, presumably including "John's" real name. However, the committee apparently already has tracked down "John from Iowa" using other means.[1040])

Somewhere around 11:15 p.m. on the Night of Benghazi, after only about five minutes or so hovering over the Mission Compound, the Predator drone reportedly is ordered to reposition over the nearby CIA Annex. According to the unnamed U.S. serviceman who claims to be this drone's camera operator, the purpose of this move is to assure the Annex also does not come under attack.

(The movement of this drone away from the Mission while the Ambassador remains missing, and before the Americans have finished evacuating, seems rather odd. Moreover, it is unclear to the author, and to "John from Iowa," what the *unarmed* drone possibly could do to prevent an attack on the Annex in any case.[1041] Subsequent events sadly will bear this out.)

Pursuant to orders, the drone's operators then remotely fly it the one-half mile or so and begin broadcasting (and recording) video from above the Annex.[1042] The RPA will transmit from there for almost the next five and one-half hours, until a second drone arrives to relieve it as its fuel runs low.[1043] ∎

[1040] Additional Views of Reps. Jordan and Pompeo, pp. 447-448; and Amanda Terkel, "Benghazi Committee Finally Interviews the Mysterious 'John From Iowa,'" *The Huffington Post* online (June 9, 2016; Updated June 10, 2016).

[1041] Hannity Radio Interview of Unnamed U.S. Serviceman ("We wouldn't have been able to do much anyways due to the Status of Forces Agreement that we had with . . . other host countries where we're located; we were not allowed to be armed that night").

[1042] *Id.*

[1043] Appendix: Key Delays on the Night of Benghazi ("Key Delays Appendix") (See September 11 entries at 5:15 p.m. and 11:00 p.m., both Washington time); and Sen. Intelligence Committee Benghazi Report, p. 29.

45

"We're Comin' In Hot!"

While Panetta and Dempsey continue to brief the president, back at the Mission Compound in Benghazi the Diplomatic Security agents and their GRS reinforcements have concluded Ambassador Chris Stevens cannot have survived the Villa fire. Their rescue attempts have evolved into a mission to recover his body.

Then, when the DSA and GRS agents still fail repeatedly to find Chris Stevens' remains in the Villa, the GRS Team Lead reportedly concludes the ambassador must have been kidnapped and removed from the Mission Compound.[1044] Perhaps the reason the attackers depart so quickly is because they have captured their objective – Ambassador Stevens. The more the Americans discuss possible scenarios, the more likely they judge a kidnapping has occurred.[1045]

(Indeed, it is entirely possible the Benghazi terrorists *do* originally plan to kidnap Stevens and hold him hostage (or execute him).[1046] If so, when they realize the Ambassador is beyond their reach in the Villa's safe haven, they likely alter their plan and elect to try to burn him to death.)

Some of the Americans at the Mission begin to discuss the possibility the attackers will return soon, and conclude they can't remain at the Mission much longer. The DSAs tell the GRS Team Lead they do not have sufficient weaponry to withstand an attack when they leave for the Annex. In response, Tig Tiegen gives his belt-fed machine gun to Dave Ubben, along with his last ammo drum. Tig keeps his assault rifle.[1047]

[1044] Sen. Intelligence Committee Benghazi Report, p. 7; and Zuckoff, *13 Hours*, Chap. 8, pp. 176-177.

[1045] Zuckoff, *13 Hours*, Chap. 8, pp. 171-172.

[1046] See, e.g., Kenneth R. Timmerman, "The Shadowy Iranian Spy Chief Who Helped Plan Benghazi," *New York Post* online (June 20, 2014) ("Their original orders [referring to Iranian "Kuds Force" operatives allegedly present in Benghazi in summer 2012] were to kidnap the U.S. ambassador while he was visiting Benghazi, and to destroy the CIA Annex. They wanted to drive the United States out of Benghazi, where they believed the CIA was supervising weapons transfers to the Syrian rebels").

[1047] *Id.*, Chap. 8, p. 168.

Meanwhile, Ubben, Jack Silva and Tanto Paronto make for the Mission's TOC to gather as many laptops and hard drives as possible before leaving for the Annex. When they return they move to an armored Land Cruiser positioned near the Main Gate. They dump the computer equipment through the open back hatch on top of some weapons already loaded there. Occasional shots begin being fired at the agents from the Back Gate area.[1048]

About this time, the Americans have begun receiving radio messages and telephone calls warning them that large groups of bad guys are reforming and moving toward the Mission. It's time to get the hell out. The DSAs enter their armored Land Cruiser and prepare to leave.[1049]

BOOM! Shortly after 11:00 p.m., an explosive device detonates inside the compound's unlocked Back Gate. A second wave of attacks on the Mission is underway. Armed militants again swarm onto the compound and open fire. (Some of the new attackers may have stayed hidden in a large grove of olive trees on the compound's grounds the entire time since the initial assault, and the GRS and 17 February searchers just missed them.[1050]) **BOOM!** Another explosion occurs to the side of the Villa building, from an RPG launched from the direction of the Mission's open Back Gate. **BOOM!** Another explosion goes off inside the compound.[1051]

Still inside the smoke-filled safe haven searching for the ambassador, Tig Tiegen hears the explosions and gunfire outside. He knows his mission must change. He quickly exits the Villa. Once outside, Tig gratefully gulps the fresh air. Then he sees a militant wielding an RPG launcher who has appeared from behind cover of the Annex wall at the Back Gate to fire another round toward the Villa. The attacker ducks back behind the wall. When this shooter reappears, Tig fires his assault weapon at the bad guy. The attacker goes down.[1052]

(None of the DSAs even have fired their weapons during these attacks on the Mission by the militants.)

[1048] *Id.*, Chap. 8, pp. 172-174.

[1049] *Id.*, Chap. 8, pp. 171 and 174-177.

[1050] Benghazi Committee Report, p. 72.

[1051] *Id.*, p. 71; and Baier, 13 Hours at Benghazi: The Inside Story (*Watch video there*; Go to 11:29-47).

[1052] Baier, 13 Hours at Benghazi: The Inside Story (*Watch video there*; Go to 11:48 - 12:11).

Team Annex remorselessly returns fire at the attackers. They provide cover while Rone and Jack load Sean Smith's body into the back of the armored Mercedes Team Annex soon will leave in. The DSAs, now all aboard their own vehicle, swiftly evacuate the Mission under fire through the Main Gate at about 11:16 p.m. Incredibly, the DSA who has inhaled the most smoke this night – Scott Wickland – ends up driving! A member of Team Annex radios to the Annex the DSAs are leaving the Mission ("State Department is leaving").[1053]

The Team Lead has learned by phone the bad guys are gathering to the right side as one leaves the Main Gate. Accordingly, he and GRS operator Rone Woods emphatically instruct Wickland to make a *left* turn out of the Mission to go to the Annex. Instead, Wickland inexplicably turns *right!*[1054]

This wrong turn leads the DSAs directly into an ambush! It is the fourth firefight of the night, but it is entirely one-sided. The good guys are on the receiving end. The DSAs change direction several times. They desperately attempt to avoid more potentially hostile large crowds and blockades. During this chaotic trip, their vehicle repeatedly comes under heavy fire from armed men they pass on the streets. But the armor and ballistic-resistant glass of their vehicle perform well. The assaults include a point-blank fusillade by militants with AK-47s standing just feet from their vehicle. Attackers throw grenades under their SUV. The blasts blow out two of their "run-flat" tires. Somehow, their vehicle keeps functioning.[1055]

Using a radio Jack Silva has given him, DSA Dave Ubben radios the Annex and the GRS operators at the Mission. He shouts, "We're taking heavy fire! We're on our run-flats!"[1056]

They have been followed from the Mission by an unidentified vehicle whose lights are off. It detours to a warehouse located near the CIA Annex. (Is this following vehicle how the terrorists learn of the Annex and its location?) As they draw near to the Annex, chief DSA Alec Henderson radios ahead to the CIA's TOC they are "Comin' in hot" (meaning *We're coming in fast, have the Annex gate open!*).[1057]

[1053] Benghazi Committee Report, pp. 71-72; Lamb Oversight Committee Prepared Testimony, p. 7; and Zuckoff, *13 Hours*, Chap. 9, p. 190.

[1054] Baier, 13 Hours at Benghazi: The Inside Story (*Watch video there*; Go to 12:20-37).

[1055] Zuckoff, *13 Hours*, Chap. 8, pp. 180-181, and Chap. 9, pp. 188-190.

[1056] *Id.*, Chap. 9, p. 189.

[1057] *Id.*, Chap. 9, pp. 190-191.

After a circuitous, seven-minute journey that seems like hours, all five very relieved survivors arrive in their bullet-ridden vehicle, unharmed, inside the CIA Annex. The gate is closed. CIA personnel standing in the courtyard are astonished at the shattered exterior condition of the DSAs' vehicle. They cannot believe anyone inside it possibly could have survived. Yet they all have. It is 11:23 p.m. in Benghazi.[1058]

Oz Geist descends the ladder from Building C's rooftop. He assumes command over the DSAs as well, even though they work for the State Department, not the CIA. Oz inspects the DSAs as they exit their vehicle, and is relieved they do not appear to be injured. He orders DSA Scott Wickland (who is covered with soot and looks to Oz like a "chimney sweep") to go inside the main building for medical care. Alec Henderson walks inside Building C to brief Chief of Base "Bob" and the other Annex managers on what happened at the Mission.[1059]

"I need people up on the roofs!" Oz commands. He directs the other DSAs to take positions on rooftops of the Annex buildings to be on guard until Team Annex returns. (*If* they return.) Oz places Ubben on the roof of Building D on the west side of the compound. Geist orders one of the Tripoli-based DSAs to the roof of Building A (near the front gate), and the other to Building B's rooftop. Then Oz himself returns to the rooftop of Building C to stand guard while awaiting his fellow GRS agents' arrival. He then radios Team Annex for a status report. When he learns they are preparing to depart the Mission, he descends the ladder to make a final check of the Annex defenses and to prepare for Team Annex's arrival.[1060]

Back at the Mission, the second-wave attack by the militants recedes. The GRS men no longer are under direct fire. Tig Tiegen later says of the lull, "It was like a light switch; everything stopped." The GRS Team Lead decides it is time to evacuate – without Stevens. He radios his men to collect and depart. They enter the armored Mercedes

---

[1058] Benghazi Committee Report, pp. 71-74, and Select Benghazi Timeline, p. 559; Lamb Oversight Committee Prepared Testimony, p. 7; Sen. Intelligence Committee Benghazi Report, p. 7; and Baier, 13 Hours at Benghazi: The Inside Story (*Watch video there*; Go to 12:25-48 and 14:06-38).

[1059] Zuckoff, *13 Hours*, Chap. 9, p. 191.

[1060] *Id.*, Chap. 9, pp. 191-192; and Baier, 13 Hours at Benghazi: The Inside Story (*Watch video there*; Go to 14:37-57).

(with Sean Smith's body in the back). They leave through the Main Gate sometime around 11:19 to 11:25 p.m.[1061]

Author Zuckoff concludes, "The moment they reached the gate, the United States Special Mission Compound in Benghazi would effectively cease to exist." Although every GRS man fears they are about to encounter an ambush, miraculously they do not. About 20 uneventful minutes later, the GRS rescue party arrives safely back at the CIA Annex.[1062]

After Team Annex leaves the Mission, terrorists reenter the compound grounds through the Back Gate. Some are armed, some not. The former discharge small arms fire, RPGs and explosives. The terrorists reset fires, loot the armored vehicles, commandeer an armored SUV, and steal papers and gear from the compound's Tactical Operations Center. Terrorists now control the former U.S. Mission Compound.[1063]

The Washington Post later reports on the prosecution of alleged terrorist leader Ahmed Abu Khatallah. Prosecutors tell the court, "Near midnight, Abu Khattala [sic] allegedly entered a mission office and oversaw the looting of data about a nearby CIA annex that soon came under mortar fire...." at around 5:15 a.m. The federal indictment against Khatallah also will claim he supervises this plunder of U.S. property at the Mission.[1064] If accurate, it is one possible explanation of how terrorists learn of the "secret" CIA Annex and its location.

Indeed, in his later testimony at Abu Khatallah's criminal trial (see Chapter 114 below), DSA Dave Ubben lends some corroboration to

---

[1061] Benghazi Committee Report, p. 74; and Baier, 13 Hours at Benghazi: The Inside Story (*Watch video there*; Go to 12:10-25 and 12:49-55). See also Sen. Intelligence Committee Benghazi Report, p. 7.

[1062] Benghazi Committee Report, p. 74; and Zuckoff, *13 Hours*, Chap. 8, pp. 186-187 and Chap. 9, pp. 192-195.

[1063] Benghazi Committee Report, p. 74; and Hicks Oversight Committee Testimony (May 8, 2013).

[1064] Khatallah Superseding Indictment, Count 1, ¶20(i), p. 8; Hsu, U.S. Will Not Seek Death Penalty for Accused Ringleader in Benghazi Attacks; Eyder Peralta, "Benghazi Suspect, Ahmed Abu Khattala [sic], Is Indicted on 17 New Charges," National Public Radio online (Oct. 14, 2014); and Hayes and Joscelyn, The Benghazi Report. See also DOJ Press Release, "Mustafa al-Imam Sentenced to 236 Months in Prison for September 2012 Terrorist Attack in Benghazi, Libya," Justice Dept. website (Jan. 23, 2020).

this *Washington Post* story. Ubben testifies that above his desk at the Mission Compound was a map which (like others at the Mission) "contained grid coordinates for the CIA post." This map reportedly was "the same size and color" of rolled-up or folded maps looters carried out of the office during the attack, according to surveillance camera video.[1065]

Later about Khatallah's trial, *The Washington Post* writes:
> Prosecutors allege it was only after Abu Khattala [sic] traveled after midnight to a militia headquarters with maps, charts, computers and other sensitive information looted from the diplomatic site that the secret CIA annex about a mile away came under small-arms fire, at about 12:45 a.m.[1066]

Because of the swiftness with which the numerous attackers have overwhelmed the lightly-defended Mission Compound in the two waves, it is clear sending military help from *outside Benghazi* could not have saved Stevens or Smith. However, Team Annex does help evacuate five Americans alive from the Mission.[1067] But the danger is far from over. ■

[1065] Hsu, Baring Grievous Wounds, Dry Humor, U.S. Agent Lays Out Key Evidence at Benghazi Trial.

[1066] *Id.*

[1067] Sen. Intelligence Committee Benghazi Report ("... U.S. personnel in Benghazi that night ... credited their lives being saved to the personnel [from the Annex] who responded to the attacks"), p. 27; and *Id.* ("The six-man CIA security team (plus an interpreter) ... did not make it in time to save Ambassador Stevens and Sean Smith, but they successfully evacuated the other Americans at the Mission facility to the Annex"), p. 29.

46

The Defenders of the Alamo

Back at the CIA Annex, come what may, by about 11:40 to 11:45 p.m. Benghazi time all the Americans from the Mission and Annex now are together – except for the missing Ambassador Stevens. Here they will "hunker down" and await Team Tripoli, which they have been told will be arriving later from the airport.

Although there is great sadness over the death of Sean Smith and apprehension over Ambassador Stevens' status, simultaneously there is an "uptick" in morale. All the security operators stationed in Benghazi now are together at the Alamo. Somehow, none have been killed or wounded during the rescue and evacuation from the Mission.[1068]

While Leon Panetta and General Dempsey are on their way back to the Pentagon from the White House, at the Annex in Benghazi staffers find a bedsheet to cover the body of Sean Smith in the back of the Mercedes. Then, as the drone overhead watches, the GRS agents rapidly join Oz Geist and the DSA agents in taking up defensive positions on the towers and rooftops. They make some adjustments in their preplanned positions to account for the addition of the DSA agents. All are exhausted. However, because they expect more attacks their adrenaline remains high.[1069]

Once at the CIA Annex, the State Department DSAs have resumed reporting back to the U.S. Tactical Operations Center in Tripoli, explaining the situation on the ground at the Benghazi Annex. They advise Tripoli that Ambassador Stevens' whereabouts and status still are unknown.

During this period, the Tripoli CIA Chief of Station contacts the Benghazi GRS Team Lead to ask if they require a "Medevac." At this time the answer is "no." (There also is discussion and uncertainty regarding exactly where in Benghazi any such Medevac even would go if needed.) Nevertheless, out of caution Tripoli prudently advises

---

[1068] Zuckoff, *13 Hours*, Chap. 9, p. 196.

[1069] Benghazi Committee Report, p. 74; Lamb Oversight Committee Prepared Testimony, p. 7; Zuckoff, *13 Hours*, Chap. 9, p. 195; and Baier, 13 Hours at Benghazi: The Inside Story (*Watch video there*; Go to 14:56 - 15:28).

AFRICOM in Stuttgart a Medevac may be needed.[1070] (Sadly, this request appears to have been ignored. No Medevac plane is readied. Still more nonchalance.)

After arriving back at the Annex, the GRS Team Lead also briefs "Bob," the Station Chief, on what has happened at the Mission. "Henry" the translator goes inside Building C for a well-earned de-compression. Within this structure, some of the CIA staff continue to destroy classified information. Others are filling "dozens of magazines" with ammunition for the defenders on the roofs and in the towers.[1071]

Rone Woods goes inside Building C to provide medical care to DSA Scott Wickland. According to author Zuckoff, Rone is the essence of confidence and swagger under pressure. One of the CIA "non-shooter" staffers later says Rone's confidence is infectious and helps lift morale. This is in complete contrast to Chief of Base "Bob," whose "defeatist" mannerisms anger Tanto Paronto. At this point Tanto has ducked into Building C quickly to get an update on what outside support and "overhead firepower" the defenders can expect to receive.[1072] (He will not be amused by the answers.)

In preparing for possible danger, one of the Tripoli DSAs is atop Building A, the building nearest the front gate. In addition to watching that gate, he also overlooks the Annex's south wall. The Annex security chief also stations himself near the front gate. D.B. Benton now stands guard on the roof of Building B on the east side of the compound. He soon is joined by an unhappy Tanto Paronto, who has heard no good news from inside Building C. D.B. and Tanto shortly are joined by the DSA agent from Building A, who wants a better vantage point if a fight comes. The CIA case officer with combat experience in Afghanistan maintains a position on the rooftop of Building C, which oversees the Annex's north wall. He soon is joined by Rone Woods, who has finished treating Scott Wickland and is now "jocked up" and ready for war. From this perch the defenders can view the area surrounding the Annex compound to the north and east – "Zombieland."[1073]

[1070] Benghazi Committee Report, pp. 74-75.

[1071] Zuckoff, *13 Hours*, Chap. 9, pp. 195-196.

[1072] *Id.*, Chap. 9, pp. 196, 200-201 and 203.

[1073] *Id.*, Chap. 9, pp. 196-197 and Chap. 11, pp. 247 and 250; and Baier, 13 Hours at Benghazi: The Inside Story (*Watch video there*; Go to 19:06-19).

THE TRUE ACCOUNT OF VALOR AND ABANDONMENT

Jack Silva stations himself on the rooftop of Building D, nearest the west wall. He is with DSA Dave Ubben and one of the Tripoli DSAs, an army veteran.[1074]

The three Libyan guards are atop the steel towers. Tig Tiegen joins two of them, taking up a position at the Annex's southeast corner. Like others who were inside the Mission Villa, Tig is still feeling the effects of smoke inhalation from his multiple search trips inside the Villa. As Zuckoff puts it, "Tig felt as though he might cough up a lung."[1075]

During this time, Oz Geist is constantly on the move. He wants to confirm every defender is in a good position and knows his field of fire. He also brings ammo and water to several of the security men. Oz climbs onto the roof of Building D and speaks with Jack Silva. Oz asks for a summary of what happened at the Mission. After, when he is satisfied with everyone's deployment, Oz takes up a position on the steel tower at the corner of the exterior wall to the northeast of Building C. In the darkness he surveys Zombieland. He also studies two large sheep pens, where two shepherds are tending to several hundred sheep.[1076]

As Zuckoff describes the defenders: "They checked their gunsights and weapons. They determined their fields of fire, so each man knew which area to be watching for attackers."[1077]

From time-to-time, some of the newly-arrived GRS agents take brief bathroom breaks. Next they restock their ammo, and grab some water and Gatorade bottles and snack bars.[1078]

At some point, the GRS Team Lead comes over the radio with answers to questions Tanto Paronto has posed to him earlier. The Team Lead (who mostly stays inside during this period) advises there is an unarmed drone above them. However, there is no word on a gunship arriving.[1079]

During this lull, since no Spectre gunship is coming Tanto wants more firepower. He descends the ladder and begins looking for a grenade launcher. He checks the vehicles without success. He radios an inquiry whether anyone knows where one is, but no one replies. Next

---

[1074] Zuckoff, *13 Hours*, Chap. 9, pp. 196-197.

[1075] *Id.*, Chap. 9, pp. 196-197 and 200.

[1076] *Id.*, Chap. 9, pp. 196 and 203-205.

[1077] *Id.*, Chap. 9, p. 201.

[1078] *Id.*, Chap. 9, p. 201.

[1079] *Id.*, Chap. 9, p. 201.

Tanto goes inside Building C. He comes out empty-handed except for some extra magazines of ammo he has crammed into his pockets.[1080] *Damn it!*

Tig Tiegen radios a request for someone to turn on the exterior floodlights aimed away from the Annex's walls. They soon go on, but so do the interior floodlights. This enables anyone watching from outside to see the defenders' positions! Equally bad, the lights blind the defenders, who can't see outside the compound. Several agents radio expletive-filled demands for someone to turn the interior floodlights off. Some GRS men badly want to shoot out the interior floodlights, but the sound of gunfire would draw unneeded attention to the Annex compound in the middle of the night. After a frustrating delay, some CIA staffer inside the buildings finally figures out how to turn the damned interior lights out.[1081]

As discussed next, five thousand miles to the west at the Pentagon Secretary Panetta just has convened a planning session with his generals. Four hundred miles to the west, Team Tripoli is preparing to depart for Benghazi. Minutes later at 12:07 p.m. Benghazi time, State is issuing an alert advising Ansar al-Sharia is claiming credit for the attacks on the Mission. They also reportedly are calling for attacks on the very Embassy Team Tripoli has just left.[1082] Despite this enhanced danger, to their credit no one in Tripoli asks Team Tripoli to return and reinforce the Embassy.

Back in the gloom on the rooftops and towers, the Benghazi Annex defenders thus far are unaware of these new developments. One of the GRS agents looks at his watch. It is eight minutes past midnight in Benghazi. The anniversary of 9/11 is over. But the Battle of Benghazi is not. ■

[1080] *Id.*, Chap. 9, p. 200.

[1081] *Id.*, Chap. 9, pp. 198-199; and Benghazi Committee Report, p. 75.

[1082] Zuckoff, *13 Hours*, Chap. 9, p. 197.

47

Panetta's Council of War

As previously indicated, after the 5:00 p.m. briefing with President Obama, Secretary Panetta and General Dempsey immediately return to the Pentagon. They arrive there about 6:00 p.m. Panetta and Dempsey then convene a meeting of "relevant members" of the Secretary's staff and the Joint Staff to assess what military assets to deploy in this crisis.

Also attending this meeting is AFRICOM Commander General Carter Ham, who happens to be in Washington (instead of at his headquarters in Stuttgart, Germany). Vice Admiral James Winnefeld and General John F. Kelly (Senior Military Assistant to the Secretary of Defense) frequently update the participants with new information. (Kelly later will become President Trump's Director of Homeland Security, and then his second White House Chief of Staff.) Winnefeld briefs the gathering on the current deployment of U.S. military forces that might be able to respond to the violence in Benghazi. According to the Select Committee, the Joint Staff surprisingly "did not keep a daily updated list of assets and their locations."[1083] (No wonder this "council of war" will drag on for an hour.)

At this meeting Panetta is not told of the two DoD special forces members stationed at a U.S. Tripoli Annex who will become a part of "Team Tripoli." Nor is he informed of four other special forces soldiers (referenced in Chapter 18, above, and discussed further below) who are part of a "training mission" at the U.S. Embassy in Tripoli.[1084]

Three Military Assets Are Chosen

"During this Pentagon meeting, three distinct capabilities are identified to deploy in response to the attacks in Benghazi": two platoons of U.S. Marines stationed in Rota, Spain – which are part of

---

[1083] Panetta, *Worthy Fights*, Chap. 16, p. 428; Benghazi Committee Report, pp. 69-70; and Rosen, Top Defense Officials Briefed Obama on "Attack" Not Video or Protest.

[1084] Benghazi Committee Report (". . . [T]he Secretary was not aware, and was not told, of any assets in Tripoli"), p. 70; and *Id.* (Regarding the DoD personnel in Tripoli, ". . . this 'asset' or 'element' was not even on the list of 'assets' and 'elements' provided to the Secretary of Defense"), p. 109.

the "Fleet Antiterrorism Security Team"; a "Commander's In Extremis Force" ("CIF"), currently on a training exercise in Croatia; and the U.S.-based Special Operations Force ("SOF") stationed at Ft. Bragg, North Carolina, "capable of response to crises worldwide."[1085]

Panetta later will write that, with the addition of "Team Tripoli": Those were all of the units that could plausibly respond. *No aircraft*, no aircraft carrier, no surface ship would have gotten there any faster, given the realities of moving those assets over the great distances needed to get them into position *in time to make a difference*.[1086]

(As discussed below, this conclusion ignores completely the options of sending an armed drone to Benghazi,[1087] or seeking help from our allies.)

We next describe briefly the three military "capabilities" Panetta has chosen tonight.

The "Fleet Antiterrorism Security Team"

According to the Select Benghazi Committee's report, there are Marine Fleet Antiterrorism Security Team (known by the inapt acronym "FAST") platoons stationed at U.S. Naval Station Rota in Rota, Spain. (Rota is a port city located in southwestern Spain on the Bay of Cadiz on the Atlantic Ocean side of the Straits of Gibraltar. It is quite near the Mediterranean Sea, and is known as the "Gateway to the Mediterranean." Naval Station Rota is approximately 1,500 air miles from Benghazi, and 1,100 miles from Tripoli.[1088])

According to *Stars and Stripes*, on the Night of Benghazi these FAST platoons each are comprised of "about 50 marines trained in crisis response operations."[1089] The Select Committee explains, "FAST

[1085] *Id.*, p. 70; and Panetta, *Worthy Fights*, Chap. 16, p. 429.

[1086] Panetta, *Worthy Fights* (emphasis added), Chap. 16, p. 429.

[1087] Additional Views of Reps. Jordan and Pompeo ("An asset that could have made a difference would have been armed drones. And as the Committee learned, it would have been relatively fast and easy to arm a drone. . . ."), p. 447.

[1088] Benghazi Committee Report, p. 7.

[1089] Chris Carroll and John Vandiver, "Marine Anti-Terrorism Team Dispatched to Libya After Diplomats Killed," *Stars and Stripes* online (Sept. 12, 2012). See also Adam Housley and Jennifer Griffin, "Facts and Questions About What Happened in Benghazi," Fox News online (Jan. 22, 2013) ("The FAST team . . . was made up of about 50 Marines . . . .").

platoons, as of September 2012, were typically used to reinforce embassy security and operated from a fixed location within an embassy."[1090]

Amazingly, in September 2012 the FAST groups (including the ones in Rota) do not have their own dedicated aircraft. (Does the Pentagon believe any terrorist problem only will occur in the greater Rota area?) They must wait for a plane to arrive from another location, most likely Germany, before being deployed onward![1091] Typically, FAST platoons and their equipment are transported by C-130s, such as those housed at Ramstein, Germany – 1,100 miles away.[1092] (However, in the days leading up to, and including, September 11, none of these C-130s are on heightened alert.[1093]) Nor do FAST teams deploy with their own vehicles, making them dependent on others for ground mobility. This further limits their effectiveness as a "quick-reaction force."[1094]

On this Night of Benghazi, the commanders of the FAST platoons in Rota issue an order for their Marines to return to base at about midnight in Rota (6:00 p.m. in Washington, just as Leon Panetta convenes his "council of war" at the Pentagon).[1095]

The "Commander's In Extremis Force"

In addition to the FAST Marine groups, the U.S. European Command also has an asset known as the "Commander's In Extremis Force" ("CIF"). European Command shares this CIF with Africa Command. The Select Committee describes it as "one of the most capable quick response forces." According to Aaron Klein of WorldNetDaily.com, the CIF consists of 40 special operators. The AFRICOM Commander, General Carter Ham, later testifies the CIF is "the force of first choice should there be an emergent situation." The

---

[1090] Benghazi Committee Report, p. 58.

[1091] *Id.*, pp. 58 and 116; and Kevin Baron, "Marines Move Crisis Response Force to Edge of Africa," ForeignPolicy.com website (April 25, 2013) ("The Marine FAST platoon in Rota, Spain, was hindered in its response because it lacked dedicated airlift at its location; the airlift was in Germany. . . .").

[1092] Benghazi Committee Report, p. 7.

[1093] *Id.*, pp. 58 and 66.

[1094] *Id.*, p. 58.

[1095] *Id.*, p. 116.

CIF is "a special operations response team that offers capabilities for emergency action in missions such as *hostage rescue, noncombatant evacuation when the security situation is uncertain, or convoy security.*" Unlike the FAST teams, CIF has its own dedicated aircraft and deploys with its own vehicles. This latter asset gives the CIF the capability to drive from an airfield upon landing to a "crisis site."[1096] (Sounds perfect for the Benghazi crisis, doesn't it?)

The CIF sometimes works with the U.S.-based Special Operations Force, discussed next. However, when that force is not feasible (due to time and distance challenges), "the CIF can assault a target immediately."[1097]

The CIF normally is stationed in Germany. However, in the days leading up to September 11, 2012, the CIF is deployed to Croatia to perform a long-planned joint training exercise. (What military genius plans such an exercise on the 9/11 anniversary? On the other hand, Croatia actually is *closer* to Benghazi than is Germany.) Sharyl Attkisson reports that from Croatia the CIF would have only a three-hour flight to Libya, and a two-hour flight to Sigonella Naval Air Station in Sicily.[1098] At one point during this Night of Benghazi, the Chief of Staff to Secretary Panetta sends an email to a State Department official, explaining that a special operations "element" that is in Croatia (no doubt referencing the CIF) ". . . can fly to Suda [sic Souda] Bay, Crete. . . . ," which is the U.S. base closest to Benghazi.[1099] As noted below, why the U.S. base at Souda Bay ultimately is excluded completely from any response to the Benghazi crisis remains baffling.

The "Special Operations Force"

Finally, the U.S. military has available its U.S.-based Special Operations Force ("U.S. SOF" or "SOF"). On this night in 2012, the SOF is based at Fort Bragg, North Carolina. The SOF "offers

---

[1096] Benghazi Committee Report, (emphasis added), pp. 58-59; Letter from Elizabeth L. King, Assistant Secretary of Defense for Legislative Affairs, to Rep. Elijah E. Cummings (D-MD) (May 7, 2013), Democrat House Oversight website, p. 1; and Klein, Secret Purpose of Benghazi Annex Still Secret.

[1097] Benghazi Committee Report, p. 59.

[1098] Attkisson, *Stonewalled*, Chap. 4, pp. 159-160.

[1099] *Id.*, pp. 59 and 83; and Letter from Elizabeth L. King, Assistant Secretary of Defense for Legislative Affairs, to Rep. Elijah E. Cummings (D-MD) (May 7, 2013), Democrat House Oversight website, p. 1.

capabilities that complement and expand upon the assets brought by the CIF. . . . If time permits, the preferred option is to hand the target over to the U.S. SOF, given its more robust capabilities." One of SOF's functions is hostage rescue. On occasion, the CIF and U.S. SOF both work together. However, given time and distance factors, the CIF typically will be able to reach an overseas target first. The U.S. SOF will have to travel more than 5,400 miles to Benghazi, compared to about 1,000 miles for the CIF platoon in Croatia. Nevertheless, tonight the Pentagon wisely launches SOF "just in case." (As events will play out, the tardy CIF will reach Sigonella, Sicily only about 90 minutes before SOF arrives there.[1100] Neither asset will proceed to Benghazi.)

NATO Military Assets

Beyond a possible armed drone deployment, there is another glaring omission in Secretary Panetta's description of the available military assets on this night. It is an omission as big as Alaska. In assessing whether military assets can reach Benghazi on this horrible night, these Pentagon chiefs (like most pundits, reporters and U.S. government officials) are considering only *United States'* military assets. However, the U.S. has allies. Lots of them.

Consider NATO. Several of our NATO allies have military bases in the Mediterranean region – Italy, Greece, France and Spain immediately come to mind. Then there is Israel, one of our closest and most vital non-NATO allies. Do none of these countries have assets that can help the U.S. in its hour of crisis on this Night of Benghazi? Does anyone at the White House, the Pentagon, Foggy Bottom or Langley even *ask* them? In fact, they do *not*.[1101] Does Secretary Panetta speak to the Supreme NATO Commander this night? If not, *why not?* (In their memoirs, Leon Panetta and Hillary Clinton do not even mention the possibility of enlisting our allies.) What good is having allies if you can't turn to them in an emergency, as the Battle of Benghazi assuredly is?

(Is it possible our allies are not consulted on this Night of Benghazi because of how weak this would make Team Obama appear to the American voters in the impending election? After all, if the Obama administration must rely upon allies to rescue U.S. government

---

[1100] Benghazi Committee Report, p. 59; and Key Delays Appendix (See September 12 entries for 1:57 p.m. and 3:28 p.m., both Washington time).

[1101] Attkisson, *Stonewalled* ("Nobody asked NATO for assistance"), Chap. 4, p. 168.

personnel abroad on the 9/11 anniversary, won't this portray Obama and the U.S. as weak and unprepared (which of course they *are*)? If this in fact is the truth, it is a pathetic reason not to seek help for three dozen Americans in mortal, real-time peril abroad.)

Delays in Pentagon Decision-Making

The fact the Defense Secretary and his top brass will take approximately an hour to identify the military assets that can be deployed this night also is disturbing. Their leisurely meeting is convened in the middle of a national security emergency. Meanwhile, in Libya events are unfolding rapidly, not waiting for Panetta and his generals to finish scratching their heads with their pistols.[1102] (Indeed, as discussed below, minutes into this council of war "Team Tripoli" leaves for the airport. Minutes later, the State Department will issue an alert advising Ansar al-Sharia is claiming credit for the Benghazi assaults, and is calling for attacks on the U.S. Embassy in Tripoli. Halfway through this council, Team Tripoli will depart Tripoli airport. And during the second half of this council, the first-wave attack at the supposedly "secret" CIA Annex in Benghazi will begin and end.[1103] However, it is unclear when Panetta and his staff actually receive word of this attack.)

When Panetta's session finally wraps up around 7:00 p.m.,[1104] well over *three hours* have elapsed since the first attack begins! (This meeting should take ten minutes, tops. And it should occur much earlier in the evening, and preferably in the White House Situation Room.)

Let us take a brief departure to assess precisely what other military assets are available to Defense chief Panetta and his generals as they conduct their 6:00 p.m. council of war on this Night of Benghazi. In other words, for those readers who wish to join us, for the next few pages let's play "Second Guess the Pentagon." ∎

[1102] Attkisson, *Stonewalled* ("Those involved in the U.S. response to the attacks tell me that the U.S. government was in sheer chaos that night. . . ."), Prologue, p. 3.

[1103] Key Delays Appendix (See September 11 entries for 6:07 p.m., 6:30 p.m., 6:34 p.m., and 6:51 p.m., all Washington time).

[1104] Benghazi Committee Report, p. 70.

48

"We Chose Not to Do It"

Beyond the three assets Secretary Panetta reportedly decides to deploy, what other military assets actually are known to be available to the Pentagon as they conduct their 6:00 p.m. planning meeting at the Pentagon? (In the interest of brevity, we principally consider U.S. assets, as our "leaders" apparently do this dreadful night.)

Theoretical Possible Military Responses:

As SecDef Panetta and General Dempsey meet with their staffs on this Night of Benghazi, on paper there are lots of U.S. military assets available. However, none are on any serious level of alert despite the 9/11 anniversary. And the military tools closest to Benghazi supposedly have no planes available to take them there, or no nearby air tankers to get any planes there and back. But perhaps most dismal of all, there seems to be an absolute lack of political and military will to launch any military assets to Benghazi.[1105]

The author has no military experience, and is far from an expert in this area. However, even an amateur can identify some of the obvious military options Panetta and his generals might want to consider deploying on this night. They include:

- A Predator drone armed with "Hellfire" missiles;[1106]
- An AC-130H Spectre gunship over Benghazi to kill and disperse the terrorists;
- Attack helicopters to do the same;
- A "flyover" by jet fighter aircraft to frighten and disperse the attackers;

[1105] Attkisson, *Stonewalled* (". . . Those with knowledge of military assets and Special Forces tell me that resources weren't fully utilized to try to mount a rescue while the attacks were under way. . . ."), Prologue, p. 3.

[1106] Additional Views of Reps. Jordan and Pompeo ("An asset that could have made a difference would have been armed drones. And as the Committee learned, it would have been relatively fast and easy to arm a drone. . . ."), p. 447.

- A flight of armed U.S. (or allied) soldiers into Benghazi airport, and from there to the Annex;
- Inserting paratroopers into the Benghazi area near the CIA Annex; and
- Surveillance aircraft to supplement the intelligence provided by the drones that do arrive.

We consider variations of several of these options below.

Actual U.S. Military Assets Available

During the Select Committee's inquiry, the Pentagon provides the panel with maps that identify then-available U.S. military assets at various locations. When the committee identifies an asset missing from the maps, its members inquire of DoD whether there are any other assets not on the maps, or that were withheld due to classified information restrictions. Defense officials refuse to reply to the Select Committee's (quite reasonable) inquiry.[1107] This refusal only adds to many other doubts concerning the Obama administration's claimed transparency relating to the Benghazi fiasco.

U.S. *Troop* Assets Nearest to Libya

AFRICOM Troops in Djibouti

As noted above, Libya is the responsibility of U.S. Africa Command. However, as bad luck will have it, AFRICOM has very few of its own assigned forces. AFRICOM's sole troop force of any size is a contingent of soldiers (of uncertain strength), stationed in the Republic of Djibouti, on the Gulf of Aden near the Horn of Africa.[1108] These troops are some 2,000 miles from Benghazi.[1109] They are farther from Benghazi than most other assets Panetta and his team are considering (including FAST and CIF, and aircraft from Souda Bay, Sigonella and Aviano). Obviously, however, these Djibouti troops are much closer to Benghazi than the U.S.-based SOF at Fort Bragg (over 5,400 miles) that Panetta has ordered to deploy to the North Africa region tonight. Apparently, however, the Djibouti troops lack air

---

[1107] Benghazi Committee Report, p. 70.

[1108] *Id.*, pp. 57-58.

[1109] *Id.*, p. 7.

transport. (A familiar refrain.) AFRICOM's assets in Djibouti therefore are useless in North Africa this night.

Thus, in order to respond quickly to any events occurring in Libya (or elsewhere in Africa), AFRICOM must rely upon troops, aircraft, ships, bases and equipment in the U.S. and European Commands. This need to rely on other military commands will exacerbate an already bad situation. We consider next the assets of those other U.S. commands.

U.S. Soldiers in Tripoli

In September 2012, the U.S. has literally only a handful of its soldiers stationed in Tripoli, Libya (a one-hour flight from Benghazi). First, the United States Embassy in Tripoli has a contingent of U.S. Marines of uncertain size.[1110] The U.S. government officials apparently do not consider moving any of these soldiers to Benghazi. (As noted, there are no Marines stationed at the Benghazi Mission Compound.)

Second, AFRICOM has six soldiers in Tripoli. Two of these are special forces soldiers working at an "annex" in Tripoli. These already have become part of the Team Tripoli rescue mission (discussed above and below). (This unit has just left the U.S. Embassy in Tripoli for the airport as Panetta convenes his council of war.) Third, there also are four special operations personnel who are part of a "training mission" at the U.S. Embassy in Tripoli.[1111] (As discussed in Chapter 80, early the following morning SOCAFRICA will order these four soldiers *not* to fly to Benghazi.)

As noted above, during the attacks, Defense Secretary Panetta does not even know these last two groups (containing six military personnel) are in Libya.[1112] As the Select Committee report summarizes, "... [T]he only U.S. military asset to actually reach Benghazi during the attacks [the two soldiers on Team Tripoli] was an asset the

---

[1110] Clinton, *Hard Choices*, Chap. 17, p. 393. In the days following Benghazi, White House Press Secretary Jay Carney appears to confirm a reporter's statement there are no Marines at the Tripoli Embassy, despite administration officials previously having said there were. Press Briefing by Press Secretary Jay Carney, The White House, Obama White House Archives (Sept. 19, 2012). However, in her book former Secretary Clinton clearly states there are Marines at the U.S. Embassy in Tripoli.

[1111] Benghazi Committee Report, pp. 70 and 109.

[1112] *Id.*, p. 70 ("... [T]he Secretary was not aware, and was not told, of any assets in Tripoli"); and *Id.* at p. 109 (Regarding the DoD personnel in Tripoli, "... this 'asset' or 'element' was not even on the list of 'assets' and 'elements' provided to the Secretary of Defense").

Secretary [of Defense] did not know about, was not told about by his subordinates, and did not learn about until after the fact."[1113]

Marine Troops at Sigonella?

At times, there has been a Marine detachment stationed at Sigonella Naval Air Station in Sicily (discussed in more detail below). This is an hour flight time from Benghazi. Based on one group photo, this unit appears to have consisted of about 80 Marines.[1114] Is there such a detachment here on this Night of Benghazi? If so, why is it not flown to Benghazi's airport this night – by charter aircraft or otherwise?

U.S. *Air* Assets Nearest to Libya

Predator Drones

One key air asset that can help in Benghazi is remotely-piloted "Predator" drones. Such drones can be armed with "Hellfire" missiles. There is a U.S. drone base at a classified location in southern Europe. On September 11, 2012, the U.S. Air Force operates four drones from this base. (The pilots are located in the U.S.) This base is only *four-hours flight time* to Benghazi. The Battle of Benghazi (including the evacuation) will last for over *twelve* hours.[1115]

As explained below, an unarmed replacement drone will arrive above the CIA Annex at 5:00 a.m. Benghazi time. This is fifteen minutes before the fatal mortar attack.[1116] *What if this second drone had been armed?* (Obviously, if the base's two other drones are on missions tonight, it will take time to fly them back to the base to arm them.)

These drones conduct missions over several nations – including Libya. However, *none of these four drones are armed on this Night of Benghazi*. The reasons they are unarmed are varied; they include: the supposed lack of need for military force after Qadhafi's takedown (Right!); the opposition of the government hosting the drone base (and

---

[1113] Benghazi Committee Report, p. 64.

[1114] Undated online photograph of Sigonella Naval Air Station.

[1115] Benghazi Committee Report, pp. 60-61; and Key Delays Appendix (See September 11 entry for 3:42 p.m. and September 12 entry 3:54 a.m., both Washington time).

[1116] Key Delays Appendix (See September 11 entries for 11:00 p.m., 11:15 p.m., and 11:17 p.m., all Washington time).

THE TRUE ACCOUNT OF VALOR AND ABANDONMENT

apparently also of the Libyan "government"); and the drones' capacity to carry more fuel without missiles, permitting longer missions.[1117]

According to *The New York Times Magazine*, one of the most influential Obama advisors on using drones against terrorists is Assistant to the President for Counterterrorism John Brennan.[1118] However, Brennan virtually is missing in action on this Night of Benghazi. The Select Committee's report virtually ignores any role by Brennan, except his efforts to withhold information from Congress after the attacks.

There supposedly are no military ground controllers in Libya this night to direct fire from a drone had one been armed. However, a GRS agent later testifies *all six* of the GRS men in Benghazi possess the military experience to call in an armed drone strike. On this Night of Benghazi this option apparently is mooted by the policy to fly only unarmed drones in the region since Qadhafi's fall.[1119]

(Tonight, a true U.S. national security emergency is playing out in Benghazi. Initially about thirty, later almost three dozen, American lives are in jeopardy – including a U.S. ambassador. The U.S. commanders should disregard the sensibilities of the drone base "host government" and Libyan government and arm a damned Predator drone or two or three and fly the damned things the four hours to Benghazi. This almost certainly can be done in time to be in position above the Annex before the fatal mortar attacks at about 5:17 a.m., Benghazi time.[1120] Instead, the U.S. possibly sacrifices two American lives (and sustains severe injuries to two other heroes) just to avoid ruffling diplomatic feathers of a few allies. In such cases, as Jed Babbin

---

[1117] Benghazi Committee Report, pp. 60-61 and 63.

[1118] Schwartz, A Spymaster Steps Out of the Shadows.

[1119] *Id.*, pp. 62-64; and Hannity Radio Interview of Unnamed U.S. Serviceman (emphasis added) ("We wouldn't have been able to do much anyways due to the Status of Forces Agreement that we had with . . . other host countries where we're located; *we were not allowed to be armed that night*").

[1120] Additional Views of Reps. Jordan and Pompeo (". . . Although a Department of Defense drone circled overhead in Benghazi during much of the attack, the military never sent an armed drone that could possibly have changed the course of events during the hours-long siege, especially as the terrorists pounded the Annex with mortar fire. An armed drone never came. Why?), p. 444; and *Id.* ("An asset that could have made a difference would have been armed drones. And as the Committee learned, it would have been relatively fast and easy to arm a drone. . . ."), p. 447.

explains, it is better to seek forgiveness later than permission now.[1121] Let them get over it.)

This failure to arm and launch Predator drones with missiles and get them to Benghazi clearly is one of the most significant failings of the U.S. military (and perhaps the State Department) on this Night of Benghazi. We have the drones and pilots available. We have missiles to put on them. They are in range to reach Benghazi within hours. Yet they are not launched.[1122] This is betrayal.

A Jet Aircraft "Flyover

As noted above, one possible military response to the Benghazi attacks is a simple "flyover" by U.S. fighter aircraft, in the hope of alarming the militants that have gathered to assault the CIA Annex enough to disperse them. It might not work. But does the Pentagon have a good reason not to at least *try* it in this crisis? (As far as the U.S. military knows this night, it may even be possible for jet aircraft to drop bombs on the attackers. Except none of its planes has any loaded.)

At least three of the GRS operators believe such a simple flyover could have helped their situation on this Night of Benghazi. In a lengthy interview with Fox News, John "Tig" Tiegen says, "I was expecting at least some kind of air support, even if it was just a flyover by a jet or whatever." His colleague Kris "Tanto" Paronto adds, "Sometimes that's all it takes; it gets the bad guys down." And Mark "Oz" Geist states, "And no doubt that would have been nice."[1123]

Investigative reporter and author Sharyl Attkisson writes that, following the Benghazi tragedy, she frequently is approached by unidentified men "affiliated with the secretive world of military Special Operations." Attkisson reports these men contend that a U.S. military plane should have gotten to Benghazi quickly and "buzzed over the

---

[1121] See, e.g., Babbin, Whitewashing Benghazi (". . . The administration tried to excuse inaction by saying it did not have Libyan permission to cross the border with armed aircraft or troops. In cases such as these, it's always better to ask forgiveness than permission").

[1122] Additional Views of Reps. Jordan and Pompeo (". . . [T]he fighter planes and armed drones never left the ground. . . ."), p. 445.

[1123] Baier, 13 Hours at Benghazi: The Inside Story (*Watch video there*; Go to 15:57 - 16:09).

site." She quotes one such source as saying, "You should see 'em scatter when a plane buzzes in low! But we didn't even try."[1124]

Gregory Hicks tells congressional investigators he, too, believes such a flyover could have worked. In April 2013, Hicks reportedly tells House Oversight investigators:

> ... I believe if we had been able to scramble a fighter or aircraft or two over Benghazi as quickly as possible after the attack commenced, I believe there would not have been a mortar attack on the annex in the morning because I believe the Libyans would have split. They would have been scared to death that we would have gotten a laser on them and killed them.[1125]

(An email Hillary Clinton sends in 2014 after she leaves office and containing classified information describes just such an effect.[1126]) However, according to the Select Committee the Commander of Africa Command determines even prior to Benghazi that if any attack is to occur on September 11, it likely would be on a small scale and "fighter aircraft would not be the right tool to respond."[1127]

[1124] Attkisson, *Stonewalled*, Chap. 4, p. 159.

[1125] Attkisson, Diplomat: U.S. Special Forces Told "You Can't Go" to Benghazi During Attacks (Greg Hicks: "... The Libyans that I talked to and the Libyans and other Americans who were involved in the war have told me also that Libyan revolutionaries were very cognizant of the impact that American and NATO airpower had with respect to their victory. They are under no illusions that American and NATO airpower won that war for them. And so, in my personal opinion, a fast-mover flying over Benghazi at some point ... as soon as possible might very well have prevented some of the bad things that happened that night"); and Gehrke, E-Mail: Military Offered to Send Rescue Team to Benghazi During Attack. See also ABC News, Hicks Sept. 2013 Interview With Stephanopoulos ("I don't know exactly what was available. ... I still don't quite understand why they couldn't fly aircraft over to Benghazi. ... I just thought that they would come. ...") (*Watch video there*; Go to 6:39 - 7:18).

[1126] Katie Pavlich, "Unsecured Podesta-Hillary Exchange Exposes Intelligence Source on the Ground in Libya," Townhall.com website (Oct. 13, 2016), quoting August 2014 Email from Former Secretary Hillary Clinton to Counselor to the President John Podesta Re "Here's What I Mentioned" (Aug. 19, 2014) ("... A source in Tripoli stated in confidence that when the U.S. Embassy was evacuated, the presence of two U.S. Navy jet fighters over the city brought all fighting to a halt for several hours, as Islamist forces were not certain that these aircraft would not also provide close ground support for moderate government forces"); and "Special Report" with Bret Baier, Fox News Channel (Oct. 21, 2016).

[1127] Benghazi Committee Report, p. 60.

The Pentagon's Excuses

After the crisis, the U.S. military will have numerous reasons why it does not deploy jet fighters to Benghazi tonight. We examine some of these briefly here.

There Are No Refueling Tankers

The jet aircraft that are available at Aviano Air Base in northeastern Italy (discussed below) will require refueling to reach Benghazi. However, the closest tankers are in Mildenhall, England, some 700 miles from Aviano![1128] The Select Committee concludes that because of the distance, the F-16s will require two air refuelings to reach Benghazi.[1129]

This absence of U.S. refueling tankers begs the question whether our NATO allies also have no such tankers in the Mediterranean region. Is the entire NATO alliance in southern Europe also as unprepared as the U.S. is this night? These allies provided tankers during the mission to topple Qadhafi in Libya. Why can't they do so again tonight?[1130]

Secretary Panetta later admits there is no air-refueling tanker available in the entire Mediterranean area. If true, this arguably is gross negligence on the part of Panetta and the Defense Department – particularly on the anniversary of 9/11. It leaves every American in North Africa vulnerable.[1131]

In any event, the unavailability of an in-air refueling tanker should not be determinative. Aviano is only about 600 miles from Sigonella Naval Air Station in eastern Sicily. U.S. F-16 fighters flying out of

---

[1128] *Id.*, pp. 59-60.

[1129] *Id.*, p. 60.

[1130] House Oversight Committee Hearings (May 8, 2013) (Remarks of Rep. Jason Chaffetz (R-UT): ". . . I think one of the hard questions we have to ask is not only about the tankers, but what was the NATO response? We flew for months over Libya. For months, we conducted an air campaign. And we have assets. We have NATO partners. We worked, for instance, with the Italians. It is stunning that our government, the power of the United States of America, couldn't get a tanker in the air"), p. 66.

[1131] Benghazi Committee Report ("These impediments to any fighter aircraft response from Aviano to North Africa were well known prior to September 11. Yet the alert posture of the aircraft at Aviano did not change in advance of that date, nor did the alert posture change after the protests in Cairo, Egypt"), p. 60.

Aviano toward Benghazi have a range of 2,000 miles.[1132] Why can't they land at Sigonella and be refueled? Sigonella is very close to the direct flight path from Aviano to Benghazi. Sigonella's landing strip can accommodate jet fighters, and it has its own fuel storage facilities. (Indeed, during Operation Odyssey Dawn against Qadhafi, discussed above, Spanish F-18 and other coalition fighters refueled at Sigonella.) Sigonella is an hour flight time from Libya.[1133] Such a landing, refueling, and takeoff can be accomplished in minutes. Under this plausible scenario, U.S. jets from Aviano could be over Benghazi and available to flyover or strafe the terrorist attackers some three hours or so after takeoff from Aviano. Yet Panetta and the entire Obama administration consistently maintain no military support is available for the entire thirteen hours of the assaults and evacuation!

(Despite the fact nearly 30 American lives are in peril, the U.S. military exhibits very little in the way of urgency or "outside-the-box" thinking on this night of September 11, 2012. Too bad the CIA's Head of Station in Tripoli isn't the Defense Secretary this night.)

Former Deputy Under Secretary of Defense Jed Babbin disagrees with Team Obama. He explains, "There were other aircraft – F-15s [sic F-16s] and more – at our airbase in Aviano, Italy, that could have been alerted. Even if it took an hour to gather intelligence and arm the aircraft, even if they had to land at Sigonella to quickly refuel because no tankers were available, they could have arrived long before the 5:00 a.m. [sic 5:15 a.m.] attack on the annex."[1134]

It Is the Middle of the Night

The Vice Chairman of the Joint Chiefs of Staff, Vice Admiral James Winnefeld, claims to the Select Committee that F-16s would do no good in Benghazi because it is "the middle of the night" there.[1135] True. But where is it written an air force cannot do a flyover at night?

Also, the odds are very good that at some point it will start to get light and the sun will rise in Benghazi. Sunrise there on September 12,

---

[1132] U.S. Air Force Fact Sheet for F-16 Fighting Falcon, Air Force website (Sept. 23, 2015).

[1133] "Operation Odyssey Dawn," Defense Dept. website (caption in photograph); and Attkisson, Could U.S. Military Have Helped During Libya Attack? (*Watch video there*).

[1134] Babbin, Whitewashing Benghazi.

[1135] Benghazi Committee Report, p. 67.

2012, occurs at 6:22 a.m.[1136] Of course, it begins getting light even earlier. The final, fatal mortar attack begins at about 5:17 a.m., Benghazi time. Again, on this Night of Benghazi the U.S. military has no way of predicting when the attacks will come or end in Benghazi. The mortar attack might have occurred at 7:17 or 8:17 a.m. instead of 5:17 a.m. (If you never launch the F-16s to get them closer to Benghazi, they will never arrive there, day or night.)

Communication Is Lacking

Vice Admiral Winnefeld later will testify, "You don't even have any communications with the people on the ground."[1137] This is entirely inaccurate. The Tactical Operations Center at the CIA Annex in Benghazi is in constant contact with Tripoli, Washington, and possibly with Stuttgart and the Pentagon.[1138] Moreover, a GRS agent stationed at the Annex says they are able to communicate with U.S. military aircraft by radio. In any event, communication may be required if a bombing or strafing is attempted. Why is it even required for a simple flyover? Is the Pentagon afraid the GRS men will shoot at the U.S. jets? (A simple telephone call to the Annex will solve this: "We're staging a flyover in ten minutes.")

Pilots Can't See "Action on the Ground"

Vice Admiral Winnefeld also testifies the F-16 pilots would not be able to see "action going on on the ground . . . [because] but for most of the night there wasn't."[1139] Again, this is after-the-fact rationalization. When Winnefeld and other Pentagon brass decide to take no decisive aircraft rescue action targeted at Benghazi, they have no way of knowing there later will be a lengthy lull in the "action on the ground." A three and one-half hour pause occurs between the second attack on the Annex (ending at about 1:40-1:50 a.m.) and the final, fatal attack (commencing at about 5:15 a.m.). This pause supposedly will lead

---

[1136] *Id.*, p. 55.

[1137] *Id.*, p. 67 (Vice Admiral James Winnefeld, Vice Chairman of the Joint Chiefs).

[1138] Griffin, CIA Operators Were Denied Request for Help During Benghazi Attack (". . . There were no communications problems at the annex, according to those present at the compound. The team was in constant radio contact with their headquarters. . . .").

[1139] Benghazi Committee Report, p. 67.

some U.S. officials to believe the battle is over![1140] The earlier lull between the second firefight at the Mission Compound and the first attack on the Annex is much shorter – about 75 minutes or so.[1141]

In any event, why must pilots see "action on the ground" for a simple flyover? All they need are GPS coordinates of the CIA Annex.

Pilots Have No Tactical Action Controllers

Another military witness tells the Select Committee there are no "tactical action controllers" in Benghazi.[1142] However, the Select Committee report states, ". . . [M]any of the GRS agents on the ground had the JTAC [joint tactical air controller] capabilities from prior military experience."[1143] In any event, JTAC is not required for a flyover.

Most of these Pentagon objections to utilizing the F-16's in Benghazi this night relate to the possibility of these aircraft dropping bombs (or shooting the aircrafts' cannon at the terrorists). Few of the objections have merit with respect to the feasibility of a simple flyover to disperse the attackers.

Are There Fighter Jets Available?

There may be no refueling tankers anywhere near Libya, but are there U.S. jets within range for at least a flyover on this Night of Benghazi? Where might jet aircraft come from to conduct such a flyover? There may be as many as three U.S. airbases with jet fighters. (This is not even counting bases of our NATO allies in the Mediterranean region.)

[1140] E.g., Griffin, CIA Operators Were Denied Request for Help During Benghazi Attack ("U.S. officials argue that there was a period of several hours when the fighting stopped before the mortars were fired at the annex, leading officials to believe the attack was over").

[1141] See Key Delays Appendix (See September 11 entries for 5:19 p.m. and 6:34 p.m., both Washington time).

[1142] Benghazi Committee Report (AFRICOM Director of Operations Rear Admiral Richard B. Landolt: ". . . [W]e don't have people on the ground that can direct targeting. There were not tactical action controllers in Benghazi, as far as I know"), p. 68.

[1143] *Id.*, p. 68.

Aviano Air Base

On this Night of Benghazi, the U.S. Air Force operates an airbase in Aviano, Italy. It is in the northeastern part of that country, about 50 miles north of Venice. In September 2012, the U.S. 31st Fighter Air Wing is stationed at Aviano Air Base. This Wing includes two squadrons of American F-16 Fighting Falcons, with a total of 42 fighter aircraft. Aviano is approximately 1,050 miles from Benghazi. The Select Committee concludes this would require two hours flight time.[1144] (One military witness tells the Select Committee the flying time from Aviano to Benghazi is "three to four hours."[1145] It is possible this is the round-trip flight time.)

Over the four decades of its production, there have been numerous varieties and models of the F-16. (It is unknown to the author which models are at Aviano on this Night of Benghazi.) According to the U.S. Air Force, F-16s have a range of about 2,000 miles (one-way).[1146] They have a maximum speed of about 1,500 miles per hour (Mach 2 +).[1147] They can be armed with missiles (air-to-air, air-to-ground and anti-ship), bombs (some laser-guided), and (on many models) an internal 20-mm cannon. Some F-16s have special capabilities for "navigation and precision attack at night and in all weather conditions . . ."[1148] The F-16 can be refueled in flight,[1149] but of course no tankers are available tonight.

Despite President Obama's supposed call for a "heightened alert" during his September 10 conference call, *not one* of the 42 F-16 "Fighting Falcons" at Aviano is on an alert status on September 11, 2012.[1150] (Even the Cairo protests earlier in the day have not changed

---

[1144] *Id.*, pp. 59-60.

[1145] *Id.* (Testimony of AFRICOM Director of Operations Rear Admiral Richard B. Landolt), p. 68.

[1146] U.S. Air Force Fact Sheet for F-16 Fighting Falcon, Air Force website (Sept. 23, 2015).

[1147] Lockheed Martin website.

[1148] Eric Hehs, "History of the F-16 Fighting Falcon," Lockheed Martin website (Feb. 19, 2014). See also "F-16 Fighting Falcon Multirole Fighter," Air Force Technology website.

[1149] "F-16 Fighting Falcon Multirole Fighter," Air Force Technology website.

[1150] Benghazi Committee Report, p. 68 (AFRICOM Director of Operations Rear Admiral Richard B. Landolt: ". . . [T]here was nothing on strip alert there in Aviano").

this status.[1151]) Aviano's F-16s are on a training and inspection posture. Nothing is pre-loaded on the aircraft. No live ordinances are assembled; bombs must be put together piece-by-piece.[1152] (This on the anniversary of 9/11.)

Sigonella Naval Air Station

As noted above, the U.S. also has a large Naval Air Station ("NAS") at Sigonella in Italy, south of Catania near the eastern coast of Sicily. It is part of NATO base Sigonella.[1153] NAS Sigonella describes itself as the "Hub of the Med." As of 2016 and 2017 it is the Navy's "second largest security command."[1154] According to its website, NAS Sigonella's air terminal operates 24 hours a day, seven days a week.[1155] Jet fighter aircraft do use Sigonella's runways. The Sigonella base is only about 450 miles from Benghazi (not much further than Tripoli is from Benghazi), at most an hour's flight time.[1156] However, it is unclear whether there are any jet fighters stationed here on the Night of Benghazi. The Defense Department suggests there are *not*. However, as noted, fighter jets from Aviano can refuel at Sigonella.

Souda Bay "Naval Support Activity"

The Select Benghazi Committee's report also briefly mentions a U.S. Naval Air Station at Souda Bay, on the northwest coast of Crete, a Greek island in the eastern Mediterranean Sea. The Pentagon describes

---

[1151] *Id.*, p. 60.

[1152] *Id.*, pp. 59-60; and Sen. Intelligence Committee Benghazi Report (Major General Darryl Roberson, Vice Director of Operations for the Joint Staff: ". . . The other fighters that might have been available were located in Aviano, Italy. They were not loaded with weapons. They were not on an alert status. We would've had to build weapons, load weapons, get tankers to support it, and get it there. There was no way that we were going to be able to do that. . . ."), pp. 28-29.

[1153] See Naval Air Station Sigonella website ("We deliver world-class ashore support to US, NATO and Coalition forces through our devotion to: vigilant preparedness, dynamic coordination, relentless follow-through and frequent assessment").

[1154] *Id.*

[1155] *Id.*

[1156] CBS Benghazi Timeline (". . . Sigonella, Sicily – less than one hour's flight away from Benghazi. . ."); and Benghazi Committee Report (Sigonella is 450 miles from Benghazi), p. 7.

"Naval Support Activity Souda Bay" as "a primary logistics hub in the eastern Mediterranean for essential U.S. and NATO missions."[1157] The NAS Souda Bay base is located at the Hellenic Air Force Base. This facility also is home to the Hellenic Air Force's 115th Combat Wing.[1158]

The base's own website currently describes NSA Souda Bay's capabilities as follows:

NSA is poised to carry out its vital mission of extending Joint and Fleet War fighting capability through Operational Support to U.S., Allied and Coalition Forces deployed within the EUCOM/CENTCOM/*AFRICOM* AOR [Areas of Responsibility] *at a moment's notice.* This installation extends the war fighting capability by providing, operating and sustaining superior facilities and services *dedicated to combat readiness and security* of ships, aircraft, detachments and personnel.[1159]

This website also states, "NSA Souda Bay Air Operations Department provides flightline support *24 hrs / 7 days a week to all military and DoD contracted aircraft.*"[1160]

NSA Souda Bay is only about 320 miles from Benghazi – closer than Tripoli is to Benghazi.[1161] This is at most a one-hour flight.[1162] According to the Defense Department's own website, this airbase at Souda Bay was used by coalition aircraft in Operation Odyssey Dawn (discussed in Part I) to fly missions over Libya against Qadhafi's forces.[1163]

According to the website Naval-Technology.com:

[1157] Defense Logistics Agency, Military Construction, Defense-Wide FY 2009 Budget Estimates, and FY 2009 Military Construction Project Data, Defense Dept. website (Feb. 2008), p. 88.

[1158] CNIC Naval Support Activity Souda Bay website.

[1159] *Id.*

[1159] *Id.* (emphasis added).

[1160] *Id.* (emphasis added).

[1161] Benghazi Committee Report, p. 7.

[1162] Attkisson, Diplomat: U.S. Special Forces Told "You Can't Go" to Benghazi During Attacks ("The U.S. Souda Bay Naval Base is an hour's flight from Libya").

[1163] "Operation Odyssey Dawn," Defense Dept. website (caption in photograph).

NSA Souda Bay operates as a Naval Operating Base, Naval Air Station and Naval Weapons Station. The facility supports joint US Navy and Air Force reconnaissance missions and other joint USN / USAF and multinational operations. . . .[1164]

(It is clear from Department of Defense and other military websites the landing strip at the U.S. base at Souda Bay can accommodate F-16 Fighting Falcons.[1165] (Are any of these aircraft stationed here this fateful night in September 2012? If so, no refueling tankers are required to get these birds over Benghazi. Souda Bay has its own jet fuel storage facilities.[1166])

The Select Committee Report devotes but a single paragraph to this facility – despite the fact it is the U.S. base closest to Benghazi! The Select Committee Report briefly notes that while they are at the base, members of the committee "received a briefing regarding *special operations aircraft* that were stationed at Souda Bay on the night of the attacks in Benghazi and *could have been utilized in response to the attacks.*" The panel's report claims the Select Committee sought confirmation of this information from the Pentagon. The Report then

---

[1164] See Naval-Technology.com.

[1165] Staff Sgt. Austin Harvill, "Airmen, F-16s Train in Souda Bay," U.S. Air Forces in Europe & Air Forces Africa website (Jan. 23, 2017) (Photograph description: "A 555th Fighter Squadron F-16 Fighting Falcon departs from Aviano Air Base, Italy on Jan. 21, 2016 to support a flying training deployment in Souda Bay, Greece. Fourteen F-16s, one KC-135 Stratotanker . . . and 280 Airmen deployed to Souda Bay to train with Greece's Hellenic air force"); Terri Moon Cronk, "Air Force Flies F-16s in Training Exercise with Greece," DoD News, Defense Media Activity, Defense Dept. website (Jan. 21, 2015) ("Air Force F-16 fighter jets are engaged in a flying training deployment in Souda Bay, Greece . . . The training exercise comprises 18 F-16s and about 300 personnel . . ."); "Morning Mission," Defense Dept. website (As of Feb. 1, 2017: "Air Force pilots taxi in F-16 Fighting Falcon aircraft on the flightline at Souda Bay, Greece, Jan. 28, 2016"); and "Fighter Pre-Flight," Defense Dept. website (As of Feb. 1, 2017: "Air Force Staff Sgt. Ryan Anderson performs preflight checks on an F-16 Fighting Falcon fighter aircraft during a training exercise at Souda Bay, Greece, Jan. 27, 2016").

[1166] As of February 2008, the military was planning to replace both fuel storage facilities at the Souda Bay base, as well as the base's own pipeline connected to the Marathi NATO main fuel depot through which it obtained "JP-5 jet fuel." Defense Logistics Agency, Military Construction, Defense-Wide FY 2009 Budget Estimates, and FY 2009 Military Construction Project Data, Defense Dept. website (Feb. 2008) (This pipeline provides the primary means of transporting jet fuel from the main NATO fuel depot at Marathi 4.3 miles away to NSA Souda Bay to support "operational and contingency requirements"), pp. 86-89. It is unknown to the author whether these improvements ever were completed.

asserts, "The Defense Department has not denied the presence of these assets."[1167] So why on earth are these nearby capabilities not deployed on this Night of Benghazi?[1168] (Of the many mysteries of Benghazi, this is among the most puzzling – and troubling.)

Following this important but cryptic paragraph, the Select Committee Report "goes dark" on Souda Bay. Astonishingly, this U.S. base is not mentioned again in the panel's exhaustive (and exhausting) report! It is one of the biggest disappointments in an otherwise excellent work product. (The author surmises U.S. intelligence agencies have told the Select Committee the less said about Souda Bay publicly, the better.) However, the committee's paragraph does confirm there *are* aircraft at Souda Bay on the Night of Benghazi, and they *could* have been deployed "in response to the attacks." (Major portions of this "puzzle piece" still remain hidden.)

According to NSA Souda Bay's current website, as of June 2018 the base has some 650 commissioned and enlisted personnel, plus about 250 civilians and contractors.[1169] Is a comparable number stationed here on the Night of Benghazi? Even if the number is far smaller than as we go to press, there must be many "shooters" who can be flown to Benghazi. And, as discussed below, there is a U.S. destroyer in port at Souda Bay tonight which must have many of its own shooters among its crew of more than 300 sailors. (Almost certainly, there are many more shooters at Souda Bay than at the Mission Compound, at the Annex, and on Team Tripoli combined. And as detailed elsewhere, Team Annex and Team Tripoli each will press a non-shooter into service during the emergency conditions this night. If necessary, why can't Souda Bay do likewise? *Why are they not sent?* (Two months after Benghazi, the Pentagon reportedly will transfer a Marine FAST platoon from Rota, Spain to Souda Bay.[1170] Good idea.)

And even if none of the U.S. air assets that are at Souda Bay tonight can perform a flyover or rescue the Americans in Benghazi, what about the Greek's aircraft? As noted above, their air force has a combat wing

---

[1167] Benghazi Committee Report (emphasis added), p. 64.

[1168] Statement of Senators McCain, Graham and Ayotte ("We do not know why . . . U.S. military units and assets in the region were not ready, alert, and positioned to respond in a timely fashion to what should have been a foreseeable emergency – despite the fact that there is a U.S. military base in Souda Bay, Crete, which is a short flight to Benghazi").

[1169] CNIC Naval Support Activity Souda Bay website.

[1170] Sen. Intelligence Committee Benghazi Report (Redacted), p. 31.

stationed at Souda Bay. Is this wing here on this Night of Benghazi? The Greeks are NATO allies of the U.S. Why can't the Greeks send their fighters to do a flyover above the Mission Compound, and especially the CIA Annex? And if the Greeks have fixed-wing aircraft at the Hellenic Air Force Base, why can't they fly a rescue party of U.S. shooters from Souda into Benghazi's airport, as Team Tripoli does? (Team Obama never answers these questions. Team Trump should.)

The Vice Chairman of the Joint Chiefs of Staff, Vice Admiral Winnefeld, later makes this stark confession to the Select Committee regarding the decision to send no jet aircraft toward Benghazi:

So I mean, it was *highly unlikely* that we were going to be able to make a difference, even if we could get there in time with air power, so *we chose not to do it*.[1171]

("Highly unlikely," not impossible. They *"chose"* not to do it! There are nearly thirty Americans in peril – soon to be joined by seven more on Team Tripoli. And what about the orders from the president and SecDef Panetta to "do everything *possible*"? Do our military chiefs "choose" not to obey these orders? Or does the White House change the orders?)

Spectre Gunships

Another possible military asset that might help this night is the AC-130H "Spectre" gunship. Tonight, the GRS contractors repeatedly will request such a gunship.[1172] The Spectre is a large, four-propeller, fixed-wing aircraft that is armed with a 30-millimeter gun (among other weapons).[1173] (The Spectre is known within the Air Force as "Heavy Metal.") The effect a Spectre can impose on a ground force has been described as "devastating."[1174] A Spectre gunship likely can remove the attackers outside the CIA Annex as a functioning assault force. Also, tomorrow morning it might prevent the terrorists from setting up their

---

[1171] Benghazi Committee Report (Testimony of Vice Admiral James A. Winnefeld, emphasis added), p. 68.

[1172] E.g., Zuckoff, *13 Hours*, Chap. 4, pp. 98 and 101.

[1173] News Transcript, Department of Defense Press Briefing by Col. Warren via Teleconference from Baghdad, Iraq, Defense Dept. website (Dec. 22, 2015).

[1174] E.g., "U.S.-Aided Syrian Forces Complete Successful Anti-ISIL Military Actions," Defense Dept. website (Nov. 4, 2015).

mortar launcher.[1175] (The assaults at the Mission Compound are over too quickly for U.S. gunships to arrive on-scene in time.)

According to two news sources there are AC-130H Spectre gunships that can reach Benghazi within hours. This almost certainly would be before the deadly mortar attack takes place beginning at 5:17 a.m., Benghazi time – some seven and one-half hours into the battle. CBS News cites "military sources" who reportedly claim AC-130H Spectre gunships are located at three military bases in the region.[1176] (These are the Naval Air Station in Sigonella, Italy, Aviano Air Base, Italy, and the Naval Air Station at Souda Bay, Crete.) As noted above, Sigonella is at most an hour's flight from Libya;[1177] the base at Souda Bay is even closer.[1178]) An *Investor's Business Daily* editorial in October 2012 claims AC-130H gunships are stationed at these bases, but the order never comes to deploy them.[1179]

According to investigative reporter Sharyl Attkisson, unidentified men affiliated with military Special Ops tell her after the crisis that the U.S. Commander's In Extremis Force training in Croatia (discussed above) "had access to an AC-130 gunship." If accurate, this would put that gunship just "a few hours' flight away" from Benghazi.[1180]

[1175] Attkisson, Could U.S. Military Have Helped During Libya Attack? ("Military sources tell CBS News that resources at the three bases [Sigonella, Aviano and Souda Bay] include fighter jets and Specter AC-130 [sic Spectre AC-130H] gunships, which the sources say can be extremely effective in flying in and buzzing a crowd to disperse it") (*Watch video there*); and Baier, 13 Hours at Benghazi: The Inside Story (*Watch video there*; Go to 36:24 - 37:03).

[1176] Attkisson, Could U.S. Military Have Helped During Libya Attack? (*Watch video there*).

[1177] *Id.* (*Watch video there*).

[1178] Attkisson, Diplomat: U.S. Special Forces Told "You Can't Go" to Benghazi During Attacks.

[1179] Ferrara, Benghazi: Obama's Actions Amount to a Shameful Dereliction of Duty, quoting Editorial, "Obama Knew Benghazi Was Terrorism And Did Nothing," *Investor's Business Daily* online (Oct. 24, 2012) ("IBD Editorial, Obama Knew Benghazi Was Terrorism And Did Nothing") ("Within an hour's flight from Libya, at the large naval air station in Sigonella, Italy, and at bases in nearby Aviano and Souda Bay, were fighters and AC 130 gunships that can be extremely effective in dispersing crowds or responding to a terrorist assault").

[1180] Attkisson, *Stonewalled*, Chap. 4, p. 159.

In sharp contrast, in her memoir Hillary Clinton will insist that on the Night of Benghazi the nearest Spectre gunship is in Afghanistan, over 1,000 miles away![1181] (Who, if anyone, is telling the truth?)

On the ground in Benghazi, the GRS agents repeatedly ask whether the Spectre gunships are on the way to help them. Eventually, they stop asking. No gunship ever comes.[1182]

Reconnaissance Aircraft

According to Jed Babbin of *The American Spectator*, yet another military air asset is available at Sigonella. Babbin claims a "former senior Navy officer" (unnamed) asserts that EA-18G "Growler" reconnaissance aircraft are "fueled and on the ramp" in Sigonella on this Night of Benghazi. These unarmed aircraft reportedly are only 40 minutes flying time (at Mach 0.7) from Benghazi. However, they could provide additional surveillance intelligence over Benghazi within an hour or two after the initial attack. Babbin poses the excellent question, "Why weren't they ordered in?"[1183]

U.S. *Naval* Assets Nearest to Libya

According to the Pentagon, on the Night of Benghazi there are almost no U.S. Navy surface ships anywhere close to Benghazi. The nearest two U.S. aircraft carriers are in the Persian Gulf. The Pentagon says it would take the closer carrier seven days to transit through the Suez Canal (assuming no delays at Suez). The large U.S. amphibious ship closest to Benghazi is underway in the Gulf of Oman, southeast of the Strait of Hormuz.[1184] It, too, cannot get to Benghazi in time. The

---

[1181] Clinton, *Hard Choices*, Chap. 17, p. 393.

[1182] E.g., Zuckoff, *13 Hours*, Chap. 9, pp. 199-200, and Chap. 10, p. 218; Baier, 13 Hours at Benghazi: The Inside Story (*Watch video there*; Go to 15:47-57); Griffin, CIA Operators Were Denied Request for Help During Benghazi Attack; Hicks Oversight Committee Testimony (May 8, 2013) (Response to questions of Rep. Ron DeSantis (R-FL)) ("AC-130 gunships were never mentioned to me, only fighter planes out of Aviano" [Aviano Air Base in northeast Italy]"), p. 95; and *Id.* ("No air support was sent"), p. 95.

[1183] Babbin, Whitewashing Benghazi.

[1184] Sen. Intelligence Committee Benghazi Report (Redacted) (Testimony of Major General Darryl Roberson, Vice Director of Operations for the Joint Staff: "There were no ships available to provide any support that were anywhere close to the facility in

location of these ships also means there is no attack helicopter available anywhere near Benghazi tonight.

But there is at least one U.S. Navy vessel near Benghazi.

The Destroyer U.S.S. Laboon

The exception is a destroyer visiting the U.S. Naval Base at Souda Bay, Crete (about 320 miles from Benghazi). According to a Department of the Navy response to a FOIA Request (posted by Judicial Watch on its website), the Destroyer Laboon is in port at the U.S. Souda Bay naval base on the Night of Benghazi. The Laboon is an "Arleigh Burke-class" guided-missile destroyer, with a speed of more than 30 knots. The Laboon has no aircraft. According to one unofficial website, the Laboon currently has a crew of nearly 340.[1185]

Even if the Laboon leaves port immediately upon hearing of the Benghazi attack (which of course it is not ready to do), it will take about eight hours (sailing at 35 knots, or about 40.3 mph) to steam to Benghazi. Hence, it will not arrive until after the final mortar attack is over. (However, yet again, the Laboon's captain – indeed the entire U.S. Navy – has no idea when the Battle of Benghazi will be over.)

Even after arriving off Benghazi, the Laboon would need permission to dock there, assuming there is an empty dock available. Then, any shooters the Laboon could deploy would have to find a secure means of transportation to enter Benghazi and move to the CIA Annex. (This is the same problem Team Tripoli is facing after landing at the Benghazi airport.)

However, the Laboon presumably does have many shooters among its crew. And there are airplanes at Souda Bay (and at the neighboring Greek Hellenic Air Force base). Could those planes carry some shooters from the Laboon's crew who are not onshore (or others among the Souda base's staff) to Benghazi? Even if planes from Souda Bay can land in Benghazi, the same problem arises. How do they securely get from the airport to the Annex? However, at a minimum the Souda base and Laboon's crews could reinforce Team Tripoli.

Benghazi. . . ."), pp. 28-29; and Map of U.S. Navy ships' positions nearest Benghazi on September 11, 2012, at Judicial Watch website.

[1185] See Map of U.S. Navy ships' positions nearest Benghazi on September 11, 2012, at Judicial Watch website; and NavySite website (stating USS Laboon (DDG 58) has crew of 23 officers, 24 Chief Petty Officers, and 291 enlisted sailors).

(Given the life-threatening emergency tonight, the author believes the U.S. should coordinate with the Greeks tonight to arrange aircraft to transport shooters from the Laboon and the U.S. base at Souda Bay to Benghazi. No such effort is made.)

Conclusions Regarding Available Military Assets

There is no doubt one or more armed Predator drones could have been sent to Benghazi before the final, fatal assault on the Annex. There simply was no desire anywhere in the U.S. government to do so.

It is highly suspect that jet aircraft capable of a flyover could not have gotten to Benghazi before this last attack.[1186] Even if there are no jet fighters based at Sigonella, jets from Aviano could have refueled at Sigonella. Further, the Obama administration has never explained why air assets from nearby Souda Bay (or the adjacent Greek airbase) could not get to Benghazi, without the necessity of the absent tankers.[1187]

The evidence regarding Spectre gunships is more uncertain. At this point, the author gives the benefit of this doubt to Team Obama. Regarding refueling tankers, the author has uncovered no evidence suggesting military commanders are misstating the tankers' unavailability. (The fact there are no tankers close enough to North Africa itself remains unacceptable.)

The evidence firmly supports the lack of any possible assistance from U.S. Navy ships (except for some of the crew of the USS Laboon being transported to Benghazi by aircraft).

Finally, until its last minutes in office, Team Obama fails completely to explain why none of America's NATO allies have assets that can help protect or even rescue Americans in peril in Benghazi on September 11, 2012.

Now, let us resume our story of this Night of Benghazi. ∎

[1186] See Attkisson, *Stonewalled* (Major General Darryl Roberson "acknowledged that aircraft could have buzzed the hostile crowd [in Benghazi] to try to scatter it. But that, too, was ruled out because it wasn't seen as a sure bet"), Chap. 4, p. 161.

[1187] See Attkisson, *Stonewalled* ("General Carter Ham, the head of [AFRICOM], would concede that assets *were* available. Just as my sources had said. But it was decided they wouldn't be used. And it was decided that a potential rescue of Americans under attack on foreign soil wasn't in line with the military's mission"), Chap. 4, p. 161.

49

Ansar al-Sharia Claims Credit

At 6:07 p.m. Washington time, the State Department Operations Center issues an alert disseminating two significant pieces of information as reported by the U.S. Embassy in Tripoli. First, on Facebook and Twitter an Islamic, anti-American militant group called "Ansar al-Sharia" reportedly has claimed responsibility for the Benghazi attacks on the Mission Compound. And second, that same group has called for an attack on the U.S. Embassy in Tripoli.[1188]

This likely comes as no surprise to those at the Mission Compound and CIA Annex. This is because the CIA agents at the Annex recently have obtained and translated documents indicating Ansar al-Sharia has established a base at one of the residential properties just east of the Mission Compound! Of course, the CIA has shared this information with State personnel at the Mission.[1189]

(Later, on September 17, Ansar al-Sharia will deny they are responsible for the Benghazi attacks.[1190] However, the U.S. government will conclude otherwise.[1191])

[1188] Hicks Oversight Committee Testimony (May 8, 3013), pp. 26-27; Tapper and Parkinson, White House Responds to Release of Real-Time Emails About Benghazi Attack, linking ABC News online (Text of email); CBS Benghazi Timeline; CBS/AP, "Assault on U.S. Consulate in Benghazi Leaves 4 Dead, Including U.S. Ambassador J. Christopher Stevens," CBS News online (Sept. 12, 2012) (Ansar al-Sharia claiming credit); and Burnett, Benghazi Timeline: "We Are Under Attack" (*Watch video there*; Go to 5:48 - 6:03). Compare Hayes, The Benghazi Talking Points (alert issued at 6:08 p.m.).

[1189] Zuckoff, *13 Hours*, Chap. 9, p. 188.

[1190] CBS News, CIA Saw Possible Terror Ties Day After Libya Hit: AP ("Intelligence officials say the leading suspected culprit is a local Benghazi militia, Ansar al-Shariah. The group denies responsibility for the attack but is known to have ties to a leading African terror group, al Qaeda in the Islamic Maghreb. . . ."); and Tapper and Parkinson, White House Responds to Release of Real-Time Emails About Benghazi Attack.

[1191] Hsu, Baring Grievous Wounds, Dry Humor, U.S. Agent Lays Out Key Evidence at Benghazi Trial.

THE TRUE ACCOUNT OF VALOR AND ABANDONMENT

Gregory Hicks later testifies that at about 12:30 a.m. Benghazi time (6:30 p.m. Washington time), diplomatic staff in Tripoli begin to see the Twitter feeds calling for an attack on the U.S. Embassy in Tripoli. (Hicks' recollection of the time is different than other sources claim, being about 23 minutes later.) In Tripoli, U.S. Embassy staff reside and work at two separate locations in the city.[1192] Hicks and his team begin to make preparations to evacuate the State Department "residential compound" in Tripoli (which includes "28 diplomatic personnel"), and to consolidate all American diplomatic personnel (about 55 people total) at "the Annex" elsewhere in Tripoli.[1193] (See Chapters 55 and 73.) According to Hillary Clinton, in a later phone call with Hicks (discussed below) she approves his recommendation to evacuate the Embassy's personnel to an "alternative compound."[1194] (*Finally, someone at Foggy Bottom makes a wise security decision.*) ∎

[1192] Wood House Oversight Prepared Testimony, p. 1.

[1193] Hicks Oversight Committee Testimony (May 8, 2013), p. 27; and *Id.* (Response to questions of Rep. Kerry Bentivolio (R-MI)), p. 94.

[1194] Clinton, *Hard Choices*, Chap. 17, p. 396.

50

Team Tripoli Departs

Before departing the capital, Team Tripoli receives updates by telephone from Embassy Tripoli officials. This will include information that Sean Smith is dead and Ambassador Stevens is missing, and the rest of the Mission personnel have evacuated to a CIA Annex facility. Everyone in this rescue group now is wondering if they are heading into a hostage situation in Benghazi.

At 12:30 a.m., the chartered aircraft takes off from the Tripoli airport carrying the brave posse to Benghazi.[1195] Team Tripoli is traveling – *on their own initiative* – to try to reinforce and evacuate the besieged Americans in Benghazi.[1196] However, even these intrepid men do not leave Tripoli until over two and one-half hours into the crisis. Although they do not know it at the time, they will be the only U.S. assets headed toward Benghazi during the entire thirteen hours of the battle and subsequent evacuation. ∎

[1195] Benghazi Committee Report, pp. 54-55.

[1196] Panetta, *Worthy Fights* (emphasis added) ("At 6:30 p.m. EST. a seven-man team in Tripoli, composed of five CIA security officers and two military men, found a private plane to fly them to Benghazi, arriving an hour later. Although the seven of them worked together, they were not a military unit that had trained together for this type of mission, but acted bravely *on their own initiative*"), Chap. 16, p. 429; Benghazi Committee Report (". . . [T]hese individuals [on Team Tripoli] went to Benghazi from Tripoli at the direction of the Chief of Station in Libya, not at the order of anyone in Washington, D.C."), p. 109; and *Id.* (emphasis added) (". . . Team Tripoli . . . acted with purpose, precision and ingenuity that night. . . . They *deployed themselves* because fellow Americans needed them"), p. 113.

51

The First Attack on the CIA Annex

While SecDef Panetta continues planning with his generals and admirals at the Pentagon, on the ground at the CIA's Benghazi Annex events are quite a bit more urgent. The GRS and DSA agents there still are deployed in their defensive posts, preparing for more trouble. They soon will get it. Over the next five hours, there will be a total of three firefights with terrorists at the Annex. Like the earlier assaults at the Mission Compound, the Annex video equipment will record these attacks.[1197]

Not long after the CIA security contractors and DSA men have mounted their Annex perches, Tanto and D.B. on the roof of Building B begin to hear Arabic chants. Then they hear squealing tire noises from nearby to the east. The watch as several cars gather at a nearby parking area about 300 yards east of the Annex. Because of the time of night, they know something unusual is occurring. They radio the GRS Team Lead to ask whether any friendly 17 February Brigade militia members are expected. The TL is uncertain. The GRS and DSA defenders must assume the new arrivals are bad guys.[1198]

The American protectors scan the area outside the Annex walls, using their night-vision equipment. Just before 12:30 a.m. Benghazi time, the CIA and DSA men see persons gathering and staging cars and gun trucks at an intersection to the east near the Annex. The Americans still don't know if these people are "friendlies" or militants. The group soon moves away from the vehicles and starts approaching the Annex on foot, "moving tactically." That is, "They're moving sideways. They're playing hide and go seek," apparently not realizing the Annex defenders have night-vision equipment.[1199] They are in fact bad guys. The GRS and DSA men decide they must engage the approaching

---

[1197] See Benghazi Committee Report, pp. 74-76.

[1198] Zuckoff, *13 Hours*, Chap. 9, pp. 198-199 and 205-206; and Baier, 13 Hours at Benghazi: The Inside Story (*Watch video there*; Go to 15:29-47).

[1199] Zuckoff, *13 Hours*, Chap. 9, p. 206; and Benghazi Committee Report, p. 75.

militants, but will allow them to get as close as possible before opening fire.[1200]

Then, at 12:34 a.m., the first attack on the CIA Annex commences. An RPG comes over a wall and soars over the heads of D.B. Benton and Tanto Paronto before exploding.[1201] **BOOM!** Attackers direct small arms fire at the Annex, hitting Building B in the compound's northeast sector. At the same time, one attacker throws an improvised explosive device over the Annex wall. **BOOM!** It explodes near Tig Tiegen, who is carrying water to Oz Geist. Tig is startled, but unhurt.

For the next fifteen minutes or so, a firefight ensues as the northeast corner of the Annex comes under small arms fire, RPG assaults and IED explosions. The American defenders aggressively return fire. They hear bullets whiz past their heads and see the attackers' muzzle flashes. The GRS men are using lasers to sight their firing, so those with night-vision equipment see three and four sets of green rays of light simultaneously dancing in the night from target to target. (Tanto later describes this visual effect as "gorgeous" and "awesome.")[1202] However, the goggles rob the agents of their peripheral vision, and much of their depth perception. Author Zuckoff describes the night-vision gear as "making it seem as though they were looking at the world through narrow cardboard tubes with green cellophane on the ends."[1203]

During this firefight the attackers attempt to shoot out the Annex floodlights that illuminate their approach. A piece of something ricochets off a light and cuts Oz Geist slightly on the bridge of his nose. This will be the only injury among the defenders during this initial fight. The assailants will incur far worse damage.[1204] (As will Oz later in the battle.)

At 12:41 a.m., attackers additionally direct fire against the Annex east wall. These likewise are aimed at Building B. This assault from the east continues for some ten minutes. The first wave incursion ends

---

[1200] Baier, 13 Hours at Benghazi: The Inside Story (*Watch video there*; Go to 17:32-38).

[1201] Benghazi Committee Report, pp. 75-76; and Baier, 13 Hours at Benghazi: The Inside Story (*Watch video there*; Go to 17:42-49).

[1202] Benghazi Committee Report, p. 76; and Baier, 13 Hours at Benghazi: The Inside Story (*Watch video there*; Go to 17:40 - 18:31).

[1203] Zuckoff, *13 Hours*, Chap. 5, p. 122.

[1204] Baier, 13 Hours at Benghazi: The Inside Story (*Watch video there*; Go to 18:31-50).

about 12:51 a.m. (6:51 p.m. Washington time, as Leon Panetta is ending the meeting with his chieftains). By 12:59 a.m., the defenders on the Annex rooftops can see militants still are present in a field to the east. However, they hold their fire because the attackers are close to a residence where a local family with children lives.[1205]

The GRS men interpret this first firefight as a mere probe. The attackers wish to get a feel for the Annex's defenses. The defenders fully expect the assailants to return with a larger force and reengage. They will be proven correct.[1206]

This attack on the CIA's "secret" Benghazi Annex should have profound implications for U.S. government officials in Washington. No doubt they begin to learn of the engagement from the CIA staff in the Annex TOC minutes after it begins. This assault proves beyond doubt the CIA's Annex no longer is a covert facility (if it actually ever was). As indicated, it is unknown whether the militants in Benghazi knew about the Annex before tonight, whether they discover it when some of them follow the DSA or GRS agents there after the Americans evacuate the Mission, or whether the terrorists uncover the Annex's existence while looting the Mission's files.

In any event, this strike on the covert CIA Annex should ratchet up considerably the exigency of the situation at the CIA, Pentagon, White House, State, and other government agencies. It should prod them to dispatch urgent relief to Benghazi. Instead, this alarming information seems to have no discernible impact on the American government's actions. ■

[1205] Benghazi Committee Report, p. 76; and Baier, 13 Hours at Benghazi: The Inside Story (*Watch video there*; Go to 17:04-16).

[1206] Baier, 13 Hours at Benghazi: The Inside Story (*Watch video there*; Go to 18:50 - 19:01).

52

Secretary Clinton Calls Libya's President

Reportedly at the request of President Obama, at 6:49 p.m., Washington time, Secretary of State Hillary Clinton calls Libya's leader, President Mohamed Magariaf.[1207] (Why doesn't Obama call him?) Because this call occurs just 15 minutes after the first-wave attack at the CIA Annex commences, it is unlikely Clinton is aware of this startling new development during this call.

In her memoir, Clinton writes she is unsatisfied with the cooperation the U.S. is getting from the Libyans, and she requests further assistance from the Libyan leader. She claims she warns Magariaf of "the possibility of additional attacks." Clinton adds, "I wanted to make sure that he and others understood the urgency of the situation [this was more than three hours after the first attack] and did not assume the threat had passed."[1208]

Clinton describes Magariaf as "deeply apologetic." Magariaf reportedly strongly condemns the attacks, and pledges his efforts to protect Americans and to pursue the perpetrators. Hillary asserts she demands "immediate action [i.e., additional security support] to protect our people in Benghazi and Tripoli."[1209]

[1207] Benghazi Committee Report, Select Benghazi Timeline, p. 559; and Zuckoff, *13 Hours*, Chap. 6, p. 146.

[1208] Clinton, *Hard Choices*, Chap. 17, p. 395.

[1209] Remarks of Secretary of State Hillary Clinton on the Deaths of American Personnel in Benghazi, Libya, State Department Treaty Room, Washington, D.C., State Dept. Archives website (Sept. 12, 2012); Clinton, *Hard Choices*, Chap. 17, p. 395; and Statement on the Attack in Benghazi, by Secretary of State Hillary Rodham Clinton, United States Department of State, State Dept. Archives website (Sept. 11, 2012; 10:07 p.m.).

THE TRUE ACCOUNT OF VALOR AND ABANDONMENT

President Obama never calls Magariaf during this long Night of Benghazi. (This is a betrayal of his duty to his U.S. government personnel imperiled there.[1210]) ∎

[1210] "Readout of the President's Call with Libyan President Magariaf, Obama White House Archives" (Sept. 13, 2012). See Connor Simpson, "Graham Threatens Hagel Confirmation Over Benghazi," *The Atlantic* online (Feb. 10, 2013) (Quoting Sen. Lindsey Graham (R-SC): "Did the president at any time during this eight-hour attack, pick up the phone and call anybody in Libya to get help for these folks? Secretary Clinton said she was screaming on the phone at Libyan officials. There's no voice in the world like that of the president of the United States. And I do believe if he had picked up the phone and called the Libyan government, these folks [presumably Team Tripoli] could have gotten out of the airport, to the annex and the last two guys may very well be alive. . . . But if he failed to call on behalf of those people under siege, then I think that's a massive failure of leadership by our commander in chief").

53

Panetta's 7:00 P.M. Order

Defense Secretary Leon Panetta later will claim that by 7:00 p.m. this night (Washington time), he gives an order to "immediately" deploy "the identified assets" ("7:00 p.m. Order"). This means deploy the FAST, CIF and SOF forces discussed above.[1211]

In his memoir, Panetta will write General Dempsey and Vice Admiral Winnefeld have advised him "those were the only units that could reach *Tripoli* within hours to effect a *rescue*."[1212] Although he refers to a "rescue," note Panetta says "reach Tripoli," *not* reach Benghazi! The Americans most in need of "rescuing" are in Benghazi. And this is well before a later interagency meeting from 7:30 to 9:30 p.m. (discussed in Chapter 59 below) officially will shift the principal focus of the U.S. response from Benghazi to Tripoli!

It appears Panetta's 7:00 p.m. Order does not direct any "special operations aircraft" or other forces to deploy from the U.S. base at Souda Bay, Crete. This is despite the fact these U.S. (and Greek) assets are some of the closest to Benghazi. (Why not?)

The Select Committee's report quotes Secretary Panetta's testimony: "My orders were to deploy those forces, period. . . . [I]t was very clear: They are to deploy."[1213] (Ah, but deploy *when?* And to *where?* And to do *what?*) The report concludes:

> He [Panetta] did not order the preparation to deploy or the planning to deploy or the contemplation of deployment. His unequivocal testimony was that he ordered the identified assets to *"deploy."*[1214]

[1211] Benghazi Committee Report, pp. 70-71.

[1212] Panetta, *Worthy Fights* (emphasis added), Chap. 16, p. 429.

[1213] Benghazi Committee Report, p. 70.

[1214] *Id.* (emphasis added), p. 70. See also *Id.* (Question: "You did not issue an order to prepare to deploy. You issued an order to deploy." Secretary Panetta's answer: "That's correct"), p. 95; and *Id.* ("Despite the Secretary of Defense's clear directive and his intention that forces would move and move quickly, no forces had yet moved" in the four hours after the initial attack), p. 83.

THE TRUE ACCOUNT OF VALOR AND ABANDONMENT

In significant respects, Panetta's testimony is contradicted by his own 2014 memoir (written closer in time to the events of Benghazi). In his book Panetta says he directs two Marine FAST teams in Rota, Spain to "*prepare* to deploy to Benghazi and Tripoli."[1215] This is consistent with the Senate Intelligence Committee's report, which states, "One [FAST] team was to go to Benghazi to respond to the attack on the Temporary Mission Facility," and "One [FAST] team was to deploy to Tripoli to protect the Embassy if it was attacked."[1216] Panetta also asserts he orders the CIF to "cease the exercise and *prepare* for a rescue mission."[1217] In contrast, Panetta writes he directs a special operations hostage rescue unit in the U.S. (the SOF at Fort Bragg) to "*load up and fly* to *Libya* in case we had an opportunity to rescue Stevens or others."[1218] (Actually, they are ordered to Sigonella in Sicily, not to Libya; they will never get to Libya.) In any event, Panetta insists his 7:00 p.m. Order "went into effect immediately and were [sic] followed up that evening with written directives."[1219] (Yes, *much* later.)

Panetta further tells the Select Committee, "I had the authority to deploy those forces. And I ordered those forces to be deployed. And I didn't have to ask anybody's permission to get those forces in place."[1220] Panetta testifies he fully expects his orders are being carried out at the time.[1221] (But does he remain at the Pentagon to assure this happens?)

Even if Panetta's testimony is true, he waits *two and one-half hours* after he first learns of the initial assault on the Mission Compound – and at least *90 minutes* after he purportedly receives the president's directive – to order assets deployed! (Moreover, unless Tripoli is the real focus (discussed in detail below), this 7:00 p.m. Order seems completely inconsistent with his later assertions no assets can get to Benghazi in time, so there is no need even to try.[1222])

[1215] Panetta, *Worthy Fights* (emphasis added), Chap. 16, p. 428.

[1216] Sen. Intelligence Committee Benghazi Report, p. 30.

[1217] Panetta, *Worthy Fights* (emphasis added), Chap. 16, p. 429.

[1218] *Id.* (emphasis added), Chap. 16, p. 429.

[1219] *Id.*, Chap. 16, p. 429.

[1220] Benghazi Committee Report, p. 94.

[1221] *Id.*, pp. 83-84.

[1222] E.g., CBS News/Associated Press, "Panetta: Unclear Early Info Slowed Benghazi Response," CBS News online (Oct. 25, 2012) ("It was really [nearly?] over before, you know, we had the opportunity to really know what was happening").

Secretary Panetta later explains to the Select Committee his 7:00 p.m. Order to "deploy now" is conveyed to the relevant forces *during* the Pentagon meeting he has convened at 6:00 p.m., and which ends around 7:00 p.m.[1223] However, in addition to Panetta's delay, the Select Committee concludes:

... [N]early two more hours elapsed before the Secretary's orders actually were relayed to those [three identified] forces.
[It is possible this means the official, written orders, as opposed to verbal orders Panetta claims he issues by the end of his 6:00-7:00 p.m. meeting with his staff.] Several more hours elapsed before any of those forces moved.[1224]

On its face, this appears to be a stark and significant contradiction. Panetta and the Select Committee both cannot be correct about when his order is relayed to the forces. If the Select Committee is accurate, this betrays a shocking degree of nonchalance on the part of the Pentagon and AFRICOM brass.

Moreover, the Select Committee correctly concludes, *"none of the orders given to the [U.S. military] assets that night contained an order to deploy to Benghazi."*[1225] Panetta's testimony aside, the two FAST platoons in Rota merely are ordered to *prepare* to deploy. (According to CBS News, and consistent with Panetta's memoir, one FAST team is ordered to prepare to deploy to Benghazi, and the second to Tripoli.) The U.S.-based SOF and the CIF in Croatia both "were ordered to deploy only to an intermediate staging base [Sigonella in Sicily], not to Benghazi or Tripoli." Again according to the Select Committee, once the decision is made to deploy the SOF from the U.S., the CIF's mission apparently changes to preparing for the SOF's arrival at the intermediate staging base, in lieu of deploying to Libya itself.[1226]

Months after Benghazi, Congress questions Leon Panetta's successor, Secretary Chuck Hagel, regarding why the CIF is not ordered to Benghazi. In May 2013, Elizabeth L. King, an Assistant Secretary at DoD, will tell Congress, "... Because exact conditions on the ground in Benghazi were unknown at the time of the order of the AFRICOM commander, the CIF immediately began to fulfill its

---

[1223] Benghazi Committee Report, p. 83.

[1224] *Id.*, p. 71.

[1225] *Id.* (emphasis added), p. 91.

[1226] *Id.*, p. 91; CBS Benghazi Timeline; and Panetta, *Worthy Fights*, Chap. 16, p. 428.

THE TRUE ACCOUNT OF VALOR AND ABANDONMENT

tasking by pre-positioning at an intermediate staging location, Naval Air Station Sigonella. . . ."[1227] ("Immediately"?)

The Select Committee later questions that AFRICOM Commander, General Ham, about whether he considers deploying the CIF directly from Croatia to Benghazi. His response is nothing short of depressing:

> ... [T]here was some consideration to ... do they go somewhere other than the intermediate staging base. Should they go to Benghazi? Should they go to Tripoli?
>
> My recollection is that the situation was certainly evolving. And ... my view was the situation, after *an initial spike, the fighting had largely subsided*, that Benghazi was probably not the right place for them to go. Get them to the staging base, where we now have many, many options. [Except the option of attempting to save the Americans under assault in Benghazi, as the President reportedly has ordered.]
>
> ... [F]or me, it was, where's the best place for that force to be right now? And, in my view, I believe ... that the best place for them would be at the intermediate staging base so that they would be well-postured for *subsequent missions*.[1228]

(What is wrong with the *current* mission – trying to rescue the many Americans already under mortal attack in *Benghazi?*)

Vice Admiral Tidd, Director of Operations for the Joint Chiefs of Staff, also is questioned by the Select Committee about why U.S. forces are ordered to the intermediate staging base, rather than directly to Libya. The Select Committee's Report states, "Tidd testified one reason the CIF and the U.S. SOF were ordered to an intermediate staging base and not to Libya directly *was due to concerns expressed by the State Department regarding the number of military personnel that would arrive in country.*"[1229] Specifically, Tidd testifies:

> ... *State* was very, very concerned about what the footprint *would look like* in *Tripoli*. They didn't want it to *look like* we were invading.
>
> That was the gist or that was the genesis of the discussion that occurred over whether or not when the FAST arrives at the airport *in Tripoli* – because they wanted to reinforce

---

[1227] Letter from Elizabeth L. King, Assistant Secretary of Defense for Legislative Affairs, to Rep. Elijah E. Cummings (D-MD) (May 7, 2013), Democrat House Oversight website, p. 1.

[1228] Benghazi Committee Report (emphasis added), pp. 99-100.

[1229] *Id.* (footnote omitted; emphasis added), p. 100.

security at the *embassy* – but there was concern that it not have *this image of a big, invading force.*

... And there was just concern of parading a bunch of trucks or buses full of Marines in uniform, *what kind of image* that would present, recognizing it was going to be daylight when they arrived.[1230]

(*So, politics and diplomatic "optics" trump trying to save nearly thirty – and soon to be three dozen – American lives in Benghazi.* And note Tidd's emphasis is completely on reinforcing Tripoli, not Benghazi.)

This extreme deference to State Department anxieties is confirmed in May 2014 hearings before the House Oversight Committee. During this hearing, the following exchange occurs between Congressman Jason Chaffetz (R-UT) and Retired Air Force Brigadier General Robert Lovell (formerly of AFRICOM):

Chaffetz: ... We had assets there in Europe. Did they actually go to the sound of the guns? Did they actually go into Benghazi?

Lovell: No, sir, those assets did not.

Chaffetz: Why not?

Lovell: Basically, *there was a lot of looking to the State Department for what it was that they wanted,* and in the deference to the Libyan people and *the sense of deference to the desires of the State Department in terms of what they would like to have.*

Chaffetz: Did they ever tell you to go save the people in Benghazi?

Lovell: Not to my knowledge, sir.

Chaffetz: We didn't run to the sound of the guns. They were issuing press releases. We had Americans dying. We had dead people, we had wounded people, and our military didn't try to engage in that fight. Would you disagree with that?

...

Lovell: Four individuals died, sir; we obviously did not respond in time to get there.

Chaffetz: Could we have?

...

Lovell: We may have been able to, but we'll never know.

[1230] *Id.* (emphasis added), p. 100.

THE TRUE ACCOUNT OF VALOR AND ABANDONMENT

Chaffetz: Because we didn't try.[1231]

Greg Hicks, number two U.S. diplomat in Libya at the time, holds a view that is in sharp contrast to the official "State" position as summarized by Vice Admiral Tidd. Hicks tells investigators:

I believe that the Libyans were hoping that we were going to come bail them out of this mess. And ... they were as surprised as we were that American ... military forces that did arrive only arrived on the evening of September 12.[1232]

Amazingly, after issuing his 7:00 p.m. Order to "deploy now," Panetta does not call Obama to advise which "Dogs of War" SecDef has unleashed.[1233] (Why not? Obama *is* the Commander in Chief.) ∎

[1231] Testimony of Brig. Gen. Robert Lovell (Ret.) before House Committee on Oversight and Government Reform, House Oversight Committee website (May 1, 2014) (emphasis added).

[1232] Attkisson, Diplomat: U.S. Special Forces Told "You Can't Go" to Benghazi During Attacks.

[1233] Panetta and Dempsey Senate Armed Services Committee Testimony (Feb. 7, 2013) (Response to questions of Sen. Kelly Ayotte (R-NH)); Benghazi Committee Report, p. 70; Additional Views of Reps. Jordan and Pompeo, p. 444; Statement of Senators McCain, Graham and Ayotte; Zuckoff, *13 Hours*, Chap. 6, p. 146; William Kristol, "Petraeus and Panetta Speak – But Not the President," *The Weekly Standard* online (Oct. 31, 2012) ("Kristol, Petraeus and Panetta Speak – But Not the President") (". . . [I]t's beyond inconceivable he [Panetta] didn't then stay in touch with the White House after he returned to the Pentagon"); Daniel Halper, "Panetta: Obama Absent Night of Benghazi," *The Weekly Standard* online (Feb. 7, 2013); and Rivera and Rivera, Where Was President Obama During Benghazi Terror Attack? (*Watch video there*; Go to 3:15-45).

54

Ambassador Stevens Is Found

Sometime between the first two firefights at the Annex, around 1:00 a.m. Benghazi time (7:00 p.m. in Washington), unidentified local Libyans (possibly looters) find the body of Chris Stevens.

Stevens is found in a bedroom within the Mission's Villa. A witness captures the scene on video. The witness claims Stevens has a pulse and is alive, but barely. A Libyan Army officer helps bring Stevens' body out of the Villa. The officer obtains Scott Wickland's cell phone, which the DSA agent had given the ambassador during the attack.[1234]

A neighbor, who knows Stevens, transports his body to nearby Benghazi Medical Center. For the next 45 to 90 minutes (accounts vary), doctors reportedly will attempt to resuscitate the diplomat.[1235]

The Libyan Army officer who helps remove Stevens' body begins calling "contact" numbers stored in the phone Stevens had. At about 1:40 a.m. Benghazi time, the Libyan reaches the U.S. Embassy in Tripoli. He conveys word Stevens' body has been found and taken to a hospital. Although the Select Committee's report is confusing on this subject, eventually U.S. officials begin to understand Stevens is at a hospital and possibly is deceased. Initially, Gregory Hicks and the rest of the Embassy staff do not know to which hospital Stevens has been taken. Four hundred miles away, the defenders at the Benghazi CIA Annex learn Ambassador Stevens is at a hospital when one of the DSA

[1234] Benghazi Committee Report, pp. 77-78; Hicks Oversight Committee Testimony (May 8, 2013), p. 24; Burnett, Benghazi Timeline: "We Are Under Attack" (*Watch video there*; Go to 6:48 - 7:02); CNN Finds, Returns Journal Belonging to Late U.S. Ambassador (*Watch video there*; Go to 0:14 - 1:36); and Baier, 13 Hours at Benghazi: The Inside Story (*Watch video there*; Go to 19:05-37).

[1235] Benghazi Committee Report, pp. 77-78; CNN Finds, Returns Journal Belonging to Late U.S. Ambassador (*Watch video there*; Go to 1:37 - 2:07); Hicks Oversight Committee Testimony (May 8, 2013), pp. 26-28; Kirkpatrick and Myers, Libya Attack Brings Challenges for U.S.; CBS/AP, "Assault on U.S. Consulate in Benghazi Leaves 4 Dead, Including U.S. Ambassador J. Christopher Stevens," CBS News online (Sept. 12, 2012) (Libyan doctor tried for 90 minutes to revive Stevens); and Baier, 13 Hours at Benghazi: The Inside Story (*Watch video there*; Go to 19:19-37).

THE TRUE ACCOUNT OF VALOR AND ABANDONMENT

agents on a rooftop with DSA Scott Wickland and GRS Jack Silva gets a call on his cell phone.[1236]

To make matters worse, David McFarland of the U.S. Embassy in Tripoli learns from his contacts in Benghazi the hospital where Stevens reportedly has been taken is under Ansar al-Sharia's control. This is the very terrorist group social media is claiming has staged the attacks on the Mission Compound! Greg Hicks later testifies this knowledge means Team Tripoli likely must become a hostage rescue team.[1237] (This is yet another good reason to deploy the F.E.S.T. crisis response team from Washington. Despite this word Stevens may be under Ansar al-Sharia's control, State's Patrick Kennedy and Charlene Lamb – and the 7:30 Meeting of "Deputies" – will elect *not* to activate F.E.S.T.)

Greg Hicks then contacts a Libyan friend in Benghazi and asks the latter to go to the hospital and explore whether this patient is in fact Ambassador Stevens. (This contact is the same Libyan who previously had assisted in rescuing a downed American Air Force pilot in 2011 during the NATO attacks on Qadhafi!)[1238]

During this time, the U.S. Embassy team in Tripoli begins receiving various calls from unknown individuals who claim to know where Stevens is. They provide few details, and are evasive in answering the diplomatic staff's questions. The mystery callers invite the Americans to come pick Stevens up. Especially given David McFarland's intelligence that Ansar al-Sharia controls the hospital where Stevens may be, Hicks and his team are extremely wary. They suspect the unknown callers are seeking to lure the Americans into a terrorist trap.

Hicks and his staff decide not to take the bait. They (and the CIA's Tripoli Chief of Station) direct Team Tripoli (still at the airport) to go to the CIA Annex instead of the hospital.[1239] (Good instinct. However, as events will play out, the Annex also is a terrorist ambush.) ■

[1236] Benghazi Committee Report, pp. 77-78 and 89, and Select Benghazi Timeline, p. 560; Hicks Oversight Committee Testimony (May 8, 2013), p. 26; and Baier, 13 Hours at Benghazi: The Inside Story (*Watch video there*; Go to 19:06-19). See also Clinton, *Hard Choices*, Chap. 17, pp. 396-397.

[1237] Hicks Oversight Committee Testimony (May 8, 2013), pp. 26-27.

[1238] Clinton, *Hard Choices*, Chap. 17, p. 396.

[1239] Hicks Oversight Committee Testimony (May 8, 2013), p. 28; Sen. Intelligence Committee Benghazi Report, p. 8; and Hsu, CIA Officers Detail Part of Bloody Benghazi Attack at Terrorism Trial (Criminal trial testimony of disguised CIA agent, pseudonym "Roy Edwards").

55

Secretary Clinton Calls Greg Hicks

At 7:05 p.m. Washington time (1:05 a.m. Tripoli time), Hillary Clinton and eight of her senior State Department officials convene a conference call with Gregory Hicks, Deputy Chief of Mission in Tripoli, Libya. None of them know Chris Stevens' body has just been found in the Benghazi Mission.

(Hicks later will testify he recalls this call took place around 2:00 a.m. in Tripoli,[1240] which would be 8:00 p.m. in Washington. However, as discussed below (Chapter 59), Clinton likely is well into a subsequent meeting by then. The author has no basis to doubt the admirable Mr. Hicks' veracity, but has chosen to base the time of this call on the State Department's Operations Center Watch Log.[1241])

State officials participating in this call include Clinton's Chief of Staff Cheryl Mills, Deputy Chief of Staff Jake Sullivan, Wendy Sherman, Steve Mull, Beth Jones, and Under Secretary for Management Patrick Kennedy.[1242] F.E.S.T.'s Mark Thompson is *not* on this conference.[1243] This call is placed almost three and one-half hours after the initial assault on the Mission, and continues during the start of the second firefight at the Annex (discussed below). (Query: Why doesn't Hillary Clinton contact Hicks almost immediately upon learning of the first attack on the Mission Compound and the ambassador going missing?)

Hicks testifies further that during this ten-minute conversation he briefs Clinton on developments in Libya. The second wave assault on the Annex commences just five minutes into this call; it is possible someone slips Hicks a note advising him of this during the call. However, remarkably it appears at this point Hicks has yet to learn

---

[1240] Hicks Oversight Committee Testimony (May 8, 2013), p. 27; *Id.* (Response to questions of Rep. Tim Walberg (R-MI)), p. 63; and *Id.* (Response to questions of Rep. Ron DeSantis (R-FL)), p. 96.

[1241] Additional Views of Reps. Jordan and Pompeo, p. 426 n. 27.

[1242] Benghazi Committee Report, Select Benghazi Timeline, p. 559; and Benghazi Committee Report, p. 151.

[1243] Benghazi Committee Report, Select Benghazi Timeline, p. 559.

THE TRUE ACCOUNT OF VALOR AND ABANDONMENT

even of the *initial* attack on the Annex that began about 30 minutes before his call with Secretary Clinton. He later testifies that at the time of this call, ". . . the first two attacks had been completed. [This likely refers to the firefights at the Mission, and possibly to the attacks on the DSAs as they drove from there to the Annex.] And there was a lull in Benghazi at the time. . . . We had at that time no expectation that there would be subsequent attacks at our annex in Benghazi."[1244]

(In attempting to understand to which "lull" Hicks is referring, note there was only about a twenty-minute gap between the first and second attacks on the Annex. In contrast, there was roughly a 70- to 75-minute "lull" between the attacks on the Diplomatic Security Agents as they fled the Mission and the first assault on the Annex.[1245])

Most of the discussion during this State conference with Greg Hicks relates to the search for Ambassador Stevens and hopefully his rescue, and also the mission of Team Tripoli.[1246] Hicks also recommends during this call the U.S. personnel in *Benghazi* should be evacuated. Clinton agrees this is the right thing to do.[1247] Surprisingly, according to Hicks during this call with Clinton and her team they do not discuss securing military assistance from the president or the Defense Secretary for these Americans in *Benghazi!*[1248] The assumption by those on the call must be they will have to evacuate on their own.

However, support for Tripoli apparently is another story. During this conference, Hicks requests security reinforcements in Tripoli and a transport aircraft to evacuate their wounded out of Libya to a medical facility. (It is unclear at this point who Hicks is referring to as being "wounded," unless he is assuming Ambassador Stevens will need medical attention if and when he is found. Oz Geist and Dave Ubben will not sustain their severe injuries for another four hours.)

Secretary Clinton indicates to Hicks a Marine FAST team is being deployed to "bolster our security posture *in Tripoli*," and a C-17 will be coming to take people back. Clinton advises the Marines will be

---

[1244] Hicks Oversight Committee Testimony (May 8, 2013) (Response to questions of Rep. Ron DeSantis (R-FL)), p. 96; and Benghazi Committee Report, pp. 151-152.

[1245] Key Delays Appendix (See September 11 entries for 5:16 p.m., 5:23 p.m., 6:34 p.m., 6:51 p.m. and 7:10 p.m., all Washington time).

[1246] Hicks Oversight Committee Testimony (May 8, 2013), p. 27; and *Id.* (Response to questions of Rep. Ron DeSantis (R-FL)), p. 96.

[1247] *Id.*, p. 27.

[1248] *Id.* (Response to questions of Rep. Ron DeSantis (R-FL)), p. 96.

arriving in *Tripoli* on September 12th.[1249] (Note at this point – even *before* the upcoming 7:30 Meeting of the "Deputies" (or "Principals") – Clinton apparently knows already no FAST Marine team is headed to Benghazi.)

Hicks claims he does not discuss the subject of a "demonstration" on this call with Clinton.[1250]

Then the call terminates. Hillary Clinton and her team have a fateful meeting to attend. ■

[1249] *Id.* (emphasis added) (Response to questions of Rep. Thomas Massie (R-KY)), pp. 88-89; and Benghazi Committee Report, p. 151.

[1250] Hicks Oversight Committee Testimony (May 8, 2013) (Response to questions of Rep. Tim Walberg (R-MI)), p. 63. See also Benson, The Damning Dozen: Twelve Revelations from the Benghazi Hearings.

56

Assault from Zombieland

It is 1:10 a.m. Benghazi time (7:10 p.m. in Washington, while Hillary Clinton and her team are speaking with Gregory Hicks). A car drives near the CIA compound from the rear and stops. A man exits and makes a motion to throw something over the Annex's back gate. From his rooftop post GRS agent Oz Geist is observing the man, training his gun sight on him. Oz engages him, shooting the thrower two or three times. The assailant goes down. The thrown object lands short of the gate and explodes. BOOM! It is the signal to launch the second-wave attack on the Annex.[1251]

The terrorists have regrouped. This second assault involves "even heavier sustained fire and a larger number of attackers" than the first wave. One GRS operator says of this second firefight, "It was a lot more force, lasted probably twice as long" as the first Annex fight. The assailants move toward the Annex in perhaps twenty cars.[1252]

BOOM! Next, an RPG strikes Annex Building 2. For the following five minutes, the defenders take heavy and persistent small arms fire from terrorists along the east perimeter wall. They also receive such fire from the northeast corner of the Annex, and RPG attacks from the field to the east of the Annex in Zombieland.[1253]

The protectors on the rooftops and towers inside the Annex return fire with a vengeance. *This is war!* But they target the advancing militants with deliberation. They use "controlled bursts," aiming individually at each target before squeezing the trigger. In contrast, the poorly-trained attackers mostly are spraying the Annex with wild, sustained shooting.

Finally, having sustained heavy, unrelenting return fire from the Annex guards, the terrorists retreat again. This second battle lasts about 30 minutes or so. None of the Americans are seriously injured.[1254]

[1251] Baier, 13 Hours at Benghazi: The Inside Story (*Watch video there*; Go to 19:57 - 20:24).

[1252] Benghazi Committee Report, p. 76; and Baier, 13 Hours at Benghazi: The Inside Story (*Watch video there*; Go to 20:25-52).

[1253] Benghazi Committee Report, p. 76.

[1254] *Id.*, p. 76.

(There are reports that, at some point, those inside the Annex capture a few of the Libyan attackers.[1255] However, the author has been unable to find credible support for these assertions.)

This is the last violence at the Annex until the final, fatal mortar attacks that will come some three and one-half hours later.[1256] This second-wave onslaught is still further, unambiguous evidence for the U.S. government officials and military leaders that the Battle of Benghazi is not over. It is sad almost none of them appear to be paying attention. ■

[1255] E.g., Griffin, CIA Operators Were Denied Request for Help During Benghazi Attack (three Libyan attackers reportedly captured).

[1256] Benghazi Committee Report, p. 76.

57

"Spinning Up"

Soon it becomes clear many officials in Washington (and at military commands abroad) are acting as if Defense Secretary Panetta never has given any order for military forces to "deploy now." Meanwhile, a high-level, interagency teleconference to discuss the crisis is being arranged to begin at 7:30 p.m. ("7:30 Meeting," discussed below in Chapter 59).

Minutes before this 7:30 Meeting starts, Panetta's Chief of Staff, Jeremy Bash, writes a brief but critical email at 7:19 p.m. No doubt in preparation for this conference, Bash sends it to several key officials at the State and Defense Departments. Recipients at State include Jacob Sullivan, Cheryl Mills and Thomas Nides, the Deputy Secretary of State for Management and Resources. DoD officials who are copied include General Dempsey, Vice Admiral James Winnefeld and Secretary Panetta's Senior Military Assistant, General John Kelly.[1257]

Bash's email states, "After consulting with General Dempsey, General Ham and the Joint Staff, we have identified the forces that could move *to Benghazi.*"[1258] Bash mentions a special operations force in Croatia and the Marine FAST team at Rota. Bash asserts (incorrectly), "They are spinning up as we speak." Bash then writes, "*Assuming Principals agree to deploy these elements*, we will ask State to secure the approval from host nation."[1259] Note this email – sent just

---

[1257] Press Release, "Judicial Watch: New Benghazi Email Shows DOD Offered State Department 'Forces That Could Move to Benghazi' Immediately – Specifics Blacked Out in New Document," Judicial Watch website (Dec. 8, 2015) ("Judicial Watch Release, New Benghazi Email Shows DOD Offered State Department 'Forces That Could Move to Benghazi' Immediately").

[1258] Benghazi Committee Report (emphasis added), p. 83; Email from Jeremy Bash to Jacob J. Sullivan, et al. Re: "Libya" (Sept. 11, 2012), Judicial Watch Document Archive (Redacted; emphasis added); Judicial Watch Release, New Benghazi Email Shows DOD Offered State Department "Forces That Could Move to Benghazi" Immediately; and Joel Gehrke, "E-mail: Military Offered to Send Rescue Team to Benghazi During Attack," National Review online (Dec. 8, 2015) ("Gehrke, E-Mail: Military Offered to Send Rescue Team to Benghazi During Attack").

[1259] Benghazi Committee Report (emphasis added), p. 83; Email from Jeremy Bash to Jacob J. Sullivan, et al. Re: "Libya" (Sept. 11, 2012) (Redacted; emphasis added);

before the 7:30 Meeting – focuses on sending rescue forces to *Benghazi*. As discussed in detail below, during and after the 7:30 Meeting the focus inexplicably will become sending military assets to *Tripoli and Sicily only*.

(For three years the Obama administration conceals the existence of Bash's "spinning up" email. It finally is disclosed in December 2015 as ordered by a judge in a Freedom of Information Act lawsuit filed by the aggressive conservative watchdog entity, "Judicial Watch."[1260])

Regarding Bash's email, why do the "Principals" need to agree to deploy the forces? Has President Obama negated or altered his own directive to do "everything possible" and deploy all available assets to help the Americans in Benghazi? Has Panetta withdrawn or modified his previous order to "deploy now"? Or have these two officials never really given the "do everything possible" and "deploy now" orders as they later will insist they have? Or, as preposterous as it sounds, do both high- and lower-level military officers (and other government officials) simply resolve not to follow or even recognize Panetta's "deploy now" order? (These frustrating alternative explanations for inexplicable actions boggle the mind.)

In his subsequent testimony before the Select Committee, Bash's statements support Panetta's version of events. However, his testimony is inconsistent with his own 7:19 p.m. "spinning up" email quoted above, where Bash himself writes, "Assuming Principals agree to deploy these elements. . . ." The Select panel's questioning of Bash includes the following unambiguous exchange:

> Bash: . . . My recollection was he [Secretary Panetta] was told of the situation, he was told about which units could respond, and he said: Go get them, do it, move.
>
> Q: So there would've been no further order necessary from him?

Judicial Watch Release, New Benghazi Email Shows DOD Offered State Department "Forces That Could Move to Benghazi" Immediately; and Gehrke, E-Mail: Military Offered to Send Rescue Team to Benghazi During Attack.

[1260] Judicial Watch Release, New Benghazi Email Shows DOD Offered State Department "Forces That Could Move to Benghazi" Immediately (Tom Fitton, Judicial Watch president: "The Obama administration and Clinton officials hid this compelling Benghazi e-mail for years. The e-mail makes readily apparent that the military was prepared to launch immediate assistance that could have made a difference, at least at the CIA Annex. The fact that the Obama Administration withheld this e-mail for so long only worsens the scandal of Benghazi"); and Gehrke, E-Mail: Military Offered to Send Rescue Team to Benghazi During Attack.

THE TRUE ACCOUNT OF VALOR AND ABANDONMENT

Bash: Correct.
Q: Wheels could have taken off and he would not have had to say another single, solitary word?
Bash: Correct. And I believe that actually was the case.
Q: All right. So he never amplified, clarified, withdrew, changed his instructions, which were deploy.
Bash: He did not.[1261]

If this is true, why eleven minutes after he transmits his "spinning up" email will Jeremy Bash participate in a two-hour 7:30 Meeting on this Night of Benghazi, listening to a bunch of gasbag representatives of "Principals" debate whether they should concur with Panetta's order to "deploy now" the "elements" identified by the Defense Secretary and his team? (More contradictions regarding vital facts.) ∎

[1261] Benghazi Committee Report, p. 96.

58

Team Tripoli Arrives in Benghazi

During the second Annex firefight, Team Tripoli's chartered aircraft lands at Benina Airport in Benghazi at 1:30 a.m. local time (7:30 p.m. Washington time).[1262]

Based upon their coordination efforts before leaving Tripoli, the rescuers expect to be met at the airport by a militia group known as the "Libyan Shield." However, no one is there to receive them. (An airport guard in his pajamas comes out and asks the Americans what the hell is going on. He sounds like some of the government officials in Washington.) At this time, one of Team Tripoli's prime missions is to locate Ambassador Stevens. As far as the Tripoli rescuers know at this point, Stevens still is missing and presumed alive.[1263]

Team Tripoli has brought no ground transport of its own. They will lose a great deal of valuable time attempting to arrange secure transportation into Benghazi (the emphasis being on "secure"). While planning their transportation, they must wrestle with the "conflicting aims of keeping a low profile while still moving in force to avoid being ambushed and needing rescuing themselves."[1264] Ultimately, they will stay at this airfield for some *three hours!*[1265]

[1262] Benghazi Committee Report, Select Benghazi Timeline, p. 560.

[1263] Benghazi Committee Report (Redacted), pp. 78-80; and Hsu, CIA Officers Detail Part of Bloody Benghazi Attack at Terrorism Trial (Criminal trial testimony of two disguised CIA agents, pseudonyms "Roy Edwards" and "Alexander Charles": "armed escort of Libyan special forces personnel" did not appear at Benghazi airport as expected to take Team Tripoli to CIA Annex).

[1264] Hsu, CIA Officers Detail Part of Bloody Benghazi Attack at Terrorism Trial (Criminal trial testimony of two disguised CIA agents, pseudonyms "Roy Edwards" and "Alexander Charles").

[1265] See Hicks Oversight Committee Testimony (May 8, 2013), p. 28; Key Delays Appendix (See September 11 entries for 7:30 p.m. and 10:30 p.m., both Washington time); and Hsu, CIA Officers Detail Part of Bloody Benghazi Attack at Terrorism Trial (Criminal trial testimony of disguised CIA agent, pseudonym "Alexander Charles": "Obviously nothing worked, because we were on the ground for approximately three hours").

THE TRUE ACCOUNT OF VALOR AND ABANDONMENT

Meanwhile, back in Tripoli the CIA Chief of Station and the Embassy's Defense Attaché are burning up the phones. They are trying to persuade the Libyan government and local militia to send vehicles and military or other security assets to aid Team Tripoli in moving from the Benghazi airport into the city. In Benghazi, the Chief of Base at the CIA Annex is doing likewise.[1266]

While at the airport, Team Tripoli's members begin to hear reports Ambassador Stevens is at a hospital. When they discuss this by phone with the CIA's Chief of Station in Tripoli, the latter fears these reports might be a terrorist trap.[1267]

Team Tripoli now faces a dilemma: when they get transportation should they travel to the hospital where Stevens may be, or to the CIA Annex where most of the Americans are? They identify a local militia willing to take them to the Annex, but it refuses to take the Americans to the hospital. The rescue party loses more time negotiating with this militia over their destination. During this period, Embassy Tripoli officials are urging Team Tripoli to go to the CIA Annex instead of the hospital.[1268] In the meantime, Team Tripoli hears reports Ambassador Stevens is deceased. At this point, they conclude they will follow the latest directive of the CIA Station Chief in Tripoli and go directly to the Annex.[1269]

While still at the Benghazi airport, Team Tripoli is "alerted" Stevens' personal tracking device is pinging "within 25 meters of their current location on the airfield." The rescue team finds this odd. They conclude it means someone nearby (perhaps one of the Libyan militia members) is in possession of some of the ambassador's belongings![1270] This is one more reason (among many) they are concerned for their own safety.

(Afterwards, it is possible someone in the White House attempts misleadingly to imply it is government officials in *Washington* who

---

[1266] Hicks Oversight Committee Testimony (May 8, 2013), pp. 26-27.

[1267] Benghazi Committee Report (Redacted), p. 79.

[1268] Hicks Oversight Committee Testimony (May 8, 2013), p. 28; and Sen. Intelligence Committee Benghazi Report, p. 8.

[1269] Benghazi Committee Report (Redacted), p. 79; Hicks Oversight Committee Testimony (May 8, 2013), p. 28; Hsu, CIA Officers Detail Part of Bloody Benghazi Attack at Terrorism Trial (Criminal trial testimony of disguised CIA agent, pseudonym "Roy Edwards"); and Miller, CIA Rushed to Save Diplomats as Libya Attack Was Underway.

[1270] Benghazi Committee Report (Redacted), pp. 79-80.

have dispatched Team Tripoli to Benghazi. On October 20, 2012, investigative correspondent Sharyl Attkisson reports, "A White House official told CBS News that a 'small group of reinforcements' *was sent* from Tripoli to Benghazi, but declined to say how many or what time they arrived."[1271] However, the Benghazi Select Committee concludes Team Tripoli goes to Benghazi on their own initiative, under the authority of the CIA's bold Chief of Station in Tripoli.[1272] Leon Panetta's memoir is consistent with this conclusion.[1273])

As detailed below, the seven valiant members of Team Tripoli will be the only American rescuers from outside Benghazi to step foot in this snake pit of a city during the entire battle and subsequent evacuation from the Annex to the airport. ∎

[1271] Attkisson, Could U.S. Military Have Helped During Libya Attack? (emphasis added).

[1272] Benghazi Committee Report ("... [T]hese individuals [on Team Tripoli] went to Benghazi from Tripoli at the direction of the Chief of Station in Libya, not at the order of anyone in Washington, D.C."), p. 109; and *Id.* (emphasis added) ("... Team Tripoli ... acted with purpose, precision and ingenuity that night. ... They *deployed themselves* because fellow Americans needed them"), p. 113.

[1273] Panetta, *Worthy Fights* (emphasis added) ("Although the seven of them worked together, they were not a military unit that had trained together for this type of mission, but acted bravely *on their own initiative*"), Chap. 16, p. 429.

59

Navel-Gazing

There is perhaps no better emblem of the Obama team's fecklessness and complete lack of urgency than the interagency "Deputies" assembly that will consume much of this Night of Benghazi.[1274] While five-thousand miles away the CIA Annex defenders are repulsing terrorists in the second-wave attacks, and Team Tripoli is landing in Benghazi, the bureaucrats in Washington "jock up" in their own unique fashion: they summon a huge meeting.

It begins at 7:30 p.m., Washington time. *This is about three hours and forty-five minutes after the assault on the diplomatic Mission Compound begins, almost three and one-half hours after Ambassador Stevens goes missing, nearly an hour after administration officials learn a second, "secret" U.S. facility in Benghazi is under attack, and one-half hour after Defense Secretary Panetta will claim he issues a "deploy now" order to his military.* Despite its tardy start, this gathering will drag on for approximately *two hours!* (Why is there no sense of *exigency? U.S. government employees are under <u>attack</u>!*)[1275]

This session entails a high-level, multi-agency video teleconference among officials from the White House, National Security Council ("NSC"), CIA, State Department, and Defense Department and Joint Chiefs of Staff (the "7:30 Meeting"). (This also sometimes is referenced in documentary evidence as the "Deputies' meeting.")[1276] Instead of this meeting of "Deputies," to address the Benghazi crisis President Obama and his National Security Advisor, Thomas Donilon, should be convening the cabinet-level National Security "Principals

---

[1274] Benghazi Committee Report (Asking "... why the urgency and ingenuity displayed by team members at the Annex and Team Tripoli was seemingly not shared by all decision makers in Washington"), p. 123.

[1275] See Key Delays Appendix; and Benghazi Committee Report ("By stark contrast [to Team Tripoli's urgent actions], in those same four hours, principals in Washington had merely managed to identify forces that could potentially deploy to Libya and convened a meeting to discuss those forces"), p. 83.

[1276] Benghazi Committee Report, p. 82, and Select Benghazi Timeline, p. 560; and Clinton, *Hard Choices,* Chap. 17, p. 396.

Committee" in the Situation Room. But none of this happens. (Indeed, as discussed below, the president never will make it there on this Night of Benghazi.)

Instead, the critical teleconference of "Deputies" is convened by Denis McDonough, then Deputy Assistant to the President for National Security Affairs. (At the beginning of the president's second term, McDonough will become Obama's Chief of Staff. At this 7:30 Meeting, does McDonough have President Obama's authorization to modify the latter's 5:30 p.m. instructions to Panetta? Or Panetta's 7:00 p.m. Order to "deploy now"? We still don't know.)

On this Night of Benghazi, to the extent any one person is coordinating the entire response of the U.S. government to the crisis underway in Benghazi, it is Denis McDonough. (McDonough has no military experience. Indeed, *The Daily Caller* reports few NSC staffers under Obama have military or intelligence experience.[1277] Fortunately, unlike many other key Benghazi decision-makers (see Chapter 66), at least McDonough is not a lawyer like his boss, Tom Donilon.)

In recent years, the operational role of the National Security Council staff expands constantly. This is a relatively new (and to some experts, alarming) attribute of the Obama administration. Throughout Obama's presidency, the ever-enlarging NSC staff increasingly will engage in micromanagement, and immerse themselves in operational details and tactics – matters traditionally handled by the Pentagon, the CIA, and other executive agencies and their officials.[1278] On this Night of Benghazi, this NSC interference and control will not end well.

[1277] Jonah Bennett, "Former Mil Officials: Obama's National Security Council Is Full of Activists," The Daily Caller website (Mar. 15, 2016) ("One Democrat with a long history in the defense industry told Breaking Defense in January that one of the most frustrating elements of the NSC is that it's staffed by people without real-world experience, either in intelligence or the military").

[1278] Mark F. Cancian, "Limiting Size of NSC Staff," Center for Strategic & International Studies website (July 1, 2016) (". . . [T]he National Security Council has assumed more of an operational role as opposed to focusing on strategic planning and interagency coordination. Both former Secretaries of Defense Robert Gates and Leon Panetta have complained about the NSC and White House staff's centralization of decision making and intrusion into operational and tactical details"); Gates, *Duty* ("The controlling nature of the Obama White House and the NSS [NSC] staff took micromanagement and operational meddling to a new level. . . ."), Chap. 10, p. 587; *Id.* ("This was part and parcel of an increasingly operational National Security Staff in the White House and micromanagement of military matters – a combination that had proven disastrous in the past"), pp. 351-352; and Interview of Robert Gates with Bret Baier, Fox News Channel (April 7, 2015) ("It was the operational micromanagement

The Participants

President Obama does not participate in this 7:30 Meeting. Neither (apparently) does his White House Chief of Staff Jack Lew or his vice president, Joe Biden. Leon Panetta does not join; the Director of the CIA, David Petraeus, isn't on the line; and the Chairman of the Joint Chiefs of Staff also doesn't participate.[1279] Neither does Thomas Donilon, the president's National Security Advisor. Nor apparently does John Brennan, the president's advisor on terrorism and future CIA Director. (Why not? What is more important for these officials tonight?)

Representing the Defense Department is Vice Admiral Kurt Tidd (then Director of Operations for the Joint Chiefs of Staff), and Jeremy B. Bash (Chief of Staff to the Secretary of Defense, a lawyer). According to the Select Committee, the Vice Chairman of the Joint Chiefs, Vice Admiral James Winnefeld, does not participate as he usually would. Instead, after attending Panetta's "Council of War" he has gone home to host a dinner party for "foreign dignitaries"! (Winnefeld reportedly receives one update on Benghazi during dinner over the soup course. Afterwards, at around 10:00 p.m. (4:00 a.m. in Benghazi) when the dessert plates have been cleared, Winnefeld goes to a "secure communications facility" in his residence to obtain the latest intelligence regarding the crisis.)

The Under Secretary of Defense for Policy, James Miller, also does not join the conference due to a family emergency. Ordinarily he, too, would be involved in such a Deputies meeting. Miller has asked Bash to participate in his stead. Miller tells Congress he tries to join the teleconference by phone from his home, but fails to connect.[1280]

The many State representatives on this conference include: Secretary Clinton; Cheryl Mills (Clinton's Chief of Staff); Patrick Kennedy (Under Secretary for Management); Jacob J. Sullivan (Deputy Chief of Staff for Policy and Planning); Stephen D. Mull (Executive Secretary); Wendy R. Sherman (Under Secretary for Political Affairs); and Beth Jones (Acting Assistant Secretary for Near Eastern

---

that drove me nuts of White House and NSC staffers calling senior commanders out in the field and asking them questions, second guessing commanders").

[1279] Benghazi Committee Report (Obama and Panetta not participating), pp. 82, 86 and 94; and Clinton, *Hard Choices*, Chap. 17, p. 396.

[1280] Benghazi Committee Report, pp. 82, 84-85 & n. 351.

Affairs).[1281] Many of these, including Clinton, participate by videophone. She takes the call in State's Operations Center.[1282] To her credit, *Clinton is the only cabinet member on this conference.*[1283] However, Mark Thompson, leader of State's F.E.S.T. counterterrorism crisis-response unit, is *not* involved in this session!

(As readers who have attended meetings this large can attest, it is guaranteed *substantial* amounts of time will be wasted. Instead, hours ago on this night the president should have gathered six or eight knowledgeable, high-level decision-makers in the Situation Room and decided everything in ten or fifteen minutes, *max*. There is a national security *crisis* underway – and a U.S. ambassador's life is at stake!)

The Context

Consider some of the key facts of which participants in this 7:30 Meeting must be aware as their conference begins: First, Sean Smith is dead; second, Ambassador Stevens still is missing; third, under fire the five surviving DSA agents have abandoned the flaming ruins of the Mission with their GRS rescuers from the Annex; and fourth, the CIA's supposedly "secret" Annex in Benghazi also has come under attack.[1284] During this 7:30 Meeting the participants also likely learn a second-wave attack at the Annex has begun (7:10 p.m. Washington time) and ended (about 7:40-7:50 p.m.). During this teleconference they no doubt are informed of the arrival of Team Tripoli in Benghazi (just as the 7:30 Meeting begins). This increases to nearly three-dozen the number of Americans who are in mortal peril in that city. Finally, it is likely during this session the officials learn of reports Ambassador Stevens has been taken to a hospital (see Chapter 54).[1285]

In other words, the participants in this horrifically long navel-gazing session have no objective, reasonable basis to believe the Battle of Benghazi is over. And yet, as explained in subsequent chapters, they will claim to believe just that.

[1281] *Id.*, pp. 82 and 90.

[1282] Clinton, *Hard Choices* Chap. 17, p. 396.

[1283] Benghazi Committee Report, pp. 82, 86 and 94.

[1284] Benghazi Committee Report, pp. 82-83 and 91-92.

[1285] Key Delays Appendix (See September 11 entries at 7:00 p.m., 7:30 p.m. and 8:05 p.m., all Washington time).

The Objectives

The Select Committee will discover the participants later describe the purpose of this 7:30 Meeting in varying ways. State's Jacob Sullivan says the objective is to "work through this issue" of deploying the identified forces. (Haven't Leon Panetta and his generals already spent an hour doing this in their council of war ending thirty minutes ago?) Vice Admiral Tidd and several other participants view the purpose of the meeting as providing "an opportunity to share information across agencies." Under Secretary Patrick Kennedy repeats this theme of sharing and "conforming" information across entities. He describes the attendees as "Trying to make sure that we all, meaning across the entire U.S. Government, had the clearest coherent understanding of what was going on in the fog of war." (Have they not heard of email?) In addition to sharing information, State's Cheryl Mills testifies the conference also is to "figure out how to coordinate resources to support our team."[1286] (Very little "support" will be forthcoming for the Americans in Benghazi; but perhaps Mills means supporting the Obama "political team" in Washington.)

Topics of Discussion and Decision

Approving Panetta's Decision "To Deploy"

The Select Committee writes that from the perspective at Defense, this 7:30 Meeting is an opportunity to notify the White House and State Department of the assets DoD "*could deploy* in response to the attacks *as ordered by the secretary* and *to seek concurrence*."[1287] (Why the hell don't the White House and State already *have* this information? Secretary Panetta makes his final "deploy" decision by 7:00 p.m., a full half-hour before this teleconference starts. In any event, as explained above, Defense's Jeremy Bash already has sent explanatory emails before the 7:30 Meeting convenes.[1288])

[1286] Benghazi Committee Report, pp. 83-85.

[1287] *Id.* (emphasis added), pp. 85-86. See also *Id.* (emphasis added) (Vice Admiral Tidd: ". . . [W]hen we got to the military, we talked about these are the type of forces that we *can deploy*, and here's what we know, here's what we think, and here's what our *recommendations are*"), pp. 84-85.

[1288] Benghazi Committee Report, p. 83; and Gehrke, E-Mail: Military Offered to Send Rescue Team to Benghazi During Attack.

Regarding Bash, recall that in his 7:19 p.m. "spinning up" email Bash writes, "*Assuming Principals [at the 7:30 Meeting] agree to deploy these elements.*" Similarly, Vice Admiral Winnefeld (who is not on the teleconference) later testifies his "sense" is that at the 7:30 Meeting "the deputies" are told what specific assets Secretary Panetta has decided to deploy, ". . . and they all concurred with that. . . ."[1289]

Why does Defense need to "seek concurrence" if Panetta has given a decisive order on behalf of the National Command Authority? Panetta insists he does not need anyone's approval of his 7:00 p.m. Order to "deploy now." Why does his own Chief of Staff (Bash) think otherwise? (It is yet another maddening contradiction concerning this Night of Benghazi.)

Yet Jeremy Bash isn't the only one representing the Pentagon at this marathon meeting who believes the military "asset selection" decision has not been finalized. The Select Committee later asks Vice Admiral Tidd what the status is of the assets "that you all discussed? Were they preparing to deploy?" Tidd's answer is astonishing in light of Secretary Panetta's position. Tidd testifies, "They were alerted. *The final decision had not yet been made definitively, as I recall*, but we came out of that [7:30] meeting basically: send everything."[1290] (Yes, "send everything." To Sicily and Tripoli, but not Benghazi; and send them tomorrow, not tonight.)

Deploying the F.E.S.T. Group

As noted above, during this entire two-hour meeting Chris Stevens still is missing. It is entirely possible Stevens has been taken hostage by the militant attackers. (Indeed, according to Defense Secretary Panetta, one early report "suggested that Stevens had been taken hostage. . . ."[1291] Also, the Senate Intelligence Committee later will write that when the DSA and GRS men fail repeatedly to find Chris Stevens in the Villa, the GRS Team Lead concludes the ambassador has been kidnapped and taken from the compound.[1292])

[1289] Benghazi Committee Report, pp. 85-86.

[1290] *Id.* (emphasis added), p. 84.

[1291] Panetta, *Worthy Fights*, Chap. 16, p. 428.

[1292] Sen. Intelligence Committee Benghazi Report, p. 7.

Despite this, apparently none of the many State officials on this 7:30 conference recommends F.E.S.T. be launched to Libya. Mark Thompson learns later on this Night of Benghazi that during this meeting Patrick Kennedy personally *discourages* F.E.S.T.'s deployment.[1293] Thompson believes State representatives' opposition to his F.E.S.T. group's deployment is sufficiently strong to persuade the "NSC committee" [presumably the 7:30 p.m. "Deputies Meeting"] not to deploy this crisis response and hostage-rescue team.[1294]

Later, according to *The Atlantic* and Fox News, rumors will surface Thompson has been "threatened and intimidated by unnamed State Department officials" not to testify that Secretary Clinton "willfully blocked out" involvement of Thompson's group on the Night of Benghazi. (To the author, Mark Thompson does not seem to be the type to be intimidated by *anyone*.) Foggy Bottom – including Thompson's boss, Daniel Benjamin – vigorously denies the rumors are true. Thompson insists his "Counterterrorism Bureau" is not excluded from any deliberations it should have been part of.[1295] However, he testifies to the House Oversight panel his own crisis-response *side* of that Bureau *is* shut out of Benghazi deliberations on September 11, 2012.[1296] Thompson later testifies that the following day, September 12, he is told *not* to participate in "VTCs" [presumably video teleconference calls] regarding Benghazi. Although Counterterrorism Bureau officials do participate, the F.E.S.T. "side" of this Bureau does not.[1297]

Vice Admiral Kurt Tidd, then Director of Operations for the Joint Chiefs of Staff, later testifies to the Select Committee that during this 7:30 Meeting at the White House F.E.S.T. deployment "was discussed

---

[1293] House Oversight Committee Hearings (May 8, 2013) (Remarks of Rep. Jason Chaffetz (R-UT), quoting email from Mark Thompson to Patrick Kennedy's deputy), p. 36.

[1294] Thompson Oversight Committee Testimony (May 8, 2013) (Response to questions of Rep. Mark Meadows (R-NC)), p. 92.

[1295] Alexander Abad-Santos, "Benghazi Whistleblowers Reveal Their Clinton Cover-up Moment," *The Atlantic* online (May 6, 2013); and Chad Pergram and James Rosen, "Clinton Sought End-Run Around Counterterrorism Bureau on Night of Benghazi Attack, Witness Will Say," Fox News online (May 6, 2013).

[1296] Thompson Oversight Committee Testimony (May 8, 2013) (Response to questions of Rep. Eleanor Holmes Norton (D-D.C.)), pp. 38-39.

[1297] *Id.* (Response to questions of Rep. Jason Chaffetz (R-UT)), p. 37.

briefly ... but dismissed."[1298] (Why isn't deployment of F.E.S.T. discussed and resolved at high levels much earlier than this 7:30 Meeting?) In his testimony before the Select Committee, Secretary Panetta supposedly does not recall *any* discussions regarding a potential F.E.S.T. deployment in response to Benghazi.[1299] (But then, he isn't part of this 7:30 Meeting. Indeed, by 8:00 p.m. he may have left the Pentagon for parts unknown.)

(The discussion of deploying F.E.S.T. may have been *very* brief. According to intrepid investigative reporter Sharyl Attkisson, following the crisis she interviews various Team Obama officials, including Denis McDonough. Attkisson writes that McDonough indicates he has not heard of F.E.S.T. before![1300])

Regarding the decision not to deploy F.E.S.T., Vice Admiral Tidd later suggests to Congress the State Department is concerned about placing individuals in Libya who are not "trigger pullers" and who potentially may need to be rescued.[1301] (Wait a minute – F.E.S.T. consists of the guys who coordinate the rescuing! State's alleged concerns regarding F.E.S.T.'s safety ignore the nature of F.E.S.T. itself. Mark Thompson testifies his group is trained to deploy to "hot spots."[1302] And don't the Pentagon and FBI have "trigger pullers" to contribute to F.E.S.T.? (Moreover, Thompson himself has pulled quite a few triggers during his 20 years with the Marines.) Besides, Washington officials don't even send *any* "trigger pullers" to Benghazi this night, *do* they? Team Tripoli is sent by U.S. officials in Tripoli, not Washington.)

(And why not at least tell F.E.S.T. members to "prepare to launch"? State officials always can call them off if the situation is clearer by the time F.E.S.T. is ready to deploy, or can order F.E.S.T.'s plane to return if that seems advisable.[1303]

[1298] Benghazi Committee Report, p. 65.

[1299] *Id.*, p. 65.

[1300] Attkisson, *Stonewalled*, Chap. 4, pp. 167 and 171.

[1301] Benghazi Committee Report, p. 65.

[1302] Thompson Oversight Committee Testimony (May 8, 2013) (Response to questions of Rep. Blake Farenthold (R-TX)), p. 80.

[1303] *Id.* (Question of Rep. Thomas Massie (R-KY): "... [W]ould it have been a reasonable thing in an uncertain situation such as this crisis, where we don't know how it is going to unfold, to go ahead and assemble that team and put them on a plane? Were there sufficient communications on the plane that you could have pulled back a mission that was ready to deploy?"; Answer: "... [T]hat [F.E.S.T.] plane ... has a

THE TRUE ACCOUNT OF VALOR AND ABANDONMENT

(From a security standpoint, there is no good reason not to deploy the F.E.S.T. group at least preliminarily on this Night of Benghazi.[1304] The only downside is cost. What price tag should we put on the lives of nearly three dozen Americans, including a U.S. ambassador? And since when does Team Obama fret about the cost of *anything?* The National Debt nearly *doubles* on its watch, by almost $10 trillion.[1305])

The Anti-Muslim Video

Much of the discussion on this teleconference reportedly addresses the anti-Muslim Video that triggers the Cairo protests earlier today.[1306] As discussed below, all participants in the Benghazi crisis on the ground in Libya will claim this Video has no relevance to events in Libya, including Benghazi. (At this juncture, this subject is a galactic waste of precious time. *A battle is ongoing!* If, as Team Obama later will assert, they are concerned the anti-Islamic film might cause unrest or "copycat attacks" *elsewhere* in the Middle East region,[1307] they should have a separate team working on this Video issue. They should not distract the group whose mission (supposedly) is to protect and rescue the Americans *in Benghazi.*)

Placating the Libyans

Participants also debate whether military troops in any rescue or reinforcement mission should wear uniforms or civilian clothes, so as not to offend the Libyans, or give the impression the U.S. is invading Libya! The consensus of the 7:30 Meeting: civvies.[1308]

---

robust communications suite. The senior communicator on there works for me. And he is very competent at his job"), p. 88.

[1304] See Attkisson, *Stonewalled* (Responding to NSC spokesperson Tommy Vietor's contention that F.E.S.T. could not have gotten to Benghazi in time: ". . . [S]ince nobody knew at the start how long the crisis would last, it doesn't explain why FEST wasn't sent in the beginning"), Chap. 4, p. 167.

[1305] Treasury Dept. website (Debt on Jan. 19, 2009: ~ $10.627 trillion; Total debt on Jan. 20, 2017: ~ $19.947 trillion).

[1306] Benghazi Committee Report, pp. 114 and 130-131.

[1307] E.g., Clinton House Select Benghazi Committee Testimony (Oct. 22, 2015) (Response to questions from Rep. Jim Jordan (R-OH)).

[1308] Benghazi Committee Report (State Department email at 9:46 p.m.: "We made a request that any deployments should be in plain clothes to avoid any impression of a

This sit-down also considers whether the U.S. needs permission of the Libyan government (such as it is) to enter Libyan airspace and send military help to the Americans under assault in Benghazi and to Americans in Tripoli. State officials insist Libyan approval is required. This is flatly inconsistent with Leon Panetta's later testimony to the Select Committee. "At no point, according to the Secretary of Defense, did a U.S. response to the attacks in Benghazi hinge on Libya agreeing with the actions ordered." The consensus of the group: Libya must approve.[1309] (Still more contradictions.)

Triggering the War Powers Act

The Deputies gathering also considers whether the War Powers Act mandates notification to Congress, *if* any troop deployment is made. The consensus: notification is required.[1310] (This is directly contrary to the administration's approach in its war against Libya, discussed in Part I. However, with Benghazi Team Obama is looking for excuses *not* to act, while they were *chomping at the bit* to overthrow Qadhafi.)

The 7:30 Meeting's Significance

The Select Committee finds some participants in this meeting "were surprisingly unable to recall details regarding the various issues and discussions during the White House meeting."[1311] (I'll bet. This likely is one of the most significant meetings many of these officials ever will attend, yet they can't remember it?)

For her part, Secretary of State Clinton apparently has no difficulty remembering what she says during this everlasting 7:30 Meeting. According to Clinton's memoir:

U.S. invasion of Libya"), p. 88 n. 376; *Id.* (State Department email at 10:40 p.m.: "Apparently Pat K [Patrick Kennedy?] expressed concern on the SVTC [secure video teleconference] about Libyan reaction if uniformed US forces arrived in country in military aircraft"); and *Id.* (Redacted) (Possibly email from Defense Department: ". . . State remains concerned that any U.S. military intervention be fully coordinated with the Libyan Government and convey Libyan concerns that [sic] about U.S. military presence, to include concerns that wheeled military vehicles should not be used and U.S. Military Forces should consider deploying in civilian attire"), pp. 89-92.

[1309] *Id.* (Redacted), pp. 86-87 and 89-90.

[1310] *Id.* (Redacted), pp. 87 and 89-90.

[1311] *Id.*, p. 86.

THE TRUE ACCOUNT OF VALOR AND ABANDONMENT

I downloaded to the group my discussions with Greg [Hicks, State's number two diplomat in Libya] and [Libyan] President Magariaf, and I stressed how critical it was to get our people out of *Benghazi* as quickly and safely as possible.[1312]

Despite its obvious vital nature, some 7:30 Meeting participants and others later downplay its significance. For example, in her memoir Hillary Clinton includes a very lengthy (and defensive) 34-page chapter focused entirely on the Benghazi attacks. She devotes only a single paragraph (just 91 words) to the 7:30 Meeting. She pens but a single sentence (quoted above) describing what she says during this conference, and not one word discussing what any of the other numerous officials involved say over a two-hour period.[1313]

As noted, Leon Panetta does not participate in the 7:30 Meeting (apparently having better things to do tonight). Interestingly, his brief, six-page discussion of Benghazi in his memoir does not even reference the pivotal two-hour videoconference his staff attends. (Indeed, the Benghazi tragedy – one of the biggest fiascos of Panetta's entire career – does not even rate its own chapter.)[1314] This despite the fact *this conference effectively modifies Panetta's claimed 7:00 p.m. Order to "deploy now" without conditions.* (But then, Leon is not seeking the presidency, and Hillary *is*.)

(Understandably, this 7:30 Meeting is one everyone on Team Obama wants to forget.) ∎

[1312] Clinton, *Hard Choices* (emphasis added), Chap. 17, p. 396.

[1313] Benghazi Committee Report ("The two-hour 'meeting' . . . was in fact much more detailed and involved than witnesses suggested and presents a new perspective on what was happening and being discussed in Washington D.C. even while an Ambassador was missing and a second U.S. facility was under attack half a world away"), p. 86; and Clinton, *Hard Choices,* Chap. 17, p. 396.

[1314] Panetta, *Worthy Fights*, Chap. 16, pp. 426-431.

60

"No One Stood Watch"

After issuing a "deploy now" directive at 7:00 p.m., what does Leon Panetta do? Does he stay at the National Military Command Center (or his office or elsewhere in the Pentagon) to ensure his orders are being carried out, and to oversee the rescue missions he testifies he has ordered? Or is the Select Committee correct he does not remain at his post to steer the Pentagon's mighty military machine? If so, where is he this night after supposedly issuing his order to "deploy now" at 7:00 p.m.? The answer is unclear.

According to Defense's own timeline, from 6:00 p.m. to 8:00 p.m. "Secretary Panetta convenes a series of meetings in the Pentagon with senior officials including General Dempsey and General Ham." This document claims they are discussing "additional response options for Benghazi and for the potential outbreak of further violence throughout the region . . ."[1315] But where is Panetta *after* 8:00 p.m.?

In his memoir Panetta writes, "General Kelly [Panetta's Senior Military Assistant], Jeremy [Bash, Panetta's Chief of Staff], and other senior members of the DoD team spent most of the evening, into the night, tracking events from the Pentagon."[1316] This implies Panetta does *not* remain with them. (*Why not?* He personally has ordered hundreds of his troops to deploy into harm's way on a potentially hazardous mission against heavily-armed militants, who already have murdered at least one American Foreign Service officer in "the most dangerous city" in Northern Africa. What is he doing that is more important than monitoring this mission from the NMCC (if not the Situation Room)?)

Panetta later even disavows he was in charge of the military mission on this night! In testimony, he is unable to answer a straightforward question. Senator Lindsey Graham (R-SC) asks, *"Would it be fair to say that you were in charge?"* on the Night of Benghazi? Panetta stammers, then mutters, "It's not that simple. . . . I think the people that

---

[1315] Benghazi Committee Report, Appendix G, Defense Dept. Timeline, p. 573.

[1316] Panetta, *Worthy Fights*, Chap. 16, p. 429.

were in charge were the people on the ground. . . ."¹³¹⁷ (*Now* it makes sense: The people who screwed up the U.S. response to Benghazi were the Americans under attack and those on Team Annex and in Tripoli who were the only ones who tried to rescue them. Unbelievable.)

As the Select Committee explains, ". . . From the moment the first attack occurred, the clock began to tick, and with each passing hour, the need to immediately deploy forces became more crucial. . . ."¹³¹⁸

Despite this truth, the U.S. Special Operations Force (SOF) – the one furthest from Benghazi – will take more than 13 hours to deploy from Fort Bragg. (As detailed below, the Americans still alive already have evacuated Benghazi by then.) "It would take nearly 18 hours for the FAST team [in Rota Spain] to move, and over 20 [actually 19.3] hours from the beginning of the attack before the CIF [Commander's In Extremis Force in Croatia] moved."¹³¹⁹ (These excessive delays in the face of mortal peril to dozens of Americans in Benghazi are incomprehensible. They are *inexcusable*. Many heads at Defense should roll. Including Leon Panetta's.)

Notwithstanding all of these inordinate delays, in May 2013 the Pentagon will paraphrase its spokesman George Little as claiming, "The U.S. military responded quickly to notifications of the attack on the Benghazi consulate [sic]."¹³²⁰ (What movie is Little watching?)

The Select Committee majority report concludes starkly:

> During those crucial hours between the Secretary's [7:00 p.m.] order and the actual movement of forces, *no one stood watch* to steer the Defense Department's bureaucratic behemoth forward to ensure the Secretary's orders were carried out with the urgency demanded by the lives at stake in Benghazi.¹³²¹

(So true. This is a devastating indictment of the incompetence of the U.S. military command this night. Above all others, it is Leon Panetta's job tonight to "stand watch." This he fails to do.) ∎

---

¹³¹⁷ "Justice with Judge Janine," Fox News Channel (Oct. 26, 20133) (Response to Sen. Lindsey Graham) (*Watch video there*; Go to 2:56 - 3:13).

¹³¹⁸ Benghazi Committee Report, p. 114.

¹³¹⁹ *Id.*, p. 83; and Key Delays Appendix (See September 12 entries for 5:00 a.m., 10:00 a.m., and 11:00 a.m., all Washington time).

¹³²⁰ Pentagon Press Release, "DOD Cooperates with Congress on Benghazi Probes."

¹³²¹ Benghazi Committee Report, p. 71.

61

Ambassador Stevens Is Pronounced Dead

While the 7:30 Meeting continues in Washington, doctors at Benghazi Medical Center have been attempting desperately to resuscitate Chris Stevens. However, Dr. Zaid Abu Zeid later explains to CNN that after these efforts the man shows no signs of life. He is pronounced dead. He has succumbed to asphyxiation.

Apparently, at this time the doctors do not even know they have been treating a U.S. ambassador. He simply is a white male in extreme distress. It is approximately 2:00 a.m. Benghazi time (8:00 p.m. Washington time). Stevens was 52.[1322]

(Later, there will be numerous reports Ambassador Stevens has been "tortured, sodomized, dragged bloody through the streets of Benghazi, and murdered."[1323] However, these sensational reports (although widespread on the web) are unsubstantiated.[1324] It would be satisfying to confirm beyond dispute exactly how Ambassador Stevens dies on this Night of Benghazi. Nevertheless, the author believes the precise manner of his demise does not alter the critical facts: Obama and Clinton recklessly have placed Stevens (and his team) in harm's way with grossly inadequate security; terrorists light the fuse that proximately results in Stevens' assassination; and (as we will document

---

[1322] Benghazi Committee Report, pp. 77-78; Kirkpatrick and Myers, Libya Attack Brings Challenges for U.S.; CNN Finds, Returns Journal Belonging to Late U.S. Ambassador (*Watch video there*; Go to 1:37 - 2:07); and Baier, 13 Hours at Benghazi: The Inside Story (*Watch video there*; Go to 19:19-37).

[1323] E.g., Ferrara, Benghazi: Obama's Actions Amount to a Shameful Dereliction of Duty.

[1324] See CBS/AP, "Assault on U.S. Consulate in Benghazi Leaves 4 Dead, Including U.S. Ambassador J. Christopher Stevens," CBS News online (Sept. 12, 2012) (Doctor Zaid Abu Zeid at Benghazi Medical Center "said Stevens had 'severe asphyxia,' apparently from smoke inhalation, causing stomach bleeding, but had no other injuries"); and Sharyl Attkisson, "Officials Instructed Benghazi Hospital to List Stevens as 'John Doe,'" CBS News online (May 30, 2013) (Stevens was autopsied at FBI facility in Dover, Delaware, "which revealed he died of asphyxia, presumably from smoke inhalation. Officials found no internal damage, no indication of assault and no mistreatment of his body. . . .").

THE TRUE ACCOUNT OF VALOR AND ABANDONMENT

below) Team Obama makes no serious attempt to rescue him or his compatriots in Benghazi.)

According to Fox News, after Stevens is pronounced dead, using Scott Wickland's phone someone (possibly the Libyan army officer again) calls contact phone numbers stored in the device. One of these numbers called reportedly is that of David McFarland, the Political Section Chief of the U.S. Embassy in Tripoli. The caller tells the Embassy staffer who answers a white man has died at the Benghazi hospital. The description the caller provides matches Ambassador Stevens. It is dreadful news.[1325]

As discussed below, the U.S. State Department will not officially confirm Ambassador Stevens' murder until some two and one-half hours later, at 10:34 p.m. Washington time (4:34 a.m. in Benghazi).[1326] ∎

[1325] Baier, 13 Hours at Benghazi: The Inside Story (*Watch video there*; Go to 19:37-55).

[1326] Benghazi Committee Report, Select Benghazi Timeline, p. 560.

62

"Deploy Now... Maybe"

Despite Secretary Panetta's supposedly clear 7:00 p.m. Order to "deploy now," most of the participants at the 7:30 Meeting and their staffs do not appear to believe actual deployment is a settled issue.[1327]

The Select Committee finds various emails summarizing the teleconference and its follow-up items. Several of these emails speak in conditional terms regarding force deployment: "getting forces ready to deploy"; "likely deployment";[1328] "possibly deploying" forces this evening;[1329] "if any deployment is made";[1330] and forces "Will not deploy until order comes to go to either Tripoli or Benghazi."[1331]

Another email (which may or may not be sent during the 7:30 Meeting) similarly signals a lack of a final deployment determination: "The U.S. military has begun notifying special units of *likely* deployment, *with ultimate disposition pending* State coordination with the Libyan government and *final approval by the White House*." (The time of this email is uncertain, because the Select Committee's report appears to cite the wrong source.[1332] Hasn't President Obama supposedly given the "final" White House approval when he meets with Leon Panetta and General Dempsey earlier in the evening, at 5:00 p.m.? Is Tom Donilon or Denis McDonough or White House

---

[1327] Benghazi Committee Report ("At the time of the White House [7:30] meeting, the final decision about which assets to deploy had apparently not been made, according to them [the participants], despite the [Defense] Secretary's recollection and testimony to the contrary"), p. 84.

[1328] *Id.*, p. 90.

[1329] *Id.* (Redacted) (E.g., email at 10:40 p.m.: "There is likely to be a deployment very quickly, possibly this evening, of forces to assist in Libya"), pp. 86 & n. 362 and 89-90.

[1330] *Id.* (Redacted), pp. 86-89.

[1331] *Id.* (Redacted), pp. 89-90.

[1332] *Id.* (emphasis added), p. 90. The Select Committee's report cites testimony of Jeremy Bash as the source for the email. See p. 91 n. 383. It is possible the report inadvertently transposed footnotes 383 and 384. If this is correct, the email in question is sent at 7:19 p.m., shortly before the 7:30 Meeting convenes.

Chief of Staff Jack Lew or someone else in a position subsequently to overrule the president? *Really?* Has Barack Obama had second thoughts after he issues his 5:30 p.m. directive to Panetta and Dempsey? Or has the president never really given a "Do Everything Possible" order in the first place? More questions and doubts.)

The Select Committee's interpretation of these various summaries is that "the conclusion from the [7:30] meeting was that forces were not going to deploy 'until order comes, to go to either Tripoli or Benghazi.'"[1333] (This drama is surreal. It is as if these officials are watching a different movie than the one Leon Panetta claims to be viewing. And isn't the urgent need to get the distant forces *started moving toward Benghazi ASAP*, and worry later about whether they should be re-routed in mid-air toward Tripoli or even turned around instead?[1334])

There also is great confusion among some of the U.S.'s top military commanders concerning the nature of their orders. Is Panetta so imprecise in issuing his 7:00 p.m. Order his commanders all misinterpret it?[1335] Or are his commanders obtuse in construing them?

The Pentagon's top uniformed brass appear to believe the "Deploy Now" order is not yet settled *going into* the 7:30 Meeting. In discussing

---

[1333] Benghazi Committee Report, p. 86.

[1334] See Thompson Oversight Committee Testimony (May 8, 2013) (Responding to questions of Rep. Tim Walberg (R-MI)) (". . . [W]e did have a need to get people pushed forward early, and even if they did not end up in Tripoli, they would be closer. Again, going back to the tyranny of distance, whether we would have landed in Frankfort or Sigonella or Crete or somewhere in the area. . . ."), p. 62.

[1335] This possibility calls to mind an infamous Civil War military directive issued by Confederate Commander General Robert E. Lee on July 1, 1863, the first day of the pivotal Battle of Gettysburg. General Lee ordered Confederate General Richard Ewell to take a Union-held area known as "Culp's Hill" "if he found it practicable." By this the genteel Lee almost certainly meant "Go take the damned hill!" But Lee's imprecision would prove costly. Ewell determined it was "not practicable" to attack the assigned objective because his men were too tired from the day's fighting. However, almost all of Ewell's subordinate commanders disagreed. They insisted they should attack Culp's Hill. The decision not to assault Culp's Hill that day probably was a key factor in allowing the Union forces to maintain the high ground for the remainder of the three-day battle. Federal troops would spend the entire evening and night fortifying Culp's Hill. The Confederate attack on the position the next day was a costly, bloody failure. The resulting Union victory at Gettysburg would prove the turning point of the Civil War. Had Ewell taken Culp's Hill on Day One as Lee intended to order, the entire battle may have turned out differently. And the South may have triumphed in the war. See Shelby Foote, *The Civil War: A Narrative*, Vol. II (Random House, New York; 1963), p. 479 et seq. Thank God Lee was inexact.

an email sent at 8:53 p.m. by Vice Admiral Tidd summarizing the orders to the combatant commands, Vice Admiral Winnefeld later testifies to the Select Committee about his own understanding of Tidd's email:

> All this is doing is reporting out what the Secretary has directed to do [sic]. And *[Tidd] would not put this out unless the deputies had concurred with it*. If the deputies [at their 7:30 Meeting] had not concurred with the SecDef deciding to do these things, that would have been a big issue, but it wasn't. The *deputies obviously concurred, so [Tidd] put it out*: Hey, this is *now official*; Secretary says do this.[1336]

(So, the Defense Secretary's 7:00 p.m. Order to "Deploy Now" had not been "official"? And the lower-level deputies – including many persons not in the military chain of command – have the power to make Panetta's orders "official"? Who is running the damned Defense Department tonight?)

Again, why do the Deputies at the 7:30 Meeting have to concur in *anything?* As the Select Committee report states:

> It is unclear why concurrence from anyone attending the White House [7:30] meeting was needed. The National Command Authority, the lawful source of military orders, consists of two people: the President and the Secretary of Defense. Neither of them attended that [7:30] meeting. Both the President and Secretary Panetta had already issued their orders [supposedly to "Do Everything Possible" and "Deploy Now," respectively]. . . .[1337]

Remarkably, there even seems to be a difference of understanding among Pentagon officials regarding the meaning of "prepare to deploy" versus "deploy now."[1338] There also is disagreement among military

---

[1336] Benghazi Committee Report (emphasis added), p. 94.

[1337] Benghazi Committee Report (footnotes omitted), p. 94; and *Id.* (Panetta further elaborates in his Select Committee testimony: "My directions were clear; those forces were to be deployed, period . . . So I wanted no interference with those orders to get them deployed"), p. 94 n. 397.

[1338] Compare Benghazi Committee Report (Testimony of Under Secretary of Defense for Policy James Miller: ". . . [I]t's a technical difference that in this instance and in any other instance has no operational impact, one form of the order says deploy to the intermediate staging base and prepare to deploy into Libya, and that additional authorization will be given prior to deployment into Libya; a second says deploy to the intermediate staging base and proceed to Libya unless given direction not to do so"), p. 95; with *Id.* (Testimony of General Carter Ham: ". . . So it's prepare to deploy, 'I think I may need you, so I want you to be ready.' A deploy order says, 'I do need you.

THE TRUE ACCOUNT OF VALOR AND ABANDONMENT

officials regarding whether another order is needed to actually move U.S. forces into Libya. In other words, *on this Night of Benghazi there is a significant dispute among military commanders regarding the extent of the authority they have to move U.S. forces into Libya!*[1339] (One would have thought the more than 200-year-old U.S. military had such basics down pat by now. Can you say "Cluster ****?" No wonder no U.S. forces except Team Tripoli – acting on their own initiative and not waiting for any muddled military orders – ever make it to Benghazi.)

On this Night of Benghazi General Carter Ham, head of AFRICOM, interprets his orders dramatically differently than does his own deputy, Vice Admiral Leidig. Ham also construes his orders differently than the description in Vice Admiral Tidd's 8:53 p.m. email relaying Panetta's orders to the combatant commands. Ham testifies:

> ... [M]y belief is the Secretary had given authority to me to do that [granting final approval to deploy FAST]. ... [M]y recollection is different than what Vice Admiral Tidd has written here. ... And my belief is that – and my recollection differs a bit from what Vice Admiral Tidd says – that when the Secretary made his decisions, my understanding of that was that *the Secretary of Defense was transferring operational control to me for those forces [the FAST platoons, the CIF and the SOF] for their deployment and employment.*[1340]

Deploy'"), p. 98; and with *Id.* (Testimony of Vice Admiral Charles Leidig, Deputy Commander for Military Operations, US Africa Command: "They are two very distinct orders in the military. The first is prepare to deploy. And that's basically ... you have permission to make every preparation necessary to execute this mission. But you do not have permission to actually to [sic] deploy them yet – you don't have permission to execute the mission"), p. 95.

[1339] Benghazi Committee Report (Testimony of Vice Admiral Charles Leidig: "We were never given an execute order to move any forces until we got to move in the C-17 to evacuate folks out of Tripoli later that next morning. There was never an execute order to move any forces from Sigonella into Africa or from Rota into Africa until later. ... [W]e did get an order eventually to move the FAST team into Tripoli to provide security, but during that evening hour, that incident, there were no execute orders to move forces into our AOR [Area of Responsibility]. ... Execute order comes from the Secretary of Defense. ... I wouldn't move those [assets – the FAST platoon or the C-17] ... without an order from the Secretary or the Chairman. They're moving across COCOM boundaries"), pp. 96-97; and *Id.* at pp. 98-99.

[1340] *Id.* (emphasis added), pp. 97-99.

THE BENGHAZI BETRAYAL

(Remember, General Ham is in the Pentagon tonight. Too bad Leon Panetta apparently doesn't stick around so Ham can ask him to clarify his supposed 7:00 p.m. Order to "Deploy Now.")

Subsequently, General Ham washes his hands of the matter. When asked by the Select Committee whether he knows if the Secretary of Defense (or, implicitly, anyone else in the chain of command) has to do anything further to deploy the identified forces, Ham demurs. He claims (preposterously), ". . . I'm just not familiar with the specifics of the order."[1341] (This is among the most important orders he ever has received in his then 37-year military career. Yet he is unfamiliar with it, despite the complete fiasco and scandal and deaths that ensue?)

To add insult to injury, according to diligent reporter Eli Lake, Congressman Jason Chaffetz (R-UT) later speaks to *The Daily Beast* regarding how General Ham explains his authority on the Night of Benghazi. Lake writes that in November 2012 Chaffetz tells *The Daily Beast* General Ham "told me directly that he had no directive to engage in the fight in Benghazi."[1342] (Still further contradictions.)

Ham's own trusted deputy, Vice Admiral Leidig, later testifies he needs to receive a subsequent "execute" order before he can deploy the FAST platoon into Libya. He claims no such "execute" order is given during this crisis![1343]

(These dramatic differences in interpreting their orders from Secretary Panetta in the middle of a national security crisis are incomprehensible. They are unforgiveable. It is dereliction of duty not to seek clarification of their precise orders when Ham and his own deputy (and others in the military) construe these directives so differently. Such is the bizarre dynamic pervading this entire, ill-fated Night of Benghazi.) ■

[1341] *Id.*, p. 99.

[1342] Eli Lake, "Benghazi Whistleblower: Requests for Military Backup Denied," *The Daily Beast* online website (May 6, 2013).

[1343] Benghazi Committee Report ("We were never given an execute order to move any forces until we got to move in the C-17 to evacuate folks out of Tripoli later that next morning. There was never an execute order to move any forces from Sigonella into Africa or from Rota into Africa until later. So, I mean, we did get an order eventually to move the FAST team into Tripoli to provide security, but during that evening hour, that incident, there were no execute orders to move forces into our AOR [Area of Responsibility, i.e., Africa]"), p. 96.

63

Inaction Items

The Select Committee reports ten "Action Items" emerge from the 7:30 Meeting.[1344] Two are redacted by the administration and not provided to Congress. The Select Committee's report discusses only some of the remaining disclosed items in any detail.

Deployment of the FAST Force in Rota

According to a State Department email, Action Item 3 asserts the FAST team of Marines in Rota, Spain "need six hours to prepare ... Will not deploy until order comes to go to either Tripoli or Benghazi." (This is false. They do *not* need six more hours to prepare. By 6:00 p.m. Washington time, the local FAST commander in Rota already is ordering his Marines to return to base. By the time the aimless 7:30 Meeting finally ends at about 9:30 p.m., the FAST platoons in Spain already have had their orders to prepare to deploy for at least 50 minutes. By 11:45 p.m. Washington time, they are ready to kick off and are sitting on a damned runway with their weapons and gear. They need six hours for a damned U.S. airplane to get from Germany to Rota to pick them up![1345])

War Powers Act Notification

Action Item 4 from the 7:30 Meeting states, "*If* any deployment is made, Congress would need to be notified under the War Powers Act...."[1346] As explained in Part I above, the Obama administration earlier blows off this legal mandate when it decides to wage war against Libya and remove Qadhafi. (Perhaps because of the warranted

---

[1344] Two of the Select Committee's Republican members assert there actually are eleven "action items." Additional Views of Reps. Jordan and Pompeo, p. 448.

[1345] Benghazi Committee Report (Redacted), pp. 89 and 116-117, and Select Benghazi Timeline, p. 560; and Key Delays Appendix (See September 11 entries at 6:00 p.m., 8:39 p.m. and 11:45 p.m., all Washington time).

[1346] Benghazi Committee Report (Redacted), pp. 86-89.

criticism following that decision, on this Night of Benghazi the Obamatons determine the War Powers Act is relevant again.)

A later State Department email sent at 10:40 p.m. Washington time, just over an hour after the 7:30 Meeting ends, states, "Options *under consideration for the deployment* include: (1) a FAST team; (2) a [U.S.-Based SOF]...; and (3) a Commander's Force...." Again, this flatly contradicts Panetta's testimony he gives a final 7:00 p.m. Order to "deploy now" *more than three and one-half hours earlier*. The 10:40 p.m. email continues, "DOD indicated they would circulate additional information on the options/decisions *in the morning* and we will need to be prepared to do a quick War Powers assessment and probably report *by COB tomorrow*."[1347] (In the morning; close of business mañana. *Absolutely no sense of urgency!*)

President Obama eventually will submit a cursory War Powers notification to Congress on September 14, days after the Battle of Benghazi is over.[1348]

Securing Libyan Approval for Deployment

During the 7:30 Meeting, State Department representatives insist the Libyan Government must approve any U.S. deployment into Libya. Thus, Action Item 4 provides, "Libya must agree to any deployment." In this regard, the Defense and State departments agree they will coordinate to get essential information to the Libyan government. (This includes plane numbers, expected arrival time, personnel numbers, types of weapons carried, airport support needed, etc. – and which Libyan city they will arrive in!)[1349]

CBS News "has been told" Secretary Clinton "did seek clearances from Libya to fly in their airspace, but the administration won't say anything further about what was said or decided on that front."[1350]

Regarding a possible jet aircraft "flyover," Gregory Hicks later testifies to the House Oversight Committee that on this Night of Benghazi the U.S. never requests permission from the Libyan

---

[1347] *Id.* (emphasis added), p. 90.

[1348] "Letter from the President Regarding the War Powers Resolution Report for Libya," The White House, Office of the Press Secretary, Obama White House Archives (Sept. 14, 2012).

[1349] Benghazi Committee Report (Redacted), pp. 86-89.

[1350] Attkisson, Could U.S. Military Have Helped During Libya Attack?

government for such a flyover above Benghazi. Hicks believes the Libyans would have granted such an application had it been made.[1351] Thus, the U.S. apparently only considers seeking clearance for military troop transport flights.

According to the Select Committee, even before the 7:30 Meeting the U.S. Defense Attaché in Tripoli informally has alerted the Libyan government of a possible request for flight clearances later this evening. The Attaché has every expectation such a request will be approved. It appears the Libyan government does preliminarily authorize the proposed deployment by 1:40 a.m., Washington time.[1352] (This is consistent with the Libyan government offering to provide a C-130 transport to take four U.S. special forces soldiers from Tripoli to Benghazi, discussed below in Chapter 80.)

It takes more than six and one-half hours from the time Panetta reportedly gives his "deploy now" order until even preliminary Libyan clearance to land in Tripoli is obtained. Unbelievably, no U.S. forces begin to move until such preliminary authorization is secured.[1353] (Why not? It is still further incompetence by our military.)

Finding Ambassador Stevens

Way down at Action Item 5 the participants in the 7:30 Meeting remember Ambassador Chris Stevens remains missing. Item 5 is to continue attempts to locate Stevens, including contacting "the hospital to confirm the identity of the patient. . . ." who reportedly has been taken there (see Chapters 54 and 61).[1354] (Why isn't this Action Item 1?) Of course, as noted above, although Washington doesn't yet know it, by the middle of the 7:30 Meeting the ambassador already has been declared dead in a Benghazi hospital.

[1351] Hicks Oversight Committee Testimony (May 8, 2013) (Response to questions of Rep. Jason Chaffetz (R-UT)), p. 66.

[1352] Benghazi Committee Report, pp. 87, 109 and 118-119.

[1353] *Id.* (". . . [T]he question still remains if the request for host nation approval from Libya was merely *pro forma* and did not delay deployment of forces, why did the forces not move until approval was obtained?"), pp. 118-119; and Babbin, Whitewashing Benghazi (". . . The administration tried to excuse inaction by saying it did not have Libyan permission to cross the border with armed aircraft or troops. In cases such as these, it's always better to ask forgiveness than permission").

[1354] Benghazi Committee Report (Redacted), p. 89.

Exorcising the Blasphemous Video

The Select Committee's Report is vague on the remaining five action items. It observes "half" the items relate to the anti-Muslim Video! The Select panel's report concludes, "... [T]he White House ... presided over a two hour meeting where half of the action items related to an anti-Muslim video *wholly unconnected to the attacks* ..."[1355] Despite the ongoing crisis, both Secretary Panetta and Deputy National Security Advisor McDonough spend some of their precious time on this Night of Benghazi addressing this Video.[1356] These arguably are the two officials most vital tonight if a military rescue mission to Benghazi is to be conducted. (Talk about "taking your eye off the ball"![1357]) ∎

[1355] *Id.* (emphasis added), p. 114. See also *Id.* ("Half of the action items that emerged from the White House meeting convened in response to the killing of an American Foreign Service Officer and an attack on an American diplomatic facility related to a video. Half. There is more of a record of phone calls from White House officials to "You Tube" and a virtually anonymous "pastor" than there were calls imploring the Defense Department to move with greater urgency. . . ."), pp. 130-131; and Additional Views of Reps. Jordan and Pompeo, p. 448.

[1356] Benghazi Committee Report (emphasis added), pp. 108-109; and *Id.* (". . . Why McDonough had time to concern himself with "You Tube" videos while an Ambassador was missing and unaccounted for remains unclear. And why the Secretary of Defense was used to call "You Tube" and a "pastor" about a video – that had not and would not be linked to the attacks in Benghazi – rather than inquiring about the status of the asset deployment he ordered five hours earlier is also unclear"), p. 130. But see Matthew Continetti, "Obama's National-Security Team of Yes Men," National Review website (June 14, 2014) (". . . To assign responsibility for American incompetence to President Obama's National Security Council is to miss the target. The NSC is a symptom of the dysfunction, not its cause. Behind our endless series of foreign-policy screw-ups – Benghazi, Snowden, Syria, Crimea, Bergdahl, Iraq – is not Obama's team. It's Obama").

[1357] Additional Views of Reps. Jordan and Pompeo (". . . At this critical moment, with lives at risk in Benghazi and military assets sitting idle, it is difficult to imagine a worse use of the Defense Secretary's time than to call Pastor Jones about a video having nothing to do with the attack. Rather than diverting the Secretary of Defense's attention, every effort should have been made to marshal assets that could have gone to Benghazi"), p. 448.

64

Not So FAST

The Select Committee asserts the State Department (Patrick Kennedy in particular) requests the FAST platoon's soldiers to arrive in Libya in civilian attire. (Are we going to a prom?)

As noted, this subject arises at the 7:30 Meeting, but the debate continues afterwards. Kennedy and perhaps others at State also are concerned about the image of U.S. soldiers arriving in military aircraft, or using wheeled military vehicles with U.S. insignia. They want to allay potential (but as yet unexpressed) Libyan government concerns about avoiding the appearance of a large-scale military invasion![1358] (Why don't they just send the damned Boy Scouts?)

However, from a military standpoint, Defense officials are concerned their forces may be *less* safe in civilian garb once they are on the ground and moving to the "target area."[1359] In other words, *the State Department is asking the U.S. military to take actions that will increase the risk to American soldiers!* (Does no one in the Pentagon have the cojones to tell the wussies at State to go to hell?)

This decision supposedly has no effect on timing, as the FAST Marines in Rota have civilian clothes in their rucksacks anyway. However, Team Obama's consideration of the putative rescuers' safety apparently occurs in the context of transiting through *Tripoli, not Benghazi.*[1360] (If this portion of the Select Committee's report is accurate, it is further evidence the Americans in Benghazi already have been abandoned by their government, discussed in the next chapter.)

The FAST platoon commander in Rota, Spain later testifies that while waiting for hours in the aircraft on a runway in Rota *the FAST soldiers reportedly change in and out of their uniforms four times!*[1361]

[1358] Benghazi Committee Report, p. 92; and Additional Views of Reps. Jordan and Pompeo, p. 448.

[1359] Benghazi Committee Report, p. 88.

[1360] *Id.* (Redacted, emphasis added) ("The Defense Department assessed the impact of the requirement [to wear civilian clothes] as quite the opposite: it created an *increased* risk to the FAST platoon members as they traveled through *Tripoli*"), pp. 87-90.

[1361] *Id.*, p. 117.

(No doubt this results from the inconclusive "navel-gazing" occurring more than five thousand miles away on the two-hour teleconference in Washington. By the second change of clothes do you doubt these Marines are wondering about the mental health of those in charge? And is it too much to ask such basic logistical issues be resolved in advance, rather than in the middle of a firefight with terrorists?)

More time is wasted discussing whether the FAST Marines will be allowed to take their "personal weapons" with them! The platoon commander insists his Marines deploy with their personal weapons because ". . . we've got a very violent thing going on the ground where we're going, so we're going to be carrying something that can protect ourselves."[1362] (What an amazing concept: Marines wanting to be armed as they deploy into a firefight with violent, heavily-armed militants! Can U.S. diplomats really be this stupid? Yes.)

One of the most disturbing aspects of the U.S. government's response on this Night of Benghazi is its overpowering desire to avoid offending the Libyans (whose sorry asses we just have ridded of the tyrant Qadhafi). Shockingly, this imperative clearly is more important to our officials than protecting the lives of Americans (both those besieged in Benghazi, and their potential military rescuers).[1363] This is a betrayal of these brave Americans by their government. ∎

[1362] *Id.*, p. 117.

[1363] *Id.* ("With the storming of the compound in Benghazi, the killing of Smith, and Stevens missing, discussing the nature of the vehicles to be used and the clothing to be worn by those seeking to provide aid seemed to place a disproportionate emphasis on how the Libyan government might respond. After all, the Libyan government was supposed to play an active role in preventing the attack in the first instance and certainly in responding afterward"), p. 125; Fox News, House Republicans Fault US Military Response to Benghazi (Select Benghazi Committee Chairman Trey "Gowdy said . . . that the report documents that the U.S. was slow to send help to the Americans in Benghazi 'because of an obsession with hurting the Libyans' feelings'"); and Ferrara, Benghazi: Obama's Actions Amount to a Shameful Dereliction of Duty (". . . Obama and his allies did not want a show of American force in the country [Libya] that would offend Muslim sensibilities. They wanted to rely instead on the host country's security that the embassy was telling them was inadequate and could not be depended upon").

65

Expendable: Abandoning Benghazi For Tripoli

It is fair to conclude from the evidence available that the most pivotal event occurring within the U.S. government on the evening of September 11, 2012, is the 7:30 Meeting in Washington. (Especially if you are holding an automatic weapon in the darkness on a rooftop or tower of the CIA Annex in Benghazi.)

The basis for this assessment is straightforward. As the 7:30 Meeting commences, the primary goal of the United States government is to send help to the embattled Americans actually being attacked by militants *in Benghazi*. However, by the time the leisurely, two-hour teleconference finally winds up at around 9:30 p.m., the primary goal has shifted. This objective is now to fortify and reinforce the U.S. Embassy in *Tripoli* in the event its personnel also come under attack (which they never do).

At some point during this meandering, two-hour discussion an implicit yet very clear decision is reached by high-level officials of the United States government: *the remaining Americans in Benghazi are expendable. They simply must fend for themselves.* This is a betrayal of these patriots. (Whether at this time any of the participants in this 7:30 Meeting acknowledge to themselves they have reached this inescapable conclusion is unknowable.)

Just over half-way into the 7:30 Meeting, at 8:39 p.m. Washington time, the Pentagon at long last begins to transmit to the combatant commands the official orders regarding the movement of the "identified assets." The FAST platoons in Spain are ordered to "*prepare* to deploy"[1364] – a direct contradiction of the 7:00 p.m. Order Panetta says he gives to "deploy now."[1365] The CIF is ordered "to deploy" to an intermediate staging base. Fourteen minutes later, at 8:53 p.m., "The NMCC conveys formal authorization *to deploy* the U.S. Based Special

---

[1364] Benghazi Committee Report (emphasis added; citing Unclassified Defense Dept. Timeline (Nov. 9, 2012)), pp. 91 and 93, and Select Benghazi Timeline, p. 560.

[1365] Benghazi Committee Report ("The orders issued to the forces that night were different from the orders the Secretary gave earlier that evening"), p. 94.

Operations Force [at Fort Bragg] to an intermediate staging base."[1366] (This "intermediate" base will prove to be Sigonella in Sicily.)

According to the Select Committee, also at 8:53 p.m. – while he is involved in the 7:30 Meeting – Vice Admiral Kurt Tidd, the Joint Chiefs Director of Operations, sends an email to various unidentified recipients. In this message, Tidd explains the Defense Secretary:

> ... has directed FAST to make all *preps* to deploy but *hold departure* until we are sure we have clearance to land in Tripoli. ... [The] ... intent is to get security force augmentation into [Tripoli] (*not Benghazi*, at least not initially) ASAP. ... [T]he point is to get the Marines on the ground securing the *embassy in Tripoli* as rapidly as we can move them.[1367]

("Rapidly?" Tidd's email is sent *more than five hours* after the Battle of Benghazi begins!)

In his 8:53 p.m. email, Tidd also asserts, "Remember *[the Secretary of Defense] holds final approval to deploy FAST*, pending receipt of *Tripoli* country clearance."[1368] In an all too familiar refrain, Tidd's understanding of the substance and timing of the orders already given yet again directly contradicts that of his boss, Secretary Panetta!

Recall at this point Ambassador Stevens is in *Benghazi*, not Tripoli, he is missing and possibly has been kidnapped, and it is not yet known he has been pronounced deceased some 50 or so minutes previously (see Chapter 61).[1369] (Indeed, minutes earlier at 8:51 p.m. Eric Pelofsky, a Senior Advisor to U.S. Ambassador to the U.N. Susan Rice, sends a hopeful email regarding Stevens' status to Rice and others. The message explains, "Post" has received a call from "a person using a RSO [Regional Security Officer] phone that Chris was given saying that the caller was with a person matching Chris's description at a hospital and that he was alive and well." Pelofsky then asks why, if this is true, Chris Stevens does not place the call himself?[1370] A mere fifteen minutes later Pelofsky emails Rice again, with a far more pessimistic

---

[1366] *Id.*, Select Benghazi Timeline (emphasis added), p. 560.

[1367] Benghazi Committee Report (emphasis added), pp. 93-94.

[1368] *Id.* (emphasis added), p. 93.

[1369] Clinton, *Hard Choices,* Chap. 17, p. 396.

[1370] Email from Eric J. Pelofsky to Susan Rice, et al. Re: Libya Update from Beth Jones (Sept. 11, 2012; 8:51 p.m.), Judicial Watch Document Archive (Posted June 9, 2014).

note: "... I'm very, very worried. In particular, that he is either dead or this was a concerted effort to kidnap him." Rice understandably responds, "God forbid."[1371])

By this time on the Night of Benghazi, U.S. officials know there already have been *two* assaults on the "secret" CIA Annex in Benghazi. *Tidd's 8:53 p.m. email demonstrates beyond doubt the Pentagon simply has written off Stevens and the three dozen Americans in Benghazi.* (Despite this truth, President Obama in October 2012 will state at a presidential debate, "... [W]e did everything we could to secure those Americans who were still in harm's way."[1372] As Tidd's email proves, it is a blatant lie.)

Regarding the possibility of a FAST team deployment to Benghazi, Vice Admiral Tidd later gives the Select Committee a remarkable explanation. Tidd testifies:

> We were looking at two FAST teams, but it *very, very soon* became *evident* that *everybody was leaving Benghazi*. And so I don't remember if it was just before the [7:30 Meeting] ... or during the [meeting] or just right after. By the time we came out of the [7:30 Meeting], it was *pretty clear* that *nobody was going to be left in Benghazi*. And so the decision – I think, at the [meeting], there was some discussion – but as I recall, we weren't going to send them to Benghazi, because everybody was going to be back in Tripoli by the time we could actually get them there.
>
> ...
>
> And I think even at this point we *knew* that everybody had moved ... from the temporary diplomatic facility ... to the Annex, and they were moving or going to be moving, if they had not already begun moving, from the Annex to the airport, and would be leaving at the airport as quickly as they *could*.
>
> So it was *pretty clear* we weren't going to be able to get anything into Benghazi before the last people left. So, I don't think we ever went beyond the notion of moving ... the FAST platoon into Tripoli.[1373]

[1371] Email from Eric J. Pelofsky to Susan Rice Re: Libya Update from Beth Jones (Sept. 11, 2012; 9:06 p.m.), Judicial Watch Document Archive (Posted June 9, 2014).

[1372] Transcript of Presidential Debate Between President Barack Obama and Former Governor Mitt Romney (Oct. 22, 2012), CBS News website; and Baier, New Revelations on Attack in Benghazi (*Watch video there*; Go to 0:07-11).

[1373] Benghazi Committee Report (emphasis added), pp. 91-93; and *Id.* (emphasis added) ("While it may have been 'pretty clear' to Tidd that 'nobody was going to be

AFRICOM Commander General Ham makes a similar (erroneous) assumption about the emergency in Benghazi being largely over.[1374] Similarly, the commander of the CIF later testifies that once he learns Ambassador Stevens is dead, he (unbelievably) concludes:

> ... And once we found out that the crisis was not what it was originally articulated in terms of a U.S. Ambassador or any Am[erican] cit[izen] missing, and that he was killed ... *that crisis was no longer occurring as originally discussed*, then it became deliberative. So from my perspective, at that point **the crisis was no longer ongoing** and it was more of a deliberate process. ... I didn't know what my mission was going to be *if there wasn't a crisis* that we were prone to look at.[1375]

(*"The crisis was no longer ongoing?"* So more than thirty still-surviving Americans under attack by heavily armed militants in "the most dangerous city" in North Africa is not a "crisis"? Is the Pentagon even *talking* to the CIA or State or the National Security Council on this Night of Benghazi? According to Joint Chiefs Chairman General Dempsey, throughout this night the "president's staff" continuously is in contact with the Pentagon's National Military Command Center.[1376] You would never know it from the results.)

Everyone in the 7:30 Meeting has convinced themselves of a "fact" for which none of them has any empirical basis. Thus it is that during the marathon 7:30 Meeting the bureaucrats and military brass manage to talk themselves out of attempting to rescue nearly three dozen Americans still in peril in Benghazi. This despite President Obama's and Secretary Panetta's supposed direct orders to the contrary. (Wanna bet Tidd and the other "deputies" do not convey this "never mind" decision to the Americans besieged in Benghazi this night?)

---

left in Benghazi,' it was not at all clear to those in Benghazi who were manning a rooftop exchanging gunfire with attackers. ... [H]ow the principals in Washington were certain U.S. personnel in Benghazi were going to be leaving Benghazi and *how* they were going to be leaving is itself unclear"), p. 92.

[1374] *Id.* ("... [M]y view was the situation, after *an initial spike, the fighting had largely subsided*, that Benghazi was probably not the right place for them [the CIF force] to go...."), pp. 99-100.

[1375] *Id.* (emphasis added), pp. 120-121.

[1376] Panetta and Dempsey Armed Services Committee Testimony (Feb. 7, 2013) (Response to questions of Sen. Kelly Ayotte (R-NH)).

THE TRUE ACCOUNT OF VALOR AND ABANDONMENT

How these military officers and other officials possibly can know everyone will have left Benghazi, or that the fighting otherwise is over, is a complete mystery. When the 7:30 Meeting finally ends at about 9:30 p.m. Washington time, it is 3:30 a.m. in Benghazi. The second firefight at the CIA Annex in Benghazi has been over for about one hour and forty minutes. However, the exhausted GRS operators and DSA agents remain in the darkness on the Annex rooftops and towers standing guard with their automatic weapons at the ready. They still have no safe way to get to the Benghazi airport (and no aircraft large enough to take them all).

The Team Tripoli rescue party has arrived in Benghazi hours ago, but remains stranded at that airport – likewise without secure transport. The bureaucrats and military officers in Washington and Stuttgart have no way of knowing how long Team Tripoli will remain there. In fact, the rescuers from Tripoli will not leave the airport for another hour or so, at 10:30 p.m. Washington time.[1377] (If it is so difficult for Team Tripoli to get from the airport into Benghazi (ultimately it takes three and one-half hours[1378]), why do Vice Admiral Tidd and the others in the U.S. military assume it will be so easy for the Americans at the Annex to get *to* that same airport?)

At the time Obama administration officials abandon Benghazi, not a single American has escaped that city!

Moreover, a member of Team Tripoli later testifies before the Select Committee their group plans to *return to the Annex* after they have conducted the nonessential CIA personnel to the airport for evacuation and the latter's plane has departed. He explains regarding who Team Tripoli planned to evacuate:

It was nonessential personnel only prior to the mortar attack happening . . . we were going to take 14 personnel back with us to the airport, let the jet take off, take them back to Tripoli. *We were going to come back to the Annex and help hold up with the GRS guys until further notice . . . the majority of*

[1377] Benghazi Committee Report, p. 100; and Key Delays Appendix (See September 11 entry at 10:30 p.m., Washington time).

[1378] Key Delays Appendix (See September 11 entries for 7:30 p.m. and 10:30 p.m., both Washington time); and Hsu, CIA Officers Detail Part of Bloody Benghazi Attack at Terrorism Trial (Criminal trial testimony of disguised CIA agent, pseudonym "Alexander Charles": "Obviously nothing worked, because we were on the ground for approximately three hours").

those people [the GRS] would have stayed there. Shooters, if you will. . . .[1379]

He further testifies Team Tripoli "didn't know how long we were going to have to stay at the Annex."[1380] He also tells the Select Committee the remaining GRS agents and the Annex Chief of Base intend to stay at the Annex after the nonessential personnel (*i.e.*, the "non-shooters") have gone.[1381]

The Annex Chief of Base also will testify to the Senate Intelligence Committee that, ". . . it was only after this third wave of attacks, when the mortars hit [at 11:17 p.m. Washington time], that he decided it was necessary to evacuate the personnel from the Annex."[1382]

(This is critical: **Team Tripoli, the Chief of Base, and the GRS contractors all are planning to stay at the Annex in Benghazi!** In sharp contrast, the U.S. military blithely assumes and acts as if the CIA's and Team Tripoli's plans are for *everyone* to *leave* Benghazi swiftly.) Further, the last, fatal firefight in Benghazi will not begin until about 11:15 p.m. in Washington – about one hour and forty-five minutes after the 7:30 Meeting ends.[1383]

Finally, the last planeload of American evacuees will not leave the Benghazi airport until almost 4:00 a.m. Washington time, some *six-and-one-half hours* after it is "pretty clear" to Tidd and the others in

---

[1379] Benghazi Committee Report (emphasis added), p. 82.

[1380] *Id.* (emphasis added) (Before the final mortar attack ". . . [W]e did not make the decisions for that [airplane] to come back. *We didn't know how long we were going to have to stay at the Annex.* . . ."), pp. 82 and 100. See also Zuckoff, *13 Hours* ("As a result [of the fact Team Tripoli's chartered commercial jet wasn't large enough to take all of the Americans], the initial evacuation wouldn't include the Benghazi operators, several other shooters, or the remains of Sean Smith. Under the plan, rather than wait in the open at the airport, the men left behind would stay in the relative safety of the Annex with Smith's body until they got word that another plane had arrived for them. When the second plane landed, the militia motorcade would return to the Annex [hopefully!] to escort the remaining men and Smith's body to the airport"), Chap. 11, p. 252.

[1381] Benghazi Committee Report (emphasis added) (". . . We were under the understanding they [the GRS agents and apparently the Annex Chief of Base] *wanted to stay. They did not want to leave.* . . . I believe it was the [CIA] Chief of Base that wanted to keep some individuals there" at the CIA Annex in Benghazi), pp. 82 and 100-101.

[1382] Sen. Intelligence Committee Benghazi Report, p. 9.

[1383] Key Delays Appendix (See September 11 entries for 9:30 p.m. and 11:15 p.m., both Washington time).

THE TRUE ACCOUNT OF VALOR AND ABANDONMENT

D.C. everybody is leaving Benghazi "as quickly as they could."[1384] There is simply no reasonable basis from which to assume the Battle of Benghazi is ending. (This unwarranted assumption by Tidd and other decision-makers is another example of the total lack of earnestness of the "leaders" in Washington and elsewhere this night. They wish something to be true, therefore it *is* true.)

Regarding this triumph of hope over actual facts, the Select Committee concludes:

> Among the questions left even in the aftermath of investigating what happened before, during and after the attacks in Benghazi is how so many decision makers in Washington and elsewhere were unaware of the Annex in Benghazi and how the Washington decision-makers expected U.S. personnel remaining in Benghazi to evacuate or defend themselves for a prolonged period of time without assistance.[1385]

Also, in the orders officially issued at 8:39 and 8:53 p.m. the CIF and the U.S.-based SOF both "were ordered to deploy only to an intermediate staging base, not to Benghazi or Tripoli."[1386] As noted, that base will prove later to be Sigonella Naval Air Station in Sicily. The Select Committee states, *". . . [N]one of the orders given to the assets that night contained an order to deploy to Benghazi."*[1387] Elsewhere the panel's report concludes, "No asset was ordered to deploy to Benghazi."[1388] And the official orders that *are* given to deploy elsewhere occur some *five hours or more* after the terrorist attacks in Benghazi begin!

The Select Committee reaches the same conclusion as the author: ". . . [I]t was clear by the end of the White House [7:30 p.m.] meeting that no forces were going to Benghazi."[1389] The Select Committee emphasizes this decision is reached despite the fact many Americans still are under siege at the CIA Annex, Ambassador Stevens remains missing (and possibly taken hostage), and Team Tripoli still is stranded

---

[1384] Benghazi Committee Report, pp. 91-92.

[1385] *Id.*, pp. 92-93.

[1386] *Id.*, p. 91. See also *Id.*, p. 93.

[1387] Benghazi Committee Report (emphasis added), p. 91, citing Appendix G, Defense Dept. Timeline.

[1388] *Id.*, p. 93.

[1389] *Id.*, p. 91.

at the Benghazi airport. (Oh, and despite the fact Obama and Panetta hours earlier supposedly have given contrary orders.)

A chilling email is sent at 9:46 p.m., Washington time – shortly after the 7:30 Meeting ends – by a Watch Officer at the State Department Operations Center. It apparently is based upon notes Ambassador Stephen D. Mull takes during the 7:30 Meeting. (At this time, Mull is the Executive Secretary of the State Department, a high-level agency official.[1390]) This email shows clearly how Washington (or at least the State Department) also effectively has abandoned Ambassador Stevens and the other Americans in Benghazi:

> Overall theme: *getting forces ready to deploy in case the crisis expands and a real threat materializes against Embassy Tripoli.* . . .
> Congressional angle: *If* any deployment is made, Congress will need to be notified under the War Powers Act. . . . Libya *must* agree to *any deployment.*[1391]

(So a series of actual, ongoing terrorist attacks in Benghazi against nearly thirty Americans – including a missing U.S. ambassador – is not a "real threat"? And doesn't this email concede at this time there is no "real threat" against Embassy Tripoli?) The Select Committee has it right: "The real threat at the time was and remained in Benghazi."[1392]

(The author is not suggesting there is no reason to worry on this Night of Benghazi about security at the U.S. Embassy in Tripoli. This is a very legitimate concern, particularly after Ansar al-Sharia calls for attacks on the U.S. facility in Tripoli. Indeed, as noted in Part I, years earlier the U.S. had abandoned its Embassy in Tripoli for many years after a mob attacked and set fire to it in December 1979.[1393] However, this night it is Americans in Benghazi who currently are under actual, ongoing assault by large groups of well-armed militants, not the Embassy personnel in Tripoli. Greg Hicks, the CIA Chief of Station, and other officials at the Embassy and CIA Annex in Tripoli recognize this fact. Despite their own risk, they are ready, willing and *do* send their own security assets to aid their comrades in Benghazi. Why can't officials in *Washington* grasp this concept and act similarly?)

[1390] State Dept. website; and Benghazi Committee Report, Select Benghazi Timeline, p. 559.

[1391] Benghazi Committee Report (Redacted; emphasis added), pp. 86-87 and 89.

[1392] *Id.*, p. 92.

[1393] See Chapter 1; and Embassy of the U.S., Tripoli, Libya website.

THE TRUE ACCOUNT OF VALOR AND ABANDONMENT

The Select Committee accurately highlights how differently Washington officials behave than the U.S. heroes in Libya:

The creativity, valor and selfless sacrifice of the Diplomatic Security Agents, the team from the Benghazi Annex and Team Tripoli stand in some contrast to the discussions held during the White House meeting occurring at roughly the same time, half a world away, in the safe confines of the U.S."[1394] ■

[1394] Benghazi Committee Report, p. 113.

66

Over-Lawyered?

Besides the desire to win an upcoming presidential election, an additional factor might help explain the near-complete dysfunction of the U.S. government on this Night of Benghazi: *It is quite possible there are just too damned many lawyers managing our nation's response to this life-threatening crisis.*

Lawyers' training does not prepare us well for emergency crisis management. We are instructed to gather as much evidence (information) as possible before making any important decision.[1395] We are warned to avoid rash judgments. We are taught to exercise caution, and err on the side of safety. We are coached always to avoid risk and minimize the exposure of our clients (and ourselves!). And we are schooled to avoid making decisions hastily, and instead to think and act with deliberation.[1396] (We also are convinced we inherently know everything about all subjects – an irritating attribute some have called "surgeons' syndrome." In truth, attorneys suffer from this affliction far more than do surgeons.)

In the midst of this national security emergency with nearly three dozen Americans under repeated armed attacks, is it possible these lawyerly traits become a hindrance rather than an advantage? The author suggests it is not merely possible, but very likely. (In contrast, military people are trained to kill people and break things, when ordered. The reader must decide which skills are more in need on this Night of Benghazi.)

These potential drawbacks of legal training might not be so significant if only a few attorneys are helping to "manage" America's response to Benghazi this evening. Such is not the case. Instead,

---

[1395] E.g., James Mann, "Obama's Gray Man," Foreign Policy online (May 28, 2013) ("The gist of the complaints is that [National Security Advisor Tom] Donilon burns out personnel with his unending requests for more and more paperwork on the details of foreign policy (he asks for extensive briefing papers, even before a meeting with a journalist) . . .").

[1396] E.g., Mark Landler, "Rice to Replace Donilon in the Top National Security Post," *The New York Times* online (June 5, 2013) (". . . A tireless student of the bureaucratic process, Mr. Donilon favors exhaustive preparation over seat-of-the-pants advice. . . .").

THE TRUE ACCOUNT OF VALOR AND ABANDONMENT

lawyers are almost everywhere tonight on the administration's crisis management team.

At the State Department, lawyers abound. Secretary Clinton of course is a lawyer, as is her Chief of Staff, Cheryl Mills. So is Jacob Sullivan, Clinton's Deputy Chief of Staff and Director of Policy Planning. As noted above, all three participate in the pivotal 7:30 Meeting. (Of course, in Libya Ambassador J. Christopher Stevens also was an attorney, but his life tragically will be snuffed out before his legal training either can help or harm him.) Patrick Kennedy and Charlene Lamb are not lawyers. (They have no excuse. Quite simply, they should know better.)

At the Defense Department, two of the very highest civilian officials involved in responding to the attacks in Benghazi are attorneys: Secretary Panetta himself, and his Chief of Staff Jeremy Bash (who helps represent Defense at the 7:30 Meeting).

The over-abundance of attorneys is especially pronounced at the White House. Both President Obama and Vice President Biden are trained as lawyers (although both practiced law only very briefly, and Obama has not been registered to practice law since in 2008[1397]). Obama's Chief of Staff, Jack Lew, is an attorney. Although key crisis manager Denis McDonough thankfully is not an attorney, his boss (National Security Advisor Tom Donilon) *is* a lawyer. Worse, much of Donilon's experience is in partisan politics, not national security.[1398] Samantha Power (also on the National Security Council staff) was trained at Harvard Law School. And if the president decides to consult one or both of his very closest personal White House advisors on this night, Senior Advisor Valerie Jarrett is an attorney and First Lady Michelle Obama formerly practiced law.[1399]

Finally, if President Obama or anyone on his team decides to consult the Department of Homeland Security tonight, that agency's Secretary, Jeh Johnson, also is an attorney.

[1397] Attorney Registration & Disciplinary Commission of the Supreme Court of Illinois website.

[1398] James Mann, "Obama's Gray Man," Foreign Policy online (May 28, 2013) (When "old pals from the Carter administration" gather, ". . . [T]he question gets asked from time to time: How did a pol [political operative] like Donilon end up as national security advisor?").

[1399] According to the Attorney Registration & Disciplinary Commission of the Supreme Court of Illinois website, Michelle Lavaughn Obama (formerly licensed as Michelle Lavaughn Robinson) has been on inactive status since 1993.

THE BENGHAZI BETRAYAL

To make matters worse, almost all of these many lawyers on Team Obama have little or no military experience. (This includes Defense Secretary Panetta, whose distant military service occurred during his few years as an Army intelligence officer way back in 1964 to 1966.) Nevertheless, tonight all of these legal counselors find themselves managing what principally should be a military rescue operation. Sadly, these administration lawyers and other incompetent managers have turned the endeavor into something quite different – little more than a mere exercise in military logistics and political survival and damage control (not necessarily in that order).

Who *in the world* would design such a national security crisis management team so completely dominated by attorneys? (Answer: attorneys.)

(Perhaps when making critical executive appointments, future presidents should ensure their top crisis-management team is not over-represented by deliberative, paper-pushing attorneys who fancy themselves as national security experts. Instead, possibly they should include more officials with military backgrounds and actual experience dealing with real-world emergencies requiring split-second, life-and-death decisions of the type the crisis in Benghazi presents. You know, folks like Mark Thompson, Lt. Col. Andrew Wood and Eric Nordstrom – all of whom are shut out of events entirely on this Night of Benghazi.) ■

67

Standing Guard on the Rooftops

It is 3:46 a.m. in Benghazi. The Americans trapped at the CIA Annex are awaiting the sunrise with foreboding. Besides Team Tripoli, no serious mission to reinforce or rescue them has arrived – or even been launched.

In Rota, Spain, 1,500 hundred miles to the west, the Marines have been mustered back to their base and still are gathering their gear for a possible deployment to Libya. (There is no rush; they have no aircraft yet.) Five thousand miles to the west of Benghazi in Washington, Vice Admiral Winnefeld's staff is clearing the tiramisu dessert plates of the admiral and his dinner guests. In Tripoli, 400 miles west of Benghazi, in between anxious calls to the Annex TOC in Benghazi for status reports, Greg Hicks is trying to cope with – and hopefully disprove – reports claiming Ambassador Stevens is dead at a Benghazi hospital.

Four hundred and fifty miles distance to the northwest of Benghazi at Sigonella in Sicily, the staff is preparing the base for the eventual arrival of large numbers of special ops troops from Fort Bragg and Croatia.

At Foggy Bottom in Washington, a Watch Officer is just sending the email concerning "getting forces ready to deploy in case the crisis expands and a real threat materializes against Embassy Tripoli." Up on the seventh floor of the State Department, after the marathon 7:30 Meeting Hillary Clinton is reviewing a draft public statement about the tragedy her department will issue shortly.

At the White House, God knows what president Obama is doing

Some 1,000 miles north of Benghazi, at the airbase in Aviano, Italy, the flight crews probably are sleeping. In Ramstein, Germany, 1,300 miles away from Benghazi, air crews apparently are trying to locate the C-130 troop transport aircraft they know they have parked somewhere at the airfield. And a mere 320 miles away to the northeast of Benghazi, at the Naval Air Station in Souda Bay, Crete, apparently nothing is happening. Except possibly for military officers there scratching their heads with their pistols wondering why in the world they are not deploying assets to Benghazi tonight.

Meanwhile in Benghazi itself, while their government in Washington is busy forsaking them the Americans wait in the darkness.

347

Down inside Building C of the Annex, some CIA staff continue destroying classified material and equipment. Others are making frantic phone calls hoping to find a friendly militia group or other force that can rescue the personnel at the Annex, and hopefully even get them to the airport. Inside other Annex buildings, some case officers and other CIA personnel (fully clothed, ready for hasty departure) are trying to catch some fitful sleep during the lull in gunfire and RPG assaults.

Outside, on the Annex rooftops and makeshift towers, the armed defenders have no such luxury. Blurry-eyed, in the darkness the tired GRS and DSA agents continue to scan Zombieland and the other areas surrounding the compound with their night-vision equipment. Zombieland features numerous bushes and small trees that can provide concealment. Along with a nearby stockyard containing many sheep, it is the area of greatest concern. Weary heads nodding, the defenders search continuously for any suspicious, threatening movements.

Unlike the Washington bureaucrats who assume the danger has passed, after the more forceful second terrorist assault about two hours ago, the Annex defenders fear an even heavier attack lies ahead.[1400]

Since the end of the second Annex firefight, the security men have stocked up on ammo, water, Gatorade, Red Bull, juices, Snickers and granola bars, and other snacks. Sometimes, these items are brought up to them by the "non-shooter" CIA personnel. Except for bathroom breaks, the guardians have not left their posts. A number of them sit on cheap plastic lawn chairs the CIA staff have brought up to them. Sitting down is a helluva lot more comfortable than kneeling or sitting on the hard rooftop. The agents are dog-tired, every muscle aching.

As they wait in the gloom, the defenders wonder, and ask each other apprehensively in hushed tones, what the dawn will bring. More attacks? Rescue? Both? Perhaps neither? The answers are unknowable.

No doubt they also are wondering, *When the hell will Team Tripoli arrive from the airport? Where is the Spectre gunship? What's the status of the FAST Marine platoon they told us was deploying from Spain? Why are there no U.S. jet aircraft flying overhead to establish military supremacy in the skies over Benghazi, and to scare the crap out of the bad guys? Where is the frigging help they promised us?*[1401] ■

[1400] Benghazi Committee Report, p. 76; and Baier, 13 Hours at Benghazi: The Inside Story (*Watch video there*; Go to 16:08-22 and 20:52 - 21:04).

[1401] See Lt. Col. Tony Shaffer (Ret.) with Jeanine Pirro on "Justice with Judge Jeanine" (Possibly Oct. 27, 2017) (When asked to speculate on what Tyrone Woods' last thoughts must be: "Where is the cavalry? I thought they'd come").

68

A Secret Order to "Not Deploy" To Benghazi?

How does one explain the numerous incoherent, spineless actions of the Obama administration civilian and military officials on this Night of Benghazi? It seems almost unfathomable so many high-level officials virtually would ignore direct and pointed commands supposedly issued by President Obama ("Do everything possible") and Defense Secretary Panetta ("Deploy now").

Unless . . . Unless a secret order is issued later – probably during or shortly after the 7:30 Meeting – that countermands the earlier directives from the National Command Authority. Does it occur? If so, who issues it? On whose authority? It can only issue from the White House. And when? And most vital of all, *why?*

Six weeks after the attacks, in October 2012, *The Weekly Standard* and later Fox News and ABC News (among others) report the CIA has issued a statement disputing "the Agency" denied help to its case officers, GRS security operators or other Americans in Benghazi. CIA spokesperson Jennifer Youngblood is quoted as claiming:

> We can say with confidence that the Agency reacted quickly to aid our colleagues during that terrible evening in Benghazi. Moreover, *no one at any level* in the CIA told *anybody* not to help those in need; claims to the contrary are simply inaccurate. . . .[1402]

(If *The Weekly Standard,* Fox and ABC are correct the CIA issues such a statement, the author could not locate it on the CIA's website as this book was written, nor as we went to press.[1403] Did the "spooks" at the

---

[1402] William Kristol, "Petraeus Throws Obama Under the Bus," *The Weekly Standard* online (Oct. 26, 2012) (emphasis added); Kristol, Petraeus and Panetta Speak – But Not the President; Baier, New Revelations on Attack in Benghazi (emphasis added) (*Watch video there*; Go to 15:18 - 16:03 and 20:07-26); Griffin, CIA Operators Were Denied Request for Help During Benghazi Attack (emphasis added); and Jake Tapper, "President Obama Begs Off Answering Whether Americans in Benghazi Were Denied Requests for Help," ABC News online (Oct. 26, 2012) (emphasis added).

[1403] E.g., see List of 2012 CIA Press Releases and Statements, CIA website.

CIA make it disappear? Did they realize it was untrue with respect to "Bob," the CIA Benghazi Annex Chief of Base?)

At this same time, President Obama is asked repeatedly by a persistent local Denver TV reporter, Kyle Clark, whether it is true Americans in Benghazi are denied requests for help on the Night of Benghazi. Twice Obama ducks the question. He explains he is awaiting the results of pending investigations before reaching any conclusions about "what went wrong."[1404]

Several weeks after the attacks, in *The Weekly Standard* conservative columnist William Kristol addresses the CIA's assertion:

> So *who* in the government did tell "anybody" [a reference to the alleged CIA statement quoted above] not to help those in need? *Someone* decided not to send in military assets to help those agency operators [in Benghazi]. Would the secretary of defense make such a decision on his own? No.
>
> *It would have been a presidential decision.* There was presumably a rationale for such a decision. What was it? *When* and *why* – and based on whose counsel obtained in what meetings or conversations – did President Obama decide against sending in military assets to help the Americans in need?[1405]

Some have suggested no military rescue is launched to Benghazi to preserve the secrecy of the CIA's operations there. A large rescue mission could well destroy any hope of continued secrecy. Townhall's Guy Benson summarizes this possible thinking by Team Obama:

> This theory may also reveal why the military seemed paralyzed for hours on end as the attack raged. Should they step in and salvage a busted, previously secret mission? Or let it play out and concoct a back story later?[1406]

[1404] Jake Tapper, "President Obama Begs Off Answering Whether Americans in Benghazi Were Denied Requests for Help," ABC News online (Oct. 26, 2012).

[1405] William Kristol, "Petraeus Throws Obama Under the Bus," *The Weekly Standard* online (Oct. 26, 2012) (emphasis added). See also Kristol, Petraeus and Panetta Speak – But Not the President (". . . Panetta's position is untenable. The Defense Department doesn't get to unilaterally decide whether it's too risky or not to try to rescue CIA operators, or to violate another country's air space. In any case, it's inconceivable Panetta didn't raise the question of what to do when he met with the national security advisor and the president at 5:00 p.m. on the evening of September 11 for an hour").

[1406] Guy Benson, "Bombshell: CIA Using 'Unprecedented' Polygraphing, 'Pure Intimidation' to Guard Benghazi Secrets," Townhall.com website (Aug. 2, 2013).

THE TRUE ACCOUNT OF VALOR AND ABANDONMENT

However, there is a major difficulty with this hypothesis: By the time the rescue mission to Benghazi is abandoned (probably sometime between 8:50 and 9:30 p.m., Washington time), there seems little hope of keeping the CIA's presence in Benghazi a secret.

Consider these facts: Nearby Benghazi residents and passersby clearly can see and hear the U.S. Mission Compound is under heavy attack (beginning 3:42 p.m., Washington time). Most of the U.S. Mission Compound is in flames (by shortly after 4:00 p.m.), and a crowd collects outside watching the fires. The CIA's seven-member Team Annex already has deployed toward the Mission under fire, and five of them arrive at the Front Gate very publicly following firefights in the streets (4:03 to 4:40 p.m.).

Chris Stevens has been reported missing (4:14 p.m.). Sean Smith has been confirmed dead (5:01 p.m.). The Mission DSAs are attacked violently, repeatedly and publicly on Benghazi city streets during their escape to the CIA Annex (5:16 to 5:23 p.m.). The militants have stolen sensitive information from the ransacked Mission buildings, which must be presumed to include the location of the CIA Annex.

Secretary Panetta already has issued his "Deploy Now" order to hundreds of U.S. service members (about 7:00 p.m.). Some of them are headed to Libya, where the public will see them.

Some 26 Americans at the CIA's formerly "secret" Benghazi Annex are surrounded by a mob of heavily-armed militants, and already have been attacked *twice* (from 6:34 to about 7:40 to 7:50 p.m.). A number of Benghazi residents from nearby homes and apartments will have heard the shooting and explosions, and gone out to see what's going on.

Team Tripoli (with five CIA personnel) already has chartered a private plane (not a secret CIA aircraft) and landed at Benghazi's public airport (7:30 p.m.). Finally, reports are arriving in the U.S. Ambassador Stevens is dead (8:05 p.m.). This quickly will become international news, shining a spotlight on this Night of Benghazi. Very likely, the "secret" CIA cat already is out of the Benghazi bag.

As this book goes to press, we still do not have answers to the above "Who" and "When" questions. *What seems inescapable is the conclusion sometime during or soon after the two-hour, multi-agency videoconference, the core military mission is changed from rescuing Americans under assault in Benghazi to reinforcing the U.S. Embassy in Tripoli.* (This is a major part of the overall Benghazi Betrayal.)

In the following chapter, the author suggests a possible answer to the question "Why" the mission is changed. ■

69

"Operation Eagle Claw"

How does one explain all these puzzling, inconsistent, feckless, illogical and indeed incoherent decisions and actions by official Washington and the U.S. military on this Night of Benghazi? The fact too many lawyers are "managing" the crisis likely is only a partial explanation. The author has an additional hypothesis to propose.

As they deliberately and methodically and ineptly try to sort out the crisis in Benghazi, it seems probable Obama and his team are recalling another American terror-related disaster that also had occurred thousands of miles away in the Middle East. It had happened thirty-two years before Benghazi. That earlier tragedy sprang out of the Iranian revolution of 1979, and the subsequent capture of the U.S. Embassy in Tehran, Iran on November 4, 1979. (This revolution would launch the Iranian regime's central role in Islamist terrorism in the world.[1407]) In all, 52 American diplomats, civilian employees and Marines were captured and taken hostage by Iranian "students." These supposed "students" were, of course, doing the bidding of their new Islamic leaders.[1408] (Six Americans managed to escape, and were given shelter by courageous Canadians in Tehran. This getaway was the subject of the book and movie of the same name, *Argo*.[1409]) This outrage was a clear act of war. However, the Carter administration refused to label it as such.

U.S. officials at the Pentagon on this Night of Benghazi ponder what assets are available for a military rescue attempt, sit through a marathon two-hour teleconference hosted by the White House, and make tense telephone calls to Tripoli and Benghazi and Rota and Sigonella and Stuttgart (and probably Souda Bay). As they do so, at

---

[1407] Interview of Former U.S. Ambassador to the United Nations John Bolton with Bill Hemmer, "America's Newsroom," Fox News Channel (Oct. 24, 2017).

[1408] William J. Bennett, *America: The Last Best Hope (Vol. II)* (Nashville: Thomas Nelson, 2007) ("Bennett, *America, The Last Best Hope*"), p. 469.

[1409] See Antonio Mendez and Matt Baglio, *Argo: How the CIA and Hollywood Pulled Off the Most Audacious Rescue in History* (New York: Viking Penguin, 2012).

least some military and civilian members of Team Obama no doubt recall how badly that Iranian hostage debacle had ended for a previous U.S. president in the run-up to a reelection bid.

Instead of declaring war on Iran, then Democrat President Jimmy Carter initially decided to adopt a "patient diplomacy" approach to the Iranian hostage crisis. Weeks, then months passed. All the while, the American hostages were beaten, tortured and threatened with execution.[1410] The Carter administration secretly reached deal after deal with the mullahs running the new Iranian regime. But each one turned to dust. More weeks passed. Carter was experiencing ever-increasing, and eventually enormous political pressure to act decisively. America and Carter looked and acted weak. (Because they were. The Soviet Union soon exploited Carter's weak position in Iran and invaded adjacent Afghanistan in late December 1979.[1411])

After the Americans had been in captivity for five months, even the passive, anemic Carter had had enough. He ordered a military rescue mission to be prepared. It would be known as "Operation Eagle Claw."

A daring but complex and exceedingly dangerous rescue operation was organized and undertaken. It was so perilous most personnel involved left "death letters" for their loved ones. As excellent historical chronicler Mark Bowden writes:

> It was unbelievably risky; everyone on the mission knew there was a very good chance they would never get home alive. ... Most of them, [mission commander Colonel Charlie] Beckwith included, had written death letters to be delivered to their spouses in the event they were killed. They were going all the way with this, to victory or to Valhalla.[1412]

President Carter gave the final order, and the mission was launched on April 24, 1980. There were just over six months to go until the election. If the unpopular Carter could rescue all (or even most) of the

---

[1410] Bennett, *America: The Last Best Hope*, pp. 469 and 472.

[1411] *Id.*, p. 470.

[1412] Mark Bowden, *Guests of the Ayatollah: The First Battle in America's War with Militant Islam* (Atlantic Monthly Press, 2006) ("Bowden, *Guests of the Ayatollah*"), pp. 435 and 438. *Guests of the Ayatollah* is an excellent history of the Iranian hostage crisis, including the failed rescue mission that helped scuttle President Carter's reelection bid.

52 American captives, he just might be able to win reelection over the surging former California governor, Republican Ronald Reagan.[1413]

To achieve the essential stealth, the plan required minimizing the number of planes utilized. As a result, some of the aircraft carried both airplane fuel and rescue troops. Effectively, these were flying bombs.

Deep in the Iranian desert at a remote, covert U.S. logistical base known as "Desert One," the operation unraveled. The decision was made to abort the mission because not enough helicopters made it to Desert One in operational condition. Then, in the middle of the night, disaster struck. As the military personnel prepared to evacuate their secret base, an American C-130 aircraft collided with a U.S. helicopter and caught fire. The C-130 held both service members and fuel. A huge, fatal fireball destroyed both aircraft.[1414]

Possibly on this Night of Benghazi President Obama and some of his officials in Washington and Langley, and his military officers at the Pentagon, Fort Bragg, Rota, Stuttgart and in Croatia replay in their minds these horrific memories. Are they remembering the jarring, grisly black-and-white Iranian propaganda photographs and videos of the charred American human remains and the wreckage of the aircraft at Desert One in the Iranian wasteland?[1415] In Eagle Claw, not one American in Tehran was rescued. During the mission, eight American military personnel perished in the conflagration.

Ultimately, the Iranians hold their American hostages for 444 days. In November 1980 – the exact one-year anniversary of the U.S. Tehran embassy seizure – Ronald Reagan wins a landslide victory over the feeble, pathetic Carter. Iran releases all 52 hostages on the day of Reagan's inauguration.[1416] (Days later, your author stood on a street corner on Pennsylvania Avenue in Washington, D.C., applauding and cheering with a huge throng as buses carried the freed hostages to the White House to meet President Reagan.) The failed Operation Eagle Claw likely put the last nail in Carter's political coffin. *He* certainly blamed it for his loss.[1417]

[1413] *Id.* ("Rescue was enormously appealing. . . . Americans would rejoice. Carter's second term would be virtually assured"), p. 409. But compare *Id.* (Defense Secretary Harold Brown: ". . . [I]f we fail, that will be the end of the Carter presidency"), p. 411.

[1414] *Id.*, pp. 431-468.

[1415] Search online for "Operation Eagle Claw photos."

[1416] Bennett, *America: The Last Best Hope*, pp. 477-478 and 481-482.

[1417] "Jimmy Carter: Iran Hostage Rescue Should Have Worked," *USA Today* online (Sept. 17, 2010) (". . . Carter mostly blamed his election loss [to Ronald Reagan in

THE TRUE ACCOUNT OF VALOR AND ABANDONMENT

Quite possibly these stark, ghastly images of the ill-fated Eagle Claw mission's outcome render any Benghazi rescue operation too dicey politically so near the 2012 election.[1418] Given the upcoming voting, perhaps better for Obama and his squad to do nothing urgent or risky, to downplay the crisis, to halt any serious Benghazi rescue mission, to avoid asking allies for help, and to "hope for the best." Whether or not they consciously remember Eagle Claw, this is what they do. ∎

1980] on his failure to win the release of U.S. hostages held captive in Iran. A day before losing the election, he observed that his pollster, Pat Caddell, was finding 'massive slippage' in his support as people realized the hostages were not coming home. Undecided voters were moving almost entirely to Ronald Reagan").

[1418] Attkisson, Could U.S. Military Have Helped During Libya Attack? (quoting Rick Nelson, Senior Fellow at Center for Strategic and International Studies: Regarding military raid missions: "A lot can go well, right, as we saw with the bin Laden raid. It was a very successful event. But also, when there are high risk activities like this, a lot can go wrong, as we saw with the Iranian hostage rescue decades ago"). Compare Clinton, *Hard Choices* (". . . Our military does everything humanly possible to save American lives – and would do more if they could. That anyone has ever suggested otherwise is something I will never understand"), Chap. 17, p. 392; and Media Matters, *The Benghazi Hoax*, Chap. XIII, p. 74 (". . . The question of what was to be gained politically by not trying to thwart an assault that killed four Americans – had such a counter-attack been logistically possible – hangs in the air"). Truly, those who cannot remember the past are condemned to repeat it. George Santayana (1863-1952), *Reason in Common Sense* (1905).

70

"Foggy Bottom" Speaks

Hillary Clinton is in her seventh floor office at the State Department, now freed after the interminable 7:30 Meeting finally is over. She has directed her staff to prepare a public statement on the Benghazi attacks, and now has approved their draft.[1419]

Before this statement is issued, close Clinton aide Jacob Sullivan confers with Ben Rhodes, Deputy National Security Advisor at the White House, regarding its contents. At 9:53 p.m., Rhodes will issue a directive by email to the Pentagon and others that the State Department's announcement is to be the only U.S. government public response tonight.[1420]

At approximately 10:07 p.m. Washington time (4:07 a.m. in Benghazi), Secretary Clinton issues the State Department's first public pronouncement on the Benghazi crisis. At this time, State knows Sean Smith is deceased. Ambassador Stevens remains missing and his fate still is unknown to officials in Washington. However, as noted above, he reportedly has been taken to a Benghazi hospital and by now there are rumors he has perished.[1421]

(Query: Before she issues her statement, has Clinton previously spoken to Denis McDonough or Ben Rhodes or someone else in the White House? Have they directed her to blame the attacks on the inflammatory anti-Islam Video that has surfaced in recent weeks? Or perhaps such a directive occurred during the Ben Rhodes – Jacob Sullivan communication. As discussed below (Chapter 97), this would be consistent with Rhodes' development three days later of secret "talking points" heavily blaming the Video.)

Clinton's brief statement reads, in its entirety:

> I condemn in the strongest terms *the attack* on our mission in Benghazi today. As we work to secure our personnel and facilities [except in Benghazi], we have confirmed that one of

---

[1419] Clinton, *Hard Choices*, Chap. 17, p. 396.

[1420] Benghazi Committee Report, pp. 158-159.

[1421] *Id.* (Redacted), p. 89.

our State Department officers was killed. We are heartbroken by this terrible loss. Our thoughts and prayers are with his family and those who have suffered in this *attack*.

This evening, I called Libyan President Magariaf to coordinate additional support to protect Americans *in Libya*. President Magariaf expressed his condemnation and condolences and pledged his government's full cooperation.

Some have sought to justify this vicious behavior *as a response to inflammatory material posted on the Internet* [here clearly referring to the anti-Muslim Video]. *The United States deplores any intentional effort to denigrate the religious beliefs of others. Our commitment to religious tolerance goes back to the very beginning of our nation. But let me be clear: There is never any justification for* violent acts *of this kind.*

In light of the *events of today*, the United States government is working with partner countries around the world to protect our personnel, our missions, and American citizens worldwide [except in Benghazi].[1422]

At the time Hillary Clinton issues this pronouncement, the U.S. government has absolutely no evidence the *Benghazi* assaults (unlike the Cairo protests) are related in any way to the anti-Islamic *Innocence of Muslims* Video posted on the internet that soon will become world famous.[1423] (Also, note Clinton's statement makes no reference to any protests in Benghazi.)

Select Benghazi Committee member Representative Jim Jordan (R-OH) later asks Secretary Clinton to explain this Video reference in her 10:07 p.m. Statement issued on this Night of Benghazi. She responds that in her statement she is attempting to warn others "in the region" there is no excuse for further violence in response to the Video.[1424]

[1422] Statement on the Attack in Benghazi, by Secretary of State Hillary Rodham Clinton, United States Department of State, State Dept. Archives website (Sept. 11, 2012; 10:07 p.m.) (emphasis added); and *The New York Times*, What They Said, Before and After the Attack in Libya.

[1423] House Select Benghazi Committee Hearings (Oct. 22, 2015) (Remarks of Rep. Jim Jordan (R-OH)).

[1424] Clinton House Select Benghazi Committee Testimony (Oct. 22, 2015) (Response to questions from Rep. Jim Jordan (R-OH)).

(Nice try, Hillary. The reference in your September 11 statement's third paragraph to attempts to "justify *this vicious behavior* as a response to inflammatory material posted on the Internet" clearly refers to the previous paragraphs one and two. Those expressly pertain to Benghazi and Libya only. They do not even reference Cairo or other areas "in the region." Nor does your fourth and final paragraph, which mentions working with partner countries to protect Americans "around the world," not "in the region.")

In testifying before the Select Committee, Ben Rhodes also will "tap dance" while attempting to explain the use of this "vicious behavior" reference in the State Department announcement.[1425]

Secretary Clinton's reference to the internet Video soon will add fuel to what becomes an international firestorm over the causes behind this Night of Benghazi. ∎

[1425] Benghazi Committee Report, pp. 158-159.

71

Assassination Confirmed

According to subsequent congressional testimony of Gregory Hicks, on September 12 at about 3:00 a.m. Tripoli time, he receives a telephone call from the Libyan Prime Minister. The latter informs Hicks Ambassador Stevens is deceased. "I'm very sorry, Greg, to tell you this but our friend Chris has passed on."[1426] Hicks' worst fears are confirmed. He testifies later "I think it's the saddest phone call I've ever had in my life." Hicks immediately calls Washington to convey the dire news.[1427]

However, this timing appears inconsistent with other events. If Hicks is correct, Washington officials know Stevens is dead shortly after 9:00 p.m., Washington time. As noted above, over an hour later at 10:07 p.m. Hillary Clinton issues a public statement confirming only one death – that of Sean Smith (who is not mentioned by name yet). (The author believes Hicks' recollection may be faulty. He has been up all night. Probably it is the result of his exhaustion, stress and grief on this early morning of September 12. This horrific call from the Libyan Prime Minister likely occurs about one hour later than Hicks remembers, shortly after 4:00 a.m. Benghazi time.)

Soon after the release of Secretary Clinton's statement – probably sometime between 10:07 p.m. and about 10:20 p.m. Washington time – some in the United States government in Washington begin receiving the tragic confirmation Ambassador Stevens is dead. It is likely Hicks informs State Department headquarters of Stevens' demise at about 10:15 p.m.[1428] The Libyan friend whom Greg Hicks has asked to investigate at the Benghazi Medical Center sadly has confirmed the Arab who called various contacts on Scott Wickland's cell phone had

---

[1426] Hicks Oversight Committee Testimony (May 8, 2013), p. 27; ABC News, Hicks Sept. 2013 Interview With Stephanopoulos (*Watch video there*; Go to 5:45 - 6:23); and Stephen F. Hayes, "U.S. Military in Tripoli Ordered Not to Go to Benghazi," *The Weekly Standard* online (May 6, 2013) ("Hayes, U.S. Military in Tripoli Ordered Not to Go to Benghazi").

[1427] Hicks Oversight Committee Testimony (May 8, 2013), p. 27.

[1428] Additional Views of Reps. Jordan and Pompeo, p. 446.

been correct. The white male who is pronounced dead shortly after 2:00 a.m. Benghazi time at the hospital is in fact Ambassador Stevens.[1429]

Stevens has not been kidnapped and taken hostage after all. He had been hiding inside the Mission's safe haven the entire time until his murder.[1430] *An American ambassador has been <u>assassinated</u>.*[1431] ■

[1429] Clinton, *Hard Choices*, Chap. 17, pp. 396-397.

[1430] Zuckoff, *13 Hours* ("The operators' early speculation that Stevens had been kidnapped was mistaken. He'd been inside the villa since the start of the attack, hidden somewhere deep within the safe haven where the DS agents and operators couldn't locate him through the fire and smoke"), Chap. 11, pp. 244-245.

[1431] Official Biography of John Christopher Stevens (1960-2012), Office of the Historian, Bureau of Public Affairs, State Dept. website.

72

The President Speaks with Secretary Clinton

Soon after issuing her public statement at 10:07 p.m., Hillary Clinton leaves the State Department and goes home.[1432] At this time, her Ambassador to Libya still is missing and rumored dead, another employee of hers has been murdered, five of her surviving diplomatic security agents are trapped at the Benghazi CIA Annex which militants have attacked *twice*, and her staff at the Embassy in Tripoli are continuing to evacuate under concerns they will be the next target of Ansar al-Sharia. (Still more leadership.)

Very likely as she is being driven home, Greg Hicks is calling the State Department to advise headquarters of Chris Stevens' death.[1433]

Shortly after Clinton arrives at her residence, President Obama calls her at 10:27 p.m. (4:27 a.m. in Benghazi). Clinton gives him the "latest updates." This occurs as Team Tripoli finally is preparing to leave the Benghazi airport. According to Clinton, "He asked me how our people were holding up and reiterated that he wanted all necessary steps taken to protect our diplomats and citizens in Libya and across the region."[1434]

Although Clinton does not confirm it in her memoir, it is possible President Obama calls Clinton because he has just been told his Ambassador to Libya has been assassinated. Just seven minutes after Obama places this call, at 10:34 p.m. Washington time, the State Department's Diplomatic Security Command Center will issue an internal alert advising the Libyans have confirmed Chris Stevens is at a

---

[1432] Clinton, *Hard Choices* (emphasis added) ("With our DS agents at the *heavily fortified* CIA post and our reinforcements from Tripoli on the ground at the airport, I decided to move from the office to my home in northwest Washington, only minutes away from Foggy Bottom. I knew the days ahead were going to be taxing on us all, with the entire Department looking to me to lead them through this shocking tragedy while keeping everyone focused on what lay ahead"), Chap. 17, p. 397.

[1433] Additional Views of Reps. Jordan and Pompeo, p. 446.

[1434] Benghazi Committee Report, Select Benghazi Timeline, p. 560. If this 10:27 p.m. time is accurate, Clinton obviously does not personally clear her agency's 10:07 p.m. public statement in advance with President Obama himself. See also Clinton, *Hard Choices*, Chap. 17, p. 397.

Benghazi hospital and is deceased.[1435] (Alternatively, perhaps the timing of Obama's call is fortuitous, and he and Clinton afterwards learn from others Stevens is dead.)

A few minutes later at 10:38 p.m., Clinton will send an email stating, "Cheryl [presumably Cheryl Mills, her Chief of Staff] told me the Libyans confirmed his death."[1436] This most likely is the first official confirmation to Clinton that her Ambassador to Libya is dead.

Two Select Committee members claim this is the first and only time Clinton speaks with the president this night. (Again, Obama and Clinton should be together in the Situation Room instead of talking by phone.) According to Clinton's own timing, this conversation does not occur until *six hours and forty-five minutes* after the initial attack commences![1437] (Recall Hillary Clinton does not speak with Defense Secretary Panetta even *once* during this entire Night of Benghazi.[1438])

At the very latest, it appears shortly after speaking with the president, Clinton learns of Chris Stevens' death. Just minutes before the final fatal attack in Benghazi, Clinton emails her daughter, Chelsea (aka "Diane Reynolds"), at 11:12 p.m. She writes, "*Two* of our officers were killed in Benghazi by an al Queda-like [sic] group. . . ."[1439]

Actual combat in the Battle of Benghazi will not conclude for another hour after Clinton goes home, as five of her employees and 28 other Americans continue to fight for their lives. And the very last State Department employee, DSA Alec Henderson (and the remains of her employees Chris Stevens and Sean Smith) will not be evacuated safely from Benghazi for over five and one-half hours after she returns to her residence.[1440] (Night, night, Madam Secretary. And she wanted to be our Commander in Chief.) ■

[1435] Benghazi Committee Report, Select Benghazi Timeline, p. 560.

[1436] *Id.*, p. 560.

[1437] Additional Views of Reps. Jordan and Pompeo, pp. 444-445; and Key Delays Appendix (See September 11 entries for 3:42 p.m. and 10:27 p.m., both Washington time).

[1438] Additional Views of Reps. Jordan and Pompeo, pp. 444-445.

[1439] Benghazi Committee Report (emphasis added), pp. 133 and 161; and Diamond and Labott, What Did We Learn About Benghazi at Marathon Meeting?

[1440] Key Delays Appendix (See September 11 entry for 11:26 p.m. and September 12 entry for 3:54 a.m., both Washington time).

73

"Bug Out" In Tripoli

After receiving the tragic confirmation of Ambassador Stevens' death, Hicks and his colleagues in Tripoli "accelerate" their efforts to organize the evacuation of State's personnel and equipment at the Embassy residence compound and move them to "a U.S. embassy annex" elsewhere in the city.[1441] Hicks describes his staff's efforts this night as exhibiting "amazing discipline and courage in Tripoli in organizing our withdrawal."[1442]

There is much to be done. Logs must be kept of the evacuation process. Vehicles must be assembled for transport to the annex, and drivers arranged. Some of the communications equipment must be disassembled so it can be taken to the annex. The classified communications capability of the equipment to be left behind must be destroyed. Hard drives will be smashed with an ax. In preparation for trouble, ammunition must be collected, loaded into magazines, and transferred to the evacuation vehicles.[1443]

Meanwhile, during this frenzy of activity David McFarland continues his constant efforts to communicate with his contacts in Benghazi, hoping to arrange help for the besieged Americans there. According to Greg Hicks, Defense Attaché Phillips, Lt. Col. Gibson and several special operations military personnel in Tripoli provide enormous assistance during this evacuation.[1444]

During this same time at the Embassy, Regional Security Officer John Martinec remains on the phone with Benghazi, keeping abreast of developments at the Alamo. According to Greg Hicks, Martinec provides a "mountain of moral support" to the beleaguered Americans.[1445]

[1441] Pentagon Press Release, "DOD Cooperates with Congress on Benghazi Probes."

[1442] Hicks Oversight Committee Testimony (May 8, 2013), p. 27.

[1443] *Id.*, pp. 27-28.

[1444] *Id.*, p. 28; and Pentagon Press Release, "DOD Cooperates with Congress on Benghazi Probes."

[1445] Hicks Oversight Committee Testimony (May 8, 2013), p. 28.

Hicks and his team plan to evacuate to the U.S. annex at dawn. They will have to get there by taking heavily-armored vehicles they are unfamiliar driving. (Locals usually drive these vehicles, but are not present at the Embassy this night.) Hicks believes waiting until dawn may help them avoid unpredictable militia checkpoints more easily. Eventually, they are ready to go and apparently decide to leave before dawn. (The evacuees will begin to arrive at the Tripoli annex at about 4:45 to 5:00 a.m., well before sunrise.[1446])

The Libyan government finally provides some external security around the U.S. Tripoli annex facility. This enhanced security posture makes it possible for Hicks and his team to consider sending more of the limited Tripoli military personnel to Benghazi as reinforcements. (However, as discussed in Chapter 80 below, the U.S. military at Special Operations Command Africa soon will override this plan.)[1447] ■

[1446] *Id.*, p. 28.

[1447] *Id.*, p. 29.

74

Team Tripoli Leaves Benghazi Airport

Meanwhile, at the Benghazi airport Team Tripoli has its own "action items" to contend with. After learning Chris Stevens is deceased, the mission of Team Tripoli changes. At this point, they determine their goal must become the evacuation of some fourteen "nonessential personnel" from the CIA Annex.

The Tripoli rescuers plan to travel to the Annex, escort these CIA people back to the airport, and move them out of Benghazi to Tripoli on the chartered plane on which the rescuers arrived three hours earlier. Team Tripoli then expects to *return to the Annex* and bolster the GRS defenders there, whom they believe intend to remain at the Annex "until further notice," pending instructions from the CIA Tripoli Chief of Station. A GRS agent later testifies he believes it is "Bob," the Benghazi Chief of Base, who wants to keep some staff at the Annex.[1448]

(Again, given these facts, how is it the U.S. military blithely is assuming all Americans in Benghazi plan to leave this hellhole as quickly as possible? Is the Pentagon even *talking* to the CIA tonight?)

Eventually, some members of a branch of the "Libyan Shield" militia appear at the Benghazi airport with several gun trucks and some Land Cruisers. By this point, Team Tripoli is totally exasperated and desperate to get to the CIA Annex. After consulting with U.S. officials in Tripoli, Team Tripoli decides this Libyan Shield group is "the less bad element of the militia" for transport to the Annex. They leave Benina Airport for the Annex with these militia members in a ten-vehicle convoy at about 4:30 a.m. Benghazi time (10:30 p.m. Washington time, just as Clinton is speaking with the president).[1449] ■

[1448] Zuckoff, *13 Hours* ("With Stevens confirmed dead, the team of Tripoli operators had no reason to venture into potentially hostile territory around the Benghazi Medical Center. Arrangements would need to be made to retrieve Stevens's remains, but only if that could be accomplished without putting anyone else in danger"), Chap. 11, p. 245; Benghazi Committee Report (Redacted), pp. 81-82; and Sen. Intelligence Committee Benghazi Report, p. 8.

[1449] Benghazi Committee Report (Redacted), pp. 81-82 and 100; and Zuckoff, *13 Hours*, Chap. 11, p. 245.

75

F.E.S.T. Is "Off the Menu"

While unbeknownst to Mark Thompson his agency's head, Hillary Clinton, is speaking with President Obama, the dejected ex-Marine still awaits a final decision on whether his F.E.S.T. unit will be activated tonight.

Earlier, at 9:58 p.m., Thompson sends an email to Kathleen Austin-Ferguson, Patrick Kennedy's deputy. Thompson tells her he has heard Kennedy discouraged the F.E.S.T. option at the earlier 7:30 Meeting. He writes, "To remind, F.E.S.T. has dedicated aircraft able to respond in 4 hours, is Department of State-led, and provides the below skills [apparently summarized in his email]." He also advises Austin-Ferguson the FBI supports F.E.S.T.'s deployment tonight.[1450]

Thompson's frustration (and quite likely his anger) must have been heightened when Austin-Ferguson communicates with him. She advises Thompson it might be "too unsafe" for F.E.S.T. to deploy to Libya![1451] (*What?* "Too unsafe" for a counterterrorism crisis response team to deploy in what is likely a terrorism crisis? Or perhaps Austin-Ferguson means too unsafe *politically*.) Charlene Lamb, State's Deputy Assistant Secretary for Diplomatic Security, also believes it is not appropriate to deploy the F.E.S.T. assets this night.[1452]

It is now after 10:30 p.m. in Washington (4:30 a.m. in Benghazi). Thompson remains very concerned a U.S. ambassador officially still is unaccounted for, and the supposedly covert CIA Annex already has been targeted *twice* by armed militants. Thompson is hoping his agency will relent even at this late hour and unchain him and his crisis response group. *F.E.S.T. wants to get into this fight!* But given events earlier this evening in Washington, he cannot be optimistic.

[1450] House Oversight Committee Hearings (May 8, 2013) (Remarks of Rep. Jason Chaffetz (R-UT), quoting email from Mark Thompson to Patrick Kennedy's deputy), p. 36.

[1451] Thompson Oversight Committee Testimony (May 8, 2013) (Response to questions of Rep. Jason Chaffetz (R-UT)), p. 37.

[1452] Benghazi Committee Report, p. 65.

THE TRUE ACCOUNT OF VALOR AND ABANDONMENT

Then, at 10:34 p.m., Thompson sees the gut-punching coup de grâce email notice from his agency's Diplomatic Security Command Center. It advises Libya has confirmed Chris Stevens is at a Benghazi hospital and has perished.[1453] Thompson is crushed. He closes his eyes and thinks of how devastated the ambassador's family soon will feel. *Damn it!*

Nine minutes later at 10:43 p.m., Kennedy himself emails Thompson – almost exactly *seven hours* into the crisis. (Thompson does not even merit a phone call.) Kennedy says he "did not feel the dispatch of such a [F.E.S.T.] team to Libya is the appropriate response to the current situation."[1454] It is now official: Ambassador Stevens is deceased and F.E.S.T. will not be going to Libya. (F.E.S.T. members should just go home, and watch events unfold on cable news channels.)

Mark Thompson later will tell the House Oversight Committee he views F.E.S.T. as "... a tool that should remain on the menu of options...." in a situation like Benghazi. Instead, he asserts, "... [I]t was early taken off the menu."[1455]

Thompson will testify further before this panel that active members of his F.E.S.T. group are stunned they are not deployed on this Night of Benghazi. Thompson states, "People who are a part of the team, a normal part of that team that deploy with us were shocked and amazed that they were not being called on their cell phones, beepers, et cetera, to go." Thompson adds he does not know if this view is shared by "very senior people" in these team members' agencies.[1456]

Thompson additionally testifies he does not know the real reason why F.E.S.T. is not called into action on this Night of Benghazi.[1457] (There is a crisis in Benghazi, and a crisis response team in the U.S. trained and eager to deploy, but never the two shall meet.) Thompson is asked by a committee member when would be the right time to deploy the F.E.S.T. team if not in response to this Benghazi crisis. Thompson responds, "There is no answer to that, sir."[1458]

[1453] *Id.*, Select Benghazi Timeline, p. 560.

[1454] Benghazi Committee Report, p. 65.

[1455] Thompson Oversight Committee Testimony (May 8, 2013) (Response to questions of Rep. John Mica (R-FL)), p. 110.

[1456] *Id.* (Response to questions of Rep. Mark Meadows (R-NC)), p. 92.

[1457] *Id.* (Response to questions of Rep. Jason Chaffetz (R-UT)), p. 37.

[1458] *Id.* (Response to questions of Rep. Thomas Massie (R-KY)), p. 88.

(The U.S. government's failure to activate a F.E.S.T. team at least *provisionally* early on this Night of Benghazi is yet another of many troubling decisions.[1459] Effectively, this is a "stand down" order by State Department and NSC leadership. It is consistent with a narrative becoming increasingly clear as readers progress through these pages: *officials in Washington are determined not to make the Benghazi attacks appear to be too significant an event.* After all, if the Counterterrorism Bureau's F.E.S.T. crisis response unit is deployed, doesn't this signal the administration thinks *terrorism* may be involved in Benghazi? And doesn't it concede Benghazi is a *crisis?* Politically, these are not useful messages to emphasize eight weeks before a presidential election. This choice to keep F.E.S.T. on the leash dovetails with the "do as little as possible and hope for the best" approach U.S. leaders seem bent on pursuing this deadly night. (See Chapters 64-65 and 68-69.)

This timidity of our government's "leaders" stands in sharp contrast to the F.E.S.T. members themselves. The latter are raring to go to Libya.[1460] At the House Oversight hearings Thompson, a 20-year Marine veteran, is asked whether there would have been any reluctance on the part of himself or any of his F.E.S.T. team members "to go to Libya or anywhere in the world that you were needed to protect Americans?" He replies, "I hang out with a very noble and brave crowd. The answer is no."[1461] ∎

[1459] Benghazi Committee Report ("... [W]ith Stevens considered missing for hours in Libya after the death of [Sean] Smith, FEST expertise could have augmented the capabilities of the U.S. Embassy in Libya"), p. 65.

[1460] Attkisson, *Stonewalled* (citing unnamed Obama administration source commenting on F.E.S.T. team members, "... Undersecretary of State Patrick Kennedy advised against sending them. They wanted to go, but weren't allowed"), Chap. 4, p.168.

[1461] Thompson Oversight Committee Testimony (May 8, 2013) (Response to questions of Rep. Blake Farenthold (R-TX)), p. 80.

76

Where Is the President?

As Commander in Chief, President Barack Obama is responsible for all the above actions (and inactions) of the U.S. government. One abiding question endures: Where *is* Barack Hussein Obama on this evening of September 11, 2012, and the early hours of the following morning?

More specifically, what is Obama doing as the five DSAs come under fire while evacuating the Mission Compound? As Obama's NSC convenes a two-hour decision meeting of "Deputies"? As Team Tripoli is stranded at the Benghazi airport? As the "secret" CIA Annex comes under attack? And (as we discuss later) what is Obama doing as Team Tripoli is riding from the Benghazi airport to the Annex with the Libyan Military Intelligence militia? As Lt. Col. Gibson and his men are being ordered not to go to Benghazi? Where is President Obama as the Annex comes under deadly mortar attack?

Official Records Are Unavailable

The author has been unable to locate an official White House schedule for the president on the Obama presidential archives for this date.[1462] Curiously, although once listed among official White House documents for September 11, 2012,[1463] the schedules for the First Lady[1464] and Vice President Biden[1465] appear to have been taken down from the Obama White House archives website.

[1462] Schedule believed previously to have been posted at http://www.whitehouse.gov/schedule/president/2012-09-11. See generally Rivera and Rivera, Where Was President Obama During Benghazi Terror Attack? (*Watch video there*; Go to 0:00-49).

[1463] Official September 11, 2012 White House Documents believed previously to have been posted at https://search.whitehouse.gov/search?query=September+11%2C+2012&op=Search&affiliate=wh.

[1464] Schedule believed previously to have been posted at https://www.whitehouse.gov/schedule/First-lady/2012-09-11.

[1465] Schedule believed previously to have been posted at https://www.whitehouse.gov/schedule/vice-president/2012-09-11.

Beyond these daily schedules, another official record exists documenting Obama's activities. A White House "diarist" keeps a detailed log of every action of the president, and of everyone with whom he meets. This log is preserved at the National Archives. However, this record has never been disclosed for this Night of Benghazi.[1466]

(In contrast, after the successful military raid that killed Osama bin Laden, the White House releases a near minute-by-minute chronology of President Obama's actions on that night.[1467] Obama had been in the Situation Room with his team during that mission.[1468] The White House widely disseminated a now-famous picture of the president and his team being briefed there on that mission.[1469] No such timetable or photograph will be released for this Night of Benghazi.[1470])

The author has been unable to find any mention of President Obama attending his Presidential Daily Briefing on September 11, 2012. However, this is not unusual. According to conservative author and commentator Marc Thiessen (former chief speechwriter for President George W. Bush), through mid-June 2012 of his presidency Obama personally attends his daily briefing only about 44 percent of the time.[1471] On other days, he reportedly reads the briefing.

One blog (of unknown reliability) called "TheRoot.com" posted a document purporting to be the White House's "Daily Guidance and Press Schedule for Tuesday, September 11, 2012."[1472] From this

---

[1466] Marc Thiessen, Opinion, "Where Was Obama During Benghazi? Ask the White House Diarist," *The Washington Post* online (May 12, 2014).

[1467] Rivera and Rivera, Where Was President Obama During Benghazi Terror Attack? (*Watch video there*; Go to 0:00-28). See also Nick Rasmussen, "The Weight of One Mission: Recounting the Death of Usama [sic] bin Laden, Five Years Later," Obama White House Archives (May 2, 2016).

[1468] "Bin Laden: Shoot to Kill" Documentary (May 16, 2012) at https://www.youtube.com/watch?v=-QBMSeNpYgE.

[1469] View photograph of the Situation Room gathering at https://obamawhitehouse.archives.gov/photos-and-video/photo/2012/08/president-and-vice-president-recieve-update-osama-bin-laden-mission.

[1470] Rivera and Rivera, Where Was President Obama During Benghazi Terror Attack? (*Watch video there*; Go to 0:00-28).

[1471] Marc A. Thiessen, Opinion, "Marc Thiessen: Why Is Obama Skipping More Than Half of His Daily Intelligence Meetings," *The Washington Post* online (Sept. 10, 2012).

[1472] The Root Staff, "Obama's Day, Sept. 11: 9/11 Anniversary Events," TheRoot.com online (Sept. 11, 2012).

TheRoot.com posting and other sources, we know at 8:45 a.m. this morning president and Mrs. Obama observe a moment of silence on the White House South Lawn in honor of 9/11. Later at 9:30 a.m. this morning the president and First Lady attend an "Observance Ceremony" for 9/11 at the Pentagon. Also, according to a blog called "White House Dossier" (reliability also uncertain) at 2:15 p.m. the president has a scheduled visit with wounded warriors at Walter Reed National Military Center. The president arrives back at the White House at 4:50 p.m. from this Walter Reed visit[1473] (just after Team Annex is reaching and beginning to clear the Mission Compound in Benghazi). This is just in time for his previously-scheduled 5:00 p.m. meeting with Secretary Panetta and others in the Oval Office (discussed in Chapter 43 above). This schedule is consistent with the information posted on "TheRoot" blog, referenced above, which lists no other presidential events for September 11.

Not in the Situation Room

In a later presidential debate, President Obama will claim, "So as soon as we found out that the Benghazi consulate [sic] was being overrun, I was *on the phone* with my *national security team* and I gave them three instructions." These were: beef up security in Libya and "the region"; investigate what happened and hold people accountable; and hunt down who did it. (Interestingly, Obama does not include "go rescue the Americans in Benghazi" among his orders.)[1474] Unless the president calls his team from the helicopter on the way back to the White House (which is possible), these calls may occur after his 5:00 p.m. meeting with Panetta and Dempsey.

We know after this 5:00 p.m. meeting the president is in the White House.[1475] When asked in May 2013 if Obama is in the Situation

---

[1473] Keith Koffler, "Obama Schedule, Tuesday, September 11, 2012," White House Dossier online (Sept. 10, 2012). See also Becky Brittain, "POTUS's Schedule for 9/11 Anniversary," The 1600 Report, CNN Politics online (Sept. 11, 2012); and Rivera and Rivera, Where Was President Obama During Benghazi Terror Attack? (*Watch video there*; Go to 2:18-30).

[1474] ABC News Transcript of Second 2012 Presidential Debate Moderated by Candy Crowley of CNN's "State of the Union" (Oct. 16, 2012), ABC News online (emphasis added).

[1475] E.g., Interview of Dan Pfeiffer with Chris Wallace, "Fox News Sunday," Fox News Channel (May 19, 2013) ("Fox News, Pfeiffer May 2013 Interview with Wallace") (*Watch video there*; Go to 3:20-22).

Room, Dan Pfeiffer (Assistant to the President and Senior Advisor) will claim he doesn't remember what room the president is in, but says "That's a largely irrelevant fact."[1476] (Persistent Fox News interviewer Chris Wallace performs a journalistic molar extraction trying to get Pfeiffer to answer whether Obama ever goes to the Situation Room during this crisis. The insistent Wallace fails.) Pfeiffer tells Fox News the president is kept up-to-date on Benghazi developments "as it was happening throughout the entire night, from the moment it started until the very end."[1477] Pressed for details, Pfeiffer replies, "... He was in constant touch that night with his national security team, and kept up-to-date as [sic] the events as they were happening."[1478]

One retired military analyst tells Fox News his sources claim President Obama is in the Situation Room watching live drone feeds from Benghazi with others.[1479] These sources appear to be wrong. Another Obama aide, National Security Council spokesperson Tommy Vietor, later claims he himself is in the Situation Room on this Night of Benghazi, and admits the president is *not* there.[1480] (Why *not*? Obama manages to make it there for Osama Bin Laden's capture in May 2011, and for Hurricane Sandy seven weeks after Benghazi.[1481])

An Early Evening Briefing

Based on a White House photograph reportedly taken on this Night of Benghazi, at some point this evening the president is briefed further

---

[1476] Fox News, Pfeiffer May 2013 Interview with Wallace (*Watch video there*; Go to 2:02-13).

[1477] *Id.* (*Watch video there*; Go to 0:37-47 and 3:20-30).

[1478] *Id.* (*Watch video there*; Go to 1:37-45).

[1479] Lt. Col. Tony Shaffer (Ret.) with Jeanine Pirro on "Justice with Judge Jeanine" (Possibly Oct. 27, 2017) (*Watch video there*; Go to 1:47 – 2:26).

[1480] Interview of Tommy Vietor with Brett Baier, "Special Report," Fox News Channel (May 1, 2014) (*Watch video there*; Go to 9:43 - 11:18). See also Rivera and Rivera, Where Was President Obama During Benghazi Terror Attack? (*Watch video there*; Go to 3:15 45); and Editorial, "Benghazi: Where Was President Waldo During Attack?" Investor's Business Daily website (May 20, 2013) ("When Clint Eastwood talked to an empty chair at the GOP National Convention last summer, everyone laughed. Well, there was an empty chair in the Situation Room the night of Sept. 11, 2012, when four Americans were being murdered by terrorists, and no one is laughing. It's called dereliction of duty ...").

[1481] "2012: A Year in Photos," Photo by White House Photographer Pete Souza, Obama White House Archives.

in the Oval Office (not the Situation Room) on developments in Benghazi.[1482] This photograph is posted online, but is not time-stamped. Hence, we do not know the time this briefing takes place. (Although it is difficult to be sure, through the glass panes of an Oval Office door it appears to be twilight outside. On this evening the sun sets in Washington, D.C. at 7:22 p.m.[1483] One blogger at "Conservative Tree House" claims the photo's metadata shows it is taken at 7:26 p.m.[1484] (Another post the next day on the same blog gives two different times, 7:26 and 7:28 p.m.[1485]) If correct, this photo is taken just 16 minutes after the second-wave attack on the CIA Annex commences, and just minutes before Team Tripoli lands in Benghazi.[1486])

Those visible in this photograph are President Obama, Vice President Joe Biden, White House Chief of Staff Jack Lew, National Security Advisor Tom Donilon, and Deputy National Security Advisor Denis McDonough, who is doing the talking as this image is captured.[1487] Biden is holding handwritten notes, but the author is unable to read them. (As discussed in Chapter 66, all except McDonough are lawyers. None of these five men have one day of military experience. Most have little national security experience prior to their present positions. These are ominous signs if you are an American in Benghazi tonight.)

Conspicuously missing from this photograph is Obama's chief advisor on counterterrorism, John Brennan. (Where is he tonight? In a June 2018 profile of Brennan, a *New York Times Magazine* article

---

[1482] "2012: A Year in Photos," Photo by White House Photographer Pete Souza, Obama White House Archives (See photo dated Sept. 11, 2012).

[1483] See timeanddate.com.

[1484] "Benghazigate: Research Help Request – White House 9-11-12 Photo During Benghazi 7 Hour Siege. . . .?" TheConservativeTreeHouse.com (Jan. 4, 2013). Note this blog contains numerous factual errors.

[1485] Sundance, "Benghazi – During Attack Denis McDonough and Tom Donilon Replace President Obama and VP Biden . . . ," The Last Refuge, TheConservativeTreeHouse.com (Jan. 5, 2013).

[1486] Key Delays Appendix (See September 11 entries for 7:10 p.m., 7:26 p.m. and 7:30 p.m., all Washington time).

[1487] "2012: A Year in Photos," Photo by White House Photographer Pete Souza (See the only photograph dated Sept. 11, 2012), Obama White House Archives.

mentions "Benghazi" only once. It simply asserts Brennan is "involved in decision-making about . . . Benghazi . . . ," with no details.[1488])

Because Denis McDonough chairs a two-hour videoconference beginning at 7:30 p.m. tonight (see Chapter 59), it is likely this meeting with the president takes place sometime in the two-hour window between about 5:30 p.m. (when his briefing by SecDef Panetta and General Dempsey likely ends), and the commencement of McDonough's 7:30 conference. (It also is possible McDonough steps out of his teleconference long enough to update the president on recent Benghazi developments.)

Phone Calls That Don't Occur

We know the president does not speak again this night with his Defense Secretary Panetta, or with General Dempsey, following their 5:00 p.m. meeting. Nor does anyone else in the White House.[1489] (Why not? Three dozen American lives are at risk. And hundreds of U.S. soldiers supposedly are being deployed into "harm's way.") Obama speaks only once with his Secretary of State, whose agency's reckless decisions have precipitated much of this crisis. According to Secretary Clinton and the Select Committee, this call does not occur until about 10:27 p.m., almost *seven hours* after the initial assault on the Mission (see Chapter 72)![1490] Does the president speak at all with David Petraeus, his CIA Director? We don't know.

Does the president telephone the Libyan president or prime minister during this emergency and demand security assistance and rescue for the Americans in Benghazi? Hillary Clinton does so. Gregory Hicks

---

[1488] Schwartz, A Spymaster Steps Out of the Shadows.

[1489] Panetta and Dempsey Senate Armed Services Committee Testimony (Feb. 7, 2013) (Response to questions of Sen. Kelly Ayotte (R-NH)); Benghazi Committee Report, p. 70; Additional Views of Reps. Jordan and Pompeo, p. 444; Statement of Senators McCain, Graham and Ayotte; Zuckoff, *13 Hours*, Chap. 6, p. 146; Kristol, Petraeus and Panetta Speak – But Not the President (". . . [I]t's beyond inconceivable he [Panetta] didn't then stay in touch with the White House after he returned to the Pentagon"); James Nye, "Panetta: President Obama Was Absent Night of Benghazi Attack and Did Not Check In Once During the Night of the Deadly Terror Assault," Daily Mail online (Feb. 8, 2013); Rivera and Rivera, Where Was President Obama During Benghazi Terror Attack? (*Watch video there*; Go to 3:15-45); and Daniel Halper, "Panetta: Obama Absent Night of Benghazi," *The Weekly Standard* online (Feb. 7, 2013).

[1490] Clinton, *Hard Choices*, Chap. 17, p. 397.

does so. Yet Barack Obama does not lift the phone to seek the Libyans' help tonight. (Why *not?* Is he too busy? Is it too much bother?[1491]) According to White House records, Obama first calls Libyan President Magariaf on September 13, long after the immediate crisis is over and all Americans are long gone from Benghazi.[1492]

A Call to Israel

White House records establish President Obama speaks "for an hour *tonight*" by telephone with Israeli Prime Minister Benjamin Netanyahu. There are indications Vice President Biden also is on this call.[1493] According to a hastily-drafted White House official "readout" of this call (which is silent on the time of the call), the two men speak mostly about Iran's nuclear program and "other security issues."[1494]

During this call, does Obama ask Netanyahu for help rescuing our people in Benghazi? True, the U.S. Naval Air Stations at Souda Bay (320 miles) and Sigonella (450 miles) are far closer to Benghazi than is Israel (about 860 miles). However, Israel is much closer to Benghazi than the U.S. FAST teams in Rota, Spain (1,500 miles), the U.S. base at Aviano (1,050 miles), and the CIF force in Croatia (1,000 miles). And, of course, much closer than the SOF at Fort Bragg, North Carolina (over 5,400 miles). In any event, the White House readout makes no mention of the leaders even discussing the Benghazi attacks.[1495]

One blog (of unknown reliability) puts Obama's call with Netanyahu at about 6:30 to 7:30 p.m., Washington time.[1496] This would

---

[1491] Statement of Senators McCain, Graham and Ayotte ("We do not know what the President did or who he was in contact with during the seven hours of the attack, and we do not know why the President did not reach out to Libyan President Magariaf during that period of time").

[1492] "Readout of the President's Call with Libyan President Magariaf," Obama White House Archives (Sept. 13, 2012).

[1493] See, e.g., Sundance, "Benghazi – During Attack Denis McDonough and Tom Donilon Replace President Obama and VP Biden . . . ," The Last Refuge (Jan. 5, 2013), theconservativetreehouse.com.

[1494] "Readout of the President's Call with Israeli Prime Minister Netanyahu," Obama White House Archives (Sept. 11, 2012).

[1495] "Readout of the President's Call with Israeli Prime Min. Netanyahu," Obama White House Archives (Sept. 11, 2012) (emphasis added).

[1496] Sundance, "Benghazi – During Attack Denis McDonough and Tom Donilon Replace President Obama and VP Biden . . . ," The Last Refuge (Jan. 5, 2013), theconservativetreehouse.com.

be 1:30 a.m. to 2:30 a.m. in Israel.[1497] (Another blog places the starting time at 7:00 p.m. Washington time, 2:00 a.m. in Israel.[1498]) Given the time difference, it seems unlikely the call occurs much later than this (assuming Netanyahu is in Israel at this time). (The handwritten notes Biden is holding in the photo noted above may relate to this call with Netanyahu – which may have just concluded when the photo is taken – rather than to Benghazi.[1499]) If the 6:30-7:30 timing is correct, both Obama and Biden effectively are "out of pocket" while the "secret" CIA Annex is coming under attack *twice*.[1500] It is possible the photo captures the five officials while the president and vice president are being updated after their lengthy call with Netanyahu.

If it does not involve seeking help for the Americans in Benghazi, what is so urgent about speaking with Netanyahu that it must occur tonight, in the middle of a U.S. national security emergency?

Some suggest the purpose of this call is entirely political, not security-related. On this September 11, news stories have been circulating President Obama has "snubbed" Netanyahu by refusing to meet with the prime minister later this month during the United Nations meeting in New York.[1501] Politically, this could be a big problem for Obama with Jewish voters just eight weeks before a presidential election. The brief (four-sentence) readout of the call devotes the final

---

[1497] See timezonesmap.org.

[1498] Jack Cashill, "What Obama Did on September 11, 2012," American Thinker online (May 5, 2014).

[1499] See Sundance, "Benghazi – During Attack Denis McDonough and Tom Donilon Replace President Obama and VP Biden . . . ," The Last Refuge, TheConservativeTreehouse.com (Jan. 5, 2013).

[1500] Key Delays Appendix (See September 11 entries for 6:34 p.m., 6:51 p.m. and 7:10 p.m., all Washington time).

[1501] E.g., The Rosett Report, "Benghazi and the Missing Obama 9/11 Timeline," Foundation for Defense of Democracies website (Nov. 5, 2012) (". . . Other than the attempt to defuse stories in the press about a snub . . . was there anything discussed in that phone call that was so desperately urgent it couldn't have waited until the white hot crisis in Benghazi was resolved? . . ."); Daniel Halper, "Panetta: Obama Absent Night of Benghazi," *The Weekly Standard* online (Feb. 7, 2013); and William Kristol, "Obama's September 11 Phone Call," *The Weekly Standard* online (Oct. 28, 2012) ("While Americans were under assault in Benghazi, the president found time for a non-urgent, politically useful, hour-long call to Prime Minister Netanyahu. And his senior national security staff had to find time to arrange the call, brief the president for the call, monitor it, and provide an immediate read-out to the media. . . . [F]or President Obama, a politically useful telephone call – and the ability to have his aides rush out and tell the media about that phone call – came first").

sentence to disavowing any snub has occurred.[1502] The president spends an hour speaking about an unrelated foreign policy matter and a political issue while a national security incident is unfolding, and his "secret" CIA Annex in Benghazi is being attacked.

Debate Preparation?

There are rumors that on this night President Obama is engaged in preparation for an upcoming presidential debate with Mitt Romney. However, that debate is not scheduled until October 3rd. Citing the White House Visitor's Log, Marc Thiessen claims three individuals enter the White House on September 11, 2012, for "debate prep." These visitors are Michael Donilon, David Ginsberg and Ron Klain. *The Wall Street Journal* describes Klain as the president's lead debate coordinator.[1503] According to Thiessen, the log states, "3 meet with Potus NO TIME LISTED 9/11/12."[1504] (The author is unable to locate this visitors log to confirm this.) Does Obama in fact meet with these men tonight? Alternatively, are the men meeting with Vice President Biden for *his* debate preparation?[1505] After all, Klain is Biden's former Chief of Staff.[1506] Is Obama joining these men as they prepare *Biden*?

Other Possibilities

But other than his (political) call with Netanyahu, where *is* Obama tonight? What is he *doing*? Where is he during the three-hour period between when the 7:26 p.m. "update" photograph is taken and the call he places to Secretary of State Clinton at 10:27 p.m. (Chapter 72)? Where is he that is more important than chairing the 7:30 Meeting? We

---

[1502] "Readout of the President's Call with Israeli Prime Minister Netanyahu," Obama White House Archives (Sept. 11, 2012) ("Contrary to reports in the press, there was never a request for Prime Minister Netanyahu to meet with President Obama in Washington, nor was a request for a meeting ever denied").

[1503] Carol E. Lee, "Obama Debate Challenge: Keeping Answers Short," *The Wall Street Journal* online (Sept. 18, 2012).

[1504] Marc Thiessen, Opinion, "Where Was Obama During Benghazi? Ask the White House Diarist," *The Washington Post* online (May 12, 2014).

[1505] See, e.g., "Visitor Logs: Obama Had 'Debate Prep' Meeting on September 11, 2012, the Day of the Benghazi Attack," Patterico's Pontifications (May 2, 2014).

[1506] Carol E. Lee, "Obama Debate Challenge: Keeping Answers Short," *The Wall Street Journal* online (Sept. 18, 2012).

know he is not monitoring the (supposed) rescue efforts from the Situation Room. Is he elsewhere in the White House watching the live drone video feeds from Benghazi? Or is he playing less deadly video games or watching television? Is he upstairs in the family quarters dissecting the adverse political ramifications of the Benghazi catastrophe with his wife, and his close confidant Valerie Jarrett, or with both? Where the hell *is* he?[1507]

(Or perhaps Obama is following the example of President Jimmy Carter during the commencement of the Iranian hostage crisis (see Chapter 69, above). At 4:30 a.m. on November 4, 1979, the president's bedside telephone rings at Camp David, the presidential retreat in northern Maryland. On the line is Carter's National Security Advisor, Zbigniew Brzezinski. He tells Carter the U.S. embassy in Tehran has been overrun, and all Americans there have been taken hostage. (Brzezinski is unaware six Americans have escaped capture.) Instead of rising and boarding his Marine One helicopter to return immediately to the White House Situation Room, Carter reportedly turns over and tries to go back to sleep.[1508] Now *that's* leadership.)

Inquiries from Congress

Near the culmination of the select Benghazi Committee's inquiry, the panel's chairman (Trey Gowdy, R-SC), sends fifteen written questions about Benghazi to President Obama for his personal response. Thirteen of these are unclassified. Some of these queries

---

[1507] Babbin, Whitewashing Benghazi ("And what of the president? We still don't know where Obama was or what he was doing on the night of the attacks. To repeat a familiar phrase, what did the president know, and when did he know it? How did he react? Did he make any decisions, and if so what were they? If not, why not?"); Michael Goodwin, "Now We Know – President Obama was MIA on Benghazi," Fox News Opinion online (Feb. 11, 2013) ("According to [Defense Secretary] Panetta, President Obama checked in with his military team early on during the attack, then checked out for the rest of the night. . . . There is still much we don't know, but Panetta, under persistent Senate probing, revealed that Obama simply wasn't involved. Did he just go to sleep?"); Kristol, Petraeus and Panetta Speak – But Not the President ("So the question remains: What did President Obama do that evening (apart from spending an hour on the phone with Prime Minister Netanyahu)? What did he know, and what did he decide, and what was the basis for his decision?"); and Editorial, "Benghazi: Where Was President Waldo During Attack?" Investor's Business Daily website (May 20, 2013).

[1508] Bowden, *Guests of the Ayatollah*, pp. 66 and 329.

concern the president's actions on this Night of Benghazi. They include the following inquiries:

...

3. What orders or direction, if any, did you give to Secretary of Defense Leon Panetta upon learning of the initial attack? Did you or anyone at your direction ever modify, withdraw, alter, or amplify the initial orders or direction you gave to Secretary Panetta?

...

5. Were you subsequently kept informed about the initial attack, subsequent attacks, and/or efforts to either send military assistance or evacuate U.S. personnel? By whom?

...

11. When did you learn individuals associated with terrorist organizations participated in the attack on the U.S. facilities in Benghazi, Libya?

...

The Obama White House arrogantly will refuse to answer any of these thirteen Select Committee questions.[1509] (More impressive leadership.)

(Now that he has departed office, doesn't Barack Obama owe his fellow Americans – and history – an answer to these basic questions? Doesn't he owe it to thirty-some American survivors who were in Benghazi? Doesn't he owe it to the families of the Fallen Four?)[1510]

Despite all the many unanswered questions, one damning, incontestable fact remains: On this Night of Benghazi, Commander in Chief Barack H. Obama never appears in the Situation Room. ■

[1509] Appendix C to Benghazi Committee Report, pp. 467-469; and Additional Views of Reps. Jordan and Pompeo ("... So while the investigation uncovered new information, we nonetheless end the Committee's investigation without many of the facts, especially those involving the President and the White House, we were chartered to obtain"), p. 417. See also Stephen F. Hayes, "Obama Did Not Ask for an Intel Brief the Day After the Benghazi Attack," *The Weekly Standard* online (June 28, 2016) ("... The White House has provided little detail on Obama's activities throughout the Benghazi attacks and their aftermath, refusing to answer to [sic] questions from journalists about the president's whereabouts and actively working to keep information from investigators with the Select Committee"); and Hank Berrien, "Where Was Obama During Intelligence Briefing the Morning After Benghazi?" The Daily Wire website (June 28, 2016).

[1510] Kristol, Petraeus and Panetta Speak – But Not the President ("... Both Petraeus and Panetta have raised more questions than they've answered. The only person who can provide the answers the American people deserve is President Obama").

77

"Welcome to the Party, We're Having a Blast!"

The exhausted Americans at the Benghazi CIA Annex heave a huge, collective sigh of relief when the Team Tripoli rescue party finally is in sight.

According to the Defense Department, just minutes earlier at 5:00 a.m. Benghazi time, a second *unarmed* Predator drone arrives on site in Benghazi above the CIA Annex to relieve the first drone, whose fuel is running low.[1511] It is just in time to view Team Tripoli's arrival. And it is just in time to record the horrors about to unfold. (Another problem for the later "Fog of War" narrative.)

Probably as the replacement drone arrives, Team Tripoli calls the Annex personnel to advise they are nearing the Annex. The GRS Team Lead radios his men, "Tripoli guys are coming in." The posse reaches the Annex at approximately 5:05 a.m., Benghazi time (11:05 p.m. Washington time). Tanto Paronto, perched on the roof of Building A, overlooks the Annex front gate. Recognizing several of the new arrivals from his time in Tripoli, Tanto gives the "all clear" to the Annex security leader to admit them into the Annex. As the Americans exit their vehicles and approach on foot Tanto calls down, "Hey, it's good to see you. Welcome to the party. We're having a blast over here." The GRS Team Lead meets Team Tripoli at the now open Annex front gate, and the rescue party walks into the Annex.[1512]

The convoy vehicles remain outside the gate. Hoping it will make the Libyan Shield members stay (not so much!), Team Tripoli invites a militia "sub-commander" inside the Annex with them. He joins them. The Annex front gate is closed again.[1513] The militia members

---

[1511] Benghazi Committee Report, Unclassified Defense Dept. Timeline, p. 574. See also CBS Benghazi Timeline.

[1512] Benghazi Committee Report, p. 101, and Select Benghazi Timeline, p. 560; and Zuckoff, *13 Hours*, Chap. 11, pp. 248-250. Compare Sen. Intelligence Committee Benghazi Report (". . . approximately 5:00 a.m. Benghazi time . . ."), p. 8.

[1513] Benghazi Committee Report, p. 101; and Zuckoff, *13 Hours*, Chap. 11, p. 250.

THE TRUE ACCOUNT OF VALOR AND ABANDONMENT

remaining with the vehicles outside are supposed to secure the perimeter of the Annex, but *do not*.

The Team Tripoli members walk to Annex Building C (which contains the Annex's TOC). There they discuss several urgent topics with the Annex Chief of Base and his deputy. These include: whether there are wounded Americans at the Annex who need medical care (there are not at this time); how Team Tripoli can bolster Annex security; and the forthcoming evacuation of nonessential personnel to the airport and related security issues. They address the details of Team Tripoli's proposed evacuation plan. Their main concern is how to avoid an ambush on the way back to the airport.[1514] (Officials at the Pentagon and in Washington seem oblivious to this issue.)

As noted above, Team Tripoli's chartered plane is not large enough to evacuate all the Americans on one flight. Instead, their plan is to evacuate fourteen "nonessential" American personnel from the Annex, and escort them to the airport in the friendly Libyan Shield militia vehicles that have brought Team Tripoli to the Annex. (Four of the five DSA agents eventually will end up leaving with these "nonessentials.") Rather than be exposed at the airport, *the Annex-based GRS operators (or at least a majority of them) plan to remain at the Annex* along with the CIA's top managers and Sean Smith's remains and "hold the Alamo." When the plane departs Benghazi, *Team Tripoli plans to return to the Annex and support the remaining GRS defenders and essential CIA personnel "until further notice."*[1515] According to author Mitchell Zuckoff, when the Annex receives word another plane has landed in Benghazi to evacuate them, the remaining Americans plan to leave with Smith's body via a militia convoy for the airport.[1516]

(As discussed above, this is completely inconsistent with the testimony and claims of officials at Foggy Bottom, the Pentagon, Langley and the White House that they abandon plans to send a FAST platoon to Benghazi because it is clear all Americans soon will have left Benghazi for Tripoli. Further, these government officials cannot know about the deadly mortar attack yet to come, which will change the plans for leaving some defenders at the Annex in Benghazi for a time.) ■

[1514] Zuckoff, *13 Hours*, Chap. 11, p. 250; and Benghazi Committee Report, p. 101.

[1515] Benghazi Committee Report, pp. 100-101; and Baier, 13 Hours at Benghazi: The Inside Story (*Watch video there*; Go to 24:00-16).

[1516] Zuckoff, *13 Hours*, Chap. 11, p. 252.

78

"Mortars! MORTARS! MORTARS!!"

It is now 5:08 a.m. in Northern Africa on September 12. The red-eyed security team members on the Annex rooftops and towers are exhausted, their muscles sore. Their clothes, body armor and skin are "caked with sweat and dirt."[1517] None of them has slept in many hours.

It is still dark, but traces of dawn are appearing on the eastern horizon. They await the sunrise with apprehension, but all are relieved that Team Tripoli is here.[1518] They listen to the Arabic chants from the loudspeakers atop the minarets of Benghazi's mosques, calling the faithful to the *Fajr* prayer.[1519]

Being ex-military, all the GRS agents are aware dawn is a classic time to launch a military attack. (Query: Have U.S. military leaders at the Pentagon and in Stuttgart figured this out?) Also, when daylight arrives, the GRS men's advantage of having night-vision goggles will be lost. Any attackers will be able to see the defenders' positions.[1520]

Atop the roof on Building C, Oz Geist and Rone Woods crouch next to each other, at the northwest corner. Their post overlooks a portion of Zombieland to the north. Oz tells Rone, "We need to get the heck out of here. It's getting light." DSA Dave Ubben also is stationed atop Building C, at the far northeast corner near the ladder to the roof. Ubben's position is only about eight or ten yards from the Annex wall. Although Ubben is only about 45 feet from Oz and Rone, he can barely see them in the early-morning darkness.

[1517] Zuckoff, *13 Hours*, Chap. 11, p. 247.

[1518] Baier, 13 Hours at Benghazi: The Inside Story (*Watch video there*; Go to 23:25-54); and Zuckoff, *13 Hours*, Chap. 11, p. 250.

[1519] Zuckoff, *13 Hours*, Chap. 11, p. 247.

[1520] *Id.*, Chap. 11, pp. 247-248 and 251; Benghazi Committee Report, pp. 100-101 (Testimony of GRS Oz Geist: "It was about 5:30 in the morning – the sun was just coming up – because me and Tyrone [Woods] had been talking about . . . if they're going to attack us, it's going to happen here shortly because usually the time to attack is right before the sun comes up. . . ."); and Baier, 13 Hours at Benghazi: The Inside Story (*Watch video there*; Go to 24:16-28).

THE TRUE ACCOUNT OF VALOR AND ABANDONMENT

Alone in Tower 3 in the Annex complex northeast corner, Tig Tiegen has spent most of the past two hours keeping watch over sheep pens outside the Annex walls. The defenders are concerned attackers might attempt to hide themselves among the sheep as they approach the Annex for another attack. Sitting in a lawn chair on his platform, Tig also surveys several dirt pathways in Zombieland for approaching hostiles.[1521]

On Building D's rooftop, Jack Silva is very pleased to see his old friend Glen "Bub" Doherty is part of the Team Tripoli rescue team. For Jack, in a bind there are few (if any) people he would rather have in his foxhole than Bub. He looks forward to catching up with his old buddy.[1522] On top of Building A, Tanto Paronto also is pleased he will again meet up with Bub. Although they are newer friends, Tanto and Bub worked together in Tripoli. Atop Building B's roof, D.B. Benton continues to stand his post.[1523]

About this time, several cars drive up near the Annex and then drive away again. Because the Annex defenders are uncertain about the drivers' identities and motives, they hold their fire. Then a man with a cell phone walks up near the Annex wall, turns, and walks away. Is he taking GPS coordinates? Or is he just out for a walk? Again, the defenders want to shoot but do not.[1524]

Most of Team Tripoli and the Annex leaders still are conferring at Building C. After a few minutes, Glen Doherty leaves the planning session and climbs to the rooftop of Building C to say hello to his old friend, Rone Woods, and join him in standing guard. As Doherty approaches the ladder to the roof, a radio call instructs the Annex personnel this is their final chance to collect their essential belongings in preparation to gather at Building C for evacuation.[1525]

Glen Doherty makes that fateful climb up the ladder, and soon reunites with Rone. The latter introduces Doherty to Oz Geist. After some brief catching-up with Rone, Doherty decides to go take a look

---

[1521] Zuckoff, *13 Hours*, Chap. 12, p. 265.

[1522] *Id.*, Chap. 11, pp. 247 and 250.

[1523] *Id.*, Chap. 11, p. 253.

[1524] Baier, 13 Hours at Benghazi: The Inside Story (*Watch video there*; Go to 22:54 - 23:24).

[1525] Zuckoff, *13 Hours*, Chap. 11, pp. 251-252; and Benghazi Committee Report, p. 101.

over the building's front door. As Doherty walks in that direction, Rone and Oz return their gazes back toward Zombieland.[1526]

Meanwhile, Tanto is back on Building A's roof after a brief bathroom break. He observes the militia motorcade that escorted Team Tripoli from the airport has remained in its original location. Tanto radios his Team Lead "to ask why the militia hadn't set up blocking positions on surrounding streets, to prevent anyone from attempting a third attack on the Annex." Just after releasing the call button, Tanto hears "a strange whooshing sound." He presses the button again and inquires, "Incoming?"[1527]

The CIA group talking with Team Tripoli is now on the patio outside Building C. They begin to hear "sporadic gunfire" whizzing over the top of Building C.[1528]

From his perch on Tower 3, Tig Tiegen hears a "thunk" from south of the compound. Then, Tig hears a follow-up "fffuuuvvv" sound. His immediate reaction is *mortar?* But Tig dismisses it, thinking surely the 17 February Brigade militia must have the city under control by now.[1529]

Then, all hell breaks loose.[1530]

BOOM!

Only minutes after Doherty reaches the roof, a mortar round explodes out in the road where the Libyan Shield vehicles remain parked, near the Annex's north perimeter wall. Some of the Libyan Shield members sustain injuries from the blast.[1531] Small arms fire continues to pass over the top of Building C. It is coming from the direction of Zombieland, but the defenders cannot see who is shooting at them. Nevertheless, Rone and Oz begin firing back in the general direction of the attackers. With just over an hour to sunrise, the third and final firefight at the Annex is underway. It is about 5:17 a.m.,

---

[1526] Zuckoff, *13 Hours*, Chap. 12, p. 255; Benghazi Committee Report, p. 101; and Baier, 13 Hours at Benghazi: The Inside Story (*Watch video there*; Go to 24:28-50).

[1527] Zuckoff, *13 Hours*, Chap. 11, p. 253.

[1528] Benghazi Committee Report, p. 101.

[1529] Zuckoff, *13 Hours*, Chap. 12, p. 265.

[1530] Hsu, CIA Officers Detail Part of Bloody Benghazi Attack at Terrorism Trial (Criminal trial testimony of disguised CIA agent, pseudonym "Alexander Charles": "All hell broke loose").

[1531] Hicks Oversight Committee Testimony (May 8, 2013), p. 28; and Benghazi Committee Report, p. 103.

THE TRUE ACCOUNT OF VALOR AND ABANDONMENT

Benghazi time (11:17 p.m. in Washington).[1532] This assault is the first time the terrorist attackers have employed mortars during the Battle of Benghazi.

After the first mortar strike hits near their convoy, the Libyan Shield militia quickly skedaddle. They immediately drive away from the Annex at high speed, leaving their commander behind inside the Annex! Soon thereafter, the commander begins calling his troops on his cell phone, demanding to know why the hell they had not secured the perimeter of the Annex, and why they have abandoned him.[1533] (Both excellent questions.)

When the first mortar explodes outside the Annex north wall, former Ranger Tanto on Building A's roof flinches, and instinctively takes a knee. He sees Rone and Oz pouring automatic weapons fire steadily toward Zombieland from Building C's roof. Rone is firing his twenty-pound machine gun. By his side, Oz is shooting his assault rifle, aiming at the muzzle flashes of the hidden assailants.[1534]

Tanto decides to join his comrades in combating the assailants from Zombieland. He moves quickly in a low combat crouch to the northern edge of Building A. He cannot see the attackers, but nevertheless begins firing into Zombieland. Then he realizes he still needs to cover the field to the south in case an assault develops from that direction. He stops firing and turns back to keep watch over the south wall. He is just in time to observe the militia convoy as they rapidly drive away from the Annex.[1535]

BOOM! A second mortar shell lands on top of the north Annex wall behind Building C and explodes, near Dave Ubben's position. The terrorists have recalibrated their mortar, their aim improved this time. Oz hears Ubben yell out, *"I'm hit! I'm hit!"* In the gradually growing dawn light, Oz can see Dave sitting down on a box beneath the ladder and holding his head. Ubben does not appear to Oz to be seriously wounded. In fact, Dave has been hit by shrapnel on his left temple. The blood from his wound is obscuring his vision. Ubben, a U.S. Army Iraq war combat veteran, has been under mortar fire "fairly frequently" in

---

[1532] Benghazi Committee Report, pp. 101-102, and Select Benghazi Timeline (first mortar strikes at 5:17 a.m.), p. 560.

[1533] Benghazi Committee Report (Redacted), pp. 103-105.

[1534] *Id.*, p. 102.

[1535] Zuckoff, *13 Hours*, Chap. 12, p. 258.

his career. He later testifies, "I heard that whistling sound so I knew we were going to get more."[1536]

Oz, kneeling, is changing his magazines and preparing to fire again. To his left, Rone drops to a three-quarter crouch position and is firing his machine gun with a vengeance. As his colleagues later describe it, Rone is "laying down hate" at the people who are trying to kill him and his comrades.[1537]

Atop his northeast tower, Tig Tiegen sees the flash of light created by the initial mortar explosion. It silhouettes the warriors on the rooftop of Building C. Then Tig sees the defenders atop Building C begin to pour a deadly fusillade toward Zombieland. When the second mortar shell slams onto the top of the north Annex wall, Tig thinks his position might well be next. He grabs his weapon and a "go-bag" Oz Geist left behind earlier, and jumps down from the tower.

Someone asks over the radio whether the Annex is under attack by RPGs. From atop Building A Tanto replies, "No, it was a mortar!" When the original caller repeats his question, Tanto replies more loudly, "Mortars! MORTARS! *MORTARS!!*"[1538]

Oz rises to resume firing at the attackers. **KABOOM!** Suddenly, at 5:18 a.m., mortar shells begin landing and exploding on the roof of Building C! Rone stops firing. The first mortar shell has hit halfway between Ubben's position in the northeast corner, and that of Rone and Oz in the northwest corner. Through a haze of black smoke, Oz sees Rone on his left go down immediately; he's been hit. Rone is lying on his side in the corner in a fetal position, motionless, his back toward Oz. The latter's heart sinks.[1539]

The mortar explosion knocks Oz backward and off balance. He catches himself before falling onto the roof surface. Oz tells himself,

---

[1536] Hsu, Baring Grievous Wounds, Dry Humor, U.S. Agent Lays Out Key Evidence at Benghazi Trial; Benghazi Committee Report, p. 102; Zuckoff, *13 Hours*, Chap. 12, pp. 255-256 and 259; and Baier, 13 Hours at Benghazi: The Inside Story (*Watch video there*; Go to 24:48 - 25:12).

[1537] Benghazi Committee Report, p. 102; Zuckoff, *13 Hours*, Chap. 12, pp. 255-256 and 259; and Baier, 13 Hours at Benghazi: The Inside Story (*Watch video there*; Go to 24:48 - 25:12).

[1538] Zuckoff, *13 Hours*, Chap. 12, p. 258.

[1539] Benghazi Committee Report (Redacted), pp. 102-103; Zuckoff, *13 Hours*, Chap. 12, pp. 259-260; Baier, 13 Hours at Benghazi: The Inside Story (*Watch video there*; Go to 25:12-38); and Hsu, Baring Grievous Wounds, Dry Humor, U.S. Agent Lays Out Key Evidence at Benghazi Trial.

THE TRUE ACCOUNT OF VALOR AND ABANDONMENT

Engage! Get your rifle up and get into the fight![1540] Oz does not realize it yet, but the first rooftop mortar shell has severely injured his left arm. His forearm literally is blown apart, though oddly he feels no pain yet. Oz's bloody left wrist and hand are dangling by a thread of muscle, hanging at a ninety-degree angle to his arm. Despite this, he valiantly attempts to use his enfeebled limb to try to help aim his automatic rifle to return fire at the attackers. But his left hand "flops uselessly" and cannot grab the gun barrel![1541]

Oz no longer can see Dave Ubben through the thick smoke the mortar shell has left behind.[1542]

KABOOM! A second mortar blast strikes the roof of Building C. "It released a blinding white ball of light."[1543] Through the smoke, over his right shoulder Oz sees Glen Doherty lying face-down on the concrete roof some four to five steps away. Initially, Oz is unsure if Bub is hit or merely is taking cover. Desperately wanting to get Building C back into the fight, Oz tries once more to employ his useless limb to steady the barrel of his weapon. Again he fails.[1544]

From atop Building A, Tanto watches Oz's heroic efforts to use his mangled arm and rejoin the battle. (Tanto later describes Oz's actions as "pretty impressive.")[1545]

Down below on the ground, Jack Silva approaches Tig and says he sees no movement on the Building C rooftop where the mortars have landed. Moving quickly in a low combat crouch, Tig heads west toward Building C.[1546]

[1540] Zuckoff, *13 Hours*, Chap. 12, p. 261; and Baier, 13 Hours at Benghazi: The Inside Story (*Watch video there*; Go to 25:18-42).

[1541] Zuckoff, *13 Hours*, Chap. 12, pp. 261-262; Benghazi Committee Report (Redacted), p. 103; Baier, 13 Hours at Benghazi: The Inside Story (*Watch video there*; Go to 25:38-56); and Chang, "Secret Soldiers of Benghazi" Discusses Real-Life Events Behind "*13 Hours*" (*Watch video there*; Go to 5:32-48), showing clip of *13 Hours: The Secret Soldiers of Benghazi* (Paramount, 2016).

[1542] Zuckoff, *13 Hours*, Chap. 12, p. 261.

[1543] *Id.*, Chap. 12, p. 262.

[1544] *Id.*, Chap. 12, p. 262; Benghazi Committee Report (Redacted), pp. 102-103; and Baier, 13 Hours at Benghazi: The Inside Story (*Watch video there*; Go to 25:54 - 26:08).

[1545] Interview of Kris "Tanto" Paronto and Other GRS Agents with Megyn Kelly, "The Kelly File," Fox News Channel (Possibly Jan. 4, 2016) (*Watch video there*; Go to 14:12-36).

[1546] Zuckoff, *13 Hours*, Chap. 12, p. 266; and Baier, 13 Hours at Benghazi: The Inside Story (*Watch video there*; Go to 26:41 - 27:20).

Moments later, ***KABOOM!*** A third mortar shell hits the roof. Oz is blasted with shrapnel. He later describes it to the Select Committee: "... [I]t felt like I got stung by a thousand bees."[1547] Oz has a hole in his neck, and several in his chest from the shrapnel. In addition to his badly wounded arm, he has numerous other, somewhat less serious shrapnel wounds up and down his side and elsewhere on his body as well.[1548] Dave Ubben later will testify a mortar round landed "very close. I could feel the heat from the blast. It was intensely painful. A lot of light."[1549]

A total of three, 81-millimeter mortar shells have discharged within a small area on this rooftop in quick succession.[1550] As discussed in the following chapter, they are not the work of amateurs.

Oz dives down behind the low wall around the roof. He has given up on his useless left arm and hand. Oz forces himself into a sitting position and moves awkwardly toward Rone. Oz tries in vain to find a pulse in Rone's femoral artery.[1551]

Then Oz realizes he had better deal with his own bleeding. He pulls out a one-piece combat tourniquet from the inside of his tactical vest and unsuccessfully begins attempting to put it on his injured arm with his remaining good hand.[1552]

One last mortar round lands near the north perimeter wall, but mercifully inflicts no further casualties.[1553] Annex video footage of the

---

[1547] Benghazi Committee Report, p. 102; Zuckoff, *13 Hours*, Chap. 12, pp. 262-263; and Baier, 13 Hours at Benghazi: The Inside Story (*Watch video there*; Go to 26:08-16).

[1548] Benghazi Committee Report (Redacted), pp. 103 and 106; Zuckoff, *13 Hours*, Chap. 12, pp. 262-263; and Baier, 13 Hours at Benghazi: The Inside Story (*Watch video there*; Go to 28:28-36).

[1549] Hsu, Baring Grievous Wounds, Dry Humor, U.S. Agent Lays Out Key Evidence at Benghazi Trial.

[1550] Benghazi Committee Report (Redacted), p. 103; and Hsu, Baring Grievous Wounds, Dry Humor, U.S. Agent Lays Out Key Evidence at Benghazi Trial (Criminal trial testimony of Dave Ubben: "They all seemed to land within meters of each other, in an area the size of maybe that conference table").

[1551] Zuckoff, *13 Hours*, Chap. 12, pp. 262-263; Benghazi Committee Report, p. 102; and Baier, 13 Hours at Benghazi: The Inside Story (*Watch video there*; Go to 26:14-18).

[1552] Benghazi Committee Report, p. 102; and Baier, 13 Hours at Benghazi: The Inside Story (*Watch video there*; Go to 28:00-10).

[1553] Benghazi Committee Report (Redacted), p. 103.

fight later will reveal all six mortar blasts occur within a span of just one minute and thirteen seconds.[1554]

Mysteriously, shortly after the sixth and final mortar round hits, the small arms gunfire from Zombieland and elsewhere outside the Annex compound suddenly ceases. The battlefield goes silent.[1555] For some unknown reason, the terrorists do not press the advantage their devastating mortar barrage on the Annex has created. They abandon the initiative.[1556] Are they out of mortar shells? Are they concerned pro-American militia units having heard the noise of the battle soon will appear and counterattack them? Now that it's getting light, are they worried U.S. warplanes will arrive and smite them from above? (Fat chance on that one.)

The militants have lost many men this night. Perhaps they feel they have bloodied the Americans enough to commemorate adequately the memory of 9/11. Astonishingly, the third and final firefight at the Annex is over as rapidly as it starts. It has lasted for only about eleven minutes.[1557] But it has inflicted a grievous toll on the Americans.

Up on the roof of Building C, the wounded Oz Geist still does not know what Dave Ubben's status is. In fact, the mortar attack has severely wounded Ubben. His lower right leg is "mostly severed." He tries but fails to apply a tourniquet to the leg from his medical kit. He later testifies "I went and looked at my left arm, and I had a grapefruit-sized chunk taken out above the elbow. . . ."[1558]

After seeing and hearing the explosions atop Building C and hearing Jack Silva's concern, Tig hurries up the ladder to that rooftop. (He later expresses his surprise the whole building has not collapsed under the mortar hits.) Through the smoke the badly-wounded Oz sees Tig climb onto the roof. Tig – a trained medic – first places two tourniquets on Dave Ubben, one on his leg and one on his arm. Tig is alarmed both nearly are severed. Tig radios to the men below for help for the injured men on the roof. Then Tig moves over to Oz. He grabs Oz's tourniquet

---

[1554] *Id.*, p. 103.

[1555] *Id.*, p. 102.

[1556] Baier, 13 Hours at Benghazi: The Inside Story.

[1557] Sen. Intelligence Committee Benghazi Report, p. 9; CBS Benghazi Timeline; and Key Delays Appendix (See September 11 entries for 11:15 p.m. and 11:26 p.m., both Washington time).

[1558] Hsu, Baring Grievous Wounds, Dry Humor, U.S. Agent Lays Out Key Evidence at Benghazi Trial; Zuckoff, *13 Hours*, Chap. 12, p. 262; and Benghazi Committee Report (Redacted), p. 103.

from him and puts it on the injured man's arm. *Ahhhhhh!!!*, Oz yells out in reaction to the excruciating pain! Tig very likely has saved the lives of both men.[1559]

Tig helps Oz stand. He asks if Oz can make it off the roof under his own power, so Tig can attend to the fallen Rone Woods and Glen Doherty. (Tig and Oz do not yet know both men are deceased.) The gutsy former-Marine Geist answers affirmatively, although he is in very bad shape.[1560]

A bloody, badly wounded and exhausted Oz somehow manages to make his way over the top of the ladder and down the rungs by himself. He nearly slips, but catches himself with his good arm. As Oz lands, he literally falls on top of a "CIA agent" (apparently a GRS agent from Team Tripoli) who is waiting to ascend the ladder to aid the injured on the roof.[1561] While Oz is on the ground, small arms fire from the attackers resumes. The CIA man drags Oz around a corner to protect him from the bullets. The CIA agent places new tourniquets on Oz's bleeding left arm. Then, Oz is helped inside Building C by the GRS agent from Team Tripoli. Oz tells the staff present Ubben is wounded up on the roof and needs help. Oz is placed on a table in the living room area. He knows he is bleeding, and asks the people around him to cut his clothes off to check his wounds. No new serious injuries are discovered, although Oz is bleeding from many small wounds. Several present patch Oz's shrapnel wounds, and then start an IV.[1562]

Meanwhile up on the roof, after getting Oz up and walking Tig quickly moves over to the still body of Rone Woods. He rolls Rone over, but there is no response. Tig removes Rone's body armor and feels for a pulse. He finds none. Tig shines his flashlight into Rone's eyes, but sees no dilation or pupil movement. Tig next puts his ear to Rone's chest, but senses no movement, hears no heartbeat. Rone is

---

[1559] Benghazi Committee Report (Redacted), pp. 102-103; Interview of Mark "Oz" Geist and Other GRS Agents with Megyn Kelly, "The Kelly File," Fox News Channel (Possibly Jan. 4, 2016) (*Watch video there*; Go to 13:47 - 14:02); and Baier, 13 Hours at Benghazi: The Inside Story (*Watch video there*; Go to 26:52-58 and 27:16 - 28:22).

[1560] Benghazi Committee Report (Redacted), pp. 102-103; and Baier, 13 Hours at Benghazi: The Inside Story (*Watch video there*; Go to 28:22-38).

[1561] Benghazi Committee Report (Redacted), pp. 103 and 106; and Baier, 13 Hours at Benghazi: The Inside Story (*Watch video there*; Go to 28:38 - 29:02).

[1562] Benghazi Committee Report (Redacted), pp. 103 and 106.

THE TRUE ACCOUNT OF VALOR AND ABANDONMENT

gone. Tig says a brief prayer for Rone: "God watch over him; guide him to where he needs to be; take care of his family."[1563]

Tig rises and swiftly moves over to the other prone man. He repeats the same procedure on Bub Doherty, and receives the same tragic results. He says a similar prayer for Doherty.[1564]

Tig knows both brave men are dead.[1565]

The two soldiers on Team Tripoli (known as the "D-Boys" for "Delta Force") now have appeared on the rooftop. They attempt to clear it quickly. None of the defenders can know whether more mortar rounds are coming. They must assume they are. Tig swiftly gathers up the weapons of the fallen and wounded. With great difficulty, some defenders who have arrived on the roof carry the badly-wounded Dave Ubben to the ladder. Despite Ubben's large size (six-foot-four-inches, 220 pounds), one of the men wearing full combat gear straps Ubben to his back and makes the difficult trek, somehow carrying Ubben down the ladder. He likely saves the injured man's life.[1566]

Down below inside Building C, Oz is moved to a couch to make room for Dave on a table in the living room area. There, tourniquets are applied, and Dave is given an IV and morphine for his intense pain. A shrapnel wound on Ubben's neck also is dressed. The Team Tripoli member who is treating Ubben and Oz calls the Americans in Tripoli and requests blood because "I didn't think he [Ubben] was going to make it much longer."[1567] (Presumably, he is asking personnel in Tripoli to locate a source in Benghazi for a blood transfusion.) By this time, the living room floor of Building C is bathed in the blood of Geist and Ubben.[1568]

[1563] Baier, 13 Hours at Benghazi: The Inside Story (*Watch video there*; Go to 29:42 - 30:02).

[1564] *Id.* (*Watch video there*; Go to 29:08 - 30:02).

[1565] As Tig Tiegen later will explain, such deaths of private U.S. security contractors are far from rare. According to Tiegen, between 2001 and 2016, some 3,500 contractors are killed. Tig adds that in 2013 alone, more security contractors are killed than active duty U.S. military personnel. *13 Hours: The Secret Soldiers of Benghazi*, Extra Features DVD, "Uncovering Benghazi's Secret Soldiers" (Paramount, 2016). Tig's colleague Oz Geist and his wife later will found a nonprofit organization "Shadow Warriors" to support wounded contractors and their families.

[1566] Hicks Oversight Committee Testimony (May 8, 2013), pp. 28-29; and Hsu, Baring Grievous Wounds, Dry Humor, U.S. Agent Lays Out Key Evidence at Benghazi Trial.

[1567] Benghazi Committee Report (Redacted), pp. 103 and 106-107.

[1568] Zuckoff, *13 Hours*, Chap. 13, p. 281.

One individual appears to have provided most of the treatment to Dave and Oz in Building C after the attacks. (Although the Select Committee report is confusing on his identity, it likely is a GRS agent on Team Tripoli.) The Select Committee later asks him whether he believes Ubben or Geist would have made it to Tripoli alive without his intervention. The witness responds, "No."[1569]

It is 5:32 a.m. in Benghazi. By now, the CIA Annex staff have reported the deadly mortar attacks to Tripoli, and have requested a medical evacuation.[1570]

Given the threat of mortar attacks resuming, the D-Boys decide to remove the bodies of the two deceased men from Building C's rooftop as expeditiously as possible. To the shock of the other Americans present, the D-Boys pick up the two bodies and unceremoniously dump them over the short wall around the roof. The heroes' remains land on the ground with a horrible, sickening "thump," jarring all who witness it. It is something no one ever wants to behold.[1571] ∎

[1569] Benghazi Committee Report (Redacted), pp. 106-108.

[1570] *Id.*, p. 105.

[1571] Baier, 13 Hours at Benghazi: The Inside Story (*Watch video there*; Go to 30:02-58).

79

Ambush

There is considerable reason to suspect the deadly mortar barrages at the CIA Annex are a planned ambush, not a mere coincidence in timing or part of an "attack at dawn" strategy.

The (unnamed) Libyan Shield sub-commander who is stranded at the Annex later tells Reuters he believes the attackers are aware Team Tripoli has been delayed at the airport while they seek transport into Benghazi. He suggests the attackers may have waited until the Tripoli party arrives at the Annex before launching their onslaught on the Americans:

> It began to rain down on us. I really believe that this attack was planned. The accuracy with which the mortars hit us was too good for any regular revolutionaries.[1572]

According to the Select Committee, one of the GRS members on Team Tripoli told the CIA in an after-action interview he was "100% confident that the enemy was waiting for the QRF [Quick Reaction Force] to arrive at the Annex so they could hit them upon arrival."[1573] Given the timing of the attack just minutes after Team Tripoli's arrival at the Annex, it is difficult to dismiss this. He also is "confident it was a well-trained mortar team that hit the [Annex] compound."[1574]

One of the two U.S. military personnel on Team Tripoli reaches a similar conclusion. He later testifies:

> I would say personally that it was probably a skilled mortar team. It's not easy. And you, being a trained mortar man,

---

[1572] Benghazi Committee Report (Redacted), pp. 103-104, citing Hadeel Al Shalchi, "Libya Rescue Squad Ran Into Fierce, Accurate Ambush," Reuters (Sept. 12, 2012) (". . . [T]wo Libyan officials, including the commander of a security force which escorted the U.S. rescuers, said a later assault on a supposedly safe refuge for the diplomats appeared professionally executed"). This Reuters article contains numerous factual errors, but so do most contemporaneous accounts of the tragedy. See CBS Benghazi Timeline ("The precision of the attacks indicates a level of sophistication and coordination").

[1573] Benghazi Committee Report, p. 105, citing CIA Document No. 1-004067, p. 71.

[1574] *Id.*, p. 105, citing CIA Document No. 1-004067, p. 71.

know how hard that would be to shoot inside the city and get something on the target within two shots. That's difficult. I would say they were definitely a trained mortar team or had been trained to do something similar to that. . . . I was kind of surprised. I had not heard of or seen anybody or talked to anyone that had been trained on mortars at all [during my time in Tripoli]. So it was unusual.[1575]

Dave Ubben, who is severely wounded by the mortars, agrees the mortar team was well-trained.[1576]

The Senate Select Intelligence Committee report reaches this conclusion: "The mortar fire was particularly accurate, demonstrating a lethal capability and sophistication that changed the dynamic on the ground that night."[1577]

This obvious mortar proficiency can yield only one conclusion: the mortar strikes are not fired by spontaneous protestors.[1578] Instead, they likely are a preplanned ambush. Indeed, one unidentified witness who was within the CIA Annex (called "Officer A") tells the Select Benghazi Committee that accused terrorist Abu Khatallah is present during this mortar attack on the Annex. Indeed, Officer A claims Khatallah is standing next to the individual who is directing the mortar launcher![1579] According to the Select Committee's Report, standing with Khatallah is Wissam bin Hamid, the commander of the same Libyan Shield militia that has escorted Team Tripoli from the airport to the Annex![1580] (Recall from Chapter 28 Khatallah also has been placed

---

[1575] *Id.*, p. 105. See also Hicks Oversight Committee Testimony (May 8, 2013) ("The accuracy was terribly precise"), p. 28.

[1576] Hsu, Baring Grievous Wounds, Dry Humor, U.S. Agent Lays Out Key Evidence at Benghazi Trial (Summarizing Dave Ubben's testimony in convicted terrorist Abu Khatallah's criminal trial: "The tight pattern [of the mortar landings], he testified, and the timing of the strikes moments after a CIA security contractor team arrived from the airport . . . suggested a precision attack by well-trained adversaries using targeting equipment").

[1577] Sen. Intelligence Committee Benghazi Report, p. 9.

[1578] Babbin, Whitewashing Benghazi (summarizing the conclusion of a former Navy ordinance expert: ". . . [T]he mortar attack could not have been accomplished by random demonstrators"); and Attkisson, *Stonewalled* (referencing "the incredibly skilled mortar hits that landed on the CIA annex – too precise to be lucky or spontaneous"), Chap. 4, p. 208.

[1579] Benghazi Committee Report, p. 104.

[1580] *Id.*, pp. 104-105 (Summarizing testimony of Officer A: "Wissam bin Hamid was standing with Abu Khattala [sic] during the attack . . .").

THE TRUE ACCOUNT OF VALOR AND ABANDONMENT

at the initial attack on the Mission Compound.) As explained below, as this book goes to press Khatallah will be one of only two persons ever apprehended for the Benghazi terror attacks. However, *The Washington Post* reports that during his criminal trial prosecutors will concede Khatallah was home by the time the mortar attack on the Annex occurs![1581] (Yet another of many discrepancies in the evidence regarding Benghazi. This is perhaps one reason Khatallah will be acquitted of most terrorism charges, as discussed in Chapter 114.)

The lack of any air support throughout the Battle of Benghazi also may have played a role with respect to these mortar attacks. Some of the surviving GRS operators believe air support might have prevented the deadly mortar assault. For example, in a 2014 interview, Oz Geist asserts, "Would it [air support] have improved our chances? Oh heck, yeah."[1582]

The American deaths and injuries at the Annex in the final mortar barrage occur more than *seven and one-half hours* after the initial attack on the Mission Compound.[1583] The Select Committee later concludes:

> What was disturbing from the evidence the Committee found was that at the time of the final lethal attack at the Annex, no asset ordered deployed by the Secretary had even left the ground. Not a single asset had launched, save the military personnel from Tripoli who did so on their own accord and whose presence no one in Washington seemed aware of when discussing which assets to deploy. Nothing was on its way to Benghazi as a result of the Secretary's initial order to deploy. . . .[1584]

Committee Chairman Trey Gowdy (R-SC) asserts, "[N]othing was en route to Libya at the time the last two Americans were killed almost eight hours after the attacks began."[1585]

[1581] Hsu, Baring Grievous Wounds, Dry Humor, U.S. Agent Lays Out Key Evidence at Benghazi Trial.

[1582] Baier, 13 Hours at Benghazi: The Inside Story (*Watch video there*; Go to 36:24 - 37:02).

[1583] Key Delays Appendix (See September 11 entries for 3:42 p.m. and 11:15 p.m., both Washington time).

[1584] Benghazi Committee Report, p. 124.

[1585] Fox News, House Republicans Fault US Military Response to Benghazi.

(Had Obama, Panetta, and the U.S. military sent air (or other) assets immediately when – or even soon after – the initial assault first commenced, could the two dead and two wounded American heroes have been saved at the Annex? We will never know.[1586] But it should have been *tried*.[1587] Instead, other than Team Tripoli, no serious rescue mission for the Americans in Benghazi even is commenced by the U.S. tonight. Should "dereliction of duty" be hyphenated?[1588]) ∎

[1586] Benjamin Bell, "Gregory Hicks: Hearing of Death of Christopher Stevens 'Saddest Moment' in My Career," ABC News online (Sept. 8, 2013) (Interview of Gregory Hicks with ABC's George Stephanopoulos) (*Watch video there*; Go to 8:20-40) (Gregory Hicks: "Sadly, I think that Ambassador Stevens and Sean Smith, maybe not. Ty and Glen of course were killed in the mortar attacks that took place eight hours after the initial attack. It's possible they could have been saved, I think").

[1587] Additional Views of Reps. Jordan and Pompeo ("The American people expect their government to make every effort to help those we put in harm's way when they find themselves in trouble. . . ."), p. 416; and National Review Editors, What We Do Know About the Benghazi Attack Demands a Reckoning (". . . Obama and his subordinates never even tried to relieve the Americans under attack. It is not that rescue craft turned around once reports led them to believe it was too late to get to Benghazi; they never left the ground in the first place").

[1588] National Review Editors, What We Do Know About the Benghazi Attack Demands a Reckoning (". . . [T]he [Select Committee majority] report is a devastating account of staggering dereliction of duty and deception by the president and his top subordinates. . . .").

80

"Bigger Balls Than the Military"

In addition to Team Tripoli, there are other American military servicemen *in Tripoli* who want to help their comrades in Benghazi this night. However, they will be one of three groups of Americans (along with Team Annex and F.E.S.T.) who *effectively* are ordered to "stand down" and not ride to the rescue in Benghazi.

This third group consists of four U.S. special forces military personnel stationed in Tripoli. As noted above, they are part of the American Embassy's "training mission."[1589] (They previously had been assigned to the SST, whose other members are withdrawn from Libya in mid-August. The four have remained behind in Libya with orders to help train local Libyan guards.) These four special operators are under General Carter Ham's AFRICOM command (not that of the Chief-of-Mission at Embassy Tripoli).[1590] Tonight they are helping Greg Hicks and his staff relocate the U.S. Embassy personnel to a separate annex location.[1591] Again, the Defense Secretary has not been made aware of their presence in Tripoli.

Sometime in the early morning hours of September 12 (after the U.S. learns Ambassador Stevens is deceased, which likely occurs around 4:05 a.m., Benghazi time), the Libyan military finally makes an offer of help. In response to the repeated pleas of U.S. Defense Attaché Lt. Col. Phillips in Tripoli, the Libyans agree to fly a C-130 aircraft from Tripoli to Benghazi "to carry additional personnel to Benghazi as reinforcements."[1592] Greg Hicks recalls this offer comes before the final mortar attack on the CIA Annex.[1593]

[1589] Hicks Oversight Committee Testimony (May 8, 2013), p. 29; and Benghazi Committee Report, pp. 70 and 109.

[1590] Hicks Oversight Committee Testimony (May 8, 2013) (Response to questions of Chairman Issa (R-CA)), p. 53.

[1591] Pentagon Press Release, "DOD Cooperates with Congress on Benghazi Probes."

[1592] Attkisson, Diplomat: U.S. Special Forces Told "You Can't Go" to Benghazi During Attacks; and Hicks Oversight Committee Testimony (May 8, 2013), p. 29.

[1593] Attkisson, Diplomat: U.S. Special Forces Told "You Can't Go" to Benghazi During Attacks (Gregory Hicks to congressional investigators: ". . . [T]he Libyan

A short while later, *after* they learn of the fatal mortar attack in Benghazi, Greg Hicks and his team in Tripoli (now at an annex) decide to send more help to the besieged Americans in Benghazi. As Hicks later testifies: "Again, we determined that we needed to send a second team from Tripoli *to secure the airport* for the withdrawal of our personnel from Benghazi *after the mortar attack.*"[1594] This decision likely is made sometime just before 5:30 a.m. Tripoli and Benghazi time.

The four U.S. special forces soldiers in Tripoli want to take this C-130 flight to Benghazi to aid the besieged Americans there.[1595] Initially, Hicks considers also sending Jackie Levesque, the Embassy's nurse, to Benghazi on the flight. But he will change his mind. Instead, he orders her to go to a nearby hospital where she has made valuable contacts. There, she will coordinate with the facility's emergency medical staff to prepare to treat any wounded among the Benghazi evacuees when (and if) they arrive in Tripoli.[1596]

This four-man special forces team in Tripoli is commanded by Lieutenant Colonel S. E. Gibson. Greg Hicks later testifies in May 2013 that he and Lt. Col. Gibson believe it is important for the special forces troops to get to Benghazi tonight because "the people in Benghazi had been fighting all night; they were tired, they were exhausted. *We wanted to make sure the [Benghazi] airport was secure for their withdrawal.*"[1597]

---

military agreed to fly their C-130 to Benghazi and carry additional personnel to Benghazi as reinforcements. . . . [A]t that time, the third attack, the mortar attack at 5:15 [a.m.], had not yet occurred, if I remember correctly").

[1594] Hicks Oversight Committee Testimony (May 8, 2013) (emphasis added) (Response to questions of Rep. Jason Chaffetz (R-UT)), p. 35.

[1595] Hicks Oversight Committee Testimony (May 8, 2013), p. 29; Attkisson, Diplomat: U.S. Special Forces Told "You Can't Go" to Benghazi During Attacks; and Hayes, U.S. Military in Tripoli Ordered Not to Go to Benghazi.

[1596] Hicks Oversight Committee Testimony (May 8, 2013), p. 29.

[1597] *Id.* (emphasis added), p. 29; and *Id.* (Response to questions of Rep. Turner (R-OH)) (". . . There was every reason to continue to believe that our personnel [in Benghazi] were in danger"), p. 52. See also Attkisson, Diplomat: U.S. Special Forces Told "You Can't Go" to Benghazi During Attacks (Greg Hicks: "We fully intended for those guys [four Special Forces] to go, because we had already essentially stripped ourselves of our security presence, or our security capability to the bare minimum. . . ."); and *Id.* ("The account from Gregory Hicks is in stark contrast to assertions from the Obama administration, which insisted that nobody was ever told to stand down and that all available resources were utilized").

(Throughout the crisis, American military leaders repeatedly appear to ignore this latter imperative of securing the Benina airport. They blithely *assume* it is secure. In reality, as discussed below, there will be a confrontation between two armed militia groups at the Benghazi airport early this Wednesday morning – including the group that will escort the evacuating Americans to the airport. Fortuitously, it will not escalate to a gunfight.)

The Libyan C-130 is scheduled to depart for Benghazi at around 6:00 or 6:30 a.m. Libyan time. (Recall this C-130 is restricted to daylight operations. Sunrise is at 6:22 a.m.[1598]) The four special forces soldiers are on their way to enter the vehicles they plan to take to Mitiga airport in Tripoli, where the C-130 is waiting. (The exact timing of these events is unclear. They likely occur sometime around or just after 5:30 a.m.) One of Gibson's soldiers has a broken foot in a cast, and limps toward the vehicle carrying a machine gun on his shoulder. Injured foot and all, he willingly is marching toward the sound of the guns. He is the last of the Embassy's military-trained medics.[1599] (Too bad his superiors at the Pentagon and in Stuttgart lack his fortitude.)

A May 2013 Pentagon press release will explain that, apparently during this time period, Lt. Col. Gibson calls Special Operations Command – Africa. Gibson tells his superiors his team has completed helping move U.S. Embassy personnel to the Tripoli annex. He also advises them of "his intention to move his team to Benghazi aboard a Libyan C-130."[1600] Then, according to Greg Hicks, Gibson tells the former the small special forces team has been told *they are "not authorized" to board the flight to Benghazi!*[1601] Hicks later tells investigators, "They were told not to board the flight, so they missed

---

[1598] Benghazi Committee Report, p. 55.

[1599] Hicks Oversight Committee Testimony (May 8, 2013), p. 29.

[1600] Pentagon Press Release, "DOD Cooperates with Congress on Benghazi Probes."

[1601] Hicks Oversight Committee Testimony (May 8, 2013), p. 29; *Id.* (Response to questions of Rep. Jason Chaffetz (R-UT)), pp. 33-34; *Id.* (Response to questions of Rep. Ron DeSantis (R-FL)), p. 95; CNN Report, Why Didn't the U.S. Military Respond in Time in Benghazi? (*Watch video there*; Go to 2:33-51); and Interview of Former U.S. Ambassador to the United Nations John Bolton with Jonathan Hunt, "On the Hunt," Fox News Channel (Circa May 2013) (*Watch video there*; Go to 4:22-33). See also Griffin, CIA Operators Were Denied Request for Help During Benghazi Attack (". . . Fox News has also learned that two separate Tier One Special operations forces were told to wait, among them Delta Force operators").

it."[1602] Investigative journalist Sharyl Attkisson reports this "stand down" command is given to Gibson during this telephone call with SOCAFRICA.[1603] Hicks – who is now the top U.S. diplomat in Libya – apparently is not given an explanation for this denial of authorization.[1604]

For the remainder of the entire Benghazi saga, the Obama administration largely will pretend this event never happens. However, according to the Democrat-controlled Senate Intelligence Committee, the Pentagon concedes it *did* happen.[1605] So does Obama and Clinton defender Elijah Cummings (D-MD) (later Ranking Member of the Select Benghazi Committee).[1606] In May 2013 the Pentagon itself confirms this incident occurs during the crisis.

According to Hicks, Lt. Col. Gibson is "furious" about the directive not to deploy.[1607] Hicks testifies, "I had told him to go bring our people home. That's what he wanted to do."[1608] Gibson tells Hicks, "I have never been so embarrassed in my life that a State Department officer [Hicks] has bigger balls than somebody in the military."[1609]

[1602] Hicks Oversight Committee Testimony (May 8, 2013) (Response to questions of Rep. Turner (R-OH): ". . . Lieutenant Colonel Gibson said, he was not to proceed to board the airplane"), p. 52; Attkisson, Diplomat: U.S. Special Forces Told "You Can't Go" to Benghazi During Attacks; Hayes, U.S. Military in Tripoli Ordered Not to Go to Benghazi; and Statement of Senators McCain, Graham and Ayotte.

[1603] Attkisson, Diplomat: U.S. Special Forces Told "You Can't Go" to Benghazi During Attacks.

[1604] Hicks Oversight Committee Testimony (May 8, 2013) (Response to questions of Rep. Robin Kelly (D-IL): "I have no idea why . . . they were not allowed to go get on that airplane"), p. 68.

[1605] Sen. Intelligence Committee Benghazi Report (Redacted) (". . . According to the DoD, the four staff under SOC-AFRICA were told by their command to stay to protect Embassy Tripoli due to concerns of a similar attack in Tripoli"), p. 29.

[1606] House Oversight Committee Hearings (May 8, 2013) (Opening Remarks of Ranking Member Elijah Cummings (D-MD)) (". . . The decision the next morning to keep four military personnel in place in Tripoli was not made by the White House or the State Department, but by the military chain of command"), p. 5.

[1607] Hicks Oversight Committee Testimony (May 8, 2013), p. 29; and Scott Shane, Jeremy W. Peters and Eric Schmitt, "Diplomat Says Questions Over Benghazi Led to Demotion," *The New York Times* online (May 8, 2013).

[1608] Hicks Oversight Committee Testimony (May 8, 2013), p. 29.

[1609] *Id.* (Response to questions of Rep. Jason Chaffetz (R-UT)), p. 36; Attkisson, Diplomat: U.S. Special Forces Told "You Can't Go" to Benghazi During Attacks; Hayes, U.S. Military in Tripoli Ordered Not to Go to Benghazi; and Eli Lake,

Greg Hicks is not told at the time who orders Gibson and his men to "stand down." He knows only the order issues from SOCAFRICA.[1610] However, we learn later this "stay in Tripoli" order is given to Gibson by his superior officer, Marine Corps Colonel George Bristol, also of Africa Command. Specifically, Bristol is Commander of Joint Special Operations Task Force – Trans Sahara (also located in Stuttgart, Germany). At the time Bristol speaks with Gibson, the former is in Dakar, Senegal.[1611] According to Fox News, Bristol (who reportedly will not be under oath) later tells a classified briefing of the House Armed Services Committee no one else tells him to give this order, it is his decision alone. Colonel Bristol explains to the committee he wants Gibson and his other three men to stay in Tripoli to help protect *the Embassy* (which is not then under attack and in fact already has been evacuated), and to assist survivors "being evacuated" from Benghazi. (Well, not quite yet; at this point, it is unknown whether there will *be* any survivors.)[1612]

However, the official then in charge of this Embassy – Hicks – as well as the CIA Chief of Station in Tripoli both want Gibson and his team to go to Benghazi! Why should *Bristol's* preference control over that of Hicks, who since 3:00 a.m. in Benghazi has been the new Chief of Mission at the Tripoli Embassy? SOCAFRICA's job is to protect the CIA and State personnel in Tripoli, but the local heads of both agencies want the SOCAFRICA team to go to *Benghazi!*

Later, on May 8, 2013 (purely coincidentally, just in time for a House Oversight hearing that day) the Pentagon issues a press release attempting to explain why these four special ops soldiers are ordered

---

"Benghazi Whistleblower: Requests for Military Backup Denied," *The Daily Beast* online website (May 6, 2013).

[1610] Hicks Oversight Committee Testimony (May 8, 2013) (Response to questions of Rep. Ron DeSantis (R-FL)), pp. 95-96; and *Id.* (Response to questions of Ranking Member Elijah Cummings (D-MD)), p. 100.

[1611] Sharyl Attkisson, "Republicans Want to Talk to Col. George Bristol About Benghazi," CBS News online (July 6, 2013); and Rosen, Top Defense Officials Briefed Obama on "Attack" Not Video or Protest.

[1612] Report of James Rosen, "The O'Reilly Factor," Fox News Channel (July 31, 2013). See also House Oversight Committee Hearings (May 8, 2013) (Opening Remarks of Ranking Member Elijah Cummings (D-MD)); and Sen. Intelligence Committee Benghazi Report (Redacted) ("... According to the DoD, the four staff under SOC-AFRICA were told by their command to stay to protect Embassy Tripoli due to concerns of a similar attack in Tripoli"), p. 29.

not to go to Benghazi. The release, quoting Pentagon Press Secretary George Little, states:
> By this time, the mission in Benghazi had shifted to evacuation. The higher command [at Special Operations Command - Africa operations center] directed the team leader [Gibson] "to continue *providing support* to *the embassy in Tripoli*. . . . We continue to believe there was nothing this team could have done to assist *during the second attack* in Benghazi. . . ."[1613]

(No doubt by "second attack" the Pentagon means the final mortar attack. But this is a red herring. Gibson's team is not asked to go to Benghazi until *after* that "second attack" is over. And there is "nothing to do" in Benghazi except help secure the airport against militias for the Americans' safe departure.

(Oh, and there is another small problem: as noted, by about 4:30 a.m. on the morning of September 12 *all of the U.S. personnel already have been evacuated from the U.S. Embassy in Tripoli!* The Embassy is empty.[1614] (*Ooops!*) Perhaps Bristol and the Defense Department both *mean* Gibson's men must stay to protect the U.S. *annex* in Tripoli, to which the Embassy staff have relocated. But this is not what they *say*. Does the U.S. military's performance this night justify according it the benefit of this doubt?

(Bristol supposedly will retire from the military in March 2013 after a 38-year career. Republicans in Congress investigating Benghazi understandably wish to talk with him, but cannot locate him. They ask the Pentagon for help. The Pentagon will not assist, claiming they "cannot compel retired members to testify before Congress"![1615] (Gee,

---

[1613] Pentagon Press Release, "DOD Cooperates with Congress on Benghazi Probes" (emphasis added); and House Oversight Committee Hearings (May 8, 2013) (Remarks of Rep. Robin Kelly (D-IL), quoting Press Release), p. 68. See also Sharyl Attkisson, "Republicans Want to Talk to Col. George Bristol About Benghazi," CBS News online (July 6, 2013) ("Administration officials contend that Gibson's team was stopped from going to Benghazi simply because it was needed more in Tripoli, and that even if it had flown to Benghazi, it wouldn't have made any difference. . . .").

[1614] See Chapter 73 and Key Delays Appendix (See September 11 entry for 10:45-11:00 p.m., Washington time).

[1615] Sharyl Attkisson, "Republicans Want to Talk to Col. George Bristol About Benghazi," CBS News online (July 6, 2013); and Jeremy Herb, "House to Hear Long-Sought Testimony About Benghazi From Task Force Chief," The Hill online (July 30, 2013) ("Herb, House to Hear Long-Sought Testimony About Benghazi From Task Force Chief") ("The Pentagon told CBS News on July 5 that Bristol, the

thanks a lot.) However, it turns out Bristol's retirement actually isn't finalized after all. He is still on active-duty status. The Pentagon later claims it is all an "administrative error."[1616] (More *Ooops!)* The dogged Select Benghazi Committee later will locate Colonel Bristol and interview him.)

Both Gibson and Bristol reportedly later tell Congress Bristol's directive is not a "stand down" order.[1617] (Seeing a pattern? When your superior officer knows your soldiers are getting on a plane – with weapons – to fly to a battlefield and he orders you not to get on the plane, how is this not effectively a "stand down" order? Apparently, anything short of a directive to "stop breathing" cannot be a "stand down" order. Such is the "Alice in Wonderland" nature of the events unfolding on this Night of Benghazi and its wake.)

The Republican-controlled House Armed Services Committee later will join this fantasy world. In June 2013 it receives testimony from various AFRICOM officers, including Gibson. A subcommittee then issues a press release stating:

> ... Contrary to news reports, Gibson was not ordered to "stand down" by higher command authorities in response to his understandable desire to lead a group of three other Special Forces soldiers to Benghazi. Rather, he was ordered to remain in Tripoli to defend Americans there in anticipation of possible additional attacks, and to assist the survivors as they returned from Benghazi. [At this time, how can they possibly be certain there even will *be* any survivors from Benghazi?] Gibson acknowledged that had he deployed to Benghazi he would have left Americans in Tripoli undefended. [But that's what those Americans *wanted!*] He also stated that *in hindsight*, he would not have been able to get to Benghazi in time to make a difference, and *as it turned*

---

commander of the Joint Special Forces Task Force-Trans Sahara, could not testify because he was retired").

[1616] David Martosko, "Pentagon Does About-Face on Key Benghazi Witness, Makes Marine Colonel Available to Talk to Congress," *Daily Mail* online (July 19, 2013); and Herb, House to Hear Long-Sought Testimony About Benghazi From Task Force Chief.

[1617] E.g., Herb, House to Hear Long-Sought Testimony About Benghazi From Task Force Chief (Gibson not given stand down order).

out his medic was needed to provide urgent assistance to survivors *once they arrived in Tripoli*.[1618] (Isn't "hindsight" wonderful? And if the magic words "stand down" are not uttered, there can be no such conduct. Further, are we supposed to believe this essential medic, if necessary, could not have returned to Tripoli on the same plane as the wounded Americans, during which flight the medic could have provided "urgent assistance" to the two wounded men? It seems reasonably clear that before Gibson speaks with Congress, he has been "re-educated" by his superior officers – likely at the behest of Team Obama.)

Also, someone at Armed Services should coordinate with Democrat Congressman Elijah Cummings, because he admits this "stand down" did happen! He just blames it on the military, not the Obama administration.

It is possible Colonel Bristol's order for Gibson's team to remain in Tripoli is defensible as a matter of military doctrine and tactics. At the same time, Bristol's directive also is consistent with the author's proposed over-arching theme – documented in these pages – that *the U.S. government is determined to send no military rescue assets to Benghazi in a craven attempt to minimize the political significance of the militants' attacks there. And to prevent any military rescue party from meeting a bad ending, as happened in Eagle Claw.*

General Dempsey later testifies to Congress that had these four special ops personnel gone to Benghazi, "they would have simply passed each other in the air."[1619] (This after-the-fact claim is *preposterous!* At the time Bristol orders Gibson and his men to stand down, neither Dempsey nor Bristol nor anyone else in the entire U.S. military command possibly can know when hostilities in Benghazi will cease, or when (or even if) the surviving Americans will be flying back to Tripoli.[1620] When Gibson's team is ordered at around 5:30 a.m. not to board the Libyan plane, it will be another hour before the Americans in

---

[1618] "Readout of House Armed Services Committee, Subcommittee on Oversight and Investigations Classified Briefing on Benghazi," House Armed Services Committee website (June 26, 2013) (emphasis added).

[1619] CNN Report, Why Didn't the U.S. Military Respond in Time in Benghazi? (*Watch video there*; Go to 2:51-55).

[1620] E.g., Additional Views of Senators Chambliss, Burr, et al. (emphasis added) (". . . General Dempsey's attempts to excuse inaction by claiming that forces were not deployed because they would not have gotten there in time does not pass the common sense test. *No one knew when the attacks against our facilities in Benghazi would end*, or how aggressive the attacks would be. . . ."), p. 11.

Benghazi even evacuate the Annex. Indeed, it will be 45 minutes before their "ride" to the airport, the Libyan Military Intelligence militia, even *arrives* at the Annex.[1621] Until that happens *no one* knows how or if the Americans can get to the Benghazi airport. And Dempsey's argument again ignores the imperative of securing the airport until all the Americans – including the second group leaving just before 10:00 a.m. – can evacuate. It is yet more ass-covering.)

Defense Secretary Panetta later will join this misdirection festival. He will claim falsely, "Any suggestion that anyone, from the president on down, *delayed*, or was indifferent to the ambassador and his staff in Benghazi is simply false." In support of his point, Panetta will invent a "straw man" argument – apparently relating to these four Tripoli special forces soldiers. In his memoir, Panetta misleadingly writes:

> One conspiracy theory held that the <u>CIA security team in Tripoli</u> had been ordered by their own chain of command to "stand down." That was not only false but directly the opposite of everyone's efforts in response to the president's orders, which was to move as quickly as possible to help.[1622]

It is not the "CIA security team" in Tripoli that is ordered to "stand down." To the contrary, it is the resourceful CIA Chief of Station in Tripoli who authorizes and organizes the Team Tripoli rescue party. Instead, it is the four special forces *military* personnel in Tripoli who are directed to "stand down" by their *military* commander. As Leon Panetta damned well knows when he authors his memoir, these soldiers are in *his own* chain of command; they do not report to the CIA or Greg Hicks. Also, as discussed above in Chapter 35, the author believes the CIA GRS operators at the Annex in *Benghazi* are in fact also effectively ordered by their CIA Chief of Base to "stand down" at a critical time as the initial assault on the Mission Compound is raging. Of course, thankfully they eventually disobey this directive. (Nice try with your literary sleight of hand, Leon. Panetta's red herring is one of many misdirection plays that will be run from the Team Obama playbook concerning the Benghazi tragedy.)

Of course, as events actually will transpire on the ground in Libya, if the C-130 does not depart for Benghazi until 6:00 a.m. or later, even if they took this flight the four special forces men would indeed be too late even to escort the Americans from the CIA Annex to the airport.

[1621] Key Delays Appendix (See September 11 entry for 11:30 p.m., and September 12 entries for 12:16 a.m., 12:34 a.m., and 12:45 a.m., all Washington time).

[1622] Panetta, *Worthy Fights* (emphasis added), Chap. 16, p. 430.

As Stephen Hayes of *The Weekly Standard* points out, the U.S. officer who gives this order, Colonel Bristol, *cannot possibly know* Gibson and his soldiers will be too late to help battle the militants.[1623]

And to repeat, at a minimum Lt. Col. Gibson and his Tripoli special forces soldiers can provide additional security for Americans at the Benghazi airport as the latter await evacuation. Greg Hicks "thinks" the Libyan C-130 lands in Benghazi about 7:30 a.m.[1624] If correct, this would have provided four more security assets (three if Gibson's medic returns with the wounded) to protect the departing Americans until the last group finally leaves Benghazi at just before 10:00 a.m. Benghazi time (discussed in Chapter 86).

Gibson and his men should be allowed to *try* to help their compatriots in Benghazi. This is yet another of many missed opportunities by the U.S. military on this long, exasperating Night of Benghazi. ∎

[1623] Hayes, U.S. Military in Tripoli Ordered Not to Go to Benghazi ("The team would have likely arrived after the fighting in Benghazi had ended, but those who made the decision not to send them had no way of knowing that when they ordered them to remain in Tripoli").

[1624] Hicks Oversight Committee Testimony (May 8, 2013), p. 29.

81

A White House in the Fog

While Americans in the CIA's Benghazi Annex brace themselves for more mortars and frantically try to stabilize the medical condition of Dave Ubben and Oz Geist, the bureaucrats in Washington continue their incompetence and nonchalance. This is despite the fact that at 11:41 p.m. Washington time (5:41 a.m. in Benghazi), the State Department's Diplomatic Security Command Center has begun to advise officials in D.C. a mortar attack has occurred at the Annex in Benghazi, causing more American casualties.[1625]

Four minutes later, at 11:45 p.m. Washington time, Deputy National Security Advisor Denis McDonough (who earlier chaired the 7:30 Meeting) is still awake and working. (One is not certain this is a positive thing.) McDonough sends an email to numerous high-level Executive Branch officials, including: Ben Rhodes at the National Security Council; Jeremy Bash and Vice Admiral James Winnefeld at the Defense Department; and Jake Sullivan and Wendy Sherman at the State Department.

The purpose of this email is to prepare for yet another interagency teleconference the following morning. (Oh great, just what the Americans in Benghazi need.) The portion of the email referenced by the Select Committee expresses absolutely no sense of urgency (except arguably about removing the anti-Muslim Video from the internet). It contains numerous mistakes and omissions. Eight hours into the crisis McDonough writes:

The situation in Benghazi remains fluid. [Wasn't it "pretty clear" more than two hours earlier everyone would be *gone* from Benghazi by now?] Amb. Chris Stevens remains unaccounted for; *one* State Department officer is confirmed dead ... [then why has Hillary Clinton told her daughter more than a half hour earlier at 11:12 p.m. *two* officers are dead?]; five State Department officers are accounted for and at another USG compound in Benghazi, which had been

---

[1625] Benghazi Committee Report, Select Benghazi Timeline, p. 560.

407

taking fire earlier in the evening (until at least 2030 EDT) [no, not 8:30 p.m., it was until about 7:40 p.m. EDT]. . . . Five DOD personnel [no, it was two DoD personnel and five others from the CIA for a total of seven men on Team Tripoli] arrived in Benghazi about an hour ago [no, they arrived *more than four hours earlier* at 7:30 p.m. Washington time] from Tripoli to reinforce security there.

On our people in *Libya* the Joint Staff *is deploying* three sets of teams into *the region* [but not into *Benghazi*] appropriate to the mission(s).

. . .

And on getting the video(s) in question taken down, I reached [out] to YouTube to ask them to take down two videos. . . . Sec. Panetta has also reached out to Pastor Jones to ask him to pull down his video . . .[1626]

(McDonough may not be a lawyer, but he still is clueless.)

The fatal third attacks on the Annex end at about 11:26 p.m., Washington time, are reported to the Tripoli Embassy at 11:32 p.m., and are known by some in Washington by 11:41 p.m.[1627] However, McDonough obviously has not yet learned of them by the time he sends his 11:45 p.m. email.

Moreover, as noted above, the Select Committee will report that by 10:34 p.m. the State Department's Diplomatic Security Command Center is announcing the Libyans have confirmed Ambassador Stevens is dead at a hospital.[1628] As discussed earlier, at 10:38 p.m. Clinton will send an email stating, "Cheryl [presumably Cheryl Mills, her Chief of Staff] told me the Libyans confirmed his death."[1629] And as also stated above, Hillary Clinton at her home emails her daughter at 11:12 p.m. two Americans have died in Benghazi. Yet by 11:45 p.m. Deputy National Security Advisor McDonough still does not yet know of Stevens' death! (The incompetence is breathtaking!)

McDonough's pathetic, error-ridden and misleading email is sent eight hours into the Battle of Benghazi. It is frightening how

---

[1626] Benghazi Committee Report (emphasis added), pp. 108-109, and Select Benghazi Timeline, p. 560.

[1627] Key Delays Appendix (See September 11 entries for 11:15-19 p.m., 11:32 p.m. and 11:41 p.m., all Washington time).

[1628] Benghazi Committee Report, Select Benghazi Timeline, p. 560.

[1629] *Id.*, p. 560.

THE TRUE ACCOUNT OF VALOR AND ABANDONMENT

ill-informed is the high-level White House official who (as much as anyone) is coordinating the entire United States government's response to the crisis in Benghazi. Perhaps most troubling, *instead of getting a rescue party to Benghazi to save American lives, McDonough and Panetta are negotiating with YouTube and a pastor over damned videos!* Yet, as the Select Committee explains, at the time of McDonough's 11:45 p.m. email ". . . [N]one of the forces the Secretary ordered to deploy had actually moved."[1630] (Imagine how the surviving heroes of Benghazi must feel years later when they learn *that*.)

Very shortly after Denis McDonough sends his mistake-filled email, word of the terrorists' deadly mortar attacks on the CIA Annex in Benghazi spreads through the White House, CIA, and the State and Defense Departments.[1631] This dreadful news is unmistakable evidence the Battle of Benghazi still rages. Yet this shocking intelligence changes *none* of the decisions made at the highest levels of the U.S. government. (It is late; they are tired; some probably are asleep. Why change such a terrific game plan now?) ∎

[1630] Benghazi Committee Report, p. 109.

[1631] *Id.* ("Moments after McDonough sent this email, word of the mortar attacks on the Annex would make its way through the State Department, the White House, and the Defense Department"), p. 109.

82

Americans Evacuate the Annex

After the third firefight ends, it is obvious the CIA Annex has no defense against further mortar attacks. Their predicament has become untenable.

The defenders do not have enough shooters, and have two seriously wounded men. They have no air support. Their plan quickly changes to a complete evacuation of the Annex.[1632] At 6:12 a.m. in Benghazi (12:12 a.m. in Washington, D.C.), speaking of the five surviving State security agents Secretary Clinton's Chief of Staff advises Deputy National Security Advisor Denis McDonough, "[W]e're pulling everyone out of Benghazi."[1633] (*Finally*, the bureaucrats in Washington will be on the same page as their fighters in Benghazi.)

Of course, at this point the State Department cannot possibly know how it will accomplish this. In part this is because the vehicles now at the Annex compound are inadequate to protect the Americans on the trip to the Benghazi airport.

Near miraculously, at 6:16 a.m. (12:16 a.m. in Washington) a 50-vehicle convoy arrives to transport the Americans to Benina airport. Unlike the previous Libyan Shield convoy, this motorcade contains "heavily-armed security vehicles," including a number of "technicals" – pick-up trucks "retrofitted with mounted machine gun-like weapons."[1634] The convoy belongs to a group known as the Libyan Military Intelligence ("LMI"). Remarkably, the CIA (like most other U.S. government personnel) does not even know of LMI's existence until this Night of Benghazi![1635] (Equally bad, in its final report on

---

[1632] Benghazi Committee Report (Redacted), pp. 109-110; Sen. Intelligence Committee Benghazi Report, pp. 8-9; and Hsu, CIA Officers Detail Part of Bloody Benghazi Attack at Terrorism Trial (Criminal trial testimony of disguised CIA agent, pseudonym "Roy Edwards": "Expecting a 'final assault to wipe us out,' . . . the Americans evacuated to the airport").

[1633] Benghazi Committee Report, Select Benghazi Timeline, p. 560.

[1634] Benghazi Committee Report (Redacted), p. 110; and Baier, 13 Hours at Benghazi: The Inside Story (*Watch video there*; Go to 31:51 - 32:24).

[1635] Benghazi Committee Report, p. 111.

THE TRUE ACCOUNT OF VALOR AND ABANDONMENT

Benghazi the House Intelligence Committee is so intelligent it thinks LMI is the Libyan Shield![1636])

Despite its name, LMI has no connection to the current Libyan government. Rather, it is a militia group consisting of former military officers from the late Colonel Qadhafi's government. Until this time, its members have been maintaining a very low profile in Benghazi for fear of being killed by the various anti-Qadhafi militias that dominate the city.[1637] (Why the pro-Qadhafi LMI elects to take this risk for the Americans who overthrew Qadhafi remains a mystery. Perhaps they conclude in the uncertain situation now enveloping chaotic Libya, it may be helpful to have the powerful Americans "owe them one.")

The GRS agents cannot help but ask themselves where this convoy had been several hours ago.[1638] *Significantly, it is not until this LMI contingent appears shortly after midnight Washington time there is a plausible path for a successful evacuation of the surviving Americans.*[1639] This is almost *three hours after* the U.S. military and other government officials in Washington determine it is "pretty clear" no Americans will be left in Benghazi for long.[1640] The Select Committee concludes the LMI "likely" saves dozens of American lives as a result of their rescue.[1641] (Maybe we should let LMI run the Pentagon.)

But LMI has not shown up at the Annex by accident or miracle. Their presence is due to the exceptional efforts and resourcefulness of one of the Annex's CIA case officers (called "Officer A" by the Select Committee). Officer A (who is not named for security reasons) has worked throughout this Night of Benghazi to attempt to reach Libyan government or other groups that may be willing to help the Americans under siege. However, none of the groups the U.S. government has

---

[1636] House Intelligence Committee Benghazi Report (Timeline at 6:33 a.m.: "Libya Shield convoy departs the Annex with all personnel en route to the airport"), p. 6.

[1637] Benghazi Committee Report (Redacted), pp. 110-111.

[1638] Baier, 13 Hours at Benghazi: The Inside Story (*Watch video there*; Go to 32:25-35).

[1639] Benghazi Committee Report ("Despite the 'assurance' some principals in Washington had that U.S. personnel in Benghazi were evacuating earlier, it was not until the rescuing convoy actually arrived . . . at the Annex that the evacuation of all U.S. personnel was fully understood by those on the ground in Benghazi"), p. 111.

[1640] Benghazi Committee Report, pp. 91-92.

[1641] *Id.* (Redacted), pp. 110-111.

spent many months cultivating relationships with during the Libyan revolution have answered the call for help. Not the Libyan government, not the 17 February Brigade, and not the Libyan National Police. *Nobody*.[1642]

However, a contact in the National Police does connect Officer A with a colonel in the LMI. Officer A first speaks with the LMI colonel by phone at about 4:30 a.m. on September 12. The colonel tells Officer A he will need time to put together a force large enough to protect and transport the Americans to the airport. Then, "immediately" after the lethal mortar attacks, Officer A calls the LMI colonel again and says the Americans urgently need the LMI to come to the Annex at once.[1643]

The Select Committee describes the irony of this surprising Libyan rescue force:

> ... This group, ironically, had close ties to the former Qadhafi regime – the very regime the United States had helped remove from power. It was also this group, not groups previously given credit by previous investigations, that came to the rescue of the Americans in those early morning hours – likely saving dozens of lives as a result.[1644]

As the sun peeks over the horizon in Benghazi at 6:22 a.m., at the Annex "non-shooters" are loaded into the "up-armored" LMI vehicles; shooters enter the "thin-skinned vehicles to be able to fire weapons out of their cars."[1645] The seriously wounded Oz Geist calls for someone to fetch his wallet, passport and phone.[1646] Geist, who remains conscious, and the unconscious Ubben are carried into LMI vehicles on stretchers. Before he is loaded into the back of a small truck, Oz catches the attention of Jack Silva. Oz tells him, "Rone shielded me. He saved my

---

[1642] Fox News, House Republicans Fault US Military Response to Benghazi (Select Benghazi Committee Chairman Trey "Gowdy said the Libyan forces that evacuated Americans from the CIA annex in Benghazi were not affiliated with any of the militias the CIA or State Department had developed a relationship with during the previous 18 months"). See also Benghazi ARB Report ("The Board found the Libyan government's response to be profoundly lacking on the night of the attacks, reflecting both weak capacity and a near total absence of central government influence in Benghazi. . . ."), p. 36.

[1643] Benghazi Committee Report (Redacted), pp. 110-111.

[1644] *Id.*, p. 111.

[1645] *Id.*, p. 111.

[1646] Zuckoff, *13 Hours*, Chap. 13, p. 281.

THE TRUE ACCOUNT OF VALOR AND ABANDONMENT

life."[1647] The GRS medic on Team Tripoli who has been treating Oz will ride in the back with him, holding on to Oz during the trip to the airport.[1648]

Eventually, at about 6:34 a.m., Benghazi time, the survivors from the Mission and the Annex depart the CIA compound.[1649] Two GRS operators, the CIA Chief of Base and another CIA staff officer stay behind at the Annex for a short time to continue destroying sensitive CIA equipment. They leave about 6:45 a.m. in a pick-up truck, and soon catch up to the rest of the convoy on the way to the airport.[1650]

Dave Ubben is resting on a litter in the back of a small SUV in the convoy. The bumpy drive restores him to consciousness. It is a good thing. Because of Ubben's large six-foot-four-inch frame, the SUV's rear hatch will not close. Ubben later will testify that throughout this ride to the airport, "The whole route I was sliding out the back." Ubben repeatedly shouts at the SUV's driver to hit the brakes so the injured man's momentum would move his body back toward the front of the vehicle. He tries to use his good leg as best he can to brace himself in position. In retrospect, Ubben's predicament has a comical aspect.[1651] At the time, however, in his condition this ride must be almost as harrowing in its own way as the DSAs' dangerous escape from the Mission Compound the previous night.

(The State Department's Charlene Lamb later will testify inaccurately to Congress regarding this rescue escort, "A large number of *Libyan government* security officers ... arrived in more than 50 vehicles and escorted the remaining Americans to the airport."[1652] Just before the upcoming presidential election, the CIA also will claim falsely the evacuation was orchestrated by a "heavily-armed Libyan military unit...."[1653] (It was the CIA's own case officer who arranged the rescue with the LMI.) Much later, in her memoir Hillary Clinton will repeat this fable that "Libyan government security forces ...

[1647] *Id.*, Chap. 13, p. 283.

[1648] Benghazi Committee Report, p. 107.

[1649] *Id.* (Redacted), pp. 107 and 112; and Baier, 13 Hours at Benghazi: The Inside Story (*Watch video there*; Go to 31:50 - 32:44).

[1650] Benghazi Committee Report (Redacted), p. 112.

[1651] Hsu, Baring Grievous Wounds, Dry Humor, U.S. Agent Lays Out Key Evidence at Benghazi Trial (Testimony of Dave Ubben: "So there's a little bit of comedy there").

[1652] Lamb Oversight Committee Prepared Testimony (emphasis added), p. 7.

[1653] Miller, CIA Rushed to Save Diplomats as Libya Attack Was Underway.

returned to provide escort to the airport."[1654] In fact, as noted, these are unofficial militia members who do so; they have no connection with the new Libyan government or its military.[1655] More misinformation.)

The Libyan Military Intelligence successfully escorts the Americans the entire way to the Benghazi airport. Mercifully, other than Dave Ubben's difficulties with the laws of physics, the trip is without incident.[1656]

The LMI convoy transporting the Americans probably arrives at Benina airport between approximately 6:55 and 7:10 a.m.[1657] Once they get there, a confrontation arises between the LMI and another, much smaller militia group currently in control of the airport. The Americans present fear a shooting incident is about to unfold. In fact, one of the Libyan militiamen accidentally discharges his weapon, causing everyone present to fear the worst. However, the unintended shot actually causes reason to prevail. The smaller militia unit eventually backs down to the larger LMI force.[1658] For the present, the Americans now are secure at the airport.

(Again, none of the officials at Langley or the Pentagon or in Washington even consider such trouble possibly might occur at the airport. They simply assume the Americans all will depart serenely so long as they stow their carry-on luggage securely in the overhead compartments, and place their tray tables in the full upright position.) ■

[1654] Clinton, *Hard Choices*, Chap. 17, p. 398.

[1655] Benghazi Committee Report (Redacted), pp. 110-111.

[1656] *Id.* (Redacted), pp. 107 and 112; and Baier, 13 Hours at Benghazi: The Inside Story (*Watch video there*; Go to 31:50 - 32:44).

[1657] The author's estimate is based in part upon time it takes for Libyan Shield militia to transport Team Tripoli from the airport to the CIA Annex, and in part upon the estimate of the House Intelligence Committee Benghazi Report, p. 6.

[1658] Baier, 13 Hours at Benghazi: The Inside Story (*Watch video there*; Go to 32:44-54).

83

Forklifts & Nap Time

Shortly after the Americans evacuate the CIA's Benghazi Annex, about 970 miles to the north at about 7:00 a.m. Croatian and Benghazi time (1:00 a.m. Washington time), the U.S. CIF in Croatia finally is ready to deploy onward.[1659] This is more than *nine hours* into the crisis. From their training site the CIF apparently has taken ground transportation on a two-hour trip to Zagreb International Airport, where their dedicated aircraft will pick them up.[1660]

The Select Committee explains the U.S. military uses a concept of "Notification hour" or "N-hour" to designate when a particular unit's operational timeframe commences. The panel's report states, ". . . The N-hour is the established time that essentially starts the clock ticking for when the forces are required to be airborne." The Select Committee puts CIF's "N-hour" at 5:00 a.m. Croatia and Benghazi time (11:00 p.m. Washington time). However, it is emblematic of this Night of Benghazi that the commander of the CIF later cannot even recall when his assigned N-hour is during this emergency![1661] In any event, the CIF commander will miss his "N-hour" – by a country mile.

Although the Select Committee's report is somewhat unclear on this aspect of Benghazi, it seems obvious the CIF experiences significant delays. First, before reaching its 7:00 a.m. readiness status, the CIF must wait for a forklift to arrive from Zadar, Croatia, some 180 miles away, so they can load their gear and ammunition onto pallets! (Given this is a national emergency with American lives in the balance, perhaps the CIF should

---

[1659] Benghazi Committee Report, p. 120, and Select Benghazi Timeline, p. 561.

[1660] Benghazi Committee Report, p. 120.

[1661] *Id.*, pp. 119-121 & n. 481 and 123.

consider departing only with the gear and ammo they can carry onto trucks and planes themselves. Somehow, it is difficult to envision Team Annex or Team Tripoli or Woods' SST unit waiting around for a forklift before heading into battle.)

But this forklift delay, while embarrassing, proves largely irrelevant. The good news is CIF has two dedicated C-130 transport aircraft on this Night of Benghazi located somewhere nearby in Croatia. The bad news is upon learning of the Benghazi attacks at approximately midnight local Croatia and Benghazi time (6:00 p.m. in Washington), the commander of the C-130s (before receiving any orders) *places their pilots and air crews on "crew rest" for eight hours, in anticipation of a possible mission!* This is shortened by Major General Michael S. Repass (Commander of U.S. Special Operations Command Europe, "SOCEUR"[1662]) from the usual twelve hours. Given the "exigent circumstances" of an ongoing, life-and-death calamity in Benghazi – including a missing U.S. ambassador who may have been taken hostage by militants – this crew rest period should be waived entirely. But despite these "exigent circumstances," it is *not* waived!

To make matters worse, it appears this CIF force and its commander are in a partial intelligence blackout. Throughout their preparation period, they do not receive vital Benghazi situation information until they learn Ambassador Stevens is deceased. For example, they are not told State Department personnel at the Mission in Benghazi have evacuated to the CIA Annex. Nor are they informed when that Annex is attacked by mortars, and two additional Americans are murdered.[1663] (Perhaps this partially explains why, as noted previously in Chapter 65, their commander incorrectly concludes the emergency has passed once CIF learns Stevens is dead.)

The CIF and its air crews train all year for an emergency. Tonight, in Benghazi, they have one. But instead of putting their air crews in a cockpit, their commanding officer puts them in

---

[1662] See Master Sgt. Donald Sparks, "Special Operations Command Europe Holds Change of Command," U.S. European Command website (Aug. 26, 2011).

[1663] Benghazi Committee Report, p. 120.

THE TRUE ACCOUNT OF VALOR AND ABANDONMENT

bed. (Yet again, the U.S. military exhibits no sense of urgency in the middle of a genuine crisis![1664] The Americans on Annex rooftops and towers in Benghazi will get no such "crew rest.")

In large part because of this mandated crew rest, the CIF's C-130s will not arrive at the CIF's location for another *nine hours* after CIF is ready to deploy. In the meantime, the CIF special ops team is sitting on a runway, ready to deploy, waiting for their transport.[1665] (A familiar refrain: there is lots of waiting by U.S. military units occurring on this Night of Benghazi.) The two C-130s finally arrive at Zagreb airport (with a fresh and happy crew) around 4:00 p.m., possibly as late as 4:21 p.m., local and Benghazi time (10:00 a.m. to 10:21 a.m. Washington time).[1666] After loading aboard their C-130s, apparently around 5:00 p.m. Croatia and Benghazi time (11:00 a.m. Washington time), the CIF team finally is airborne for Sigonella Naval Air Station in Sicily.[1667] This is *twelve hours* after CIF's "N-hour"![1668]

The Select Benghazi Committee later will learn one reason for CIF's lackadaisical attitude is because early on it is determined CIF will not be going to Libya in any event. Rather, they supposedly are being transported to be ready if other trouble develops "in the region." Specifically, Vice Admiral James Winnefeld, Vice Chairman of the Joint Chiefs, testifies regarding why the military's actions morph from crisis response to deliberative planning:

[1664] *Id.* (". . . [T]he lack of urgency in responding to what was actually happening on the ground in Benghazi is difficult to reconcile"), p. 124.

[1665] *Id.* (Testimony of CIF Commander: "So, in terms of the air, . . . I was waiting on the aircraft. . . . [F]or us, we packed up every [sic very] quickly and then we were waiting at the airfield. . . . So once we were sitting at the airfield about seven o'clock in the morning on September 12th, I had limited communications with what was going on. I was just waiting for the aircraft to show up"), p. 120.

[1666] *Id.*, p. 123, and Select Benghazi Timeline, p. 561.

[1667] Benghazi Committee Report, Select Benghazi Timeline (C-130 departs for Sigonella at 11:00 a.m., Washington time), p. 561.

[1668] The Select Committee puts this delay at eleven hours. Benghazi Committee Report, p. 123.

417

> ... [I]t wasn't a matter of not having enough urgency, I think it was more a matter of posture, coupled with the fact *the focus was on regional challenges, not on something additional was going to happen in Benghazi later that night.* And so when there was not the perception of an immediate threat right there ... people are going to operate safely.
> ...
> And remember, the reason we were moving the CIF, we were moving it to ... Sigonella. ... *It was not because they were going to Benghazi.*
> ...
> *We were worried about the copycat attacks elsewhere in the region.* And so ... it wasn't a lack of urgency, but it was ... they keep safety in mind. It was, okay, there could be a copycat attack; we need to reposition ourselves in theater. *Let's do it, but let's not kill ourselves doing it.*
> ... [I]n 20/20 hindsight, if anybody had *known* there was going to be a second attack [actually third attack at the Annex] and that potentially the CIF could end up going there, maybe they would have asked that question that you're asking [why actions become deliberate]. But again, their mindset was we're moving the CIF to Sigonella because *something else could happen in the region.*[1669]

(Of course, this is somewhat inconsistent with other evidence discussed above (Chapter 65). According to the Select Committee, Vice Admiral Tidd testifies "one reason the CIF and the U.S. SOF were ordered to an intermediate staging base and not to Libya directly was due to concerns expressed by the State Department regarding the number of military personnel that would arrive in country."[1670] But who in the highest chain-of-command decided State's concerns should override the Pentagon's orders?)

[1669] Benghazi Committee Report (emphasis added), p. 128.

[1670] *Id.*, p. 100.

THE TRUE ACCOUNT OF VALOR AND ABANDONMENT

U.S. military commanders later agree that, regardless of its mission, the CIF fails to meet its required timelines. Subsequently, AFRICOM Commander General Ham will testify to the Select Committee:

... [T]he reality is they [the CIF] should have made their timelines. And ... *there's no excuse for that.* ... They should have been postured for subsequent use. As it turns out, they would not have been needed, but *we didn't know that at the time.* ...[1671]

(Would not have been needed? What about defending the airport in Benghazi?) Defense Secretary Leon Panetta will agree with General Ham. He later tells the Select Committee, "I think it's a legitimate area to ask why did it take that long" for CIF to be transported from Croatia to Sigonella.[1672] (And what is *your* answer, Mr. Secretary? *You* were in charge.)

According to a Democrat member of the House Oversight Committee, months after the Benghazi tragedy, on or about April 30, 2013, Fox News airs a controversial interview with an alleged Special Ops soldier whose identity is concealed. This soldier disagrees with General Ham's conclusion the CIF "would not have been needed." He claims the CIF force in Croatia could have prevented the final mortar attacks on the CIA Annex in Benghazi. He asserts the CIF has the ability to be "there" (presumably Benghazi) in four to six hours.[1673] Critics dismiss this unidentified soldier's claims as absurd.[1674] (The author is not so sure.)

[1671] *Id.* (emphasis added), p. 123.

[1672] *Id.*, p. 123.

[1673] House Oversight Committee Hearings (May 8, 2013) (Remarks of Rep. Danny Davis (D-IL)), p. 86; and "Pentagon Denies Claims That Help Could Have Been Sent During Benghazi Attack," Fox News online (May 7, 2013). The author has been unable to locate a video of this program on the Fox News website or on other sources.

[1674] E.g., Billy Birdzell, "Benghazi (II): A Military Analysis of the Fox Mystery Man's Fantasy Rescue Plan," ForeignPolicy.com website (May 2, 2013) ("... Forty operators armed with rifles and light-machine guns can neither stop mortar rounds nor determine from where the mortar is being fired. The only thing the CIF would have done had they gotten to the annex before 0515 [5:15 a.m., Benghazi time] is created more targets and overcrowded the consulate"). The author notes Mr. Birdzell's article contains numerous factual errors. Also, like nearly all Team Obama officials, Birdzell is assuming

A week after this interview airing on Fox News, the Defense Department issues a letter responding to the Oversight Committee's Ranking Democratic Member, Elijah Cummings (D-MD), rejecting this anonymous soldier's claim. DoD says, "... [T]he time needed from alerting the CIF to landing at the Benghazi airport is greater than the approximately 7.5 hours between the initiation of the first attack [at the Mission] and that of the second one [the final attack at the Annex]." The Pentagon's letter adds, "The time requirements for notification, load, and transit alone prevented the CIF from being at the [Benghazi CIA] Annex in time to change events."[1675] (Defense's letter "forgets" to discuss missing forklifts and crew rest periods.)

(Once again, the Pentagon – like almost everyone else in the Obama administration – misses (or deliberately obscures) the key point: *On this Night of Benghazi, at the time no one knows when the Battle of Benghazi will be over! No one knows when or if another fight is coming, and no one knows what it will look like.* (For example, almost everyone involved will be surprised the militants are able to show up with, and accurately use, mortars.) During this crisis, everyone in the U.S. military should be acting as if they *can* make a difference. Instead, almost none of them do.)

While this tardy CIF force limps slowly toward Sigonella, Sicily, let us return to the saga of the imperiled Americans still in Benghazi. ■

---

everyone connected with the CIF knows exactly when the fighting at the Annex will be over (at 5:26 a.m., Benghazi time), and when the last Americans will depart Benghazi (9:54 a.m.). In fact, when the CIF is ordered into action, no one possibly can know these times. Again like Team Obama, Birdzell also ignores the importance of securing the Benghazi airport for the Americans' evacuation.

[1675] Letter from Elizabeth L. King, Assistant Secretary of Defense for Legislative Affairs, to Rep. Elijah E. Cummings (D-MD) (May 7, 2013), Democrat House Oversight website, p. 1; and House Oversight Committee Hearings (May 8, 2013) (Remarks of Rep. Danny Davis (D-IL)), pp. 86-87.

84

"I'm Going to Frigging Walk Out Of This Town"

The aircraft chartered by Team Tripoli is still on the tarmac at Benina Airport. As noted above, it is not large enough to transport all the nearly three dozen Americans in Benghazi to Tripoli on one flight. The two badly wounded defenders, the Team Tripoli GRS medic who is treating them, several other State Department Diplomatic Security Agents, and the nonessential CIA personnel will go on this first trip.[1676]

The severely wounded Dave Ubben is taken aboard the aircraft on a stretcher. The Americans have to strap him to the stretcher so they can turn him sideways to get him through the plane's very narrow doorway.[1677]

When his comrades begin to lift his stretcher, Mark Geist stops them. Oz insists, "Hell no. I walked into this country, and I'm going to frigging walk out of this town." He does. (Oz later explains, ". . . It's who I am. . . . I'm not gonna lose.") As Oz walks slowly, painfully and deliberately toward the plane, the flight attendants of the chartered jet see the blood continue to drip down Oz's badly-wounded left arm. Some of them run into the jet and frantically begin to lay towels down so the blood does not stain the private aircraft's carpet and seats.[1678]

After everyone is aboard, and as the Americans sit on the aircraft awaiting takeoff, someone clears his pistol improperly and a round accidentally goes off, startling everyone. No one is hurt. However, the pilot refuses to take off until he can determine whether the fuselage has been compromised by the bullet. If the delay is long, Dave Ubben almost certainly will die. He simply has lost too much blood.

[1676] Benghazi Committee Report (Redacted), pp. 107 and 112.

[1677] Zuckoff, *13 Hours*, Chap. 13, p. 286.

[1678] Baier, 13 Hours at Benghazi: The Inside Story (*Watch video there*; Go to 32:54-33:21) (Oz Geist: "I walked into Benghazi, I'm going to walk out of here"); Zuckoff, *13 Hours*, Chap. 13, pp. 286-287; and Interview of Mark "Oz" Geist and Other GRS Agents with Megyn Kelly, "The Kelly File," Fox News Channel (Jan. 4, 2016) (*Watch video there*; Go to 14:58 - 15:20).

Oz's morphine is wearing off, and he is again experiencing excruciating pain in his arm. But he is more concerned about Ubben, lying next to him on the floor, than himself. According to author Zuckoff, Oz thinks to himself, *I'm going to get up with my pistol and frigging tell the captain he's flying one way or the other. We got to get Dave to a hospital or he's gonna die.*[1679]

Finally, the errant round is found embedded in a seat. The craft's exterior is undamaged. This flight leaves Benghazi at about 7:31 a.m. local time (1:31 a.m. Washington time).[1680] Dave Ubben is alive.

During this flight, Ubben moves in and out of consciousness. The medic GRS from Tripoli gives Ubben more morphine. They land in Tripoli at about 8:38 a.m.[1681]

As part of her valiant efforts to mobilize emergency medical care in Tripoli, the U.S. Embassy's nurse, Jackie Levesque, has an ambulance waiting at the airport for the wounded men from Benghazi. Ubben must deplane without the stretcher the ambulance crew has brought because it is too big to fit through the aircraft door. (Apparently the crew lacks the straps needed to lash Ubben to their stretcher, which were used to carry him onto the plane when departing Benghazi.) During this process, Ubben actually stops breathing. The GRS agent gives Ubben CPR, and manages to get him breathing again.[1682]

Ubben and Oz Geist are taken by that ambulance to Afia Hospital in Tripoli. There, the waiting emergency room doctors at a minimum save Dave Ubben's leg, and probably his life as well.[1683] They also provide vital preliminary care to Oz's mangled forearm and hand.

Back at Benghazi airport, at 8:25 a.m. Ambassador Stevens' remains are brought from a Benghazi hospital to the remaining U.S. personnel at the airport. (These are the uninjured GRS men, the survivors of Team Tripoli, and lead DSA agent Alec Henderson.) According to the Select Committee, the diplomat's body is delivered by "individuals delegated by the Libyan Ministry of Foreign Affairs." The

---

[1679] Zuckoff, *13 Hours*, Chap. 13, pp. 288-289.

[1680] Baier, 13 Hours at Benghazi: The Inside Story (*Watch video there*; Go to 33:27 - 34:00); Benghazi Committee Report (Redacted), p. 112, and Select Benghazi Timeline, p. 561; and Clinton, *Hard Choices*, Chap. 17, p. 398. Compare CBS Benghazi Timeline (plane left Benghazi at approximately 7:40 a.m.).

[1681] Benghazi Committee Report, pp. 107-108.

[1682] *Id.*, pp. 107-108.

[1683] *Id.* Report (Redacted), pp. 107-108 and 112; and Hicks Oversight Committee Testimony (May 8, 2013), p. 29.

THE TRUE ACCOUNT OF VALOR AND ABANDONMENT

State Department subsequently claims it has coordinated this transfer of Stevens' remains to the airport.[1684]

However, a CIA GRS agent from Team Tripoli who testifies later at alleged terrorist Abu Khatallah's criminal trial tells a different story than this "official" State Department party line. (Imagine that, another factual discrepancy.) According to this CIA agent's testimony (under oath), at the Benghazi airport this GRS agent happens to walk near two of the "Libyan revolutionary militiamen" guarding the Americans. He testifies he hears one of the militia ask the other, "Should we tell them about this dead American at the hospital?" The GRS agent claims he offers all the money in his backpack for the dead American's remains. However, the militiamen's commander declines the offer of payment. He promises to "see what I can do." About fifteen minutes later, Ambassador Stevens' body reportedly is delivered to the Americans at the airport.[1685] (Who does the reader believe is telling the truth regarding this event? Me, too.)

Lead DSA Alec Henderson lifts the sheet covering the body and identifies the ambassador. There no longer is any doubt Chris Stevens is deceased.[1686]

Meanwhile, back in the United States news about the Benghazi attacks has begun to find its way onto television screens. Some relatives of the Americans in Benghazi first learn of the crisis from TV news, not from the government that sent their family member into harm's way. While at the Benghazi airport waiting for a second plane, the survivors make quick calls home telling their spouses and other loved ones they are alive. When their phones ring in the U.S., these families do not know if it will be their loved one on the other end of the line, or an official with a notification of death. Four families will receive no such calls from their now departed loved ones.[1687]

After calling their spouses, some of the exhausted Americans stretch out on the tarmac to try to get some rest. However, they keep their

---

[1684] Benghazi Committee Report (Redacted), p. 112; Zuckoff, *13 Hours*, Chap. 13, p. 289; Lamb Oversight Committee Prepared Testimony, p. 7; and Sen. Intelligence Committee Benghazi Report, p. 9.

[1685] Hsu, CIA Officers Detail Part of Bloody Benghazi Attack at Terrorism Trial (Criminal trial testimony of disguised CIA agent, pseudonym "Alexander Charles").

[1686] Benghazi Committee Report, Select Benghazi Timeline, p. 561; and Zuckoff, *13 Hours*, Chap. 13, p. 290.

[1687] Baier, 13 Hours at Benghazi: The Inside Story (*Watch video there*; Go to 34:10-42); and Zuckoff, *13 Hours*, Chap. 13, pp. 290-291.

loaded weapons nearby. They are not out of the woods yet. After all, this is Benghazi.[1688]

The Libyan government – not the United States – sends a Libyan Air Force C-130 *cargo* plane to transport to Tripoli the second and final group of Americans. This aircraft also will take the bodies of Chris Stevens, Sean Smith, Tyrone Woods and Glen Doherty. According to one of the Team Tripoli CIA operators who takes this flight, this aircraft is so dilapidated he actually fears for his life boarding it. "I really felt that was how I was going to die."[1689]

(There is no band. There is no honor guard. No 21-gun salute. There are no flags fluttering in the breeze to salute these Heroes of Benghazi. They even lack enough blankets to cover the remains of Bub Doherty and Rone Woods.[1690] There is just a damned, decrepit Libyan cargo plane. Note neither of the two evacuation planes belongs to the U.S. government.)

The final group of warriors and the remains of the deceased Americans take off from Benghazi for Tripoli at about 9:54 a.m., Benghazi time (3:54 a.m. in Washington). During this flight, although Rone Woods is deceased, his body continues to drain blood. According to a GRS agent on the plane, "I remember it made a stream of blood from the bodies all the way to the ramp of the plane."[1691]

As the Libyan cargo jet lifts from the Benghazi runway, almost twelve and one-quarter hours have elapsed since the initial terrorist assault. Yet the United States military – the mightiest on the globe – has failed to muster a single armed air asset into the skies above Benghazi. Not one jet fighter aircraft flyover, not a single AC-130H

[1688] Zuckoff, *13 Hours*, Chap. 13, p. 290.

[1689] Benghazi Committee Report (Redacted), p. 112; and Hsu, CIA Officers Detail Part of Bloody Benghazi Attack at Terrorism Trial (Criminal trial testimony of disguised CIA agent, pseudonym "Roy Edwards").

[1690] Hsu, CIA Officers Detail Part of Bloody Benghazi Attack at Terrorism Trial (Criminal trial testimony of disguised CIA agent, pseudonym "Alexander Charles").

[1691] Hsu, CIA Officers Detail Part of Bloody Benghazi Attack at Terrorism Trial (Criminal trial testimony of disguised CIA agent, pseudonym "Alexander Charles"); Benghazi Committee Report (Redacted), p. 112, and Select Benghazi Timeline (second plane departs around 10:00 a.m. Benghazi time), p. 561; and CBS Benghazi Timeline (second plane departs about 10:00 a.m. Benghazi time). Compare Zuckoff, *13 Hours*, (second plane departs about 10:30 a.m.), Chap. 13, p. 292.

THE TRUE ACCOUNT OF VALOR AND ABANDONMENT

Spectre gunship, not one lone attack helicopter. Not even one armed drone. In twelve hours. *Nothing*.[1692] The Select Committee concludes: More than twelve hours had passed since the first attack happened at the Mission compound, . . . yet in that time, the greatest military on earth was unable to launch one single asset toward the sound of the guns.[1693]

After a flight spent in reflective silence, the second group of Americans lands in Tripoli at 11:33 a.m. local time. Some members of the U.S. Embassy staff are at the airport to greet the Heroes of Benghazi. One of the D-Boys obtains some body bags. He and Jack Silva place the remains of Rone Woods and Glen Doherty inside, and zip them up.[1694] It is a heartbreaking end of the saga.

The Battle of Benghazi is history. This sordid, tragic Benghazi chapter of U.S. history is closed. As this book goes to press, America's diplomats still have not returned to Benghazi. (Good riddance.) ■

[1692] Key Delays Appendix (See September 12 entry for 3:54 a.m., Washington time); Sen. Intelligence Committee Benghazi Report (Redacted) ("DoD moved aerial assets, teams of Marines, and special operations forces toward Libya as the attacks were ongoing, but in addition to the seven-man reinforcement team from Tripoli, the only additional resources that were able to arrive on scene were unmanned, unarmed aerial surveillance assets. . . ."), p. 28; and Hicks Oversight Committee Testimony (May 8, 2013) (Response to questions of Rep. Ron DeSantis (R-FL)) ("No air support was sent"), p. 95. The U.S. may not have learned enough lessons from Benghazi. In October 2017, four American soldiers were killed and two wounded in Niger following a reported denial of a request for an armed drone. *The Wall Street Journal*, "US Forces in Niger Sought Armed Drone Before Deadly Ambush," Fox News online (Oct. 28, 2017) (". . . [T]he request [for an armed drone] was blocked in a chain of approval that snakes through the Pentagon, State Department and the Nigerien government, according to officials briefed on the events").

[1693] Benghazi Committee Report, p. 124.

[1694] *Id.* (Redacted), p. 112; and Zuckoff, *13 Hours*, Chap. 13, p. 292.

85

Libyan Flight Clearance Is Received

Eventually, by 7:40 a.m. Benghazi time (1:40 a.m. in Washington), the Libyan government has given *preliminary* approval for U.S. military assets to fly into *Tripoli* (not Benghazi). This will permit the FAST Marine platoon in Rota, Spain to fly into the Libyan capital.[1695] (*Oh joy!*) The U.S. never seeks clearance for a Benghazi rescue attempt.[1696]

However, by this time no U.S. military assets have yet deployed – despite Secretary Panetta's "deploy now" orders supposedly issued almost *seven hours earlier!* After evacuating the CIA Annex, the first planeload of U.S. Benghazi refugees has just taken off for Tripoli.[1697]

Incomprehensibly, the two American C-130 transport planes in Ramstein, Germany still have not taken off for Rota! *They have awaited Libyan flight clearance before even beginning to move toward the FAST assets that are their mission!* They will not take off from Ramstein for another twenty minutes, at about 8:00 a.m., on a flight that is scheduled to take another *three hours and forty minutes.*[1698]

Final, official flight clearance will take still longer. The U.S. Defense Attaché in Tripoli later testifies the U.S. does not even provide the paperwork required for the final flight clearance request to the Libyans until "sometime midmorning to noon on the 12th. It could have been a little bit after that."[1699] Noon will have been more than *fourteen hours* after the first attack, and comes after all Americans in Benghazi already have evacuated from Benina airport and are en route to Tripoli. (Should "halfhearted" be hyphenated?) ∎

[1695] Benghazi Committee Report, pp. 118-119.

[1696] Attkisson, *Stonewalled*, Chap. 4, p. 168.

[1697] *Id.* (Redacted), pp. 109, 112 and 119; and Clinton, *Hard Choices*, Chap. 17, p. 398.

[1698] Benghazi Committee Report, pp. 109 and 116-119.

[1699] *Id.*, pp. 87 and 118.

86

The Evacuation Out of Tripoli

On Wednesday, September 12 at 6:05 a.m. Benghazi time, a U.S. C-17 medical airplane has been ordered to prepare to deploy to Tripoli to evacuate the wounded, deceased, and other American citizens.[1700] The plane will not leave Germany until about 2:15 p.m., Benghazi time. This is more than *eight hours* after AFRICOM orders the C-17 to prepare to deploy as part of the medivac! The C-17 lands in Tripoli at about 5:15 p.m.[1701]

Departing Tripoli at approximately 7:17 p.m. local time, the surviving Benghazi personnel (including the wounded), and the remains of the four deceased Americans are flown to the U.S. military base in Ramstein, Germany. "Non-essential" personnel from the U.S. Embassy in Tripoli also leave.[1702]

They land in Ramstein at about 10:19 p.m., Benghazi (and Ramstein) time.[1703] At Ramstein, the wounded will be treated at Landstuhl Regional Medical Center and the dead examined. The healthy survivors are put up until they can be debriefed and their future status determined.

It is a heart-rending end to the entire Benghazi saga. In a later interview, Tig Tiegen, Oz Geist and Tanto Paronto are asked if they would do it all again. They all reply, "Yes, definitely."[1704] ∎

[1700] Benghazi Committee Report (Redacted), pp. 97 and 112-113, and Select Benghazi Timeline, p. 560; and CBS Benghazi Timeline.

[1701] Benghazi Committee Report (Redacted), pp. 112-113; and Select Benghazi Timeline, p. 561.

[1702] *Id.*, p. 113; CBS Benghazi Timeline; and September 12 Special Briefing.

[1703] Benghazi Committee Report, p. 113, and Select Benghazi Timeline, p. 561; and CBS Benghazi Timeline.

[1704] Baier, 13 Hours at Benghazi: The Inside Story (*Watch video there*; Go to 34:59 - 35:08).

87

Better Late Than Never?

As an anti-climactic afterthought, eventually the three U.S. military forces the Pentagon has deployed will arrive in the Mediterranean region (but none in Benghazi).[1705]

The Commander's In-Extremis Force

At approximately 7:57 p.m. Croatia and Benghazi time (1:57 p.m. in Washington) on Wednesday, September 12, the CIF team that has deployed from Croatia finally lands at Sigonella Naval Air Station in Sicily.[1706] *This is over 22 hours after the Battle of Benghazi begins*, and some 43 minutes after the surviving U.S. personnel from Benghazi already have left Tripoli for Germany. And this is the U.S. military asset of the three the Pentagon has chosen that is *closest* to Benghazi when the crisis begins![1707] (It is a pathetic response time.) The CIF never will deploy on to Libya.[1708]

The FAST Marine Platoons

The C-130s land in Rota, Spain at around noon, local (and Benghazi) time. It will take the (not-so-) FAST Marines about one hour to load their personnel and gear onto the aircraft. (One hopes *they* have

---

[1705] For an excellent diagram comparing the (lack of) progress of the three U.S. military assets, see Additional Views of Reps. Jordan and Pompeo, pp. 445-446.

[1706] Benghazi Committee Report, Select Benghazi Timeline, p. 561.

[1707] Benghazi Committee Report, p. 121 (CIF is ". . . the closest military asset capable of quickly deploying to Benghazi . . ."); Attkisson, Could U.S. Military Have Helped During Libya Attack? (*Watch video* there); and CNN Report, Why Didn't the U.S. Military Respond in Time in Benghazi?

[1708] Benghazi Committee Report, pp. 96-97; *Id.*, Appendix G, Defense Dept. Timeline, pp. 573-574; CNN Report, Why Didn't the U.S. Military Respond in Time in Benghazi?; and Adam Housley and Jennifer Griffin, "Facts and Questions About What Happened in Benghazi," Fox News online (Jan. 22, 2013) ("Members of . . . the Commander's In Extremis Force in nearby Croatia say they were never given permission to enter Libya, even though some were just a short flight way in Europe").

428

THE TRUE ACCOUNT OF VALOR AND ABANDONMENT

enough forklifts.) The C-130s are loaded and ready for takeoff by 1:00 p.m. However, the first C-130 does not depart Rota for *another three hours!*[1709] (As noted in Chapter 64, above, some of this delay involves the FAST Marines changing in and out of uniform four times, and U.S. officials debating whether these warriors should be allowed to take their personal weapons into a battle. By any measure, this delay is gross incompetence. It is fortunate there is no national security crisis tonight.)

More than ten hours after they are ready to deploy, and after sitting on a fully-loaded airplane on a runway for three hours, a Marine FAST platoon finally departs Rota for Tripoli. It is 4:00 p.m. Benghazi time (10:00 a.m. Washington time). At 8:56 p.m. Libyan time on September 12 (2:56 p.m. in Washington), this FAST team finally lands at Tripoli, Libya (which still has not been attacked by terrorists). This is over *twenty-three hours* after the initial attack, and about one hour and forty minutes after the American refugees from Benghazi have departed Tripoli for Germany.[1710]

In its subsequent report, the Senate Intelligence Committee states:

Because all Americans were evacuated from Benghazi before the first FAST platoon could *arrive*, it was *diverted* to protect the *U.S. Embassy* in Tripoli and arrived at 8:56 p.m. Tripoli time, on September 12, 2012.[1711]

This statement is misleading in the extreme. (Let us give the senators the benefit of the doubt by assuming when they say "U.S. Embassy in Tripoli" (which probably is evacuated by around 4:45 a.m., Benghazi time) they really mean the U.S. annex in Tripoli.) By using the word "diverted," the Senate panel seems to suggest FAST's aircraft is re-routed to Tripoli – perhaps even while in flight to Benghazi.

However, as explained above, FAST never really is destined to go to Benghazi at all. *FAST's first plane does not even depart Rota for over six hours after all Americans have evacuated Benghazi!*[1712] As explained in Chapter 65 above, the Pentagon has decided as early as

---

[1709] Benghazi Committee Report, pp. 116-117, and Select Benghazi Timeline, p. 561.

[1710] Benghazi Committee Report, pp. 114 and 116-117, and Select Benghazi Timeline, p. 561; CNN Report, Why Didn't the U.S. Military Respond in Time in Benghazi?; and Key Delays Appendix (See September 12 entries for 1:17 p.m. and 2:56 p.m., both Washington time).

[1711] Sen. Intelligence Committee Benghazi Report (Redacted; emphasis added), p. 30.

[1712] Key Delays Appendix (See September 12 entries for 3:54 a.m. and 10:00 a.m., both Washington time).

2:53 a.m. Benghazi time to abandon the besieged Americans who are still there and focus instead on securing Americans in Tripoli. Any "diversion" of FAST has nothing to do with FAST not being able to arrive in Benghazi in time. Rather, FAST's orders are changed early on to exclude any possible Benghazi rescue attempt. *Remember, by the time the White House 7:30 Meeting of "Deputies" has ended at 3:30 a.m. Benghazi time, "everyone" knows no troops are headed to Benghazi. This occurs twelve and one-half hours before FAST's aircraft lifts off from Rota bound for Tripoli.*[1713]

Later, Leon Panetta testifies to the Select Committee that when he issues his 7:00 p.m. Order he does not expect it will take this long for FAST to arrive *in Tripoli.*[1714] (But ponder this, dear reader: when Panetta issues his 7:00 p.m. Order, doesn't he supposedly expect at least one platoon is bound for Benghazi, not Tripoli?[1715]) Further, the Select Committee asks the head of AFRICOM, General Carter Ham, whether he knows why it takes so long for the FAST platoon to get to Tripoli. His reply: "I do not."[1716] (And he was in charge. No wonder he soon will be forced into retirement (discussed in Chapter 113).)

The Special Operations Force

About ninety minutes after CIF arrives, on September 12 at 9:28 p.m. Libyan time (3:28 p.m. in Washington), the U.S.-based SOF forces from Fort Bragg land at Sigonella.[1717] This is almost eighteen and one-half hours after SOF receives its orders to deploy on September 11 at 8:53 p.m. Washington time, "nearly 12 hours *after* all U.S. personnel had evacuated from Benghazi," and nearly a full day after the crisis begins. And it is more than two hours after the Americans have evacuated Tripoli for Germany! Despite the fact it has traveled some 4,500 miles farther than CIF, SOF arrives at Sigonella

---

[1713] Key Delays Appendix (See September 11 entries for 9:30 p.m. and 11:45 p.m., and September 12 entry for 10:00 a.m., all Washington time).

[1714] Benghazi Committee Report, p. 115.

[1715] See Sen. Intelligence Committee Benghazi Report (". . . One [FAST] team was to go to Benghazi to respond to the attack on the Special Mission Facility"), p. 30.

[1716] Benghazi Committee Report, pp. 117-118.

[1717] Benghazi Committee Report, p. 123, and Select Benghazi Timeline, p. 561; Sen. Intelligence Committee Benghazi Report (Redacted), p. 31; and CNN Report, Why Didn't the U.S. Military Respond in Time in Benghazi?

THE TRUE ACCOUNT OF VALOR AND ABANDONMENT

only about ninety minutes after CIF. Like CIF, SOF never will deploy on to Libya.[1718] (But then, Sicily is lovely in September.)

Conclusions Regarding Military Performance

In his subsequent testimony before the Select Committee, Leon Panetta is completely unable to explain this deplorable performance by his military. He claims he simply assumes his military units are moving as fast as they can. (Why doesn't he stay at the Pentagon on this Night of Benghazi to guarantee this?) And he invokes the ever-popular "tyranny of time and distance" excuse.[1719]

(This appallingly slow and ineffectual performance by the U.S. military – on the anniversary of 9/11 – is inexcusable. Leon Panetta, and many others who serve under him, are to blame. Panetta should take responsibility and resign, but does not. President Obama should sack him immediately, but will not. Congress should impeach him, but apparently cannot. And the entire fiasco should cost Barack Obama the upcoming election, but of course does not.

(The conduct of our top government and military leaders in Washington on this Night of Benghazi is a complete disgrace.) ∎

[1718] Benghazi Committee Report (emphasis in original), pp. 96-97 and 123; CNN Report, Why Didn't the U.S. Military Respond in Time in Benghazi?; Adam Housley and Jennifer Griffin, "Facts and Questions About What Happened in Benghazi," Fox News online (Jan. 22, 2013) ("Members of the Special Operations teams sent from Fort Bragg N.C. . . . say they were never given permission to enter Libya . . ."); and Key Delays Appendix (See September 11 entries for 3:42 p.m. and 8:53 p.m., and September 12 entries for 3:54 a.m., 1:17 p.m., 1:57 p.m. and 3:28 p.m., all Washington time).

[1719] Benghazi Committee Report, pp. 114-115.

PART IV:

AFTER THE ATTACKS

88

Chaos in the Obama Kingdom

Following the disaster in Benghazi, as is usual in the initial hours following such chaotic situations, there appears to be a great deal of confusion among many in our government regarding exactly what has happened in Benghazi – and who is responsible.

Appropriately, President Obama quickly orders heightened security at U.S. diplomatic posts, especially in Libya.[1720] Among other specific actions, the U.S. Embassy in Tripoli is taken down to "emergency staffing levels," and two U.S. Navy warships reportedly are sent to positions off the Libyan coast.[1721]

Describing the immediate aftermath of the crisis, President Obama will tell a press conference in May 2013, ". . . What we have been very clear about throughout was that immediately after this event happened we were not clear who exactly had carried it out, how it had occurred, what the motivations were. . . . And nobody understood exactly what was taking place during the course of *those first few days.*"[1722]

Stated somewhat less charitably, in the hours, days and weeks following the Benghazi debacle Obama administration officials appear entirely bumfuzzled. (That's a legal term.) They desperately will seek to assemble a coherent explanation. Different officials issue inconsistent or downright conflicting public statements. They utter

---

[1720] Kirkpatrick and Myers, Libya Attack Brings Challenges for U.S. (President Obama ". . . ordered tighter security at all American diplomatic installations. The administration also sent 50 Marines [the FAST Platoon from Rota] to the Libyan capital, Tripoli, to help with security at the American Embassy there, ordered all nonemergency personnel to leave Libya and warned Americans not to travel there. . . .").

[1721] September 12 Special Briefing; NBC News Staff and Wire Services, "Ambassador Rice: Benghazi Attack Began Spontaneously," NBC News online (Sept. 16, 2012); and Kirkpatrick and Myers, Libya Attack Brings Challenges for U.S. ("A senior defense official said that the Pentagon sent two warships toward the Libyan coast as a precaution").

[1722] Remarks by President Obama and Prime Minister Cameron of the United Kingdom in Joint Press Conference, Obama White House Archives (May 13, 2013) (emphasis added) ("Obama-Cameron Joint Press Conference"); and CBS News, "Benghazi Timeline: How the Probe Unfolded," CBS News online (Undated) (emphasis added).

433

public assertions that differ from simultaneous private emails and other non-public remarks.[1723] And their public statements sometimes change and shift as days or even hours pass.[1724] This is true both within the same agency and across different departments.[1725] And in many instances, Obama officials utter statements that prove to be flat out false.[1726]

[1723] E.g., Additional Views of Reps. Jordan and Pompeo (". . . With the presidential election just 56 days away, rather than tell the American people the truth and increase the risk of losing an election, the administration told one story privately and a different story publicly. They publicly blamed the deaths on a video-inspired protest they knew had never occurred"), p. 416; *Id.* (". . . Secretary Clinton and the administration told one story privately – that Benghazi was a terrorist attack – and told another story publicly – blaming a video-inspired protest"), p. 420; Jeremy Diamond and Elise Labott, "What Did We Learn About Benghazi at Marathon Meeting?" CNN online (Oct. 22, 2015) ("Diamond and Labott, What Did We Learn About Benghazi at Marathon Meeting?") ("Like the [sic] her call to the Egyptian prime minister, [Hillary] Clinton's apparent certainty [in an email to her daughter] that the attack was carried out by a known terrorist group contradicted some administration officials' public statements in the wake of the attack"); *Id.* ("In response to the revelations at the [Select Benghazi Committee] hearing, Clinton chalked up the differences in her accounts and the administration's repeated references to a spontaneous demonstration to shifting intelligence assessments during a chaotic period"); Hemingway, 5 Big Takeaways From the House Benghazi Report ("The [Select] Benghazi committee shows that the administration told a public story designed to connect the attack to the video and protests in Cairo and a private story that acknowledged the reality that it was a terrorist attack . . . Each day it goes on like this: Clinton tells family members of those killed in Benghazi that the video was to blame, while privately admitting their deaths had nothing to do with a spontaneous protest of a video. Administration members' public statements all talk about the video, while most private statements don't"); and Attkisson, *Stonewalled* ("Why was the conversation with the American public so starkly different than the one taking place behind the scenes – the accurate one – unless the narrative was being seriously manipulated?"), Chap. 4, p. 211.

[1724] E.g., "Clinton on Benghazi: We All Had the Same Intel," CBS News online (Oct. 16, 2012) ("CBS News, We All Had the Same Intel") ("Over time, the Obama administration changed its characterization of the attacks, calling it a planned terrorist assault – fueling Republican charges of a political cover-up"); and CBS News, House Probes Security Leading Up to Libya Attack ("Republican [Oversight] committee members sought to take the witnesses to task for that shifting explanation of what happened in Benghazi, suggesting that the administration was trying to cover up that it was unprepared for the 11th anniversary of the Sept. 11, 2001, terrorist attacks").

[1725] Attkisson, *Stonewalled* (Regarding "The Benghazi mystery," ". . . The feds are keeping a suspiciously tight clamp on details. . . . What they do reveal sometimes contradicts information provided by their sister agencies. . . ."), Prologue, p. 2.

[1726] E.g., Judicial Watch: State Department Documents Show Its Security Contractor Operating Without a License in Benghazi on Day of Terrorist Attack (". . . State Department spokesperson Victoria Nuland emphatically denied on September 18, 2012,

THE TRUE ACCOUNT OF VALOR AND ABANDONMENT

Sometimes, officials (including President Obama himself) refuse to repeat conclusions they have asserted publicly just hours or days before. Some statements are made in an official capacity, while others involve anonymous leaks.[1727] In certain cases, it is possible good intelligence obtained at lower levels within an agency is not passed promptly up the agency's chain of command. It is no wonder the public, the media and the Congress all become thoroughly confused by the political "Tower of Babel" the administration erects (intentionally or otherwise) in Benghazi's wake.

Of course, there are several alternative explanations for these post-attack discrepancies and confusion. First, the Obama administration may be receiving inconsistent, incomplete and otherwise flawed intelligence reports. Second, at least some in the administration may be attempting to mislead the public (and the media) with misdirection to minimize the political fallout from Benghazi with the approaching presidential election just weeks away.[1728] And third, some (perhaps

---

that State had hired any private firm to provide security at the American mission in Benghazi. The department later retracted that claim"); Diamond and Labott, What Did We Learn About Benghazi at Marathon Meeting? (noting Susan Rice later "walked back" her comments on CBS's "Face the Nation" that spontaneous protests in Benghazi arose in response to a video defaming the Prophet Muhammad); and Attkisson, *Stonewalled* ("The State Department said it did not refuse security requests prior to the September 11, 2012, attacks on Americans in Benghazi, Libya"), Chap. 1, p. 18.

[1727] E.g., CBS News, CIA Saw Possible Terror Ties Day After Libya Hit: AP ("The officials who told the AP [Associated Press] about the CIA cable [indicating the Benghazi attacks are the work of "militants," not a "spontaneous mob"] spoke anonymously because they were not authorized to release such information publicly"); and CBS News, House Probes Security Leading Up to Libya Attack (". . . The officials spoke on condition of anonymity because they weren't authorized to speak publicly on the matter, and provided no evidence that might suggest a case of spontaneous violence or angry protests that went too far").

[1728] E.g., Interview of Rep. Trey Gowdy (R-SC) on "America's Newsroom," Fox News online (Circa Oct. 3, 2012) (". . . You have another dichotomy. Either they [the Obama administration] intentionally misled the American people and Congress, *or* they are so negligent and reckless that they didn't bother to get the facts before they tried to explain it") (*Watch video there*; Go to 1:56 - 2:08); Hayes, The Benghazi Talking Points ("Even as the [Obama] White House strove last week to move beyond questions about the Benghazi attacks of Tuesday, September 11, 2012, fresh evidence emerged that senior Obama administration officials knowingly misled the country about what had happened in the days following the assaults . . . Senior administration officials . . . sought to obscure the emerging picture and downplay the significance of attacks that killed a U.S. ambassador and three other Americans"); Opinion, L. Brent Bozell and Tim Graham, "L. Brent Bozell: Susan Rice Is Still Lying," *Investor's Business Daily* online (April 5, 2017) ("On Sept. 16, 2012 — five days after radical Islamic terrorists killed four Americans in Benghazi, Libya – Susan Rice lied through her teeth on five

many) high-level Obama officials may demonstrate considerable incompetence (as also has occurred before and during the assaults[1729]).

Obviously, these three possibilities are not mutually exclusive. It is conceivable members of Team Obama are both bungling *and* deceptive.[1730] It also is possible the initial intelligence is flawed *and* Obama officials seek to take advantage of this fact to mislead the voters. Or that inept officials do not react responsibly to imperfect intelligence.[1731]

There is evidence (discussed in detail below) arguably supporting each of these explanations. The author believes all three scenarios contribute to create the utter chaos reflected in the post-Benghazi Obama administration's actions. However, the conclusion seems inescapable the "deceive the voters and the media" alternative plays a major role in the ensuing muddle.[1732]

Sunday news programs that this preplanned attack with rocket launchers was somehow a 'spontaneous reaction' to a 'hateful and offensive video' on YouTube. . . . Everyone knows that is patently false. Evidence flowed in that she and the president and then-Secretary of State Hillary Clinton knew it was a terrorist attack. But everyone claimed otherwise for more than a week. They had an election to win. The media gently helped them lie"); and Hemingway, 5 Big Takeaways From the House Benghazi Report ("Even though U.S. officials – including Hillary Clinton – knew immediately that the siege in Benghazi was a highly coordinated terror attack, they chose to mislead the public with statements about spontaneous protests caused by a YouTube video. The [Select Committee] report indicates that political considerations were on the minds of State Department officials learning about the attack. . . .").

[1729] E.g., Hicks, What the Benghazi Attack Taught Me About Hillary Clinton (". . . Despite the fact that Sydney Blumenthal had alerted her to the increasing danger for Americans in Benghazi and Libya, Mrs. Clinton apparently never asked security professionals for an updated briefing on the situation in Libya. Either she could not correlate the increased tempo of attacks in Libya with the safety of our diplomats, demonstrating fatal incompetence, or she was grossly negligent").

[1730] E.g., Rep. Mike Rogers (R-MI), House Intelligence Committee Chairman, Op-Ed for *The Hill* (Dec. 10, 2014) ("The Obama administration's White House and State Department actions before, during, and after the Benghazi terrorist attack on September 11, 2012, ranged from incompetence to deplorable political manipulation in the midst of an election season"); Compare CBS News, Clinton on Benghazi: We All Had the Same Intel (Senator Lindsey Graham (R-SC) on "Face the Nation" (Date unspecified) (emphasis added): "Either they are misleading the American people, *or* are incredibly incompetent") (*Watch video there*; Go to 1:54 - 2:10).

[1731] E.g., Interview of Senator John McCain, "Face the Nation," CBS News (Oct. 28, 2012) (emphasis added) (". . . [N]obody died in Watergate. But this is either a massive cover-up *or* incompetence that is not acceptable service to the American people").

[1732] E.g., National Review Editors, What We Do Know About the Benghazi Attack Demands a Reckoning ("The attack on the facility . . . threatened to destroy the

In their separate statement, two insightful members of the Select Benghazi Committee also reach this "deception" conclusion. Congressmen Mike Pompeo (R-KS) and Jim Jordan (R-OH) write: And so on this highly charged political stage – just 56 days before the presidential election – events forced the administration to make a choice about what to tell the American people: Tell the truth that heavily armed terrorists had killed one American and possibly kidnapped a second – and increase the risk of losing the election. Say we do not know what happened. Or blame a video-inspired protest by tying Benghazi to what had occurred earlier in the day in Cairo. The administration chose the third, a statement with the least factual support but that would help the most politically.[1733]

We consider below some of the actual evidence relating to these three alternatives. However, the author first sets forth his opinion regarding the considerable strength of the "deception" and "misdirection" hypothesis. ∎

---

president's campaign claims. . . . [T]he White House was very concerned about the politics. Clinton, already plotting her 2016 campaign, had similar worries, given her portrayal of post-Qaddafi Libya as an Arab Spring success story where a stable, representative government was taking shape"); Hayes, The Benghazi Talking Points (Last week "fresh evidence emerged that senior Obama administration officials knowingly misled the country about what had happened in the days following the assaults. . . . Senior administration officials . . . sought to obscure the emerging picture and downplay the significance of attacks that killed a U.S. ambassador and three other Americans"); Michael Goodwin, "Now We Know – President Obama was MIA on Benghazi," Fox News Opinion online (Feb. 11, 2013) (". . . Even before the bodies of the four Americans came home, the White House was eager to tell any story except the real one. Aides twisted and turned to create the false narrative that a protest over an anti-Muslim video was spontaneously hijacked by radicals. . . ."); Guy Benson, "Bombshell: CIA Using 'Unprecedented' Polygraphing, 'Pure Intimidation' to Guard Benghazi Secrets," Townhall.com website (Aug. 2, 2013) (emphasis added) (". . . [T]he White House . . . labeled the catastrophe 'phony,' *deceived the public at every turn*, and promoted several key players involved in the political cover-up. . . ."); and Editorial, "Military Support Offered in Benghazi – Why Would White House Say No?" Investor's Business Daily online (Dec. 10, 2015) ("So, it appears a White House decision was made to let the violence play out without intervention, then make up a lie that the attacks weren't terrorism but merely a protest over an anti-Islamic video that just got out of hand").

[1733] Additional Statement of Congressmen Jordan and Pompeo, p. 424.

89

Spinning the "Benghazi Narrative"

In the author's interpretation of the evidence, after the Benghazi attacks are over the deception, misdirection and cover-ups from the Obama administration begin almost immediately. They swiftly attempt to put diplomatic lipstick on a national security disaster pig. Their public statements about the attacks can fairly be described as schizophrenic, as the administration scrambles to craft a coherent narrative that will cover Obama's butt politically – at least until after the upcoming voting.[1734] When the Battle of Benghazi ends, this tough election is only eight weeks away.

The Obama White House immediately grasps it desperately needs to explain why on Obama's watch there are multiple, successful, fatal terror attacks on two American installations in a foreign city well known to be extremely dangerous – *all on the anniversary of 9/11, a highly symbolic and perilous date.*[1735] The attacks are even more politically damaging because they result from another major foreign policy blunder by Obama's administration (summarized in Part I): overthrowing Qadhafi's regime and allowing Libya to sink into a quagmire of chaos, civil war and terrorism. Further, the Benghazi assaults run counter to the administration's insistent campaign claims that Obama has weakened al Qaeda and other terrorist groups.[1736]

[1734] E.g., IBD Editorial, Obama Knew Benghazi Was Terrorism And Did Nothing ("Could it be the cover story [about a spontaneous mob upset about the anti-Islam Video] was necessary so no one would ask the obvious question of why a rescue or relief mission was not mounted?").

[1735] CBS News, House Probes Security Leading Up to Libya Attack (*Watch video there*) ("Republican [Oversight] committee members sought to take the witnesses to task for that shifting explanation of what happened in Benghazi, suggesting that the administration was trying to cover up that it was unprepared for the 11th anniversary of the Sept. 11, 2001, terrorist attacks").

[1736] Scott Wilson and Karen DeYoung, "Benghazi E-mails Show Clash Between State Department, CIA," *The Washington Post* online (May 10, 2013) ("Wilson and DeYoung, Benghazi E-mails Show Clash Between State Department, CIA") ("During the 2012 presidential campaign, Republican nominee Mitt Romney accused the White House of downplaying the [Benghazi] attackers' links to Ansar al-Sharia for political

THE TRUE ACCOUNT OF VALOR AND ABANDONMENT

Obama's officials must make Americans believe the Benghazi attacks are spontaneous, unforeseeable and not preventable. Barack Obama's administration cannot be seen to be at fault. And they must prop up their overall foreign policy theme that al Qaeda is on the decline.[1737] *They have to buy time until the election is over.*[1738]

Team Obama swiftly develops a story line to contain the political fallout of the Benghazi disaster. In the author's view, this "Benghazi Narrative" has at least 19 key components:

(1) The United States has vital national interests for being in Libya in general, and in Benghazi in particular;[1739]

(2) Prior to September 11, 2012, the president has placed the U.S. military and national security assets on a "heightened" state of alert;

(3) Security at the Benghazi Mission Compound on September 11, 2012, is "robust";[1740]

---

reasons given Obama's campaign argument that he had severely weakened the terrorist group").

[1737] E.g., *The New York Times* Transcript of Third 2012 Presidential Debate Moderated by Bob Schieffer of CBS News, *The New York Times* online (Oct. 22, 2012) ("... The truth, though, is that al-Qaida is much weaker than it was when I came into office, and they don't have the same capacities to attack the U.S. homeland and our allies as they did four years ago"); "Remarks by the President at a Campaign Event – Las Vegas, NV," White House website (Sept. 12, 2012) ("A day after 9/11, we are reminded that a new tower rises above the New York skyline, but al Qaeda is on the path to defeat and bin Laden is dead"); Leigh Ann Caldwell, "Sen. Graham: Libya Is 'Exhibit A of a Failed Foreign Policy,'" CBS News online (Oct. 18, 2012) (Senator Lindsey Graham (R-SC) "... said the Obama administration tried to blame the attacks on an American-made anti-Muslim video, which had prompted violent demonstrations across the Muslim world, because they are 'trying to sell a narrative' that fits into their message that al Qaeda is on the decline"); and *Wall Street Journal* Opinion, The Missing Benghazi Email ("... Mr. Obama's campaign said al Qaeda was on the run and it was time for 'nation-building at home.' The terror attack on Americans in Benghazi didn't fit this story....").

[1738] E.g., Interview of Charles Krauthammer with Sean Hannity, "Hannity," Fox News Channel (Oct. 22, 2012) (Krauthammer: "... So they [the Obama administration and campaign] think they've got the media in their pocket, the election is coming up, they simply have to run out the clock and they'll be scott free, ... they'll be home free ... and now [because of coverage by Fox News and others] the mainstream media had been shamed into covering it themselves") (*Watch video there*; Go to 1:42 – 2:46).

[1739] E.g., Kennedy House Oversight Prepared Testimony ("... The United States is better off because Chris Stevens went to Benghazi"), p. 3.

[1740] September 12 Special Briefing (emphasis added) ("We had a physical perimeter barrier, obviously. And then we had a *robust* American security presence inside the compound, including a strong component of regional security officers...."); Lamb Oversight Committee Prepared Testimony ("In terms of armed security personnel, there

(4) The DoD's SST team that was withdrawn from Libya was restricted to Tripoli, and could not have helped in Benghazi;[1741]

(5) This is a "regular" visit by Stevens to Benghazi that he makes "periodically" (just business as usual);[1742]

(6) At least initially, in part because of the "fog of war," we don't know for certain whether the Benghazi attacks involve *terrorism*;[1743]

---

were five Diplomatic Security agents on the Compound on September 11th. There were also three members of the Libyan 17th February Brigade. In addition, stationed nearby at the embassy annex was a well-trained U.S. quick reaction security team"), p. 3; CBS News, House Probes Security Leading Up to Libya Attack (*Watch video there*) (Charlene Lamb, Deputy Assistant Secretary of State for diplomatic security: "We had the correct number of assets in Benghazi at the time of 9/11"); "This Week," ABC News (Sept. 16, 2012) (emphasis added) (Susan Rice responding to why security at the Mission Compound wasn't better: "First of all, *we had a substantial security presence* . . . with our personnel and the consulate in Benghazi. Tragically, two of the four Americans who were killed were there providing security. That was their function. And indeed, there were many other colleagues who were doing the same with them") (*Watch video there*; Go to 1:49 - 2:48).

[1741] E.g., Lamb House Oversight Committee Testimony (Oct. 10, 2012) (Because Lt. Col. Wood's team was based in Tripoli, and spent most of its time there, "It [the Libya SST] would not have made any difference in Benghazi"), pp. 56-57; Tapper, Security Team Commander Says Ambassador Stevens Wanted His Team to Stay in Libya Past August (*Watch video* there; Go to 1:38-50); and Schmitt and Landler, Focus Was on Tripoli in Requests for Security in Libya ("This [the SST] was not a SWAT team with a DC-3 on alert to jet them off to other cities in Libya to respond to security issues").

[1742] September 12 Special Briefing (emphasis added) ("With regard to Chris's trip to Benghazi, as you know, *he made regular and frequent trips to Benghazi* so that he could check up on developments in the east. You know that he had been our representative – the Secretary's representative and the President's, to the Transitional National Council before the fall of Qadhafi and had spent a lot of time in Benghazi and built deep contacts there. So this was one of his *regular visits* that he made *periodically*").

[1743] CBS News, CIA Saw Possible Terror Ties Day After Libya Hit: AP ("U.S. intelligence officials say in this case, the delay [in sharing raw intelligence reports] was due in part to the time it took to analyze various conflicting accounts. One official [speaking anonymously] . . . explained that it 'was clear a group of people gathered that evening' in Benghazi, but that the early question was 'whether extremists took over a crowd or they were the crowd'"); *Id*. ("Secretary of State Hillary Rodham Clinton blamed the 'fog of war' for the early conflicting accounts"); CBS News, Clinton on Benghazi: We All Had the Same Intel (Hillary Clinton: ". . . I think it's part of what the 'fog of war' causes") (*Watch video* there; Go to 1:34-54); Erik Wemple, Opinion, "Univision's Ramos Picked the Wrong Benghazi Question for Hillary Clinton," *The Washington Post* online (Mar. 10, 2016) (Clinton: "This was fog of war. This was complicated"); Clinton, *Hard Choices* ("The events of that September occurred in what is often called the 'fog of war,' with information hard to come by, and conflicting or

THE TRUE ACCOUNT OF VALOR AND ABANDONMENT

(7) The Benghazi attacks grow out of *protests in Benghazi*;[1744]
(8) These protests are in response to an anti-Islamic *Video*;[1745]
(9) The release of this Video is *very recent*;[1746]

---

incomplete reports making it difficult to tell what was actually happening on the ground, especially from thousands of miles away in Washington. To a frustrating degree, that fog persisted so long, in part because of continuing turmoil in Libya"), Chap. 17, p. 385; Benghazi Committee Report (Under Secretary of State Patrick Kennedy: One purpose of 7:30 Meeting was "Trying to make sure that we all, meaning across the entire U.S. Government, had the clearest coherent understanding of what was going on in the fog of war"), p. 85; and Panetta, *Worthy Fights* ("In hindsight, we as a government could have made that point [that Benghazi involved terrorism] more clearly publicly following the attack, but not doing so was merely prudent reluctance to go beyond the official intelligence assessments. . . Like everyone else at that point, I was working from initial reports that could only be verified by a fuller investigation"), Chap. 16, p. 431.

[1744] CBS News, CIA Saw Possible Terror Ties Day After Libya Hit: AP (". . . [O]n Saturday [September 15] of that week, briefing points sent by the CIA to Congress said 'demonstrations in Benghazi were spontaneously inspired by the protests at the U.S. Embassy in Cairo and evolved into a direct assault'"); and *Id.* ("The Obama administration maintained publicly for a week that the attack on the diplomatic mission in Benghazi . . . was a result of the mobs that staged less-deadly protests across the Muslim world around the 11th anniversary of the 9/11 terror attacks on the U.S.").

[1745] E.g., Press Briefing by Press Secretary Jay Carney, The White House, Obama White House Archives (Sept. 19, 2012); CBS News, CIA Saw Possible Terror Ties Day After Libya Hit: AP (". . . Republicans say he [Obama] was speaking generally and didn't specifically call the Benghazi attack a terror attack until weeks later, with the president and other key members of his administration referring at first to the anti-Muslim movie circulating on the Internet as a precipitating event"); CBS News, House Probes Security Leading Up to Libya Attack (*Watch video there*) ("In statements immediately after the attack, neither President Barack Obama nor Secretary of State Hillary Rodham Clinton mentioned terrorism. [This is incorrect as to Obama.] And both gave credence to the notion that the attack was related to protests about an anti-Islam video"); CBS News, Dispute Over Nature of Libya Attack Continues ("The Obama administration has called the attack more impulsive than planned. . . . U.S. officials have said since the immediate aftermath of the attack that it originally started as an Anti-American protest against an amateurish online video made in the U.S. that insults the Muslim Prophet Muhammad"); and Erik Wemple, Opinion, "Univision's Ramos Picked the Wrong Benghazi Question for Hillary Clinton," *The Washington Post* online (Mar. 10, 2016) (Quoting Patricia Smith on Fox News: "Hillary and Obama and Panetta, Biden and Susan Rice all told me that it was a video when they knew . . . it was not the video"; "Those comments by Patricia Smith have played into the much-discussed accusation that Obama administration officials, in the immediate aftermath of Benghazi, attempted to blame the attacks on an anti-Muslim video instead of terrorism – as part of a scheme to insulate themselves from criticism in advance of the 2012 presidential election").

[1746] E.g., Email from Benjamin J. Rhodes to Dag Vega, NSC Deputy Press Secretary, et al., Re: "PREP CALL with Susan: Saturday at 4:00 p.m. ET (Sept. 14, 2012)"

(10) These protests are *"spontaneous"* and "opportunistic," not preplanned;[1747]

(11) The U.S. has no "actionable intelligence" a terror attack is planned for Benghazi on September 11;[1748]

(12) Because of these factors, there is no way the Obama administration reasonably can be expected to foresee the Benghazi terror attacks coming;[1749]

(13) The U.S. justifiably relies on Benghazi locals for security, and they heroically help battle the attackers;[1750]

(emphasis added) ("The protests we've seen *these last few days* were sparked by a disgusting and reprehensible video. . . ."), pp. 1-2, Judicial Watch Document Archive (posted June 16, 2014).

[1747] E.g., Attkisson, Diplomat: U.S. Special Forces Told "You Can't Go" to Benghazi During Attacks ("Ambassador Susan Rice and Secretary of State Hillary Clinton initially indicated the attacks were not planned acts of terror, but an outgrowth of a spontaneous protest over an anti-Islamic YouTube video"); CBS News, CIA Saw Possible Terror Ties Day After Libya Hit: AP (". . . [O]n Saturday [September 15] of that week, briefing points sent by the CIA to Congress said 'demonstrations in Benghazi were spontaneously inspired by the protests at the U.S. Embassy in Cairo and evolved into a direct assault'"); CBS News, Clinton on Benghazi: We All Had the Same Intel (Susan Rice on September 16: ". . . [W]e do not have information at present that leads us to conclude that this was premeditated or preplanned"); and CBS News, Dispute Over Nature of Libya Attack Continues ("The Obama administration has called the attack more impulsive than planned").

[1748] E.g., Panetta Senate Armed Services Prepared Testimony; Kennedy House Oversight Committee Testimony (Oct. 10, 2012), p. 105; Attkisson, 8 Major Warnings Before Benghazi; and CBS News, U.S. Memo Warned of High Risk of Libya Violence ("The State Department also has continued to cite the threat assessment conducted by the Director of National Intelligence which stated that there was, "no actionable intelligence that an attack on our post in Benghazi was planned or imminent").

[1749] Analysis/Opinion by Charles Hurt, "If Voters Look Past Hillary's History of Lies, They'll Get What They Deserve in the White House," *The Washington Times* online (June 28, 2016) (". . . Hillary Clinton . . . immediately dismissed the attacks as some sort of unforeseeable, instantaneous reaction to some obscure anti-Muslim internet video that nobody had ever heard of – at least not until Secretary Clinton made it instantly famous around the globe by blaming it for Benghazi"); and Attkisson, *Stonewalled* (". . . the administration advanced the narrative that it couldn't have predicted the Benghazi attacks. (That was to explain why it denied security requests and had no military help accessible.) . . ."), Chap. 4, p. 213.

[1750] E.g., "Remarks by the President on the Deaths of U.S. Embassy Staff in Libya," The Rose Garden, The White House, Obama White House Archives (Sept. 12, 2012) ("Libyan security personnel fought back against the attackers alongside Americans . . ."); and Lamb Oversight Committee Prepared Testimony (". . . [O]ver the course of the attack, two local Libyan security personnel were beaten, and two were shot."), p. 4.

(14) On the Night of Benghazi the U.S. government has little real-time information regarding the situation on the ground in Benghazi until the battle is over;[1751]

(15) Due to the "tyranny of time and distance" and other factors, no U.S. military assets possibly can make it to Benghazi in time to prevent any attacks or save lives there;[1752]

(16) No "stand down" order is given to anyone in the U.S. military or the CIA on this Night of Benghazi;[1753]

(17) Therefore, Barack Obama and his administration cannot be held morally or militarily or diplomatically or politically responsible for the unforeseeable terror attacks and the resulting deaths of four Americans, including an ambassador, and the serious injuries to two more Americans;

(18) The FBI (and later the "independent" State Accountability Review Board) investigation of Benghazi (discussed below) are continuing; some or all of the above "facts" may change as a result of these inquiries;[1754] and

(19) Obama will move heaven and earth to assure "those responsible" for this "crime" are "brought to justice."[1755]

[1751] E.g., Panetta Armed Services Committee Testimony (Feb. 7, 2013) (Response to questions of Sen. Kelly Ayotte (R-NH) ("The biggest problem that night, Senator, was that nobody knew really what was going on there") (*Watch video there*; Go to 2:48-53).

[1752] E.g., Benghazi Committee Report (The Pentagon: "The fact remains – as we have repeatedly indicated – that United States forces could not have arrived in time to mount a rescue of those Americans killed or injured that night"), pp. 66-69 and 114-115; Press Release, "DOD Cooperates with Congress on Benghazi Probes"; and Prepared Statement of General Martin Dempsey, Chairman, Joint Chiefs of Staff, before Senate Armed Services Committee (Feb. 7, 2013) ("Our military was appropriately responsive. We acted quickly once notified of the attacks on the Temporary Mission Facility. . . . We did what our posture and capabilities allowed").

[1753] Attkisson, Diplomat: U.S. Special Forces Told "You Can't Go" to Benghazi During Attacks ("The account from Gregory Hicks is in stark contrast to assertions from the Obama administration, which insisted that nobody was ever told to stand down and that all available resources were utilized").

[1754] Hayes, The Benghazi Talking Points.

[1755] E.g., "Remarks by the President on the Deaths of U.S. Embassy Staff in Libya," The Rose Garden, The White House, Obama White House Archives (Sept. 12, 2012) (emphasis added); Remarks by the President in Golden, Colorado, Obama White House Archives (Sept. 13, 2012); Matt Compton, "President Obama Discusses the Attack in Benghazi, Libya," Obama White House Archives (Sept. 12, 2012) (emphasis added) (*Watch video* there); ABC News Transcript of Second 2012 Presidential Debate Moderated by Candy Crowley of CNN's "State of the Union" (Oct. 16, 2012), ABC News online (". . . [W]e are going to find out who did this and we're going to hunt

THE BENGHAZI BETRAYAL

(*Whew!* This Benghazi Narrative will prove to be quite a mouthful for the American public to swallow and digest.) Team Obama's highest officials possibly begin to craft this Benghazi Narrative during their lengthy 7:30 Meeting on this night of September 11 (or perhaps even sooner). This Benghazi Narrative has many moving parts. It will prove difficult to sell to the public and Congress – in part because most of its components will prove to be patently untrue.[1756]

Fortunately for President Obama, a compliant mainstream media will aid greatly the marketing campaign supporting the Benghazi Narrative snake oil as these "news" outlets seek to protect him going into the final weeks of the 2012 election campaign.[1757] (The author

---

them down, because . . . when folks mess with Americans, we go after them"); and Sen. Intelligence Committee Benghazi Report, p. 43.

[1756] E.g., Benghazi Committee Report, pp. 114 and 130-131 (many "action items" from 7:30 Meeting pertain to anti-Muslim Video); Eli Lake, "Obama's Shaky Libya Narrative," *The Daily Beast* online (Sept. 21, 2012) ("Ten days after the attack on the U.S. consulate [sic] in Benghazi, Libya, the White House's official story about the incident appears to be falling apart. . . . Now there is mounting evidence that the White House's initial portrayal of the attacks as a mere outgrowth of protest was incorrect – or, at the very least, incomplete. The administration's story itself has recently begun to shift. . . . [O]ther indications that the White House's early narrative was faulty are also beginning to emerge. . . ."); Attkisson, *Stonewalled* ("In the early days after the Benghazi attacks, high-ranking Obama administration officials seem to be on the very same page. But it's a page pulled from a work of fiction"), Chap. 4, p. 195; Lucy Madison, "Congress to Investigate CIA Talking Points on Benghazi," CBS News online (Nov. 19, 2012) ("Madison, Congress to Investigate CIA Talking Points on Benghazi") (quoting Mike Rogers (R-MI) on "Meet the Press": "I know the narrative was wrong and the intelligence [attributing the Benghazi attacks to terrorist assaults] was right"); *Id.* (quoting Sen. Lindsey Graham (R-SC) on "Meet the Press" as calling Rice a "bit player" responsible largely for "passing on a narrative that was misleading to the American people"); and Rosen, Top Defense Officials Briefed Obama on "Attack" Not Video or Protest (". . . The new evidence [showing Panetta and Dempsey initially were told Benghazi attack likely was 'terrorist attack'] raises the question of why the top military men . . . allowed him and other senior Obama administration officials to press a false narrative of the Benghazi attacks for two weeks afterward . . . the Obama administration ultimately acknowledged that its early statements on Benghazi were untrue").

[1757] E.g., Remarks of K.T. McFarland on "Lou Dobbs Tonight," Fox Business Channel (Nov. 6, 2012) (*Watch video there*; Go to 1:12-33 and 3:33 – 4:02) (". . . [A] majority of Americans now think that there is a cover up. The tragedy of all this is the mainstream media is part of that cover-up. . . We now have a mainstream media that doesn't want to fight for the truth at all. That is really the press office of an Obama campaign . . ."); Klein, *The Amateur* (". . . [T]he presidential nominee of the Republican Party will not only have to run against Barack Obama in 2012; he will also

444

THE TRUE ACCOUNT OF VALOR AND ABANDONMENT

agrees with those commentators who believe the close family, marital, and other personal ties between Team Obama and members of the mainstream news media help shield Obama during the throes of the 2012 election battle.[1758] See this book's website for a partial listing of these tight Team Obama-media relationships.[1759]) ■

---

have to run against the full force and power of the liberal mainstream media and the cultural establishment"), Chap. 20, p. 229; and Remarks of Charles Krauthammer with Bret Baier, "Special Report," Fox News Channel (May 2, 2014) (". . . [W]hat's changed now . . . is I think the other media are somewhat embarrassed by the fact that, unlike Fox, they allowed themselves to be stoned and spun and rolled for a year and a half and now the memo [in an email from Ben Rhodes dated September 14, 2012 discussing Susan Rice's upcoming Sunday Shows appearances] appears and it's obvious that they missed the story") (*Watch video there*; Go to 2:24-53).

[1758] E.g., Paul Farhi, "Media, Administration Deal with Conflicts," *The Washington Post* online (June 12, 2013) ("Conservatives have suggested that these relationships may play a role in how the media cover Obama, specifically in their supposedly timid approach to reporting on the White House's handling of the terrorist attacks last year on American facilities in Benghazi, Libya. . . .").

[1759] *Visit* www.TheBenghaziBetrayal.com.

90

"Fog of War"

Following the carnage in Benghazi, Obama administration officials frequently will invoke the "fog of war" excuse for much of the confusion, errors, inconsistencies, misstatements, contradictions, and downright foolishness that occur during and after the attacks.

For example, in February 2013 former Secretary of Defense Leon Panetta will testify to the Senate: "The biggest problem that night, Senator, was that nobody knew really what was going on there."[1760] It is a lie. Panetta, the Pentagon, the CIA, the State Department, the White House and others are receiving extensive, "near-constant" information regarding the situation on the ground in Benghazi.[1761]

In assessing the credibility of administration statements like Panetta's, it is useful to recall some of the considerable "real-time" information U.S. government officials are receiving from Benghazi and Tripoli on this night, as documented above:

- Almost immediately after the initial attack, a DSA in the Mission Compound TOC sets up an open radio link to the Benghazi CIA Annex, permitting continuous communication between the two Benghazi facilities;[1762]

[1760] Panetta Armed Services Committee Testimony (Feb. 7, 2013) (Response to questions of Sen. Kelly Ayotte (R-NH)). See also Attkisson, *Stonewalled* (". . . the 'fog of war,' a phrase that Obama officials first evoked in the weeks after the attacks – and often repeated – to help explain why it didn't mount an outside military rescue of the trapped Americans that night"), Chap. 4, p. 208.

[1761] See Benghazi ARB Report ("Washington-Tripoli-Benghazi communication, cooperation, and coordination on the night of the attacks were effective, despite multiple channels of communication among Washington, Tripoli, Benghazi, and AFRICOM headquarters in Stuttgart, as well as multiple channels of communication within Washington itself. . . . Overall, communications systems on the night of the attacks worked, with a near-constant information flow among Benghazi, Tripoli, and Washington"), pp. 36-37.

[1762] Benghazi Committee Report, pp. 32-33.

- One DSA in the Mission TOC keeps Tripoli Embassy security on speakerphone "almost the whole time" of the attack on the Mission;[1763]
- That same DSA in the TOC passes much of the attack in real-time by phone to State's "Diplomatic Security Command Center";[1764]
- From the time the initial attack begins, senior DSA Alec Henderson in the Mission TOC claims he "updated officials in Washington every 15 to 30 minutes throughout the night – giving the State Department virtually a front-row seat to the attack";[1765]
- Deputy Chief of Mission Greg Hicks in Tripoli is in communication with Washington "all night long ... reporting ... what was happening to Washington by telephone";[1766]
- The State Department's top diplomatic security official in Washington, Charlene Lamb, is in State's DSCC with her "liaison" at State, who "had constant contact with the Annex";[1767]
- Lamb: "We had almost full-time connection to the DS agents that were on the ground . . .";[1768]
- Lamb is "monitoring *multiple open lines* with our agents for much of the attack";[1769]

[1763] *Id.*, p. 33.

[1764] *Id.*, p. 142.

[1765] *Id.* (" . . . [The] Diplomatic Security agent in charge at the Benghazi Mission compound [Alec Henderson] testified he was in constant contact with the Diplomatic Security Command Center"; Henderson: ". . . Much of the [initial] attack was passed in real-time through my phone to DS command center"), p. 142; and Additional Views of Reps. Jordan and Pompeo, p. 426.

[1766] Attkisson, Diplomat: U.S. Special Forces Told "You Can't Go" to Benghazi During Attacks (Gregory Hicks to congressional investigators). See also Hicks Oversight Committee Testimony (May 8, 2013) (Hicks: "During the night I'm in touch with Washington, keeping them posted of what's happening in Tripoli and to the best of my knowledge what I'm being told in Benghazi"), p. 27.

[1767] Benghazi Committee Report, p. 145.

[1768] *Id.*, p. 145.

[1769] Lamb Oversight Committee Prepared Testimony (emphasis added), p. 4; and CBS Benghazi Timeline.

- Lamb is able to listen in "almost real time" over a listen-only, audio-only feed;[1770]
- State's Regional Security Officer John Martinec in Tripoli remains on the phone with Benghazi almost constantly, keeping abreast of developments there with the beleaguered Americans;[1771]
- Throughout this Night of Benghazi CIA personnel in the Benghazi CIA Annex are in constant telephone and internet communication with the CIA Station Chief in Tripoli and CIA headquarters in Langley, Virginia;[1772] and
- About 90 minutes after the initial attack, an unmanned, unarmed surveillance drone arrives on station over Benghazi, and just before the final mortar attack on the CIA Annex a second drone arrives to relieve the first craft; these drones transmit live video feeds to Tripoli, Washington and Europe, which are recorded and viewed in real-time at the National Military Command Center, AFRICOM, European Command, the White House Situation Room, the CIA, and at various other agencies.[1773] Of these drones a CIA cable will state, "ISR [drone] coverage was [a] crucial resource [Redacted]... ISR was also crucial to provide situational awareness to Benghazi Base and Team Tripoli efforts on the ground."[1774]

[1770] Lamb Oversight Committee Prepared Testimony, p. 5.

[1771] Hicks Oversight Committee Testimony (May 8, 2013), p. 28.

[1772] E.g. Griffin, CIA Operators Were Denied Request for Help During Benghazi Attack ("... There were no communications problems at the annex, according to those present at the compound. The team was in constant radio contact with their headquarters...."). Compare Goldman and Miller, Former CIA Chief in Benghazi Challenges the Story Line of the New Movie '13 Hours' (Annex Chief of Base ("Bob") claims to *The Washington Post* he only speaks with CIA headquarters in a single phone call on this Night of Benghazi, and after a mere two minutes "I just cut it short").

[1773] Benghazi Committee Report, p. 71; Miller, CIA Rushed to Save Diplomats as Libya Attack Was Underway; Clinton, *Hard Choices*, Chap. 17, p. 394; CBS Benghazi Timeline; and Griffin, CIA Operators Were Denied Request for Help During Benghazi Attack ("... Both [drones] were capable of sending real time visuals back to U.S. officials in Washington, D.C. Any U.S. official or agency with the proper clearance, including the White House Situation Room, State Department, CIA, Pentagon and others, could call up that video in real time on their computers").

[1774] Sen. Intelligence Committee Benghazi Report (Redacted), p. 32.

THE TRUE ACCOUNT OF VALOR AND ABANDONMENT

This extensive real-time data from these multiple sources, including Charlene Lamb's almost-real-time monitoring, make highly questionable the later assertions from officials in Washington the "fog of war" just makes it too difficult to tell what is happening in Benghazi.[1775] As discussed below (Chapter 109), even the deeply flawed Benghazi Accountability Review Board later will concede, "On the night of the attacks, Benghazi, Tripoli, and Washington communicated and coordinated effectively with each other...."[1776]

(On this Night of Benghazi U.S. officials are in a fog, alright. But it isn't the fog of war. As demonstrated above in Part III, it appears the challenge is not a lack of information about what is happening on the ground in Benghazi. Rather, the problem is incompetence, indecisiveness, timidity, vacillation and a failure of will in Washington and elsewhere in *processing* and *failing to react properly* to the considerable information that *is* received in actual or near real-time.[1777]) ∎

[1775] CBS News, CIA Saw Possible Terror Ties Day After Libya Hit: AP ("Secretary of State Hillary Rodham Clinton blamed the 'fog of war' for the early conflicting accounts" of what triggered the Benghazi attacks); Clinton, *Hard Choices* ("The events of that September occurred in what is often called the 'fog of war,' with information hard to come by, and conflicting or incomplete reports making it difficult to tell what was actually happening on the ground, especially from thousands of miles away in Washington. To a frustrating degree, that fog persisted so long, in part because of continuing turmoil in Libya"), Chap. 17, p. 385; Benghazi Committee Report (Under Secretary of State Patrick Kennedy: One purpose of 7:30 Meeting was "Trying to make sure that we all, meaning across the entire U.S. Government, had the clearest coherent understanding of what was going on in the fog of war"), p. 85; and Panetta Armed Services Committee Testimony (Feb. 7, 2013) (Response to questions of Sen. Kelly Ayotte (R-NH): "The biggest problem that night, Senator, was that nobody knew really what was going on there").

[1776] Benghazi ARB Report Briefing for the Media (Remarks of ARB Vice-Chairman Michael Mullen).

[1777] See House Oversight Committee Hearings (May 8, 2013) (Remarks of Rep. Kerry Bentivolio (R-MI)) ("... The fog of battle is easily blamed when mistakes are made at the highest level...."), p. 93.

91

Thorns in the Rose Garden

Early on the morning of September 12, President Barack Hussein Obama will begin his personal implementation of the Benghazi Narrative.

First, however, he orders all U.S. flags to be flown at half-staff in honor of the Americans who died in Benghazi.[1778] He also orders increased security at U.S. diplomatic posts around the world.[1779]

Then, sometime this morning the White House releases a brief written statement by the president on the tragedy. In it he states, "I strongly condemn the *outrageous attack* on our diplomatic facility in Benghazi, which took the lives of four Americans, including Ambassador Chris Stevens." The president then commiserates with the families of the fallen. Next he asserts, "While *the United States rejects efforts to denigrate the religious beliefs of others*, we must all unequivocally oppose the kind of *senseless violence* that took the lives of these public servants."[1780] (Note the attackers didn't take the lives, "the violence" took the lives. And if you are an Islamist terrorist bent on chasing evil Americans out of eastern Libya, this violence is anything but "senseless.") This written statement does not mention "terror" or "terrorists." As discussed below, this statement's reference to "denigrat[ing] the religious beliefs of others" will be the first of many Obama allusions in the coming days and weeks to the anti-Muslim Video that is so important to the Benghazi Narrative.

Later this morning, flanked by Secretary of State Clinton, at 10:43 in a Rose Garden event to address the Benghazi calamity President Obama states, in part:

... Yesterday, four of these extraordinary Americans [working in U.S. diplomatic efforts] were killed in an *attack* on our diplomatic post in Benghazi. ... The United States

---

[1778] "Presidential Proclamation – Honoring the Victims of the Attack in Benghazi, Libya," by President Barack Obama, Obama White House Archives (Sept. 12, 2012).

[1779] "Statement by the President on the Attack in Benghazi," The White House, Obama White House Archives (Sept. 12, 2012).

[1780] *Id.* (emphasis added).

THE TRUE ACCOUNT OF VALOR AND ABANDONMENT

condemns in the strongest terms this *outrageous and shocking attack*. We're working with the government of Libya to secure our diplomats. . . . And make no mistake, we will work with the Libyan government to *bring to justice* the *killers* who *attacked* our people. Since our founding, the United States has been a nation that *respects all faiths. We reject all efforts to denigrate the religious beliefs of others.* But there is absolutely no justification to [sic] this type of *senseless violence. None.* . . .

Libyan security personnel fought back against the *attackers* alongside Americans [well, a few of them fought]. . . .

Of course yesterday was already a painful day for our nation, as we marked the solemn memory of *the 9/11 attacks*. We mourn with the families who were lost on that day. . . . And then last night we learned of the news of *this attack in Benghazi*.

As Americans let us never, ever forget that our freedom is only sustained because our people who are willing to fight for it, to stand up for it, and in some cases lay down their lives for it. Our country is only as strong as the character of our people, and the service of those – both civilian and military – who represent us around the globe. *No acts of terror* will ever shake the resolve of this great nation, alter that character, or eclipse the light of the values that we stand for. . . . We will not waiver in our commitment to see that *justice* is done for *this terrible act*. And make no mistake, *justice* will be done. . . .[1781]

Although President Obama makes one reference in this statement to "acts of terror," in these remarks he never expressly refers to the Benghazi attack as a terrorist deed. (The official White House summary of these remarks does not include Obama's "No acts of terror" quote,

---

[1781] "Remarks by the President on the Deaths of U.S. Embassy Staff in Libya," The Rose Garden, The White House, Obama White House Archives (Sept. 12, 2012) (emphasis added); and Matt Compton, "President Obama Discusses the Attack in Benghazi, Libya," Obama White House Archives (Sept. 12, 2012) (emphasis added) (*Watch video there*). See also David Martin, "Piecing Together White House Response to Benghazi," CBS News online (Oct. 19, 2012) ("Martin, Piecing Together White House Response to Benghazi"); and CBS News, CIA Saw Possible Terror Ties Day After Libya Hit: AP.

451

and itself does not mention "terror" or "terrorists."[1782]) As discussed below, for this the president later will be demonized by some – including Republican presidential candidate Mitt Romney.[1783] Again, this statement's further reference to denigrating religious beliefs is another oblique reference to the blasphemous Video. Note this presidential Rose Garden statement does not reference a protest or demonstration in Benghazi, as many subsequent administration remarks will.

(Oh, and again, Mr. President, the violence in Benghazi is not "senseless." It is *purposeful*. Its purpose is for our terrorist enemies to punish and weaken and malign the United States of America and its people on the 9/11 anniversary. And *you* in particular, Mr. President. And to chase the United States out of eastern Libya. And it succeeds.)

After these remarks, a national debate will arise concerning whether the president's reference to "No acts of terror" refers to the Benghazi attacks, to the original 9/11 attacks in 2001 (which Obama references in the previous paragraph), or to both. Bizarrely, this seemingly trivial uncertainty will form the basis of one of the most contested issues in the remainder of the 2012 presidential election campaign.[1784]

[1782] Matt Compton, "President Obama Discusses the Attack in Benghazi, Libya," Obama White House Archives (Sept. 12, 2012).

[1783] Martin, Piecing Together White House Response to Benghazi ("The attack on the U.S. consulate [sic] in Benghazi, Libya, has become a contentious issue in the presidential race, with Mitt Romney accusing the president of misleading the public about whether the attack was an act of terrorism"); CBS News, CIA Saw Possible Terror Ties Day After Libya Hit: AP (". . . Republicans say he [Obama] was speaking generally and didn't specifically call the Benghazi attack a terror attack until weeks later, with the president and other key members of his administration referring at first to the anti-Muslim movie circulating on the Internet as a precipitating event"); and CBS News, House Probes Security Leading Up to Libya Attack ("In statements immediately after the attack, neither President Barack Obama nor Secretary of State Hillary Rodham Clinton mentioned terrorism. And both gave credence to the notion that the attack was related to protests about an anti-Islam video").

[1784] E.g., Dylan Byers and Mackenzie Weinger, "CBS Under Fire for Withholding Obama's Benghazi Remarks," On Media, POLITICO website (Nov. 5, 2012) ("Byers and Mackenzie, CBS Under Fire for Withholding Obama's Benghazi Remarks") ("Confusion over when Obama called the [Benghazi] attack an 'act of terror' was one of the most significant moments of the second presidential debate on Oct. 16"); Bret Baier, "What President Obama Really Said in That '60 Minutes' Interview About Benghazi," Fox News online (Nov. 5, 2012) ("Baier, What President Obama Really Said in That '60 Minutes' Interview About Benghazi") ("That moment [when Romney challenged Obama's claim he had called Benghazi terrorism in his Rose Garden statement] was one of the most intense exchanges in the second presidential debate. Romney was on the offensive on what conservatives believed was a serious

THE TRUE ACCOUNT OF VALOR AND ABANDONMENT

(To be fair to the president – and unlike many of Obama's detractors – the author believes on its face this reference to "acts of terror" reasonably can be construed as a reference to Benghazi.[1785] After all, Benghazi is the only act of terror to have occurred the previous day. Cairo is a chaotic, violent and disturbing demonstration, but is not an act of terror. Alternatively, Obama's phrase might be interpreted as a reference to *both* the original 9/11 in 2001 and to Benghazi on its eleventh anniversary. The president's statement mentions *both* events in earlier paragraphs before the "No acts of terror" quote. However, as discussed in the following chapter, in an interview later this same day President Obama surprisingly will concede (in a segment suppressed by CBS News for seven and one-half weeks) he does *not* call Benghazi a terrorist attack in his Rose Garden remarks!)

After this Rose Garden statement, President Obama is driven to the State Department, where he offers condolences to the personnel there. He speaks for about twenty minutes regarding the important work America's diplomats like Chris Stevens perform to advance America's national security.[1786] Then, before leaving Washington for a campaign event, Obama will sit for a previously-scheduled "60 Minutes" interview with Steve Kroft of CBS News, as discussed in detail in Chapter 92.

(The author believes during the coming weeks Mitt Romney's campaign and Obama's other detractors make a foolish and significant political miscalculation in insisting Obama has not linked Benghazi to terrorism in his Rose Garden statement. This challenge badly damages

---

vulnerability of Obama – the handling of the Benghazi attack and what he called it from the beginning"); and Jonah Goldberg Op Ed, "Goldberg: Benghazi's Smoking Guns," *Los Angeles Times* online (May 14, 2013) ("Goldberg: Benghazi's Smoking Guns") (". . . The president said Monday [in May 2013 remarks] that he immediately referred to the Benghazi attacks as 'terrorism.' This is at best a brutal bending of the truth. He used the word 'terror' generically in the Rose Garden on Sept. 12. . . .").

[1785] Compare Martin, Piecing Together White House Response to Benghazi (". . . Obama stepped into the Rose Garden and spoke of the killing of four Americans as if it were a terrorist attack"), to Ferrara, Benghazi: Obama's Actions Amount to a Shameful Dereliction of Duty (". . . The transcript [of Obama's Rose Garden statement] in plain black and white shows that Obama was not even talking about Benghazi when he mentioned terror, but about terrorism more generally, as displayed on 9/11. Do you see precisely the further 'calculated deception'").

[1786] "President Obama Greets State Department Employees," Obama White House Archives (Sept. 12, 2012); Matt Compton, "President Obama Discusses the Attack in Benghazi, Libya," Obama White House Archives (Sept. 12, 2012); and Clinton, *Hard Choices*, Chap. 17, pp. 400-401.

the credibility of Obama's critics over the next few weeks. Equally important, even though arguably true it shifts the focus away from other salient points for which Obama, Clinton and Panetta have no good response. Romney and the media should be focusing instead on other issues, including: why Obama's administration denies repeated requests for more security in Libya, and in fact removes significant security assets from Libya shortly before the attacks; why Stevens is allowed to go to Benghazi with woefully inadequate security on the 9/11 anniversary (especially when, as we later learn, the State Department has decided to replace its local Blue Mountain security force and anti-U.S. protests are planned in Egypt); and why no serious military rescue effort for three dozen Americans is mounted on the Night of Benghazi.[1787]

(Further, Obama and his team should be faulted for their undisputed, repeated and deliberate refusals *in subsequent days* to characterize the Benghazi attacks as terrorism. Obsessing over these Rose Garden remarks instead is one of many serious blunders the Romney campaign and Obama's other political adversaries will commit. Romney has aimed for Obama's rhetorical capillaries, instead of focusing on his exposed terrorism policy jugular. It will be a fatal political error.

(In the author's view, as demonstrated in these pages Barack Obama is answerable for far more serious transgressions relating to Benghazi than his imprecise language in the Rose Garden.) ■

[1787] E.g., Goldberg, Benghazi's Smoking Guns (". . . [T]he true core of this story has nothing to do with media vanity or talking points – or a political circus. The real issue is that for reasons yet to be determined – politics? ideology? incompetence? all three? – the administration was unprepared for an attack on Sept. 11, of all dates. When the attack came, they essentially did nothing as our own people were begging for help – other than to tell those begging to help that they must 'stand down'").

92

The "60 Minutes" Interview

After he returns to the White House from the State Department on September 12, President Obama sits in the Blue Room for a previously-scheduled interview with the CBS News program "60 Minutes." This interview mostly involves economic and other domestic issues. However, the crisis in Benghazi the previous night inevitably comes up. Without explaining to its viewers it is doing so, CBS actually releases the Benghazi discussion in three different installments. The final one is disclosed (online only) just two days before the election.

The September 23 Package:

In the version of the "60 Minutes" interview CBS originally broadcasts (on September 23), interviewer Steve Kroft asks the president, "Have recent events in the Middle East given you any pause about your support for the governments that have come to power following the Arab Spring?" Obama responds, in part:

"Well, I'd said even at the time that this is going to be a rocky path.... I was pretty certain and continue to be ... pretty certain that *there are going to be bumps in the road* because ... in a lot of these places, the one organizing principle has been Islam. ... There are strains of extremism, and anti-Americanism, and anti-Western sentiment. ... This is a tumultuous time that we're in."[1788]

(*Please* tell me the president is not describing the death of four American government servants the previous night as "bumps in the road.")

Despite the Benghazi tragedy having occurred just hours before, subsequently there is only a passing reference by Kroft to the Benghazi attacks. He states (in part), "Since the Benghazi tragedy, your opponent has attacked you as being weak on national defense and weak on

---

[1788] Fox News Transcript of Obama on '60 Minutes,'" Fox News online (Sept. 24, 2012) ("Fox 60 Minutes Transcript").

foreign policy...." Kroft pauses for Obama to react. President Obama's response does not even mention Benghazi! That's it. No more Benghazi. Even casual viewers are left wondering why Kroft does not ask the president a number of follow-up questions about this lethal attack on Americans, and the death of our ambassador. This cursory mention of an American tragedy just hours old seems odd to many.[1789]

By sheer luck in timing, CBS has a major "scoop" – the very first televised interview of the president the day after the Benghazi attacks in which four Americans are murdered, including an ambassador. Yet for some reason, on "60 Minutes" CBS initially does not air the entire portion of the interview dealing with Benghazi. As explained next, without any disclaimer CBS withholds a segment for another 26 days, and keeps secret from the public an even more critical portion for a total of 42 days. It is all quite bizarre. Why does CBS do it?

The October 19 Package:

Later, on October 19, three days after the second presidential debate on October 16 (discussed below in Chapter 107), CBS will release more of the September 12 "60 Minutes" interview. In the debate, Obama will claim in his Rose Garden statement he *had* called Benghazi a terrorist attack.

This second package of footage CBS airs includes the following exchange. Kroft asks, "But there are reports that they were very heavily armed with grenades, that doesn't sound like your normal demonstration." President Obama responds:

... [W]e're still investigating exactly what happened. I don't want to jump the gun on this. But you're right that this is not a situation that was exactly the same as what happened in [Cairo] Egypt. And my suspicion is there are folks involved in this who were looking to target Americans from the start....[1790]

[1789] E.g., Fox News Transcript of Obama on '60 Minutes,'" Fox News online (Sept. 24, 2012). See also, e.g., Baier, "What President Obama Really Said in That '60 Minutes' Interview About Benghazi" ("Whatever your politics, there are a lot of loose ends here, a lot of unanswered questions and a lot of strange political maneuvers that don't add up").

[1790] Interview of President Obama with Steve Kroft, "60 Minutes" (Sept. 12, 2012); Baier, What President Obama Really Said In That "60 Minutes" Interview About Benghazi; and Sharyl Attkisson, "Emails Detail Unfolding Benghazi Attack," CBS News online (Oct. 24, 2012).

THE TRUE ACCOUNT OF VALOR AND ABANDONMENT

However, in this interview clip, Obama does not explicitly characterize the Benghazi attacks as terrorism.[1791]

As discussed next, this package CBS releases on October 19 omits a vital portion of the "60 Minutes" interview that *directly contradicts* Obama's statement made in the October 16 debate.[1792]

The November 4 Package:

Then, 16 days later on November 4 at about 6:00 p.m. – a day and one-half before polling places open – CBS releases online at CBS.com (but not on television news programs) a final, previously-withheld portion of Kroft's original September 12 interview with the president.[1793] (This is after many millions of Americans already have voted by mail or otherwise in "early voting," or have made up their minds and likely no longer are following campaign news.)

In this last fragment of the original interview released online, interviewer Kroft asks, "Mr. President, this morning you went out of your way to avoid the use of the word 'terrorism' in connection with the Libya attack." Off camera in the background, President Obama's voice apparently can be heard saying, "Right." Kroft then asks, "Do you believe that this was a terrorist attack?" The president responds, "Well, *it's too early to know exactly how this came about, what group was involved*. But obviously it was an attack on Americans. . . ."[1794]

[1791] Baier, What President Obama Really Said In That "60 Minutes" Interview About Benghazi.

[1792] Byers and Weinger, CBS Under Fire for Withholding Obama's Benghazi Remarks.

[1793] Baier, What President Obama Really Said In That "60 Minutes" Interview About Benghazi; and Byers and Weinger, CBS Under Fire for Withholding Obama's Benghazi Remarks ("CBS News is continuing to draw fire for withholding footage of a Sept. 12 interview with President Barack Obama in which he said it was 'too early to tell' whether or not the previous day's attack in Benghazi, Libya, had been an act of terror"); and Attkisson, *Stonewalled*, Conclusion, p. 380.

[1794] Byers and Weinger, CBS Under Fire for Withholding Obama's Benghazi Remarks; Baier, What President Obama Really Said In That "60 Minutes" Interview About Benghazi; "Lou Dobbs Tonight," Fox Business Channel (Nov. 6, 2012) (emphasis added) (*Watch video there*; Go to 0:20-38); Goldberg, Benghazi's Smoking Guns (". . . In a segment that "60 Minutes" helpfully sat on for almost two months, Obama told Steve Kroft that 'it's too early to know' whether the attack was terrorism. . . ."); and Attkisson, *Stonewalled*, Chap. 4, p. 196 and Conclusion, p. 378.

In this final sliver of the September 12 interview, President Obama thus acquiesces in Steve Kroft's assertion Obama in his Rose Garden Statement has *not* called the Benghazi attacks terrorism. (As noted previously, the author believes Obama *has* called it an "act of terror.") Thus, this last-minute footage would appear to confirm the charges Mitt Romney and other Republicans have been making for weeks on this point.[1795] It is exactly the opposite of what Obama says in the second presidential debate on October 16 with Mitt Romney. (Small wonder Americans are confused about Benghazi.)

Had CBS released this portion of this "60 Minutes" interview shortly after the October 16 presidential debate, it would have been a blockbuster news story.[1796] CBS supposedly is in the news business. Why in the world does CBS keep this major news item a secret for 16 more days of the campaign?[1797]

[1795] Baier, What President Obama Really Said In That "60 Minutes" Interview About Benghazi (". . . Right after getting out of the Rose Garden, where, according to the second debate and other accounts he definitively called the attack terrorism, Obama is asked point blank about not calling it terrorism. He blinks and does not push back. Understand that this ["60 Minutes"] interview is just hours after he gets out of the Rose Garden"); Remarks of K.T. McFarland on "Lou Dobbs Tonight," Fox Business Channel (Nov. 6, 2012) (*Watch video there*; Go to 1:12-23); and Becket Adams, "Flashback: '60 Minutes' Edits Obama's Answer on Benghazi," *Washington Examiner* online (June 28, 2016) (Quoting former House Speaker Newt Gingrich: "The thing that is most egregious about CBS is that they edited out the part of the interview that would have undermined him [Obama] after the second debate. . . .").

[1796] Baier, What President Obama Really Said In That "60 Minutes" Interview About Benghazi ("Why wasn't it news after the president said what he said in the second debate, knowing what they had in that '60 Minutes' tape – why didn't they use it then? . . ."); Attkisson, *Stonewalled* ("President Obama acknowledged in a *60 Minutes* interview that day that he had intentionally avoided calling them terrorist attacks"), Chap. 4, p. 222; *Id.*, Conclusion, p. 379; Byers and Weinger, CBS Under Fire for Withholding Obama's Benghazi Remarks (Quoting interview with former House Speaker Newt Gingrich: "The thing that is most egregious about CBS is that they edited out the part of the [September 12 '60 Minutes'] interview that would have undermined him [Obama] after the second debate. . . . [W]hy didn't they decide to release it after the debate? They only released half of his remarks, which was explicitly misleading"); and *Id.* (Quoting interview with former White House press secretary Ari Fleisher: ". . . It's astounding that CBS would sit on this instead of releasing it the morning after the second debate when the major focus was on Benghazi and whether or not the president declared it an act of terror. . . .").

[1797] Byers and Weinger, CBS Under Fire for Withholding Obama's Benghazi Remarks (". . . [S]ources at rival television networks, who declined to speak on the record, expressed confusion over CBS's decision. 'It's surprising they held on to any of it,' one source said. 'If [we had the interview], we would've put that stuff out the second it became news – again – after the debate. All of it'") (bracketed editing in original

THE TRUE ACCOUNT OF VALOR AND ABANDONMENT

(There is only one plausible answer: CBS is attempting to protect President Obama until it is too late for Romney's campaign to discover and react to Obama's admission in a manner that might affect the election.[1798] By releasing it online late on November 4, CBS still can claim it discloses the damaging footage before the election (barely).[1799] By the way, have we mentioned that Deputy National Security Advisor Ben Rhodes is the brother of David Rhodes, president of CBS News?)

After the Interview

Following his "60 Minutes" interview, President Obama boards Air Force One and travels to a political fund raiser in Las Vegas, Nevada.[1800] (Out of decency and respect for the fallen Americans he should cancel this political event, but does not.[1801]) At the campaign

---

article); and *Id.* ("Former White House press secretary Ari Fleisher said he was 'dumbstruck' by the network's decision not to report on such a newsworthy item").

[1798] Byers and Weinger, CBS Under Fire for Withholding Obama's Benghazi Remarks ("In interviews with POLITICO, former House Speaker Newt Gingrich said CBS had been 'explicitly misleading' in order 'to protect President Obama.'. . . [C]onservative columnist Byron York wrote on Twitter that the network had 'a scandal on their hands'"); *Id.* (Former Speaker Gingrich: "This is part of the elite media's extraordinary protection of Barack Obama and I think it's the most distorted journalism in modern times"); *Id.* (Describing Senator John McCain (R-AZ) also as seeing CBS's actions as "an attempt by the network to protect the president"; McCain: "This is not the first action of this nature by a major network, but it is what it is. . . . It's in their DNA"); and Attkisson, *Stonewalled* (". . . [U]pper-level journalists at CBS had been a party to misleading the public. *Why wouldn't they have immediately released the operative sound bite after Romney raised the issue in the debate? It would have been a great moment for CBS. The kind of break that news organizations hope for. We had our hands on original material that no other news outlet had that would shed light on an important controversy. But we hid it* ") (emphasis in original), Conclusion, p. 379.

[1799] Byers and Weinger, CBS Under Fire for Withholding Obama's Benghazi Remarks (Quoting interview with former White House Press Secretary Ari Fleisher: ". . . I think somebody smart at CBS figured out, if we don't release it today, before the election, we'll be in huge trouble. . . .").

[1800] "Remarks by the President at a Campaign Event – Las Vegas, NV," Obama White House Archives website (Sept. 12, 2012).

[1801] ABC News Transcript of Second 2012 Presidential Debate Moderated by Candy Crowley of CNN's "State of the Union" (Oct. 16, 2012), ABC News online (Mitt Romney: "But I find more troubling than this, that on . . . the day following the assassination of the United States ambassador, the first time that's happened since 1979, . . . when we have four Americans killed there, when apparently we didn't know what happened, that the president, the day after that happened, flies to Las Vegas for a political fund-raiser, then the next day to Colorado for another . . . political event").

rally in Las Vegas, the president mentions the attacks in Benghazi, and praises the four dead Americans. As in the Rose Garden this very morning, Obama does not explicitly call the Benghazi assaults an act of terrorism, but he does mention "terror" in a general manner.[1802]

(On September 12, President Obama may have time to deliver remarks in the Rose Garden, visit the State Department, be interviewed by "60 Minutes," and fly to Las Vegas for a fund-raiser, but not for his Presidential Daily Briefing ("PDB"). According to the Select Benghazi Committee Report, Obama does not take his in-person daily briefing the day after the fatal Benghazi terrorist attacks. (This is not unusual when the president is in the White House, as opposed to traveling – when he usually does receive it in-person. Today of all days, one would think he would make an exception.) Instead, only his Chief of Staff Jack Lew receives the PDB in-person.[1803])

Barack Obama is back on the campaign trail. And the Benghazi Narrative is in motion. ∎

[1802] "Remarks by the President at a Campaign Event – Las Vegas, NV," Obama White House Archives website (Sept. 12, 2012) (emphasis added) (". . . And we want to send a message all around the world – anybody who would do us harm: No *act of terror* will dim the light of the values that we proudly shine on the rest of the world, and no act of violence will shake the resolve of the United States of America") (*Watch video there*; Go to 7:28 - 10:30). (There are claims that after this campaign event President Obama attends subsequent parties with Beyonce and Jay-Z. See, e.g., Ferrara, Benghazi: Obama's Actions Amount to a Shameful Dereliction of Duty. However, the author is unable to confirm this. Indeed, such rumors seem inconsistent with Obama's official schedule, which states he makes a late flight to another political rally in Colorado.)

[1803] Benghazi Committee Report, p. 167; *Id.*, Appendix H, pp. 575 and 580-581; Stephen F. Hayes, "Obama Did Not Ask for an Intel Brief the Day After the Benghazi Attack," *The Weekly Standard* online (June 28, 2016) (". . . Barack Obama skipped his daily intelligence briefing one day after the Benghazi attacks on September 11, 2012. . . ."); and Hank Berrien, "Where Was Obama During Intelligence Briefing the Morning After Benghazi?" The Daily Wire website (June 28, 2016) ("Where was Barack Obama on September 12, 2012, one day after the Benghazi terror attack that killed four Americans? Not at his daily intelligence briefing, according to documents secured by the Benghazi Select Committee; Obama skipped that meeting").

93

The "Special Briefing" for Reporters

Sometime during the evening of September 12, 2012 – after the president's Rose Garden statement – the State Department holds a "Special Briefing" via teleconference for reporters from major news outlets. The purpose is to update them on the unfolding events in Benghazi and Libya.

Three "senior" Obama administration officials conduct this briefing. Their names are not identified in the official transcript of the Special Briefing that is posted on State's website. (Obviously, all the reporters participating know who the briefers are.) The principal briefer appears to be from the State Department. At least one of the other briefers is from the Defense Department. The third senior official leaves the teleconference before speaking.[1804]

The Special Briefing begins with an administration official making the following disclaimer:

> ... First of all, we want to make clear that we are still here today operating within the confusion of first reports. Many details of what happened in Benghazi are still unknown or unclear. The account we're going to give you endeavors to reconstruct the events of last night to the best of our ability now. And again, this reflects our current accounting of events. These are first reports, and so the facts could very well change as we get a better understanding.[1805]

(Sure enough, like most other "first reports" the Special Briefing gets many of the true facts wrong. It is unknowable whether this is intentional, inadvertent, or some of both.)

The U.S. officials conducting the Special Briefing advance several components of the Benghazi Narrative: Security at the Mission Compound is "robust"; this is a "regular" visit by Stevens to Benghazi that he makes "periodically"; we can't say yet if it is terrorism; and in preparing for the 9/11 anniversary in Benghazi, "... there was *no*

[1804] September 12 Special Briefing.

[1805] *Id.*

information and there were *no threat streams* to indicate that we were insufficiently postured."[1806] (Oh, *brother!*)

However, in response to specific questions, the briefers defer answering whether or when there are protests in Benghazi, and whether the Benghazi attacks are related to the inflammatory internet Video. In one very revealing admission, one of the briefers makes a significant assertion. When asked which agency directs "the operation" to respond to the attacks, the State Department briefer declares:

> It was very much an inter-agency effort ... while the violence was ongoing and in the aftermath and throughout the day today, <u>led</u> in the usual way by the National Security Council with the participation of all of us. Obviously, the State Department had a huge piece of that, but all agencies – all relevant agencies were involved.[1807]

Note there is no specific mention of the Pentagon! Also, the National Security Council is part of the Executive Office of the President.[1808] In other words, the *White House – not* the Pentagon – is running the Benghazi operation during this crisis. And as noted above, it is Denis McDonough – not his boss, the National Security Advisor, Tom Donilon – who is supervising the NSC's actions concerning Benghazi. (Again, McDonough has no military experience.)

(Where *is* Tom Donilon on this Night of Benghazi? The Select Benghazi Committee's massive report barely mentions him! A lengthy profile of Donilon published in *Foreign Policy* in May 2013 does not even contain the word "Benghazi."[1809] He is the Stealth National Security Advisor. He cannot be detected, even by radar.) ■

[1806] *Id.* (emphasis added) ("We had a physical perimeter barrier, obviously. And then we had a *robust* American security presence inside the compound, including a strong component of regional security officers. . . .").

[1807] *Id.* (emphasis added).

[1808] Presidential Memorandum: Organization of the National Security Council and the Homeland Security Council, White House website (Jan. 28, 2017); and Obama White House Archives.

[1809] See Jeffrey Lord, "Benghazi: What Was Tom Donilon Doing?" The American Spectator online (May 6, 2014); Mark Landler, "Rice to Replace Donilon in the Top National Security Post," *The New York Times* online (June 5, 2013) ("Critics have faulted Mr. Donilon, whose background is in Democratic Party politics, for not functioning as a strategic adviser to Mr. Obama"); and James Mann, "Obama's Gray Man," Foreign Policy online (May 28, 2013).

94

Massaging the Talking Points

Almost immediately after the attacks, disagreements arise among top Obama administration officials regarding how to describe the Benghazi debacle to Congress, the media, and the public. They must agree on a consistent, plausible-sounding version of the Benghazi Narrative's many details and moving parts. Given this Narrative's many flaws, this will prove a difficult task.

The Washington Post later reports:

> ... [A]n intense bureaucratic clash took place between the State Department and the CIA over which agency would get to tell the story of how the tragedy unfolded. That clash played out in the development of administration talking points that have been at the center of the controversy over the handling of the incident...[1810]

(If only it were just an "incident.") The *Post* will claim further that in the five days following the attacks "senior officials from the Central Intelligence Agency and the State Department argued over how much information to disclose about the assault..."[1811]

"Senior" Obama administration officials will insist "none of Obama's political advisers were involved in discussions around the *original* talking points, only national security staff officials."[1812] The use of the word "original" may limit this assertion to the initial draft of the "Talking Points," which almost everyone agrees the CIA drafts ("CIA Talking Points"). Moreover, "national security staff" includes personnel of the National Security Council, who are part of the White House staff. And as explained above, under Barack Obama a number of these staffers very much function as political advisors. (These include National Security Advisor Thomas Donilon, his deputies Denis McDonough and Ben Rhodes, NSC spokesperson Tommy Vietor, and other NSC aides such as Samantha Power.)

[1810] Wilson and DeYoung, Benghazi E-mails Show Clash Between State Department, CIA.

[1811] *Id.*

[1812] *Id.* (emphasis added).

Subsequent reports will establish these CIA Talking Points are revised at least a dozen times. ABC News publishes these twelve different versions in May 2013.[1813] The Senate Intelligence Committee formally releases these twelve edited variants in its January 2014 report.[1814]

The CIA Talking Points' Significance

There is nothing sinister or inappropriate for administrations to prepare and use talking points. Probably every government in history has done so. The issue with the Benghazi CIA Talking Points is whether in the weeks leading up to a national election Team Obama deliberately crafts them to misstate some facts, and to hide others. As we discuss here, the evidence is overwhelming Obama's people will do both.

Eight months after Benghazi, President Obama will dismiss the importance of the CIA Talking Points brouhaha. He asserts, "We dishonor them [the Americans who died in Benghazi] when we turn things like this into a political circus." He continues, ". . . the whole issue of talking points, throughout this process, frankly, has been a sideshow. . . . There's no there there."[1815]

For somewhat different reasons than President Obama, the author agrees the news media, the Republicans, and presidential candidate Mitt Romney's campaign all make far too much of the CIA Talking Points' many inadequacies. We already have established Obama administration officials repeatedly have lied about what happened before, during and after the Benghazi terror attacks. And we discuss in later chapters still further evidence of this boundless mendacity. Hence, it no longer is necessary to rely exclusively upon the development of the infamous CIA Talking Points to prove this vital point. Also, as conservative commentator Jonah Goldberg of *National Review* points out, ". . . [I]t's worth remembering that Obama and then-Secretary of State Hillary Rodham Clinton didn't get their information from the talking points. They got their information earlier and from much higher

---

[1813] See ABC News online (May 10, 2013); and Wilson and DeYoung, Benghazi E-mails Show Clash Between State Department, CIA.

[1814] Sen. Intelligence Committee Benghazi Report, Appendix I, pp. 43-52.

[1815] Obama-Cameron Joint Press Conference; and Goldberg, Benghazi's Smoking Guns.

THE TRUE ACCOUNT OF VALOR AND ABANDONMENT

authorities, like then-CIA Director David H. Petraeus. . . ."[1816] (And, as discussed below in Chapter 97, from close presidential advisor Ben Rhodes.)

Even more significant, as documented elsewhere in this book Team Obama has far more grievous Benghazi sins to atone for than drafting misleading and useless speaking points. Accordingly, we provide here only a relatively brief overview of the CIA Talking Points' confusing evolution. (Readers interested in a more detailed dissection of the formulation of the CIA Talking Points can find them in multiple sources, including those referenced in the notes.[1817])

The CIA's Initial Talking Points Drafts

On Thursday, September 13, after being briefed about Benghazi by CIA Director Petraeus, the ranking Democrat on the House Intelligence Committee, C.A. "Dutch" Ruppersberger (D-MD), reportedly asks for guidance concerning what members of Congress can say publicly regarding the attacks without disclosing classified information. General Petraeus agrees to have his agency prepare such a document.[1818]

According to *The Washington Post*, across the Potomac River from Washington at Langley, Virginia, CIA Deputy Director Mike Morell is given responsibility for overseeing the preparation of the CIA Talking Points.[1819] The CIA's Office of Terrorism Analysis is tasked with

---

[1816] Goldberg, Benghazi's Smoking Guns (". . . The talking points drafted by the State Department, the CIA, and the White House and given to congressional Republicans and, most famously, to U.N. Ambassador Susan Rice are not the center of this story. . . . More central are the talking points – written or unwritten – that Obama and Clinton used for weeks after the attacks").

[1817] Sen. Intelligence Committee Benghazi Report, pp. 37 and 43-52; Hayes, The Benghazi Talking Points; Drafts of CIA Talking Points, ABC News online (Possibly May 10, 2013); Jonathan Karl and Chris Good, "The Benghazi Emails, Talking Points Changed at State Dept.'s Request," ABC News online (May 15, 2013); and "The Benghazi Attack of September 11, 2012," A Judicial Watch Special Investigative Report (Jan. 22, 2013; Updated April 29, 2014), pp. 12-13.

[1818] Hayes, The Benghazi Talking Points; and House Intelligence Committee Benghazi Report, Executive Summary (Nov. 21, 2014) ("Fifth, the Committee finds that the process used to generate the talking points HPSCI asked for – and which were used for Ambassador Rice's public appearances – was flawed. HPSCI asked for the talking points solely to aid Members' ability to communicate publicly using the best available intelligence at the time . . ."), p. 1.

[1819] Wilson and DeYoung, Benghazi E-mails Show Clash Between State Department, CIA ("Behind the scenes, as a then-close presidential campaign entered its final stretch,

465

drafting a written response for use by congressmen. (Ponder this: Why would the CIA early on assign this task to a unit with "Terrorism" in its name unless the Agency already believes or at least suspects at the time Benghazi likely is an act of terrorism?) It is this responsive CIA document that will morph through numerous edits into the infamous CIA Talking Points.

The first draft, containing six paragraphs (or "bullet points"), reportedly is distributed internally within the CIA for comment at about 11:15 a.m. on Friday, September 14. Within the agency, the CIA Talking Points are edited (in order) by the Office of General Counsel, the Offices of Public Affairs and Congressional Affairs, and then Deputy Director Mike Morell (finishing his edits at around 5:09 p.m.). It is important to note at this point Morell is sufficiently satisfied with this relatively long version (still containing all six bullet-points) he authorizes its distribution for *interagency* comment within the administration in the early evening this same Friday. The State Department reportedly gets its first crack at them later this evening.[1820]

This September 14 circulated CIA version specifically mentions Ansar al-Sharia's possible involvement, and also references al Qaeda.[1821] At some point, "Unidentified government officials removed references to terrorism and al Qaeda" from the version of the CIA Talking Points released to the public.[1822]

Changes Made by Other Agencies

A number of other revisions are made to the CIA Talking Points in the next 24 hours. After Deputy Director Mike Morell signs off on

---

State Department officials found themselves at a disadvantage in debating the CIA, whose deputy director, Mike Morell, took charge of organizing days of internal agency discussions into a coherent set of talking points for members of Congress").

[1820] Sen. Intelligence Committee Benghazi Report, Appendix I, pp. 45-48; Wilson and DeYoung, Benghazi E-mails Show Clash Between State Department, CIA; and Hayes, The Benghazi Talking Points ("The talking points were first distributed to officials in the interagency vetting process 6:52 p.m. on Friday [September 14]").

[1821] Sen. Intelligence Committee Benghazi Report, Appendix I, pp. 47-48; Hayes, The Benghazi Talking Points ("This initial CIA draft included the assertion that the U.S. government 'know[s] that Islamic extremists with ties to al Qaeda participated in the attack'"); and Benson, Petraeus: We Knew Benghazi Was Terrorism "Almost Immediately."

[1822] Attkisson, Diplomat: U.S. Special Forces Told "You Can't Go" to Benghazi During Attacks.

THE TRUE ACCOUNT OF VALOR AND ABANDONMENT

them at the CIA, the Director of National Intelligence makes revisions. Although DNI later confirms its Director, James Clapper, has revised the CIA Talking Points, members of the intelligence community testify before the House Intelligence Committee they do not know who has changed the CIA Talking Points.[1823] (*Ooops!* More contradictions.) Then the CIA Talking Points go to the FBI, whose suggested changes all are incorporated by the CIA.[1824]

At various times, administration officials tell the media the changes to the CIA Talking Points are made for intelligence reasons (to protect classified information) or legal ones (don't compromise the FBI investigation),[1825] or for purely "stylistic" purposes. Senate Intelligence Committee Chair Diane Feinstein (D-CA) assures the media the only change the White House makes to the CIA Talking Points is to clarify the Mission Compound is not a "consulate," as has been reported erroneously earlier, and substituting the term "diplomatic post" or "mission."[1826] (However, Feinstein's own committee's report later will refute her claim a bit, and disclose Tommy Vietor (on behalf of White House counterterrorism guru John Brennan) makes other minor changes.[1827])

Later, on November 28, Obama's Press Secretary Jay Carney will repeat Feinstein's inaccurate assertion from the White House Press Briefing Room – with respect to changes by both the White House *and*

[1823] "Sources: Office of the DNI Cut 'al Qaeda' Reference from Benghazi Talking Points, and CIA, FBI Signed Off," CBS News online (Nov. 20, 2012).

[1824] Sen. Intelligence Committee Benghazi Report, Appendix I, pp. 50-51; "Sources: Office of the DNI Cut 'al Qaeda' Reference from Benghazi Talking Points, and CIA, FBI Signed Off," CBS News online (Nov. 20, 2012); and Hayes, The Benghazi Talking Points (Discussions regarding CIA Talking Points involve "senior officials" from National Security Council, CIA, Office of Director of National Intelligence, State Department and the White House).

[1825] Eric Schmitt, "Petraeus Says U.S. Tried to Avoid Tipping Off Terrorists After Libya Attack," *The New York Times* online (Nov. 16, 2012) (Regarding identifying the terrorist groups likely involved in the Benghazi attacks, ". . . Justice Department lawyers expressed concern about jeopardizing the F.B.I.'s criminal inquiry in the attacks. . . ."); and Wilson and DeYoung, Benghazi E-mails Show Clash Between State Department, CIA.

[1826] Madison, Congress to Investigate CIA Talking Points on Benghazi (Sen. Feinstein: ". . . I've checked into this. I believe it to be absolute fact. And that was the word consulate was changed to mission. That's the only change that anyone in the White House made, and I've checked this out"); and Wilson and DeYoung, Benghazi E-mails Show Clash Between State Department, CIA.

[1827] Sen. Intelligence Committee Benghazi Report, Appendix I, pp. 49-50.

the State Department![1828] (Does anyone believe this?) Far more plausibly, *The Washington Post* later concludes in May 2013, "... White House officials were *directly involved in developing the talking points* through discussions with the CIA, the State Department, the FBI, the Justice Department, and elements of the Pentagon."[1829] (In the author's view, the Pentagon appears to play little, if any, role, in modifying the CIA Talking Points.)

The eventual modifications made by (or at the request of) other agencies to the original CIA Talking Points include the following, substantive changes (among others):

- Changing characterizations of the "attacks" to "demonstrations" and "violent demonstrations";[1830]
- Removing references to terrorism;[1831]
- Eliminating references to al Qaeda, including prior CIA warnings concerning al Qaeda in Libya;[1832]
- Excising references to Ansar al-Sharia;[1833]
- Deleting references to "Islamic extremists";[1834]

[1828] White House Press Secretary, Daily Press Briefing, The White House (Nov. 28, 2012) (Carney: "... The White House and State Department have made clear that the single adjustment that was made to those Talking Points by either of these two institutions were [sic] changing the word 'consulate' to 'diplomatic facility' because 'consulate' was inaccurate") (*Watch video there*; Go to 3:44 - 4:46).

[1829] Wilson and DeYoung, Benghazi E-mails Show Clash Between State Department, CIA (emphasis added). See also Attkisson, *Stonewalled* ("... [T]he 'extensive public record' shows that White House officials and the State Department had significant input into editing the talking points into their final, scrubbed version"), Chap. 4. p. 214.

[1830] Sen. Intelligence Committee Benghazi Report, Appendix I, pp. 46-47; Wilson and DeYoung, Benghazi E-mails Show Clash Between State Department, CIA; and Hayes, The Benghazi Talking Points.

[1831] House Foreign Affairs Benghazi Majority Staff Report, p. 14; and Attkisson, Diplomat: U.S. Special Forces Told "You Can't Go" to Benghazi During Attacks.

[1832] "Sources: Office of the DNI Cut 'al Qaeda' Reference from Benghazi Talking Points, and CIA, FBI Signed Off," CBS News online (Nov. 20, 2012); Attkisson, Diplomat: U.S. Special Forces Told "You Can't Go" to Benghazi During Attacks; Hayes, The Benghazi Talking Points; and Fox News, Pfeiffer May 2013 Interview with Wallace (references to terror and al Qaeda removed from CIA Talking Points by CIA, not by White House or State Department) (*Watch video there*; Go to 6:15-27).

[1833] Wilson and DeYoung, Benghazi E-mails Show Clash Between State Department, CIA; and Hayes, The Benghazi Talking Points.

[1834] Hayes, The Benghazi Talking Points.

THE TRUE ACCOUNT OF VALOR AND ABANDONMENT

- Eliminating mention of prior CIA warnings to State about extremism in eastern Libya;[1835]
- Removing mention of the possible surveillance of the U.S. facility in Benghazi;[1836] and
- Omitting the fact "unknown gunmen had carried out at least five recent attacks in and around Benghazi against 'foreign interests.'"[1837]

The first bullet adding the notion of "demonstrations" to the document could have been disproven at any point on September 12 or thereafter by anyone on Team Obama making a single phone call to any of the thirty Americans in Germany who survived Benghazi.

The CIA claims references to Ansar al-Sharia are removed because this information is classified.[1838] If classified, why does the CIA's Office of Terrorism Analysis initially even put it in their original draft? They know they are preparing a document congressmen desire to use in speaking to the public and the media about Benghazi.[1839] And why does CIA Deputy Director Morell approve a version that mentions Ansar al-Sharia twice?[1840] The Justice Department and FBI reportedly have a concern about referring to Ansar al-Sharia and terrorism because it poses a problem for the FBI's criminal inquiry.[1841] If true, why does the U.S. government later designate as a terrorist one of the only two men arrested for Benghazi in January 2014, and label Ansar al-Sharia as a "terrorist organization"?[1842] Before the first criminal trial even occurs. (More inconsistencies.)

[1835] House Foreign Affairs Benghazi Majority Staff Report, p. 14.

[1836] Hayes, The Benghazi Talking Points.

[1837] Wilson and DeYoung, Benghazi E-mails Show Clash Between State Department, CIA; Babbin, Whitewashing Benghazi; and Hayes, The Benghazi Talking Points.

[1838] Miller, CIA Rushed to Save Diplomats as Libya Attack Was Underway; and Wilson and DeYoung, Benghazi E-mails Show Clash Between State Department, CIA.

[1839] Wilson and DeYoung, Benghazi E-mails Show Clash Between State Department, CIA (Ansar al-Sharia not mentioned in final CIA Talking Points because information was classified, "even though the early versions . . . showed that the agency initially intended to name the group").

[1840] Sen. Intelligence Committee Benghazi Report, Appendix I, pp. 47-48.

[1841] Wilson and DeYoung, Benghazi E-mails Show Clash Between State Department, CIA.

[1842] Hsu, U.S. Will Not Seek Death Penalty for Accused Ringleader in Benghazi Attacks.

Many months later, former National Security Council spokesperson Tommy Vietor is interviewed on Fox News. Host Bret Baier of Fox asks Vietor if he was the person who changed the word "attacks" in the CIA Talking Points to "demonstrations." (In fact, he apparently was not.[1843]) In typical Team Obama fashion, Vietor deflects the question and answers "Maybe," but he does not really remember. Vietor adds dismissively, "Dude, this was [is?] like two years ago."[1844] Vietor then suggests it may have been Mike Morell, CIA Deputy Director, who didn't like the CIA Talking Points, took them back, and changed them.[1845] (No, Morell on September 14 already has signed off on a version of the CIA Talking Points in which the CIA internally has substituted "demonstrations" for "attacks."[1846] Morell apparently "took them back" on September 15 to make *other* changes Team Obama wanted.) The Senate Intelligence Committee later will report it is the CIA's Offices of Public Affairs or Congressional Affairs (or possibly both jointly) that change Benghazi "attacks" to the inaccurate word "demonstrations" in the CIA Talking Points.[1847]

Regarding the varying earlier drafts of the CIA Talking Points, *The Washington Post* reports, ". . . State Department officials raised concerns that the CIA-drafted version could be used by members of Congress to criticize diplomatic security preparedness in Benghazi."[1848] These concerns apparently are voiced in emails sent by State's chief spokesperson, Victoria Nuland, to national security staff in the White House and other agencies that are editing the CIA Talking Points. According to *The Weekly Standard*, Nuland reportedly expresses her "serious concerns" congressmen "would use the talking points to criticize the State Department for 'not paying attention to Agency

---

[1843] But see Attkisson, *Stonewalled* (". . . Vietor acknowledges that, while at the White House, he made at least one substantive change to the talking points. That change was to add a line that seemed to advance the notion that the attacks were born from spontaneous demonstrations"), Chap. 4, p. 217.

[1844] Interview of Tommy Vietor with Brett Baier, "Special Report," Fox News Channel (May 1, 2014) (*Watch video there*; Go to 5:48 – 6:40).

[1845] *Id.*, (*Watch video there*; Go to 6:40-59).

[1846] Sen. Intelligence Committee Benghazi Report, Appendix I, pp. 47-48.

[1847] *Id.*, Appendix I, pp. 46-67.

[1848] Wilson and DeYoung, Benghazi E-mails Show Clash Between State Department, CIA.

warnings,' so "why do we want to feed that?"[1849] (Well, *yeah*. Sometimes the shoe fits and the truth hurts.) The changes made in response to State's objections are hardly "stylistic."

Yet Nuland apparently has a difficult time getting others to address fully her department's "serious concerns." The CIA makes some changes (including dropping all references to Ansar al-Sharia). But Nuland remains unhappy. At 9:24 p.m. on Friday, September 14, she sends an email asserting the edits made thus far don't ". . . resolve all my issues or those of my building leadership. They are consulting with NSS," likely referring to National Security Council staff.[1850] In this regard, *The Weekly Standard* reports Ben Rhodes, a Deputy National Security Advisor, quickly responds to Nuland's latest email, stating the matter must be resolved the following morning at a high-level Saturday meeting *at the White House*.[1851] But, of course, the White House supposedly is making *no* "substantive" changes to the CIA Talking Points!

Despite all these State Department complaints and requests for changes, in November 2012 a spokesman for the Director of National Intelligence outrageously will claim to reporters the "intelligence community" ("IC") is solely responsible for "substantive" changes in the CIA Talking Points.[1852] (So if CIA or DNI staff type in the State Department's or FBI's or White House's requested changes on a CIA or DNI computer, the IC is solely responsible for the changes? More

---

[1849] Hayes, The Benghazi Talking Points; Guy Benson, "Surprise: Obama Promotes Another Benghazi Scandal Player," Townhall.com website (May 24, 2013); House Foreign Affairs Benghazi Majority Staff Report ("Perhaps the most troubling aspect of this interagency correspondence is the extent to which senior State Department officials repeatedly objected to the inclusion of any information that might cast the Department in an unflattering light"), p. 14; and *Id.* ("The actions of State Department officials in this episode demonstrate a troubling preference for political self-preservation over embracing the culture of accountability necessary for protecting its personnel serving abroad. . . . Department leadership focused on how to avoid or mitigate damage to their reputations"), p. 14.

[1850] Hayes, The Benghazi Talking Points; and Karl Rove, "Benghazi Emails Reveal Obama White House's Obsession With Spin Control," Fox News Opinion online (May 17, 2013).

[1851] Hayes, The Benghazi Talking Points.

[1852] Wilson and DeYoung, Benghazi E-mails Show Clash Between State Department, CIA (". . . [DNI Director James] Clapper, CIA, FBI and State Department counterterrorism officials told the [Senate Homeland Security] committee that 'changes characterizing the attacks as "demonstrations" and removing references to al-Qaeda or its affiliates were made within the CIA and the' intelligence community").

lies.) The rest of Team Obama is happy to agree with the DNI's claims of the IC's parentage of the CIA Talking Points. As it becomes clear over the next few weeks the CIA Talking Points are inaccurate and incomplete, other Obama officials cheerfully will blame the IC.[1853]

Crafting the "Final" CIA Talking Points

It is the morning of Saturday, September 15. Over the past day it has become painfully obvious the current draft CIA Talking Points are inconsistent with what various members of the intelligence community are telling Congress and even the media.[1854] According to reporting by Stephen Hayes of *The Weekly Standard*, on this Saturday Obama administration officials continue to scramble to revise the CIA Talking Points that supposedly will form the basis for its message on the next day's Sunday news talk shows (see Chapter 103). (These are the same speaking points then former Secretary of State Clinton later will claim the intelligence community purportedly has no idea Susan Rice will use on the Sunday news shows.[1855] The Select Committee's Report backs up Clinton on this issue.[1856])

[1853] Transcript of Vice Presidential Debate Between Vice President Joe Biden and Rep. Paul Ryan (R-WI), *The New York Times* online (Oct. 11, 2012) (Asked why the Obama administration talked about protests in Benghazi when there were none, Vice President Biden replied: "Because that's exactly what we were told . . . by the intelligence community. The intelligence community told us that. As they learned more facts about exactly what happened, they changed their assessment"), referenced in Daily Press Briefing by State Department Spokesperson Victoria Nuland, State Dept. Archives website (Oct. 12, 2012); Hayes, The Benghazi Talking Points (". . . After pushing the intelligence community to revise its talking points to fit the administration's preferred narrative, administration officials would point fingers at the intelligence community when parts of that narrative were shown to be misleading or simply untrue"); *The Wall Street Journal* Opinion, The Missing Benghazi Email ("The White House also found a scapegoat in the intelligence community, blaming the CIA for drawing up the faulty 'talking points' used by Administration officials. . . ."); and Josh Rogin, "State Department: No Video Protest at the Benghazi Consulate [sic]," ForeignPolicy.com (Oct. 9, 2012) ("[Susan] Rice has since attributed those [erroneous] statements [blaming protests triggered by the Video] to information given to the administration by intelligence officials").

[1854] Madison, Congress to Investigate CIA Talking Points on Benghazi ("Democrats and Republicans alike . . . have noted that there were discrepancies between the talking points being distributed by the CIA to Obama administration officials and the way intelligence officials were speaking about the matter . . .").

[1855] Clinton, *Hard Choices* ("None of the intelligence officials working on that request [from congressmen for information they could use in making public statements about

472

At the September 15 morning White House meeting the Obama inner circle apparently decides that, given the Benghazi Narrative's many flaws and discrepancies, the less said about it in the "official" CIA Talking Points, the better. At this Saturday conference the "final" contents of the draft CIA Talking Points is agreed upon. *The Weekly Standard* will claim these revisions involve substantial deletions, which a later Senate Intelligence Committee report will confirm. It is now a much shorter (and far less informative) version than the CIA's original product.[1857] CIA Deputy Director Morell reportedly will make most of the finishing touches (principally deletions).[1858] The fact Morell signed off late the previous afternoon on his Agency's behalf on a much longer, more detailed version of the CIA Talking Points suggests strongly that in his final two edits on September 15 he is implementing changes desired by *others* on Team Obama from *outside* the CIA.[1859]

The final unclassified CIA Talking Points version (after minor edits by Ben Rhodes at the White House and Jake Sullivan at State) is both misleading and virtually devoid of useful information.[1860] According to the House Foreign Affairs Committee majority staff, CIA Director Petraeus remarks of the final product, "[f]rankly, I'd just as soon not use this then. . . ."[1861] The single remaining substantive bullet paragraph reads (in its entirety):

> The currently available information suggests that the *demonstrations* in Benghazi were *spontaneously* inspired by the protests at the U.S. Embassy in Cairo and *evolved into a*

Benghazi] had any idea the talking points would be used two days later by Susan [Rice]"), Chap. 17, p. 413.

[1856] Benghazi Committee Report ("No CIA witness the Committee interviewed had any knowledge the HPSCI [House Intelligence Committee] talking points were going to be shared with Rice to be used on the Sunday talk shows"), p. 206.

[1857] Hayes, The Benghazi Talking Points (CIA Deputy Director Morell will cut all or part of four of the CIA Talking Points' six paragraphs, reducing the total word count by 148 words from 248 words).

[1858] *Id.*; and Sen. Intelligence Committee Benghazi Report, Appendix I, pp. 51-52.

[1859] Hayes and Joscelyn, The Benghazi Report.

[1860] Goldberg, Benghazi's Smoking Guns ("According to ABC News correspondent Jonathan Karl, when [then-CIA Director David] Petraeus saw the talking points, he thought they were useless").

[1861] House Foreign Affairs Benghazi Majority Staff Report, p. 14, citing Email from Director of Central Intelligence David Petraeus, Subject: Hill Talking Points (Sept. 15, 2012).

direct assault against the U.S. diplomatic post and subsequently *its* annex. There are *indications* that *extremists* participated in the violent *demonstrations*.[1862]

The remaining final two bullets of the shortened CIA Talking Points assert the investigation is ongoing, updates will follow, and the U.S. is working with the Libyan government to bring "those responsible" to justice.[1863]

The Obama administration provides its final, bare-bones, unclassified CIA Talking Points to both the House and Senate intelligence committees later on September 15.[1864] No doubt they send them to Susan Rice the same day, for her (mis)use the next morning on the Sunday news shows (discussed in Chapter 103 below). However, as demonstrated below (see Chapter 97), the "real" speaking points used by Rice are contained in a secret email Ben Rhodes already has crafted the previous day, September 14. (The House Intelligence Committee's November 2014 report manages to miss this minor detail, although they do mention Rhodes' email.[1865])

Clearly, in these final CIA Talking Points Team Obama wants to emphasize "demonstrations" are at the heart of the Benghazi tragedy. The following chapter proves this assertion is completely lacking in factual support. Equally obvious, the CIA, State, and probably others know the referenced "annex" belongs to the CIA, and is not a State Department facility as the CIA Talking Points falsely claim. (Interestingly, this last erroneous statement has remained in the CIA Talking Points throughout all twelve iterations, including the initial effort by the CIA's Office of Terrorism Analysis.[1866] Undoubtedly, the U.S. government is attempting to shield the fact the CIA also is operating in Benghazi. Yet this same (perhaps worthy) objective could have been accomplished without lying by saying "an annex" instead of "its annex," or simply referencing a "second facility.")

[1862] Sen. Intelligence Committee Benghazi Report (emphasis added), p. 43; and Hayes, The Benghazi Talking Points (emphasis added).

[1863] Sen. Intelligence Committee Benghazi Report, p. 43; and Hayes, The Benghazi Talking Points.

[1864] Sen. Intelligence Committee Benghazi Report, p. 43.

[1865] See House Intelligence Committee Benghazi Report, Executive Summary (Nov. 21, 2014) (referencing only CIA's Taking Points), p. 1; and *Id.* ("For her public comments, Ambassador Rice used talking points developed at the request of HPSCI"), p. 28.

[1866] Sen. Intelligence Committee Benghazi Report, pp. 43-52.

The Omission of the Video

Among the most interesting aspects of the CIA Talking Points evolution is the curious fact *none of the many drafts contains any mention of an anti-Islamic Video!*[1867] This fact is especially puzzling in light of the importance Ben Rhodes accords to this Video in his crucial email of September 14 (discussed below in Chapter 97), written to prepare for Susan Rice's September 16 appearances on the Sunday television news programs.[1868] If Team Obama really believes the Video plays a key role in the Benghazi attacks, how is it possible none of the twelve CIA Talking Points iterations even *mentions* the Video? Despite this glaring omission, as explained below this Video nonetheless almost immediately will become a central component of Team Obama's exposition of the Benghazi Narrative. ∎

[1867] *Id.*, pp. 43-52; Hayes, The Benghazi Talking Points ("There is no mention of any 'video' in any of the many drafts of the talking points"); and *The Wall Street Journal* Opinion, The Missing Benghazi Email (". . . [T]hose [CIA-drafted] talking points never mentioned a video . . .").

[1868] Email from Benjamin J. Rhodes to Dag Vega, NSC Deputy Press Secretary, et al., Re: PREP CALL with Susan: Saturday at 4:00 p.m. ET (Sept. 14, 2012) (emphasis added), p. 1, Judicial Watch Document Archive (posted June 16, 2014).

95

"The Protest of All Ages"

A major tenet of the Benghazi Narrative is the fantasy that a "spontaneous demonstration" in Benghazi somehow "morphed" into a mob of extremists attacking Americans at two different facilities with heavy weapons, RPGS and (eventually) mortars. As explained in the previous chapter, the CIA implants this error into its talking points early on and it remains in the final version.

(In the interest of brevity, we discuss here (and in subsequent chapters) only selected examples of the administration's implementation of the Benghazi Narrative's themes.)

In her memoir, Hillary Clinton later emphasizes the North African and Middle East protests against the "offensive internet video" that occur in Cairo on September 11, 2012, and on September 12 in various cities in Morocco, Egypt, and Mauritania. She also points to other protests in Tunisia, Yemen, Kuwait, India, Sudan, Pakistan, the Philippine Islands and Indonesia.[1869] By September 16, ABC News has identified protests in 33 countries.[1870]

In truth, at the time there is evidence known by at least some within Obama's administration that there is no "spontaneous protest" in Benghazi objecting to the supposedly blasphemous Video. Rather, they quickly realize the Benghazi terrorist attacks are preplanned, and have not evolved from any protest or demonstration there.

Indeed, the written Presidential Daily Briefing ("PDB") prepared for President Obama on the morning of September 12, 2012, the day after the Benghazi attacks, disputes the "protest" theory. The Select Committee calls this PDB "The very first written piece produced by CIA analysts regarding the Benghazi attacks..."[1871] The "Executive

---

[1869] Clinton, *Hard Choices*, Chap. 17, pp. 401-402. See also Kirkpatrick and Myers, Libya Attack Brings Challenges for U.S. ("Their attack [in Benghazi] followed by just a few hours the storming of the compound surrounding the United States Embassy in Cairo by an unarmed mob protesting the same video. On Wednesday [September 12], new crowds of protesters gathered outside the United States Embassies in Tunis and Cairo").

[1870] "This Week," ABC News (Sept. 16, 2012) (*Watch video there*; Go to 4:08 - 6:45).

[1871] Benghazi Committee Report, Appendix H, p. 575.

Coordinator" of the PDB (who apparently is from the Defense Intelligence Agency, not the CIA) adds a critical conclusion to this written PDB (which a CIA analyst originally has prepared). After speaking with sources in Libya, the coordinator adds this significant (and correct) line: ". . . [T]he presence of armed assailants from the outset suggests this was an intentional assault and *not the escalation of a peaceful protest.*"[1872] (As noted above, the president does not attend his oral PDB this morning; instead, only his Chief of Staff Jack Lew is briefed. It is unknown to the author whether Obama ever reads the written PDB for September 12.)

(It is interesting that the Executive Coordinator's addition of this completely accurate sentence to the PDB is viewed with alarm within the CIA. The two CIA analysts who prepare the draft PDB strongly oppose her making the truthful change, and argue with the coordinator about it. The manager of the analysts also disagrees with the change. This manager calls the Executive Coordinator's conduct an analytic "cardinal sin" and a "big deal." CIA Deputy Director Mike Morell also thinks it is a major mistake. He calls it a "bureaucratic screw-up" and a "big no-no."[1873] (Have I mentioned the added sentence – which merely leaves open the possibility Benghazi might be an intentional, planned assault – proves to be 100 percent accurate, and everyone else involved at the CIA is proven wrong?) If this is how the CIA works, no wonder the Night of Benghazi is such a complete disaster. Thankfully, at least the Executive Coordinator is never disciplined for getting it right – unlike Gregory Hicks at State.[1874])

No American who is on the ground in Benghazi on September 11-12 claims this night or later there is a protest. Gregory Hicks later testifies Ambassador Stevens surely would have reported a protest had one occurred.[1875] Hicks testifies further he and his diplomatic team in

---

[1872] Benghazi Committee Report, p. 167 (emphasis added); and *Id.,* Appendix H, pp. 575, 579-580 and 584 (emphasis added); and Stephen F. Hayes, "Obama Did Not Ask for an Intel Brief the Day After the Benghazi Attack," *The Weekly Standard* online (June 28, 2016) (". . . That assessment [in the September 12 PDB] would prove accurate – the Benghazi attack was an intentional, planned assault and was not the escalation of a peaceful protest, because no such protest took place. . . .").

[1873] Benghazi Committee Report, Appendix H, pp. 576-578 and 581-583.

[1874] *Id.,* p. 584.

[1875] Hicks Oversight Committee Testimony (May 8, 2013) (Response to questions of Rep. Patrick McHenry (R-NC)) (". . . I am confident that Ambassador Stevens would have reported a protest immediately if one appeared on his door. . . ."), p. 59.

Libya this night consistently describe the crisis as an attack, not a protest.[1876]

As noted above, privately Secretary Clinton earlier has revealed this in an email she sends to her daughter, Chelsea, this same night of the initial attacks on the Mission Compound. There, Clinton describes the mob's assault as an attack by "an al Queda-like [sic] group."[1877] Clinton also admits to a foreign leader the attack is a planned terror event, not a spontaneous reaction to an amateur Video. At 7:19 p.m. on Wednesday, September 12, she tells the Egyptian Prime Minister, Hesham Kandil, "We know that the attack in Libya had nothing to do with the film. It was a planned attack – not a protest."[1878] According to a *New York Times* article published the day after the attacks, "A senior Obama administration officials [sic] told reporters during a conference call that 'it was clearly a complex attack,' but offered no details."[1879] (This almost certainly is a reference to the administration's "Special Briefing" on September 12, discussed above in Chapter 93.)

A contrary view attributed to CIA Director David Petraeus is presented by Defense Secretary Leon Panetta in his memoir. According to Panetta, on September 12 Petraeus is supporting the conclusion by some of his agency's analysts that "the attack in Benghazi was the work of a mob of protestors rather than an organized assault."[1880] Panetta asserts Petraeus reportedly supports this "mob of protestors" theory of his analysts during a high-level meeting of national security officials in the Situation Room. Panetta claims he disagreed with this hypothesis, in part because spontaneous protestors usually don't appear at a demonstration bearing rocket-propelled grenade launchers. Also, the mortar attack the next morning at the Annex certainly is not from a

---

[1876] *Id.* (Response to questions of Rep. Patrick McHenry (R-NC)) ("... The only report that our mission made through every channel was that there had been an attack on a consulate... No protest."), p. 59.

[1877] Benghazi Committee Report, pp. 133 and 161; and Diamond and Labott, What Did We Learn About Benghazi at Marathon Meeting?

[1878] Unclassified and Redacted Email from Lawrence Randolph to "S_CallNotes" Re Call Notes: S-Egyptian PM Kandil, The Secretary's Call with Egyptian PM Kandil (Sept. 12, 2012; 7:11 p.m.), released by Select Benghazi Committee; Hemingway, 5 Big Takeaways From the House Benghazi Report; and Diamond and Labott, What Did We Learn About Benghazi at Marathon Meeting? (*Watch video there*; Go to 1:15 - 2:00).

[1879] Kirkpatrick and Myers, Libya Attack Brings Challenges for U.S.

[1880] Panetta, *Worthy Fights*, Chap. 16, p. 430.

THE TRUE ACCOUNT OF VALOR AND ABANDONMENT

"mob of protestors." Petraeus supposedly replies his analysts' scenario is plausible given Libya at the time is awash with such deadly weapons.[1881]

On September 12, even the pro-Obama and pro-Clinton *New York Times* seems to question the "protest" narrative, although its editorial staff cannot quite bring themselves to call the Benghazi tragedy a "terrorist" attack. Rather, "The violence . . . was apparently the work of a relatively small group of radicals *not associated with any legitimate protest*."[1882]

In a televised interview with Al Jazeera on Friday, September 14, Libyan President Mohamed Magariaf isn't buying the "spontaneous protest of the Video" lines of the administration's Benghazi Narrative. He reportedly concludes, "I think this was al-Qaeda."[1883] He further states:

> It's clear from the timing on September 11th and from the detailed planning of the attacks that behind it there were experienced masterminds. It was not a spontaneous act in protest of a movie. This has been prepared for a long time on this specific day. . . . If you take into account the weapons used, like RPGs and other heavy weapons, it proves that it was pre-planned. It's a dirty act of revenge that has nothing to do with religion.[1884]

(Two days earlier, Libya's Deputy Interior Minister had claimed Qadhafi "loyalists" were responsible for the attack, but in his

---

[1881] *Id.*, Chap. 16, pp. 430-431. See also CBS News, Dispute Over Nature of Libya Attack Continues (CBS correspondent John Miller on Libya: ". . . There's all kinds of weapons and militias with cars and weapons, so it's the one kind of place this could happen spontaneously").

[1882] Opinion, "Murder in Benghazi" (emphasis added), *The New York Times* online (Sept. 12, 2012) ("Religious fundamentalists, moderates and liberal secularists are all jockeying for power in Middle East nations after the Arab Spring. The violence done on Tuesday [in Benghazi] was apparently the work of a relatively small group of radicals not associated with any legitimate protest").

[1883] Yasmine Ryan, "Libya Says US Consulate Attack 'Pre-Planned,'" Al Jazeera online (Sept. 14, 2012).

[1884] Yasmine Ryan, "Libya Says US Consulate Attack 'Pre-Planned,'" Al Jazeera online (Sept. 14, 2012); Judicial Watch Investigative Report, citing Ryan Yasmine, "Libya Says U.S. Consulate Attack 'Pre-Planned,'" AlJazeera.com website (Sept. 15, 2012).

Al Jazeera remarks Magariaf reportedly says there is "no chance" this was the case.[1885])

The Obama administration will resist Magariaf's conclusions regarding advanced planning.[1886] On January 4, 2013, then Acting CIA Director Michael Morell writes to the Senate Intelligence panel, "[t]he nature of the attacks suggested they did not involve significant pre-planning."[1887] This committee's subsequent report then speculates, "... [I]t is possible that the individuals and groups involved in the attacks had not planned on conducting those attacks until that day, meaning that specific tactical warning would have been highly unlikely."[1888] (This hypothesis is consistent with the Benghazi Narrative's tenet "there's no way we could have seen this coming.")

According to CBS News, on Saturday, September 15, 2012, the CIA sends its talking points to Congress. Citing The Associated Press, CBS reports: "... [O]n Saturday [September 15] of that week, briefing points sent by the CIA to Congress said 'demonstrations in Benghazi were spontaneously inspired by the protests at the U.S. Embassy in Cairo and evolved into a direct assault'" against the U.S. diplomatic post in Benghazi and subsequently "its" annex.[1889] The Associated Press says the CIA Talking Points add, "'There are indications that extremists participated in the violent *demonstrations*' but did not mention eyewitness accounts that blamed militants alone."[1890] (A separate CBS report states the CIA Talking Points are given to

---

[1885] Yasmine Ryan, "Libya Says US Consulate Attack 'Pre-Planned,'" Al Jazeera online (Sept. 14, 2012).

[1886] *Wall Street Journal* Opinion, The Missing Benghazi Email ("In fact the attack on the diplomatic compound and CIA annex was a planned and well-coordinated assault by Islamist groups with ties to al Qaeda . . . Within hours, State and CIA officials at the Embassy in Tripoli, Libya's president and video footage made that clear. Yet the Administration settled on deceptive spin and stuck to it for over a week").

[1887] Sen. Intelligence Committee Benghazi Report (Redacted), p. 24, citing Letter from Acting CIA Director Michael Morell to SSCI Chairman Dianne Feinstein (Jan. 4, 2013).

[1888] *Id.* (Redacted), p. 24.

[1889] CBS News, CIA Saw Possible Terror Ties Day After Libya Hit: AP; and Sen. Intelligence Committee Benghazi Report, p. 52.

[1890] CBS News, CIA Saw Possible Terror Ties Day After Libya Hit: AP (emphasis added).

Congress a day earlier, on September 14th.[1891] However, this date appears to be erroneous, unless a draft version was provided.)

An email reportedly sent this same day, September 15, by the CIA's Station Chief in Libya also addresses the issue of whether there has been a "protest" in Benghazi. According to the Senate intelligence panel's report and *The Washington Times*, that Station Chief writes to various CIA officials, including Mike Morell, then still CIA Deputy Director, that no such anti-American demonstrations have occurred in Benghazi.[1892] (Does the CIA receive this intelligence before, or after, it sends its talking points to Congress? And does the CIA pass this information along to the White House and, if so, when? Is it before or after Susan Rice appears on the Sunday news programs on September 16, as discussed in Chapter 103 below?)[1893]

In the aftermath of the U.S. evacuation from Benghazi, FBI agents debrief the survivors in Germany. These sessions do not commence until September 15.[1894] According to three Republican Senators, the reports of these interviews make clear "there never was a spontaneous protest outside of the U.S. Mission in Benghazi."[1895] However, it apparently takes "multiple days" before these FBI reports are shared with the rest of the U.S. intelligence community.[1896] (Has the U.S. government learned *nothing* from the original September 11 about the importance of promptly sharing intelligence and information across agencies?[1897])

[1891] "Sources: Office of the DNI Cut 'al Qaeda' Reference from Benghazi Talking Points, and CIA, FBI Signed Off," CBS News online (Nov. 20, 2012).

[1892] Sen. Intelligence Committee Benghazi Report (Redacted), p. 33; and Guy Taylor, "CIA Officer Confirmed No Protests Before Misleading Benghazi Account Given," *The Washington Times* online (Mar. 31, 2014).

[1893] See Fox News, House Republicans Fault US Military Response to Benghazi ("There has been finger-pointing on both sides [Republicans and Democrats] over security at the U.S. diplomatic outpost in Benghazi and whether the White House initially tried to portray the assault as a protest over an offensive, anti-Muslim video, instead of a calculated terrorist attack").

[1894] Sen. Intelligence Committee Benghazi Report, p. 33.

[1895] Statement of Senators McCain, Graham and Ayotte.

[1896] *Id.*

[1897] *Id.* ("We do not know whether this failure [to share in a timely fashion the Benghazi evacuees' story with the intelligence community] reflects obstacles that still exist to the free sharing of information across executive branch agencies, which was a key concern of the 9/11 Commission"); "The 9/11 Commission Report: Final Report of the National Commission on Terrorist Attacks Upon the United States" ("We have

(GRS Kris "Tanto" Paronto later will explain that when he is "debriefed" by the FBI agents he feels he is being *interrogated*, not interviewed. According to Paronto, the FBI appears to be interested only in why the CIA security men fire their weapons, who they shoot at, and whether civilians are nearby. In other words, the FBI appears to be investigating whether the Heroes of Benghazi use excessive force in defending their fellow Americans from the deadly attackers! Paronto calls these FBI interviews "ridiculous."[1898])

Subsequently, all five DSAs who were in Benghazi will testify to the Select Committee no protest ever occurs at the Mission Compound prior to the terrorist attacks. Greg Hicks will do likewise.[1899]

On Sunday, September 16, Libyan President Mohamed Magariaf appears on "Face the Nation" (just before Susan Rice's appearance the same day). As he had on Al Jazeera two days earlier, he says of the evidence regarding the execution of the assault in Benghazi, "This leaves us with no doubt that this has [sic] pre-planned, determined, pre-determined."[1900]

According to the Senate Intelligence Committee, "On September 18, the FBI and CIA reviewed the closed circuit television

---

already stressed the importance of intelligence analysis that can draw on all relevant sources of information. The biggest impediment to all-source analysis – to a greater likelihood of connecting the dots – is the human or systemic resistance to sharing information"), pp. 416-417; and Richard A. Best, Jr., Report for Congress: "The National Counterterrorism Center (NCTC) – Responsibilities and Potential Congressional Concerns," Congressional Research Service (Dec. 19, 2011) (". . . Investigations of the 9/11 attacks had demonstrated that information possessed by different agencies had not been shared and thus that disparate indications of the looming threat had not been connected and warning had not been provided. . . .") (Summary page).

[1898] Interview of Kris "Tanto" Paronto with Sean Hannity, "Sean Hannity Radio Show" (Mar. 22, 2018).

[1899] Additional Views of Reps. Jordan and Pompeo, pp. 426-427.

[1900] CBS Benghazi Report, (May 6, 2013), Replaying "Face the Nation" video (*Watch video there*; Go to 1:42-56). See also David Morgan, "Libyan President: 50 Arrests in Consulate Assault," "Face the Nation," CBS News online (Oct. 18, 2012) ("Morgan, Libyan President: 50 Arrests in Consulate Assault") ("It was planned, definitely, it was planned by foreigners, by people who entered the country a few months ago, and they were planning this criminal act since their arrival") (*Watch video there*); and CBS News, Dispute Over Nature of Libya Attack Continues ("Witnesses of last week's deadly attack on a U.S. consulate in Libya have told CBS News that the alleged anti-American protest that U.S. officials say morphed into the assault never actually took place").

video from the Mission facility that showed there were no protests prior to the attacks."[1901]

On September 19, Matthew Olsen, then director of the National Counterterrorism Center, testifies about the attacks. (The National Counterterrorism Center is a component of the Office of the Director of National Intelligence.[1902]) According to CBS News (citing Reuters), Olsen reportedly tells a Senate committee that U.S. intelligence agencies do not have specific intelligence the assault was preplanned. He reportedly adds, "The attack began and evolved and escalated over several hours." Although Olsen calls the attack "opportunistic," as discussed in the next chapter he does describe it as a "terrorist attack."[1903]

Despite Olsen's testimony and the CIA Station Chief's email of September 15, various Obama administration officials – including the president himself – publicly keep the "spontaneous protest" narrative alive.[1904] For example, on September 20, President Obama sits for an

---

[1901] Sen. Intelligence Committee Benghazi Report (Redacted), p. 33.

[1902] Office of the Director of National Intelligence website; and Richard A. Best, Jr., Report for Congress: "The National Counterterrorism Center (NCTC) – Responsibilities and Potential Congressional Concerns," Congressional Research Service (Dec. 19, 2011) (Summary page).

[1903] CBS News, Dispute Over Nature of Libya Attack Continues; and CBS News, House Probes Security Leading Up to Libya Attack (". . . [W]itnesses in Benghazi later told CBS News that no protest had occurred at all, a fact the State Department acknowledged Tuesday in a briefing with reporters").

[1904] Attkisson, Diplomat: U.S. Special Forces Told "You Can't Go" to Benghazi During Attacks ("Ambassador Susan Rice and Secretary of State Hillary Clinton initially indicated the attacks were not planned acts of terror, but an outgrowth of a spontaneous protest over an anti-Islamic YouTube video"); CBS News, CIA Saw Possible Terror Ties Day After Libya Hit: AP ("The Obama administration maintained publicly for a week that the attack on the diplomatic mission in Benghazi that killed U.S. Ambassador Chris Stevens and three other Americans was a result of the mobs that staged less-deadly protests across the Muslim world around the 11th anniversary of the 9/11 terror attacks on the U.S."); CBS News, Dispute Over Nature of Libya Attack Continues ("The Obama administration has called the attack more impulsive than planned. . . . U.S. officials have said since the immediate aftermath of the attack that it originally started as an Anti-American protest against an amateurish online video made in the U.S. that insults the Muslim Prophet Muhammad"); and Sowell, Hillary 2.0 and Benghazi ("Obviously the truth about this attack could have totally undermined the image that Obama was trying to project during the election campaign ["as someone who had defeated Al Qaeda and suppressed the terrorist threat in the Middle East"], and perhaps cost him the White House. So a lie was concocted instead. The lie was that the attack was not by terrorists . . . but was a spontaneous protest demonstration against an American video insulting Islam, and that protest just got out of control").

interview on the Spanish-language Univision television network, done as part of his reelection campaign. Despite Matthew Olsen's admission the previous day, Obama declines to label the Benghazi attacks as terrorism, citing the ongoing investigation.[1905] He continues, "What we do *know* is that *the natural protests that arose* because of the outrage over the video were used as an excuse by extremists to see if they can also directly harm U.S. interests."[1906]

Quite simply, Barack Obama, Hillary Clinton and others in the administration are attempting to transplant the protests in Cairo (and other Muslim nations) onto Benghazi.[1907] It is an astounding effort in political legerdemain. Yet it largely succeeds, at least for the present.

Despite all the evidence it possesses, it is not until September 24 the Intelligence Community formally admits in its written reports "there were no demonstrations or protests at the Temporary Mission Facility prior to the attacks."[1908]

Finally, however, on October 9, 2012, "Senior State Department officials" anonymously admit to the media there is no demonstration in Benghazi prior to the attacks on the Mission. This reversal comes the day before lower-level State Department officials will testify in a key public hearing before the House Oversight Committee.[1909] No doubt State's senior management realizes the administration's "Benghazi Protest" narrative will be shattered to smithereens in this testimony.

Weeks later, in December 2012, the Benghazi Accountability Review Board Report (discussed in detail in Chapter 109) will conclude there was no protest in Benghazi prior to the attacks.[1910]

[1905] Christi Parsons, "Obama Defends Embassy Security During Univision Town Hall," Los Angeles Times online (Sept. 20, 2012).

[1906] Interview of President Barack Obama on Univision (Sept. 20, 2012) (emphasis added) (*Watch video there*; Go to 0:00-40); Christi Parsons, "Obama Defends Embassy Security During Univision Town Hall," Los Angeles Times online (Sept. 20, 2012); and "Administration Statements on the Attack in Benghazi," *The New York Times* online (Possibly Sept. 27, 2012).

[1907] See Additional Views of Reps. Jordan and Pompeo, pp. 426-427.

[1908] Sen. Intelligence Committee Benghazi Report (Redacted), p. 34.

[1909] Bradley Klapper, "State Dept Reveals New Details of Benghazi Attack," Associated Press, Yahoo online (Oct. 10, 2012) ("All was quiet outside the U.S. Consulate [sic] as evening fell on Benghazi and President Barack Obama's envoy to Libya was retiring after a day of diplomatic meetings. . . . The situation was calm, the officials said, and there were no protests. . . .").

[1910] Benghazi ARB Report, pp. 4 and 29.

THE TRUE ACCOUNT OF VALOR AND ABANDONMENT

Indeed, ARB Chairman Thomas Pickering will tell the media the intelligence community has "clearly concluded" by October 4 there was no protest, and advises the Board of this conclusion at the ARB's first meeting on that date.[1911]

Finally, it is also interesting to consider the comments of an unnamed U.S. serviceman who claims to have operated the Predator drone's camera system for the first ninety minutes above the Mission Compound and the Annex over Benghazi. He asserts the drone videos of what he watched this horrible night help debunk the protest narrative. He tells conservative radio talk show host Sean Hannity:

> ... [T]he video footage would at least clear up, and to [sic] help discern, that if this was a protest, that this would have been the protest of all ages. I mean it was unbelievable. There was too much activity going down. . . .[1912] ∎

[1911] Benghazi ARB Report Briefing for the Media.

[1912] Hannity Radio Interview of Unnamed U.S. Serviceman.

96

"Terrorists? _What_ Terrorists?"

Naturally, everyone wants to know immediately whether the Benghazi assaults are the acts of terrorists. However, the Benghazi Narrative maintains it may take a while before the Obama administration can be certain about this issue. This should surprise no one, because Obama and his officials have a long history of avoiding the "terrorism" conclusion.[1913]

Almost immediately afterwards, a number of news reports assert the assaults in Benghazi have been instigated and carried out by Islamist terror groups. As early as September 12, such reports appear in *The New York Times*.[1914] However, given how highly inaccurate most contemporary news accounts of Benghazi will prove to be, this reporting can be given little weight.

[1913] E.g., Additional Views of Senators Chambliss, Burr, et al. (summarizing other Obama administration efforts to avoid attributing terrorist attacks as Islamic terrorism), pp. 4-5; Jonah Bennett, "Former Mil Officials: Obama's National Security Council Is Full of Activists," The Daily Caller website (Mar. 15, 2016) ("The White House has repeatedly tried to avoid classifying terror-inspired incidents as terrorism, which was brought into sharp relief by the Fort Hood shootings [in November 2009]. It took Obama six years to admit that the shootings committed by Major Nidal Malik Hasan were not in fact examples of workplace violence, but were terrorism"); and Hayes and Joscelyn, The Benghazi Report (". . . President Obama and his closest advisers have consistently defined al Qaeda down. And Benghazi is a perfect example of this pattern of behavior. The president's erroneous descriptions of the Benghazi attackers continued long after September 2012").

[1914] E.g., Kirkpatrick and Myers, Libya Attack Brings Challenges for U.S. ("Islamist militants armed with antiaircraft weapons and rocket-propelled grenades stormed a lightly defended United States diplomatic mission in Benghazi, Libya, late Tuesday, killing the American ambassador and three members of his staff and raising questions about the radicalization of countries swept up in the Arab Spring. . . . [O]fficials cautioned that it was too soon to tell whether the attack was related to the anniversary of the Sept. 11 attacks. . . . [T]he assault . . . was spearheaded by an Islamist brigade formed during last year's uprising against Col. Muammar el-Qaddafi . . .").

THE TRUE ACCOUNT OF VALOR AND ABANDONMENT

According to CBS News, months later Gregory Hicks will tell House Oversight Committee investigators, "I think everybody in the mission thought it was a terrorist attack from the beginning."[1915]

As discussed above in Chapter 91, on September 12 President Obama in his Rose Garden remarks references "no act of terror," but it is unclear if he is referring to the original 9/11, to Benghazi, or to both. (As noted previously, the author believes Obama is referring to Benghazi.) Obama does not explicitly refer to Benghazi as terrorism, and later this same day tells "60 Minutes" it is too early to tell if it is terrorism (see Chapter 92).

On Wednesday, September 12, Secretary of State Clinton is somewhat ambiguous about the identity of the attackers. She reads a formal statement from the State Department Treaty Room, asserting:

> Yesterday, our U.S. diplomatic post in Benghazi, Libya was attacked. *Heavily armed militants* assaulted the compound and set fire to our buildings. American and Libyan security personnel battled *the attackers* together. Four Americans were killed. They included Sean Smith, . . . and our Ambassador to Libya Chris Stevens. . . .
>
> This is an attack that should shock the conscience of people of all faiths around the world. We condemn in the strongest terms this *senseless act of violence*, . . .
>
> . . .
>
> The mission that drew Chris and Sean and their colleagues to Libya is both noble and necessary, and we and the people of Libya honor their memory by carrying it forward. This is not easy. *Today, many Americans are asking – indeed, I asked myself – how could this happen? How could this happen in a country we helped liberate, in a city we helped save from destruction? This question reflects just how complicated and, at times, how confounding the world can be.* [And how incompetent and clueless and reckless the Obama administration can be.]
>
> . . . This was an attack by *a small and savage group* [not so small, actually] – not the people or Government of Libya. . . .
>
> The friendship between our countries, borne out of shared struggle, will not be another casualty of this attack. A free

---

[1915] Lindsey Boerma, "Official: We Knew Benghazi Was a Terrorist Attack 'From the Get-Go,'" CBS News online (May 5, 2013).

487

and stable Libya is still in America's interest and security [sic], and we will not turn our back on that, nor will we rest until *those responsible* for these attacks are found and *brought to justice*. [As this edition goes to press almost seven years later, a total of only two individuals will be captured, charged, and prosecuted.] We are working closely with the Libyan authorities to move swiftly and surely. . . .

. . . *We are working to determine the precise motivations and methods of those who carried out this assault. Some have sought to justify this vicious behavior, along with the protest that took place at our Embassy in Cairo yesterday, as a response to inflammatory material posted on the internet.* America's commitment to religious tolerance goes back to the very beginning of our nation. But let me be clear – there is no justification for this, none. *Violence* like this is no way to honor religion or faith. And as long as there are those who would take innocent life in the name of God, the world will never know a true and lasting peace.

. . . Every year on that day [September 11], we are reminded that our work is not yet finished, that the job of putting an end to *violent extremism* and building a safe and stable world continues. . . .[1916]

(Hillary Clinton does not invoke the term "spontaneous protest" in this statement. However, she again advances the Benghazi Narrative's nexus between the attacks in Benghazi and the internet Video, as she has done in her statement the previous evening. Nowhere in her lengthy September 12 statement does Secretary Clinton mention the words "terror" or "terrorist." And of course she does not use the phrase "radical Islamic terrorism," which the Obama administration has banned from its lexicon. Instead, she employs one of the Obama administration's favorite euphemisms, "violent extremism." She speaks of the attack as "a senseless act of violence." (Madam Secretary, if you are an Islamist terrorist hoping to chase America out of eastern Libya the Benghazi attacks are anything but "senseless.") And there is the obligatory reference to bringing the attackers "to justice," as if the assaults in Benghazi are a mere law enforcement problem, like a violent liquor store robbery in Colorado Springs.)

[1916] Remarks of Secretary of State Hillary Clinton on the Deaths of American Personnel in Benghazi, Libya, State Department Treaty Room, Washington, D.C., State Dept. Archives website (Sept. 12, 2012) (emphasis added).

Also on September 12, Beth Jones, then Acting Assistant Secretary of State for Near Eastern Affairs, sends an email to various state department officials. In it, Jones states she has spoken with the Libyan ambassador. Jones continues that when he said his government suspected that former Qadhafi regime elements carried out the attacks, "I told him that the group that conducted the attacks – Ansar Al Sharia – is affiliated with Islamic extremists."[1917] (Apparently, Jones hasn't yet been given her secret decoder ring containing the official Benghazi Narrative.[1918])

At a "Special Briefing" for reporters on September 12 (discussed above in Chapter 93), an unidentified "senior" Obama administration official refers to "attackers" who are "unidentified Libyan extremists," and who begin to fire on the Benghazi diplomatic post. However, the briefers expressly decline to identify the attacks as terrorism, saying only that "It was clearly a complex attack."[1919]

According to CBS News (citing The Associated Press), two unnamed "U.S. officials" claim that late on September 12 the CIA Station Chief in Libya writes a report citing evidence that the Benghazi attacks are carried out by "militants," not spontaneous protesters. CBS cites "intelligence officials" as saying that the Station Chief's report reaches U.S. intelligence agencies in Washington on September 13.[1920]

[1917] Benghazi Committee Report, p. 428; Hicks Oversight Committee Testimony (May 8, 2013) (Response to questions of Rep. Trey Gowdy (R-SC)), pp. 33 and 93; "Gowdy: Sept. 12 Email Said Benghazi Strike was 'Affiliated with Islamic Terrorists,'" CBS News online (May 8, 2013); Benson, The Damning Dozen: Twelve Revelations from the Benghazi Hearings; and Attkisson, *Stonewalled,* Chap. 4, p. 210.

[1918] See Attkisson, *Stonewalled* ("The private account between Jones and the Libyan government was entirely at odds with the messaging that President Obama, Clinton, Rice, and White House press secretary Carney delivered to the American public"), Conclusion, p. 402.

[1919] September 12 Special Briefing.

[1920] CBS News, CIA Saw Possible Terror Ties Day After Libya Hit: AP ("The CIA station chief in Libya reported to Washington within 24 hours of last month's deadly attack on the U.S. Consulate [sic] that there was evidence it was carried out by militants, not a spontaneous mob upset about an American-made video ridiculing Islam's Prophet Muhammad, U.S. officials have told The Associated Press. . . . [T]he CIA station chief in Libya compiled intelligence reports from eyewitnesses within 24 hours of the assault on the consulate that indicated militants launched the violence, using the pretext of demonstrations against U.S. facilities in Egypt against the film to cover their intent"). See also Hayes, The Benghazi Talking Points ("A cable sent . . . September 12, by the CIA station chief in Libya, reported that eyewitnesses confirmed the participation of Islamic militants and made clear that U.S. facilities in Benghazi had come under terrorist attack. It was this fact, along with several others, that top Obama

Reuters also will report that "within hours of the attack, the Obama administration received about a dozen intelligence reports suggesting militants connected to al Qaeda were involved."[1921]

At a campaign event on September 13 in Golden, Colorado, President Obama clearly appears to label the Benghazi attacks as terrorism. Obama first praises the four fallen Americans, and then makes the obligatory reference to "bring those who killed our fellow Americans to justice." The president then states, "I want people around the world to hear me: To all those who would do us harm, *no act of terror* will go unpunished...."[1922] Mysteriously, in the coming days Obama will appear hesitant to repeat this characterization of Benghazi.

In February 2013 Defense Secretary Leon Panetta tells Congress, "there was no question in my mind that this was a terrorist attack."[1923] In his memoir, he states that earlier, on Friday, September 14, 2012, he tells the Senate Armed Services Committee in a closed-door hearing:

> ... [I]t certainly looked like terrorism to me. Storming a diplomatic facility and killing a U.S. ambassador was an act of terrorism, as the president noted in the Rose Garden the day after the attack. In hindsight, we as a government could have made that point more clearly publicly following the

---

officials would work so hard to obscure"); and Leigh Ann Caldwell, "Sen. Graham: Libya Is 'Exhibit A of a Failed Foreign Policy,'" CBS News online (Oct. 18, 2012) ("On 'Face the Nation' Sunday, [Senator Lindsey Graham (R-SC)] said he was told by members of the intelligence community who are on the ground in Libya that the administration knew 'within 24 hours' that the attacks in Benghazi that killed four Americans, including Ambassador Chris Stevens, were coordinated and were conducted by an al Qaeda-associated group").

[1921] Cornwell and Zakaria, U.S. Security at Benghazi Mission Called "Weak." See also Hayes, The Benghazi Talking Points ("As intelligence officials pieced together the puzzle of events unfolding in Libya, they concluded even before the assaults had ended that al Qaeda-linked terrorists were involved...."); and *Wall Street Journal* Opinion, The Missing Benghazi Email ("In fact the attack on the diplomatic compound and CIA annex was a planned and well-coordinated assault by Islamist groups with ties to al Qaeda ... Within hours, State and CIA officials at the Embassy in Tripoli, Libya's president and video footage made that clear. Yet the Administration settled on deceptive spin and stuck to it for over a week").

[1922] Remarks by the President in Golden, Colorado, Obama White House Archives (Sept. 13, 2012) (emphasis added).

[1923] Testimony of Sec. of Defense Leon Panetta before Senate Armed Services Committee (Feb. 7, 2013) (Response to questions of Sen. James Inhofe (R-OK)); Statement of Senators McCain, Graham and Ayotte; and Rosen, Top Defense Officials Briefed Obama on "Attack" Not Video or Protest.

attack, but not doing so was merely prudent reluctance to go beyond the official intelligence assessments. . . . Like everyone else at that point, I was working from initial reports that could only be verified by a fuller investigation.[1924]
(One news report suggests Panetta may not have been entirely consistent on this conclusion.[1925])

General Carter Ham, leader of AFRICOM, also states the military quickly reached the terrorism conclusion. He asserts, ". . . I think at the command, I personally and I think the command very quickly got to the point that this was not a demonstration, this was a terrorist attack."[1926]

There is conflicting evidence regarding what then CIA Director David H. Petraeus initially tells Congress about the attacks. Petraeus later testifies the U.S. government knows "almost immediately" the assaults in Benghazi are premeditated attacks.[1927] (Democrat Senator Diane Feinstein (D-CA) supports Petraeus' assertion. According to her, the transcript of a September 14, 2012 meeting between Petraeus and members of the House Permanent Select Committee on Intelligence indicates "Petraeus very clearly said that it was a terrorist attack."[1928])

[1924] Panetta, *Worthy Fights*, Chap. 16, p. 431.

[1925] CBS News, U.S. Memo Warned of High Risk of Libya Violence (" . . . [Obama] administration officials have since classified it [Benghazi] as a terrorist act, though Defense chief Leon Panetta said it took him 'a while' to even reach that conclusion").

[1926] Testimony of Gen. Carter Ham, AFRICOM Commander, before House Armed Services Subcommittee (April 2013); Interview of Rep. Brad Wenstrup (R-OH) with Bill Hemmer, Fox News Channel (*Watch video there*); and Rosen, Top Defense Officials Briefed Obama on "Attack" Not Video or Protest.

[1927] Guy Benson, "Petraeus: We Knew Benghazi Was Terrorism 'Almost Immediately,'" Townhall.com website (Nov. 16, 2012) ("Benson, Petraeus: We Knew Benghazi Was Terrorism 'Almost Immediately'"); and "Petraeus Knew 'Almost Immediately' Terrorists Responsible for Benghazi Attack," *The Washington Free Beacon* online (Nov. 15, 2012) ("CNN reports that former Central Intelligence Agency director David H. Petraeus wants to tell Congress that he knew 'almost immediately' that the attack on the U.S. Mission in Benghazi was perpetrated by terrorists"). See also CBS News, CIA Saw Possible Terror Ties Day After Libya Hit: AP ("The CIA station chief in Libya reported to Washington within 24 hours of last month's deadly attack on the U.S. Consulate [sic] that there was evidence it was carried out by militants, not a spontaneous mob upset about an American-made video ridiculing Islam's Prophet Muhammad, U.S. officials have told The Associated Press. . . . [T]he CIA station chief in Libya compiled intelligence reports from eyewitnesses within 24 hours of the assault on the consulate that indicated militants launched the violence, using the pretext of demonstrations against U.S. facilities in Egypt against the film to cover their intent").

[1928] Statement of Senators McCain, Graham and Ayotte; and Madison, Congress to Investigate CIA Talking Points on Benghazi.

However, this is different than how Leon Panetta describes Petraeus' initial position two days before, on September 12, as discussed above.[1929] (More discrepancies.)

Moreover, CBS News reports (again citing the AP): "Two officials who witnessed Petraeus' closed-door testimony to lawmakers in the week after the attack said that during questioning he acknowledged that there were some intelligence analysts who disagreed with the conclusion that an unruly mob angry over the video had initiated the violence." According to the same sources, Petraeus reportedly warns the account could change as more intelligence becomes available.[1930]

In briefing congressmen in the first days after Benghazi, Director Petraeus apparently uses his own set of notes or "talking points" in explaining the tragedy from an intelligence standpoint. These no doubt were prepared by Petraeus and his CIA staff. They do not appear to have been approved by any other agencies, including the Director of National Intelligence ("DNI"), the head of the U.S. "intelligence community." (DNI oversees and coordinates 16 other U.S. intelligence agencies and organizations, eight of which are within the Defense Department.) This later will create confusion when the CIA subsequently creates a more formal set of talking points for dissemination to others in the Obama administration and Congress – discussed earlier in detail in Chapter 94. As explained above, these CIA Talking Points will be reviewed, edited and approved by various other agencies. The discrepancies between the two sets of "speaking points" forms part of the confusing mosaic that is the Benghazi aftermath.[1931]

On September 16, U.S. Ambassador to the U.N. Susan Rice appears on five Sunday television news programs (discussed in detail in Chapter 103). Rice repeatedly emphasizes the "spontaneous protest" narrative and declines to label the Benghazi attacks as terrorism, insisting further investigation is necessary to make that determination.

In another CBS report, that outlet states Shawn Turner, a spokesperson for DNI, tells CBS, "The intelligence community

---

[1929] Panetta, *Worthy Fights*, Chap. 16, pp. 430-431 (Petraeus initially defended his CIA analysts' view that a "mob of protestors" was responsible for the assault).

[1930] CBS News, CIA Saw Possible Terror Ties Day After Libya Hit: AP.

[1931] E.g., "Petraeus Knew 'Almost Immediately' Terrorists Responsible for Benghazi Attack," *The Washington Free Beacon* online (Nov. 15, 2012) ("... [A]ccording to CNN, Petraeus had separate talking points from [Susan] Rice's and that her talking points came from somewhere else in the administration"); and Office of the Director of National Intelligence website.

assessed from the very beginning that what happened in Benghazi was a terrorist attack." CBS further reports this information is "shared at a classified level – which [Susan] Rice, as a member of President Obama's cabinet, would have been privy to."[1932] (*Ooops!*)

On September 17, the president reportedly sends a cable to the president of Libya. In it, Obama thanks the Libyan leader for responding quickly to the "outrageous attack." According to a House Oversight Committee transcript of Greg Hicks' testimony, Obama's cable does not mention terrorism.[1933]

On September 18, President Obama appears on the "Late Show with David Letterman." During this appearance, he refers to an "extremely offensive video directed at Muhammad and Islam." He discusses the Video and its impact at length. The president asserts *"extremists and terrorists* used this as an excuse to attack a variety of our embassies, including the ... consulate [sic] in Libya."[1934] This appears to be the first time the president publicly has described Benghazi unambiguously as a terrorist attack.

Three days after Susan Rice's "performance," on September 19 Matthew Olsen, head of the U.S. National Counterterrorism Center, testifies to Congress about the Benghazi deaths. Astonishingly, Olsen's twelve-page, single-spaced prepared remarks do not even mention the Benghazi attacks![1935] However, in response to questioning about the murders of Americans in Benghazi, Olsen asserts, "... [T]hey were killed in the course of a terrorist attack on our embassy [sic]."[1936] As discussed above, this has been the view of many in the U.S. intelligence

---

[1932] "Sources: Office of the DNI Cut 'al Qaeda' Reference from Benghazi Talking Points, and CIA, FBI Signed Off," CBS News online (Nov. 20, 2012).

[1933] Hicks Oversight Committee Testimony (May 8, 2013) (Response to questions of Chairman Darrell Issa (R-CA)), pp. 78-79.

[1934] "Late Show with David Letterman" (Sept. 18, 2012) (*Watch video there*; Go to 0:01 - 3:10).

[1935] Prepared Testimony of Matthew G. Olsen, Director of National Counterterrorism Center, "The Homeland Threat Landscape and U.S. Response," before Senate Homeland Security and Government Affairs Committee, SHSGAC website (Sept. 19, 2012).

[1936] Testimony of Matthew G. Olsen, Dir. of National Counterterrorism Center, before Senate Homeland Security and Govt. Affairs Committee (Sept. 19, 2012); Katrina Trinko, "Why Won't Obama Call Libya Attacks on Terrorism?" The Corner, *National Review* online; and CBS News, Dispute Over Nature of Libya Attack Continues.

agencies since shortly after the attacks.[1937] Olsen then elaborates on the possible identity of the assailants:

> At this point, what I would say is that a number of different elements appear to have been involved in the attack, including individuals connected to militant groups that are prevalent in eastern Libya, particularly in the Benghazi area.
> ... As well, we are looking at indications that individuals involved in the attack may have had connections to al Qaeda or al Qaeda's affiliates, in particular al Qaeda in the Islamic Maghreb.[1938]

Olsen appears to be the first Obama administration official to confirm unequivocally and publicly to Congress that Benghazi involves a terrorist attack.

Olsen's public references to al Qaeda and its affiliates directly contradicts the administration's insistence that such mentions were removed from the CIA Talking Points just a few days earlier in order to protect the FBI's investigation.[1939] What has changed during this brief period so that the FBI's probe no longer is jeopardized by mentioning al Qaeda?

The next day, Thursday, September 20, presidential spokesperson Jay Carney partially confirms Olsen's assertions, but seems to split the baby: it was kind of a preplanned terror attack, but the "Video protest" door is still cracked open. During a press gaggle aboard Air Force One, Carney states:

> It is, I think, self-evident that what happened in Benghazi was a terrorist attack. Our embassy [sic] was attacked

---

[1937] Martin, Piecing Together White House Response to Benghazi (In his Rose Garden remarks, "The president was reflecting the judgment of U.S. intelligence, which, according to one official, concluded in the hours immediately after the attack that it was an act of terror"); and CBS News, CIA Saw Possible Terror Ties Day After Libya Hit: AP ("The CIA station chief in Libya reported to Washington within 24 hours of last month's deadly attack on the U.S. Consulate that there was evidence it was carried out by militants, not a spontaneous mob upset about an American-made video ridiculing Islam's Prophet Muhammad, U.S. officials have told The Associated Press").

[1938] Testimony of Matthew G. Olsen, Director of National Counterterrorism Center, before Senate Homeland Security and Government Affairs Committee (Sept. 19, 2012); and CBS News, Dispute Over Nature of Libya Attack Continues (Citing Reuters).

[1939] E.g., Eric Schmitt, "Petraeus Says U.S. Tried to Avoid Tipping Off Terrorists After Libya Attack," *The New York Times* online (Nov. 16, 2012) (Regarding identifying the terrorist groups likely involved in the Benghazi attacks, "... Justice Department lawyers expressed concern about jeopardizing the F.B.I.'s criminal inquiry in the attacks. ...").

violently, and the result was four deaths of American officials. ... Mr. Olsen said ... that at this point it appears that a number of different elements were involved in the attack, including individuals connected to militant groups that are *prevalent in Eastern Libya* [later Carney added *"particularly in the Benghazi area"*].

He [Matthew Olsen] also made clear that at this point, based on the information he has – and he is briefing the Hill on the most up-to-date intelligence – we have no information at this point that suggests that this was a *significantly preplanned attack*, but this was the result of *opportunism*, taking advantage of and exploiting what was happening as a result of *reaction to the video* that was found to be offensive.

... [A]ccording to the best information we have now, we believe it was an *opportunistic attack* on our mission in Benghazi. It appears that some well-armed militants *seized on the opportunity* as the events unfolded that evening. We do not have any specific intelligence that there was *significant advanced planning or coordination* for this attack.[1940]

(Jay, if you knew such militant groups were "prevalent," "particularly in the Benghazi area," why the hell didn't the administration provide more security in Benghazi as your diplomats had requested? And what the heck is the difference between "significantly preplanned" and "preplanned"? And isn't every successful terrorist attack "opportunistic"? What absolute *gibberish*.)

At a "town hall" style campaign event broadcast on the Univision television network and co-hosted by Facebook on September 20 – the same day his White House spokesperson is calling Benghazi a terrorist attack – President Obama himself declines to utter the "T Word," although he comes close. According to the *Los Angeles Times*, ". . . In response to a direct question, Obama said he did not know whether Iran or al Qaeda was behind the attacks on the embassies." Falling back on the Benghazi Narrative, the president adds, "What we do *know* is that the natural *protests* that arose because of the outrage over the video were used as an excuse by *extremists* to see if they can also directly harm U.S. interests. . . ."[1941]

[1940] "Press Gaggle by Press Secretary Jay Carney En Route Miami, FL, 9/20/2012," Air Force One, White House website (Sept. 20, 2012) (emphasis added).

[1941] Katrina Trinko, "Why Won't Obama Call Libya Attacks on Terrorism?" The Corner, *National Review* online (emphasis added); CBS News, Dispute Over Nature of Libya Attack Continues (emphasis added); Christi Parsons, "Obama Defends Embassy

The next day, September 21, 2012, Secretary of State Clinton finally describes Benghazi as being a terrorist attack. In remarks to reporters Clinton states, ". . . What happened in Benghazi was a terrorist attack, and we will not rest until we have tracked down and brought to justice the terrorists who murdered four Americans."[1942] Clinton will repeat this assertion days later in a meeting with the Libyan president.)

A few days afterward when he is taping the daytime television show "The View" on September 24 (in an episode airing the next day), the president yet again passes up the opportunity to label Benghazi a terrorist attack. In response to a question whether he agrees with Hillary Clinton's assertion Benghazi involves terrorism, Obama explains, ". . . [W]e're still doing an investigation. There's no doubt that the kind of weapons that were used, the ongoing assault, that it wasn't just a mob action. . . . Now we don't have all the information yet and so we're still gathering it. . . ."[1943]

The following day in remarks to the United Nations General Assembly on September 25, President Obama discusses the Benghazi attacks extensively. He uses words like "killers," "violence," "extremism," "hatred," "anger," "conflict" and "intolerance." Although he references Iran's support for "terrorist groups abroad," he never utters the words "terror" or "act of terror" or "terrorism" when referencing Benghazi.[1944] (Why in the world not? His administration already publicly and repeatedly has confirmed Benghazi was an act of terror. Is it because Obama doesn't want to remind voters of how often during the current campaign he has claimed he has Islamic terrorism (oops, excuse us, violent extremism) on the run?)

Security During Univision Town Hall," *Los Angeles Times* online (Sept. 20, 2012) (emphasis added) (*Watch video there*; Go to 0:00 – 1:00); and Attkisson, *Stonewalled*, Chap. 4, p. 210.

[1942] Amber Phillips, "The Political Fight Over Benghazi, Told in 16 Quotes," *The Washington Post* online (Oct. 22, 2015); and "Administration Statements on the Attack in Benghazi," *The New York Times* online (Possibly Sept. 27, 2012).

[1943] Interview of President and Mrs. Obama on "The View," ABC Television (Sept. 24, 2012) (*Watch video there*; Go to 0:00-46); Mark Knoller, "Obama Quips on 'The View': I'm Just 'Eye Candy,'" CBS News online (Sept. 25, 2012); Katrina Trinko, "Why Won't Obama Call Libya Attacks on Terrorism?" The Corner, *National Review* online; CBS News, Dispute Over Nature of Libya Attack Continues; Interview of Charles Krauthammer with Sean Hannity, "Hannity," Fox News Channel (Oct. 22, 2012) (*Watch video there*; Go to 0:18-26); and Rosen, Top Defense Officials Briefed Obama on "Attack" Not Video or Protest.

[1944] Goldberg, Benghazi's Smoking Guns (". . . At the United Nations he [President Obama] condemned a 'crude and disgusting' video but didn't mention terrorism").

THE TRUE ACCOUNT OF VALOR AND ABANDONMENT

By September 26th, Eli Lake reports the following:
Within 24 hours of the 9-11 anniversary attack on the United States consulate [sic] in Benghazi, U.S. intelligence agencies had strong indications al Qaeda-affiliated operatives were behind the attack, and had even pinpointed the location of one of those attackers. Three separate intelligence officials who spoke to *The Daily Beast* said *the early information was enough to show that the attack was planned and the work of al Qaeda affiliates operating in Eastern Libya*. Nonetheless, it took until late last week for the White House and the administration to formally acknowledge that the Benghazi assault was a terrorist attack. . . .[1945]

Not long thereafter, the Obama administration is forced to abandon completely the "spontaneous demonstration" theme, and admit terrorists were the perpetrators.[1946] (Later in 2017, at the criminal trial of Libyan terrorist and militia leader Ahmed Abu Khatallah, the government's evidence shows that in *early September* 2012 Khatallah and "other members of his group mobilized for an attack by stockpiling truckloads of weaponry."[1947]) On September 28 Secretary of Defense Panetta publicly asserts the Benghazi attacks "clearly" are conducted by terrorists.[1948] There are just five weeks to the election. ∎

[1945] Eli Lake, "U.S. Officials Knew Libya Attacks Were Work of Al Qaeda Affiliates," *The Daily Beast* online (Sept. 26, 2012) (emphasis added) ("Another U.S. intelligence official said, 'There was very good information on this in the first 24 hours. These guys [the terrorists] have a return address. There are camps of people and a wide variety of things we could do [presumably to target or capture the attackers]'").

[1946] CBS News, CIA Saw Possible Terror Ties Day After Libya Hit: AP (As of October 19, 2012, "The White House now says the attack probably was carried out by an al Qaeda-linked group, with no public demonstration beforehand").

[1947] DOJ Press Release, "Abu Khatallah Found Guilty of Terrorism Charges."

[1948] "Defense Secretary Says Libya Attack Was Terrorism," CBS News online (Sept. 28, 2012) (*Watch video there*).

97

"Sparked": The Video Did It

Whether the attackers are terrorists or protestors, whether their actions are spontaneous or preplanned, are they motivated by an anti-Muslim Video as the Benghazi Narrative claims?

From the get-go, the president, Secretary of State Hillary Clinton, and others in the Obama administration insist the assault in Benghazi (like the violent protest in Cairo) is caused by an obscure, anti-Islamic video, *Innocence of Muslims* ("the Video"). This film is made by a California man named Mark Basseley Youssef, and has been posted on the internet.[1949] Even the United Nations immediately jumps on the blasphemous Video bandwagon.[1950]

"Festering Outrage" Over the Video

Another, related component of the Benghazi Narrative is the implication the offensive Video is a new development, a surprise to which the administration understandably has had no time to react. It is unforeseen. However, according to *The New York Times*, the Video is not newly-released. It has been posted online in the U.S. a full *two months* prior to Benghazi, and reportedly has been "dubbed into Arabic for the first time" *eight days* before Benghazi![1951]

Again according to *The New York Times*, the Video "began attracting attention in the Egyptian news media" the *week before*

[1949] E.g., Randy Kreider, "'*Innocence of Muslims*' Film Maker Ordered Back to Prison," ABC News online (Nov. 8, 2012). This article explains Youssef also has used the aliases "Nakoula Basseley Nakoula" and "Sam Bacile" (both spelled in various ways).

[1950] "Statement Attributable to the Spokesperson for the Secretary-General on Attack Against United States Consulate in Benghazi, Libya," United Nations website (Sept. 12, 2012) ("The United Nations rejects defamation of religion in all forms. At the same time, nothing justifies the brutal violence which occurred in Benghazi yesterday. . . .").

[1951] Kirkpatrick and Myers, Libya Attack Brings Challenges for U.S. See also Burton & Katz, *Under Fire*, Chap. 3, p. 33 (*Innocence of Muslims* video first posted on YouTube on July 1, 2012).

Benghazi. *The Times'* article adds, "At that point, American diplomats in Cairo *informed the State Department of the festering outrage* in the *days* before the Sept. 11 anniversary, . . . But *officials in Washington declined to address or disavow the video*, . . ." citing an unnamed source.[1952]

Gregory Hicks later testifies before the Select Committee he believes the U.S. Embassy in Tripoli begins monitoring within Libya for any type of reaction to the film on about September 8, *before* Ambassador Stevens leaves for Benghazi.[1953] Hillary Clinton's memoir also uses this date.[1954] According to Leon Panetta, by September 10 the Defense Department also is "tracking" the Video.[1955] *Despite this "festering outrage" in Cairo over the Video, Clinton's agency does not stop Stevens going to Benghazi on September 10 with a minimal security detail. Moreover, State makes no changes in the security posture of the Special Mission Compound because of the Video.*

White House Statements on the Video

President Obama and his White House staff do their part to push the "Video" component of the Benghazi Narrative. As noted above, the president's reference in his September 12 Rose Garden statement rejecting "all efforts to denigrate the religious beliefs of others" is an oblique reference to the Video. And two days later on September 14, presidential Press Secretary Jay Carney tells reporters at the White House, "These protests were in reaction to a video. We have no information to suggest that it was a pre-planned attack."[1956] (Uh, Jay,

---

[1952] Kirkpatrick and Myers, Libya Attack Brings Challenges for U.S. (emphasis added).

[1953] Benghazi Committee Report, p. 24.

[1954] Clinton, *Hard Choices*, Chap. 17, p. 386 ("On September 8, an inflammatory fourteen-minute video that purported to be a trailer for a full-length movie called *Innocence of Muslims* was aired on an Egyptian satellite TV network widely available across the Middle East").

[1955] Panetta, *Worthy Fights*, Chap. 16, p. 427 (emphasis added) ("We were already tracking an inflammatory anti-Muslim video that was circulating on the Internet and inciting anger across the Middle East against the United States – even though the U.S. government had nothing to do with it. We braced for demonstrations in Cairo and *elsewhere across the region . . .*" – but not in Benghazi).

[1956] "Administration Statements on the Attack in Benghazi," *The New York Times* online (Possibly Sept. 27, 2012); and Baier, New Revelations on Attack in Benghazi (*Watch video there*; Go to 29:58 - 30:13).

what about the written Presidential Daily Briefing two days earlier indicating the tragedy may involve an intentional assault, not the escalation of a peaceful protest? And what about that professionally-conducted mortar attack on the CIA Annex?) Four days later on September 18, Carney asserts, "Our belief based on the information we had was that it was the video that caused the unrest in Cairo and the video that – and the unrest in Cairo that helped – that precipitated some of the unrest in Benghazi and elsewhere."[1957]

Conservative analyst Jonah Goldberg of *National Review* provides this summary of Barack Obama's fixation with the Video:

> And then for the next two weeks [following his Rose Garden remarks], he [President Obama] went on a media blitz blaming a video, including in an interview recorded that day with "60 Minutes." ... He then went on "The View," Univision and David Letterman pushing the idea that it was all about a video. At the United Nations, he condemned a "crude and disgusting" video but didn't mention terrorism.[1958]

Regarding Goldberg's last reference, as late as September 25, 2012 – a mere 42 days before the election – President Obama delivers a speech to the United Nations focusing principally on Benghazi. Obama tells the U.N. General Assembly:

> [I]n the last two weeks, ... a crude and disgusting *video* sparked outrage throughout the Muslim world. Now, I have made it clear that *the United States government had nothing to do with this video*. ... We understand why *people take offense to this video* because millions of our citizens are among them. I know there are some who ask why we don't just ban *such a video*. ... [T]here's *no video* that justifies an *attack* on an *embassy* [sic]. ... The future must not belong to those who slander the prophet of Islam. ...[1959]

(Five, count them, five references to the Video. (Actually, there is a sixth reference in a later portion of the speech.) Of course, when Obama refers to "an attack on an embassy" everyone assumes he is referring to the deadly attack on the unofficial Benghazi diplomatic

---

[1957] "Administration Statements on the Attack in Benghazi," *The New York Times* online (Possibly Sept. 27, 2012).

[1958] Goldberg, Benghazi's Smoking Guns.

[1959] Remarks by President Barack Obama to the UN General Assembly, United Nations Headquarters, New York, New York, Obama White House Archives (Sept. 25, 2012) (emphasis added) (*Watch video there*; Go to 10:20 – 14:02).

post (which of course is not an embassy), not to the (non-deadly) demonstration in Cairo at the American embassy, although that protest does involve violence to property. The only true "attack" occurs in Benghazi. The numerous "Video" references are a complete ruse, but tie in nicely with the Benghazi Narrative.[1960])

The Ben Rhodes Email

Among the most important White House statements relating to the Video's role is a closely-held email created on the evening of Friday, September 14. It is written by Deputy National Security Advisor Ben Rhodes ("Rhodes 9/14 Email"). The stated purpose of this email is to discuss preparing Susan Rice for her upcoming Sunday TV news programs on September 16 (discussed in detail in Chapter 103 below). The unstated purpose is to get everyone on Team Obama singing from the same hymnal. Although it is absent from the CIA Talking Points, the Video issue is a principal focus of the Rhodes 9/14 Email.

(It is worth pausing to consider the key role Rhodes plays in the Obama White House. Along with Denis McDonough, Ben Rhodes is one of the president's closest advisers on foreign policy matters. He is among Obama's principal propaganda apparatchiks. David Samuels discusses this Obama-Rhodes connection in a lengthy, glowing profile of Rhodes in 2016 in *The New York Times Magazine*. (Although the article goes on for thousands of words, "Benghazi" somehow is not among them.) According to Samuels, "He is, according to the consensus of the two dozen current and former White House insiders I talked to, the single most influential voice shaping American foreign policy aside from Potus himself." Samuels quotes McDonough as claiming Rhodes may spend as much as *two to three hours daily* with Obama in person! In addition, McDonough says Rhodes and the president also "communicate remotely throughout the day via email and phone calls." Samuels grandly concludes, "On the largest and smallest questions alike, the voice in which America speaks to the

---

[1960] IBD Editorial, Obama Knew Benghazi Was Terrorism And Did Nothing ("How could emails be sent to the White House Situation Room in real time describing a terrorist attack on sovereign U.S. territory in which four Americans were killed as it happened, and as a drone flew overhead recording the truth of the carnage, and the president and secretary of state insist that it was all about a video and there was no evidence to the contrary?").

world is that of Ben Rhodes."[1961] In other words, when someone on Team Obama receives an email from Ben Rhodes, they know it is a presidential directive. No doubt this is true of the Rhodes 9/14 Email as well.)

At 8:09 p.m. on September 14, Rhodes circulates his lengthy email to numerous high-level White House and other *communications officials* (read "spin-meisters"). (The Rhodes 9/14 Email is not addressed to anyone in the intelligence community or the Pentagon.) Recipients include then-White House Communications Director Dan Pfeiffer and his then-deputy Jennifer Palmieri, Press Secretary Jay Carney and his then-deputy Josh Earnest, Director of Broadcast Media Dag Vega, and then-White House Senior Advisor David Plouffe. (Interestingly, Susan Rice is not listed as a recipient, despite the fact Rhodes' email is all about a briefing for *her*. However, the email is sent to Erin Pelton, then a spokesperson for Ms. Rice, who no doubt forwards it to Rice.)

It is unknown to the author whether, when Rhodes sends this email, he already has seen the CIA Talking Points draft that has by then been circulating for several hours among administration officials outside the CIA. (The odds are Rhodes *has* seen this draft.) In any case, *Rhodes' detailed email is a virtual blueprint explaining the administration's Benghazi Narrative* and (to a far lesser extent) amplifying the bare bones CIA Talking Points.[1962] Indeed, *for Team Obama this Rhodes' email is the true, behind-the-scenes talking points. The manner in which Rhodes crafts this email "... allow[s] ... for easy connection and conflation of the video and the Benghazi attacks."*[1963] His email will call for emphasizing the protest and Video stories, and

---

[1961] David Samuels, "The Aspiring Novelist Who Became Obama's Foreign-Policy Guru," *The New York Times Magazine* online (May 5, 2016) ("... He doesn't think for the president, but he knows what the president is thinking, which is a source of tremendous power. ...").

[1962] *Wall Street Journal* Opinion, The Missing Benghazi Email ("The Rhodes email shows a White House political operative trying to protect his boss two months before Election Day") (*Watch video* there). In similar fashion, Ben Rhodes later will play a pivotal role in successfully packaging and marketing the media campaign to sell the Obama administration's nuclear agreement with Iran. (This man could sell compressed air to the New England Patriots.) The author discusses Rhodes' role on the Iran deal in detail in his forthcoming book, *The Emperor Obama: An American Betrayal; Book I – Foreign Policy, National Security and Terrorism* (to be available at www.amazon.com).

[1963] Benghazi Committee Report, p. 203.

THE TRUE ACCOUNT OF VALOR AND ABANDONMENT

deemphasizing the role of terrorism (if any). As noted above, although the House Intelligence Committee's report on Benghazi mentions the Rhodes 9/14 Email in passing, this panel does not appear to understand this document is the "real" talking points that undergirds the entire Benghazi Narrative.[1964]

The subject line of the Rhodes 9/14 Email is, "RE: PREP CALL with Susan: Saturday at 4:00 p.m. ET." This refers to a telephone conference set to occur the following day to prepare Susan Rice for her scheduled appearance on the Sunday television news shows. Rhodes' email enumerates the following as the second of four stated "Goals": "To understand that these *protests* are *rooted in an Internet video*, and *not a broader failure of policy.*" This one sentence is the heart of the Benghazi Narrative. In his message, Rhodes references the Video or "movie" five times. Rhodes later will testify to the Select Committee, "... [W]e wanted to convey that, again, the protests were rooted in this video."[1965] He later adds, "... I believe in this specific bullet I'm referring to the ongoing protests that are taking place across the Middle East which were very much still going forward on that Friday [September 14]."[1966]

Rhodes' email also contains proposed responses to anticipated questions regarding various issues beyond Benghazi. These include: "The Arab Spring" (discussed in Chapter 3), Egypt, Iran, and Israel and its Prime Minister, Benjamin Netanyahu.

The email also refers *eight times* to "protests" (once expressly relating only to Cairo) or "demonstrations." Although it mentions an "attack" twice and "violence" several times, Rhodes' email never uses the words "terror" or "terrorism" or "act of terror." It does mention "destroying al Qaeda" once, but this is part of a general discussion of the "Arab Spring" and does not relate to Benghazi specifically.

Rhodes' document includes the following discussion regarding Benghazi and the Video:

... Top-lines: • Since we began to see *protests in response to this Internet video*, the President has directed the

---

[1964] House Intelligence Committee Benghazi Report (Nov. 21, 2014), pp. 1 and 24-30.

[1965] Email from Benjamin J. Rhodes to Dag Vega, et al., Re: PREP CALL with Susan: Saturday at 4:00 p.m. ET (Sept. 14, 2012) (emphasis added), p. 1, Judicial Watch Document Archive (posted June 16, 2014); *The Wall Street Journal* Opinion, The Missing Benghazi Email; and Benghazi Committee Report (Testimony of Ben Rhodes), p. 201.

[1966] Benghazi Committee Report (Testimony of Ben Rhodes), p. 201.

Administration to take a number of steps. . . . • Third, we've made our views on this *video* crystal clear. The United States government had nothing to do with it. We reject its message and its contents. We find it disgusting and reprehensible. But there is absolutely no justification at all for responding to this *movie* with *violence*. And we are working to make sure that people around the globe hear that message. . . .

[In Question and Proposed Answers Section:] The *protests* we've seen these last few days were *sparked by a disgusting and reprehensible video. . . . We are not aware of any actionable intelligence indicating that an attack on the U.S. Mission in Benghazi was planned or imminent.* The currently available information suggests that the <u>demonstrations in Benghazi</u> were spontaneously inspired by the protests at the US Embassy in Cairo and *evolved into a direct assault* against the US Consulate [sic] and subsequently <u>its</u> *annex*.[1967]

Like many others, this Rhodes 9/14 Email is obtained in 2014 in Freedom-of-Information Act litigation brought by the conservative watchdog group, Judicial Watch.[1968] The administration has not voluntarily disclosed it to Congress.[1969] (I wonder why? Perhaps because it is a tissue of lies.[1970] It is instructive to note Ben Rhodes will

---

[1967] Email from Benjamin J. Rhodes to Dag Vega, et al., Re: "PREP CALL with Susan: Saturday at 4:00 p.m. ET (Sept. 14, 2012)" (emphasis added), pp. 1-2, Judicial Watch Document Archive (posted June 16, 2014).

[1968] *The Wall Street Journal* Opinion, The Missing Benghazi Email.

[1969] Additional Views of Reps. Jordan and Pompeo ("Despite its claims, we saw no evidence that the administration held a sincere interest in helping the [Select] Committee find the truth about Benghazi. . . . So while the investigation uncovered new information, we nonetheless end the Committee's investigation without many of the facts, especially those involving the President and the White House, we were chartered to obtain"), p. 417; Guy Benson, "Boom: New Benghazi Emails Show WH Coordinated False Talking Points," Townhall.com website (April 29, 2014) ("Previously unreleased internal Obama administration emails show that a coordinated effort was made in the days following the Benghazi terror attacks to portray the incident as 'rooted in [an] internet video, and not [in] a broader failure or [sic of] policy"); and *Wall Street Journal* Opinion, The Missing Benghazi Email (". . . The Rhodes email was subpoenaed last August [2013], but the White House blocked release until it seemed obvious it would lose its attempts to keep them secret").

[1970] National Review Editors, What We Do Know About the Benghazi Attack Demands a Reckoning (" . . . And when it came time to explain themselves, administration officials lied: Obama, Clinton, Rice, Rhodes, Carney, and the rest – serially and systematically. . . ."); and *Wall Street Journal* Opinion, The Missing

THE TRUE ACCOUNT OF VALOR AND ABANDONMENT

come under further criticism later for allegedly misleading the American public to promote President Obama's Iran Nuclear Deal. In crafting his works of "spin" for the media, Rhodes is contemptuous of many in the media. Referring to the "average reporter" he deals with, Rhodes asserts, "They literally know nothing."[1971])

As much or more than any other factor, the disclosure of this Rhodes 9/14 Email in April 2014 will lead to the House of Representatives' (very tardy) creation of the House Select Benghazi Committee the following month.[1972]

Hillary Clinton's Statements

As noted above (Chapter 95), at 7:19 p.m. on Wednesday, September 12, Clinton tells the Egyptian Prime Minister, Hesham Kandil, "We know that the attack in Libya had nothing to do with the film. It was a planned attack – not a protest."[1973]

In contrast to her accurate *private* statements, in the coming days publicly Hillary Clinton consistently clings to the "blasphemous Video" element of the official Benghazi Narrative.[1974] As discussed in Chapter 70 above, even before the Battle of Benghazi is over, at 10:07 p.m. on September 11 Secretary Clinton issues an official State Department statement blaming the Video. (". . . Some have sought to justify this vicious behavior as a response to *inflammatory material*

Benghazi Email (*Watch video there*) (". . . We can see why the Administration tried to keep them [withheld emails] under wraps").

[1971] David Samuels, "The Aspiring Novelist Who Became Obama's Foreign-Policy Guru," *The New York Times Magazine* online (May 5, 2016).

[1972] Jeffrey Lord, "Benghazi: What Was Tom Donilon Doing?" The American Spectator online (May 6, 2014).

[1973] Unclassified and Redacted Email from Lawrence Randolph to "S_CallNotes" Re Call Notes: S-Egyptian PM Kandil, The Secretary's Call with Egyptian PM Kandil (Sept. 12, 2012; 7:11 p.m.), released by Select Benghazi Committee; Hemingway, 5 Big Takeaways From the House Benghazi Report; and Diamond and Labott, What Did We Learn About Benghazi at Marathon Meeting? (*Watch video there*; Go to 1:15 - 2:00).

[1974] Additional Views of Reps. Jordan and Pompeo ("Officials at the State Department, including Secretary Clinton, learned almost in real time that the attack in Benghazi was a terrorist attack. With the presidential election just 56 days away, rather than tell the American people the truth and increase the risk of losing an election, the administration told one story privately and a different story publicly. They publicly blamed the deaths on a video-inspired protest they knew had never occurred"), p. 416.

posted on the Internet...."[1975]) On Thursday, September 13, Hillary Clinton delivers additional remarks at a State Department event involving "U.S.-Morocco Dialogue." In her prepared statement Clinton says:

> I also want to take a moment to address the video circulating on the internet that has led to these protests in a number of countries.... [She then condemns the video and disassociates the United States from it.] To us, to me personally, this video is disgusting and reprehensible. ... But as I said yesterday, there is no justification, none at all, for responding to this video with violence. We condemn the violence that has resulted, in the strongest terms . . .[1976]

Clinton asserts that violence against diplomatic facilities is "especially wrong."[1977]

As noted above in Chapter 95, in her *Hard Choices* book Clinton references numerous protests that occur following Benghazi in various cities in Africa, the Middle East, and Asia. While these protests may involve the inflammatory Video, what they do *not* involve is Benghazi or further American deaths. Yet the administration clings to its Benghazi Narrative that, because there are demonstrations opposing the Video in various cities in Africa and elsewhere, then Benghazi – at least in part – also *must* involve protests and *must* be motivated in part by the Video, too. This is because Obama and his team need an alibi for Benghazi, where the danger to Americans probably is greatest and where all four of the fatalities occur. They need political cover for Benghazi – at least until after the election.[1978]

[1975] Statement on the Attack in Benghazi, by Secretary of State Hillary Rodham Clinton, United States Department of State, State Dept. Archives website (Sept. 11, 2012; 10:07 p.m.) (emphasis added); and *The New York Times*, What They Said, Before and After the Attack in Libya.

[1976] Remarks of Hillary Rodham Clinton at the Opening Plenary of the U.S.-Morocco Strategic Dialogue (Sept. 13, 2012), State Dept. Archives website; Mary Lu Carnevale, "Hillary Clinton Denounces the Video and the Violence," *The Wall Street Journal* online (Sept. 13, 2012) (*Watch video there*); and Baier, New Revelations on Attack in Benghazi (*Watch video there*; Go to 29:40-58).

[1977] Remarks of Hillary Rodham Clinton at the Opening Plenary of the U.S.-Morocco Strategic Dialogue (Sept. 13, 2012), State Dept. Archives website.

[1978] E.g., CIA Saw Possible Terror Ties Day After Libya Hit: AP (Rep. William Thornberry (R-TX), member of House Intelligence and Armed Services Committee, "voiced skepticism over how sure intelligence officials, including CIA David Petraeus, seemed of their original account when they briefed lawmakers on Capitol Hill. 'How could they be so certain immediately after such events, I just don't know,' he said.

Thus it is that in her subsequent book Hillary Clinton, with both eyes on her own future presidential run, feels she has no choice but to "double down" on the Video as the cause of the whole damned Benghazi mess. She writes:

I know there are some who don't want to hear that an internet video played a role in *this upheaval*. But it did. *Pakistani* protestors even beat an effigy of Terry Jones, the Florida pastor associated with the film. And American diplomats, far from the politics of Washington, felt the impact up close.

What about the attack in Benghazi? In the heat of the crisis we had no way of knowing for sure what combination of factors motivated *the assault* or whether and how long it had been planned. I was clear about this in my remarks the next morning, and in the days that followed administration officials continued to tell the American people that we had incomplete information and were still looking for answers. There were many theories – but still little evidence. *I myself went back and forth on what likely happened, who did it, and what mix of factors – like the video – played a part.* But it was unquestionably *inciting the region and triggering protests all over*, so it would have been strange not to consider, as days of protests unfolded, that *it might have had the same effect here, too.* [Except Gregory Hicks already has assured you otherwise. As have all of the DSA and GRS agents who are eyewitnesses in Benghazi.] That's just common sense. *Later investigation and reporting confirmed that the video was indeed a factor.* All we knew *at that time* with complete certainty was that Americans had been killed and others were still in danger. [We also knew with "complete certainty" Chris Stevens, Sean Smith and Dave Ubben were in danger and had been killed or severely wounded because *you* sent them there on the 9/11 anniversary with minimal security.] Why we were under attack or what the attackers were thinking or doing earlier that day was not

---

'That raises suspicions that there was political motivation'"); and Michael Hastings, "Libya Threatens Clinton's Legacy – and State Does Damage Control," *Buzzfeed* (Sept. 23, 2012) ("... Foggy Bottom is now in full-on damage control mode, with the primary goal of keeping Hillary Clinton's legacy in Libya – and in Washington – intact"). See also Interview of Kris "Tanto" Paronto with Sean Hannity, "Sean Hannity Radio Show" (April 5, 2017).

at the forefront of anyone's minds. All that mattered to us was saving lives. [Unless those lives were in Benghazi, not Tripoli.] Nothing else made a difference.[1979]

Thus does Hillary Clinton compress responses all throughout Africa, the Middle East and even Asia as part of the same mosaic. There are "protests" involved, and the Video is a factor. Except Benghazi is different. There, *no* protests occur. And the attacks are preplanned, not spontaneous. But if Clinton and the Obama administration can convince the American public Benghazi is part of the same Video-spontaneous protest "casserole" as the rest of the Middle East, then perhaps they can persuade us Benghazi cannot have been foreseen or predicted or prevented, or the Americans there rescued.[1980]

The Intrepid "Reporters" in Benghazi

In her memoir, *Hard Choices*, to support her claims former Secretary Clinton also cites several news reports from Benghazi in which reporters allegedly speak with individuals who claim the Video plays a role in the Benghazi attacks. For example, Clinton's book correctly quotes at length from a detailed *New York Times* article published online on September 12, 2012. (It will appear in print on page A1 of the New York edition the following day.) It states, "Interviewed *at the scene* on Tuesday night, *many attackers and those who backed them* said they were determined to defend their faith from the video's insults."[1981] The same rambling article (which covers both the Cairo protests and the Benghazi attacks) also asserts:

Fighters involved in the *assault*, which was *spearheaded by an Islamist brigade* formed during last year's uprising against

---

[1979] Clinton, *Hard Choices* (emphasis added), Chap. 17, p. 402.

[1980] IBD Editorial, Obama Knew Benghazi Was Terrorism And Did Nothing (". . . Obama, Secretary of State Clinton, Press Secretary Jay Carney [and] U.N. Ambassador Susan Rice . . . proceeded for weeks to pursue a lie agreed upon: that a video offensive to Islam prompted the assault that killed our Libyan ambassador and three other Americans"); and *Wall Street Journal* Opinion, The Missing Benghazi Email ("In fact the attack on the diplomatic compound and CIA annex was a planned and well-coordinated assault by Islamist groups with ties to al Qaeda . . . Within hours, State and CIA officials at the Embassy in Tripoli, Libya's president and video footage made that clear. Yet the Administration settled on deceptive spin and stuck to it for over a week").

[1981] Clinton, *Hard Choices* (emphasis added), Chap. 17, p. 402, quoting *New York Times* reporting.

Col. Muammar al-Qaddafi, said in *interviews during the battle* that they were moved to the mission by anger over a 14-minute, *American-made video* that depicted the prophet Muhammad, Islam's founder, as a villainous, homosexual and child-molesting buffoon.[1982]

These reports appear to support Hillary Clinton's (and later Susan Rice's) version of Benghazi. However, the same *New York Times* article also contains a number of inaccuracies (as do almost all contemporaneous accounts).

Beyond these errors, the *Times* piece also states:

American and European officials said that while many details about the *attack* remained unclear, the assailants seemed *organized, well trained and heavily armed*, and they appeared to have *at least some level of advanced planning*. But the officials cautioned that it was too soon to tell whether the *attack* was related to the anniversary of the Sept. 11 attacks.[1983]

Thus, this *Times* article appears to say the attack is preplanned (and thus not a spontaneous protest, although the article does discuss "protests"), and is (at least partially) motivated by the blasphemous Video. By using the term "Islamist brigade" the article also arguably suggests terrorism may be involved. No doubt the CIA officers who are drafting the Agency's initial CIA Talking Points version have read this prominent article. However, by the time the CIA Talking Points edits are finished on September 15, one would never know this high-visibility *Times* article ever existed.

(Weeks later, *The Huffington Post* questions *The New York Times* about the accuracy of this September 12, 2012 article. According to *The Huffington Post*, in an email from the *Times'* foreign editor, Joseph Kahn, the paper reportedly "stands by its original report that there were demonstrators and attackers responding to the video in Benghazi that night."[1984])

In her memoir, Hillary Clinton also quotes a Reuters' reporter "on the ground that night" who writes, "The attackers were part of a mob blaming America for a film they said insulted the Prophet

---

[1982] Kirkpatrick and Myers, Libya Attack Brings Challenges for U.S. (emphasis added).

[1983] *Id.* (emphasis added).

[1984] Michael Calderone, "*New York Times* Stands By Early Report of Demonstrators at Libya Consulate Attack," *The Huffington Post* online (Updated Oct. 15, 2012).

Muhammad."[1985] (It seems the streets of Benghazi literally are teeming with intrepid journalists on the Night of Benghazi. Some of these "journalists" likely are actually local Libyans who serve as so-called "fixers," who help foreign journalists get stories in Benghazi and elsewhere in Libya by offering translating and other services.[1986]) This quoted phrase does indeed appear in a number of online news reports.[1987] (However, even if its original source is Reuters, it is not clear to the author whether the Reuters' reporter is "on the ground that night.")

In *Hard Choices*, Hillary Clinton also cites a *New York Times* article published in December 2013 purporting to analyze what really happened in Benghazi. The *Times'* "investigation" concludes, "Contrary to claims by some members of Congress, it was *fueled in large part* by anger at an American-made *video* denigrating Islam."[1988] The *Times* asserts, "Anger at the video motivated the initial attack . . . [and] *there is no doubt that anger over the video motivated many attackers*."[1989] (By the way, *The New York Times* had endorsed Hillary Clinton for president in 2008,[1990] and will do so again in 2016.[1991])

Conclusions About the Video

One of the many ironies of Benghazi is that the Obama administration's obsessive focus on the Video actually may have fueled some of the subsequent protests against it. Prior to Benghazi, the Video

---

[1985] Clinton, *Hard Choices*, Chap. 17, p. 402.

[1986] E.g., "Unbylined, A Q&A with a Libyan Fixer," Roads & Kingdoms website (July 11, 2017) (interviewing self-described Libyan "fixer" Suliman Ali Zway).

[1987] E.g., "Obama Vows to 'Bring to Justice' Ambassador's Killers," NDTV (Sept. 13, 2012) (citing Reuters); and "US Investigating Embassy Attacks Planned to Mark 9/11," Newsmax Wires (Sept. 12, 2012) (not citing Reuters).

[1988] Clinton, *Hard Choices* (emphasis added), Chap. 17, p. 403, citing *New York Times* article (Dec. 2013).

[1989] *Id.*, Chap. 17, p. 403, citing *New York Times* article (Dec. 2013).

[1990] Editorial Opinion, "Primary Choices: Hillary Clinton," *The New York Times* online (Jan. 25, 2008) ("As Democrats look ahead . . . The Times's editorial board strongly recommends that they select Hillary Clinton as their nominee for the 2008 presidential election").

[1991] By the Editorial Board, "Hillary Clinton for President," *The New York Times* online (Sept. 24, 2016) ("Our endorsement is rooted in respect for her intellect, experience and courage").

was little-known in most parts of the Muslim world.[1992] Team Obama's serial assertion of the Benghazi Narrative made the Video infamous worldwide. Some commentators have argued that this in turn encourages additional protests against the Video and the United States (where the Video-maker lived).[1993]

The evidence regarding the role (if any) of the blasphemous Video in the Benghazi debacle is mixed. In any event, in the author's view the debate over any Video role is largely irrelevant. Regrettably, the political back-and-forth over the Video issue is allowed to obscure far more significant facts and conclusions regarding Benghazi. (We summarize these in Part V, below.)

Given the evidence assembled in this book, whether some or many or most or even *all* of the terrorist attackers in Benghazi have been motivated by the insulting Video, it is difficult to see how this should insulate the Obama administration from its culpability for the tragic outcome there. *If* the Video *is* a factor in "sparking" the terrorist attacks, this just means there is one less of many lies Team Obama tells the American people in its Benghazi Narrative. Video or no Video, in fall 2012 the Islamist terror groups in and around Benghazi are a ticking bomb ready to explode in America's face at the slightest excuse. And Barry and Hillary and Leon and David must know this. ■

[1992] Katie Pavlich, "White House Stoked Violence with Benghazi Blame Game," Townhall.com website (Oct. 25, 2012) (". . . Obama administration officials decided to push the argument that the amateur YouTube video insulting Islam, with just 300 views at the time, was the reason for the violence. A spontaneous protest of the film that spun out of control was the talking point").

[1993] E.g., Katie Pavlich, "White House Stoked Violence with Benghazi Blame Game," Townhall.com website (Oct. 25, 2012) (emphasis in original) (". . . *[A]fter* Obama administration officials repeatedly blamed the YouTube video, the Muslim world erupted, with U.S. Embassies in multiple countries coming under siege, just as we saw with the Danish cartoon fiasco. On September 14, White House Press Secretary Jay Carney said, 'The cause of the unrest was a video,' adding 'The reason there is unrest is because of the film.' In this case, Carney was actually telling the truth. The cause of the unrest was a result of a video, a video the Obama administration cynically promoted. . . . [T]he Obama administration successfully enraged radical Muslims around the world in more than 25 countries . . . The administration's efforts to blame the video fanned the deadly flames of anti-American sentiment around the world. . . ."). See also Analysis/Opinion by Charles Hurt, "If Voters Look Past Hillary's History of Lies, They'll Get What They Deserve in the White House," *The Washington Times* online (June 28, 2016) (". . . Hillary Clinton . . . immediately dismissed the attacks as some sort of unforeseeable, instantaneous reaction to some obscure anti-Muslim internet video that nobody had ever heard of – at least not until Secretary Clinton made it instantly famous around the globe by blaming it for Benghazi").

98

The Fallen Come Home

On Friday, September 14, while the CIA is drafting its talking points and the FBI is cranking up its investigation, President Obama, Vice President Biden, and Secretaries Clinton and Panetta attend a "Transfer of Remains" ceremony at Andrews Air Force Base to receive the bodies of the Fallen Four.

(Remarkably, CIA Director David Petraeus apparently does not participate in this ritual.[1994] This is despite the fact Rone Woods and Glen Doherty (as well as the seriously injured Oz Geist, who is still in a hospital in Germany) worked for his agency! Has the General stayed behind in his office because he is overseeing the drafting of the CIA Talking Points? No, he has not. His deputy, Mike Morell, is doing that. Perhaps word has reached David Petraeus through one or more of his many government contacts the FBI is investigating whether he unlawfully has given classified information to his mistress and biographer, Paula Broadwell (discussed in Chapter 113, below). It is a crime to which he later will plead guilty.[1995])

U.S. Ambassador to the United Nations Susan Rice also attends this observance. Before she appears on the Sunday Shows to tell the world all about the Benghazi crisis, this will be her closest involvement with this subject.[1996]

The administration has arranged for the remains of the four heroes to be brought to the Washington, D.C. area, instead of the military mortuary at Dover, Delaware, the normal procedure. As a result, numerous State Department employees are able to be in attendance to honor their departed brothers.

As a military band solemnly and slowly plays "Nearer My God to Thee," Marine pallbearers in immaculate dress uniforms deliberately,

---

[1994] Clinton, *Hard Choices*, Chap. 17, p. 405.

[1995] Michael Pearson, "The Petraeus Affair: A Lot More Than Sex," CNN online (Nov. 14, 2012) ("Pearson, The Petraeus Affair: A Lot More Than Sex"); and Adam Goldman, "Petraeus Pleads Guilty to Mishandling Classified Material, Will Face Probation," *The Washington Post* online (April 23, 2015).

[1996] Benghazi Committee Report, pp. 197-198.

THE TRUE ACCOUNT OF VALOR AND ABANDONMENT

reverently carry the four caskets from a plane to a large hangar where the observance will take place. There is hardly a dry eye in the huge structure.

At this ceremony inside the hangar, Secretary Clinton initially makes the following remarks from a podium:[1997]

> ... This has been a difficult week for the State Department and for our country. We've seen the heavy assault on our post in Benghazi that took the lives of those brave men. We've seen *rage and violence directed at American embassies over an awful internet video that we had nothing to do with*. It is hard for the American people to make sense of that because it is *senseless* and it is totally unacceptable. ... There will be more difficult days ahead, but it is important that we don't lose sight of the fundamental fact that America must keep leading the world. We owe it to those four men to continue the long, hard work of diplomacy. . . .[1998]

Thus does Clinton play the Video card again at this solemn ceremony, as she has daily since the attacks.

Clinton then introduces President Obama. After praising each of the four American heroes, the president states:

> ... [T]he United States of America will never retreat from the world. We will never stop working for the dignity and freedom that every person deserves, *whatever their creed, whatever their faith*.
>
> That's the essence of American leadership. That's the spirit that sets us apart from other nations. This was their work in Benghazi, and this is the work we will carry on.
>
> To you – their families and colleagues – to all Americans, know this: Their sacrifice will never be forgotten. *We will bring to justice those who took them from us*. We will stand fast against the *violence* on our diplomatic missions. *We will*

[1997] To her credit, earlier on the morning following the disaster, Secretary Clinton has called the families of Chris Stevens and Sean Smith to convey her condolences. Clinton, *Hard Choices*, Chap. 17, p. 399; and Remarks of Secretary of State Hillary Clinton on the Deaths of American Personnel in Benghazi, Libya, State Department Treaty Room, Washington, D.C., State Dept. Archives website (Sept. 12, 2012).

[1998] Secretary of State Hillary Clinton's Remarks at Transfer of Remains Ceremony for Americans Killed in Libya (Transcript), *The Washington Post* online (Sept. 14, 2012) (emphasis added) (*Watch video there*; Go to 5:56 - 7:37); and Diplomatic Security, 2012 Year in Review," U.S. Department of State, Bureau of Diplomatic Security, State Dept. website (June 2013) (emphasis added), p. 27.

continue to do everything in our power to protect Americans serving overseas . . . [J]ustice will come to those who harm Americans. . . .[1999]

Unlike Clinton, President Obama is silent on the Video, except for a general reference to the dignity and freedom of every person, whatever their "creed" or their "faith." In his remarks, Obama does not mention terrorism; Clinton quotes the phrase "an act of ugly terror" in reading from a letter from a Palestinian leader praising Ambassador Stevens. Neither official publicly references any protest or demonstration.

The band next plays the National Anthem. All stand at rigid attention, saluting or with hands over hearts. (Mercifully, no one takes a knee.) Finally, a military chaplain gives a very brief benediction. Then, as the band slowly performs "America the Beautiful," the Marine guards respectfully, ceremoniously place the four caskets into waiting hearses. The rear doors are closed. The Transfer of Remains ceremony is over. The Heroes of Benghazi are home.

However, during another part of this ceremony, as is customary the administration officials meet privately at a reception with the family members of the fallen. To their faces both Obama and Clinton reportedly claim the Video was the cause of the attacks. According to two of the deceased's parents – Patricia "Pat" Smith, mother of Sean Smith, and Charles Woods, father of Tyrone Woods – Obama and Clinton promise, in effect, "we will prosecute the person who made this Video."[2000] (As James S. Robbins will ask, since when is Hillary Clinton in charge of the Justice Department? And since when did it become a crime in America to criticize Islam? And wouldn't the Fallen Four's families prefer to hear the U.S. officials promise to get the terrorist bastards who murdered their loved ones, rather than to pursue a filmmaker?[2001])

[1999] Remarks by the President at Transfer of Remains Ceremony for Benghazi Victims, Andrews Air Force Base, Obama White House Archives (Sept. 14, 2012) (emphasis added) (*Watch video there*; Go to 14:50 - 16:15).

[2000] Glenn Kessler, "What Benghazi Family Members Say Hillary Clinton Said About the Video," Fact Checker, *The Washington Post* online (Jan. 4, 2016) ("Kessler, What Benghazi Family Members Say Hillary Clinton Said About the Video"). Kessler's article contains a detailed summary of the *Post's* fact-checking inquiry into who said what at the private reception. See also Attkisson, *Stonewalled*, Chap. 4, pp. 211-212.

[2001] James S. Robbins, "TRR: Is a General Losing His Job Over Benghazi?" The Robbins Report, *The Washington Times* online (Oct. 28, 2012; Updated Oct. 29, 2012); and Attkisson, *Stonewalled* (". . . Why focus the families' attention on the producer of a perfectly legal video instead of the actual killers? Why not instead say, *We'll find whoever killed your loved one?*") (emphasis in original) Chap. 4, p. 197.

Charles Woods later asserts he knows at the time Clinton isn't telling the truth about the Video.[2002] He writes in his journal this day Clinton has told him they are going to arrest the Video maker who caused the death of his son.[2003] Sean's mother Pat Smith also insists *Clinton* and the other Obama officials lie to the families' faces.[2004] (GRS agent Tanto Paronto, who speaks with these surviving relatives afterwards, also supports Smith's and Woods' assertions.[2005]) However, other family members at the ceremony did not hear any discussion of the Video in their own, separate conversations with the administration officials.[2006]

Patricia Smith also claims repeatedly the State Department refuses to provide her with information regarding how her son died, because

---

[2002] Interview of Charles Woods with Sean Hannity on "Hannity," Fox News online (May 9, 2013) ("... When I was approached by Hillary Clinton at the coming home ceremony of the bodies at Andrews Air Force Base and she said, 'We're going to go out and we're going to prosecute the person that made the video,' I knew that she wasn't telling the truth. And I think the whole world knows that now....") (*Watch video there*; Go to 1:10 - 2:00). See also "Special Report," Fox News online (Aug. 2, 2016) (Charles Woods: "There are two options: One is either Mrs. Clinton is lying. Or she has a bad memory because of her age or her head injury that she suffered.... She stood in front of my son's casket and blamed the rage directed at U.S. embassies" on an internet video); and Cortney O'Brien, "Father of Benghazi Victim: Either Hillary Is a Liar, or Has a Bad Memory From Head Injury," Townhall.com website (Aug. 2, 2016).

[2003] Kessler, What Benghazi Family Members Say Hillary Clinton Said About the Video (Includes image of journal entry); and Cortney O'Brien, "Benghazi Widow Wonders If Hillary Never Mentioned YouTube Video to Her Because There Was a Navy SEAL Behind Her," Townhall.com website (Aug. 4, 2016).

[2004] Interview of Patricia Smith with Trish Regan, Fox Business News (Mar. 10, 2016) (*Watch video there*; Go to 0:00 - 2:54); and Erik Wemple, Opinion, "Univision's Ramos Picked the Wrong Benghazi Question for Hillary Clinton," *The Washington Post* online (Mar. 10, 2016) (Quoting Pat Smith on Fox News: "Hillary and Obama and Panetta, Biden and Susan Rice all told me that it was a video when they knew ... it was not the video." "Those comments by Patricia Smith have played into the much-discussed accusation that Obama administration officials, in the immediate aftermath of Benghazi, attempted to blame the attacks on an anti-Muslim video instead of terrorism – as part of a scheme to insulate themselves from criticism in advance of the 2012 presidential election").

[2005] Interview of Kris "Tanto" Paronto and Other GRS Agents with Megyn Kelly, "The Kelly File," Fox News Channel (Possibly Jan. 4, 2016) (*Watch video there*; Go to 15:32 - 16:32).

[2006] Kessler, What Benghazi Family Members Say Hillary Clinton Said About the Video.

she is not a member of the "immediate family."[2007] (A *mother* is not immediate family? *Really?*) Smith asserts at this Transfer of Remains ceremony the Secretary of State "absolutely" promises she will get back to Patricia Smith when more information is available. But Clinton never does.[2008] Smith claims Secretary Panetta also promises to "tell her what happened," but never does.[2009]

Kate Quigley, sister of Glen Doherty, later will tell Fox News and *The Washington Post* that at this casket ceremony Hillary Clinton (and only Clinton) *privately* blames the four Americans' deaths on a protest. Quigley tells Fox:

> ... She [Hillary Clinton] clearly came in with a script and an agenda and talked about, you know, in her moments with my family, that we should feel sad for the Libyan people because they're uneducated and that breeds fear which breeds violence which ultimately led to the *protest* that took my brother's life....[2010]

When the interviewer presses whether Clinton really blames the attacks on a protest, Quigley responds, "Absolutely."[2011]

In December 2015, during her presidential campaign Hillary Clinton appears on ABC's "This Week" with George Stephanopolous (a former presidential aide to her husband). Clinton again invokes the "fog of

---

[2007] Interview of Patricia Smith with Carol Costello, CNN News (Oct. 21, 2015) (*Watch video there*; Go to 0:00-30 and 1:22-53); and Interview of Patricia Smith with Trish Regan, Fox Business News (Mar. 10, 2016) (*Watch video there*; Go to 0:44-59 and 2:32-44).

[2008] Interview of Patricia Smith with Trish Regan, Fox Business News (Mar. 10, 2016) (*Watch video there*; Go to 8:00-22).

[2009] Kessler, What Benghazi Family Members Say Hillary Clinton Said About the Video.

[2010] "Benghazi Victim's Sister Shocked by Bill Clinton's Comments...," "The Kelly File," Fox News online (Jan. 22, 2016) (emphasis added) (*Watch video there*; Go to 1:24 - 3:26); and Kessler, What Benghazi Family Members Say Hillary Clinton Said About the Video (emphasis added).

[2011] "Benghazi Victim's Sister Shocked by Bill Clinton's Comments...," "The Kelly File," Fox News online (Jan. 22, 2016) (*Watch video there*; Go to 2:56 - 3:26). See Marina Fang, "Sister of Benghazi Victim: Hillary Clinton's Marathon Hearing Failed to Provide 'Real Answers,'" *The Huffington Post* online (Oct. 22, 2015; Updated Jan. 3, 2017) ("... Quigley criticized Clinton's initial response to the attack. She said when Clinton met with relatives of the victims, she expressed regret for Libyan protests against an anti-Islam video, which at the time was reported to have stirred the attack. State Department officials later revealed the protests never happened"); and Kessler, What Benghazi Family Members Say Hillary Clinton Said About the Video.

war" excuse and denies even making these statements about the Video to the Fallen Four's families.[2012] She will accuse the victims' parents of lying about her statements to them, and insist she herself is being honest about the incident. When asked three weeks later who is lying about what happened at this casket ceremony, Hillary Clinton will insist it is "Not me, that's all I can tell you."[2013]

Still later, at a Democrat primary debate in March 2016, Univision host Jorge Ramos asks Clinton if she lied to the families of the fallen by claiming the Benghazi attacks were the result of the blasphemous Video, rather than a terrorist attack as Clinton had told her daughter in a contemporaneous email. (Some in the audience boo Ramos for his perfectly reasonable question.) Clinton claims Patricia Smith is "absolutely wrong" in saying blaming the Video was a lie. Clinton further responds, "This was fog of war. This was complicated," asserting the intelligence on what happened kept shifting hourly. (Some in the audience cheer her wildly.)[2014]

In contrast to Smith, Woods and Quigley, Chris Stevens' mother wants no part of any "blame game." Mary Commanday calls on Republicans at their 2016 convention to cease invoking her son's death for "opportunistic and cynical" political reasons.[2015] Earlier, just weeks after the attacks, she tells CBS News, "I don't think it's productive to lay blame on people" over her son's death.[2016] (Really? Not even if it might prevent future deaths by removing incompetent government officials so they can't make the same fatal mistakes again?) ∎

[2012] Interview of Hillary Clinton with George Stephanopolous, "This Week," ABC News online (Dec. 6, 2015) (*Watch video there*; Go to 14:15 – 16:06); and Kessler, What Benghazi Family Members Say Hillary Clinton Said About the Video.

[2013] Megyn Kelly, "The Kelly File," Fox News Channel (Possibly Jan. 4, 2016) (*Watch video there*; Go to 0:36 - 1:39); and Kessler, What Benghazi Family Members Say Hillary Clinton Said About the Video.

[2014] Erik Wemple, Opinion, "Univision's Ramos Picked the Wrong Benghazi Question for Hillary Clinton," *The Washington Post* online (Mar. 10, 2016) (*Watch video there*); and Ben Wolfgang, "Jorge Ramos Booed for Asking Clinton Question About Benghazi," *The Washington Times* online (Mar. 9, 2016).

[2015] E.g., Harper Neidig, "Benghazi Victim's Mother Calls on Trump, GOP to Stop Invoking Son's Death," msn.com online (July 23, 2016).

[2016] Interview of Mary Commanday with Ben Tracy, "Mother of Slain Ambassador Speaks Out," "CBS This Morning," CBS News website (Oct. 18, 2012) (*Watch video there*; Go to 2:30-35).

99

"It Was 9/11 Everywhere"

Protest or no protest, spontaneous or preplanned, Video or no Video, after the tragedy much of the Obama administration's time and effort is spent advancing a key justification for its failed actions in Benghazi. Team Obama and their supporters repeatedly maintain no military assets from outside Libya possibly can get to *Benghazi* in time to aid the Americans there.[2017] The argument is entirely bogus.

The "Tyranny of Time and Distance"

The series of assaults at or near the Mission Compound and (later) at the CIA Annex, and the subsequent evacuation of Americans from Benghazi, will continue for more than twelve hours. *At the commencement of the violence, of course, no one in the U.S. government possibly can know how long it will last.* Despite this obvious fact, Defense Secretary Leon Panetta later claims it is not possible to send help to the besieged Americans in Benghazi because any rescue mission could not have arrived in time. In a nutshell, Panetta and other officials invoke the "tyranny of time and distance" excuse.[2018]

Although never part of the CIA Talking Points, this "tyranny of time and distance" excuse is a critical component of the Benghazi Narrative. Certainly it is valid with respect to the rapid murders of Ambassador Stevens and Sean Smith at the Mission Compound. But is it true of the deaths of Rone Woods and Glen Doherty (and the severe wounding of Dave Ubben and Mark Geist) at the CIA Annex over *seven hours later*? And is it true with respect to the protection of the Americans at the Benghazi airport as the second group waits over a *two*

[2017] E.g., House Oversight Committee Hearings (May 8, 2013) (Opening Remarks of Ranking Member Elijah Cummings (D-MD)) (". . . We have the best military in the world, but even with all of their technological advances, they could not get there in time"), p. 4.

[2018] Additional Views of Senators Chambliss, Burr, et al., p. 11; and Benghazi Committee Report, pp. 66, 115 and 130.

THE TRUE ACCOUNT OF VALOR AND ABANDONMENT

and one-half hour period to be evacuated to Tripoli? (This last departure will not be completed until *nearly five hours* after the deaths of Woods and Doherty.[2019])

Numerous military witnesses before the Select Committee, other congressional panels, and elsewhere repeat some variation of the "tyranny of time and distance" explanation for not acting swiftly on this Night of Benghazi.[2020] We summarize here only some of those variations.

Benghazi Is Too Far Away

Panetta invokes the "distance" theme in his memoir, *Worthy Fights*. There, he claims:

> ... The simple, sad fact of Benghazi is that we did not have intelligence that such an attack might occur, and as a result did not have forces close enough when the violence struck to be able to save our people from harm. We moved as quickly as we could, but this took place too far away for our forces to reach them in time.[2021]

Panetta acts as if he and the Pentagon have not known in advance of September 11, 2012, that "It's a Long Way to Benghazi." The Pentagon supposedly has a military plan for every contingency. Where is the military plan to respond to a terrorist attack in North Africa – especially on the anniversary of 9/11? (You have to plan for these contingencies *in advance!* Why don't you at least have a damned plane at the FAST base in Rota, Spain? (Seven months after Benghazi, the Pentagon finally transfers six "Osprey" transport aircraft (and additional troops) to Spain.[2022] Too late.) Instead, one has to fly there from Germany,

---

[2019] Key Delays Appendix (See September 11 entry for 11:17 p.m. and September 12 entry for 3:54 a.m., both Washington time).

[2020] E.g., Benghazi Committee Report (CIF Commander: "tyranny of distance"), p. 66; *Id.* (Secretary of Defense Panetta: "tyranny of time and distance"), p. 67; *Id.* (Under Secretary of Defense for Policy Dr. James Miller: "The logistical issues were the tyranny of distance and time, first and foremost... So there is, first, the distance to be traveled, the fact that it takes time...."), p. 67; and *Id.* (Vice Admiral James Winnefeld: Referencing "...[T]he tyranny of distance and how long it takes to get there..."), p. 69.

[2021] Panetta, *Worthy Fights*, Chap. 16, pp. 429-430.

[2022] Kevin Baron, "Marines Move Crisis Response Force to Edge of Africa," ForeignPolicy.com website (April 25, 2013).

1,100 miles away. And why don't you have a tanker closer to North Africa than England?)

It Happened Too Quickly

In February 2013 Secretary Panetta testifies before Congress, "And frankly without an adequate warning, there was not enough time given the *speed of the attack* for armed military assets to respond. . . . Time, distance, the lack of an adequate warning, *events that moved very quickly on the ground* prevented a more immediate response. . . ." In his later book, Panetta doubles-down on this claim: ". . . That time and distance were simply too much to overcome should never be mistaken for a lack of swift and honest effort to help our people. . . ."[2023]

On their face, Panetta's "time and distance" assertions are preposterous. Certainly, Benghazi is a long way from many places. But how can Panetta – or the president or Clinton or the CIA or *anyone* – possibly know in advance how *long* the attacks will last? At the time, even the terrorist *attackers* probably cannot even know. *Why don't our commanders at least initiate a rescue mission to Benghazi, even though it ultimately might prove too late?* The operation always can be turned back, or re-routed to Tripoli or Sigonella or Souda Bay, or otherwise halted. According to the Select Benghazi Committee, other than Team Tripoli no such rescue mission *to Benghazi* ever is *begun!*[2024]

It is interesting Panetta asserts events "moved very quickly on the ground." In fact, there are significant lulls in the attacks on the Night of Benghazi. The second wave assaults on the Mission Compound come more than 80 minutes after the initial attacks. And there is a lull of some 90 minutes between the second Mission assault and the first attack on the CIA Annex. Later, there is a prolonged gap of three and

---

[2023] Panetta Senate Armed Services Prepared Testimony; and Panetta, *Worthy Fights*, Chap. 16, p. 430.

[2024] Benghazi Committee Report, pp. 91 and 99-100; Additional Views of Reps. Jordan and Pompeo, p. 421; *Id.* ("We are now convinced, contrary to the administration's public claim that the military did not have time to get to Benghazi, that the administration never launched men or machines to help directly in the fight. . . . None of the three assets that Secretary Panetta ordered to deploy were intended to join the fight against terrorists at the Annex"), pp. 445-447; and The Editors, "What We Do Know About the Benghazi Attack Demands a Reckoning," National Review online (June 28, 2016) (". . . Obama and his subordinates never even tried to relieve the Americans under attack. It is not that rescue craft turned around once reports led them to believe it was too late to get to Benghazi; they never left the ground in the first place").

one-half hours between the second Annex assault and the final, fatal mortar attack. Indeed, as noted in Chapter 48 above, one of Panetta's top military commanders emphasizes these lulls, and cites them as a reason why any U.S. military jets over Benghazi would not be able to see events happening on the ground.[2025] (Even Team Obama's pathetic excuses for their inaction are tripping over each other.)

Weeks after the attacks, on October 25 at a joint press event with General Dempsey, Panetta utters the following astonishing statement: "It was really [nearly?] over before, you know, we had the opportunity to really know what was happening."[2026] (Seriously? The last two Americans to die will not fall until around 11:18 p.m. Washington time – about *seven and one-half hours* into the battle.[2027] And you had a surveillance drone overhead for over six hours of that period.)

Two months later, the State Department announces the release of the Benghazi Accountability Review Board Report (addressed in detail in Chapter 109). The Board's Vice-Chairman, retired Admiral Michael Mullen, also emphasizes "the battle was over swiftly" excuse. He tells reporters, ". . . This was over in a matter of about 20 or 30 minutes with respect to the Special Mission specifically."[2028] Note Mullen here conveniently ignores the Annex attacks and severe casualties there, which this Board does not investigate.

Later still on May 8, 2013 (purely coincidentally, the very day the House Oversight Committee holds public hearings on Benghazi), the Pentagon issues a press statement about Benghazi. (Defense is now under the new management of the incompetent Secretary Chuck Hagel.) Pentagon Press Secretary George Little is quoted in this statement as asserting, "The fact remains – as we have repeatedly

---

[2025] Key Delays Appendix (See September 11 entries for 7:40 p.m. and 11:17 p.m., both Washington time); and Benghazi Committee Report (Vice Admiral Winnefeld testifies the F-16 pilots would not be able to see "action going on on the ground . . . [because] but for most of the night there wasn't"), p. 67.

[2026] Karen Parrish, "Secretary, Chairman Respond to Reporters on Benghazi Attack," DoD News, American Forces Press Service, Defense Dept. Archives (Oct. 25, 2012); CBS News/Associated Press, "Panetta: Unclear Early Info Slowed Benghazi Response," CBS News online (Oct. 25, 2012); and Baier, New Revelations on Attack in Benghazi (*Watch video there*; Go to 0:11-15).

[2027] See Key Delays Appendix (See September 11 entries for 3:42 p.m. and 11:17 p.m., both Washington time).

[2028] Benghazi ARB Report Briefing for the Media.

indicated – that *United States forces* could not have arrived in time to mount a rescue of those Americans killed or injured that night."[2029]

(Note even this dubious disclaimer is limited to "United States forces"; it is silent on whether Greece or Italy or other NATO forces or Israel or other allies could have attempted a timely rescue. Also, does "forces" include a jet aircraft flyover? At an absolute minimum, as we have discussed previously, an *armed* predator drone *could* have arrived above Benghazi before the final deadly mortar attack.)

We Lacked Sufficient Information

As noted above, in February 2013 former Secretary of Defense Leon Panetta testifies to the Senate: "The biggest problem that night, Senator, was that nobody knew really what was going on there."[2030] At his October 25, 2012, press conference with General Dempsey, Panetta further claims:

[The] basic principle is that *you don't deploy forces into harm's way without knowing what's going on*; *without having some real-time information* about what's taking place. . . . And as a result of *not having that kind of information, the commander who was on the ground in that area*, Gen. Ham, Gen. Dempsey and I felt very strongly that *we could not put forces at risk in that situation.*[2031]

There are so many lies and half-truths in these short statements it is difficult deciding where to begin. First, let's all agree there is no commander "on the ground in that area." The commanders are in Washington, D.C. (including General Ham) and Stuttgart, but they are not even in Libya, much less Benghazi. Moreover, as discussed in Chapter 80 above, the closest thing to a "commander on the ground" in Libya – Lt. Col. S. E. Gibson in Tripoli – wants to take his small, four-man squad to Benghazi but is ordered *not* to by SOCAFRICA.

[2029] Pentagon Press Release, "DOD Cooperates with Congress on Benghazi Probes" (emphasis added).

[2030] Panetta Armed Services Committee Testimony (Feb. 7, 2013) (Response to questions of Sen. Kelly Ayotte (R-NH)).

[2031] Karen Parrish, "Secretary, Chairman Respond to Reporters on Benghazi Attack," DoD News, American Forces Press Service, Defense Dept. Archives (Oct. 25, 2012) (emphasis added); Associated Press, "Panetta: Military Lacked Enough Information to Intervene During Benghazi Attack," Fox News online (Oct. 26, 2012) (emphasis added) (*Watch video there*; Go to 2:32 - 3:09); and Kristol, Petraeus and Panetta Speak – But Not the President (emphasis added).

Second, you *do* deploy U.S. forces into harm's way when U.S. government personnel are being mortally attacked by heavily-armed militants.[2032] That's what the U.S. military is *for*; they volunteer and train for just such dire situations. (Can you imagine Israel not sending an urgent rescue party if there were nearly three-dozen Israelis under attack in Benghazi?)

Third, you never have perfect information about what's happening in a combat zone. But you and other U.S. officials at the Pentagon, State, the CIA, the White House, in Stuttgart, in Tripoli and in Benghazi have *lots* of real-time information on this Night of Benghazi, Mr. Secretary.[2033] (See Chapter 90.) (No wonder Benghazi gets so screwed up when your Defense Secretary is starting from such a flawed "basic principle.")

As noted elsewhere (see Chapters 53 and 62), these Pentagon statements seem inconsistent with other assertions that Secretary Panetta has ordered his forces "at risk" by directing them at 7:00 p.m. to "deploy now." Remember, according to the evidence cataloged above, this directive is issued *before* the U.S. government's focus shifts away from Benghazi and towards Tripoli (and Sicily). And in his email of 7:19 p.m., your Chief of Staff Jeremy Bash claims forces are "spinning up" to go to *Benghazi.* Is that not "into harm's way"? (Leon, did you, or did you not, issue that 7:00 p.m. Order to deploy? Still further contradictions.)

(Make up your mind. Did you not move forces to Benghazi because militarily it was not possible? Or did you not move them because you lacked sufficient real-time information, making it too risky to move? Get your excuses straight.[2034])

[2032] Babbin, Whitewashing Benghazi ("... There is simply no excuse for inaction. When Americans are under fire, our military has a moral obligation to fly into the fight as fast as it can...."). Jed Babbin is a former Air Force officer and Deputy Under Secretary of Defense.

[2033] Kristol, Petraeus and Panetta Speak – But Not the President ("... Indeed, since there seems in fact to have been 'real-time information' available from those fighting on the ground, Panetta's excuse for inaction would at least require considerable elaboration to be convincing").

[2034] E.g., Kristol, Petraeus and Panetta Speak – But Not the President (emphasis in original) ("Panetta's statement only makes sense if there were those in the military or elsewhere who considered or urged deploying forces into harm's way, and that those individuals were overruled because of the lack of real-time information.... In other words, Panetta is acknowledging forces *could* have been put at risk, but that a decision was made not to do so....").

We Did Everything We Could

In February 2013, Panetta further testifies to Congress, "Despite the uncertainty at the time, the Department of Defense and the rest of the United States government *spared no effort to do everything we could* to try to save American lives. Before, during and after the attack, every request the Department of Defense received we did, we accomplished. . . ." This is demonstrably untrue. Greg Hicks alone asks the U.S. Defense Attaché in Tripoli for jet flyovers above Benghazi; and Hicks asks Lt. Col. Gibson to take his four-man special forces team to Benghazi. Panetta's Defense Department denies both requests.[2035]

Panetta's claim can only be true if Defense is asked to do *nothing* regarding *Benghazi*. Because the Pentagon does *nothing* – except to send a plane to *Tripoli* after the battle is over to retrieve four caskets and evacuate the wounded and other Benghazi survivors to Germany.

Two Republican members of the Select Committee write:

> The American people expect their government to make every effort to help those we put in harm's way when they find themselves in trouble. The U.S. military never sent assets to help rescue those fighting in Benghazi and never made it into Libya with personnel during the attack. And contrary to the administration's claim that it could not have landed in Benghazi in time to help, the administration never directed men or machines into Benghazi.[2036]

According to CBS News, an unnamed "White House official" claims Panetta and Dempsey "looked at the available options, and the ones we exercised had our military forces *arrive* in less than 24 hours, well ahead of timelines laid out in established policies."[2037] (Arrive *where?* Benghazi? Tripoli? Sigonella? And to do *what?* If true, the

---

[2035] Panetta Senate Armed Services Prepared Testimony (emphasis added); and Eli Lake, "Benghazi Whistleblower: Requests for Military Backup Denied," *The Daily Beast* online website (May 6, 2013).

[2036] Additional Views of Reps. Jordan and Pompeo, p. 416.

[2037] Attkisson, Diplomat: U.S. Special Forces Told "You Can't Go" to Benghazi During Attacks (emphasis added); and Attkisson, Could U.S. Military Have Helped During Libya Attack?

Pentagon's timelines for dealing with life-and-death emergencies threatening U.S. personnel in North Africa are a *disgrace*.[2038])

Joint Chiefs Chair Dempsey also will claim to Congress, "Our military was appropriately responsive. We *acted quickly* once notified of the attacks on the Temporary Mission Facility. . . . We did what our posture and capabilities allowed."[2039]

The Select Committee writes, "Although Dempsey told the U.S. Senate that once forces began moving, 'nothing stopped us, nothing slowed us,' it appears the U.S. Military's response that night was delayed – because it started too late."[2040]

As the Key Delays Appendix demonstrates, Dempsey's claims are absurd, and the Select Committee is spot on.[2041] Regarding why the Pentagon was so unprepared for trouble in North Africa, Dempsey later will use the excuse, "It was 9/11 everywhere in the world."[2042] ∎

[2038] Babbin, Whitewashing Benghazi (". . . [G]iven the terrorist presence in Benghazi and the inadequate security there (not to mention the importance of the date), Dempsey is guilty of '. . . either a profound inability or clear unwillingness to prevent problems before they arise'"), quoting Additional Views of Senators Chambliss, Burr, et al., p. 11.

[2039] Prepared Statement of General Dempsey, Joint Chiefs Chairman, before Senate Armed Services Committee (Feb. 7, 2013) (emphasis added), p. 4.

[2040] Benghazi Committee Report, p. 118.

[2041] See Additional Views of Senators Chambliss, Burr, et al. (". . . General Dempsey's attempts to excuse inaction by claiming that forces were not deployed because they would not have gotten there in time does not pass the common sense test. No one knew when the attacks against our facilities in Benghazi would end, or how aggressive the attacks would be. . . ."), p. 11.

[2042] Karen Parrish, "Secretary, Chairman Respond to Reporters on Benghazi Attack," DoD News, American Forces Press Service, Defense Dept. Archives (Oct. 25, 2012); and Prepared Statement of General Dempsey, Joint Chiefs Chairman, before Senate Armed Services Committee (Feb. 7, 2013) (". . . [W]e must not forget that it was 9-11 everywhere. . . ."), p. 4.

100

Coulda, Shoulda, Woulda, Souda

One aspect of the U.S. military's posture on the Night of Benghazi is not easily dismissed by the Pentagon's "tyranny of time and distance" defense. Following the Benghazi tragedy, the U.S. military establishment repeatedly claims its assets at the U.S. Souda Bay Naval Air Station on Crete are not "appropriate" to address the national security crisis on this Night of Benghazi. These apparently are secret "special operations" assets. (So secret they are unusable!)

Souda is the U.S. military installation closest to the Americans besieged in nearby Benghazi. How can it possibly worsen the situation in Benghazi to deploy some of these secret assets to the sound of the guns in nearby Benghazi, just 320 miles away?

Joint Chiefs Chairman General Martin Dempsey later will testify the military assets at Souda Bay "wasn't the right tool for the particular threat we faced." More specifically, Dempsey claims the U.S. aircraft there are not on "heightened alert" (sound familiar?). Also, he asserts any "boots on the ground" deployed from Souda Bay will have arrived too late.[2043] (Arrived too late with a less-than-one-hour flight time to Benghazi? Arrived too late to at least secure the Benghazi airport? This is not credible. Yet again, how can Panetta and Dempsey possibly know how long the Battle of Benghazi will last? Dempsey almost certainly is lying to Congress.)

We know there are shooters with guns at Souda Bay tonight because the destroyer USS Laboon is docked here. It has a large crew, some of whom can board a U.S. or Greek plane and fly the 45 minutes or so to Benghazi. Benghazi has an international airport, which Team Tripoli manages to find.

As noted above (Chapter 48), the Select Committee discloses there are "special operations aircraft" of some unspecified type at Souda Bay on this Night of Benghazi.[2044] The Greek air base next door to Souda

---

[2043] Testimony of Gen. Martin Dempsey before Senate Armed Services Committee on Terrorist Attacks on U.S. Facilities in Benghazi, Libya (Feb. 7, 2013), cited in Sen. Intelligence Committee Benghazi Report (Redacted), p. 31.

[2044] Benghazi Committee Report, p. 64.

Bay very likely has aircraft that can help. Can our Greek ally's planes not carry U.S. military shooters from the Laboon to the defense of the beleaguered Americans? (We train with these guys in NATO exercises.)

Why even *have* a military base at Souda Bay if it has no useful military assets? And if you have such assets but don't deploy them in the middle of a national security emergency threatening dozens of American lives nearby, when *would* you use them? In training exercises? *What good are they?*

Given the paucity of information available about the Souda Bay assets, it is difficult to analyze why they are not deployed to Benghazi this tragic night. (There's something fishy about DoD's lack of transparency regarding its Souda Bay assets. Significantly, Leon Panetta *does not even reference Souda Bay* in his memoir's relatively brief discussion of Benghazi. And there's something very odd about the Select Committee's cryptic, minimalist discussion of Souda Bay, all but ignoring its potential role.)

Of the many unanswered questions regarding this Night of Benghazi, these involving Souda Bay are among the most puzzling and vexing. The Trump administration should make it a priority to release non-classified information concerning why these Souda Bay military assets cannot be, or otherwise are not, deployed to Benghazi to aid the Americans there in September 2012. ∎

101

"They Stood & They Watched & Our People Died"

In retrospect, the excuses and explanations given by top U.S. military brass for their failure to launch any serious rescue attempt appear completely lame. ("Africa is too big. Benghazi is too far. The night is too dark. We don't have enough time. It's all happening too quickly. Our planes are not on alert (on the 9/11 anniversary). We don't know the mission. We don't have radio contact with those on the ground. We don't have enough information. The ambassador is dead so the crisis is over. We don't want it to appear an invasion....") One gets the strong sense the Pentagon just doesn't *want* to go to Benghazi this night.[2045] Or, they are ordered *not* to go (see Chapter 68).

Two Select Committee members reject these excuses:

...What is troubling is that the administration never set in motion a plan to go to Benghazi in the first place. It is one thing to try and fail; it is yet another not to try at all. In the end, the administration did not move heaven and earth to help our people in Benghazi, as Americans would expect. The contrast between the heroic actions taken in Benghazi and the inaction in Washington – highlights the failure.[2046]

These two congressmen further conclude:

Our brave soldiers were ready, willing and able to fight for their fellow countrymen but leaders in Washington held them back.... We cannot say whether the military could have saved lives in Benghazi. We can say with certainty that our nation's leaders did not move heaven and earth to send military help with the urgency that those Americans deserved.

[2045] See Benghazi Committee Report ("There was nothing new about the time and distance concerns in Africa or the positioning of U.S. assets that might be called upon to respond"), p. 68.

[2046] Additional Views of Reps. Jordan and Pompeo, p. 421.

We will never know if a more vigorous, comprehensive, and urgent response could have saved lives.[2047]

Congressman Mike Pompeo (R-KS), elaborates further:

We expect our government to make every effort to save the lives of Americans who serve in harm's way. That did not happen in Benghazi. Politics were put ahead of the lives of Americans, and while the administration had made excuses and blamed the challenges posed by time and distance, the truth is that they did not try.[2048]

Later, Pompeo will expound further on the government's failure to mount a rescue attempt during the Benghazi attacks:

I find it morally reprehensible, and behavior that if it was your son, or your daughter, or one of your family members or friends, who were on the ground that night, and you watched the actions in Washington, D.C., you'd have every right to be disgusted.[2049]

(Congressman Pompeo later will become President Trump's CIA Director,[2050] and subsequently his Secretary of State.)

In this regard, House Oversight Committee member Paul Gosar (R-AZ) poses an excellent question. In essence he asks, "What would the military and diplomatic response have been if Chelsea Clinton had been a CIA case officer working in the CIA Annex on the Night of Benghazi?"[2051]

Another Republican on the Select Committee also is critical of Team Obama's conduct. Representative Jim Jordan (R-OH) tells CNN, "[T]oo little effort was made to protect" Ambassador Stevens and the other Americans in Benghazi. "We didn't move Heaven and Earth to get help to the people who were fighting for their lives."[2052]

[2047] *Id.*, pp. 444 and 448.

[2048] Press Release, "Select Committee on Benghazi Releases Proposed Report," Benghazi Committee website (Updated July 8, 2016).

[2049] Catherine Herridge Report, "Special Report," Fox News Channel (Nov. 18, 2016) (*Watch video there*; Go to 1:26-39).

[2050] Press Release, "Mike Pompeo Takes Helm as Director of the Central Intelligence Agency," CIA website (Jan. 24, 2017).

[2051] Betsy Woodruff, "Gosar on Benghazi: 'What if it had happened to Chelsea?'" National Review online (Sept. 11, 2013).

[2052] House Republicans Fault US Military Response to Benghazi; and Interview of Rep. Jim Jordan (R-OH) with Chris Cuomo, CNN (June 28, 2016) (*Watch video there*; Go to 4:50 – 6:18).

Former career Marine Mark Thompson, head of the benched F.E.S.T. group, also provides a powerful rejoinder to the tiresome "tyranny of time and distance" excuse:

> ... We live by a code. That code says you go after people when they're in peril when they're in the service of their country. We did not have the benefit of hindsight in the early hours. And those people who are in peril in the future need to know that we will go get them and we will do everything we can to get them out of harm's way. That night unfolded in ways that no one could have predicted when it first started. And it is my strong belief then, as it is now, that we needed to demonstrate that resolve even if we still had the same outcome.[2053]

CBS News subsequently interviews retired CIA Officer Gary Berntsen regarding this lack of military help on the Night of Benghazi. (Berntsen commanded CIA counterterrorism missions that had targeted Osama bin Laden. He also led the U.S. team that responded after U.S. embassies were bombed in East Africa in 1998.) He believes help could have come to Benghazi much sooner than Team Obama suggests:

> You find a way to make this happen. There isn't a plan for every single engagement. Sometimes you have to be able to make adjustments. They made zero adjustments in this. They stood and they watched and our people died.[2054] ■

[2053] Thompson Oversight Committee Testimony (May 8, 2013) (Response to questions of Rep. Jason Chaffetz (R-UT)), p. 67. See also James S. Robbins, "TRR: Is a General Losing His Job Over Benghazi?" The Robbins Report, *The Washington Times* online (Oct. 28, 2012; Updated Oct. 29, 2012) ("... The Army's ethos is to leave no man behind, but that is not shared by a president accustomed to leading from that location").

[2054] Attkisson, Could U.S. Military Have Helped During Libya Attack?; and IBD Editorial, Obama Knew Benghazi Was Terrorism And Did Nothing.

102

Looting the Mission Compound... Again

As Obama administration officials honor the victims of Benghazi in Washington, six thousand miles to the east the Mission Compound is being looted again. **As noted above, during the Battle of Benghazi terrorists and others loot the Mission after the Americans have departed to the CIA Annex. Among other things, they steal computers, documents and vehicles. Following this pilfering, the Compound lays in ruins.**[2055]

But the Mission still is a crime scene. Two American government officials have been murdered here, major acts of arson have transpired, and U.S. government property has been destroyed and stolen. Some American documents, equipment and other property still remain behind.

Despite this, after the battle neither the local Benghazi government (such as it is), the anemic national Libyan government, nor the U.S. make any serious effort to secure the Mission Compound. The American FBI will not arrive in Benghazi for many days (discussed in Chapter 105). Meanwhile, militia members, sightseers, looters, journalists, neighbors, and basically anyone with the interest and some time to kill are permitted to roam through the demolished Mission grounds. Still more U.S. property disappears.

Journalists in particular rummage through the documents strewn across the floors of the burned-out Mission buildings.[2056] For example, on or about September 14th, a CNN reporter recovers Ambassador Stevens' journal, in which he is writing as, or shortly before, the attacks

---

[2055] Birnbaum, Sensitive Documents Left Behind With Little Security at U.S. Diplomatic Post in Libya ("The compound still reeked of smoke Wednesday [September 12th], and all of the buildings had been looted. Overturned furniture, broken glass and strewn documents were everywhere. Chandeliers lay on the floor. In kitchens, food was rotting").

[2056] "Sensitive Documents Left Behind at US Consulate in Benghazi, Libya," NBC News online (Oct. 3, 2012); and Birnbaum, Sensitive Documents Left Behind With Little Security at U.S. Diplomatic Post in Libya.

commence.[2057] CNN publishes the seven-page handwritten diary. (According to left-leaning *Buzzfeed* (an outlet of dubious reliability), a spokesperson for Secretary of State Clinton reportedly "slammed CNN for its 'disgusting' handling" of Stevens' journal. However, because it reveals Stevens' concerns over his own security, the diary is legitimate news. Virtually any news media outlet would have published at least non-personal portions of this document.[2058])

On October 3, *The Washington Post* publishes other sensitive papers left behind in the smoldering Mission ruins. Some of these disclose the identity, contact information and other personal data of many of the Libyan private security guards who worked for the U.S. at the Mission. As a result, some of these men now fear for their lives.[2059]

As discussed in Chapter 114 below, this disappearance of evidence and contamination of the crime scene will render far more difficult an already daunting task of prosecuting any of the Benghazi terrorist attackers in U.S. courts.[2060] ∎

[2057] CNN Finds, Returns Journal Belonging to Late U.S. Ambassador. See also Hicks Oversight Committee Testimony (May 8, 2013) (Response to questions of Rep. Trey Gowdy (R-SC)), p. 95.

[2058] Michael Hastings, "Libya Threatens Clinton's Legacy – and State Does Damage Control," *Buzzfeed* (Sept. 23, 2012); and *Id.* (". . . To publish material against a grieving family's wishes is a tough call. But in this case, CNN behaved responsibly, and was clearly within any reasonable journalistic standards. . . .").

[2059] Birnbaum, Sensitive Documents Left Behind With Little Security at U.S. Diplomatic Post in Libya; Burton & Katz, *Under Fire*, Chap. 7, p. 81 n. d; and *Failed Choices*, Chap. 2, Kindle Edition, Locations 438-449.

[2060] See, e.g., House Oversight Committee Hearings (May 8, 2013) (Remarks of Rep. Trey Gowdy (R-SC)) (". . . I was an average prosecutor, but I did it for a long time. . . . Trust me when I tell you crime scenes do not get better with time. They are unsecured, which means people have access to them. They can walk through them, they can compromise the evidence"), pp. 94-95.

103

"Poisoned Chalice"

On September 16, the Obama administration sends Susan Rice, then U.S. Ambassador to the United Nations, to appear on the five major Sunday television news shows ("Sunday Shows"). Before this, Susan Rice has had *no* involvement with the Benghazi tragedy – in *any* respect, at *any* stage. It is one of the most conspicuous, memorable, and enduring incidents of the entire post-Benghazi period.

Why Is Rice Selected?

As U.S. Ambassador to the United Nations, Susan Rice has absolutely no operational role in supervising the security or any other aspects of the Benghazi diplomatic mission, or the Embassy in Tripoli. Moreover, she plays no part in responding to the attacks on the Night of Benghazi. She is not involved in preparing the CIA Talking Points or the Rhodes 9/14 Email. Rice does not even know the CIA has (make that had) a facility in Benghazi, or that two Americans have been murdered there! Her sole connection to Benghazi is attending the "Transfer of Remains" ceremony on September 14 at Andrews Air Force Base.[2061] Thus, the selection of Rice as the administration's spokesperson on the Sunday Shows (apparently a decision by Ben Rhodes) is highly questionable. As her later mistaken use of the term "consulate" on multiple Sunday Shows will betray, she apparently knows very little about the U.S. Special Mission post in Benghazi.[2062]

[2061] Rice, *Tough Love*, Chap. 16, p. 306.

[2062] Benghazi Committee Report (". . . [T]he administration selected someone to talk to the American people about the Benghazi attacks who was neither involved in the security of any U.S. facilities in Benghazi nor involved in any way with the operational response to the attacks. In fact, the administration selected an individual who did not even know there was a CIA presence in Benghazi, let alone the fact that two Americans had died there. . . ."), p. 197. See also Opinion, K. T. McFarland, "The Real Reason Obama Tapped Susan Rice for National Security Adviser," Fox News online (June 5, 2013) ("Susan Rice was the one senior administration official who knew nothing about events leading up to Benghazi and the attack itself, yet the White House asked her to go on those shows? Alarm bells should have gone off in her head!").

President Obama later admits Rice has "nothing to do with Benghazi."[2063] Then why does he allow her to speak on this subject on national television as his administration's spokesperson? Why doesn't Hillary Clinton herself appear? (She is the White House's first choice, but she apparently does not return Ben Rhodes' inquiry.) Or National Security Advisor Tom Donilon?[2064] Or Defense Secretary Panetta? Or Under Secretary Patrick Kennedy? Or President Obama, for that matter?

Why *Rice*? (Probably in part because Hillary refuses to do it, Donilon declines (possibly because he "doesn't like the uncontrolled nature of television interviews"[2065]), Kennedy likely is barricaded in his bomb shelter, and Obama is lying low until the election passes. And Rice unwisely says "Yes" to Rhodes.[2066]) In her memoir, Rice describes Ben Rhodes as "one of my closest friends."[2067] Thus, perhaps a frustrated Rhodes felt his close friend never would refuse his request to do the Sunday Shows.

Regarding her own absence from these Sunday Shows, Hillary later bizarrely writes, "I don't see appearing on Sunday-morning television as any more of a responsibility than appearing on late-night TV." (Let us help you with this, Madam Secretary. The former involves a forum used by the national government's officials to disseminate information to the American people regarding a fatal terrorist attack on Americans at U.S. government facilities in a hazardous foreign country; the latter involves monologues by comedians about unimportant trivia, chit-chat by mostly airhead celebrities, and little-known, second-rate musicians entertaining people as they are drifting off to sleep. Got it?)

Clinton wasn't always this shy. In the past her attitude has not prevented her from appearing on the Sunday news shows. For example, in the previous 20 months she made three Sunday appearances, all to discuss issues involving stability and security in North Africa. In January 2011 during the "Arab Spring," she appears on all five Sunday

---

[2063] Kirsten Powers, "President Obama's Silly, Sexist Defense of Susan Rice," Fox News Opinion, Fox News website (Nov. 15, 2012); and Madison, Congress to Investigate CIA Talking Points on Benghazi.

[2064] Benghazi Committee Report, pp. 196-197.

[2065] James Mann, "Obama's Gray Man," Foreign Policy online (May 28, 2013).

[2066] Benghazi Committee Report, pp. 196-197.

[2067] Rice, *Tough Love*, Prologue, p. 2. See also *Id.*, Chap. 18, p. 372 (". . . Like another brother, Ben [Rhodes] always had my back, and I will always have his").

news programs to declare President Obama supported an "orderly transition" in Egypt. Thus, as summarized in Chapter 3, does Clinton help the president publicly pull the American rug out from under its long-time ally, Hosni Mubarak.[2068] In March 2011, Clinton takes part in three Sunday Shows to discuss America's (unconstitutional) military intervention in Libya, which she supports strongly. And in October 2011, she is interviewed on four Sunday programs to discuss Qadhafi's recent death and the "path forward" in Libya.[2069]

Is Susan Rice selected as the administration's Benghazi spokesperson on the Sunday Shows because no one else is available? Or perhaps the White House reasons Susan Rice does not know enough about Benghazi to be dangerous? Is she designated because she doesn't know enough to realize the Rhodes 9/14 Email and CIA Talking Points she has been given to parrot are a complete crock? Too clueless to realize she has been handed a "poisoned chalice?"[2070]

It is interesting that in her memoir, Rice claims her own mother tries to talk her daughter out of appearing on the Sunday Shows. Rice writes that, after informing her mother of her daughter's planned appearances, her mother warned, "I smell a rat. This is not a good idea. Can't you get out of it?" Rice unwisely tells her mother that the latter is being "ridiculous."[2071] (Always listen to your mother.)

Who Briefs Rice?

On Friday, September 14, Rice attends a "standing meeting" with Secretary Clinton that occurs each week whenever Rice is in Washington.[2072] Both Rice and Cheryl Mills believe this meeting took

---

[2068] Lizza, The Consequentialist.

[2069] Benghazi Committee Report, pp. 196-197.

[2070] Opinion, K. T. McFarland, "The Real Reason Obama Tapped Susan Rice for National Security Adviser," Fox News online (June 5, 2013) ("I checked their schedules and most of the other senior officials were in Washington and available that morning. It's just that they were smarter than Rice and realized it was a poisoned chalice"); and Rice, Tough Love (". . . In retrospect, while I don't think – as some have suggested (including my mom) – that I was set up, I do believe that Hillary Clinton and Tom Donilon appreciated what I did not. The first person to tell the public about a highly political tragedy was likely to pay a price. The opposition typically wants a scapegoat. . . ."), Chap. 16, p. 334.

[2071] Rice, Tough Love, Prologue, p. 11 and Chap. 16, p. 307.

[2072] Rice, Tough Love, Chap. 16, p. 306.

THE BENGHAZI BETRAYAL

place, although neither has a specific recollection of it when talking to Select Committee staff. Rice is certain they do not discuss appearing on the Sunday Shows because it is only later in the day when Ben Rhodes first asks her if she is available to do the Sunday Shows.[2073]

Rice later tells the Select Committee she begins to prepare for the Sunday Shows on Saturday, September 15. She receives her daily intelligence briefing in the morning. Then she reviews a briefing book her staff has prepared for her to prep for the Sunday programs. According to both Rice and her aide, Erin Pelton, the briefing book contains "little to no information about the Benghazi attacks." (However, the book does include public statements by President Obama and Secretary Clinton regarding the tragedy.)

Both Rice and Pelton claim to the Select Committee they did not focus on gathering information regarding Benghazi because they are expecting to receive unclassified CIA Talking Points from the "intelligence community" soon. They apparently assume these will contain whatever Rice needs to know about Benghazi before her Sunday interviews. Also, Pelton previously has asked Rhodes for a memo "regarding the objectives of the Sunday show appearances." Rhodes will respond with his now infamous Rhodes 9/14 Email (discussed in detail in Chapter 97).[2074]

Prior to her appearances, on a September 15 conference call at 4:00 p.m., Ben Rhodes and other White House communications staff (including David Ploufe) brief Rice. (The briefers include at least one individual, NSC spokesperson Tommy Vietor, who was not named as a recipient of the Rhodes 9/14 Email.[2075]) Only a small group of White House staff and Rice and her staff are on the call. No one else from the State Department participates. No one from the Defense Department, the CIA, or the FBI joins in this briefing.[2076] Although Congress possibly has them by now, by the time of this 4:00 p.m. briefing, Rice has yet to receive the unclassified CIA Talking Points!

(One almost gets the sense White House spinmeisters intentionally are seeking to place Susan Rice in an intelligence-free zone. Doesn't

---

[2073] Benghazi Committee Report, p. 198.

[2074] Benghazi Committee Report, pp. 198-200.

[2075] Interview of Tommy Vietor with Brett Baier, "Special Report," Fox News Channel (May 1, 2014) (*Watch video there*; Go to 5:12-38 and 13:10-19).

[2076] Benghazi Committee Report, p. 204.

THE TRUE ACCOUNT OF VALOR AND ABANDONMENT

one? On the other hand, Rice is free to seek out further information about Benghazi on her own, and apparently refrains from doing so.[2077])

This absence of intelligence officials is telling. This is especially so, given the largely phony claim Rice is using the CIA Talking Points (refuted in detail below). In this briefing, someone almost certainly directs Rice to emphasize the important role of the *Innocence of Muslims* Video in "sparking" the "demonstrations" in Benghazi that ultimately turn violent. (You know, the Video that is not even mentioned in the CIA Talking Points.)

According to Gregory Hicks, he is not involved in this briefing of Rice. Hicks asserts that before these Sunday Shows Rice does not even speak with him about what happened in Benghazi five days earlier. This is despite the fact he is then the highest-ranking surviving diplomat in Libya.[2078]

Incredibly, the Select Committee Report later will explain, "... [M]ultiple witnesses testified Benghazi was barely mentioned on the prep call." No one discusses a humiliating national security disaster just three days old in which a U.S. ambassador is assassinated for the first time in thirty-three years, three other Americans are murdered, and two are severely wounded, and two U.S. facilities are torched – all on the 9/11 anniversary and very likely by terrorists? Instead, they all breathlessly await the (useless and erroneous) CIA Talking Points.[2079] (Yes, those will solve everything.)

No doubt Rice is expecting a more thorough and polished work product from the CIA before she goes before the cameras on Sunday. (Picture her reaction when she finally receives the lame, worthless final CIA Talking Points. *Kaboom!*)

Given the paucity of information about Benghazi Rice is provided prior to her Sunday interviews, it is little wonder she will, as explained next, virtually "parrot" the Rhodes 9/14 Email during her Sunday appearances. It is all she has.

Rice's Sunday Show Performances

Susan Rice's appearance on each of the five Sunday Shows is not so much an interview as a "performance." It is theater, and she has learned

---

[2077] *Id.*, pp. 204-205.

[2078] Hicks Oversight Committee Testimony (May 8, 2013) (Response to questions of Rep. Trey Gowdy (R-SC)), pp. 32-33.

[2079] Benghazi Committee Report, p. 205.

her few lines well. During these Sunday Shows, Rice dutifully repeats the "spontaneous protest" and "anti-Islam Video" components of the Benghazi Narrative, as reflected in the Rhodes 9/14 Email (as to the Video and protests), and the CIA Talking Points (regarding the protests).[2080] Rice's story is essentially identical on all five networks.[2081] She goes "Full Video," even though it is not mentioned in the CIA Talking Points. Her clear implication that the (nonexistent) Benghazi protest arises out of a hateful Video is pure fabrication.[2082]

For example, on NBC's "Meet the Press," Ambassador Rice tells her interviewer, David Gregory:

> But putting together the best information that we have available to us today, our current assessment is what happened in Benghazi was *in fact* initially a *spontaneous* reaction to what had just transpired hours before in Cairo, almost a copycat of the *demonstrations* against our facility in Cairo, prompted by *the video*. What we think then transpired in Benghazi is that *opportunistic extremist elements* came to the *consulate* [sic] as this was unfolding.[2083]

Rice insists to her interviewers this tale is based on the administration's "best information currently available."[2084] Trey Gowdy (R-SC), who

---

[2080] Martin, Piecing Together White House Response to Benghazi; Morgan, Libyan President: 50 Arrests in Consulate Assault; Analysis/Opinion by Charles Hurt, "If Voters Look Past Hillary's History of Lies, They'll Get What They Deserve in the White House," *The Washington Times* online (June 28, 2016) ("[Susan] Rice was simply setting up mirrors and fanning the diversionary smoke set ablaze by her Secretary of State, Hillary Clinton . . ."); and Opinion, K. T. McFarland, "The Real Reason Obama Tapped Susan Rice for National Security Adviser," Fox News online (June 5, 2013) ("Either she [Rice] knew what really happened and deliberately lied to the American people or she was a mere actress who read the script she was given and didn't know enough to question whether the words she spoke were accurate").

[2081] For a more detailed summary of Ambassador Rice's statements on the Sunday Shows, see Benghazi Committee Report, pp. 208-226.

[2082] Hemingway, 5 Big Takeaways From the House Benghazi Report ("None of these public statements [by Susan Rice about the protests caused by a Video] were true. . . .").

[2083] Interview of Amb. Susan Rice with David Gregory, "Meet the Press," NBC News (Sept. 16, 2012) (emphasis added) (*Watch video* there); and NBC News Staff and Wire Services, "Ambassador Rice: Benghazi Attack Began Spontaneously," NBC News online (Sept. 16, 2012) (emphasis added).

[2084] Interview of Amb. Susan Rice with Jake Tapper, "This Week," ABC News (emphasis added) (*Watch video* there; Go to 0:47 – 1:51); and Morgan, Libyan President: 50 Arrests in Consulate Assault (Susan Rice on CBS "Face the Nation": "Based on the best information we have to date . . . spontaneous protests" began

THE TRUE ACCOUNT OF VALOR AND ABANDONMENT

later will become Chairman of the House Select Benghazi Committee, will be unimpressed. At a House Oversight Committee meeting, Gowdy levels a blistering attack on Rice.[2085] He later tells Fox News host Greta Van Susteren:

> I would love the chance to ask follow-up questions of Susan Rice because David Gregory apparently did not avail himself of that opportunity. Greta, I just listened to the ... clip. I get tougher questions in the Bojangles drive-thru than he asked her.[2086]

On ABC's "This Week," Rice will claim "a small number of people" seeking to "replicate" the violent protests in Cairo gathered outside the "consulate" in Benghazi in "a *spontaneous, not a premeditated*" protest of the Video. Rice asserts this protest "seems to have been *hijacked*, let us say, by *some individual clusters of extremists who came with heavier weapons*, ... and it then evolved from there...."[2087]

On "Face the Nation" this same morning on CBS, Rice says:

> What our assessment is as of the present is in fact what it [sic] began *spontaneously* in Benghazi as a reaction to what had transpired some hours earlier in Cairo where ... there was a violent protest outside of our Embassy sparked by this hateful *video*. But soon after that *spontaneous protest* began outside of our *consulate* [sic] in Benghazi, we believe that it looks like *extremist elements*, individuals, joined in that ... effort with heavy weapons of the sort that are, unfortunately, readily now available in Libya post-revolution. And that it spun from

---

outside the Benghazi "consulate" [sic] after demonstrations erupted in Cairo regarding an anti-Islam video) (*Watch video there*; Go to 0:45-1:35). Compare Hemingway, 5 Big Takeaways From the House Benghazi Report ("None of these public statements [by Susan Rice about the protests caused by a Video] were true. Also, despite claims to the contrary, they did not accurately reflect changing intelligence reports, House members say").

[2085] *Watch video* at https://www.youtube.com/watch?v=YP2axws-xR8 (Go to 0:00 – 2:24).

[2086] Brendan Bordelon, "'Stunningly Arrogant': Trey Gowdy Furious Over Susan Rice's Lack of Regret Over Benghazi Comments," The Daily Caller website (Feb. 24, 2014) (Quoting interview on Fox News Channel).

[2087] Interview of Amb. Susan Rice with Jake Tapper, "This Week," ABC News (emphasis added) (*Watch video there*; Go to 0:47 – 1:51).

there into something much, much more violent.[2088] . . . We do not . . . have information at present that leads us to conclude that this was premeditated or preplanned.[2089]

CBS reports that over this weekend U.S. intelligence "began to uncover evidence" that there has not been a protest outside the Mission Compound, but claims "That new intelligence did not get to Rice before she appeared on the Sunday talk shows . . ."[2090]

However, the real story isn't this simple. *Four days before her Sunday appearance* – on Wednesday, September 12 – Susan Rice and others within the U.S. Mission to the United Nations receive an email from Payton Knopf, Rice's deputy spokesperson for the U.S. Mission. In this email, Knopf summarizes what State Department spokesperson Victoria ("Toria") Nuland has disclosed in a press briefing about the Benghazi attacks. Like most early accounts of the tragedy, Nuland's briefing (and hence Knopf's summary) contains numerous factual errors. (For example, at this time Nuland apparently thinks the CIA Annex is in the same compound as the Mission's Villa.) Knopf writes:

> . . . 4pm EST: Compound begins taking fire from *Libyan extremists*. . . . Responding to a question about whether it was an organized terror attack, Toria said that she couldn't speak to the identity of the perpetrators but that it was *clearly a complex attack*. . . .[2091]

Knopf's email does not mention the words "protest" or "demonstration."

Whether or not Rice knows her "spontaneous protest" comments on the Sunday Shows are erroneous, during these appearances she makes

---

[2088] Martin, Piecing Together White House Response to Benghazi (emphasis added); Morgan, Libyan President: 50 Arrests in Consulate Assault (*Watch video there*; Go to 0:45-1:35); and "'Face the Nation' Transcripts, September 16, 2012: Libyan Pres. Magariaf, Amb. Rice and Sen. McCain," CBS News online (Sept. 16, 2012) (transcript partially missing).

[2089] "'Face the Nation' Transcripts, September 16, 2012: Libyan Pres. Magariaf, Amb. Rice and Sen. McCain," CBS News online (Sept. 16, 2012) (emphasis added); CBS News, Clinton on Benghazi: We All Had the Same Intel (emphasis added) (*Watch video there*; Go to 0:57 - 1:11); and Morgan, Libyan President: 50 Arrests in Consulate Assault (emphasis added) (*Watch video there*; Go to 1:35-47).

[2090] Martin, Piecing Together White House Response to Benghazi.

[2091] Email from Payton L. Knopf to Susan E. Rice, et al., Re Toria Nuland Backgrounder on Libya (Sept. 12, 2012) (emphasis added), p. 1, Judicial Watch Document Archive (posted Aug. 24, 2015).

THE TRUE ACCOUNT OF VALOR AND ABANDONMENT

further false statements.[2092] These include her assertion "We've decimated al Qaeda,"[2093] and her claim the U.S. has a strong security presence in Benghazi.[2094] (What movie is *she* watching?)

Rice also incorrectly describes the deaths of Tyrone Woods and Glen Doherty. On ABC's "This Week" on this Sunday, Jake Tapper logically asks Rice to respond to the question why there wasn't better security *at the Mission Compound in Benghazi*. Adhering to the Benghazi Narrative, Rice misleadingly replies:

First of all, *we* had a *substantial security presence* . . . with our personnel and the *consulate [sic] in Benghazi*. Tragically, two of the four Americans who were killed *were there providing security. That was their function.* And indeed, there were *many other colleagues* who were doing the same with them.[2095]

Rone Woods is in Benghazi providing security to the *CIA case officers* at the *CIA Annex*, not "there" at the "consulate." Bub Doherty's assignment is providing security *in Tripoli*; he is "there" in Benghazi as part of the volunteer Team Tripoli to help rescue the beleaguered Americans. Neither man is in Benghazi to protect Ambassador Stevens and Sean Smith at the Mission,[2096] as Rice clearly (and falsely) implies.

[2092] Hayes and Joscelyn, The Benghazi Report (". . . Rice's presentation to the public was inaccurate in virtually every key detail").

[2093] "'Face the Nation' Transcripts, September 16, 2012: Libyan Pres. Magariaf, Amb. Rice and Sen. McCain," CBS News online (Sept. 16, 2012); Morgan, Libyan President: 50 Arrests in Consulate Assault ("Face the Nation") (*Watch video* there; Go to 3:49-58); Statement of Senators McCain, Graham and Ayotte ("Her [Rice's] statement that 'we've decimated al Qaeda' was not in the talking points and was patently false"); and Brendan Bordelon, "'Stunningly Arrogant': Trey Gowdy Furious Over Susan Rice's Lack of Regret Over Benghazi Comments," The Daily Caller website (Feb. 24, 2014) (Quoting interview on Fox News Channel: "'. . . [W]e were in the midst of a [presidential] campaign,' with President Obama touting the effective defeat of al-Qaida. 'Al-Qaida was not on the run,' he said, 'they were at the front door of our facility in Benghazi getting ready to kill our ambassador and burn it down'").

[2094] Statement of Senators McCain, Graham and Ayotte (". . . Ambassador Rice repeatedly suggested that the United States had a strong security presence in Benghazi. That statement was also not in the talking points and was proven false by the successful attack and the subsequent whistleblower testimony").

[2095] "This Week," ABC News (Sept. 16, 2012) (emphasis added) (*Watch video there*; Go to 1:49 - 2:48).

[2096] Eli Lake, "Obama's Shaky Libya Narrative," *The Daily Beast* online (Sept. 21, 2012) (". . . [T]wo former special operators and a former intelligence officer, two of whom had worked with Doherty, told *The Daily Beast* that Doherty and Wood's job was not to protect Ambassador Chris Stevens . . . 'Glen died for Tyrone and Tyrone

Susan Rice also will claim on "This Week" the United States is "quite popular in Libya, as you might expect, having been a major partner in their revolution."[2097] (The author prays he never becomes "quite popular" in Libya.)

(GRS operator Kris "Tanto" Paronto is listening to Rice's Sunday Shows performance from an Air Force base in Germany, to where he and his fellow heroes have been evacuated from Tripoli. Paronto later explains to conservative radio talk show host Sean Hannity he "definitely" knows Rice is telling a lie. He states he becomes "pissed" as he hears Rice spin what the author (not Paronto) calls the Benghazi Narrative.[2098]

(However, over time Tanto will become more philosophical about this mendacity. He later will tell the makers of the movie *13 Hours*:

Again, it is what it is. What are you gonna do? Shit happens. It's war. Shit happens, people die. And politicians lie about it when it's over. What are you gonna do?[2099]

(According to an anonymous U.S. serviceman "whistleblower" who claims to have operated the drone cameras for ninety minutes in the skies above Benghazi, he has a similar reaction to Tanto's initial one. He tells Sean Hannity he knows "immediately" Susan Rice and others in the Obama administration are not being truthful in explaining to the American people what happened on the Night of Benghazi.[2100])

What Speaking Points Does Rice Use?

During her Sunday appearances, Rice has relied on the Rhodes 9/14 Email, and (to a far lesser extent) the CIA's stripped-down talking points. Almost immediately following Rice's efforts, the basis for her dubious performance is subjected to close scrutiny: why has Rice said what she did? In response to this criticism, a spokesperson for Rice reportedly tells CBS News Rice "was given those speaking points

---

died for Glen,' one of the former special operators told *The Daily Beast*. 'They fought bravely, but they did not die protecting the ambassador'").

[2097] "This Week," ABC News (Sept. 16, 2012) (*Watch video there*; Go to 5:54 - 6:44).

[2098] Interview of Kris "Tanto" Paronto with Sean Hannity, "Sean Hannity Radio Show" (April 5, 2017).

[2099] *13 Hours: The Secret Soldiers of Benghazi*, Extra Features DVD, "Uncovering Benghazi's Secret Soldiers" (Paramount, 2016).

[2100] Hannity Radio Interview of Unnamed U.S. Serviceman.

THE TRUE ACCOUNT OF VALOR AND ABANDONMENT

by the *intelligence community*, not by the State Department."[2101] As demonstrated above in Chapter 94, by the time poor Susan Rice gets them the CIA Talking Points have been sliced, diced, chopped, grilled, fried, baked, stirred, shaken, puréed, sautéed, and flambéed.[2102] (One might even say they have been *tortured*.) However, they are by now so skeletal as to be virtually worthless as Benghazi background – for *anyone*. And the CIA personnel drafting the talking points (allegedly) do not even know the White House is planning to use them to brief Rice for the Sunday talk shows.[2103]

Hillary Clinton later will write that the talking points Rice uses are authored by "intelligence officials."[2104] Clinton, too, claims these officials have no idea Rice will be using them on the Sunday Shows.[2105] (Wait a minute; Rice's spokesperson says Rice is *"given"* her talking points *"by the intelligence community."* This almost certainly happens on Saturday, September 15, when Congress gets them. Why else but for the Sunday Shows would Rice need them? The Sunday talk shows are her first, last, and *only* involvement with Benghazi. Once again, someone is not telling the truth.)

Speaking of telling fibs, in her 2019 memoir, *Tough Love*, Susan Rice will "double down" on her claim she relied *only* on the CIA Talking Points during her Sunday Shows interviews. In her book,

---

[2101] CBS News, Clinton on Benghazi: We All Had the Same Intel (emphasis added); and Josh Rogin, "State Department: No Video Protest at the Benghazi Consulate [sic]," ForeignPolicy.com (Oct. 9, 2012) ("Rice has since attributed those [erroneous] statements [blaming protests triggered by the Video] to information given to the administration by intelligence officials").

[2102] Eli Lake, "Republican Benghazi Report Alleges State Department Coverup," *The Daily Beast* online (April 23, 2013); Goldberg, Benghazi's Smoking Guns ("I think there was a lot of mischief behind those talking points, which we now know were sanitized, folded, spindled and mutilated to fit a political agenda"); and Guy Benson, "Whoa: US Hasn't Detained Five Benghazi Terrorists Due to Trial-Related Evidentiary Concerns," Townhall.com website (May 21, 2013) (". . . [T]he State Department and White House contorted Susan Rice's talking points beyond recognition for political reasons . . .").

[2103] Benghazi Committee Report, p. 206.

[2104] Clinton, *Hard Choices*, Chap. 17, p. 412 ("The extensive public record now makes clear that Susan was using information that originated with and was approved by the CIA. . . . It was written by intelligence officials" for use by congressmen who asked what they could say publicly about Benghazi).

[2105] *Id.*, Chap. 17, p. 413 ("None of the intelligence officials working on that request [from congressmen for information they could use in making public statements about Benghazi] had any idea the talking points would be used two days later by Susan").

Rice repeatedly will claim she relied only on the "so-called 'talking points' written by the CIA," "the CIA's talking points," "the unclassified talking points provided by the Intelligence Community," "CIA-drafted talking points," and "the talking points provided by the IC." Rice adds, ". . . I had relied solely on the information provided to me by the Intelligence Community."[2106] For the reasons we have discussed, this is a blatant, demonstrable lie.

President Obama later will claim, "Keep in mind, . . . these so-called talking points that were *prepared for* Susan Rice five, six days after the event occurred pretty much matched the assessments that I was receiving at that time in my presidential daily briefing."[2107] (Either this is a blatant lie, or Obama is receiving complete drivel in his daily briefing. As discussed in Chapter 95 above, it *is* a lie. In the Presidential Daily Briefing for September 12, the day after Benghazi, the "executive coordinator" of the PDB adds a critical conclusion to the written PDB. It reads, ". . . [T]he presence of armed assailants from the outset suggests this was an intentional assault and *not the escalation of a peaceful protest.*"[2108] Of course, this is the *opposite* of the Rhodes 9/14 Email and CIA Talking Points given to Rice.)

Also, Obama's assertion the CIA Talking Points are prepared *for* Rice is directly contradicted by Hillary Clinton (as noted above) and Leon Panetta. In his memoir, Panetta writes, "Although they [the CIA Talking Points] weren't intended for use by UN ambassador Susan Rice, she used them during several interviews she gave that weekend [on September 16]."[2109] Panetta (like others on Team Obama) is raising a largely phony issue. If the talking points are accurate, what *difference* does it make whether they are "intended" to be used by Susan Rice?

[2106] E.g., Rice, *Tough Love*, Chap. 16, pp. 307-309, 311, 314 and 322. See also Michal Conger, Opinion, "Clinton 'Didn't Want to' Talk on Sunday Shows After Benghazi, Rice Says," *Washington Examiner* online (Feb. 15, 2013) ("I shared the best information that our intelligence community had at the time, and they provided the talking points that I used").

[2107] Obama-Cameron Joint Press Conference (emphasis added); and Fred Lucas, "Obama: State Dept. That Didn't Interview Clinton 'Investigated Every Element' of Benghazi," CNSNews.com website (May 13, 2013) ("Lucas, Obama: State Dept. That Didn't Interview Clinton 'Investigated Every Element of Benghazi'") (emphasis added).

[2108] Benghazi Committee Report (emphasis added), p. 167; *Id.*, Appendix H, p. 575; and Stephen F. Hayes, "Obama Did Not Ask for an Intel Brief the Day After the Benghazi Attack," *The Weekly Standard* online (June 28, 2016).

[2109] Panetta, *Worthy Fights*, Chap. 16, p. 431.

THE TRUE ACCOUNT OF VALOR AND ABANDONMENT

What's the problem if she uses them so long as they convey the truth and don't disclose classified information? (More incongruities.)

Later, in detailed testimony Susan Rice repeatedly will insist to the Select Committee that the CIA Talking Points *"closely mirrored . . . the intelligence product that I received at the same time. . . ."* There's one slight problem: Rice's intelligence briefing refers to "attacks," while the CIA Talking Points reference "demonstrations."[2110] (*Ooops!*)

Several weeks later in an interview with Margaret Brennan of CBS News, Hillary Clinton will duck her interviewer's question regarding whether she has "approved" the talking points Rice uses. Clinton answers, "I think she very clearly said, 'Here's what we know now, but this is going to change.'. . . 'This is what we have at present but it will evolve – and the intelligence community has said the same thing.'"[2111] However, Clinton claims she does not speak to Rice prior to the latter's appearance on the Sunday Shows.[2112] (This actually is plausible, given Susan Rice is a close friend and confidant of the president, while Hillary Clinton most assuredly is not.)

How does one make sense of all these inconsistences regarding Rice's speaking points? The answer is as straightforward as it is devious: *contrary to the clear implications of Team Obama, the real "talking points" Susan Rice uses on the Sunday Shows are not the CIA-drafted version, but the Rhodes 9/14 Email prepared inside the White House.* (Remember, on Sunday Rice emphasizes the Video, which is not even in the CIA Talking Points, while the Rhodes 9/14 Email strongly emphasizes the Video.) Remarkably, however, in her memoir's 32-page chapter on Benghazi, Rice does not even *mention* the Rhodes 9/14 Email.[2113]

The Rhodes 9/14 Email is a blatantly political document. It is prepared to minimize the short-term political consequences of a disastrous national security crisis involving a predictable terrorist attack in a highly-dangerous North African city on the 9/11 anniversary. It cannot be discovered by the media – and especially not by Mitt Romney and the GOP – prior to the election.

[2110] Benghazi Committee Report, pp. 206-208.

[2111] CBS News, Clinton on Benghazi: We All Had the Same Intel (*Watch video there*; Go to 0:34-54).

[2112] *Id.* (*Watch video* there; Go to 1:11-19).

[2113] Rice, *Tough Love*, Chap. 16, pp. 306-337.

545

(In fact, as noted above, it will remain hidden for two years until a court orders the Obama administration to disclose it in litigation. As noted, the Rhodes 9/14 Email is not sent to anyone in the intelligence community (at least not originally). One must wonder whether the CIA and DNI even know of its existence until a judge orders it released.)

So, Team Obama attempts to create confusion and ambiguity *in order to conceal the existence and role of the Rhodes 9/14 Email*. Thus, in all their diversionary public comments, President Obama and his officials instead will appear to be referring to the CIA Talking Points, which they emphasize came from the intelligence community, but which are virtually worthless as a briefing document for Rice (or anyone).[2114] A perhaps ignorant media dutifully cooperates.[2115] Congress also is fooled.[2116] It is a brilliant bit of "trickeration."[2117] And for two years it works.

Only by understanding this deft and effective series of misdirection moves concerning the Rhodes 9/14 Email by Obama, Rhodes, Clinton, Rice, Panetta and their staffs can one make sense of the aftermath of Rice's Sunday Show performances, and the perplexity surrounding Rice's speaking points.

[2114] *Wall Street Journal* Opinion, The Missing Benghazi Email (". . . On Wednesday [September 19], Mr. Carney still insisted Ms. Rice had 'relied on points about the Benghazi attack that were produced by the CIA.' He must think the press corps is stupid" [Yep]).

[2115] E.g., Mark Landler, "Rice to Replace Donilon in the Top National Security Post," *The New York Times* online (June 5, 2013) (emphasis added) ("Ms. Rice, *using talking points drafted by the C.I.A.*, said the assault appeared to be a protest gone awry rather than a premeditated terrorist attack. That proved incorrect, and though Ms. Rice cautioned that the account could change with further intelligence, Republicans accused her of sanitizing the truth for political reasons"); and Guy Benson, "Surprise: Obama Promotes Another Benghazi Scandal Player," Townhall.com website (May 24, 2013) (emphasis added) (". . . Specifically, [Victoria] Nuland asked that references to al Qaeda and previous CIA warnings about threats posed to U.S. diplomats in Libya be scrubbed from *the document that was used by U.N. Ambassador Susan Rice on news talk shows* to explain the administration's understanding of events in Libya").

[2116] E.g., House Intelligence Committee Benghazi Report, Exec. Summary (Nov. 21, 2014) (emphasis added) ("Fifth, the Committee finds that the process used to generate the talking points HPSCI asked for – *and which were used for Ambassador Rice's public appearances* – was flawed. HPSCI asked for the talking points solely to aid Members' ability to communicate publicly *using the best available intelligence* at the time . . ."), p. 1.

[2117] The author stole this invented word from radio talk show host Rush Limbaugh.

"Circling the Wagons" Around Rice

Following all this misinformation Susan Rice unloads on the Sunday Shows, the negative reactions are almost instantaneous. Some (including Republican congressmen) call for Rice to resign as U.S. Ambassador to the U.N.[2118] In reaction, Team Obama "circles the wagons" around its loyal soldier. On Tuesday, September 18, Rice's claims are the subject of numerous questions at presidential spokesperson Jay Carney's daily press briefing. In response, the White House attempts to provide some political "cover" to poor Susan Rice for the firestorm that has erupted over her erroneous Sunday claims. Carney gamely tells reporters:

... [W]e have provided information about what we believe was the precipitating cause of the *protest* and the violence, based on the information that we have had available. ... I think what I am making clear and what Ambassador Rice made clear on Sunday is that *reaction to the video was the precipitating factor* in *protests* in violence *across the region*.

... I'm simply saying based on what we knew at the time, knew initially, what we know now, the facts that we have, *the video was a precipitating cause* to the unrest in the region and *specifically in Libya*."

... I'm saying that based on ... – our initial information, and that includes all information – we saw *no evidence to back up claims by others that this was a preplanned or premeditated attack*; that we saw *evidence that it was sparked by the reaction to this video*. And *that is what we know thus far based on the evidence, concrete evidence* – *not supposition – concrete evidence that we have* thus far....[2119]

In a statement issued on September 28, Foreign Relations Committee Chairman John Kerry (D-MA) supports Rice. "I'm particularly troubled by calls for Ambassador Rice's resignation." He then praises her skills and experience. Then, Kerry repeats the refrain

---

[2118] E.g., Press Release, "Kerry Defends Ambassador Rice Against Attacks," Senate Foreign Relations Committee website (Sept. 28, 2012) (Statement supporting Rice issued in response to demand by Rep. Peter King (R-NY) for Rice to resign).

[2119] Press Briefing by Press Secretary Jay Carney, The White House, Obama White House Archives (Sept. 18, 2012) (emphasis added); and Judicial Watch Investigative Report (emphasis added). Rep. Trey Gowdy (R-SC) later will excoriate Susan Rice and Jay Carney for what he believes to be their misleading statements about the protests and the Video. *Watch video* at https://www.youtube.com/watch?v=YP2axws-xR8.

that everyone should wait for the Accountability Review Board's Report before drawing conclusions about Benghazi.[2120] (The final unclassified ARB Report (discussed in detail in Chapter 109 below) will be silent on Susan Rice's performance on the Sunday Shows. Indeed, it will not even mention the Video!) Just a few months after this statement by Kerry, of course, he will succeed the departing Clinton as President Obama's Secretary of State.

In his subsequent testimony on October 10 before the House Oversight Committee, Under Secretary Patrick Kennedy also defends Rice. Kennedy claims any administration official appearing on September 16 news programs would have made the same statements Rice has. He further asserts Rice's intelligence was the same as Kennedy had "at that point."[2121] In his testimony to the Oversight Committee, Kennedy denies "on my honor" any political pressure was brought to bear on him to assert the Benghazi attacks were the result of the inflammatory Video, rather than a terrorist attack. Kennedy maintains this includes anyone in the State Department, the National Security Council, or at the White House.[2122] (All readers who believe this, please close this book; you are excused.)

In an interview with Margaret Brennan on October 16, Hillary Clinton also will defend Rice's Sunday Shows statements, asserting:
Everybody had the same information. [No, "everybody" did *not* have the secret Rhodes 9/14 Email.] . . . Everybody in the administration has tried to say what we knew at the time with the caveat that we would learn more and that's what's happened. So I think I've seen it before not just in respect to this. I think it's part of what the "fog of war" causes.[2123]

Later in her memoir, Hillary Clinton again addresses Susan Rice's appearance (and Clinton's own non-appearance), on the Sunday Shows. Clinton asserts, "Susan stated what the intelligence community

---

[2120] Press Release, "Kerry Defends Ambassador Rice Against Attacks," Senate Foreign Relations Committee website (Sept. 28, 2012).

[2121] Kennedy House Oversight Prepared Testimony, p. 2; and House Oversight Committee Testimony (May 8, 2013) (Remarks of Rep. Patrick McHenry (R-NC)), p. 59. See also Kennedy October 10 Briefing (*Watch video* there; Go to 5:29 - 6:58).

[2122] Kennedy House Oversight Committee Testimony (Oct. 10, 2012) (Response to questions of Rep. Dennis Ross (R-FL)). See also Tapper, Security Officer: "For Me the Taliban Is Inside the Building."

[2123] CBS News, Clinton on Benghazi: We All Had the Same Intel (*Watch video there*; Go to 1:19-53).

THE TRUE ACCOUNT OF VALOR AND ABANDONMENT

believed, rightly or wrongly, at the time. That was the best she or anyone could do." (Except that by September 16 this is *not* what the intelligence community believes.[2124] And again, Rice mainly is not repeating the CIA Talking Points, but rather the Rhodes 9/14 Email.)

On October 18, during a television interview on "The Daily Show," comedian Jon Stewart inquires of the president regarding why there is so much confusion following the attacks among members of Obama's administration about what happened. With just 19 days before the election, Obama responds in a general fashion:

> ... [N]obody is more interested in figuring this out than I am. When a tragic event like this happens on the other side of the world immediately a whole bunch of intelligence starts coming in and people try to piece together exactly what happens [sic]. And what I've always tried to do is make sure that we just get all the facts, figure out what went wrong and *make sure it doesn't happen again* and we're still in that process now. But every piece of information that we get as we got *it* we laid *it* out for the American people, and the picture eventually gets fully filled in and we know exactly what happens and then we ... make sure we *prevent it in the future*.[2125]

(As we will discuss further below, note President Obama's repeated use of "it" to describe the fatal terror attacks, almost as if they are an abstraction.) Stewart then explicitly asks about the accuracy of Susan Rice's statement concerning the Video:

> Jon, the truth is that information comes in, folks put it out throughout the process, people say it's still incomplete. What I was always clear about was we are going to do an investigation and figure out exactly what happened.[2126]

[2124] Clinton, *Hard Choices*, Chap. 17, p. 412; Madison, Congress to Investigate CIA Talking Points on Benghazi ("But at some point between Petraeus' briefing [of the House Intelligence Committee on September 14th, where he very clearly said it was a terrorist attack] and Rice's appearance on the Sunday morning talk shows, that narrative changed"; Senator Diane Feinstein (D-CA) "vowed to find out where the discrepancies came from, and why the narrative seemed to have changed").

[2125] Barack Obama on "The Daily Show," Comedy Central website (Oct. 18, 2012) (emphasis added) (*Watch video there*; Go to 2:50 – 4:16); and Brian Montopoli, "Obama to Jon Stewart: Benghazi Response 'Not Optimal,'" CBS News online (Oct. 19, 2012) (emphasis added).

[2126] Barack Obama on "The Daily Show," Comedy Central website (Oct. 18, 2012) (*Watch video there*; Go to 4:16-45).

549

The Continued Backlash Against Rice

Team Obama's defensive gambit does not succeed. As *The New York Times* explains of Rice, "The furor over her remarks on Capitol Hill was so intense that it led her to withdraw her name from contention to be secretary of state" when Hillary Clinton resigns in early 2013.[2127] Instead, to reward Rice for being his "spear catcher" on the Benghazi crisis, Obama appoints her as his National Security Advisor. (Rice does not require Senate confirmation for this White House position.[2128]) However, her credibility will remain damaged for the remainder of Obama's presidency.[2129] Of course, as noted, instead of Rice, Obama will nominate Senator John Kerry to succeed Clinton as head of State.

[2127] Benghazi Committee Report, p. 195; and Mark Landler, "Obama Aide Defends Remarks on Bergdahl's Honor," *The New York Times* online (June 6, 2014). See also Madison, Congress to Investigate CIA Talking Points on Benghazi ("Since then [her appearance on the Sunday news shows], Rice's characterization [of events in Benghazi] has been proven inaccurate, and Republicans like [Senator Lindsey] Graham [R-SC] and Sen. John McCain, R-Ariz., have vowed to block her nomination to replace Hillary Clinton as Secretary of State, a position for which she is thought to be a top contender"); Sean Sullivan, "Who Is Jack Lew?" The Fix, *The Washington Post* online (Jan. 9, 2013) (". . . [C]riticism over the Sept. 11 attack on a U.S. diplomatic post in Libya prompted U.N. Ambassador Susan Rice to withdraw from consideration as secretary of state"); and Mark Landler, "Rice to Replace Donilon in the Top National Security Post," *The New York Times* online (June 5, 2013) ("Ms. Rice, using talking points drafted by the C.I.A., said the assault appeared to be a protest gone awry rather than a premeditated terrorist attack. That proved incorrect, and though Ms. Rice cautioned that the account could change with further intelligence, Republicans accused her of sanitizing the truth for political reasons").

[2128] Brendan Bordelon, "'Stunningly Arrogant': Trey Gowdy Furious Over Susan Rice's Lack of Regret Over Benghazi Comments," The Daily Caller website (Feb. 24, 2014) (emphasis added) (Quoting interview on Fox News Channel: ". . . [S]he [Susan Rice] opted to protect her career and parrot the talking points that were provided to her *by the White House*"); Mark Landler, "Rice to Replace Donilon in the Top National Security Post," *The New York Times* online (June 5, 2013); and Laura Ingraham on "Special Report," Fox News Channel (April 4, 2017) ("Remember, she wanted to be Secretary of State, and she wasn't going to be confirmed. So they had to put her over at National Security. And that was rewarding her, to the extent that they could reward her, after Benghazi").

[2129] E.g., Victor Davis Hanson, "Is the American Elite Really Elite," Townhall.com website (Mar. 2, 2017) ("Rhodes Scholar and former U.N. Ambassador Susan Rice lied repeatedly on national television about the Benghazi debacle"). At House Oversight Committee hearings on October 10, 2012, Congressman Trey Gowdy (R-SC) levels a blistering accusation of deception against Susan Rice (and Jay Carney). See also Brendan Bordelon, "'Stunningly Arrogant': Trey Gowdy Furious Over Susan Rice's

THE TRUE ACCOUNT OF VALOR AND ABANDONMENT

Historian and scholar Victor Davis Hanson later analyzes Rice's deceptive Benghazi role as follows:

> What the Benghazi scandal, the Bowe Bergdahl swap, and the Iran [Nuclear] Deal[2130] all had in common was their reliance on ruse. If the White House and its allies had told the whole truth about all these incidents, Americans probably would have widely rejected the ideological premises that framed them.
>
> In the case of Benghazi, most Americans would not fault an obscure video for causing scripted rioting and death at an American consulate [sic] and CIA annex. They would hardly believe that a policy of maintaining deliberately thin security at U.S. facilities would encourage reciprocal local good will in the Middle East. They would not agree that holding back American rescue forces was a wise move likely to forestall an international confrontation or escalation.
>
> In other words, Americans wanted their consulate [sic] in Benghazi well fortified and protected from seasoned terrorists, and they favored rapid deployment of maximum relief forces in times of crisis – but, unfortunately, these were not the agendas of the Obama administration. So, to disguise that unpleasant reality, Americans were treated to Susan Rice's yarns about a spontaneous, unexpected riot that was prompted by a right-wing video, and endangered Americans far beyond the reach of U.S. military help.[2131] ■

Lack of Regret Over Benghazi Comments," The Daily Caller website (Feb. 24, 2014) (Quoting interview on Fox News Channel: "There is no evidence to support that false narrative of a video. Not a scintilla of evidence. All of the evidence pointed exactly to what she claimed it wasn't: a preplanned, coordinated attack. So she [Susan Rice] was fabulously wrong when she said it the first time, and stunningly arrogant in her refusal to express any regret for lying to our fellow citizens").

[2130] The author addresses the Bowe Bergdahl exchange and the Iranian Nuclear agreement in detail in his forthcoming book, *"The Emperor Obama: An American Betrayal, Book I – Foreign Policy, National Security and Terrorism* (to be available at www.amazon.com).

[2131] Victor Davis Hanson, "You Gotta Lie," National Review online (May 2, 2017) (footnote added).

104

Hero Hicks Is Demoted

Within days of Benghazi, Gregory Hicks will fall from Hero to Goat in the eyes of Team Obama.

Hicks later testifies that when he hears Susan Rice blame the attacks on the Video, "I was stunned. My jaw dropped. And I was embarrassed."[2132] In a telephone call with Beth Jones of State, Hicks asks her why Ambassador Rice has asserted there was a protest, when the Tripoli Embassy has reported only an attack. Jones reportedly tells Hicks "I don't know." Hicks testifies he gets the sense he should drop this line of questioning.[2133]

In hindsight, Hicks believes his questioning of Rice's use of the CIA Talking Points marks the point at which the State Department higher-ups begin to turn hostile towards him.[2134] Hicks also will testify the contradiction between Susan Rice's Sunday Shows interviews and the public statements made by the Libyan president angers the latter and harms his credibility with the Libyan people.[2135] As discussed

---

[2132] Hicks Oversight Committee Testimony (May 8, 2013) (Response to questions of Rep. Trey Gowdy (R-SC)), p. 32.

[2133] *Id.* (Response to questions of Rep. Jim Jordan (R-OH)), p. 44; *Id.* (Response to questions of Rep. Paul Gosar (R-AZ)), p. 70; and Scott Shane, Jeremy W. Peters and Eric Schmitt, "Diplomat Says Questions Over Benghazi Led to Demotion," *The New York Times* online (May 8, 2013).

[2134] Hicks Oversight Committee Testimony (May 8, 2013) (Response to questions of Rep. Scott DesJarlais (R-TN)), p. 77; and *Id.* (Response to questions of Rep. Doc Hastings (R-WA)), pp. 81-82.

[2135] *Id.* (Response to questions of Rep. Paul Gosar (R-AZ)) ("President Magarief [sic Magariaf] was insulted in front of his own people, in front of the world. His credibility was reduced. His ability to lead his own country was damaged. He was angry. . . ."), p. 70; *Id.* (Response to questions of Rep. Trey Gowdy (R-SC)), pp. 33-34; and Statement of Senators McCain, Graham and Ayotte ("On September 16, 2012, U.S. Ambassador to the United Nations, Susan Rice, claimed the attack was a spontaneous reaction to the disgusting video, immediately after the President of the Libyan General National Congress said clearly that it was a preplanned attack that included members of al Qaeda"). See also CBS News, Dispute Over Nature of Libya Attack Continues (referencing ". . . the widening rift between U.S. and Libyan accounts of the attack. . . .").

THE TRUE ACCOUNT OF VALOR AND ABANDONMENT

below, Hicks also expresses his belief this issue complicates efforts to get FBI investigators into Benghazi after the attacks.[2136]

In the aftermath of Benghazi, a congressional investigator, Congressman Jason Chaffetz (R-UT) of the House Oversight Committee, takes a trip to Libya to investigate what happened on the Night of Benghazi. Hicks claims State Department lawyers and "unnamed higher-ups at State" have instructed him by telephone not to be interviewed alone about Benghazi by Chaffetz and his staff. Hicks is supposed to give the same directions to two other State employees in Tripoli, John Martinec (then the new Regional Security Officer for Libya) and also David McFarland (then the acting deputy chief of mission in Tripoli).[2137] When Hicks rejects this "request," the State Department provides a lawyer whose function is to serve as a "minder" (baby-sitter) for Hicks. This attorney is supposed to be present at all meetings and other events associated with Congressman Chaffetz's visit. Hicks asserts this never has happened before in his diplomatic career of more than twenty years.[2138]

Moreover, Hicks testifies before the House Oversight Committee that Hillary Clinton's Chief of Staff, Cheryl Mills, later calls him and is "very upset." Mills excoriates Hicks for attending a classified briefing

---

[2136] Hicks Oversight Committee Testimony (May 8, 2013) (Response to questions of Rep. Paul Gosar (R-AZ)), pp. 70-71; and *Id.* (Remarks of Rep. Trey Gowdy (R-SC) to Gregory Hicks: "You have made a compelling case today for why it is important to tell other countries the truth. You made a compelling case that the decision not to tell the truth on Sunday morning talk shows adversely impacted our ability to get to Benghazi. You made a compelling case . . . ."), p. 107.

[2137] *Id.* (Response to questions of Rep. Trey Gowdy (R-SC)), p. 106; *Id.* (Response to questions of Rep. Jim Jordan (R-OH)), pp. 44-45; *Id.* (Response to questions of Rep. Jackie Speier (D-CA)) ("We were not to be personally interviewed by Congressman Chaffetz"), p. 57; *Id.* (Response to questions of Chairman Darrell Issa (R-CA)) (Question: ". . . So it was, in fact, people sent by the State Department told you to breach protocol and not to provide anything, even if requested by my personal emissary, Mr. Chaffetz, on that CODEL [congressional delegation], told you not to talk to him privately even if he asked?" Answer: "That's correct"), pp. 98-99; and *Id.* (Response to questions of Ranking Member Elijah Cummings (D-MD)) (". . . I recall also stating that I was not to allow personal interviews between Congressman Chaffetz, the RSO [Regional Security Officer], the Acting DCM [Deputy Chief of Mission] or me. . . . [Related questions omitted.] They said not to have a personal interview with him"), pp. 99-100.

[2138] *Id.* (Response to questions of Rep. Jim Jordan (R-OH)), pp. 44-45; *Id.* (Response to questions of Rep. Doc Hastings (R-WA)), p. 81; *Id.* (Response to questions of Rep. Jim Jordan (R-OH)), p. 98; and Benson, The Damning Dozen: Twelve Revelations from the Benghazi Hearings.

with Congressman Chaffetz without Hicks' assigned "minder" being present. (State's lawyer lacked a sufficient security clearance to attend the briefing.)[2139]

According to Hicks, apparently during a visit to Tripoli Beth Jones, then Acting Assistant Secretary for Near Eastern Affairs, tells Hicks he needs to improve his management style, and says "people were upset." When he returns to Washington, D.C. following Chris Stevens' funeral, Beth Jones calls Hicks into her office at the State Department and delivers a "blistering critique" to him regarding his "management style." She tells Hicks she doesn't know why anyone in Libya would want him to come back.[2140] Hicks describes this as the worst management disagreement he ever had with his superiors (a "10" on a 10-point scale).[2141]

Hicks later will testify he is required to go through the "normal process" like everyone else to find another job at State.[2142] He is given no special consideration despite his heroic performance on the Night of Benghazi. He further testifies he has been "effectively demoted" from Deputy Chief of Mission to "Desk Officer." The State Department denies Hicks has been demoted.[2143]

[2139] Hicks Oversight Committee Testimony (May 8, 2013) (Response to questions of Rep. Jim Jordan (R-OH)), p. 45; *Id.* (Response to questions of Rep. Jackie Speier (D-CA)), p. 58; *Id.* (Response to questions of Rep. Carolyn Maloney (D-NY)) ("She [Cheryl Mills] was unhappy that her minder, the [State Department] lawyer that came with Congressman Chaffetz, was not included in that meeting [a classified briefing]"), pp. 104-105; Scott Shane, Jeremy W. Peters and Eric Schmitt, "Diplomat Says Questions Over Benghazi Led to Demotion," *The New York Times* online (May 8, 2013); and Benson, The Damning Dozen: Twelve Revelations from the Benghazi Hearings.

[2140] Hicks Oversight Committee Testimony (May 8, 2013) (Response to questions of Rep. Scott DesJarlais (R-TN)), p. 77; and *Id.* (Response to questions of Rep. Doc Hastings (R-WA)), p. 82. See also Benson, "Yes, Hillary's Benghazi 'Investigation' Was a Whitewash".

[2141] *Id.* (Response to questions of Rep. Doc Hastings (R-WA)), p. 82.

[2142] *Id.* (Response to questions of Rep. Doc Hastings (R-WA)), p. 82.

[2143] *Id.* (Response to questions of Rep. Scott DesJarlais (R-TN)) (". . . I've been effectively demoted from deputy chief of mission to desk officer"), p. 78; Scott Shane, Jeremy W. Peters and Eric Schmitt, "Diplomat Says Questions Over Benghazi Led to Demotion," *The New York Times* online (May 8, 2013); Benson, The Damning Dozen: Twelve Revelations from the Benghazi Hearings; ABC News, Hicks Sept. 2013 Interview With Stephanopoulos (*Watch video there*; Go to 7:19 - 8:11); and Wilson and DeYoung, Benghazi E-mails Show Clash Between State Department, CIA.

THE TRUE ACCOUNT OF VALOR AND ABANDONMENT

Hicks later will tell ABC News, "Yes, I feel that I have been punished [for speaking out]. I don't know why I was punished. I don't know why I was shunted aside – put in a closet, if you will." In a responsive statement, the State Department again insists it has not punished Hicks in any way.[2144] (Right.)

Remember, Gregory Hicks is one of the few U.S. officials who does everything *right* on the Night of Benghazi. Indeed, at later congressional hearings it is revealed both President Obama and Secretary of State Clinton have called Hicks to compliment him on his excellent performance during this crisis. Within the State Department, he also receives praise from Deputy Secretary Burns, Under Secretary Wendy Sherman, Executive Secretary Steven Mull, and the new incoming U.S. Chargé in Libya, Larry Pope. According to Hicks, Pope praises the former's performance as "near-heroic." AFRICOM Commander General Carter Ham also expresses his appreciation to Hicks.[2145] (How many foreign service officers in State Department history ever have received such high-level accolades over an entire career, much less for their conduct on one night? We sure don't want people like Greg Hicks working at State.)

After a distinguished career, Greg Hicks retires from the State Department in August 2016.[2146] He must leave with a very bad taste in his mouth. ∎

[2144] ABC News, Hicks Sept. 2013 Interview With Stephanopoulos (*Watch video there*; Go to 7:19 - 9:30).

[2145] Prepared Statement of Gregory Hicks, House Oversight Committee Hearings (May 8, 2013), p. 11; Hicks Oversight Committee Testimony (May 8, 2013) (Remarks of Rep. Scott DesJarlais (R-TN)), p. 77; and *Id.* (Response to questions of Rep. Jim Jordan (R-OH)), pp. 43-44.

[2146] Interview of Gregory Hicks with Megyn Kelly, "The Kelly File," Fox News Channel (Sept. 13, 2016) (*Watch video there*; Go to 0:19-47).

105

The FBI "Investigates"

Following the Benghazi tragedy, President Obama directs the Federal Bureau of Investigation to, well, "investigate." The FBI endeavors to send its investigators to Benghazi to attempt to find relevant evidence at the Mission Compound and the Annex, and to interview witnesses. The stated purpose is to locate evidence that will help apprehend and *prosecute* at least some of the attacking terrorists. By dispatching the FBI – as if Benghazi were a kidnapping or a bank robbery – President Obama has accorded law enforcement a preeminent role over the military in addressing this act of terrorism on foreign soil.

(President Obama could have sent special operations commandos to Libya to hunt down and kill the perpetrators. You know, the way Israel's Mossad found and killed the Munich Olympics murderers of Israeli athletes in 1972.[2147])

The case is investigated by the Joint Terrorism Task Force at the FBI's New York Field Office. This Task Force will receive "substantial assistance" from other government agencies, including the CIA and the State Department.[2148]

At first, the FBI's inquiry appears to ramp up swiftly. By Saturday, September 15, FBI agents already are in Germany, interviewing American survivors of Benghazi at Ramstein Air Base.[2149] On September 16, the Libyan government reportedly issues the FBI agents visas for travel to Libya. The next day, Libya grants flight clearance. FBI agents land in Tripoli the following day, September 18.[2150] Then, things grind to a halt.

Gregory Hicks later testifies he feels Susan Rice's appearance on the Sunday Shows on September 16 could have been used to facilitate

---

[2147] Bennett, *America: The Last Best Hope*, p. 427 n. *.

[2148] DOJ Press Release, "Abu Khatallah Found Guilty of Terrorism Charges."

[2149] Sen. Intelligence Committee Benghazi Report, p. 33.

[2150] House Oversight Committee Hearings (May 8, 2013) (Remarks of Rep. Carolyn Maloney (D-NY)), pp. 105-106.

THE TRUE ACCOUNT OF VALOR AND ABANDONMENT

and expedite getting the FBI team on the ground in Benghazi.[2151] Instead, following Rice's Sunday performance there is a lengthy delay resulting from "bureaucratic resistance" before FBI agents even are allowed into Benghazi. As noted above, during this time the "crime scenes" are unsecured. Looters, journalists and other interlopers pick through the property left behind by the Americans, and remove whatever they wish.[2152] In the meantime, the FBI agents attempt to gather as much evidence as possible from their temporary perch in Tripoli.[2153]

Other FBI agents apparently are working from Tunis, Tunisia, a nation adjacent to Libya's western border. Matters do not go well there. The FBI team members reportedly are confronted by protestors, who take photographs of the FBI agents. According to the State Department, these photos then begin to appear on Islamist websites.[2154] (What a swell neighborhood.)

One of the reasons Libyans give for the delay is the situation in Benghazi is just "too dangerous" for FBI agents to enter.[2155]

[2151] Hicks Oversight Committee Testimony (May 8, 2013) (Response to questions of Rep. Trey Gowdy (R-SC)), pp. 33-34.

[2152] *Id.* (Response to questions of Rep. Trey Gowdy (R-SC)), pp. 33-34; and *Id.* (Response to questions of Rep. Paul Gosar (R-AZ); Question: "Was the crime scene secured during that time [the 17 days before the FBI arrived]?" Hicks: "No it was not. We repeatedly asked the Government of Libya to secure the crime scene and prevent interlopers, but they were unable to do so"), pp. 70-71.

[2153] *Id.* (Response to questions of Rep. Paul Gosar (R-AZ)), p. 71.

[2154] "Diplomatic Security, 2012 Year in Review," U.S. Department of State, Bureau of Diplomatic Security (June 2013), State Dept. website, p. 43.

[2155] Morgan, Libyan President: 50 Arrests in Consulate Assault (Libyan President Magariaf on whether it was safe enough for the FBI to come to Libya to pursue their investigation of Benghazi: "Maybe it is better for them [the FBI] to stay for a little while, for a little while . . . until we do what we have to do ourselves"); Scott Shane, Jeremy W. Peters and Eric Schmitt, "Diplomat Says Questions Over Benghazi Led to Demotion," *The New York Times* online (May 8, 2013) ("A State Department official said the delays [in Libyan cooperation with FBI investigators] were caused by security concerns in Benghazi"); Birnbaum, Sensitive Documents Left Behind With Little Security at U.S. Diplomatic Post in Libya ("Concerns about safety in Benghazi have confined a team of FBI investigators to the Libyan capital, Tripoli, which is hundreds of miles away, and local security officials say they cannot guarantee that Americans would be safe here"; and military head of a militia providing security in Benghazi: ". . . If the Americans come, I'm not sure they'll be completely safe"); and Hicks Oversight Committee Testimony (May 8, 2013) (Response to questions of Rep. Carolyn Maloney (D-NY): ". . . [T]he Libyan Government did not want any of our personnel to go to Benghazi because of the security situation there"), p. 106.

(Congressman Trey Gowdy (R-SC) – later appointed chair of the House Select Benghazi Committee – reasonably inquires how it is that Benghazi is safe enough for diplomats to be there, but is "too dangerous" for trained law enforcement officials to enter.[2156])

Gregory Hicks believes there is a different reason for the difficulties in admitting FBI agents. The Libyan president has publicly stated the Benghazi attacks involve "Islamic extremists, possibly with terror links." According to Hicks, President Mohamed Magariaf never mentions any spontaneous protests in Benghazi that are a response to the Video. Hicks testifies bureaucratic delays develop in getting the FBI team into Benghazi to investigate when Obama administration officials (including Susan Rice on the Sunday Shows) contemporaneously blame the attacks on protests of the blasphemous anti-Islam internet Video.[2157] Hicks asserts the Libyan leader feels insulted and embarrassed by Team Obama's public statements that contradict him. Hicks blames the problems in the FBI inquiry on Susan Rice's statements regarding the Video.[2158] Magariaf says, "It may be

---

[2156] House Oversight Committee Hearing (May 8, 2013) (Remarks of Rep. Trey Gowdy (R-SC)), p. 106; and Interview of Rep. Trey Gowdy (R-SC) on "America's Newsroom," Fox News online (Circa Oct. 3, 2012) (". . . And it's interesting to note that the investigation that is supposed to tell us who's responsible for these murders, that area is so violent the FBI cannot go in and conduct their investigation right now. So I want you to imagine this backdrop, that the area is too dangerous for the FBI, but it wasn't dangerous enough for this administration to increase security") (*Watch video there*; Go to 2:48 - 3:15).

[2157] Hicks Oversight Committee Testimony (May 8, 2013) (Response to questions of Rep. Trey Gowdy (R-SC)), p. 32; and *Id*. (Question by Rep. Trey Gowdy (R-SC): ". . . So Ambassador Rice is telling the media that the FBI investigation has begun, when she is also talking about a video. And the reality is . . . it was a direct result of what she said that the Bureau did not get to Benghazi in a timely fashion. Is that true or is that not true?" Gregory Hicks: "That is my belief. . . . [Hicks responding to a related question:] So it [Susan Rice's statements] made achieving the objective of getting the FBI to Benghazi very, very difficult, and the ability of them to achieve their mission more difficult"), p. 95.

[2158] *Id*. (Response to questions of Rep. Paul Gosar (R-AZ): "President Magarief [sic Magariaf] was insulted in front of his own people, in front of the world. His credibility was reduced. His ability to lead his own country was damaged. He was angry. . . ."), p. 70; and *Id*. (Remarks of Rep. Trey Gowdy (R-SC) to Gregory Hicks: "You have made a compelling case today for why it is important to tell other countries the truth. You made a compelling case that the decision not to tell the truth on Sunday morning talk shows adversely impacted our ability to get to Benghazi. You made a compelling case . . . ."), p. 107. See also Statement of Senators McCain, Graham and Ayotte ("On September 16, 2012, . . . Susan Rice, claimed the attack was a spontaneous reaction to the disgusting video, immediately after the President of the Libyan General National

better for them to stay away for a little while until we do what we have to do ourselves."[2159]

Eventually, after 17 or 18 days (depending on who is counting) the Libyans allow the FBI agents into Benghazi. The Libyan government finally organizes a military escort to accompany the FBI personnel and the U.S. Special Forces troops that go with them.[2160]

The difficulty getting into Benghazi is just the beginning of the FBI's problems. Another major obstacle is disappearing witnesses. Anyone in Libya cooperating with the FBI literally is taking their life in their hands. Then FBI Director Robert Mueller explains this challenge to Congress. According to a report by the Senate Select Committee on Intelligence, in testimony before this panel Mueller explains, "as many as 15 individuals supporting the investigation or otherwise helpful to the United States have been killed in Benghazi since the attacks, underscoring the lawless and chaotic circumstances in eastern Libya." The committee's report adds, "It is unclear whether their killings were related to the Benghazi investigation."[2161] (Unclear to *whom?*)

Interestingly, under its "Rewards for Justice" program the U.S. State Department – not the FBI – offers a monetary reward of up to $10 million for information leading to the arrest or conviction of any

---

Congress said clearly that it was a preplanned attack that included members of al Qaeda"); and Guy Benson, "Whoa: US Hasn't Detained Five Benghazi Terrorists Due to Trial-Related Evidentiary Concerns," Townhall.com website (May 21, 2013) (". . . Because the State Department and White House contorted Susan Rice's talking points beyond recognition for political reasons, she appeared on national television and directly contradicted Libyan officials' (accurate) assessments with false information. This infuriated the Libyans, who proceeded to drag their feet on granting the FBI access to the attack site [sic sites]. . . .").

[2159] NBC News Staff and Wire Services, "Ambassador Rice: Benghazi Attack Began Spontaneously," NBC News online (Sept. 16, 2012).

[2160] Hicks Oversight Committee Testimony (May 8, 2013) (Response to questions of Rep. Carolyn Maloney (D-NY)), p. 106; and *Id.* (Response to questions of Rep. Trey Gowdy (R-SC)), p. 33.

[2161] Sen. Intelligence Committee Benghazi Report, p. 41, citing Robert S. Mueller III Testimony before the Senate Appropriations Subcommittee on Commerce, Justice and Science (May 16, 2013). See also Adam Goldman, "Former Guantanamo Detainee Implicated in Benghazi Attack," *The Washington Post* online (Jan. 7, 2014) ("Goldman, Former Guantanamo Detainee Implicated in Benghazi Attack") ("Lawless conditions in eastern Libya have frustrated U.S. efforts to investigate the attack in Benghazi and capture those responsible").

perpetrator of Benghazi.[2162] (This program offers rewards ranging from $500,000 to $25 million for tips leading to the location of terrorists.[2163]) Later, State will claim the reward takes effect in January 2013, but inexplicably it is not made public until November 2013![2164] (It is unclear to the author (and to House investigators) how a "secret" reward is supposed to generate any investigative leads.[2165])

The FBI does not even bother to interview Gregory Hicks (at least not as of May 8, 2013, *eight months* after launching its inquiry).[2166] (Perhaps the FBI is worried Hicks will claim State's $10 million reward!)

In the course of its investigation, the FBI publishes on its website the photos of a number of "suspects" in the attacks, whose images appear on the recordings from the surveillance cameras at the U.S. facilities in Benghazi.[2167] In the case of three suspects, it takes the FBI nearly eight months to post their photos.[2168] (Some "investigation." All of these clues strongly suggest the FBI is not conducting a serious criminal probe. As terrorism analyst Erick Stakelbeck will tell Fox News, "The Obama administration . . . is fundamentally unserious

---

[2162] State Department Rewards for Justice website; and Media Note, "Terrorist Designations of Three Ansar al-Shari'a Organizations and Leaders," Office of the Spokesperson, State Dept. Archives website (Jan. 10, 2014).

[2163] See State Department Rewards for Justice website.

[2164] Compare Jake Miller, "U.S. Offers Up to $10 Million Reward for Benghazi Info," CBS News online (Nov. 15, 2013); with Lucas Tomlinson and Catherine Herridge, "Benghazi Suspects Not on State Department's 'Rewards for Justice' List," Fox News online (Oct. 24, 2013) (reporting "The State Department's 'Rewards for Justice' program – which offers multi-million-dollar payouts for tips leading to wanted terrorists – does not include suspects in the Benghazi terror attack"; and quoting comment by State Department spokesperson Marie Harf: "This is nothing at all to do with politics. We've made crystal clear that we want to find these people and bring them to justice. . . . Whether we pay a couple million dollars isn't the point – the point is we believe it's a priority . . . and whether they are on a website or not doesn't change that").

[2165] House Foreign Affairs Benghazi Majority Staff Report ("It remains unclear to Committee investigators how the RFJ offer can be effective if it is not publicized or promoted"), p. 19.

[2166] Hicks Oversight Committee Testimony (May 8, 2013) (Hicks' Response to questions of Rep. Paul Gosar (R-AZ): "No, I was never interviewed by the FBI"), p. 71.

[2167] FBI website.

[2168] "FBI Posts New Pictures of Benghazi Suspects," CBS News online (May 2, 2013).

THE TRUE ACCOUNT OF VALOR AND ABANDONMENT

about this Benghazi investigation . . . In my estimation, they just want Benghazi to *go away*. . . ."[2169])

The FBI's inquiry is not entirely useless, however. Its existence provides a convenient excuse for why Obama administration officials are unable to respond authoritatively before the election to Benghazi-related questions: "Well gosh, we are awaiting the results of the FBI's investigation!"[2170]

In just one press briefing on September 19, White House Press Secretary Jay Carney invokes the ongoing FBI probe at least *eleven times* as a reason he can't definitively answer certain Benghazi-related questions. In the process, Carney misleadingly suggests the FBI's investigation will cover *all issues* pertaining to Benghazi. He claims:

> . . . I think it [the FBI investigation] encompasses *everything that happened*. I'm sure that they [the FBI] will look at *everything that happened there* [in Benghazi]. . . . I think the FBI is leading an investigation that will encompass *all of the information* available to the White House and to the intelligence community and to the broader diplomatic community. . . .[2171]

[2169] Interview of Erick Stakelbeck and Lt. Col. Tony Shaffer (Ret.) with Judge Jeanine Pirro, "Justice with Judge Jeanine," Fox News Channel (Date unknown) (*Watch video there*).

[2170] E.g., Press Briefing by Press Secretary Jay Carney, The White House, Obama White House Archives (Sept. 18, 2012) (emphasis added) (". . . [T]he incidents that took place [in Benghazi on the 9/11 anniversary] . . . are under investigation, and the cause and motivation behind them will be decided by that investigation . . . This is a matter that's under investigation in terms of what precipitated the attacks, what the motivations of the attackers were, what role the video played in that. . . . I am not, unlike some others, going to prejudge the outcome of an investigation . . . I'd rather wait, and the President would rather wait, for that investigation to be completed"); and Kennedy House Oversight Prepared Testimony (". . . In addition [to the Accountability Review Board inquiry], of course, there is an open criminal investigation being conducted by the Federal Bureau of Investigation. Until these investigations conclude, we are dealing with an incomplete picture. And, as a result, our answers today will also be incomplete"), p. 2. See also Benghazi ARB Report, Introduction (". . . The key questions surrounding the identity, actions and motivations of the perpetrators remain to be determined by the ongoing [FBI] criminal investigation"), p. 1.

[2171] E.g., Press Briefing by Press Secretary Jay Carney, The White House, Obama White House Archives (Sept. 19, 2012) (emphasis added) (". . . There is an ongoing investigation led by the FBI, now going back to specifically what happened in Benghazi, and we await the results of that investigation for more information about the protests and the attacks and what precipitated them and who participated in them, with the primary objective here of fulfilling the President's commitment that those people responsible for the deaths of four Americans be brought to justice. . . . Again, there is

Of course, in truth the FBI has no intention of investigating such issues as the role of the White House, the State Department, or the Pentagon in the Benghazi debacle. The FBI's only assignment is to identify the perpetrators, gather evidence against them, and (hopefully) apprehend them so they can be criminally prosecuted. The FBI manifestly is not investigating U.S. military officers, State's diplomats, or the National Security Council staff. (And Jay Carney knows it.)

The FBI's doomed, non-serious criminal inquiry will not end with a "bang," but mostly will "peter out" with a whimper. As of October 30, 2017, according to *The New York Times* prosecutors reportedly have charged "at least a dozen people under seal in the attacks."[2172] But such non-public charges are of little consequence in the real world. The entire investigation has resulted in only two arrests, both made in commando-style "snatch-and-grab" raids in Libya, and both involving FBI agents and the military. And as of June 2019, there are but two, disappointing partial convictions in U.S. federal court. (We address these subjects below in Chapter 114.)

(In retrospect, we should not have sent FBI Hostage Rescue and Special Agents to investigate and arrest the bad guys in Benghazi. We should have sent Seal Team Six to kill the bastards.) ■

---

an investigation – I think a broad investigation into what happened and how and why in Benghazi. And we will await the results").

[2172] Savage and Goldman, At Trial, a Focus on the Facts, Not the Politics, of Benghazi; and Adam Goldman and Eric Schmitt, "Benghazi Attacks Suspect Is Captured in Libya by U.S. Commandos," *The New York Times* online (Oct. 30, 2017).

106

"Not Optimal"

As noted above, five weeks after the attacks in Benghazi – just 19 days before the election – President Obama makes a televised appearance with comedian Jon Stewart on October 18. It will not go well.

Probably Obama expects this appearance on "The Daily Show" will be a "patty-cake" interview. (*Ooops!*) Among other topics, Obama and Stewart discuss how the administration performs during the Benghazi assaults. Stewart comments even the president ". . . would admit it was not the optimal response – at least to the American people as far as all of us being on the same page."[2173]

President Obama's response is astonishing:

> Here's what I'll say, *if four Americans get killed it's not optimal*. And we are going to fix *it*, . . . all of *it*. And what happens during the course of a presidency, is that *the government is a big operation,* at any given time some*thing* screws up and you make sure that you find out *what's* broken and you fix *it*. . . .[2174]

(Feast on these appalling words for a moment: *"Not optimal."* Benghazi is a human and national security tragedy; four Americans are dead (three of whom left a wife and young children), including one of your ambassadors whom you sent into harm's way. Chris Stevens is *your personal representative* to Libya.[2175] Two other Americans still in hospital are gravely wounded. Benghazi is an international humiliation for the nation you lead. And all you can say is it's "not optimal"?

[2173] Montopoli, Obama to Jon Stewart: Benghazi Response "Not Optimal" (*Watch video there*; Go to 0:00-34).

[2174] Barack Obama on "The Daily Show," Comedy Central website (Oct. 18, 2012) (Jon Stewart's interjections omitted) (*Watch video there*; Go to 4:44 – 5:48); and Montopoli, Obama to Jon Stewart: Benghazi Response "Not Optimal" (emphasis added).

[2175] ABC News Transcript of Second 2012 Presidential Debate Moderated by Candy Crowley of CNN's "State of the Union" (Oct. 16, 2012), ABC News online (emphasis added) (". . . And these [U.S. diplomats] aren't just representatives of the United States, *they are my representatives. I send them there,* oftentimes into harm's way. . . .").

THE BENGHAZI BETRAYAL

(And how about asking <u>who</u> broke *"it"* and firing their sorry asses? Obama sounds like he just has discovered for the first time on the Night of Benghazi the U.S. government is a "big operation." Apparently, you can't really expect anyone to be able even to manage (much less *control*) such a "big operation" efficiently. A "big operation" that for four years as President Barack Obama has expanded at every opportunity. (Inside his own White House, Obama reportedly explodes the size of his National Security Council staff. It alone increases from an estimated 40 to 200 under President George W. Bush, to more than 350 by 2014,[2176] and to an estimated 400 by 2015 and 2016![2177]) And didn't Obama assure America he was the very man to control "it" when he was running for president in 2007-2008? And currently for reelection in 2012?

(Further, Obama makes it sound as if the four Americans die and two others are severely injured because a wheel on their car falls off ("some*thing* screws up"). We just need to put the wheel back on. No, Barry, these four Americans are really, really *dead*, and it isn't a loose lug nut that causes this. People in *your* administration broke "it." You and Hillary Clinton wrongly sent diplomats and other Americans into grave danger in Benghazi, without adequate protection.[2178] And Leon

---

[2176] Gates, *Duty*, Chap. 15, p. 587.

[2177] Jonah Bennett, "Former Mil Officials: Obama's National Security Council Is Full of Activists," The Daily Caller website (Mar. 15, 2016) ("President Barack Obama's National Security Council (NSC) is far too big and engages in too much aggressive activism, former military officials said Monday. . . . NSC's explosion in size, from 40 staffers under former President George W. Bush to 400 under Obama, has coincided with its self-granted expansion in jurisdiction over policy. . . ."); and Mark F. Cancian, "Limiting Size of NSC Staff," Center for Strategic & International Studies website (July 1, 2016) (". . . size of NSC staff approaching 400, up from 40 in 1991 . . ."). Compare Karen DeYoung, "White House Tries for a Leaner National Security Council," *The Washington Post* online (June 22, 2015) (NSC staff was about 200 at end of George W. Bush administration and is estimated at 400 in June 2015).

[2178] E.g., Additional Views of Reps. Jordan and Pompeo (". . . The American people expect that when the government sends our representatives into such dangerous places they receive adequate protection. . . ."), p. 416; and House Oversight Committee Hearings (May 8, 2013) (Remarks of Rep. James Lankford (R-OK)) ("We have got to learn the lessons of the past. This happened in 1998. We allowed it to happen again. The State Department has to put into practice their own standards and put into place the things we know to be right. We cannot allow a place that is listed as critical and high risk to our personnel to be ignored. It did not have the support they need. If there's . . . any one way to be able to honor those that have fallen is that we actually do learn the lesson and we protect our diplomats with what is required"), p. 109.

Panetta and his Defense Department screw up in a pathetically feeble (indeed phony) attempt to "rescue" them. *They* broke *"it."*)

As president, all of "it" is *your* responsibility.[2179] ■

[2179] ABC News Transcript of Second 2012 Presidential Debate Moderated by Candy Crowley of CNN's "State of the Union" (Oct. 16, 2012), ABC News online (emphasis added) (". . . [W]hen I say that we are going to find out exactly what happened, everybody will be held accountable. And *I am ultimately responsible* for what's taking place there because these are my folks, and I'm the one who has to greet those coffins when they come home. . . ."); and *Id.* ("Secretary Clinton . . . works for me. I'm the president and *I'm always responsible* . . .").

107

Politicizing Benghazi: Taking Candy from a Romney

Both Democrats and Republicans attempt to use the Benghazi tragedy for political purposes. In addition to the usual political antics, the Benghazi scandal specifically becomes an important issue in the 2012 presidential election. And properly so.

An administration asking for four more years in power has made a clear and fatal miscalculation regarding the security of its diplomatic and intelligence personnel in a destabilized foreign country. (Indeed, a country this administration helps to destabilize.) Then, this administration has failed completely to send any military aid to the Americans under attack and in danger in Benghazi over a nearly 13-hour period. And afterwards they have deceived and confused the American people about it in the weeks leading up to the election. How can it *not* become an election issue?

Of course, this phenomenon is nothing new. An opposition party inevitably tries to take advantage of the Benghazi screw-ups because they *always* do this with scandals. (The examples are legion: The Bay of Pigs, the Vietnam War TET Offensive, Chappaquiddick, Watergate, Operation Eagle Claw, Iran-Contra, Whitewater, Monica Lewinsky, no weapons of mass destruction found in Iraq, Fast-and-Furious, Hillary Clinton's rogue email scandal, etc.).

Politics Before the Election

Obama and the Democrats try mightily to downplay the significance of the Benghazi attacks until the 2012 presidential elections are over.[2180] Democrats also blame the Republicans in Congress for not adequately funding State Department security.[2181]

[2180] Jeremy Herb, "House to Hear Long-Sought Testimony About Benghazi From Task Force Chief," The Hill online (July 30, 2013) ("Republicans have accused the Obama administration of downplaying or covering up the attack amid the heat of the 2012 presidential election, and they criticized the military's posture in the run-up to the Sept. 11 anniversary"); Benson, Petraeus: We Knew Benghazi Was Terrorism "Almost Immediately" ("Given the administration's reckless series of decisions leading up to the

THE TRUE ACCOUNT OF VALOR AND ABANDONMENT

Republicans insist they simply are trying to pry the truth out of an inept and corrupt administration that has withheld information, stalled, and told half-truths and downright lies about what happened in Benghazi and its aftermath.[2182]

The Obama-Romney Debates

There is perhaps no more significant illustration of the important political role the Benghazi tragedy plays in the 2012 election than the presidential debates. We summarize here briefly how the crisis factors into those events.

The First Debate

On October 3 in Denver, President Obama and his Republican challenger Mitt Romney face off in their first of three debates. Because this debate is about domestic issues, it is not an ideal opportunity for Romney to address the tragedy. Accordingly, Romney decides to "stay in his lane" and Benghazi is not mentioned.[2183]

---

attack, its chaotic and woefully inadequate response during the attack, and its evolving misdirection and scape-goating in its wake, is it any surprise that they're now lashing out at critics for 'politicizing' this bloody debacle of their own making?"); and Guy Benson, "New Benghazi Emails Show WH Coordinated False Talking Points," Townhall.com website (April 29, 2014) (". . . There can now be no remaining doubt. The administration's public response to the Benghazi attack was tainted by political considerations and deprived the American people of the truth").

[2181] Babbin, Whitewashing Benghazi (". . . during the vice-presidential debate on October 11, Joe Biden made the absurd claim that budget cuts had made responding to Steven's requests impossible *and* that the requests had never been received in the first place. . . .") (emphasis in original). Compare Schmitt and Landler, Focus Was on Tripoli in Requests for Security in Libya (In a debate Vice President "Biden accused . . . Republicans of cutting the administration's request for embassy security and construction. House Republicans this year [2012] voted to cut back the administration's request, but still approved more than was spent last year").

[2182] E.g., Attkisson, Could U.S. Military Have Helped During Libya Attack? ("The closer we get to the election, the harder Republicans in Congress are pushing for answers to a big question: What really happened in the attack on the U.S. Consulate [sic] in Benghazi, Libya last month that killed the U.S. Ambassador Christopher Stevens and three other Americans?").

[2183] CNN Transcript of First 2012 Presidential Debate Moderated by Jim Lehrer of PBS NewsHour, CNN online (Oct. 3, 2012).

The Second Debate

On October 16, the president and his challenger meet for their second debate in Hemstead, New York. The debate is held in a "town hall" format. CNN's Candy Crowley is the moderator. During the debate, an audience member poses a question about security in Benghazi.

In response, Romney first claims Obama has misled Americans by claiming the Benghazi attacks involved a "demonstration" (which of course Obama has). He asks, "How could we not have known?" Romney then accurately asserts, "... It was very clear this was not a demonstration. This was an attack by terrorists." Romney also properly slams Obama for going to Las Vegas for a political event on the day after the tragedy, and on to Colorado the next day for another such event. Then, Romney unwisely veers off Benghazi and discusses Obama's mistakes elsewhere in the Middle East.

Obama then responds:

> The day after the attack, governor, I stood in the Rose Garden and I told the American people in [sic] the world that we are going to find out exactly what happened. *That this was an act of terror* and I also said that we're going to hunt down those who committed this *crime*. ... And the suggestion that anybody in [sic] my team, whether the Secretary of State, our U.N. ambassador, anybody on my team would play politics or mislead when we've lost four of our own, governor, is offensive. That's not what we do. That's not what I do as president, that's not what I do as Commander in Chief.[2184]

(Actually, that's precisely what you do.)

Then, one of the most dramatic episodes of the 2012 presidential debates unfolds. Based on a transcript by ABC News, the following contentious exchange takes place among a wimpy Obama ("BO"), an inarticulate Romney ("MR"), and an aggressive moderator Candy Crowley ("CC"):

> MR: ... I think [sic] interesting the president just said something ... which is that on the day after the attack he

---

[2184] ABC News Transcript of Second 2012 Presidential Debate Moderated by Candy Crowley of CNN's "State of the Union" (Oct. 16, 2012), ABC News online (emphasis added); YouTube (*Watch video there*; Go to 1:12:28 – 1:13:23); and Interview of Mary Commanday with Ben Tracy, "Mother of Slain Ambassador Speaks Out," "CBS This Morning," CBS News website (Oct. 18, 2012) (*Watch video there*).

THE TRUE ACCOUNT OF VALOR AND ABANDONMENT

went into the Rose Garden and said that this was an act of terror.

BO: That's what I said.

MR: You said in the Rose Garden the day after the attack, it was an act of terror. It was not a spontaneous demonstration, is that what you're saying?

BO: Please proceed governor.

MR: I want to make sure we get that for the record because it took the president 14 days before he called the attack in Benghazi an act of terror.

BO: Get the transcript.

CC: It – it – it – he did in fact, sir. So let me – let me call it an act of terror . . .

BO: Can you say that a little louder, Candy?

CC: He – he did call it an act of terror. It did as well take . . . two weeks or so for the whole idea there being a riot out there about this tape to come out. You are correct about that.

MR: . . . [T]he administration indicated this was a reaction to a video and was a spontaneous reaction.

CC: It did.

MR: It took them a long time to say this was a terrorist act by a terrorist group. And to suggest – am I incorrect in that regard, on Sunday, the – your secretary –

BO: Candy?

MR: Excuse me. The Ambassador of [sic] the United Nations went on the Sunday television shows and spoke about how –

BO: Candy, I'm –

MR: – this was a spontaneous –

CC: Mr. President, let me –

BO: I'm happy to have a longer conversation –

CC: I know you –

BO: – about foreign policy.

CC: Absolutely, but I want to . . . move you on and also –

BO: OK. I'm happy to do that too.[2185]

. . .

[2185] ABC News Transcript of Second 2012 Presidential Debate Moderated by Candy Crowley of CNN's "State of the Union" (Oct. 16, 2012), ABC News online (emphasis added); and YouTube (*Watch video there*; Go to 1:13:27 – 1:14:52).

Mitt Romney goes for Obama's terrorism jugular – and misses. Some of his supporters lamely attempt later to paint this as "Romney's Finest Hour."[2186] In the author's view, however, the Obama-Crowley "tag team" has triumphed. Romney becomes completely flummoxed; he is the proverbial "deer in the headlights." He is unable to assemble a complete sentence.[2187] Crowley's running "interference" for the president totally knocks all the wind out of Romney's Benghazi sails – in front of an estimated 65 million viewers.[2188]

As the final debate will reveal, after this exchange Romney all but abandons the offensive against Obama on Benghazi.[2189] Arguably, this debate fiasco will prove the decisive moment of the 2012 election campaign. Truly, the Bard's words apply to this debate exchange:

> There is a tide in the affairs of men
> Which, taken at the flood, leads on to fortune;
> Omitted, all the voyage of their life
> Is bound in shallows and in miseries.
> On such a sea are we now afloat;
> And we must take the current when it serves,
> Or lose our ventures.[2190]

Mitt missed the tide.

The Third Debate

Prior to the third and final debate, some Republicans in Congress are scrambling to obtain documents about the Benghazi attack. They want to compare what the intelligence agencies knew versus what the Obama administration is telling the public. They hope it can help swing

---

[2186] E.g., Ferrara, Benghazi: Obama's Actions Amount to a Shameful Dereliction of Duty (referencing Romney's debate performance: "Romney alone among the three, ever sharp as a tack, and fully on top of the facts, persisted in recalling the truth. . . . But Romney maintained his control and his ever classy demeanor . . .").

[2187] Rice, *Tough Love* (". . . Romney appeared flummoxed and deflated. That was the last time Romney tried directly to bury Obama with Benghazi"), Chap. 16, p. 317.

[2188] Jack Mirkinson, "Second Presidential Debate Ratings: 65.6 Million Tune In," *The Huffington Post* online (Oct. 17, 2012) (citing Nielsen ratings of 65.6 million viewers).

[2189] Attkisson, *Stonewalled* (". . . After being smacked down by Crowley, Romney would hesitate to raise the specter of Benghazi again during the rest of the campaign"), Conclusion, p. 375.

[2190] William Shakespeare, *Julius Caesar*, Act 4, Scene 3, lines 217-223.

the election to Romney.[2191] It is too late. They are in for a serious disappointment from their candidate.

On Monday, October 22, Obama and Romney square off again in their last nationally-televised presidential debate in Boca Raton, Florida. The principal subject is foreign policy, and the moderator is Bob Schieffer of CBS News.

During this final debate, it doesn't take long for Benghazi to surface. Indeed, to Schieffer's credit, what went wrong in Benghazi, and were Americans deceived, is his first question to the candidates. Romney is first to answer. Amazingly, his response doesn't even mention Benghazi! Instead, he discusses nearly every other nation involved in the "Arab Spring" (which is not the question).[2192]

For his part, instead of ignoring Benghazi as Romney has, President Obama chooses to answer the question (albeit deceptively). He asserts:

> ... Now, with respect to Libya, as I indicated in the last debate, when we received that phone call, I immediately made sure that, number one, *we did everything we could to secure those Americans who were still in harm's way* [which Obama does *not* say in the second debate]; number two, that we would investigate exactly what happened; and number three, *most importantly*, that we would go after those who killed Americans, and we would bring them to justice, and that's exactly what we're going to do.[2193]

(Why is bringing the killers "to justice" more important than saving the Americans still in harm's way?) Obama then takes a bow for having gotten rid of the "despot" Qadhafi "who had killed Americans." Later in this debate, Obama "doubles down" on the wisdom of removing Qadhafi. He claims:

> ... And so we were going to make sure that we finished the job. That's part of the reason why *the Libyans stand with us.* But *we did so in a careful, thoughtful way,* making certain

---

[2191] CBS News, CIA Saw Possible Terror Ties Day After Libya Hit: AP (As of October 19, 2012: "Congressional aides say they expect to get the documents [showing what the intelligence agencies knew] by the end of this week to build a timeline of what the intelligence community knew and compare that to what the White House was telling the public about the attack. That could give Romney ammunition to use in his foreign policy debate with Obama on Monday night").

[2192] *The New York Times* Transcript of Third 2012 Presidential Debate Moderated by Bob Schieffer of CBS News, *The New York Times* online (Oct. 22, 2012).

[2193] *Id.* (emphasis added).

that we knew who we were dealing with, that those *forces of moderation on the ground* were ones that we could work with. . . .[2194]

Romney responds with an inexplicable (and erroneous) concession to the president. He states, ". . . It's wonderful that Libya seems to be making some progress, despite this terrible tragedy . . ."[2195] (*What* progress? What movie is Mitt watching? Libya is a complete "S**t Show.")

Still later the president asserts, "In Libya we stood on the side of the people. And as a consequence *there is no doubt that attitudes about Americans have changed.*"[2196] (Someone should break this good news to the Libyan terrorists.)

Remarkably, in this final debate Barack Obama is more interested in addressing his administration's own failures in Libya and Benghazi than is Romney! (Perhaps the latter is afraid Bob Schieffer will put on his "Candy Crowley mask" if Romney gets too aggressive on Benghazi.) Even in his closing statement when Schieffer and Obama (who has gone first) no longer can challenge him, *Romney is silent on Benghazi!* When it comes to this tragedy, Romney has been neutered politically. He has thrown in the towel on Benghazi. There are 15 days until the election.

Politics After the Election

After the election President Obama and his supporters assert Benghazi is "just politics" that is "old news" and there is "nothing new to see," so let's "move on."[2197] However, largely because of the

---

[2194] *Id.* (emphasis added).

[2195] *Id.*

[2196] *Id.* (emphasis added).

[2197] E.g., Scott Shane, Jeremy W. Peters and Eric Schmitt, "Diplomat Says Questions Over Benghazi Led to Demotion," *The New York Times* online (May 8, 2013) (quoting White House spokesperson Jay Carney: "This is a subject that has, from its beginning, been subject to attempts to politicize it by Republicans"); *Id.* ("Elijah E. Cummings of Maryland, the [House Oversight] committee's senior Democrat, accused the Republicans and [Chairman] Mr. Issa in particular of distorting the facts of the inquiry for partisan purposes"); and Benson, The Damning Dozen: Twelve Revelations from the Benghazi Hearings ("For their part, many [House Oversight] committee Democrats were focused on unseemly efforts to attack, distract and smear – all employed as they cynically groused about *Republicans* 'politicizing' the investigation") (emphasis in original).

ongoing congressional probes Obama's administration expresses frustration over the continuing political focus on Benghazi. For example, at a joint press conference with British Prime Minister David Cameron in May 2013, President Obama will refer to the congressional investigations as "political games" and a "political circus."[2198] In the same month presidential spokesperson Jay Carney joins in the fun, reportedly claiming, "It is a simple fact that from [the] first hours of [the] Benghazi attack there have been attempts by Republicans to politicize it."[2199]

Congressional and other supporters of the president also continue to argue the Benghazi tragedy is all about politics. There are too many examples to summarize here. Consider just one typical instance: Again in May 2013, Senator Robert Menendez (D-NJ), Chairman of the Senate Foreign Relations Committee, accuses Republicans on his panel of playing politics with Benghazi. Menendez asserts on the Senate floor:

> Let's be honest about what's happening here. It's not about doing all we can to find the truth and making sure it never happens again. It's about political-gamesmanship and finding someone to blame. ... [I]t's the rhetoric and the political calculus of my friends on the other side ... that has changed. They want to make this a political issue to drive a purely political agenda.[2200]

Still later, when the Select Benghazi Committee issues its report in July 2016, Democrats in Congress will insist its purpose is to prevent Hillary Clinton from becoming president.[2201]

Throughout his second term, Obama's administration continues to minimize the adverse nature of the Benghazi tragedy. Barack Obama has a legacy to burnish. He repeatedly will claim he is proud his administration has no significant scandals. Before leaving office, Obama brags in his final "60 Minutes" interview as president, "I'm

---

[2198] Obama-Cameron Joint Press Conference.

[2199] Thomson / Reuters, "Whistleblower's Emotional Testimony on Benghazi: More Could Have Been Done," NewsMax.com website (May 8, 2013).

[2200] Statement of Chairman Robert Menendez (D-NJ), "Menendez Speaks Out on Benghazi: 'We Have Fully Vetted This Issue,'" Senate Foreign Relations Committee website (May 16, 2013).

[2201] Fox News, House Republicans Fault US Military Response to Benghazi ("Democrats have said the goal of the [Select Committee majority] report is to undermine [Hillary] Clinton's presidential bid").

proud of the fact that, with two weeks to go, we're probably the first administration in modern history that hasn't had a major scandal in the White House."[2202] Shortly after leaving office, Obama will claim to a large gathering, "We didn't have a scandal that embarrassed us."[2203] As usual, in this endeavor Team Obama will receive a massive assist from a willing mainstream media.[2204] (Other problems aside, the Benghazi fiasco is not a scandal?[2205] And Barack is not embarrassed by it? Perhaps it was all just a bad dream.)

For four years, at every turn the administration downplays the role of Benghazi in Obama's presidency. We discuss below (Chapter 112) how Team Obama will do so in response to the various congressional investigations and critiques. In addition, many in the government will

---

[2202] Glenn Kessler, "Has the Obama White House Been 'Historically Free of Scandal'?" *The Washington Post* online (Jan. 19, 2017); Matt Margolis, "Obama Not Embarrassed by His Scandals?" Townhall.com website (Feb. 28, 2018); and Bre Payton, "Stop Pretending the Obama Administration Was 'Scandal Free.' It Wasn't," The Federalist website (Jan. 17, 2017) (*Watch video* of "60 Minutes" Interview there).

[2203] Matt Margolis, "Obama Not Embarrassed by His Scandals?" Townhall.com website (Feb. 28, 2018) (Quoting leaked Obama remarks in February 2018 before 12th Annual MIT Sloan Sports Analytics Conference).

[2204] E.g., David Brooks, Opinion, "I Miss Barack Obama," *The New York Times* online (Feb. 9, 2016) ("... The "Obama administration has been remarkably scandal-free. . . ."); CNN Transcript of Interview of Bakari Sellers with Dave Briggs, "New Day," CNN online (Sept. 4, 2017) (describing Obama as "eight years scandal free . . ."); and Paul Blumenthal, "In 2 Terms, Barack Obama Had Fewer Scandals Than Donald Trump Has Had in the Last 2 Weeks," *The Huffington Post* online (Jan. 13, 2017) (While "Scandal has consumed the final four years of every two-term president in modern history . . . Obama's administration is the exception. . . . It's not an accident that Obama's presidency was largely scandal-free. . . ."). Compare Matt Margolis, "Obama Not Embarrassed by His Scandals?" Townhall.com website (Feb. 28, 2018) ("[T]here were over two dozen scandals over the course of Obama's presidency, and they were all downplayed or ignored by the mainstream media. . . . And the media should be embarrassed at how they failed the American public by pretending these scandals [specifically including Benghazi] didn't exist, or weren't important").

[2205] Matt Margolis, "Obama Not Embarrassed by His Scandals?" Townhall.com website (Feb. 28, 2018) (emphasis added) (". . . Obama's presidency was the most scandalous in history. Obama may not be embarrassed by Fast and Furious, Benghazi, the IRS scandal, the VA scandal, Solyndra, the OPM hacking scandal, the GSA scandal, the Iran Ransom scandal, Uranium One, or the FISA abuse scandal currently being unraveled, but he should be. . . ."). The author discusses these (and other) Obama administration scandals in his forthcoming work, *The Emperor Obama: An American Betrayal*, Books I and II.

try to portray Benghazi in a light least damaging to Obama's historical image.

Consider just one illuminating example. An official State Department summary of attacks on U.S. diplomatic facilities from 2006 to 2015 spends only a single sentence (albeit a long one) on the entire Benghazi tragedy – the most momentous of all such attacks. One sentence. Somehow, there is not room in this sentence for the words "terror" or "terrorist." Nor does this sentence manage to mention the name of assassinated Ambassador Chris Stevens, nor of the other three murdered Americans.[2206] (In fairness, other administration documents do acknowledge Benghazi involved terrorism, and some reference Ambassador Stevens and the other fallen men by name.[2207])

Overall, however, Team Obama's goal is to minimize the import of the Benghazi crisis whenever possible.

Politics in the 2016 Election

This is not a book about Hillary Clinton specifically, nor about Donald J. Trump in any sense. However, it is clear Benghazi continues to cast a long political shadow over Hillary Clinton in her quest to become president in the 2016 election.

[2206] "Significant Attacks Against U.S. Diplomatic Facilities and Personnel 2006-2015," U.S. Department of State, Bureau of Diplomatic Security, State Dept. website (emphasis added) ("*Attackers* used arson, small arms, machine guns, rocket-propelled grenades and mortars against the U.S. Special Mission, a mission annex, and U.S. personnel en route between both facilities, killing the U.S. ambassador to Libya and three other U.S. government personnel, wounding two U.S. personnel, and three Libyan contract guards, and destroying both facilities"), p. 25. See also "Political Violence Against Americans," U.S. Department of State, Bureau of Diplomatic Security (July 2013), State Dept. website (emphasis added) ("Four U.S. government personnel, including the U.S. Ambassador to Libya, were killed during a *series of attacks* focused on the U.S. Special Mission Compound and Annex, as well as on U.S. personnel en route to both facilities. . . ."), p. 4; and *Id.* (emphasis added) (Referencing a "*series of attacks* . . . directed at the U.S. Special Mission compound and Annex"; a caption of a photograph does refer to "a terrorist mob" penetrating the Mission and setting it on fire), pp. 8-9.

[2207] E.g., "Diplomatic Security, 2012 Year in Review," U.S. Dept. of State, Bureau of Diplomatic Security (June 2013), State Dept. website (emphasis added) (". . . [I]n 2012, *terrorists attacked* our U.S. Special Mission in Benghazi, where U.S. Ambassador to Libya J. Christopher Stevens lost his life, along with Foreign Service Officer Sean Smith and former Navy Seals Glen Doherty and Tyrone Woods. . . ."), p. 2; and *Id.* at p. 26.

THE BENGHAZI BETRAYAL

Both Republican candidate Donald Trump[2208] and Republican members of Congress explicitly use Benghazi as a politically advantageous issue in the 2016 campaign. For example, then Republican House Majority Whip Tim McCarthy stupidly says the Benghazi Select Committee has hurt Hillary Clinton in the polls.[2209] (This blunder partially explains why McCarthy does not succeed John Boehner as Speaker – and does not deserve to.)

In the end Hillary Clinton does not escape completely from the Benghazi scandal. Although she receives her party's nomination for president in 2016, ultimately she will lose that election in an upset to long-shot Republican candidate Trump. Is it possible her failings concerning Benghazi play a role in her defeat? Her private email system uncovered by the Select Benghazi Committee almost certainly does. However, numerous other factors also will contribute to her defeat.[2210] ∎

[2208] See Conor Gaffey, "Who Is Mustafa Al-Islam [sic]? Benghazi Attack Suspect Captured in Libya to Face Trial in U.S.," Newsweek online (Oct. 31, 2017) ("The attack on the U.S. mission in Benghazi sparked political soul-searching in the United States and became a campaign flashpoint during the 2016 presidential election, with Trump frequently citing the incident – which occurred while Democratic candidate Hillary Clinton was secretary of state – as evidence of his opponent's unfitness for office").

[2209] David M. Herszenhorn, "House Democrats Release Benghazi Report to Blunt Republican Inquiry," *The New York Times* online (June 27, 2016) (quoting Representative Kevin McCarthy: "Everybody thought Hillary Clinton was unbeatable, right? But we put together a Benghazi special committee, a select committee. What are her numbers today? Her numbers are dropping. Why? Because she's untrustable [sic]. But no one would have known any of that had happened, had we not fought").

[2210] See, e.g., Matt Vespa, "Here's What FBI Director James Comey Admits in His New Book – And Why Some Liberals Are Infuriated by It," Townhall.com website (April 13, 2018) ("Still, the fact remains that pollsters really don't know if the letter [from FBI Director James Comey to Congress eleven days before the election revealing the discovery of new emails from Clinton] had any impact at all. Clinton still had no message, no charisma, no political skill, and called roughly half the country deplorable for supporting Donald Trump. She didn't campaign as hard in the Rust Belt. She didn't laser focus on winning back working class voters – all of this contributed to her defeat. It's her fault, which she admits after blaming The DNC [Democratic National Committee], Comey, [the] FBI, the Media, Russia, sexism, misogyny, Obama, Biden, and Sanders").

108

"The Agency" to the Rescue

On November 1, 2012 – just five days before the election – the Central Intelligence Agency is ordered to parachute its people into the middle of a national U.S. political campaign. This action is contrary to both the law and past practice. However, Republican supporters of candidate Mitt Romney are continuing to hammer President Obama and his team on the failures connected to Benghazi.[2211] Someone high in the Obama campaign decides it is time for drastic action.

On this Thursday the CIA holds a highly unusual briefing for reporters. The Agency tells the media of the heroic exploits of "the CIA" in rescuing the Americans in Benghazi. According to *The Washington Post's* coverage of this briefing:

The CIA rushed security operatives to an American diplomatic compound in Libya *within 25 minutes* [no, more like 53 minutes after as much as a fifteen-minute delay caused by the CIA Chief of Base[2212]] of its coming under attack and played a more central role in the effort to fend off a night-long siege than has been acknowledged publicly, U.S. intelligence officials said Thursday. *The agency* mobilized the evacuation effort, took control of an unarmed U.S.

[2211] E.g., Associated Press, "Panetta: Military Lacked Enough Information to Intervene During Benghazi Attack," Fox News online (Oct. 26, 2012) (". . . Republicans have criticized the Obama administration's failure to more quickly acknowledge that intelligence suggested very early on that it was a planned terrorist attack, rather than spontaneous violence erupting out of protests over an anti-Muslim film. House and Senate Republicans as well as presidential candidate Mitt Romney, have criticized President Barack Obama and administration officials over the response to the attack and whether officials failed to provide enough security at the consulate"); and Miller, CIA Rushed to Save Diplomats as Libya Attack Was Underway ("The decision to give a comprehensive account of the attack five days before the election is likely to be regarded with suspicion, particularly among Republicans who have accused the Obama administration of misleading the public by initially describing the assault as a spontaneous eruption that began as a protest of an anti-Islamic video").

[2212] See Key Delays Appendix (See September 11 entries at 3:47 p.m. and 4:40 p.m., both Washington time).

military drone to map possible escape routes, dispatched an emergency security team from Tripoli, the capital, and chartered aircraft that ultimately carried surviving American personnel to safety [well, chartered one of the two aircraft used in the evacuation to Tripoli], U.S. officials said.[2213]

The *Post* further reports the CIA decides to provide these further details of "the CIA's" role "to rebut media reports that have suggested that agency leaders delayed sending help to State Department officials seeking to fend off a heavily armed mob." (Yes, because these partially accurate "media reports" are harming Obama's reelection chances.)

The Obama campaign and the CIA briefers almost certainly hope to convey the (mis)impression all of this activity is ordered and coordinated by President Obama's top CIA officials at their Langley, Virginia headquarters. Of course, the truth is virtually all of it is initiated by *local* CIA people on the ground in Libya. As discussed above in Chapter 37, Team Tripoli is self-deployed at the direction of the CIA Chief of Station in *Tripoli*. (To their credit, the CIA briefers do disclose two of this Team Tripoli group's members are military, not CIA personnel.) Local CIA personnel in *Tripoli* charter the jet aircraft, not anyone at Langley. Moreover, as explained in Chapter 35, Team Annex – five of whom are independent security contractors, not CIA employees – likely defy the "wait" and "stand down" orders of the CIA Chief of Base at the CIA Annex to go rescue the State Department employees at the Mission Compound.

Regarding this last point, *The Washington Post* writes, ". . . U.S. intelligence officials insisted that *CIA operatives* in Benghazi and Tripoli made decisions *rapidly* throughout the assault and *with no interference from Washington*."[2214] (Perhaps, but without much *help* from Washington, either. And GRS agents on Team Annex have insisted the Annex CIA Chief of Base *does* order them to wait some 10 to 15 minutes before leaving for the Mission. Not so rapid.)

Significantly, one major news outlet is not invited to this CIA briefing party on November 1: Fox News Channel.[2215] Fox has been covering this tragedy as much or more than any other media entity. And

---

[2213] Miller, CIA Rushed to Save Diplomats as Libya Attack Was Underway (emphasis added).

[2214] Miller, CIA Rushed to Save Diplomats as Libya Attack Was Underway (emphasis added).

[2215] Erik Wemple, "Why Exclude Fox News from Benghazi Intel Briefing?" *The Washington Post* online (Nov. 5, 2012).

the network has broadcast a string of news and analysis pieces highly critical of the U.S. government's response (including the CIA's) on the Night of Benghazi.[2216] (Probably there is no connection between Fox's aggressive coverage and its non-invitation. For sure.)

There is absolutely no proper governmental reason for the CIA to conduct this unusual (and misleading) media briefing. But it works. Five days later, Barack H. Obama wins reelection as President of the United States. ∎

[2216] See, e.g., Jennifer Griffin, "EXCLUSIVE: CIA Operators Were Denied Request for Help During Benghazi Attack, Sources Say," Fox News Channel online (Oct. 26, 2012).

109

The ARB Report: "You Are on Your Own"

After Benghazi the obligatory investigations begin almost at once. Federal law requires that after the death of any State Department employee overseas, an investigation must be initiated by an "Accountability Review Board." On September 19, Secretary Hillary Clinton approves her agency personnel's recommendation to create a Benghazi Accountability Review Board ("ARB" or "Board").[2217]

Because the ARB's inquiry is the Obama administration's principal investigation of its own conduct relating to Benghazi, we discuss it here in considerable detail.

There have been many State ARBs in the past. The agency adopted detailed procedures for the creation, staffing and operation of ARBs. However, the Benghazi ARB will not follow much of this normal process. The top career official involved in creating ARBs will write to the department's Executive Secretary Stephen Mull and his deputy, "I would appreciate knowing how this [Benghazi] ARB is going to work since it is not going in the normal way. . . ."[2218]

As will be seen next, given how its Members and staff are selected, to a considerable extent *the State Department is investigating itself*.

The ARB Members and Staff

As mandated by law, Hillary Clinton personally names four of the ARB's five members. (Two of these are former State Department employees.) The Director of National Intelligence (then James Clapper)

[2217] Omnibus Diplomatic Security and Antiterrorism Act of 1986, codified at Title 22, United States Code, Sections 4831-4835; and Benghazi Committee Report, Appendix K, pp. 620-621.

[2218] Benghazi Committee Report, Appendix K, p. 624.

names the fifth member from the ranks of the intelligence community.[2219]

The Board Members

State Department procedures require an internal, seven-person "Permanent Coordinating Committee" ("PCC") to recommend whether an ARB should be convened following an overseas security incident such as Benghazi. On September 19, the PCC recommends the Secretary convene such a board for Benghazi. Clinton does so the same day.[2220] (All of this is inevitable, given what a fiasco Benghazi is.)

State's procedures also require if the PCC recommends an ARB, ". . . [I]t will forward a list of potential board members to the Secretary for approval." For the Benghazi ARB, the PCC ignores this requirement. The Select Committee concludes, "The PCC did not prepare or send a list of prospective members to the Secretary because the [State Department] senior staff were already in the process of identifying panelists to serve." (Indeed, Clinton's senior team has begun this effort at least as early as September 18, *before* the PCC even recommends an ARB.) As the Managing Director of the PCC later explains to the Select Committee, "Well, because they went for option two and did more of the *celebrity approach* as I would say. . . ." (In other words, Team Hillary does not want career bureaucrats restricting its ability to hand-pick the ARB Members.) The Select Committee observes Clinton's senior team wants ". . . individuals who would *understand the Secretary's narrative of expeditionary diplomacy. . . .*").[2221] (I'll bet.)

It appears three of Clinton's top aides principally are responsible for assembling a list of prospective ARB Members for the Secretary. They are Clinton's Chief of Staff, Cheryl Mills, Deputy Secretary William Burns, and our old friend – you guessed it – Under Secretary Patrick Kennedy![2222]

Free of PCC constraints, Secretary Clinton selects a retired State Department Foreign Service Officer, Ambassador Thomas R.

[2219] Title 22, United States Code, Section 4832(a); Benghazi ARB Report, p. 1; and Benghazi Committee Report, Appendix K, p. 621.

[2220] Benghazi Committee Report, Appendix K, pp. 620-621.

[2221] *Id.*, Appendix K (emphasis added), pp. 621-622.

[2222] *Id.*, Appendix K, p. 621.

Pickering, to chair the Benghazi ARB. At this time, Pickering is 80 years of age. Pickering is recommended by Deputy Secretary Burns, who believes Pickering is "... very experienced and fair minded and understand[s] entirely [the] demands of expeditionary diplomacy."[2223]

At the time he is named to the ARB, Pickering also serves on the Secretary of State's "Foreign Affairs Policy Advisory Board." This group advises top State managers on foreign policy issues. Pickering has served in the Foreign Service for four decades.[2224] (In other words, Pickering already is one of Clinton's favorite, most trusted people in the diplomatic world.) Hillary Clinton's husband, then President Bill Clinton, previously has appointed Pickering to be what some consider the third highest State Department official, Under Secretary of State for Political Affairs (under then Secretary Madeleine Albright). Thus, Pickering owes his highest government position to Hillary Clinton's husband, Bill. Pickering previously has served as U.S. ambassador to Russia, India, Jordan, Israel, Nigeria, El Salvador and the United Nations.

Clinton names retired Admiral Mike Mullen, a former Chairman of the Joint Chiefs of Staff, as Vice Chairman. Like Pickering, when selected Mullen already is serving on the Secretary's "Foreign Affairs Policy Advisory Board."[2225]

The other two members of the ARB named by Clinton are Richard Shinnick and Catherine Bertini.[2226] Shinnick is a retired long-time foreign service officer at the State Department. He has served in various capacities, including as Director for the Bureau of Overseas Buildings and Operations, and in the Under Secretariat for Management (Patrick Kennedy's unit). (Detecting a pattern?)

Amazingly, Under Secretary Patrick Kennedy – who should be a principal subject of the ARB's inquiry – actually recommends at least one (possibly two) of the ARB members, who in fact Secretary Clinton appoints! Thus, the man as responsible as anyone for the Benghazi debacle is helping to appoint those who will investigate him.[2227] The

---

[2223] *Id.*, Appendix K, p. 621.

[2224] *Id.*, Appendix K, p. 622.

[2225] Benghazi Committee Report, Appendix K, p. 622; Benghazi ARB Report, Introduction, p. 1; and Benghazi ARB Report Briefing for the Media.

[2226] Benghazi ARB Report, Introduction, p. 1.

[2227] Benson, "Yes, Hillary's Benghazi 'Investigation' Was a Whitewash" ("... [K]ennedy played a key role in selecting the members of the ARB and the staff that helped the ARB do its works [sic] . . .") (emphasis deleted).

target selects the investigator. (Conflict of interest? *What* conflict of interest?)

Like nearly every other aspect of the Benghazi fiasco, the evidence relating to Kennedy's role in selecting ARB Members is contradictory. Kennedy himself later will insist to the Select Committee he recommends only one Board Member, Richard Shinnick. Cheryl Mills, on the other hand, remembers things differently. Mills will testify to the Select panel she recalls Kennedy recommending Catherine Bertini for the ARB. Kennedy denies this before the committee. He admits he knows Bertini, but claims he recommends only Shinnick, but not Bertini. He explains, "Cheryl Mills asked me for the name of someone who knew about State Department facilities management and construction."[2228] (Yet again, someone appears to be lying.) Whatever the truth, Kennedy's admitted role in recommending even a single Board Member obviously is *one Member too many*.

At the time of her appointment, Catherine Bertini is on the faculty of Syracuse University. She is a Professor of Public Administration and International Affairs. She is a former Executive Director of the United Nations World Food Programme, and former Assistant Secretary for Food and Consumer Services at the U.S. Department of Agriculture.[2229] Her primary expertise appears to be organizing food relief to prevent famine in conflict-torn countries. Food security aside, Bertini has no experience with national security, intelligence, the military, or counterterrorism. (It is unclear to the author why her admirable experience in combating famine qualifies Bertini to serve on the Benghazi ARB.)

DNI James Clapper names Hugh J. Turner III to represent the intelligence community on the ARB. Turner is a retired senior official in the intelligence community. He has formerly served as the Deputy Director of Operations for the CIA.[2230]

The ARB Executive Secretary

Clinton's senior staff also is involved in selecting the Benghazi ARB's "Executive Secretary." This Executive Secretary coordinates

---

[2228] Benghazi Committee Report, Appendix K, pp. 622-623.

[2229] House Oversight Interim Report on Benghazi ARB, p. 5.

[2230] Benghazi Committee Report, Appendix K, p. 623; Benghazi ARB Report, Introduction, p. 1; Kennedy House Oversight Prepared Testimony, p. 2; and House Oversight Interim Report on Benghazi ARB, p. 5.

and facilitates the Board's work, including supervising its staff. Depending upon whose account one believes, either Cheryl Mills or Deputy Secretary Burns reportedly selects Foreign Service Officer Uzra S. Zeya as the Board's assigned Executive Secretary. As the PCC Managing Director describes it, this person acts as "the bridge from the ARB to the [State Department] building." (Think "gatekeeper.") Among other duties, the ARB Executive Secretary arranges the Board Members' interviews with State personnel, and sits in on the interviews.

(For past ARBs, the PCC Managing Director "nominates" a candidate to be the ARB's Executive Secretary. "Normally" her nominee has been selected.[2231] But not for Benghazi.)

During her career at State, Zeya has held many positions. Just prior to working for the Benghazi ARB, Zeya has served as Chief of Staff to Deputy Secretary William Burns, and as Deputy Executive Secretary to – wait for it – Hillary Clinton![2232] (Is Zeya assigned to the ARB as a personal spy for State's top management? If Burns or Clinton asks Zeya what the ARB is up to, would Zeya not tell them?)

The ARB Staff

As demonstrated previously, Under Secretary Patrick Kennedy has made many of the key security decisions relating to Libya generally and Benghazi specifically. Nevertheless, it is Kennedy who supervises the selection of the Benghazi ARB's temporary staff! Apparently, all these ARB staff members are State employees! This despite the fact the ARB statute expressly permits the Board to utilize federal employees from other agencies, or the military.[2233]

As one congressional report observes, although legally permissible, "Using Department employees in this capacity is problematic because they could end up investigating friends, coworkers, or even themselves." Also, after the ARB's inquiry is completed, all these staff members will return to their permanent State jobs. There, Clinton's

---

[2231] Benghazi Committee Report, Appendix K, pp. 624-625; and Benghazi ARB Report Briefing for the Media.

[2232] Letter from Chairman Ed Royce (R-CA), Chairman, House Foreign Affairs Committee, to Harold W. Geisel, Acting Inspector General, State Department, House Foreign Affairs Committee website (May 10, 2013).

[2233] House Foreign Affairs Benghazi Majority Staff Report, pp. 15-16; and Title 22, United States Code, Section 4832(b)(2).

management team (including Kennedy) will approve (or not) their performance evaluations and possible bonuses and promotions. It takes one House committee "months" before it can even learn these ARB staffers' identities.[2234]

(In fact, Patrick Kennedy should be recused from any involvement whatsoever in the selection of Members, staff, or the work of the Benghazi ARB. Instead, he is involved up to his *eyebrows*. It all is a galactic conflict of interest.)

The ARB's "Investigation"

The Benghazi ARB's statutory mandate principally is to investigate the *State Department's* role in the debacle. Under the ARB statute, *to a limited extent* the ARB assesses the role of the CIA and others in the intelligence community by addressing "the impact of intelligence and information availability...."[2235] In the course of its inquiry the ARB speaks with members of the intelligence community and the military.[2236] (The ARB does not claim to have spoken with President Obama, or to have interviewed anyone else in the White House or National Security Council about Benghazi.)

In fact, the Board does *not* actually investigate the actions and performance of the president, the White House and National Security Council staff, the Defense Department, the FBI, the CIA and the rest of the intelligence community, or others in the U.S. government. The ARB does not examine who perpetrated the attacks or why. Also, the Board does not assess the State Department's role in the development of the CIA Talking Points.[2237] Despite these enormous limitations,

---

[2234] House Oversight Interim Report on Benghazi ARB ("Witnesses testified that Senior State Department officials who were involved in discussions about Benghazi security were responsible for the process of selecting Board members and staff. The ARB staff consisted of State Department employees who subsequently returned to their posts"), pp. 23-29; Attkisson, Benghazi Accountability Review Board Comes Under Renewed Criticism; and House Foreign Affairs Benghazi Majority Staff Report, p. 16.

[2235] Title 22, United States Code, Section 4834(a)(4); Benghazi ARB Report, Introduction, p. 1; and Benghazi Committee Report, Appendix K, p. 618.

[2236] Benghazi ARB Report Briefing for the Media; and Benghazi Committee Report, Appendix K, pp. 630-631 n. 72.

[2237] E.g., Benghazi ARB Report, Introduction, p. 1; Benghazi ARB Report Briefing for the Media ("... We were not asked to conduct an investigation into the attacks to find out who the perpetrators were or their motives. That is the statutory role of the Federal Bureau of Investigation and the intelligence community...."); and Alexis Simendinger, "IRS, Benghazi, AP: The Problems Pile Up for Obama," Real Clear

President Obama later will claim the ARB already has investigated "every element" of the Benghazi disaster!²²³⁸

According to its report, the ARB "interviewed over 100 individuals, reviewed thousands of pages of documents, and viewed hours of video footage." State claims the ARB reviewed "more than 7,000 documents." According to *The Washington Free Beacon*, Secretary Clinton's Chief of Staff, Cheryl Mills, later testifies to the Select Benghazi Committee she was "in contact with the review board regarding witness selection. . . ." This same source asserts Vice Chair Admiral Mullen has "tipped" Mills off regarding a "potentially problematic witness." This turns out to be (no surprise) Charlene Lamb. However, although Admiral Mullen can remember this communication with Cheryl Mills about Lamb not being a good witness for State, Mills tells the Select Committee she cannot recall it.²²³⁹

Also, it is Cheryl Mills who oversees the process of identifying, collecting, organizing, reviewing and (for some documents) redacting the documents that will be made available to the ARB. (State already has begun to collect many of these relevant documents to respond to requests from Congress and others.) Certain particularly sensitive documents are set aside for Mills to review personally.²²⁴⁰ (Are we sensing another pattern here?)

The Select Committee concludes, "The ARBs [sic] access to information from the Secretary and her senior staff was extremely limited." According to the Select Committee, the Benghazi ARB did not review "documents and emails sent to or by the Secretary or her senior staff. . . ."²²⁴¹

(For example, the ARB did not have access to at least 3,000 pages of emails that were provided only to the Select Committee. Senior State officials have their own email system (not to be confused with Hillary's

---

Politics website, (May 14, 2013) ("Pickering and Mullen have said . . . they were tasked to examine the administration's security failures, not the drafting of controversial talking points that initially blamed a mob uprising, rather than terrorists, for the deaths of the Americans").

²²³⁸ Obama-Cameron Joint Press Conference.

²²³⁹ Benghazi ARB Report, Finding 2, p. 29; Alana Goodman, "Questions Raised About Independence of Benghazi Review Ahead of Clinton Hearing," *The Washington Free Beacon* online (Oct. 22, 2015); and Benghazi Committee Report, Appendix K, pp. 628 and 631-632. See also Benghazi ARB Report Briefing for the Media.

²²⁴⁰ Benghazi Committee Report, Appendix K, pp. 625-628.

²²⁴¹ *Id.*, Appendix K, pp. 628-629.

homebrew system). During the ARB's "investigation, this separate system even lacks archiving capability. This separate system makes it more likely the ARB did not have access to records stored there.[2242]

(Also, Jake Sullivan, Clinton's Deputy Chief of Staff and Director of Policy Planning, tells the Select Committee he does not think he provides *any* documents to the ARB.[2243] Recall from previous chapters that Sullivan participates in the critical two-hour 7:30 Meeting, confers with Ben Rhodes before State issues its first public statement on the Night of Benghazi, is a recipient of Denis McDonough's error-laden 11:45 p.m. email, and helps edit the CIA Talking Points. Nope, wouldn't want to see any of *his* documents.)

Congress later will issue a subpoena to the State Department, seeking all documents reviewed or created by the Benghazi ARB. For two and one-half years, State simply blows this subpoena off. In January 2015, the Select Committee reissues the subpoena for the ARB records. Soon, State begins to trickle out a handful of ARB interview summaries to the Select Committee. In April 2015, State dumps nearly 4,300 *pages* of responsive records on the Select panel.[2244] (Wait a minute. I thought State bragged the Benghazi ARB had reviewed more than *7,000 documents*? This is Team Obama's idea of "cooperation" with Congress.)

To a considerable extent, the persuasiveness of the ARB's work can be assessed by considering one fact: *the Board does not even bother to interview Hillary Clinton herself.* That's correct, the ARB does not even interview the Secretary of State who is responsible for sending Chris Stevens to Benghazi, for the political desire to name the Benghazi outpost a formal U.S. "consulate," and ultimately for the (hazardously low) level of security in that highly risky, high-threat post on the dangerous anniversary of 9/11.[2245]

[2242] *Id.*, Appendix K, p. 629.

[2243] *Id.*, Appendix K, p. 629.

[2244] *Id.*, Appendix K, pp. 629-630.

[2245] *Id.*, Appendix K, pp. 630-631; Attkisson, Benghazi Accountability Review Board Comes Under Renewed Criticism; Lucas, Obama: State Dept. That Didn't Interview Clinton 'Investigated Every Element' of Benghazi ("The ARB . . . never interviewed Clinton, who was secretary of State when the Benghazi attacks occurred and oversaw the denial of requests for more security"); and Toensing, Administration Relying on Shoddy Benghazi Report to Absolve Itself of Blame (Note: Toensing is legal counsel for Gregory Hicks).

Nor does the ARB interview certain other key members of Clinton's inner circle at State, including Deputy Secretaries of State Thomas Nides and William Burns, and Clinton's top aide Cheryl Mills. This is despite the fact Admiral Mullen later will admit to the Select Committee that initially both he and Ambassador Pickering planned "to interview everybody up the chain of command, including the Secretary..."[2246] (Apparently, the ARB members and staff later develop difficulty pushing the elevator button for the seventh floor of the State Department headquarters building.)

It appears from the Select panel's report in early November the ARB requests Deputy Secretary Nides to appear before the ARB. He emails Cheryl Mills for permission. She emails him back "Y," presumably meaning "Yes."[2247] Ultimately, however, the ARB does not interview Nides.

In her memoir, Clinton will claim of the ARB's members, "They had unfettered access to anyone and anything they thought relevant to their investigation, including me if they had chosen to do so."[2248] ARB Chairman Thomas Pickering later tells CBS News on "Face the Nation" that he does not think it necessary to interview Hillary Clinton "because in fact we knew where the responsibility rested."[2249]

(This is ludicrous. There is only one reason an ARB does not interview the head of the agency and her closest advisers whose actions they are investigating: they obviously are directed *not* to ask Clinton and her team for an interview. No other explanation passes the laugh test. Quite possibly this is done during Cheryl Mills' admitted conversations with the Board regarding "witness selection." Had the ARB conducted a tough-but-fair interview of Hillary and her immediate team, there likely would have been the scent of a resignation or an impeachment in the wind.)

[2246] Benghazi Committee Report, Appendix K, pp. 630-631; House Foreign Affairs Benghazi Majority Staff Report (ARB does not interview Clinton, Burns or Nides), p. 15; and Attkisson, Benghazi Accountability Review Board Comes Under Renewed Criticism.

[2247] Benghazi Committee Report, Appendix K, p. 635.

[2248] Clinton, *Hard Choices*, Chap. 17, p. 407. See also Gibbons Aug. 23, 2013 Letter to Chairman Issa ("The ARB has made clear that it had unfettered access to documents, individuals, and other resources to ensure a thorough review"), p. 1.

[2249] CBS News, "Benghazi Timeline: How the Probe Unfolded," CBS News online (Undated).

Significantly, the ARB also *declines* two requests by Mark Thompson (head of the F.E.S.T. team) to be interviewed. Thompson testifies he does not know why the ARB decided not to interview him. (Why on earth *would* they do that?) Although the ARB does manage to interview Under Secretary for Management Patrick Kennedy and Charlene Lamb, you would never know it from the ARB's final Report.[2250]

Although the ARB does not interview Clinton and Cheryl Mills, the Board reportedly briefs them at least once during the investigation regarding its progress. This briefing will last for two hours. However, at this briefing the ARB supposedly does not discuss any conclusions concerning accountability.[2251]

Beyond the issue of which witnesses are questioned, the ARB process is plagued by other failings. On the good side of the ledger, it appears at least some witness interviews are recorded. However, no stenographer is present to take notes; only handwritten notes are used. Also, at least if other witnesses are treated like Greg Hicks, witnesses are not allowed to review and (if necessary) correct the ARB's summary of their statements. Moreover, they apparently are not allowed to review either the unclassified or the classified version of the ARB Report before their release.[2252]

[2250] Thompson Oversight Committee Testimony (May 8, 2013) (Response to questions of Rep. John L. Mica (R-FL)), p. 48; *Id.* (Response to questions of Rep. John Duncan, Jr. (R-TN), p. 55; Benson, The Damning Dozen: Twelve Revelations from the Benghazi Hearings (*Watch video there*); Daily Press Briefing by Deputy Spokesperson Marie Harf, State Dept. Archives website (Sept. 19, 2013); and Toensing, Administration Relying on Shoddy Benghazi Report to Absolve Itself of Blame (Note: Toensing is legal counsel for Gregory Hicks). See also Nordstrom Oversight Committee Testimony (May 8, 2013) (Response to questions of Rep. John L. Mica (R-FL)) (". . . My issue [with the ARB] is that they stopped short of interviewing people that I personally know were involved in key decisions that led to how those events unfolded, specifically how those buildings were staffed and constructed and in variance with existing standards. . . ."), p. 49.

[2251] Benghazi Committee Report, Appendix K, p. 633; and Alana Goodman, "Questions Raised About Independence of Benghazi Review Ahead of Clinton Hearing," *The Washington Free Beacon* online (Oct. 22, 2015).

[2252] Hicks Oversight Committee Testimony (May 8, 2013) (Response to questions of Rep. John Duncan, Jr. (R-TN)) (". . . I was never allowed to review the recording of my testimony to the board"), p. 56; *Id.* (Response to questions of Rep. Tim Walberg (R-MI)), p. 63; and Toensing, Administration Relying on Shoddy Benghazi Report to Absolve Itself of Blame (Note: Toensing is legal counsel for Gregory Hicks).

On the positive side, according to the State Department the ARB has available a "digital forensic exam" of computers recovered from the Benghazi Mission (at least the ones that have not been stolen or incinerated). These exams are conducted by State's computer investigations and forensics teams. On the negative side, these forensic exams are performed by State employees, not independent experts. This is despite the fact the ARB statute expressly permits the ARB to utilize outside experts and consultants. (More conflicts of interest.) The ARB also reviews video footage obtained from the Mission Compound's security cameras.[2253]

The State Department later insists to Congress the ARB "conducted a rigorous investigation into the attacks."[2254] However, the ARB's quickie inquiry lasts only three months, including the time needed to write the ARB Report. During this intervening period, the ARB's existence will afford much-needed "political relief" to the State Department and the White House. Obama administration officials conveniently are able to put off answering some difficult questions until the ARB has completed its work – after the election.[2255]

[2253] Title 22, United States Code, Section 4832(b)(3); and "Diplomatic Security, 2012 Year in Review," U.S. Department of State, Bureau of Diplomatic Security (June 2013), State Dept. website, p. 43.

[2254] Gibbons Aug. 23, 2013 Letter to Chairman Issa, p. 1.

[2255] E.g., Daily Press Briefing by Department Spokesperson Victoria Nuland, State Dept. Archives website (Oct. 12, 2012) (Responding to a question why Secretary Clinton declined to answer an inquiry how she was following matters on the Night of Benghazi: "Well . . . obviously, she knows what she was doing on that night. I think that, from her perspective, the focus needs to be on the ARB, on the lessons we learned from this, rather than on her personal tick-tock. . . ."); *Id.* (emphasis added) (Responding to a question why Clinton did not address whether there was a demonstration in Benghazi: ". . . I think she wants to have the full accounting from the ARB and from the FBI. . . . [A]s she said today, there are still things we don't know and we need to let these two investigations play through. . . . *[S]he wants to get a full accounting, as a result of these investigations, before she speaks any more in public about any of these details.* . . ."); Herridge, State Department Stayed Out of Contractors' Dispute Over Consulate Security ("Asked about that letter [from a State Department official to a Benghazi security contractor] Tuesday, State Department spokeswoman Victoria Nuland said the department's investigation likely would address the issue"); and Herridge, Classified Cable Warned Consulate Couldn't Withstand Coordinated Attack (State Department Deputy Spokesman Mark Toner regarding a classified cable discussing security in Benghazi: "An independent board is conducting a thorough review of the assault on our post in Benghazi. Once we have the board's comprehensive account of what happened, findings and recommendations, we can fully address these matters") (*Watch video there*).

The ARB's Report

Five weeks after the election, the Benghazi ARB releases the unclassified version of its report on December 19, 2012. One of the most shocking features of the ARB's Report is how thin it is. Only about 20 of the report's 39 pages (including its lengthy executive summary) contain the Board's findings and analysis of what went wrong at State before and during the crisis. A full ten pages are devoted to a timeline of events, summarizing Ambassador Stevens' arrival in Benghazi, his activities there, the attacks on the Mission and the Annex, and the subsequent evacuation of the Americans from Benghazi. Some five pages contain a series of moderately-detailed recommendations to prevent "it" from happening again.

Another interesting facet of the ARB Report is how little mention it makes of the CIA Annex in Benghazi. It contains only a brief summary of the attacks there.[2256] This is despite these facts: three terrorist attacks occur there over a five-hour period on the Night of Benghazi; far more Americans reside and work there than at the Mission; the five surviving Special Mission DSAs take refuge there; and more American casualties are sustained there than at the Mission, including a State Department DSA, David Ubben. (Almost certainly, the CIA has asked the Board to downplay the Agency's Annex facility, at least in the unclassified ARB Report.)

Among the most staggering attributes of the ARB Report is *it mentions almost no names of State Department personnel* – except for the victims Chris Stevens and Sean Smith! As discussed below, the Board concludes "certain senior State Department officials" showed a lack of "leadership" and "management ability." *But the Board's report won't tell us who they are!* Nowhere are the names Patrick Kennedy, Charlene Lamb, Beth Jones, or Hillary Clinton mentioned![2257] Not even the valiant Greg Hicks or the diligent Eric Nordstrom merit a reference. Despite this failure to name any names, State spokesperson Marie Harf later will claim the ARB's findings are "hard-hitting."[2258] (Perhaps

---

[2256] Benghazi ARB Report Briefing for the Media.

[2257] Benghazi ARB Report, Finding 5, p. 39; and Jennifer Ruben, "Ambassador Thomas Pickering: There Is No Equal," *The Washington Post* online (May 24, 2013) (Speaking of Amb. Pickering, "He gets selected for a critical State Department review of Benghazi, doesn't interview the secretary or high-level advisers, and writes a report identifying no one in particular").

[2258] Daily Press Briefing by Deputy Spokesperson Marie Harf, State Dept. Archives website (Sept. 19, 2013).

these and other names are mentioned in the classified version of the ARB's Report? But why are they not disclosed in the unclassified version?)

(Going "nameless" is not easy to accomplish when you are supposed to be writing a report on how *people working at State* conducted themselves regarding the Benghazi crisis. Truly, it is a "Stealth Report."

(By way of contrast, the House Select Benghazi Committee takes two years to investigate and prepare its 800-page report. And it names names. *Hundreds* of names.)

Another troubling fact concerning the ARB Report is the Board reportedly shares an advance draft with Hillary Clinton's Chief of Staff, Cheryl Mills. (Mills will testify the Secretary herself does not review a draft report.) Mills also apparently has "multiple exchanges" with the ARB regarding her "proposed edits." Mills subsequently testifies to the Select Benghazi Committee:

> ... [A]s they were preparing their report, they reached out to say, "We have a draft of the report." They shared that draft with me. I shared back my observations of instances where there were issues or facts that I thought were relevant for their consideration. They took them, or they didn't. Ultimately, they had to make that judgment.
>
> ...
>
> I certainly made representations for places where I thought there were inaccuracies or misstatements or other information that might not be fully reflective of what the information was that was there. I certainly made those, yes.[2259]

According to *The Washington Free Beacon*, Cheryl Mills also tells the Select Committee:

> I remember having engagements with [ARB staff leader] Uzra Zeya about the changes, not about how per se they were coming. But it was quite plausible that could have happened. I just don't remember that.[2260]

[2259] Benghazi Committee Report, Appendix K, pp. 633-634. See also Rachael Bade, "What Cheryl Mills Told Benghazi Investigators," POLITICO website (Sept. 3, 2015) ("... Mills, Clinton's former Chief of Staff at the State Department, also told the House Select Committee on Benghazi that she reviewed and made suggestions for changes to the government's official, final report on what happened in Benghazi . . .").

[2260] Alana Goodman, "Questions Raised About Independence of Benghazi Review Ahead of Clinton Hearing," *The Washington Free Beacon* online (Oct. 22, 2015).

According to POLITICO, ARB Chairman Pickering reportedly explains, "[T]hey [apparently Cheryl Mills and Secretary Clinton] provided us with three or four or five thoughts that they would like us to consider. They had no editorial rights. And we reviewed those, all of us at the end, and some we thought were acceptable and some we thought were not acceptable."[2261]

We turn now to selected portions of the Report's findings.

Security Is "Grossly Inadequate"

The ARB's Report finds security at the Benghazi Mission is "grossly inadequate" to confront the attacks that occur. (S*hock!*) It also concludes the attacks are a preplanned terrorist attack, not a spontaneous protest. In perhaps the understatement of the decade, the ARB Report correctly determines there is a "pervasive realization among personnel who served in Benghazi that the Special Mission was not a high priority for Washington when it came to security-related requests, especially those relating to staffing."[2262]

The ARB summarizes one of its key findings:

> Security in Benghazi was not recognized and implemented as a "shared responsibility" by the bureaus in Washington charged with supporting the post, resulting in stove-piped discussions and decisions on policy and security. That said, *Embassy Tripoli did not demonstrate strong and sustained advocacy with Washington for increased security for Special Mission Benghazi.*[2263]

(Are you *kidding* us? So despite all his pleas for enhanced security, it is *Ambassador Stevens'* fault he is assassinated? Stevens and former Ambassador Cretz's many requests for additional security (and petitions not to reduce security levels) in Libya is not "strong and

---

[2261] Rachael Bade, "What Cheryl Mills Told Benghazi Investigators," POLITICO website (Sept. 3, 2015).

[2262] Benghazi ARB Report, Finding 2, p. 29; *Id.*, Executive Overview, Finding 1, pp. 4-5 and 33, and Finding 2, p. 5; and Benghazi ARB Report Briefing for the Media (ARB Chairman Thomas Pickering: ". . . Frankly, the State Department had not given Benghazi the security, both physical and personnel resources, it needed. . . ."); and Lucas, Obama: State Dept. That Didn't Interview Clinton 'Investigated Every Element' of Benghazi.

[2263] *Id.*, Executive Overview, Finding 2 (emphasis added), p. 4. See also *Id.*, p. 29; and Lucas, Obama: State Dept. That Didn't Interview Clinton 'Investigated Every Element' of Benghazi.

sustained advocacy with Washington for increased security" in Benghazi? Are the ARB members out of their ever-loving *minds*? And just one page later the ARB finds the Mission lacks a sufficient number of Diplomatic Security staff on September 11 and in the months and weeks before the tragedy, *"despite repeated requests from Special Mission Benghazi and Embassy Tripoli for additional staffing."*[2264] Is the ARB even reading its own report?)

This "strong and sustained advocacy" sentence quoted from the ARB Report is an artful bit of deflection by the ARB. By finding a lack of advocacy for enhanced security in *Benghazi* specifically, the ARB is able to downplay all of the undeniable "strong and sustained advocacy" for enhanced security in Tripoli specifically, and Libya generally. Recall the commander of the SST testified his 16-man force was available to respond to security threats in Benghazi (before State approved its withdrawal). And recollect also Ambassador Stevens took Tripoli security assets to Benghazi with him (and could have taken far more had his multiple requests for more security personnel at the Tripoli Embassy been granted).

Finally, let us remember the officials at State were uncertain for a time whether their department even would continue operating any facility in Benghazi past December 2012. This is another reason to place most of your security assets primarily in Tripoli, and take them to Benghazi *as needed*. (Of course, as discussed in previous chapters, this last fact changes when Hillary Clinton decides she wants to open a "permanent consulate" in Benghazi – a major reason Chris Stevens goes to Benghazi on dangerous September 11.)

The Libyan Guards Are Inadequate

The Benghazi ARB also finds that "reliance on February 17 for security in the event of an attack was misplaced . . ." The ARB Report states, "The Board found the responses by both the BML [Blue Mountain] guards and February 17 to be inadequate." The ARB finds "little evidence" the armed February 17 guards provided "any meaningful defense" or successfully summoned reinforcements from its militia members expeditiously. The ARB Report further concludes, "The four assigned February 17 guards were insufficient and did not have the requisite skills and reliability to provide a reasonable level of security on a 24/7 basis for an eight-acre compound with an extended

---

[2264] Benghazi ARB Report, Executive Overview, Finding 2 (emphasis added), p. 5.

perimeter wall. . . ." The ARB concluded the unarmed Blue Mountain guards "were also poorly skilled," and "found the responses by both [Blue Mountain] and February 17 to be inadequate" when the assault began.[2265] (There is not much doubt about this. But *whose idea* is it to hire these local Libyan guards? It is *Foggy Bottom's* idea, not the diplomats in Tripoli and Benghazi.)

It is unsurprising the ARB found security lapses in Benghazi. All previous ARBs have made such findings. The security consulting firm Stratfor describes the typical process:

> Predictably, the review boards, including Pickering's, always conclude that inadequate funding and insufficient security personnel are partly to blame for the security breaches. In response to the reports, Congress appropriates more money to diplomatic security programs to remedy the problem. Over time, funds are cut, and the cycle begins anew.[2266]

Failures of "Senior" State Management

As noted above, the ARB Report asserts, "The Board found that *certain senior State Department officials* within two bureaus in critical positions of authority and responsibility *in Washington demonstrated a lack of proactive leadership and management ability.*"[2267] The Board's Report similarly finds:

> *Systemic failures and leadership and management deficiencies* at *senior* levels within two bureaus of the State Department resulted in a Special Mission security posture that was inadequate for Benghazi and *grossly inadequate* to deal with the attack that took place.[2268]

These two bureaus are the Bureau of Diplomatic Security and the Bureau of Near Eastern Affairs. The former bureau is under the ultimate supervision of Under Secretary Patrick Kennedy.[2269] However, the ARB Report is silent on the identity of the responsible "senior" officials in these two bureaus! (Must not name names!)

[2265] *Id.*, Executive Overview, Finding 3, p. 6; *Id.*, Findings 2 and 3, pp. 32-33 and 35; and Benghazi ARB Report Briefing for the Media.

[2266] Stewart, The Benghazi Report and the Diplomatic Security Funding Cycle.

[2267] Benghazi ARB Report, Finding 5, p. 39.

[2268] *Id.*, Finding 2, p. 29.

[2269] House Foreign Affairs Benghazi Majority Staff Report, p. 6.

The U.S. Response Is "Appropriate"

The executive summary of the Benghazi ARB's report concludes, "The Board members believe every possible effort was made to rescue and recover Ambassador Stevens and Sean Smith."[2270] (This may have been true of most or all Americans inside Libya, but not of Americans elsewhere. As shown, by 9:46 p.m. Washington time at the latest, State has abandoned this goal of rescuing Stevens in Benghazi. The military has thrown in the Benghazi towel even earlier, by 8:53 p.m.[2271]

Later in its report the ARB clarifies that its conclusion regarding "every possible effort" pertains to the DSAs and Team Annex in their efforts to find Stevens and Smith inside the burning Villa.[2272] Hillary Clinton, the Department of Defense and some later media articles misleadingly will imply this ARB conclusion applies to *the entire U.S. government's efforts as a whole* on the Night of Benghazi![2273])

Almost offhandedly – *without citing any supporting evidence* – the ARB Report asserts, "The interagency response was timely and appropriate, but there simply was not enough time given the speed of the attacks for armed U.S. military assets to have made a

---

[2270] Benghazi ARB Report, Executive Overview, Finding 3, p. 7.

[2271] Key Delays Appendix (See September 11 entries at 8:53 p.m. and 9:46 p.m.); and Additional Views of Reps. Jordan and Pompeo ("The American people expect their government to make every effort to help those we put in harm's way when they find themselves in trouble. The U.S. military never sent assets to help rescue those fighting in Benghazi and never made it into Libya with personnel during the attack. And contrary to the administration's claim that it could not have landed in Benghazi in time to help, the administration never directed men or machines into Benghazi"), p. 416.

[2272] Benghazi ARB Report, Finding 3, p. 36.

[2273] E.g., Clinton, *Hard Choices*, Chap. 17, p. 409; Letter from Elizabeth L. King, Assistant Secretary of Defense for Legislative Affairs, to Rep. Elijah E. Cummings (D-MD) (May 7, 2013) (". . . [T]he time requirements for notification, load, and transit alone prevented the CIF from being at the [Benghazi CIA] Annex in time enough to change events. This analysis is consistent with the findings of the Accountability Review Board," citing ARB Report, p. 7), p. 1 n. 1; and Eugene Kiely, "Boehner and Benghazi," FactCheck.org (Feb. 17, 2015), reprinted in the following: "John Boehner Demands Answers for Benghazi Questions That Have Already Been Answered," *The Huffington Post* online (Feb. 17, 2015; Updated Dec. 6, 2017); "Fact Check: Boehner's 'Unanswered Questions' on Benghazi, *USA Today* online (Feb. 18, 2015). See also Alexis Simendinger, "IRS, Benghazi, AP: The Problems Pile Up for Obama," Real Clear Politics website (May 14, 2013).

difference."[2274] The evidence notwithstanding, in his memoir Panetta effectively endorses these fallacious ARB conclusions. He writes:

> ... [L]et me be crystal clear: We made every effort to help the U.S. personnel *in Benghazi*. I wish we could have saved them, and I am heartbroken that we could not. Nothing we say or do can ever bring them back to their loved ones, and all of us charged with defending the security of our country own that responsibility. But there was no conspiracy to sacrifice them and no conspiracy to cover up our actions. We did our best. Our best is not always enough. *That's been confirmed by the reports of the commission assigned to investigate the tragedy [referring to the ARB]* and by the Senate Intelligence Committee. The responsibility now, for both Democrats and Republicans, is to make sure it never happens again and to ensure that *those responsible* are brought to justice.[2275]

(Does "those responsible" include incompetent and negligent Pentagon and other U.S. government employees? To be charitable, the author notes Panetta's conclusions are written prior to the Select Benghazi Committee's report.)

Whether or not one agrees with the above dubious ARB assessments, the Board then goes out of its way to destroy its own credibility. Specifically, the ARB Report concludes:

> ... [T]he *safe evacuation of all U.S. government personnel* from *Benghazi* twelve hours after the initial attack and subsequently to Ramstein Air Force Base was the result of *exceptional U.S. Government coordination and military response* and helped save the lives of two severely wounded Americans. . . .[2276]

(Oh, *good grief!* The U.S. government's coordination and response is exceptional, alright – exceptionally *bad*. As we have demonstrated, this coordination among Team Obama's members (to the extent it is even attempted) is a disaster – both across agencies, and within the Defense Department itself. Moreover, it is only Team Tripoli, Team

---

[2274] Benghazi ARB Report, Finding 3, p. 37, and Executive Overview, p. 7; and Panetta, *Worthy Fights*, Chap. 16, p. 430.

[2275] Panetta, *Worthy Fights* (emphasis added), Chap. 16, p. 431.

[2276] Benghazi ARB Report, Finding 3 (emphasis added), p. 37, quoted at House Oversight Committee Hearings (May 8, 2013) (Remarks of Rep. Danny Davis (D-IL)), p. 87.

Annex and the staffs of the Tripoli Embassy and CIA offices in Tripoli and Benghazi that coordinate exceptionally well this night. The rest of the U.S. government's performance is *pathetic*.)

Moreover, the four dead Americans are *not* safely evacuated; their corpses are in body bags. (Correction: the evacuating Americans at Benghazi airport lack even enough blankets to cover Rone Woods' and Glen Doherty's bodies.) Only their remains are "safely evacuated."[2277]

The Board's conclusion the "military response" also was "exceptional" is similarly flawed. The Pentagon does not even know it has two military personnel on Team Tripoli until the battle is over. And AFRICOM orders four other special ops soldiers in that city not to go to Benghazi during the battle. The Libyan Military Intelligence group that transports the Americans to the Benghazi airport has no interaction with the U.S. military, which does not even know of LMI's existence until September 12, 2012. Finally, neither of the two aircraft that evacuate the Americans from Benghazi belongs to the U.S. government, much less to its military.

No Undue Delays

As if the Board is determined to shred any remaining particle of its trustworthiness, the ARB Report then preposterously concludes, "The Board found no evidence of any undue delays in decision making . . . *from Washington or from the military combatant commanders.*"[2278]

This claim is absurd on its face. For example, as the Select Committee's Report and this book document, the National Military Command Center is not alerted of the attack until *50 minutes* after the first assault. Panetta and Dempsey don't brief Obama until more than *75 minutes* into this attack. In the best case, SecDef Panetta and his advisers then take *another hour and one-half* to identify possible rescue forces. Panetta does not issue his verbal "deploy now" orders until more than *three hours* after the initial attack. It will be more than another *one and one-half hours* before those orders officially are conveyed in writing to the three chosen military forces.

[2277] House Oversight Committee Hearing (May 8, 2013) (Remarks of Rep. Jason Chaffetz (R-UT)) (". . . There are four people that were not safely evacuated" . . . "[W]e can't allow this ARB to say that everybody was safely evacuated, because they weren't. . . ."), p. 103.

[2278] Benghazi ARB Report, Finding 3 (emphasis added), p. 37.

The 7:30 Meeting alone lasts for *two hours!* The FAST Marines' C-130 aircraft does not even arrive in Rota, Spain for more than *14 hours* into the crisis. Then, they sit on a runway for another *four hours* before taking off – for Tripoli, *not Benghazi*. The military's medivac plane does not reach Tripoli until *over 19 hours* after the initial attack. Yet the Board cannot find any evidence of "undue delays"! (Dear ARB Members: Please see the Key Delays Appendix for a detailed summary of these and numerous further "undue delays" by the U.S. government on this Night of Benghazi.)

No Denial of Support

The ARB Report further states, "The Board found no evidence of ... denial of support from Washington or from the military combatant commanders."[2279] This claim also is flawed. In addition to the four special forces soldiers in Tripoli who are ordered not to fly to Benghazi, recall the U.S. jet fighters that never leave the runways at Souda Bay and Sigonella and Aviano. And what about the armed Predator drones that never are sent from the bases in southern Europe? Or the F.E.S.T. crisis-response team that never deploys?

Certainly there is no "denial of support" from the Americans in *Tripoli*. Quite the contrary. However, the three dozen Americans in Benghazi must think otherwise regarding Americans outside Libya. No support from Washington or the Defense Department or the CIA at Langley ever reaches them, or even is *ordered* to reach them. Only the self-directed Team Tripoli and the rogue Team Annex CIA security agents do.

(If the ARB members "found no evidence" on these key issues it can only be because they didn't *want* to find any. As the ARB findings summarized above make clear, the members of the Benghazi ARB have most of the administration's Benghazi Narrative down pat.)

The Administration Saves Lives?

Finally, Clinton's memoir claims the ARB Report found the response of the administration "saved American lives, and it did."[2280] The ARB didn't actually say that. The Board's report was referring to the laudable actions of medics and staff in Libya, and the military C-17

[2279] *Id.*, Finding 3, p. 37.

[2280] Clinton, *Hard Choices*, Chap. 17, p. 409.

evacuation, not to "the administration." Dave Ubben's and Oz Geist's lives are saved by the medics who treat them on the ground in Benghazi and during the flight to Tripoli, and by the medical staff on the C-17 medivac and at the hospitals in Tripoli and Ramstein.[2281]

(The author challenges Clinton to name a single other American in Benghazi whose life State – or anyone else on Team Obama – saves on this Night of Benghazi. Please, give us one name. The truth is the opposite. They abandon these Americans, and the survivors' lives are saved by other Americans – all of whom are in Libya or in Germany.)

The Libyan Government's Response Is Lacking

Although the ARB thinks the U.S. government did just fine on the Night of Benghazi, it reaches the opposite conclusion regarding the Libyan government. The ARB Report states, "The Board found the Libyan government's response to be *profoundly lacking* on the night of the attacks . . ." The Board attributes this to both "weak capacity" and a "near absence of central government influence and control in Benghazi."[2282] (This sounds about right.)

The ARB then erroneously over-credits the Libyan government with "facilitating assistance" with the Libyan Military Intelligence militia in evacuating the Americans from the Annex to the Benghazi airport. It also mistakenly describes the LMI as a "quasi-governmental militia," when in fact (as discussed in Chapter 82) LMI has no connection with the Libyan government.[2283] However, compared to the ARB's colossal mistakes on much more significant issues as demonstrated above, these errors seem trivial.

The ARB's Recommendations

Inconsistently, after finding deficiencies with *senior level* management, the Benghazi ARB Report concludes:

. . .[T]he Board did not find *that any individual U.S. Government employee* engaged in misconduct or willfully ignored his or her responsibilities, and, therefore did not find reasonable cause to believe that an individual breached his or

---

[2281] Benghazi ARB Report, pp. 27 and 37.

[2282] *Id.*, Executive Overview, Finding 3 (emphasis added), pp. 6-7.

[2283] *Id.*, Executive Overview, Finding 3, p. 7.

her duty so as to be the subject of a recommendation for disciplinary action."[2284]

(Note the sweeping scope of this absolution: it covers "*any individual U.S. Government employee.*" No one in the Obama administration screwed up regarding Benghazi! This is despite the fact the ARB supposedly only examines the performance of *State Department* personnel!)

Both Eric Nordstrom and Gregory Hicks later will testify they believe the relevant security decisions are made at a level more senior than Assistant Secretary and below. Nordstrom believes the ARB "absolutely" ignores many of State's higher-level decision makers.[2285] *Nordstrom explicitly names Patrick Kennedy as the official responsible for many of these fateful security decisions concerning Benghazi.*[2286]

Although Hicks and Nordstrom do not say it explicitly, the author will: *It is inconceivable the ARB does not recommend Under Secretary Patrick Kennedy's dismissal.* The State Department later will claim the ARB lacks the authority to recommend anyone's termination.[2287] (This is silly; the ARB can recommend any damned thing it wants to. Who in the world can prevent them? Will someone arrest or fine them?) However, the ARB statute only requires the Board to find an individual has "engaged in misconduct or *unsatisfactorily performed the duties of employment* of that individual," and that this has contributed to the serious "breach of security" being investigated.[2288] While this is a fairly high bar, it manifestly is cleared by such State officials as Kennedy and

---

[2284] *Id.*, Finding 5, p. 39, and Executive Overview, Finding 5, p. 7.

[2285] Nordstrom and Hicks Oversight Committee Testimony (May 8, 2013) (Response to questions of Rep. Mark Meadows (R-NC)), p. 92; and *Id.* (". . . I don't believe it is fair [that all the blame is assigned to the Diplomatic Security component]. . . . I think that certainly those resource determinations are made by the Under Secretary for Management. . . . I mean you affix blame for the three people underneath the Under Secretary for Management, but nothing to him. So that either means he didn't know what was going on with his subordinates or he did and didn't care"), pp. 92-93.

[2286] *Id.* (Response to questions of Rep. Tammy Duckworth (D-IL)) ("It's not lost on me that . . . I look at where those [security recommendation] messages seem to stop: the Under Secretary for Management. . . ."); and *Id.* (Response to questions of Rep. James Lankford (R-OK)) (". . . [S]o many of these decisions [concerning security requests] seem to be at Ambassador Kennedy's level or higher. . . ."), p. 108.

[2287] See, e.g., Nordstrom Oversight Committee Testimony (May 8, 2013) (Response to questions of Rep. Mark Meadows (R-NC)); and Gibbons Aug. 23, 2013 Letter to Chairman Issa, p. 2.

[2288] Title 22, United States Code, Section 4834(c) (emphasis added).

Lamb. Sadly, Patrick Kennedy will remain as Under Secretary for Management for the next four years.

An Oversight Committee member later asks Nordstrom and Hicks what message this ARB conclusion regarding who at State is responsible for Benghazi sends to the agency's employees. Nordstrom dramatically replies:

> I think the basic message is that whether or not you are sitting out at the post requesting resources, preparing for testimony before this committee, or standing on a building surrounded by an armed mob attacking you, the message is the same: *You are on your own.*

Greg Hicks concurs in Nordstrom's assessment.[2289]

The Benghazi ARB comes up with 29 specific recommendations to address the many security deficiencies the Board has identified. (The unclassified version of the ARB Report contains only 24 of these.[2290]) These include:

- "... [U]rgently review[ing] the proper balance between acceptable risk and expected outcomes in high risk, high threat areas";
- Adopting new State procedures and standards to address "high risk, high threat posts," including combating fire as a weapon and extending minimum tour-of-duty assignments;
- Procuring critical security assets, including increased diplomatic security personnel;
- Working with Defense to deploy more Marine security guard detachments to diplomatic facilities;
- Expanding Arabic language training of diplomats;
- Co-locating all State and other government agencies' facilities in the same metropolitan areas (unless a waiver is approved); and
- Securing more funding for embassy security.[2291]

Fortunately, the ARB's recommendations are far superior to its factual findings.

[2289] Nordstrom Oversight Committee Testimony (May 8, 2013) (Response to questions of Rep. John Mica (R-FL)) (emphasis added), p. 110; and Hicks Oversight Committee Testimony (May 8, 2013) (Response to questions of Rep. John Mica (R-FL)) ("I share what Mr. Nordstrom had to say"), p. 110.

[2290] Benghazi ARB Report Briefing for the Media.

[2291] Benghazi ARB Report, Key Recommendations, pp. 8-12; Benghazi ARB Report Briefing for the Media; and Gibbons Aug. 23, 2013 Letter to Chairman Issa, p. 1.

State's Reaction to the ARB Report

Secretary Clinton releases a statement responding to the ARB Report. She "embraces" all 29 of the Board's proposals. She also sets up an "Implementation Team" to effectuate them. She creates a new position within the Diplomatic Security Bureau, a "Deputy Assistant Secretary of State for High Threat Posts." She also announces she will ask Congress for more money for diplomatic security.[2292]

In contrast to the ARB Report (which can't find the heart to recommend discipline for anyone), the State Department sanctions four *mid-level* career State officials (all later rescinded). However, it fails to hold any of State's *senior-level officials or political appointees* accountable.[2293] Secretary Clinton places the four employees – including Charlene Lamb – on *paid* administrative leave, where they will remain for eight months. Aside from Lamb, these suspended officials are: Eric Boswell, Assistant Secretary for Diplomatic Security; Scott Bultrowicz, Director of Diplomatic Security Service; and Raymond D. Maxwell, a twenty-year foreign service officer who then is serving as Deputy Assistant Secretary of State for Maghreb Affairs. Three of the four (all except Maxwell) are subordinates of – yup – Patrick Kennedy.[2294]

[2292] "Secretary Clinton's Response to the Accountability Review Board Report" (Undated), State Dept. Archives website.

[2293] Nordstrom Oversight Committee Testimony (May 8, 2013) (Response to questions of Rep. John Duncan, Jr. (R-TN)) ("... [A]s Ambassador Pickering said, he has decided to fix responsibility on the Assistant Secretary level and below. How I see that is, that's fine. It's an accountability of mid-level officer review board and the message to my colleagues is that if you are above a certain level, no matter what your decision is, no one is going to question it. And that is my concern with the ARB"), p. 56; House Oversight Committee Hearings (May 8, 2013) (Remarks of Rep. John Mica (R-FL)) ("... Finally, for the ARB, you put in here to ignore the role ... senior department leadership played before, during and after the September 11th attack sends a clear message to all State Department employees. It looks like they are whitewashing the folks at the higher pay grades and levels and you all [the witnesses] are taking the blame...."), p. 110; *Id.* (Response to questions of Rep. Mark Meadows (R-NC)), p. 92; and Attkisson, Benghazi Accountability Review Board Comes Under Renewed Criticism (A House Oversight Committee "report says that the fact that the ARB recommended discipline for officials who later were cleared of breaching their duties calls into question the ARB's findings and the State Department's 'faith in the work of the ARB'").

[2294] Benghazi Committee Report, Appendix K, p. 636; "Kerry Clears 4 State Staffers Put on Leave Over Benghazi Attack to Return to Work," CBS News online (Aug. 20,

(The senior officials screw up big time, so let's punish the mid-level guys. Guess we know in what direction crap flows in Washington, D.C. – *downhill!* The four employees are given no due process rights, and have no right to appeal their suspension. Maxwell insists, "I had no involvement to any degree with decisions on security and the funding of security at our diplomatic mission in Benghazi." While on leave, Maxwell writes several poems implying he unfairly has been made a scapegoat.[2295] (Sounds right.) According to the majority staff report of the House Foreign Affairs Committee, Maxwell appears to have had "no role in the review or approval of recommendations related to security in Libya." Maxwell's "immediate superior" confirms this.[2296] According to supervisor, Beth Jones, the ARB interviews her twice, but never even asks her about Maxwell![2297] (Maxwell barely warrants mention in the nearly 1,000 pages of the Select Committee's reports.) Of the four sanctioned, only Charlene Lamb and possibly Eric Boswell appear to have significant culpability for the Benghazi debacle.)

Hillary Clinton's successor as Secretary of State, John Kerry, later reinstates all four of the individuals. He asserts none of them "breached their duty or should be fired...." State later will advise Congress, "Consistent with the findings of the Benghazi ARB, the Department has determined that there was no breach of duty and no basis to pursue formal disciplinary action." However, when they return to State all four are reassigned to other positions that do not involve diplomatic security.[2298] (Good idea.)

2013); Gibbons Aug. 23, 2013 Letter to Chairman Issa, p. 2; and Attkisson, Benghazi Accountability Review Board Comes Under Renewed Criticism.

[2295] *Id.*, Appendix K, pp. 636-637; and Guy Benson, "Hillary's Benghazi Scapegoat," Townhall.com website (May 21, 2013) ("... To this day, he [Maxwell] says, nobody from the State Department has ever told him why he was singled out for discipline"). One of Maxwell's poems is entitled "Trapped in a purgatory of their own deceit." For samples, see Sharyl Attkisson, "Benghazi-Disciplined Diplomat a Prolific Poet," CBS News online (May 19, 2013).

[2296] House Foreign Affairs Benghazi Majority Staff Report, p. 13; and Sharyl Attkisson, "Benghazi-Disciplined Diplomat a Prolific Poet," CBS News online (May 19, 2013) ("It's unclear as to exactly what Maxwell and the other disciplined managers allegedly did wrong or how they were chosen for discipline").

[2297] House Oversight Interim Report on Benghazi ARB, pp. 53-55.

[2298] Gibbons Aug. 23, 2013 Letter to Chairman Issa, pp. 2-3; "Kerry Clears 4 State Staffers Put on Leave Over Benghazi Attack to Return to Work," CBS News online (Aug. 20, 2013); and Attkisson, Benghazi Accountability Review Board Comes Under Renewed Criticism.

Clinton's memoir will claim all ARB recommendations are being addressed by the time she leaves Foggy Bottom on February 1, 2013. By August 2013, the State Department also claims it "has taken action to substantially address all of the ARB's recommendations."[2299]

The ARB's Alleged "Independence"

The Select Committee Democrat minority,[2300] other Democrats in Congress,[2301] Hillary Clinton,[2302] her State Department,[2303] and the mainstream media and others supporting the Obama administration,[2304] repeatedly will refer to the Benghazi ARB as an "independent"

[2299] Clinton, *Hard Choices*, Chap. 17, pp. 409-410; Press Release, State Dept. website (Jan. 31, 2013); and Gibbons Aug. 23, 2013 Letter to Chairman Issa, p. 1.

[2300] Benghazi Committee Report, Minority Report ("... [T]he evidence obtained by the Select Committee demonstrates that the ARB members conducted their investigation with complete independence, thoroughness, and patriotism. Their final report was piercing and penetrating, assigning accountability where it was due ..."), p. 803.

[2301] E.g., House Oversight Committee Hearings (May 8, 2013) (Remarks of Rep. Elijah E. Cummings (D-MD) (referencing ARB's "thorough independent investigation"), p. 101.

[2302] Clinton, *Hard Choices* (emphasis added) (referencing "the *independent* review board charged with determining the facts and *pulling no punches*"), Chap. 17, p. 385; and *Id.* ("... an independent Accountability Review Board ...").

[2303] E.g., Daily Press Briefing by Deputy Spokesperson Marie Harf, State Dept. Archives website (Sept. 19, 2013) (emphasis added) ("... [W]e need to focus on the Accountability Review Board, who [sic] *took an independent, objective look* at what happened, and now focus, quite frankly, on moving forward to enhance our security and, hopefully, prevent situations ... like this from happening in the future.... In short, *there is no question that it was independent*"); and Herridge, Classified Cable Warned Consulate Couldn't Withstand Coordinated Attack (emphasis added) (State Department Deputy Spokesman Mark Toner regarding a classified cable discussing security in Benghazi: "An *independent board* is conducting a thorough review of the assault on our post in Benghazi. Once we have the board's comprehensive account of what happened, findings and recommendations, we can fully address these matters") (*Watch video* there).

[2304] E.g., Olivia Marshall, "How the Newest House Benghazi Report Should Change Media's Approach to Gowdy's Select Committee," Media Matters for America website (Aug. 4, 2014) (referencing State's "independent" Accountability Review Board); and Herb, House to Hear Long-Sought Testimony About Benghazi From Task Force Chief ("... [A]n independent review board released its findings").

body.[2305] However, numerous facts discussed above strongly indicate otherwise. They include:

- The Secretary of State selects four of five Board Members;
- Normal procedures to nominate Board Members are bypassed; Clinton's senior staff controls the selection process and other aspects of the inquiry;
- Patrick Kennedy recommends at least one (and possibly two) of the five Board Members;
- Only State's career staff – all overseen by Kennedy – is used to assist the Board Members;
- Kennedy approves which State employees are assigned as ARB staff;
- Former Clinton aide Uzra Zeya plays a key role in supervising this staff;
- Clinton Chief of Staff Cheryl Mills oversees the collection and review of relevant documents, and apparently determines which ones are available to the ARB;
- Mills has input into who is interviewed;
- The manner in which the ARB conducts its inquiry, including a failure to interview many key high officials, including Clinton and Mills;
- The Board provides an interim briefing to Clinton and Mills; and
- Mills is given an advance copy of the draft ARB Report, and "suggests" proposed edits.

Given these and other related facts, the Benghazi ARB seems anything but independent.[2306]

[2305] E.g., Herridge, Classified Cable Warned Consulate Couldn't Withstand Coordinated Attack (Quoting State Department Deputy Spokesman Mark Toner: "An independent board is conducting a thorough review of the assault on our post in Benghazi. . . ."); Catherine Chomiak, "Benghazi Report: 'Grossly Inadequate' Security but Also 'Remarkable Heroism,'" MSNBC online (Dec. 19, 2012; Updated Sept. 13, 2013) ("An independent Accountability Review Board . . ."); and Eugene Kiely, "Boehner and Benghazi," FactCheck.org (Feb. 17, 2015) ("an independent board"; "the independent Accountability Review Board"), reprinted at "John Boehner Demands Answers for Benghazi Questions That Have Already Been Answered," *The Huffington Post* online (Feb. 17, 2015; Updated Dec. 6, 2017). See also Blake Hounshell, "Benghazi Panel Rebuts Conspiracy Theorists," ForeignPolicy.com website (Dec. 19, 2012) (referring to Benghazi ARB Report as "an independent look" at Benghazi).

[2306] See, e.g., House Foreign Affairs Benghazi Majority Staff Report (The ARB "Was assisted by State Department employees, raising concerns about the ARB's independence. . . . [It] is questionable whether it was appropriate for the Department to

The Benghazi Select Committee similarly concludes:
Notwithstanding the processes already in place [under which "career personnel" oversee the conduct of an ARB inquiry], the Secretary's senior staff oversaw the Benghazi ARB process from start to finish. The senior staff's participation ranged from selecting the ARB members to shaping the ARB's outcome by editing the draft final report. The decisions to deviate from longstanding processes raise questions about the ARB's independence, thoroughness, and therefore the fullness of their findings of accountability.[2307]

Responding to this lack of objectivity, Congressman Trey Gowdy (R-SC) reportedly observes:
There's a reason that students don't grade their own papers. There's a reason defendants don't sentence themselves. And there's the [sic] reason the State Department doesn't get to investigate itself, determine whether or not it made errors in Benghazi. That is Congress's job.[2308]

Conclusions Regarding the ARB Report

Whether one believes the Benghazi ARB fairly can be viewed as "independent," for the reasons summarized above many of the slapdash ARB Report's key conclusions clearly are erroneous. The Report is little more than a whitewash.[2309] (We did not get our "money's worth.")

---

assign them to what should be an 'independent' investigative panel...."), p. 15; and Rachael Bade, "What Cheryl Mills Told Benghazi Investigators," POLITICO website (Sept. 3, 2015) ("One of the biggest surprises to the right was that she [Cheryl Mills] said she made suggestions to change State's accountability review board report. The report was supposed to be independent from state officials that may be involved, and the GOP argues top officials should not have had input, long questioning how independent the findings were").

[2307] Benghazi Committee Report, Appendix K, p. 617.

[2308] "Trey Gowdy Quotes," BrainyQuote.com website.

[2309] E.g., Benson, "Yes, Hillary's Benghazi 'Investigation' Was a Whitewash" (citing House Oversight Committee, "The State Department's investigation into the Sept. 11, 2012 attack on the U.S. mission in Benghazi was not independent and failed to hold senior State Department officials accountable for the failures that led to the death of four Americans . . ."); and Toensing, Administration Relying on Shoddy Benghazi Report to Absolve Itself of Blame (". . . In fact, the [ARB] report was purposefully incomplete and willfully misleading. . . . Instead of letting the facts lead the direction of the investigation, the report appears designed to protect the interests of Hillary Clinton, the State Department higher ups, and the president. . . . [T]he ARB's shoddy report is

Naturally, the State Department disputes this.[2310] General Martin Dempsey, incompetent Chairman of the Joint Chiefs, also praises the ARB's work.[2311]

It will be three and one-half years before numerous of the ARB's errors are put to rest by the Benghazi Select Committee's far more authoritative and accurate report. (And, of course, still later by this book. Perhaps in retrospect we should not call it the "ARB Report." We should call it the "Kennedy-Mills Report.") ∎

---

an insult to the memory of four dead Americans. . . ."; Note: Toensing is legal counsel for Gregory Hicks).

[2310] See, e.g., Jennifer Ruben, "Ambassador Thomas Pickering: There Is No Equal," *The Washington Post* online (May 24, 2013) (Speaking of Pickering's work on the ARB investigation, "In a milieu where double-talk, evasion and protecting the powerful are rewarded there is no one better. . . [H]e's a trusted ally of the Foggy Bottom set, knowing just how to handle unpleasantries like the death of four Americans, including an ambassador"); and Daily Press Briefing by Deputy Spokesperson Marie Harf, State Dept. Archives website (Sept. 19, 2013) (". . . The ARB's work has been described by those who appeared before it as penetrating, specific, critical, . . . very tough . . . and, quote, 'the opposite of a whitewash'").

[2311] Prepared Statement of Gen. Martin Dempsey, Chairman, Joint Chiefs of Staff, before Sen. Armed Services Committee (Feb. 7, 2013) ("I commend Ambassador Tom Pickering and my predecessor Admiral Mike Mullen for their valuable work"), pp. 4-5.

110

Speak No Evil

In early 2013, something odd happens regarding Benghazi. A State Department official allegedly will try to muzzle a private security firm to prevent it from discussing Benghazi with U.S. officials or reporters.

As noted above (see Chapters 19 and 20), Torres Advanced Enterprise Solutions ("Torres AES") is a private embassy security provider. Torres is an unsuccessful bidder in January 2012 for the security contract at the Benghazi Mission Compound. Also recall that in late August 2012 – just two weeks before the terrorist attacks – the State Department allegedly has second thoughts and asks Torres AES to take over security at this Mission from the U.K.'s Blue Mountain Group, which originally won the contract.

Fast forward five years. In September 2017, officials at Torres AES will claim sometime in early 2013 a State Department official "absolutely" directs them to remain silent regarding the attacks on the Benghazi Mission. Jerry Torres, CEO of Torres AES, will claim to Fox News that in "early 2013" Jan Visintainer, the State Department's security contract officer responsible for the Benghazi Mission, meets with Torres face-to-face in the lobby of a State Department building in Rosslyn, Virginia (across the Potomac River from Washington). Visintainer allegedly instructs Torres that he and his firm should not talk to the media *or government officials* about "the Benghazi program"! Torres claims to Fox that Visintainer "absolutely" is attempting to silence him.[2312]

(Back in December 2013, when asked earlier at a State Department press briefing about a report of this alleged attempt by Visintainer to "muzzle" Torres AES, a State spokesperson nimbly dances the "Potomac two-step" and largely evades the question. While pleading ignorance of some of the facts, State's Marie Harf suggests it is "standard practice" for State to ask its contractors to refer *media*

[2312] Catherine Herridge Report, "Happening Now," Fox News online (Sept. 13, 2017); and Herridge et al., Clinton State Department Silenced Them on Benghazi Security Lapses, Contractors Say (*Watch video there*).

inquiries regarding the contractors' work for State to that agency.[2313] However, even if accurate regarding media inquiries, this facile response does not answer whether State asks Torres AES not to talk to *government* officials about Benghazi and, if so, whether this is appropriate or legal.)

For the next five years, Torres AES claims it acquiesces in Visintainer's directive. Jerry Torres explains the livelihood of Torres AES's 8,000 employees depends on his company continuing to do business with the State Department.[2314]

If true, these warnings by Visintainer raise a serious legal issue whether she has attempted to commit obstruction of Congress[2315] and perhaps obstruction of justice,[2316] both federal felonies. As discussed above (Chapter 105), the FBI probe has commenced by September 15, 2012, and will last for years. Several congressional investigations also already are underway, including the House Oversight Committee's probe, which is quite active by October 2012. (In contrast, the Select Benghazi Committee is not even created until 2014, and will not finish its work until July 2016. As noted in the previous chapter, the ARB already has finished its lame "investigation" by mid-December 2012.)

In this same interview in September 2017, Jerry Torres further tells Fox News that in early 2013 Jan Visintainer also asks Torres to support Visintainer's position that local guards at State Department "embassies" should not be armed.[2317]

[2313] Daily Press Briefing by Marie Harf, Deputy Spokesperson, State Dept. Archives website (Dec. 12, 2013).

[2314] Catherine Herridge Exclusive Report, "Tucker Carlson Tonight," Fox News Channel (Sept. 12, 2017); and Herridge et al., Clinton State Department Silenced Them on Benghazi Security Lapses, Contractors Say (*Watch video there*).

[2315] See Title 18, United States Code, Section 1505 ("... Whoever corruptly ... influences, obstructs, or impedes or endeavors to influence, obstruct, or impede ... the due and proper exercise of the power of inquiry under which any inquiry or investigation is being had by either House, or any committee of either House or any joint committee of the Congress – Shall be fined under this title, imprisoned not more than 5 years ..., or both").

[2316] See Title 18, United States Code, Section 1505 ("... Whoever corruptly ... influences, obstructs, or impedes or endeavors to influence, obstruct, or impede the due and proper administration of the law under which any pending proceeding is being had before any department or agency of the United States ... Shall be fined under this title, imprisoned not more than 5 years ..., or both").

[2317] Herridge et al., Clinton State Department Silenced Them on Benghazi Security Lapses, Contractors Say (*Watch video* there).

THE TRUE ACCOUNT OF VALOR AND ABANDONMENT

Is this Torres AES story true? Does it happen? It is a bit odd to see why State should attempt to muzzle Torres AES *after* President Obama has won reelection, and the Accountability Review Board at State has finished its work. As explained earlier, Torres AES may be motivated by sour grapes at having lost numerous subsequent bidding contests for State Department facilities abroad.

On the other hand, Jerry Torres claims he comes forward in 2017 because a new administration is in place. Also, with Hillary Clinton no longer involved in government, the politics supposedly have been removed from the Benghazi saga.[2318] (Then why does Torres wait for seven months after Donald Trump is inaugurated, and nine months after Clinton loses her election bid?) Torres' story certainly is consistent with other after-the-fact Herculean efforts of Team Obama to minimize the adverse political fallout emanating from the Benghazi debacle.[2319] With the true facts under a cloud, for the present this alleged incident must remain yet another unresolved issue concerning the Benghazi tragedy.

In any event, the Trump administration's new Secretary of State, Mike Pompeo, should order an investigation of these very serious allegations of Torres AES (and Judicial Watch) against the Obama State Department. ∎

[2318] *Id.* (*Watch video* there).

[2319] E.g., Hayes, The Benghazi Talking Points ("Senior administration officials . . . sought to obscure the emerging picture and downplay the significance of attacks that killed a U.S. ambassador and three other Americans").

111

The Congressional Investigations

Naturally, in addition to the Benghazi ARB Congress also investigates Benghazi. Again and again. And it sorely deserves to be investigated. It is, after all, a major foreign policy and national security catastrophe for America. Not to mention a huge international embarrassment.

In the week after the attacks the Obama administration attempts to limit the likelihood and extent of congressional inquiries by sending Team Obama up to "The Hill" to brief members of Congress. Secretary of State Clinton and numerous defense, intelligence, national security and law enforcement officials brief the entire Senate and House of Representatives, and respond to their questions.[2320]

It doesn't work. Many in Congress aren't satisfied with the administration's answers. There are too many contradictions, gaps in knowledge, circumlocutions, inconsistencies and logic-defying assertions. Congress decides to investigate for itself. Eight different congressional committees eventually will investigate aspects of the Benghazi tragedy. (Isn't *that* efficient? After six, do we get eggrolls?) Because we already have cited and quoted the resulting congressional reports hundreds of times in this book, we summarize only a selection of these inquiries very briefly here.

Benghazi is so serious and so obviously tragic and mismanaged, and the administration so clearly is systematically misleading our people, that it deserves an immediate, joint select committee comprised of both Senators and representatives to conduct one, broad, exhaustive investigation. (But this would have required principled, decisive, courageous leadership from the Republican and Democrat leaders in Congress. This is something as rare as purple unicorns.)

When the Benghazi tragedy occurs, the American national government is divided politically. The Democrats control the White House and the Senate, while the Republicans rule the House of Representatives. Hence, the Senate committees investigating Benghazi predictably lean toward defending the Obama administration's response

---

[2320] Clinton, *Hard Choices*, Chap. 17, pp. 410-411.

to Benghazi, while the House panels naturally tend to attack Team Obama's actions concerning the crisis. Unsurprisingly, this gulf is especially wide in a presidential election season such as that existing in fall 2012. This sharp political divide goes far in explaining some of the dramatically different approaches and conclusions regarding Benghazi reached in the two houses of Congress.

During these congressional inquiries, in addition to attempting to prevent a recurrence of the tragedy, the Republicans tend to focus on what went wrong in Benghazi and who is responsible.[2321] In contrast, like a broken record (the author is dating himself) the Democrats emphasize ensuring "it" never happens again, without addressing who or what caused "it" in the first place.[2322]

[2321] E.g., Thomson / Reuters, "Whistleblower's Emotional Testimony on Benghazi: More Could Have Been Done," NewsMax.com website (May 8, 2013) ("Republicans focused their criticism on security, early accounts of the report and the conduct of the [ARB] investigation, such as witness Eric Nordstrom not being questioned by the board probing Benghazi although he had first-hand knowledge of the attacks"); House Oversight Committee Hearings (May 8, 2013) (Remarks of Chairman Darrell Issa (R-CA)) (". . . We . . . want to make certain that our government learns the proper lessons from this tragedy so it never happens again and so that the right people are held accountable"), p. 2; *Id.* (Remarks of Rep. Scott DesJarlais (R-TN)), p. 77; *Id.* (Remarks of Rep. Blake Farenthold (R-TX)), p. 81; *Id.* (Remarks of Rep. Doug Collins (R-GA)), pp. 89-90; *Id.* (Remarks of Rep. Kerry Bentivolio (R-MI)), p. 93; and *Id.* (Remarks of Rep. Ron DeSantis (R-FL)), p. 95.

[2322] E.g., Kennedy House Oversight Prepared Testimony (". . . [W]e are here today to answer your questions and participate in a constructive discussion about *how we can mitigate the risk of this tragedy ever happening again*. . . "), p. 1; Fox News, Pfeiffer May 2013 Interview with Wallace (emphasis added) (". . . And so the question here is not what happened that night. The question is what are we going to do to move forward and *ensure that this doesn't happen again*") (*Watch video there*; Go to 1:12-18 and 2:25-28); House Oversight Committee Hearings (May 8, 2013) (Remarks of Ranking Member Elijah Cummings (D-MD)) (emphasis added) (". . . And we'll hopefully be getting that complete picture very soon so that we can get to the point that we . . . reform so that these kinds of things *are prevented from happening again*"), p. 101; *Id.*, p. 30; *Id.* (Remarks of Rep. John Tierney (D-MA)), p. 42; *Id.* (Remarks of Rep. Jackie Speier (D-CA)), p. 57; *Id.* (Remarks of Rep. Mark Pocan (D-WI)), p. 60; *Id.* (Remarks of Rep. Tammy Duckworth (D-IL)), pp. 63-64; *Id.* (Remarks of Rep. Steven Horsford (D-NV)), p. 71; and *Id.* (Remarks of Rep. Tony Cardenas (D-CA)), p. 77. See also Interview of Tommy Vietor with Brett Baier, "Special Report," Fox News Channel (May 1, 2014) (emphasis added) (". . . What we should be worried about is making sure that [an ambassador's death] *never happens again*. . . .") (*Watch video there*; Go to 4:25-44); and Panetta, *Worthy Fights*, Chap. 16, p. 431 (emphasis added) (". . . The responsibility now, for both Democrats and Republicans, is to *make sure it never happens again* and to ensure that those responsible are brought to justice").

Foolishly, Speaker John Boehner (R-OH) and other weak Republican leaders in control of the House of Representatives approach their inquires in a disjointed, scattershot, jurisdictionally-limited and half-hearted fashion.[2323] Like the ARB inquiry (focusing almost entirely on State's conduct), the various different congressional inquiries are "stove-piped": each committee's focus is constrained severely by its own jurisdictional limitations. (For example, the House and Senate Intelligence Committees principally investigate possible *intelligence failures* involved in the tragedy. Only cursorily or tangentially do they address White House or Pentagon or other military or diplomatic or political failures or other such issues.[2324] Similarly, the Armed Services panels concentrate on the military response. However, to their credit, five House committees investigating Benghazi – Foreign Affairs, Oversight, Intelligence, Judiciary and Armed Services – at least combine their investigative staffs in a joint effort.)[2325]

However, as this book demonstrates, many pieces of the Benghazi Narrative are interconnected. (Hip bone connected to the thigh bone.) For example, the White House (including NSC) oversees all involved agencies; DoD provides military resources to State before and after (but not during) the attacks; DoD ostensibly prepares to send military assets to "protect" or "rescue" (or something) the State and CIA personnel under assault; and the CIA and the rest of the intelligence community provide their product to everyone involved – before, during and after the attacks. Perhaps most critically, as we have demonstrated the NSC and State officials severely constrain the military's actions on the Night

---

[2323] E.g., *Wall Street Journal* Opinion, The Missing Benghazi Email (". . . Congressional Republicans have been less than skillful in their probes. . . . The several congressional investigations into Benghazi have been undermined by turf battles and shoddy work. We long ago advised that a select committee could focus the effort and bring overdue clarity to a shameful episode in American history. . . .").

[2324] E.g., Sen. Intelligence Committee Benghazi Report (emphasis added) (This report ". . . *focuses primarily* on the analysis by and actions of the Intelligence Community (IC) leading up to, during, and immediately following the attacks. The report also addresses, *as appropriate*, other issues about the attacks as they relate to the Department of Defense . . . and Department of State . . ."), p. 1; House Intelligence Committee Benghazi Report, Executive Summary (Nov. 21, 2014) ("The nearly two-year investigation focused on the activities of the Intelligence Community ("IC") before, during, and after the attacks"), p. 1; and *Id.*, Introduction ("As the Committee focused its review on the U.S. Intelligence Community, this report does not assess State Department or Defense Department activities other than where those activities impact, or were impacted by, the work of the Intelligence Community"), p. 3.

[2325] House Foreign Affairs Benghazi Majority Staff Report, p. 7.

of Benghazi. These separate components must be viewed as part of an entire mosaic, as we have attempted to do in this book. It is a serious mistake for Congress to seek to investigate and analyze separate portions of the tragedy in isolation. (But then, the U.S. Congress is renowned for such epic blunders, no matter which political party is in control of which house.)

We summarize in this chapter just some of the messy results of this fragmented, scattershot approach by Congress.

The Senate Foreign Relations Committee

This panel has principal Senate jurisdiction over matters concerning the U.S. State Department. Members of this committee receive at least two classified briefings on Benghazi by administration officials. This panel also receives a classified briefing by the Benghazi Accountability Review Board. Beginning in December 2012, this committee will hold several public hearings on Benghazi.[2326] As in many other cases, Secretary of State Clinton is a principal witness. Indeed, it is at one of these hearings Clinton will utter her infamous "What difference, at this point, does it make?" question.

By May 2013, this committee's chairman, Senator Robert Menendez (D-NJ), has had enough of Benghazi. On the Senate floor he proclaims, "We have fully vetted this issue."[2327] The same month, Menendez introduces the "Embassy Security and Personnel Protection Act of 2013." It is intended to implement many of the Benghazi ARB Report's 29 recommendations.[2328] The measure is approved by

---

[2326] Statement of Chairman Robert Menendez (D-NJ), "Menendez Speaks Out on Benghazi: 'We Have Fully Vetted This Issue," Senate Foreign Relations Committee website (May 16, 2013).

[2327] Statement of Chairman Robert Menendez (D-NJ), "Menendez Speaks Out on Benghazi: 'We Have Fully Vetted This Issue," Senate Foreign Relations Committee website (May 16, 2013) ("I would remind my friends – and the American people, nothing has changed. The facts remain the facts. They're the same today as they were in September, October, November, December and January – it's the rhetoric and the political calculus that has changed").

[2328] Press Release, "Menendez Introduces Embassy Security and Personnel Protection Act of 2013," Senate Foreign Relations Committee website (May 16, 2013).

the full Foreign Relations Committee in August 2013.[2329] It will not become law.

The House Foreign Affairs Committee

On the House side, its Foreign Affairs Committee also investigates the Benghazi tragedy. This panel holds four hearings from November 2012 through September 2013. High-level State Department witnesses include Secretary Clinton, Deputy Secretaries Nides and Burns, and Undersecretary for Management Patrick Kennedy. Two classified briefings are held for committee members. The panel claims it reviews 25,000 pages of documents, albeit under "highly restrictive circumstances," interviews numerous witnesses, and issues 14 requests for information to various government agencies.[2330] As noted, the committee's investigative staff works in conjunction with the staffs of four other House panels investigating the Benghazi crisis.[2331]

Apparently on September 19, 2013, the committee releases a 29-page report prepared by the panel's majority (i.e., Republican) staff members. (Why the full committee itself does not issue this report is unclear.) The investigation, and the report, principally focus on the State Department's actions relating to Benghazi – particularly on the lack of accountability of senior State officials and the flaws in the Benghazi ARB Report.[2332] The most significant of this report's findings are referenced in previous chapters, and need not be repeated here. One of the more insightful findings in this report, however, is that during the deteriorating security situation in Libya the CIA Annex in Benghazi *increases* its security, while State *decreases* its security in Libya overall.[2333] (Why is it these two sister agencies – reading the same intelligence reports and located less than a mile apart in the same city in eastern Libya – can't get on the same page on security?)

[2329] Press Release, "Bipartisan Embassy Security, Threat Mitigation and Personnel Protection Act of 2013 Passes Senate Foreign Relations Committee," Senate Foreign Relations Committee website (Aug. 2, 2013).

[2330] House Foreign Affairs Benghazi Majority Staff Report, pp. 7 and 21.

[2331] *Id.*, p. 7.

[2332] *Id.*, pp. 2-5.

[2333] *Id.*, p. 8.

THE TRUE ACCOUNT OF VALOR AND ABANDONMENT

The Intelligence Committee Investigations

The House Committee

The House Intelligence Committee Chairman, Mike Rogers (R-MI), and Ranking Democrat Member, C.A. Dutch Ruppersberger (D-MD), issue a report on Benghazi in November 2014. Although the full committee does not issue this report, it nonetheless purports to summarize the findings of "the Committee."[2334] Also, the intelligence committees (like other congressional panels at the time) reportedly do not obtain the videos of the Predator drone feeds that record much of the Battle of Benghazi, and do not interview the operators of these two unmanned aircraft.[2335]

This House committee report (including its timeline[2336]) contains numerous factual errors and omissions.[2337] Accordingly, we do not rely upon it to any significant extent. Among other findings, this report by Rogers and his Democrat counterpart contains the following conclusions:

- There is no intelligence failure prior to the attacks;
- A "mixed group of individuals," including those affiliated with al Qaeda, perpetrates the attacks;
- After the attacks, early intelligence assessments and the Obama administration's "initial public narrative" are "not fully accurate";

[2334] House Intelligence Committee Benghazi Report, Executive Summary (Nov. 21, 2014), pp. 1-2.

[2335] Interview of Unnamed U.S. Serviceman with Sean Hannity.

[2336] House Intelligence Committee Benghazi Report, Timeline of Events (Nov. 21, 2014), pp. 4-6.

[2337] E.g., Hayes and Joscelyn, The Benghazi Report (". . . Although it adds to our overall understanding of Benghazi, even a cursory read reveals sloppy errors of fact and numerous internal contradictions. . . . Those are minor errors, however, compared with the major omissions and mischaracterizations that mar the report. . . ."); *Id.* ("The absence of [Wissam] bin Hamid, the exclusion of the Khattala [sic] indictment, the whitewashing of intelligence failures, the spinning of NDAs [non-disclosure agreements], the reliance on discredited witnesses, and the mistreatment of credible ones – these are just some of the problems with the House Intelligence Committee's report on Benghazi"); and *Id.* (Quoting Oz Geist: "I would like to sit down with Rogers and go over the report line by line and have him defend what's in there. He couldn't do it").

617

- There is no protest in Benghazi, which the CIA does not admit publicly until September 24th;
- The process for generating the CIA Talking Points is "flawed" and "mistakes were made"; and
- "The Committee also found no evidence that the CIA conducted unauthorized activities in Benghazi and no evidence that the IC shipped arms to Syria."[2338]

The Rogers-Ruppersberger report is widely criticized. According to Stephen Hayes of *The Weekly Standard*, a number of committee Republicans disavow it (some off the record). Some of them claim the report does not even represent a consensus of the Republican members on the panel.[2339] Hayes quotes GRS security agent Tig Tiegen as commenting:

If this was a high school paper, I would give it an F. . . . There are so many mistakes it's hard to know where to begin. How can an official government report get so many things wrong?[2340]

One of the issues the House Intelligence panel investigates is whether some of the surviving CIA security contractors on Team Annex (and perhaps Team Tripoli) are asked by the CIA to sign new Non-Disclosure Agreements ("NDAs") to prevent them from discussing Benghazi with Congress or the media. On May 21, 2013, the CIA holds a memorial service at CIA headquarters for the late CIA contractors Glen Doherty and Tyrone Woods. According to Stephen Hayes of *The Weekly Standard*, at that service at least two (and possibly "several") former security contractors are asked to sign new NDAs to supplement others they have signed previously.

CIA Director John Brennan later will insist to the House Intelligence Committee these NDAs are not targeted at events in Benghazi. (Like many of Brennan's assertions over the Obama years, this seems disingenuous.[2341] Although these NDAs reportedly do not

---

[2338] *Id.*, Executive Summary (Nov. 21, 2014), pp. 1-2.

[2339] Hayes and Joscelyn, The Benghazi Report (Committee member Tom Rooney (R-FL): "I don't think this is the official government report. It's Mike Roger's report. The members of his own committee don't even agree with it").

[2340] Hayes and Joscelyn, The Benghazi Report.

[2341] For a good (if partial) summary of false assertions John Brennan makes during his service in the Obama administration, see Victor David Hanson, "The Distortions of Our Unelected Officials," Townhall.com website (Mar. 29, 2018). See also Schwartz, A Spymaster Steps Out of the Shadows ("Few things bother Brennan more than being

contain the word "Benghazi," they apparently are only given to security contractors who fought in Benghazi and are proffered at a ceremony honoring two agents who fell there. Also, Mark Zaid, a lawyer for three (and possibly five) of the security agents, reportedly believes these new NDAs are all about Benghazi.[2342])

On this NDA issue, the House intelligence panel ultimately finds "no evidence that any official was intimidated, *wrongly* forced to sign a nondisclosure agreement or otherwise kept from speaking to Congress, or polygraphed because of their presence in Benghazi."[2343] (Note the interesting word "wrongly." This does not rule out the possibility the contractors *are* asked or even forced to sign a supplemental NDA. This intelligence report notwithstanding, if counselor Zaid is right, CNN also may be correct when its Jake Tapper reports in August 2013, "CNN has learned the CIA is involved in what one source calls an unprecedented attempt to keep the spy agency's Benghazi secrets from ever leaking out."[2344])

The Senate Committee

The Democrat-controlled Senate Intelligence Committee also investigates the intelligence available regarding the Benghazi attacks. (We have cited its work product frequently in the preceding pages, and need not repeat them here.) It is interesting to note that both before and

---

called a liar. . . . [F]rom time to time, he bent the truth in ways that are not uncommon for C.I.A. directors and high-ranking presidential aides. Brennan's evasions differ from Trump's lies – they are smaller, less frequent, more deniable. . . . He gave the public a sanitized version of the truth [regarding a C.I.A. probe into computers of Senate staff members] and withheld the full one. He did things that the president wanted done but not known. . . .").

[2342] Stephen F. Hayes, "Benghazi Survivors Given NDAs at CIA Memorial Service for Woods, Doherty," *The Weekly Standard* online (Nov. 14, 2013); and Hayes and Joscelyn, The Benghazi Report.

[2343] House Intelligence Committee Benghazi Report (Nov. 21, 2014) (emphasis added), p. 2.

[2344] "Exclusive: Dozens of CIA Operatives on the Ground During Benghazi Attack," The Lead Blog with Jake Tapper, CNN online (Aug. 1, 2013); Stephen F. Hayes, "Benghazi Survivors Given NDAs at CIA Memorial Service for Woods, Doherty," *The Weekly Standard* online (Nov. 14, 2013); and Guy Benson, "Bombshell: CIA Using 'Unprecedented' Polygraphing, 'Pure Intimidation' to Guard Benghazi Secrets," Townhall.com website (Aug. 2, 2013).

after she returns to duty, Charlene Lamb reportedly will refuse on three occasions to meet with investigators from this intelligence panel.[2345]

The committee concludes the terrorist attacks were preventable. Among other things, the committee's report determines, "Individuals affiliated with terrorist groups, including AQIM [Al Qaeda in the Islamic Maghreb], Ansar al-Sharia, AQAP [Al Qaeda in the Arabia Peninsula], and the Mohammad Jamal Network, participated in the September 11, 2012, attacks."[2346]

As occurs often, Senator Feinstein (D-CA) and the Democrats in control of this panel rush out their report on January 14, 2014, just days before Republicans assume control over the panel and its chairmanship. Hence the Democrats, not the Republicans, control the report's contents and conclusions.

The House Oversight Committee Investigations

The Republican-controlled House Oversight Committee also investigates Benghazi in detail. As early as October 18, 2012, the top Democrat on the committee already is calling their inquiry a "witch-hunt," and claims the Republicans are treating Benghazi like a "political football."[2347]

We have cited this committee's work numerous times in prior chapters, and do not repeat most of this panel's findings here. A worthwhile exception is the Oversight Committee's analysis of the Benghazi ARB's inquiry and final product.

House Oversight Investigates the ARB Report

The Benghazi Accountability Review Board report (discussed in detail above in Chapter 109) is so suspect the House Oversight Committee decides to investigate the ARB, its personnel and its

---

[2345] Additional Views of Senators Chambliss, Burr, et al., p. 8.

[2346] Sen. Intelligence Committee Benghazi Report, p. 40; and Guy Benson, "Bipartisan Senate Benghazi Report: Attacks Were 'Preventable,'" Townhall.com website (Jan. 15, 2014).

[2347] Leigh Ann Caldwell, "Rep. Cummings: Benghazi Probe Turning Into Witch-Hunt," CBS News website (Oct. 18, 2012).

THE TRUE ACCOUNT OF VALOR AND ABANDONMENT

procedures.[2348] (Good call.) ARB Chairman Ambassador Pickering and Vice-Chair Admiral Mullen initially decline to testify about their ARB investigation and findings before the Oversight Committee! Pickering and Mullen refuse even to speak with the committee informally.[2349] (Wow, that's leadership. They must be really proud of their ARB work product.) Moreover, according to the Oversight panel's chairman, the State Department fails even to respond to (much less acquiesce in) an April 2013 Oversight Committee request that State make nine of its current and former officials available to testify at the committee's hearing (or at a separate transcribed interview) on the ARB Report.[2350]

Ultimately, both Pickering and Mullen will agree to appear before the Oversight Committee in a public hearing.[2351]

Among other findings, in its analysis of the ARB Report the Oversight Committee concludes, "The ARB downplayed [Under Secretary Patrick] Kennedy's role in the decision-making that led to the inadequate security posture in Benghazi."[2352] In response, Democrats yet again accuse the Republicans on the Oversight Committee of playing politics with the ARB's report.[2353] In turn, Republicans on the panel accuse the Obama administration of withholding information regarding the ARB's work.[2354] (In fact, they are both right.)

[2348] See, e.g., Babbin, Whitewashing Benghazi ("... According to a source close to the State Department who tried to approach the ARB about the security laxity in Benghazi, the board was dismissive and really didn't want to know....").

[2349] House Oversight Committee Hearings (May 8, 2013) (Introductory Remarks of Chairman Darrell Issa (R-CA)), p. 2.

[2350] Id. (Introductory Remarks of Chairman Darrell Issa (R-CA)), pp. 2-3.

[2351] Daily Press Briefing by Deputy Spokesperson Marie Harf, State Dept. Archives website (Sept. 19, 2013).

[2352] House Oversight Interim Report on Benghazi ARB, p. 32; and Attkisson, Benghazi Accountability Review Board Comes Under Renewed Criticism.

[2353] Attkisson, Benghazi Accountability Review Board Comes Under Renewed Criticism (Rep. Elijah Cummings (D-MD): "Rather than focusing on the reforms recommended by the ARB, Republicans have politicized the investigation by engaging in a systematic effort to launch unsubstantiated accusations against the Pentagon, the State Department, the president, and now the ARB itself").

[2354] House Oversight Committee Hearings (May 8, 2013) (Introductory Remarks of Chairman Darrell Issa (R-CA)), ("When five House committee chairmen wrote the White House and requested relevant documents about the Benghazi attacks, we were refused"), pp. 2-3; and House Oversight Interim Report on Benghazi ARB ("The State Department obstructed the congressional investigation: The State Department's refusal

On September 16, 2013, the Oversight Committee issues an interim investigative report. It properly questions the independence of the ARB's report. The Oversight report then asks why the ARB does not discipline Under Secretary Kennedy, who is "deeply involved" in security decisions, including the decision not to approve requests for additional security in Benghazi.[2355] (An excellent question. Kennedy should have been fired.)

The House Select Benghazi Committee

As noted above, in May 2014 then Speaker of the House John Boehner *at long last* figures out he needs to create a select House committee to investigate Benghazi from top to bottom. (He should have done so on September 12, 2012.) This Select Committee is created on the House of Representatives side of Congress only; it includes no Senators.

However, it is so late and there have been so many congressional inquiries already, most of the public (including the author at the time) are afflicted with "Benghazi fatigue." Politically, this House panel's creation is "too much, too late."

In addition, the Select Committee's work is frustrated by a severe lack of cooperation from the Obama administration. Two of the committee's members state, ". . . The White House in particular left large holes in the investigation by denying the Committee access to documents and witnesses . . ."[2356] Mollie Hemingway of *The Federalist* accurately summarizes the conclusions of committee members Mike Pompeo (R-KS) and Jim Jordan (R-OH): "The Obama administration

---

to turn over ARB documents has made an independent evaluation of the ARB's review difficult"), pp. 21-22.

[2355] E.g., Sen. Intelligence Committee Benghazi Report (Redacted) (". . . [S]ome senior Foreign Service officers and DS agents who met with the [later-created Independent Panel on Best Practices] identified the Under Secretary for Management (M) as the senior security official in the Department responsible for final decision making regarding critical security requirements," even though such a role was "not identified by Congress in the Diplomatic Security Act of 1986"), pp. 16-17.

[2356] Additional Views of Reps. Jordan and Pompeo, p. 419; and *Id.* ("Despite its claims, we saw no evidence that the administration held a sincere interest in helping the [Select] Committee find the truth about Benghazi. . . . So while the investigation uncovered new information, we nonetheless end the Committee's investigation without many of the facts, especially those involving the President and the White House, we were chartered to obtain"), p. 417.

wouldn't let the committee speak with anyone who was in the White House Situation Room on the night of the attacks or see [all] the email communication between White House staffers."[2357]

According to Deputy Chief of Mission Greg Hicks, when he testifies before the Select Committee it is "readily apparent" to him the committee does not receive all of the information on Benghazi that is available. Hicks will tell Fox News members of the Democrat minority on the panel show him "deliberative documents" the committee's majority does not have. For example, some deliberative documents from the State Department are not shared with the committee's majority.[2358]

Obama administration supporters quickly dismiss the House Select Committee's probe as repetitive and purely political. Democrats on the Select Committee call the majority's report "a conspiracy theory on steroids – bringing back long-debunked allegations with no credible evidence whatsoever."[2359] As noted above, the Democrats on the Select Committee issue their own 339-page report in an effort to blunt the power of the majority report. (A full 53 pages are devoted to a political attack on the Republican members of the committee and the House.[2360]) The Select panel's minority report concludes the U.S. military could not possibly have saved the lives of Americans in Benghazi that night, even had it acted differently.[2361] House Republicans reportedly describe it as "padded with bizarre non-sequiturs. . . ." It is so lame it mentions the name of Donald J. Trump a reported 23 times! (According to Mollie Hemingway of *The Federalist*, this is more than the minority report mentions two of the four murdered Americans.) Donald Trump, of course, has absolutely nothing to do with the Benghazi tragedy.[2362]

From the author's reading of the final majority report, the Select Committee conducts a principled, serious inquiry, headed by a principled, serious man, former federal prosecutor Trey Gowdy (R-SC). This is why so much of this book is based upon this committee

---

[2357] Hemingway, 5 Big Takeaways From the House Benghazi Report; and Additional Views of Reps. Jordan and Pompeo, pp. 419-429.

[2358] Interview of Gregory Hicks with Martha MacCallum, "America's Newsroom," Fox News Channel (Sept. 14, 2016) (*Watch video there*; Go to 5:50 – 6:40).

[2359] Fox News, House Republicans Fault US Military Response to Benghazi.

[2360] Benghazi Committee Report, Minority Report, pp. 907-960.

[2361] Fox News, House Republicans Fault US Military Response to Benghazi.

[2362] Hemingway, 5 Big Takeaways From the House Benghazi Report.

majority's final work product. (The panel Democrats' claim the majority report contains "no credible evidence whatsoever" is so ludicrous one wonders if they even read the majority report.)

However, in addition to intriguing the author about the Benghazi debacle, the Select Committee's work has another significant by-product, which we discuss next.

Secretary Clinton's Illicit Email System

As part of its probe, the Select Committee appropriately requests from the State Department all correspondence between Secretary Clinton and her aides relating to the Benghazi attacks. According to *The New York Times*, in its response in February 2015, State submits to the committee some 300 emails (about 900 pages) relating to the terrorist attacks. Apparently in the process of reviewing these documents, the Select Committee uncovers the fact that *throughout her entire tenure as Secretary of State, Hillary Clinton has not used State's official email system!*

The New York Times catches wind of this.[2363] In March 2015, *The Times* publishes an article revealing the Select Committee's discovery of Hillary Clinton's use of an unauthorized, private email server while she is Secretary of State.[2364] This becomes an immediate problem for President Obama. This is because he has communicated with Clinton on official business over this private server! If Clinton is prosecuted over this offense, how can President Obama also not be held accountable – and perhaps even impeached?

The Select Committee promptly issues subpoenas to Hillary Clinton seeking any and all of these private emails that relate to Benghazi. But it may be too late. To the Select panel's chagrin, it will learn that back in 2013 Team Hillary already has thrown a "Let's-Delete-the-Emails" party. Clinton's staff, her lawyers, and her private computer consultants *already have deleted more than 33,000 emails from her "homebrew"*

[2363] Hemingway, 5 Big Takeaways From the House Benghazi Report ("... The [Select Benghazi] committee did manage to uncover Secretary Clinton's breathtaking use of a private email account and server, something no previous investigative or oversight committee had known. . . .").

[2364] Michael S. Schmidt, "Hillary Clinton Used Personal Email Account at State Dept., Possibly Breaking Rules," *The New York Times* online (Mar. 2, 2015) ("Mrs. Clinton did not have a government email address during her four-year tenure at the State Department").

server! She will assure the Select Committee – and the world – only personal emails are deleted.[2365] (Right.)

Later, it will be revealed Clinton's lawyers and computer techies do more than just click on the "delete" button 33,000 times. Instead, to make certain the emails never can be recovered Clinton (no doubt through her henchmen) authorizes her techies to use a software application known as "BleachBit." This application takes extra steps permanently to "scramble" or "blow up" the actual data in the text of the emails.[2366] BleachBit reportedly is akin to an electronic shredder. As Select Committee Chairman Trey Gowdy (R-SC) later describes the result, "even God can't read them" once you have deleted computer files using BleachBit.[2367]

(Clinton and her people really, *really* want these emails gone. You know, the "non-business" ones supposedly discussing Clinton's yoga classes and her daughter's wedding. And her emails with her husband (who does not use email). However, as Chairman Gowdy queries: Who would use a tool like BleachBit to destroy innocuous personal emails discussing yoga or bridesmaids?[2368] Wouldn't using BleachBit more likely suggest an intent to destroy government records, and possibly constitute the crime of "Obstruction of Congress"?[2369]

(There is something entirely rotten about Clinton's deletion and digital destruction of all these emails while her conduct is under investigation. The Obama Department of Justice later will conduct a sham "investigation" of Clinton's use of her unauthorized email server,

---

[2365] Katie Pavlich, "Techies Instructed to Delete Hillary's Emails: This Looks Like Covering Up a Lot of Shady Sh*t," Townhall.com website (Sept. 13, 2013).

[2366] See BleachBit website (". . . Beyond simply deleting files, BleachBit includes advanced features such as shredding files to prevent recovery, wiping free disk space to hide traces of files deleted by other applications . . .").

[2367] See *Id.* ("Delete your private files so completely that 'even God can't read them' according to South Carolina Representative Trey Gowdy"); and Interview of Rep. Trey Gowdy (R-SC) with Martha MacCallum, Fox News Channel (Date unknown, possibly Aug. 2016) (*Watch video there*; Go to 1:09 - 2:02).

[2368] Interview of Rep. Trey Gowdy (R-SC) with Martha MacCallum, Fox News Channel (Date unknown, possibly Aug. 2016) (*Watch video there*; Go to 1:46 - 2:02).

[2369] See Title 18, United States Code, Section 1505 (". . . Whoever corruptly . . . influences, obstructs, or impedes or endeavors to influence, obstruct, or impede . . . the due and proper exercise of the power of inquiry under which any inquiry or investigation is being had by either House, or any committee of either House or any joint committee of the Congress – Shall be fined under this title, imprisoned not more than 5 years . . . , or both").

but will absolve her of criminal conduct – after President Obama publicly endorses her for president. Nevertheless, it is possible her use of this illicit email server contributes to her surprising presidential election loss in 2016.[2370] But that is a subject for another book.[2371]) ∎

[2370] E.g., Paul Blumenthal, "In 2 Terms, Barack Obama Had Fewer Scandals Than Donald Trump Has Had in the Last 2 Weeks," *The Huffington Post* online (Jan. 13, 2017) ("The years-long investigations into former Secretary of State Hillary Clinton's response to the attack on a U.S. diplomatic mission in Benghazi revealed that she kept a private email server. While that did not lead to any charges or convictions, it may have contributed to her election defeat").

[2371] See the author's forthcoming book *The Emperor Obama: An American Betrayal, Book I – Foreign Policy, National Security and Terrorism* (to be available at www.amazon.com).

112

Team Obama Reacts to Congress

President Obama and his senior officials harshly criticize the congressional investigations into Benghazi. There are too many examples to summarize them all here. A few should suffice.

Obama himself ridicules the inquiries as a "political circus," "political games," and a politically-motivated "sideshow" that "defies logic." He claims there is "no there, there."[2372] As noted previously, Obama also asserts the State Department ARB already has "investigated *every element* of this."[2373] (This last proclamation is a blatant lie. For example, Obama knows this ARB does not even interview Hillary Clinton and some of her top aides. Also, the ARB considers principally the State Department's role in the Benghazi fiasco. The Board does not investigate the CIA Talking Points, or the White House's or National Security Council's role in the tragedy. *It never interviews Obama.* It briefly summarizes (but does not analyze) the attacks on the CIA Annex.)

Obama's subordinates also ridicule the congressional inquiries. At one committee hearing, Defense Secretary Panetta testifies, "The United States military, as I've said, is not – and frankly should not be – a 9-1-1 service capable of arriving on the scene within minutes to every possible contingency around the world. The U.S. military has neither the resources nor the responsibility to have a fire house next to every U.S. facility in the world."[2374]

(Well, Leon, we are not talking about asking the Pentagon to go rescue some silly American tourists who on their own volition wonder into a dangerous area of a marginal country, like Iran or North Korea or Syria. This tragedy does not involve some intoxicated American tourist

---

[2372] Obama-Cameron Joint Press Conference (emphasis added); and Lucas, Obama: State Dept. That Didn't Interview Clinton 'Investigated Every Element' of Benghazi.

[2373] Obama-Cameron Joint Press Conference (emphasis added).

[2374] Panetta Senate Armed Services Prepared Testimony; "Justice with Judge Janine," Fox News Channel (Oct. 26, 2013) (*Watch video there*; Go to 1:50 - 2:15); and CNN Report, Why Didn't the U.S. Military Respond in Time in Benghazi? (*Watch video there*; Go to 1:24-33).

who gets lost sightseeing in Bangkok, takes a wrong turn, and wonders into a bad neighborhood. This is not some lunatic pacifist who enters North Korea believing he is the only person who can understand and communicate with their crazy dictator. This is a United States ambassador (and his staff) representing his country and sent by his president and Secretary of State on an official and damned dangerous diplomatic mission into a vital conflict region – a region Barack Obama's government has ruined through a reckless, unconstitutional war. And we are talking about CIA agents and their American bodyguards who work for the U.S. government and are *ordered* to go into harm's way in a foreign country known to be exceedingly dangerous.

(And if not the Pentagon, who or what *is* the appropriate 911 service when a reckless administration practicing "expeditionary diplomacy" wrongly sends American diplomats and CIA agents into extreme danger for largely political reasons, and then they foreseeably are attacked by terrorists? Should the Americans in Benghazi call their mothers? The Boy Scouts? (Excuse me, the Scouts.) Or perhaps the League of Women Voters? Or Patrick Kennedy or Charlene Lamb at the State Department, who deny them adequate security in the first place? Or possibly they should ask the American Civil Liberties Union to send some lawyers? What the hell *is* the U.S. military if not a "911 service" in times of terrorist enemy attacks abroad on *American government personnel performing in the line of duty? Of course you're the damned 911 service! That's your job, fool!* Your brave people *train* every damned day at great risk for such rescues and similar missions.[2375] *You* are who we call when the proverbial stuff hits the proverbial fan, endangering American officials' lives in a foreign land! It's what your warriors get paid for! (Not enough.) Oh, *good grief!*)

Secretary of State Hillary Clinton also criticizes the congressional investigators. In her memoir she writes, "Others [in Congress] remained fixated on chasing after conspiracy theories that had nothing

---

[2375] See, e.g., Associated Press, "12 U.S. Paratroopers Hospitalized After Night Jump," NBC News online (July 23, 2017) (12 U.S. paratroopers hospitalized after sustaining minor injuries during night time non-combat parachute jump in Romania during "a very rigorous exercise, which carries a certain level of risk"); Amanda Lee Myers, "4 Marines Killed in Helicopter Crash in California," The Associated Press, Military.com website (April 4, 2018) (Crash of Marine "Super Stallion" helicopter near El Centro, California on April 3, while practicing desert landings, killing all four crew members); and "F-16 Crashes at Nevada Training Range," *Id.* (April 4, 2018) (Crash of Air Force jet during training mission at Nellis Air Force Base, Nevada, killing the pilot).

THE TRUE ACCOUNT OF VALOR AND ABANDONMENT

to do with how we could prevent future tragedies. And some only showed up because of the cameras."[2376] In January 2013, Senator Ron Johnson (R-WI) asks Secretary Clinton at a Senate Foreign Relations Committee hearing what is the true reason for the Benghazi terrorist attacks – a spontaneous demonstration against the Video, or a preplanned terrorist assault? Astonishingly, Clinton famously will respond:

> With all due respect, the fact is we had four dead Americans. Was it because of a protest or was it because of guys out for a walk one night who decided they'd go kill some Americans? *What difference at this point does it make?* It is our job to figure out what happened, and do everything we can to prevent it from ever happening again, Senator.[2377]

(One difference it makes, Madam Secretary, is whether you are competent to be the Commander in Chief of the United States of America.[2378] Another difference it makes is whether the American government is lying to its people for political reasons. And specifically, whether the president himself is lying in order to get reelected.

(One is left to ponder whether, as much as or more than any other factor, it is this outrageous, callous, widely-disseminated question by Hillary Clinton that perhaps costs her the White House in November 2016.[2379]) ■

[2376] E.g., Clinton, *Hard Choices*, Chap. 17, pp. 411-412.

[2377] Testimony of Hillary Clinton Before Senate Foreign Relations Committee (Jan. 23, 2013) (Response to questions of Sen. Ron Johnson (R-WI)) (emphasis added); and Anne Geran and William Branigan, "Hillary Clinton's Benghazi Testimony Was Sprinkled with Heated Exchanges," *The Washington Post* online (Jan. 23, 2013).

[2378] E.g., *Wall Street Journal* Opinion, The Missing Benghazi Email ("All of this bears directly on Mrs. Clinton's qualifications to be President. Her State Department overlooked repeated warnings about a growing militant threat in Benghazi, denying requests for improved security. . . .").

[2379] See, e.g., Conor Gaffey, "Who Is Mustafa Al-Islam [sic]? Benghazi Attack Suspect Captured in Libya to Face Trial in U.S.," Newsweek online (Oct. 31, 2017) ("The Benghazi attacks loomed large over Clinton's campaign. Critics accused Obama administration officials of covering up the attack's apparently premeditated nature and State Department officials for rejecting requests for additional security at the Benghazi compound prior to the attacks").

113

Unaccountable

No one in the United States government is held publicly, meaningfully accountable for the Benghazi fiasco.[2380] President Obama fires no one. No one resigns in disgrace. And Congress impeaches no one in the government over Benghazi. No one.

The White House

Insofar as we know, no one in the White House is sanctioned for the Benghazi debacle. To the contrary, fifty-six days after Benghazi the American voters reelect Barack Obama and Joe Biden for a second, four-year term as president and vice president.

Shortly after the crisis, Jack Lew leaves his position as White House Chief of Staff. Far from being punished for the Benghazi tragedy, however, Lew is promoted by being nominated to become Secretary of the Treasury, one of Obama's most prestigious cabinet members. He is nominated in January 2013, confirmed by the Senate, and sworn in on February 28.[2381]

The National Security Council

The author is unaware of any individual on the NSC or its staff who is sanctioned for their performance concerning Benghazi. A few months after the president is reelected, National Security Advisor Thomas Donilon leaves his position, effective July 2013. Although it is possible he is asked to depart, the author has found no evidence Donilon's departure is related to Benghazi. As noted below, Susan Rice will be promoted to succeed Donilon.

Contrary to sanctioning Donilon's deputy, Denis McDonough, Obama names him to replace Jack Lew as his White House Chief of

---

[2380] E.g., House Foreign Affairs Benghazi Majority Staff Report ("... [N]o one has been held responsible in a meaningful way for the grossly inadequate security in Benghazi"), p. 20.

[2381] CNN Library, "Jack Lew Fast Facts," CNN online (Aug. 22, 2017).

Staff. This is a major promotion for the man who, as Deputy National Security Advisor, effectively supervises the entire U.S. government's response (or lack thereof) on the Night of Benghazi.

John Brennan resigns as President Obama's senior advisor on counterterrorism in January 2013. However, he is not disciplined for Benghazi but also is promoted, being nominated to become the new Director of the CIA. The Senate confirms Brennan and he is sworn in as Director in March 2013. He will serve in this position for the remainder of Obama's presidency.

Ben Rhodes will remain in his same position as lead national security "spin doctor" extraordinaire for the entire second Obama term.

The State Department

As discussed above (Chapter 109), following the ARB Report four mid-level employees of the State Department are placed on paid "administrative" leave because of the Benghazi disaster. Two of the four – Eric Boswell and Raymond Maxwell – are allowed to resign "voluntarily" from their management positions on December 19, 2012, the day after the ARB Report is issued.[2382] (However, they do not then resign as federal employees of the State Department. Moreover, Boswell keeps his other, concurrent position as Director of the Office of Foreign Missions.) The four employees placed on administrative leave are allowed to return eight months later in August 2013, although supposedly to different positions of "lesser responsibility" at the agency that do not involve diplomatic security.[2383]

Eric Boswell voluntarily retires from the agency in November 2013. However, State leaves open the possibility of "continuing to employ him for temporary assignments"! Scott Bultrowicz is reassigned to the Office of the Executive Director of Diplomatic Security. As this book goes to press, he no longer is listed in the agency's telephone directory.

Charlene Lamb enrolls in training for her "next assignment." She subsequently retires from the agency, and also is gone from the phone directory.

[2382] Stephanie Condon, "State Dept. Officials Resign Following Benghazi Report," CBS News online (Dec. 19, 2012); "Security Chiefs Resign Over Benghazi Probe That Blamed 'Grossly Poor' Security and State Department's 'Systemic Failures' for Attack That Killed U.S. Ambassador," *The Daily Mail* online (Dec. 18, 2012; Updated Dec. 19, 2012); and Zuckoff, *13 Hours*, Epilogue, p. 295.

[2383] House Foreign Affairs Benghazi Majority Staff Report, pp. 8-10.

Raymond Maxwell briefly becomes an advisor to the Bureau of African Affairs. Three months later, he voluntarily retires from foreign service, which he had planned to do in summer 2012, but had postponed to help deal with the "Arab Spring" convulsions. (Truly, no good deed goes unpunished.) Not one of these four misses a paycheck while still employed at State.[2384]

According to the House Foreign Affairs Committee majority staff, several mid-level State officials involved in Benghazi will be promoted after the debacle. For example, Elizabeth Dibble (Raymond Maxwell's immediate supervisor) is awarded a prestigious assignment as Deputy Chief of Mission at the U.S. Embassy in London. Victoria Nuland (of CIA Talking Points fame) will be nominated and confirmed in September 2013 as State's Assistant Secretary for European and Eurasian Affairs. Jake Sullivan (a key Clinton lieutenant who also edited the CIA Talking Points) is appointed in February 2013 as Vice President Biden's National Security Advisor.[2385]

No *senior* State Department official is fired or even sanctioned. Not even the feckless, irresponsible, dangerous Patrick Kennedy.[2386]

President Obama should ask Hillary Clinton to resign as Secretary of State over the Benghazi ignominy or just fire her, but does neither.[2387] (She is, after all, assumed by everyone to be Obama's successor as president.) Congress should impeach her, but makes no such attempt. Clinton has little concern about being investigated by the State Department's Inspector General's office for her Benghazi-related conduct. This is because for 1,989 days – covering Clinton's entire

---

[2384] *Id.*, pp. 10 and 20.

[2385] *Id.*, p. 13; and Guy Benson, "Surprise: Obama Promotes Another Benghazi Scandal Player," Townhall.com website (May 24, 2013).

[2386] Herridge et al., Clinton State Department Silenced Them on Benghazi Security Lapses, Contractors Say ("Jerry Torres [CEO of the Torres AES diplomatic security firm] remains haunted by the fact that specific bureaucrats and policies remain in the State Department after the Benghazi attack despite the change in administration. 'A U.S. ambassador is dead and nobody is held accountable for it. . . .'"); *Id.* (Brad Owens of Torres AES: Those "who made the poor choices that actually, I would say, were more responsible for the Benghazi attacks than anyone else, they're still in the same positions, making security choices for our embassies overseas now") (*Watch video there*).

[2387] Anne Geran and William Branigan, "Hillary Clinton's Benghazi Testimony Was Sprinkled with Heated Exchanges," *The Washington Post* online (Jan. 23, 2013) (Senator Rand Paul (R-KY) tells Secretary Clinton that had he been president he would have demanded her resignation over Benghazi).

THE TRUE ACCOUNT OF VALOR AND ABANDONMENT

tenure as Secretary of State – President Obama has not filled the vacant Inspector General position at State![2388] (How convenient for Hillary.) Clinton finally resigns on February 1, 2013. (She has a presidential campaign to prepare for. Also, she needs to get out of State before another diplomatic-national security humiliation occurs on her watch. No doubt she wishes she had left office before Libya, and especially Benghazi.[2389])

Susan Rice is not fired for repeatedly misleading the American people on the Sunday Shows.[2390] Instead, President Obama wants to reward her by promoting her to become Secretary of State following Clinton's departure. However, Republicans in Congress are so angry with Rice she has become too politically toxic and never can be confirmed by the Senate. Instead, Obama promotes her to replace the departing Tom Donilon as his National Security Advisor. This position requires no Senate confirmation. Rice will serve in this post for the last four years of Obama's second term.

On a more pleasant note, in a secret ceremony the State Department will honor the GRS members of Team Annex. This will consist of awarding medals (bearing the word "Heroism"), citations (signed by Secretary Clinton), and plaques. The plaques' wording honors:

> [T]he heroism displayed by members of the security team, under fire in the face of extreme risks to their personal safety during the deadly attack against US facilities in Benghazi, Libya, on September 11-12, 2012. The heroic actions of these

---

[2388] House Foreign Affairs Benghazi Majority Staff Report, pp. 16-17.

[2389] Editorial, "Military Support Offered in Benghazi – Why Would White House Say No?" Investor's Business Daily online (Dec. 10, 2015) (". . . It was Secretary of State Clinton's war, so she owns Libya and every disaster related to it"); and Hemingway, 5 Big Takeaways From the House Benghazi Report (". . . Hillary Clinton's signature policy achievement was her push to invade Libya, so the political ramifications were serious for her as well. As her Deputy Chief of Staff and Director of Policy Jacob Sullivan characterized it in 2011, Clinton had 'leadership/ownership/stewardship of this country's Libya policy from start to finish'. . . ."). See also Sowell, Hillary 2.0 and Benghazi (discussing ". . . the utter disaster created by the Obama administration's foreign policy, carried out by Hillary Clinton as Secretary of State").

[2390] E.g., Victor David Hanson, "The Distortions of Our Unelected Officials," Townhall.com website (Mar. 29, 2018) ("Former National Security Adviser Susan Rice lied about the Benghazi tragedy, the nature of the Bowe Bergdahl/Guantanamo detainee exchange, the presence of chemical weapons in Syria, and her role in unmasking the identities of surveilled Americans").

professionals were selfless, valorous, and representative of the highest standards of bravery in federal service.[2391]
(Yep.)

The Pentagon

No civilian Pentagon official or military officer is punished (at least not publicly) for their performance in responding to the Benghazi attacks. (As the House Foreign Affairs Committee staff report indicates, this is in contrast to situations in which military commanders have been relieved when their failure to provide adequate security resulted in soldiers' deaths.[2392])

In October 2012, just weeks after Benghazi, U.S. Africa Command Commander General Carter F. Ham announces his "retirement" after forty years in the military. Rumors quickly surface Ham is being relieved of his command for pursuing a rescue mission to Benghazi too aggressively on the Night of Benghazi, in effect refusing to obey a supposed "stand down" order.[2393] The author is unable to confirm these rumors. The Pentagon adamantly denies them. Joint Chiefs Chairman General Dempsey asserts, "The speculation that General Carter Ham is departing Africa Command due to events in Benghazi, Libya on [September 11,] 2012 is absolutely false...."[2394] (Translation: Possibly true.) The Pentagon's press secretary adds, "General Ham is doing an exceptional job leading Africa Command. He has the full confidence of

---

[2391] Zuckoff, *13 Hours*, Epilogue, p. 300.

[2392] House Foreign Affairs Benghazi Majority Staff Report (Summarizing decision of top Marine Corps officer to relieve two senior Marine generals from command for failure to provide "adequate force protection measures," resulting in September 2012 Taliban ground attack in Afghanistan that killed two marines, wounded eight personnel, and destroyed six Harrier jets), pp. 17 and 20.

[2393] E.g., James S. Robbins, "TRR: Is a General Losing His Job Over Benghazi?" The Robbins Report, *The Washington Times* online (Oct. 28, 2012; Updated Oct. 29, 2012) ("Is an American General losing his job for trying to save the Americans besieged in Benghazi? This is the latest potential wrinkle in the growing scandal surrounding the September 11, 2012 terrorist attack that left four men dead and President Obama scrambling for a coherent explanation").

[2394] Army Sgt. 1st Class Tyrone C. Marshall Jr., "Pentagon Has Full Confidence in Africom Commander, Little Says," American Forces Press Service, Defense Dept. website (Oct. 31, 2012); and James S. Robbins, "TRR: Is a General Losing His Job Over Benghazi?" The Robbins Report, *The Washington Times* online (Oct. 28, 2012; Updated Oct. 29, 2012).

the secretary of defense and the chairman of the Joint Chiefs of Staff."[2395] (Translation: Ham is damaged goods.) James Robbins of *The Washington Times* reasonably inquires if Ham is such as great leader of AFRICOM, why is his tenure there (less than two years) so much shorter than that of most other combatant commanders?[2396] (In the author's view, Ham's retirement follows too rapidly after the Night of Benghazi to be coincidence.)

(There also will be reports on various websites that, like Ham, one Rear Admiral Charles M. Gaouette, is fired or otherwise disciplined for his conduct on the Night of Benghazi. On this night, Admiral Gaouette is the Commander of U.S. Strike Force Three, which includes the Aircraft Carrier USS John C. Stennis. According to these rumors, Gaouette supposedly ignores a "stand down" order and instead attempts to launch help towards Benghazi in an effort to aid the beleaguered Americans there. However, these rumors appear to be entirely false. According to a U.S. Navy map of surface ships deployed on the Night of Benghazi, the USS Stennis is not among the naval ships in the Mediterranean or Persian Gulf.[2397] (The author believes the Stennis and its strike group likely is supporting the U.S. war in Afghanistan.[2398] According to the Pentagon, the Stennis is underway in "the Gulf region" as of October 4, 2012.[2399] Two months after Benghazi, the Stennis is stationed in the Arabian Sea, possibly off of Pakistan.[2400]) Hence, the carrier Stennis is nowhere close enough to Benghazi for its aircraft to be able to reach Benghazi – even on a one-way flight.

[2395] Army Sgt. 1st Class Tyrone C. Marshall Jr., "Pentagon Has Full Confidence in Africom Commander, Little Says," American Forces Press Service, Defense Dept. website (Oct. 31, 2012).

[2396] James S. Robbins, "TRR: Is a General Losing His Job Over Benghazi?" The Robbins Report, *The Washington Times* online (Oct. 28, 2012; Updated Oct. 29, 2012).

[2397] For a U.S. Navy map of ship placements in the regions nearest Benghazi on September 11, 2012, see Judicial Watch website at http://www.judicialwatch.org/wp-content/uploads/2014/02/NavymapBenghazi.pdf.

[2398] See, e.g., Jim Garamone, DoD Press Release, "Panetta Accelerates Stennis Carrier Strike Group Deployment," Defense Dept. website (July 16, 2012) ("The Navy will deploy the aircraft carrier USS John C. Stennis and its strike group four months early and shift its destination to the U.S. Central Command area of responsibility . . .").

[2399] Navy Petty Officer 2nd Class Scott A. McCall, "Dempsey Thanks Service Members in Pacific Northwest," DoD News, Defense Dept. website (Oct. 4, 2012).

[2400] Photograph Caption, "Travels with Dempsey," Defense Dept. website (Dec. 13, 2012).

(Also, *The New York Times* reports the Navy disciplines Admiral Gaouette in March 2013 for allegedly abusive conduct in chastising a commanding officer who was "driving" the carrier Stennis too fast in a crowded sea passage, for making "racially insensitive comments," and for using profanity in a public setting. This censure effectively ends Gaouette's chances of further promotion in his naval career.[2401])

Higher up the food chain in the Pentagon, Leon Panetta is not asked to resign as Defense Secretary after Benghazi. This is despite his agency's complete failure to get any U.S. military forces anywhere near the besieged Americans on the Night of Benghazi until the latter are well on their way to Germany. The same is true for Joint Chiefs Chairman General Dempsey. If President Obama truly gives them orders to "Do everything possible" to save American lives in Benghazi (Chapter 43), both should be fired by the president or impeached by Congress. But as noted above, they are not. Panetta also should be investigated for perjury before Congress, but is not. Instead, Panetta resigns as Secretary of Defense in February 2013 and returns to the private sector.[2402] (Like Hillary Clinton, no doubt he regrets not leaving a few months earlier.)

General Dempsey will serve out the remainder of his two-year term as Chairman of the Joint Chiefs of Staff. Incredibly, despite the military's poor performance on the Night of Benghazi, President Obama will reappoint Dempsey for a second term! He will retire from the military in September 2015.

But not everything at the Pentagon is a cluster mess. On the bright side, GRS security agent Mark "Oz" Geist will be returned to "active duty status" in the military. This will allow the Pentagon to fund the extensive surgeries and rehabilitation he requires as a result of the serious injuries Oz sustains on the Night of Benghazi. (Well done.)

According to journalist-author Mitchell Zuckoff (citing *The Washington Times*), the two military Delta Force members of Team Tripoli will be decorated for their valor on the Night of Benghazi. One Marine on the team is awarded the Navy Cross for heroism. The second member, an Army master sergeant, is awarded the Army's second-highest honor, the Distinguished Service Cross.

[2401] C. J. Chivers and Thom Shanker, "Admiral at Center of Inquiry Is Censured by Navy," *The New York Times* online (Mar. 26, 2013).

[2402] Leon E. Panetta, Former Secretary of Defense, Defense Department Official Biography.

Because they are not on "active duty" status at the time of Benghazi, none of the GRS members are eligible for such military honors.[2403]

The Central Intelligence Agency

Insofar as we know, no CIA official is sanctioned directly in connection with the Benghazi attacks.

In the weeks following Benghazi, CIA Director David Petraeus wisely decides to travel to Libya himself to investigate what has happened there. In Libya he reportedly interrogates his resolute Chief of Station in Tripoli about the attacks. However, Petraeus will never have a chance to write a report on what he learns there. Also, Petraeus is scheduled to testify before Congress in mid-November, but this will be postponed. This is because David Petraeus resigns suddenly as CIA Director effective November 9, 2012 – just over eight weeks after Benghazi, and a mere three days after the election. He has held this job for only 14 months.[2404]

David Petraeus' hasty departure likely has nothing to do with Benghazi.[2405] Rather, his resignation is a response to reports he is under criminal investigation by the FBI for unlawfully providing classified information to his mistress, Paula Broadwell. She is a fellow West Point graduate who is married and a mother of two. She also is Petraeus' biographer, who uses the classified data as background research, but apparently does not publish any of it.[2406]

(During the FBI's criminal probe of Petraeus, investigators reportedly find a video of a speech by Broadwell at the University of Denver. In it, she bizarrely suggests the terrorist attacks in Benghazi are "targeting a secret prison" located in the CIA Annex, and are an attempt to free Libyan militia members being held prisoner there! (Then why do they first attack the Mission, not the Annex? And aren't the later mortar attacks on the Annex likely to kill any Libyan prisoners along with the Americans?) A "senior intelligence official" speaking with CNN denies Broadwell's assertion. Moreover, the author has

---

[2403] Zuckoff, *13 Hours*, Epilogue, pp. 300-301.

[2404] Pearson, The Petraeus Affair: A Lot More Than Sex; and Central Intelligence Agency website.

[2405] Pearson, The Petraeus Affair: A Lot More Than Sex (Quoting anonymous "senior" U.S. official: "Any suggestion that his [Petraeus'] departure has anything to do with criticism about Benghazi is completely baseless").

[2406] *Id.*

found no evidence supporting such a theory. But then, they *are* a bunch of spies who are good at keeping secrets.[2407])

Petraeus later pleads guilty to a misdemeanor charge (mishandling classified information) relating to this sex and national security scandal.[2408] (Conservative radio talk show host Rush Limbaugh humorously will ridicule attempts by some Obama supporters to deflect political attention away from Benghazi and toward Petraeus' marital infidelities.[2409])

As noted above, Petraeus is succeeded at the CIA by John Brennan, President Obama's senior White House advisor on counterterrorism on the Night of Benghazi, who largely goes missing in action during the crisis. This is yet another key promotion for a senior Obama official in charge at the time of Benghazi.

Michael Morell temporarily will become Acting CIA Director until John Brennan can be confirmed. After this, Morell will continue to serve as Deputy Director for only three more months. He resigns in June 2013, about one month after the Obama administration finally releases emails demonstrating it is Morell who deletes the references to al Qaeda from the CIA Talking Points (explained in Chapter 94, above). New Director Brennan will assert Morell is departing from the Agency so he can spend more time with family and "pursue other professional opportunities," and his leaving is unrelated to the Benghazi CIA Talking Points.[2410] (*Hmmm.*)

[2407] *Id.*

[2408] Adam Goldman, "Petraeus Pleads Guilty to Mishandling Classified Material, Will Face Probation," *The Washington Post* online (April 23, 2015).

[2409] Compare Pearson, The Petraeus Affair: A Lot More Than Sex ("The scandal also is rumbling through the halls of Congress, where leaders in both parties are seeking answers about the FBI investigation and there's much speculation about the impact Petraeus' resignation will have into the inquiry into the Benghazi attack. . . . Petraeus' resignation also presents challenges to the congressional inquiry into the Benghazi attack. . . . Some Republicans have criticized the administration's response to the Benghazi attack and have speculated that Petraeus' departure was linked to the congressional inquiry. . . ."); with "Petraeus Scandal and Benghazi," Transcript of Rush Limbaugh Radio Show (Nov. 13, 2012) ("Yeah, they've turned Benghazi into a sex scandal. They've turned Benghazi into an episode of the Real Housewives of West Point. I'm not kidding. We've got four dead Americans. We have an actual dereliction of duty and responsibility and it's been turned into a sex scandal. . . .").

[2410] Reid J. Epstein, "Deputy CIA Director Morell Retires," POLITICO website (June 12, 2013; Updated June 13, 2013).

According to Mitchell Zuckoff (citing *The Daily Beast*), "Bob" the CIA Chief of Base at the Benghazi Annex, reportedly will receive a "prestigious intelligence service medal." Also according to Zuckoff, the GRS Team Leader at the Annex (again, a CIA employee, unlike the contractors he supervises) receives the "Distinguished Intelligence Cross, the highest honor bestowed by the CIA." Zuckoff explains this award is given to clandestine service members for "a voluntary act or acts of extraordinary heroism involving the acceptance of existing dangers with conspicuous fortitude and exemplary courage."[2411]

Because they are not CIA employees, the five surviving GRS security contractor heroes are ineligible for such CIA awards. However, the CIA does honor each of them with a newly-created "medal of valor." Tyrone Woods and Glen Doherty are given these awards posthumously.

(Except for Oz Geist, all of these surviving GRS security agents present in Benghazi later will continue to do security contracting for the CIA. (Oz is too badly injured to resume his security work.) Three of these GRS agents – Tig Tiegen, Tanto Paronto and Oz Geist – "go public" by 2014 when they collaborate openly with Zuckoff on the book *13 Hours*. This decision effectively ends Paronto's and Tiegen's ability to serve as "secret soldiers" for the CIA. Two other GRS agents remain nonpublic, although they do collaborate on the book using pseudonyms ("Jack Silva" and "Dave 'D.B.' Benton"). By the time the *13 Hours* book is published in 2014, all five of the surviving GRS contractors have retired from government security contracting and moved into the private sector.[2412])

Conclusions Regarding Accountability

A clear pattern emerges regarding how government players on the Night of Benghazi are treated afterwards. Obama and Biden are reelected for another four-year term. Senior cabinet-level members (Panetta, Clinton, Petraeus and Donilon) all are allowed to resign – all but Petraeus after a decent interval. All depart with no stated

---

[2411] Zuckoff, *13 Hours*, Epilogue, p. 300.

[2412] Interview of Kris "Tanto" Paronto with Sean Hannity, "Sean Hannity Radio Show" (April 5, 2017); and Zuckoff, *13 Hours*, Epilogue, p. 301. Tiegen, Paronto and Geist also will serve as advisers on the Paramount movie based on the book. *13 Hours: The Secret Soldiers of Benghazi*, Extra Features DVD (Paramount, 2016).

connection to Benghazi. Only Petraeus leaves under an official cloud – a sex and classified-information-breach scandal, not a terrorism one.

A number of key players at the "Deputy" or similar level below cabinet rank (Lew, McDonough, Brennan, Rice and Morell temporarily) will be *promoted* following Benghazi. Most of the senior officials who are not promoted (Dempsey, Kennedy, Rhodes and Morell after Brennan is confirmed) are allowed to retain their existing positions. Some mid-level managers are promoted or otherwise rewarded (Dibble, Nuland and Sullivan).[2413] A few mid-level employees (Lamb, Boswell, Bultrowicz and Maxwell) are sanctioned, suspended, and moved to other positions. But even *they* are not fired and never miss a paycheck. Two officials (General Ham and later Morell) possibly are pushed out of government because of Benghazi. However, Team Obama publicly denies their departures are related to the debacle. Lower-level officials who have the nerve to criticize their government's handling of Benghazi (Nordstrom and Hicks) are marginalized or effectively demoted and (in Hicks' case) eventually forced out of government service.

(Some accountability.) ∎

[2413] Guy Benson, "Surprise: Obama Promotes Another Benghazi Scandal Player," Townhall.com website (May 24, 2013) (". . . Loyal soldiers must be rewarded for protecting the castle, after all. . . . The message is clear: The president could not care less about what other people think about his administration's actions. Indeed, it's such a non-scandal to the White House that they're conspicuously promoting its key players. The arrogance and 'you can't touch me' attitude speaks for itself. . . .").

114

Bringing the Terrorists "To Justice"

If we cannot hold culpable Obama administration officials accountable for Benghazi, can we at least apprehend and punish the terrorists who actually perpetrated the deadly and destructive attacks? Sadly, the answer mostly is "No."

Later, in May 2013, Barack Obama will claim, "The day after it happened, I acknowledged that this was an act of terrorism. And what I pledged to the American people was that we would find out what happened, we would make sure that *it* did not happen again, and we would make sure we held accountable those who had perpetrated this terrible *crime*."[2414]

(It is yet another pitiful example of President Obama viewing terrorism largely as a law enforcement challenge.[2415] Can anyone imagine British Prime Minister Winston Churchill in 1940-1941 describing German Chancellor Adolph Hitler's bombing of London during the "Blitz" as a "terrible crime" and promising to arrest him, rather than an act of war and terror, or at least a "war crime"? Very few individuals actually are held accountable for terrorism against the U.S. during President Obama's administration.[2416] Regrettably, Attorney General Jeff Sessions in the *Trump* administration later adopts this same "crime" attitude.[2417])

[2414] Obama-Cameron Joint Press Conference (emphasis added); and Lucas, Obama: State Dept. That Didn't Interview Clinton 'Investigated Every Element' of Benghazi. See also FBI Most Wanted Notice, "Seeking Information on Attacks in Benghazi," FBI website (Undated) ("We need your help to solve this crime. . . .").

[2415] Guy Benson, "Whoa: US Hasn't Detained Five Benghazi Terrorists Due to Trial-Related Evidentiary Concerns," Townhall.com website (May 21, 2013) (emphasis in original) (". . . Our government / military / intelligence community has the information and capacity to haul in at least five of the suspected Benghazi terrorists, but eight months after the deadly raid, they remain free men *entirely* because of the Obama administration's ideological obsession with furnishing foreign terrorists with civilian trials. . . .").

[2416] *The Emperor Obama: An American Betrayal, Book I – Foreign Policy, National Security and Terrorism* (to be available at www.amazon.com).

[2417] DOJ Press Release, "Libyan National Charged with Federal Offenses in 2012 Attack on U.S. Special Mission and Annex in Benghazi," Justice Dept. website

In his October 18 "Comedy Central" appearance, Obama tells Jon Stewart, "I wasn't confused about the fact that we were going to hunt down whoever did *it* and *bring them to justice.*"[2418] He will repeat this refrain nearly every time he speaks of Benghazi in public.

In August 2013, the State Department tells Congress:

> ... [T]he ARB Report [discussed above in Chapter 109] was very clear in stating that the only people responsible for the lethal attack on our Special Mission Compound in Benghazi were the terrorists who orchestrated the attack. These terrorists must be brought to justice; the entire U.S. Government remains committed to doing just that.[2419]

(The emphasis again is on law enforcement, not combating terrorism and killing terrorists. "Deploy lawyers to *attack!*")

However, despite this and many similar promises by Team Obama, out of scores of terrorists who attack the three-dozen Americans in Benghazi, only two people – Ahmed Abu Khatallah and Mustafa al-Imam – ever are apprehended for playing any role in the attacks. And as this edition goes to press nearly eight years later, only those two men have been convicted of any Benghazi-related crimes.[2420]

Ahmed Abu Khatallah

Ahmed Abu Khatallah (aka Ahmed Mukatallah, age believed to be 46) is a Libyan national who lives in Benghazi. Khatallah allegedly is a leader of a "brigade" related to the Ansar al-Sharia militia group. The State Department will describe him as a "senior leader" of Ansar al-Sharia in Benghazi. His group is known as "Ubaydah bin Jarrah."

(Oct. 30, 2017) (emphasis added) (". . . The United States will continue to investigate and identify all those who were involved in the [Benghazi] attack – and we will hold them accountable *for their crimes*"); and DOJ Press Release, "Attorney General Jeff Sessions Delivers Statement on the Apprehension of Mustafa Al-Imam for His Role in 2012 Attack in Benghazi, Libya," Justice Dept. website (Oct. 30, 2017) (". . . [W]e will hold them accountable for their crimes").

[2418] Montopoli, Obama to Jon Stewart: Benghazi Response "Not Optimal" (emphasis added).

[2419] Gibbons Aug. 23, 2013 Letter to Chairman Issa, p. 3.

[2420] DOJ Press Release, "Libyan National Found Guilty of Terrorism Charges in 2012 Attack on U.S. Facilities in Benghazi," Justice Dept. website (June 17, 2019); and Jessica Donati and Del Quentin Wilber, "Libyan Extremist Is Found Guilty in Benghazi Attacks," *The Wall Street Journal* online (Nov. 28, 2017) ("Donati and Wilber, Libyan Extremist Is Found Guilty in Benghazi Attacks").

The U.S. government says one goal of this group is to establish Sharia law in Libya. For a time, the U.S. reportedly defers apprehending Khatallah "for fear that American action could trigger unrest and destabilize the Libyan government."[2421] (A tad late to worry about that.)

Khatallah finally is seized in Libya on June 15, 2014, in a secret raid by U.S. special operations forces working in conjunction with the FBI, after he is "lured to a villa south of Benghazi." The operation reportedly is code-named "Greenbrier River." Khatallah, armed with a handgun, resists strenuously. But he is no match for the Delta Force soldiers and FBI hostage rescue agent. Bruised and cut, he is taken to the coast, where U.S. Navy Seals take him by boat to a waiting U.S. warship. For five days on the voyage to the U.S., Khatallah is interrogated (without a lawyer). The Libyan government protests the raid and snatching as a violation of its sovereignty![2422] (Remind us, to what country does the "new" Libya owe its sovereignty?)

Abu Khatallah has been charged earlier, in July 2013, in a sealed (nonpublic) federal criminal complaint for his alleged role in the Benghazi assaults. Eleven months later, his luck runs out.[2423]

[2421] Khatallah Superseding Indictment, Count 1, ¶9, pp. 3-4; Media Note, "Terrorist Designations of Three Ansar al-Shari'a Organizations and Leaders," Office of the Spokesperson, State Dept. Archives website (Jan. 10, 2014); Eyder Peralta, "Benghazi Suspect, Ahmed Abu Khattala [sic], Is Indicted on 17 New Charges," National Public Radio online (Oct. 14, 2014); Goldman, Former Guantanamo Detainee Implicated in Benghazi Attack; Savage and Goldman, At Trial, a Focus on the Facts, Not the Politics, of Benghazi; and Adam Goldman and Eric Schmitt, "Benghazi Attacks Suspect Is Captured in Libya by U.S. Commandos," *The New York Times* online (Oct. 30, 2017).

[2422] Department of Defense Briefing by Rear Admiral Kirby, Defense Dept. website (June 17, 2014); Savage and Goldman, At Trial, a Focus on the Facts, Not the Politics, of Benghazi; Press Release, "Pentagon Announces Capture of Key Figure in Benghazi Attacks," DoD News, Defense Dept. website (June 17, 2014); Press Release, "Libyan National Charged with Federal Offenses in 2012 Attack on U.S. Special Mission and Annex in Benghazi," Justice Dept. website (June 17, 2014); DOJ Press Release, "Abu Khatallah Found Guilty of Terrorism Charges"; Dave Boyer and Maggie Ybarra, "Capture of Benghazi Suspect in Secret Raid Fuels Debate on Prisoner's Legal Status," *The Washington Times* online (June 17, 2014); Hsu, U.S. Will Not Seek Death Penalty for Accused Ringleader in Benghazi Attacks; and Hsu, CIA Officers Detail Part of Bloody Benghazi Attack at Terrorism Trial (Criminal trial testimony of two disguised CIA agents using pseudonyms "Roy Edwards" and "Alexander Charles").

[2423] DOJ Press Release, "Libyan National Charged with Federal Offenses in 2012 Attack on U.S. Special Mission and Annex in Benghazi," Justice Dept. website (June 17, 2014); and DOJ Press Release, "Abu Khatallah Found Guilty of Terrorism Charges." For a description of the detailed and elaborate capture and interrogation of Abu Khatallah, see Spencer S. Hsu, "Thirteen Days in the History of the Accused Leader of the Benghazi Attacks," *The Washington Post* online (June 9, 2017).

THE BENGHAZI BETRAYAL

A rational American leader would order Abu Khatallah taken to the U.S. military prison at Guantanamo Bay, Cuba as a terrorist "enemy combatant" captured abroad. There, he should be subject to rigorous "enhanced interrogation" to learn more about his fellow terrorist attackers and the groups that support them. Then, he should be tried by a military tribunal.[2424] If found guilty, he should be executed.[2425]

Unfortunately, on his second full day in office President Obama has discontinued enhanced interrogations.[2426] Moreover, this same day Obama also has ordered Guantanamo closed.[2427] For his entire presidency, Barack Obama will make every effort possible to move detainees *out* of Guantanamo, not *into* it.[2428] So instead of "Gitmo,"

[2424] Savage and Goldman, At Trial, a Focus on the Facts, Not the Politics, of Benghazi ("A recurring debate has emerged over whether such suspects should instead be held and interrogated at the military prison at Guantánamo Bay, Cuba, then prosecuted before the military commissions system there").

[2425] Interview of Kris "Tanto" Paronto with Sandra Smith, "America's Newsroom," Fox News Channel (Nov. 29, 2017) (His reaction to the verdict in Khatallah's trial: ". . . Disgusted. To be honest with you, it should never have gotten into a criminal court. To allow a terrorist to have due process and to be covered under our constitution is completely ridiculous. That's why I didn't testify. . . . [A]t the very best Khatallah should have got a military tribunal. . . . In the very best in my case, the extraction team should have put a bullet in his head. . . . This is ridiculous; it's a travesty"); and Katie Pavlich, "Kris Paronto: A Bullet Should Have Been Put in Benghazi Terrorist's Head," Townhall.com website (Nov. 29, 2017) (Tanto Paronto: "You don't bring a terrorist and waste taxpayer money and give him a criminal trial. You put him in GITMO or you interrogate him and you execute him. That's how you deal with terrorists. . . . You don't give animals due process and that's what terrorists are").

[2426] Executive Order 13491 by President Barack Obama – Ensuring Lawful Interrogations, Obama White House Archives (Jan. 22, 2009); and Michael Isikoff, "Obama's Order Ends Bush-Era Interrogation Tactics," Newsweek online (Jan. 21, 2009) (". . . President Obama overruled the pleas of senior U.S. intelligence officials and signed a new executive order that bars the CIA from using harsh interrogation methods beyond those permitted by the U.S. military").

[2427] Executive Order by President Barack Obama – Closure of Guantanamo Detention Facilities, Obama White House Archives (Jan. 22, 2009).

[2428] E.g., Victor Davis Hanson, "The Next President Unbound," Townhall.com website (Sept. 28, 2016) ("Rebuffed by Congress, Obama is now slowly shutting down the Guantanamo Bay detention center by insidiously having inmates sent to other countries"); "Obama to Unveil Guantanamo Bay Closure Plan," CNN online (Feb. 22, 2016); Interview of Department of State Special Envoy Lee Wolosky with CNN (Feb. 2016) (emphasis added); "Obama to Unveil Guantanamo Bay Closure Plan," CNN online (Feb. 22, 2016) (Special Envoy Wolosky: "This is hard. It's a difficult ask of the U.S. to make, to say please take these individuals whom the world has branded as terrorists. . . . We work to put in place mechanisms that are intended to keep *pretty close track* of them in order to mitigate any threat these resettled detainees may pose to

THE TRUE ACCOUNT OF VALOR AND ABANDONMENT

Obama orders Abu Khatallah removed to Washington, D.C.![2429] As a result, the alleged terrorist immediately is cloaked with numerous constitutional protections, including being provided with a team of lawyers and other "due process" rights, such as the rights to remain silent and to a jury trial by his supposed "peers."

The decision to accord Khatallah all the rights of a U.S. citizen caught robbing a Dairy Queen in Des Moines has other consequences. Had he been taken to Guantanamo and treated as the enemy combatant he is, he could have been interrogated – rigorously. He would receive no *Miranda* warning. It is entirely possible his interrogators could have learned the names of at least some of his co-conspirators.[2430]

The father of slain Tyrone Woods, Charles Woods, later will tell Fox News, "I am very bothered by the fact the U.S. government gave constitutional rights and due process rights to a foreign national who allegedly killed Americans outside the U.S." He adds, "This is what bothered me from the very beginning."[2431] (Yep, Charles has nailed it.)

For multiple reasons, any criminal prosecution of Khatallah in U.S. federal court is destined to be difficult. To begin, in recent years success in prosecuting foreign terrorists in U.S. courts has been mixed.[2432] Among other challenges, years have passed, classified information will be needed for evidence, much of the crime scene evidence has been looted or tainted, and many of the witnesses who might still be located are in the dysfunctional, violence-torn, failed

---

the receiving country or the United States"); and Savage and Goldman, At Trial, a Focus on the Facts, Not the Politics, of Benghazi ("Although Mr. Khatalla [sic] is not an American citizen, the Obama administration chose not to send him to Guantánamo both because it was trying to close the prison and because he lacked strong ties to Al Qaeda").

[2429] DOJ Press Release, "Abu Khatallah Found Guilty of Terrorism Charges."

[2430] Additional Views of Reps. Jordan and Pompeo ("... It is ... certain that the Obama administration's decision to treat Abu Khatallah and other terrorists as ordinary criminals – affording them the full panoply of legal protections available under U.S. law – has made it harder to capture Abu Khatallah's co-conspirators. . . ."), p. 449 n. 119.

[2431] Samuel Chamberlain, "Benghazi Victims' Relatives Outraged Over Khatalla [sic] Verdict," Fox News online (Nov. 28, 2017).

[2432] E.g., Savage and Goldman, At Trial, a Focus on the Facts, Not the Politics, of Benghazi (In 2010 jury trial of former Guantanamo detainee Ahmed Ghailani, charged with Al Qaeda's 1998 bombings of two American embassies in East Africa, Ghailani was convicted only of "conspiring to destroy American buildings but acquitted of 284 other charges, including every murder count").

nation of Libya (or in some cases, probably dead). (Citing a military spokesperson, Al Jazeera reports the Libya authorities do not even get around to examining the crime scene at the Mission Compound until "late on Friday afternoon . . . ," September 14.) Indeed, in Khatallah's eventual trial out of 30 witnesses only four persons from Libya will testify![2433] One of these effectively must be "bribed" with $7 million to do so. This likely is paid through the State Department's "Rewards for Justice" program, discussed above. (Lotsa luck, prosecutors!)

In October 2014, a federal grand jury in Washington indicts Abu Khatallah on an additional 17 counts. The federal charges, as enhanced, include: murder of an internationally-protected individual (Ambassador Stevens); murders of officers and employees of the U.S.; killing persons during an assault involving a firearm on a U.S. facility; attempted murder of an officer and employee of the U.S.; conspiracy to support terrorism; "providing material support and resources" to terrorists that results in death; damaging U.S. government facilities by means of fire and an explosive causing death; and discharging, brandishing, using, carrying and possessing a firearm during a crime of violence. Some of these charges are death-penalty-eligible.[2434] The Indictment claims Khatallah undertook the Benghazi attacks because he had discovered the U.S. had a facility collecting intelligence located in that city, and was "going to do something about this facility."[2435] Khatallah pleads not guilty to all charges.[2436]

[2433] Hsu, U.S. Will Not Seek Death Penalty for Accused Ringleader in Benghazi Attacks; Savage and Goldman, At Trial, a Focus on the Facts, Not the Politics, of Benghazi ("Adding to the complexity of the case, the F.B.I. was not able to swiftly secure the crime scene and conduct a typical forensic investigation because Benghazi was too dangerous"); and Yasmine Ryan, "Libya Says US Consulate Attack 'Pre-Planned,'" Al Jazeera online (Sept. 14, 2012); and DOJ Press Release, "Abu Khatallah Found Guilty of Terrorism Charges."

[2434] Khatallah Superseding Indictment, Counts 1-18, pp. 2-20; DOJ Press Release, "Libyan National Charged with Federal Offenses in 2012 Attack on U.S. Special Mission and Annex in Benghazi," Justice Dept. website (June 17, 2014); DOJ Press Release, "Ahmed Abu Khatallah Indicted on Additional Charges for September 2012 Attack in Benghazi, Libya," Justice Dept. website (Oct. 14, 2014); and Eyder Peralta, "Benghazi Suspect, Ahmed Abu Khattala [sic], Is Indicted on 17 New Charges," National Public Radio online (Oct. 14, 2014).

[2435] Khatallah Superseding Indictment, Count 1, ¶20(a), p. 6; and Eyder Peralta, "Benghazi Suspect, Ahmed Abu Khattala [sic], Is Indicted on 17 New Charges," National Public Radio online (Oct. 14, 2014).

[2436] Hsu, U.S. Will Not Seek Death Penalty for Accused Ringleader in Benghazi Attacks.

THE TRUE ACCOUNT OF VALOR AND ABANDONMENT

As proof of how seriously the U.S. government takes its duty to "bring to justice" those responsible for Benghazi, in May 2016 the Obama administration determines it will not even seek the death penalty against Abu Khatallah![2437] This is contrary to what federal prosecutors recently have done in the trial in the 2013 Boston Marathon bombing. There, the government seeks and obtains a death sentence against Dzhokhar Tsarnaev. Unlike Khatallah, Tsarnaev is an American citizen living in the U.S., who commits his terrorism on U.S. soil.[2438] (*Why the hell is a foreign terrorist who murders American government officials abroad treated more leniently than a U.S. citizen terrorist who murders U.S. civilians at home?*)

In October 2015, President Obama tells an interviewer, "I've not been opposed to the death penalty in theory, but in practice it's deeply troubling."[2439] According to *The Washington Post*, ". . . no D.C. jury has ever imposed the death penalty."[2440] (*Is this is why Obama orders Abu Khatallah transferred to D.C.?* In reality, it probably doesn't matter; the U.S. government has executed only three federal inmates since 1964, and not a single person on the federal death row is put to death during the entire eight years of Obama's presidency.[2441])

[2437] *Id.* ("The Justice Department announced Tuesday that it will not seek the death penalty against Ahmed Abu Khattala [sic], 54, a U.S.-designated terrorist whom prosecutors accuse of leading the 2012 attacks in Benghazi, Libya, that killed four Americans"); and Additional Views of Reps. Jordan and Pompeo ("After the attacks, President Obama promised 'justice will be done.' There is no doubt our nation can make good on that commitment. Yet, almost four years later [as of June 2016], only one of the terrorists has been captured and brought to the United States to face criminal charges. Even that terrorist will not receive the full measure of justice after the administration chose not to seek the death penalty. The American people are owed an explanation"), p. 416.

[2438] Hsu, U.S. Will Not Seek Death Penalty for Accused Ringleader in Benghazi Attacks.

[2439] Steven Mufson and Mark Berman, "Obama Calls Death Penalty 'Deeply Troubling,' But His Position Hasn't Budged," *The Washington Post* online (Oct. 23, 2015) ("This is something I've struggled with for quite some time. . . . There are certain crimes that are so beyond the pale that I understand society's need to express its outrage").

[2440] *Id.*; and Hsu, U.S. Will Not Seek Death Penalty for Accused Ringleader in Benghazi Attacks.

[2441] Hsu, U.S. Will Not Seek Death Penalty for Accused Ringleader in Benghazi Attacks ("Federal prosecutors have sought the death penalty for an accused terrorist at least 14 times since 1993, but only one was executed – Timothy McVeigh, the 1995 Oklahoma City federal-building bomber"); and Steven Mufson and Mark Berman,

Khatallah's federal criminal trial begins in October 2017. The Justice Department claims that in the months prior to the Benghazi attacks, Khatallah "sought to incite violence by his and other militia groups against the presence of the United States in Libya."[2442] The prosecutors summarize their evidence against Khatallah as follows:

> Before, during and after the attack, Khatallah maintained contact with his group in a series of cellphone calls. Also, according to the government's evidence, for much of the attack, he positioned himself on the perimeter of the [Mission] compound and kept others, including emergency responders, from getting to the scene. The government's evidence also showed that Khatallah made calls to leaders of other militia groups warning them not to interfere with the attack.[2443]

In contrast, according to *The Washington Post*, during the trial "... [D]efense lawyers said Abu Khattala [sic] came to the mission out of curiosity, was directing traffic to keep bystanders safe and entered only after the fighting was over and Americans had left." This same *Post* article said prosecutors conceded Khatallah was home by the time of the final deadly mortar attacks on the CIA Annex (at about 5:17 a.m., Benghazi time).[2444] (As noted in Chapter 79, this contradicts the congressional testimony of one American inside the CIA Annex, who claims to have observed Khatallah at the mortar assault.)

After six weeks of trial, on November 28 *a federal jury acquits Khatallah of 14 of the 18 charges (including the most serious murder ones)!* It convicts him only of four lesser offenses. Khatallah is found guilty on one count each of: conspiracy to provide (and actually providing) material support to terrorists; maliciously destroying dwellings and property and placing lives in danger within U.S. territorial jurisdiction; and using and carrying a semiautomatic weapon during a crime of violence.[2445] (Wow, the jury really let him have it.)

"Obama Calls Death Penalty 'Deeply Troubling,' But His Position Hasn't Budged," *The Washington Post* online (Oct. 23, 2015).

[2442] DOJ Press Release, "Abu Khatallah Found Guilty of Terrorism Charges."

[2443] *Id.* See also Khatallah Superseding Indictment, Count 1, ¶20(e), p. 7.

[2444] Hsu, Baring Grievous Wounds, Dry Humor, U.S. Agent Lays Out Key Evidence at Benghazi Trial.

[2445] DOJ Press Release, "Abu Khatallah Found Guilty of Terrorism Charges"; and Donati and Wilber, Libyan Extremist Is Found Guilty in Benghazi Attacks.

Even on these few conviction charges, Khatallah theoretically remains subject to a possible sentence of life in prison, with a mandatory minimum of ten years.[2446])

(Perhaps the jury took objection to the evidence the U.S. paid one Libyan witness a whopping $7 million to fly to America and testify against Khatallah! Nice work if you can get it.[2447] What genius in the Justice Department thinks *this* is a good idea? Possibly this registers just a tad high for the jurors on the "self-interest" and "bias" scales.)

Sean Smith's mother, Pat Smith, will tell Fox News she is "not happy" with the verdict, but "not surprised." She adds, "I think the people who bear responsibility – Secretary of State Hillary Clinton – aren't even touched."[2448]

The Khatallah jury's decision is strong evidence of how misguided is the Obama administration's policy of prosecuting non-citizen terrorists captured abroad – who are enemy combatants in every sense – in American federal civilian courts. Khatallah is treated like any other federal prisoner, as if he has knocked off a credit union in Sparks, Nevada, or taken a stolen car across the Alabama-Georgia border.

In late June 2018, presiding Judge Christopher R. Cooper sentences Khatallah to only 22 years in prison.[2449] This is just 5.5 years per murder. (So 5.5 years is the punishment for assassinating a U.S. ambassador? It is a disgrace.)

(Given how lengthy and inefficient is the terrorism military tribunal system established by the George W. Bush administration – as modified by the courts – perhaps it doesn't much matter. Under either inept option, the American government betrays its citizens' safety. The Trump administration should fix this.)

Mustafa al-Imam

In Libya in late October 2017, during the Trump administration, a U.S. commando squad captures a second alleged Libyan terrorist suspected of taking part in the Benghazi attacks. He is Mustafa

---

[2446] DOJ Press Release, "Abu Khatallah Found Guilty of Terrorism Charges"; and Donati and Wilber, Libyan Extremist Is Found Guilty in Benghazi Attacks.

[2447] For what it's worth, the author would have been willing to do it for $6 million.

[2448] Samuel Chamberlain, "Benghazi Victims' Relatives Outraged Over Khatalla [sic] Verdict," Fox News online (Nov. 28, 2017).

[2449] DOJ Press Release, "Ahmed Abu Khatallah Sentenced to 22 Years in Prison for September 2012 Attack in Benghazi, Libya," Justice Dept. website (June 27, 2018).

al-Imam (age then about 46). According to *The New York Times*, al-Imam is captured in a surprise raid near the coastal city of Misrata, Libya (between Tripoli and Benghazi). It is conducted by a commando team comprised of members of Seal Team Six and the FBI's Hostage Rescue Team. The mission reportedly has been planned for months, and is authorized by President Trump.[2450]

Al-Imam reportedly has been captured on surveillance cameras at the Mission Compound on the Night of Benghazi. Prosecutors also believe he is involved in the later attacks on the CIA Annex.[2451] *The Washington Times* reports al-Imam communicates frequently by phone with Ahmed Abu Khatallah before and during the attacks.[2452] Prosecutors later confirm "a series of cellphone calls" during the attack, including an 18-minute call "during the height of the attack."[2453]

In October 2017, Fox News will report "U.S. forces on the ground then" assert al-Imam had been observed by U.S. forces *as early as December 2012*. Sources reportedly claim U.S. commandos have been ordered *twice* not to "snatch and grab" al-Imam! Some five years later, President Trump wisely reverses Barack Obama's earlier decisions.[2454]

Unfortunately, the Trump administration then repeats the errors of Team Obama and brings al-Imam back to the U.S. to stand trial in a

---

[2450] "Statement of President Donald J. Trump on the Apprehension of Mustafa al-Imam for His Alleged Role in the September 11, 2012 Attacks in Benghazi, Libya Resulting in the Deaths of Four Americans," White House website (Oct. 30, 2017).

[2451] DOJ Press Release, "Libyan National Charged with Federal Offenses in 2012 Attack on U.S. Special Mission and Annex in Benghazi," Justice Dept. website (Oct. 30, 2017); Conor Gaffey, "Who Is Mustafa Al-Islam [sic Imam]? Benghazi Attack Suspect Captured in Libya to Face Trial in U.S.," Newsweek online (Oct. 31, 2017) (*Watch video* there); Adam Goldman and Eric Schmitt, "Benghazi Attacks Suspect Is Captured in Libya by U.S. Commandos," *The New York Times* online (Oct. 30, 2017); and "Special Report," Fox News Channel (Oct. 30, 2017). See also DOJ Press Release, "Attorney General Jeff Sessions Delivers Statement on the Apprehension of Mustafa Al-Imam for His Role in 2012 Attack in Benghazi, Libya," Justice Dept. website (Oct. 30, 2017).

[2452] Andrea Noble, "Second Suspect Arrested in Benghazi Attack on U.S. Mission Held Without Bond," *The Washington Times* online (Nov. 9, 2017).

[2453] DOJ Press Release, "Mustafa al-Imam Sentenced to 236 Months in Prison for September 2012 Terrorist Attack in Benghazi, Libya," Justice Dept. website (Jan. 23, 2020).

[2454] "Special Report," Fox News Channel (Oct. 30, 2017).

federal civilian court.²⁴⁵⁵ As with Khatallah, he should have been removed to Guantanamo for interrogation and a military tribunal.²⁴⁵⁶ Earlier, in May 2015, al-Imam has been charged in a sealed criminal complaint filed in Washington, D.C. on three counts: conspiracy to provide material support and resources to terrorists, resulting in death; killing a person in the course of an attack on a U.S. government facility involving the use of a firearm and dangerous weapon; and possessing and using a firearm during a crime of violence.²⁴⁵⁷ A later indictment contains only a single charge of conspiring to provide material support to terrorists resulting in death. Eventually, al-Imam will be tried on 17 criminal counts. Al-Imam pleads not guilty.²⁴⁵⁸

The federal criminal trial of al-Imam begins on May 8, 2019. During a four-week trial, the jury hears evidence from 27 witnesses. These include the wounded defenders, as well as a number of other survivors. On June 13, the jury finds al-Imam guilty on only two counts: (1) Conspiracy to provide material support and resources to terrorists; and (2) Maliciously destroying and injuring a dwelling and placing lives in jeopardy. *The jury fails to reach a verdict on the remaining 15 counts!* This results in the judge declaring a mistrial on

---

[2455] DOJ Press Release, "Attorney General Jeff Sessions Delivers Statement on the Apprehension of Mustafa Al-Imam for His Role in 2012 Attack in Benghazi, Libya," Justice Dept. website (Oct. 30, 2017).

[2456] Adam Goldman and Eric Schmitt, "Benghazi Attacks Suspect Is Captured in Libya by U.S. Commandos," *The New York Times* online (Oct. 30, 2017) ("The arrest shows that Mr. Trump, who vowed during his campaign to fill the wartime prison at Guantánamo Bay with 'bad dudes,' is willing to use civilian courts to prosecute terrorism suspects captured overseas. . . ."); and Lolita C. Baldor, Josh Lederman and Matthew Lee (Associated Press), "Militant Accused in Benghazi Attack on His Way to US Jail," Fox News online (Oct. 31, 2017) ("Al-Imam will face court proceedings in U.S. District Court, officials said, in an apparent departure from Trump's previously expressed desire to send militants to the U.S. detention center at Guantanamo Bay, Cuba").

[2457] DOJ Press Release, "Libyan National Charged with Federal Offenses in 2012 Attack on U.S. Special Mission and Annex in Benghazi," Justice Dept. website (Oct. 30, 2017); Donati and Wilber, Libyan Extremist Is Found Guilty in Benghazi Attacks; Special Report, Fox News Channel (Nov. 8, 2017); Conor Gaffey, "Who Is Mustafa Al-Islam [sic]? Benghazi Attack Suspect Captured in Libya to Face Trial in U.S.," Newsweek online (Oct. 31, 2017) (*Watch video* there); Adam Goldman and Eric Schmitt, "Benghazi Attacks Suspect Is Captured in Libya by U.S. Commandos," *The New York Times* online (Oct. 30, 2017); and "Special Report," Fox News Channel (Oct. 30, 2017).

[2458] Jake Gibson, "Benghazi Attack Suspect Pleads Not Guilty," Fox News online (Nov. 9, 2017).

those counts. On January 23, 2020, Judge Christopher Cooper sentences al-Imam to 236 months imprisonment.[2459] (This is similar to the sentence he gives Ahmed Abu Khatallah, discussed above). As this edition goes to press, it is unclear whether the government will seek to retry al-Imam on the 15 unresolved charges.

(This unsatisfying outcome again exemplifies why it is a mistake to try terrorist non-citizen enemy combatants in civilian U.S. courts.)

Abu Sufian bin Qumu

Another suspected participant in the terror attack is Abu Sufian bin Qumu (54), another Libyan national. On the Night of Benghazi, Qumu reportedly is the leader of Ansar al-Sharia in the Libyan coastal city of Darnah, located about 150 miles east of Benghazi. He is a former Guantanamo Bay detainee, whom the George W. Bush administration unwisely releases to the custody of Qadhafi's government in 2007. Libya reportedly frees Qumu the following year. Among other militant activities, *The Washington Post* reports Qumu trained in 1993 at a terrorist camp in Afghanistan run by Osama bin Laden. There, Qumu apparently fought with the Taliban against the U.S. Qumu later moved to Pakistan, where he was captured and turned over to the U.S., which sent him to Guantanamo.[2460] (And Bush released him *why?*)

In January 2014, the State Department designates Qumu as a "Specially Designated Global Terrorist." (This prohibits persons from engaging in transactions with Qumu, or providing him with "material support or resources.")[2461]

[2459] DOJ Press Release, "Mustafa al-Imam Sentenced to 236 Months in Prison for September 2012 Terrorist Attack in Benghazi, Libya," Justice Dept. website (Jan. 23, 2020).

[2460] Fox News, "Al Qaeda, Ex-Gitmo Detainee Involved in Consulate Attack, Intelligence Sources Say," Fox News online (Sept. 20, 2012); Media Note, "Terrorist Designations of Three Ansar al-Shari'a Organizations and Leaders," Office of the Spokesperson, State Dept. Archives website (Jan. 10, 2014); CBS News, Dispute Over Nature of Libya Attack Continues (Quoting CBS News senior correspondent John Miller: "He's a great suspect on paper. There is some intel about him but it's way too early to verify these reports we've seen that he is the prime suspect or the prime mover. Way too early") (*Watch video* there); Goldman, Former Guantanamo Detainee Implicated in Benghazi Attack; and Zuckoff, *13 Hours*, Epilogue, p. 299.

[2461] Media Note, "Terrorist Designations of Three Ansar al-Shari'a Organizations and Leaders," Office of the Spokesperson, State Dept. Archives website (Jan. 10, 2014).

THE TRUE ACCOUNT OF VALOR AND ABANDONMENT

As of January 2016, Qumu remains in Libya. An article in *Egypt Today* dated June 11, 2018, claims bin Qumu has been seen in Libya in "Derna" (Darnah) on May 20, 2018.[2462] As this edition goes to press, bin Qumu still has been neither apprehended nor cleared.

Faraj al Chalabi

Another possible Benghazi suspect is Faraj al Chalabi. *The Washington Post* describes him as "a Libyan extremist who might have fled the country." Libya's government reportedly arrests him in March 2013 in connection with the Benghazi attack. While Chalabi is in custody, the FBI apparently interrogates him. For unknown reasons, the Libyans release Chalabi by May 2013. CNN will report in October 2015 that Chalabi has been killed (probably by militia members holding him in custody) in the east Libyan town of Marj.[2463]

General Qasem Soleimani

Some analysts believe Iranian General Qasem Soleimani (sometimes spelled Qassem Suleymani) also played a role in providing money and support for the Benghazi attacks. Soleimani was the commander of Iran's elite "Quds Force" (part of its "Islamic Revolutionary Guard Corps"). The Quds Force has been described as a "combination CIA and Green Berets for Iran. . . ."[2464] (We note the Benghazi Select Committee could find "no evidence" Iran's Revolutionary Guard played any role in Benghazi.[2465]) The U.S. government has designated the IRGC and its Quds Force as a "foreign

---

[2462] Goldman and Miller, Former CIA Chief in Benghazi Challenges the Story Line of the New Movie '13 Hours'; and Egypt Today Staff, "Militant, Abu Abdullah al-Masry, Killed in Libya's Derna," Egypt Today online (June 11, 2018).

[2463] Goldman, Former Guantanamo Detainee Implicated in Benghazi Attack; and Jomana Karadsheh, Holly Yan, and Michael Pearson, "Where Are the Benghazi Suspects?" CNN online (Updated Oct. 21, 2015).

[2464] Kenneth R. Timmerman, "The Shadowy Iranian Spy Chief Who Helped Plan Benghazi," *New York Post* online (June 20, 2014) (citing Timmerman's own book, *Dark Forces: The Truth About What Happened in Benghazi* (Broadside Books; 2014)).

[2465] Benghazi Committee Report, p. 34 n. 135 ("The committee found no evidence of involvement by the Iranian government, specifically the Iranian Revolutionary Guard-Quds Force (IRGC-QF) as has been reported. . . .").

terrorist organization."[2466] Many regarded Soleimani as the most effective terrorist mastermind on the planet.[2467] However, any consideration of apprehending Soleimani as a Benghazi planner now is moot. On the order of President Trump, on January 2, 2020, Soleimani was killed by a U.S. military precision drone strike near the airport in Bagdad, Iraq. President Trump asserted, "Soleimani was plotting imminent and sinister attacks on American diplomats and military personnel, but we caught him in the act and terminated him."[2468] (Astonishingly, many Democrats claim it was "provocative and disproportionate" to eliminate Soleimani[2469] – despite Soleimani's group having "targeted, injured, and murdered hundreds of American civilians and servicemen."[2470])

Other Possible Suspects

The Washington Post further reports that for "more than a week" after the attack on the Mission Compound, members of Ansar al-Sharia live openly in Benghazi. (Indeed, *Newsweek* and other outlets report Ahmed Abu Khatallah himself lives openly in Benghazi following the

---

[2466] Foreign Terrorist Organizations, Bureau of Counterterrorism, State Dept. website (April 15, 2019).

[2467] E.g., Kenneth R. Timmerman, "The Shadowy Iranian Spy Chief Who Helped Plan Benghazi," *New York Post* online (June 20, 2014) ("[Soleimani's] the Wizard of Oz of Iranian terror, the most dreaded and most effective terrorist alive").

[2468] "Remarks by President Trump on the Killing of Qasem Soleimani," White House website (Jan. 3, 2020) (describing Soleimani as "the number-one terrorist anywhere in the world").

[2469] E.g., "Pelosi Statement on Airstrike in Iraq Against High-Level Iranian Military Officials," House Speaker website (Jan. 2, 2020) (". . . [W]e cannot put the lives of American servicemembers, diplomats and others further at risk by engaging in provocative and disproportionate actions. Tonight's airstrike risks provoking further dangerous escalation of violence. . . ."); and Allan Smith, "Democrats Demand Answers on Soleimani Killing: 'This Is Not a Game,'" NBC News website (Jan. 5, 2020).

[2470] "Remarks by President Trump on the Killing of Qasem Soleimani," White House website (Jan. 3, 2020). See also DOD Press Release, "Statement by the Department of Defense," Defense Dept. website (Jan. 2, 2020) (". . . General Soleimani and his Quds Force were responsible for the deaths of hundreds of American and coalition service members and the wounding of thousands more. . . .").

THE TRUE ACCOUNT OF VALOR AND ABANDONMENT

attack, and gives "multiple interviews" to U.S. media members, in which he denies any connection to the attacks.[2471])

Soon after the event, some within our intelligence community claim they know who some of the other attackers are. According to *The Daily Beast*, as of September 26, 2012, one U.S. intelligence official asserts, "I can't get into specific numbers but soon after the attack we had a pretty good bead on some individuals involved in the attack."[2472]

Indeed, as early as September 14, Al Jazeera reports Libyan authorities already have made four arrests in the Benghazi attacks. By September 16, NBC News is reporting (quite imprecisely), "Libyan officials are holding 30 to 40 suspecting [sic] in the deadly attack of a the [sic] US embassy [sic] in Libya . . ." That same day, Libyan President Mohammed Magariaf tells CBS's "Face the Nation" about "50 people, not all Libyans, have been arrested in connection with the Benghazi attack, which he said was planned by al-Qaida linked foreigners, some from Mali and Algeria."[2473]

Whatever happens to all these arrested individuals? It is certain they are not extradited to the United States.

According to Guy Benson of Townhall.com, by May 2013:

"... [A]t least five Benghazi attackers have been identified and located by the U.S. government. None of them have been detained, however, because the administration is trying to build a legal case against them that could hold up in a civilian American courtroom. Madness. . . ."[2474]

[2471] Birnbaum, Sensitive Documents Left Behind With Little Security at U.S. Diplomatic Post in Libya; and Conor Gaffey, "Who Is Mustafa Al-Islam [sic]? Benghazi Attack Suspect Captured in Libya to Face Trial in U.S.," Newsweek online (Oct. 31, 2017) (*Watch video there*).

[2472] Eli Lake, "U.S. Officials Knew Libya Attacks Were Work of Al Qaeda Affiliates," *The Daily Beast* online (Sept. 26, 2012).

[2473] "Libya Makes Arrests Over Benghazi Attack," Al Jazeera online (Sept. 14, 2012); and NBC News Staff and Wire Services, "Ambassador Rice: Benghazi Attack Began Spontaneously," NBC News online (Sept. 16, 2012).

[2474] Guy Benson, "Surprise: Obama Promotes Another Benghazi Scandal Player," Townhall.com website (May 24, 2013), citing Benson, "Whoa: US Hasn't Detained Five Benghazi Terrorists Due to Trial-Related Evidentiary Concerns," Townhall.com website (May 21, 2013) (citing Associated Press: "U.S. officials . . . say they have enough evidence to justify seizing them by military force as suspected terrorists – but not enough proof to try them in a U.S. civilian court as the Obama administration prefers. So the officials say the men remain at large while the FBI gathers more evidence. . . ."). See Sen. Intelligence Committee Benghazi Report (". . . The IC has identified several individuals responsible for the attacks. Some of the individuals have

If any or all this is true, does Team Obama pass up possible strikes on the terrorists identified? Does it fail to insert the FBI or military intelligence or special ops commandos into Benghazi quickly enough to make swift captures? (Given the Libyan government's objection to the later U.S. raid to snatch Khatallah, it is far from certain the U.S. could obtain Libyan permission for other arrests or strikes on the terrorists. But again, in such matters perhaps it is better to ask for forgiveness later than for permission today.) These possible missed opportunities to take out some of the perpetrators merely add to the many frustrations enfolding the entire Benghazi saga.

Conclusions About Holding the Terrorists Responsible

With only two persons apprehended by the U.S. for a series of attacks involving several scores of perpetrators at least, the Obama administration's vow to "seek justice" for the victims rings hollow.[2475] (One of these two is captured during the Trump administration.) Each day, the chances of apprehending any more of the attackers dwindle.

The terrorists have assassinated a U.S. ambassador, murdered three other American government workers, and severely wounded two others. They have destroyed an American diplomatic post and a CIA facility, both of which now are abandoned. They have captured sensitive U.S. intelligence data. And they have chased the mighty United States out of eastern Libya. Most of the scores of surviving terrorists largely will escape any punishment for this evil they have wrought upon America.

The Libyan terrorists have won the Battle of Benghazi.[2476] ■

---

been identified with a strong level of confidence. . . ."), p. 40; and Additional Views of Reps. Jordan and Pompeo (". . . [T]he United States does know the identity of many of the attackers. Yet, the resources devoted to bring them to justice have proven inadequate"), p. 449.

[2475] Hayes and Joscelyn, The Benghazi Report ("The Obama administration has been lax in its efforts to kill or capture the dozens of terrorists who assaulted the U.S. mission and annex. . .").

[2476] House Foreign Affairs Benghazi Majority Staff Report (". . . This tactical defeat at the hands of Islamist terrorists has been made worse by President Obama's failure to honor his vow to bring the perpetrators to justice"), p. 20.

Part V:

Conclusions

115

The Corrected "Benghazi Narrative"

We still don't know the whole truth about Benghazi. Probably, we never will. However, based upon the known evidence summarized in this book, we confidently can revise and update the Obama administration's "Benghazi Narrative" (described in Chapter 89) as follows:

(1) The U.S. has no vital national security interest in overthrowing Qadhafi, or in continuing to maintain a diplomatic outpost in treacherous Benghazi after the Libyan revolution;[2477]

(2) The supposed "heightened" state of alert on September 11, 2012, is mostly public relations theater as it pertains to Europe, the Mediterranean and North Africa;

(3) Security at the Benghazi Mission Compound on September 11, 2012, is not "robust" but is "grossly inadequate";[2478]

(4) The Defense Department's SST unit did travel to Benghazi when necessary, and some or all of its members could have accompanied Stevens to Benghazi had they not been removed from Libya by decision of the State Department headquarters (by Patrick Kennedy);[2479]

(5) Stevens does not travel to Benghazi "regularly" or "periodically," has not been able to go there since his return to Libya in

---

[2477] E.g., Catherine Herridge Report, "Special Report," Fox News Channel (Nov. 18, 2016) (Select Committee member Mike Pompeo (R-KS) chastises Hillary Clinton and her State Department team for ignoring the rising terror threat in Libya because it did not fit the Obama administration's "political narrative") (*Watch video there*; Go to 1:15-23).

[2478] E.g., Benghazi ARB Report, Finding 2, p. 29; Statement of Senators McCain, Graham and Ayotte ("... Ambassador Rice repeatedly suggested that the United States had a strong security presence in Benghazi. That statement was also not in the talking points and was proven false by the successful attack and the subsequent whistleblower testimony"); and House Foreign Affairs Benghazi Majority Staff Report ("Systemic failures at the State Department during Secretary Clinton's tenure resulted in a grossly inadequate security posture in Benghazi. . . ."), p. 20.

[2479] Attkisson, *Stonewalled*, Chap. 4, pp. 221-222.

THE TRUE ACCOUNT OF VALOR AND ABANDONMENT

May 2012, and in fact has cancelled trips there in June and (due to security concerns) in August;[2480]

(6) The violent Benghazi attacks involve *terrorism*, as many in the Obama administration know almost immediately;[2481]

(7) These terror attacks do not grow out of *protests* because there are no protests in Benghazi on September 11 – spontaneous or otherwise – regarding the blasphemous anti-Muslim Video or anything else; a demonstration occurs in Cairo earlier in the day, and in a number of African and Middle Eastern cities on ensuing days, but none in Benghazi;[2482]

[2480] E.g., Benghazi Committee Report, pp. 10-11; *Id.* (Stevens had not visited Benghazi since he became ambassador four months earlier, and had postponed his planned August 2012 visit to Benghazi because of security concerns), p. 19; and Tapper, Security Team Commander Says Ambassador Stevens Wanted His Team to Stay in Libya Past August (emphasis added) ("Stevens didn't typically travel to Benghazi during Wood's rotation in Libya, Wood said, though the ambassador made some attempts to travel there in June . . . Ultimately, plans fell through and Stevens' schedule kept him in Tripoli") (*Watch video there*; Go to 1:50-58).

[2481] Benghazi Committee Report (Remarks of Rep. Trey Gowdy (R-SC), reading email from Beth Jones dated September 12: "When he [the Libyan ambassador to the U.S.] said his government suspected that former Qadhafi regime elements carried out the attacks, I told him that the group that conducted the attacks, Ansar al-Sharia, is affiliated with Islamic terrorists"), p. 33; Hicks Oversight Committee Testimony (May 8, 2013) (Response to questions of Rep. Trey Gowdy (R-SC), pp. 33 and 93; "Gowdy: Sept. 12 Email Said Benghazi Strike was 'Affiliated with Islamic Terrorists,'" CBS News online (May 8, 2013); CBS News, CIA Saw Possible Terror Ties Day After Libya Hit: AP ("The CIA station chief in Libya reported to Washington within 24 hours of last month's deadly attack on the U.S. Consulate [sic] that there was evidence it was carried out by militants, not a spontaneous mob upset about an American-made video ridiculing Islam's Prophet Muhammad, U.S. officials have told The Associated Press"); Hayes, The Benghazi Talking Points ("A cable sent . . . September 12, by the CIA station chief in Libya, reported that eyewitnesses confirmed the participation of Islamic militants and made clear that U.S. facilities in Benghazi had come under terrorist attack. It was this fact, along with several others, that top Obama officials would work so hard to obscure"); Leigh Ann Caldwell, "Sen. Graham: Libya Is 'Exhibit A of a Failed Foreign Policy,'" CBS News online (Oct. 18, 2012) ("On 'Face the Nation' Sunday, [Senator Lindsey Graham (R-SC)] said he was told by members of the intelligence community who are on the ground in Libya that the administration knew 'within 24 hours' that the attacks in Benghazi that killed four Americans, including Ambassador Chris Stevens, were coordinated and were conducted by an al Qaeda-associated group"); Benson, The Damning Dozen: Twelve Revelations from the Benghazi Hearings; and Lindsey Boerma, "Official: We Knew Benghazi Was a Terrorist Attack 'From the Get-Go,'" CBS News online (May 5, 2013).

[2482] E.g., Benghazi Committee Report, pp. 26-27; Additional Views of Reps. Jordan and Pompeo ("Officials at the State Department, including Secretary Clinton, learned

(8) These Benghazi terrorist attacks may (or may not) be (at least in part) a response to the anti-Islamic Video;

(9) The release of this Video has occurred two months before Benghazi, the State Department has advance warning it is provoking unrest in North Africa and the Middle East, yet makes no changes in the Mission's security posture in Benghazi, or in Stevens' travel plans to that city;[2483]

(10) The Benghazi attacks are complex and preplanned, not spontaneous;[2484]

(11) It appears correct the U.S. has no specific intelligence an attack in Benghazi will be launched on September 11-12;[2485]

(12) Despite this, because of the numerous recent terror attacks against western governments and interests in and around Benghazi, and because of Chris Stevens' and his staff's warnings to the State

---

almost in real time that the attack in Benghazi was a terrorist attack. With the presidential election just 56 days away, rather than tell the American people the truth and increase the risk of losing an election, the administration told one story privately and a different story publicly. They publicly blamed the deaths on a video-inspired protest they knew had never occurred"), pp. 426-427; *Id.*, p. 416; Josh Rogin, "State Department: No Video Protest at the Benghazi Consulate [sic]," ForeignPolicy.com (Oct. 9, 2012) ("Prior to the attack on the U.S. mission in Benghazi late in the evening of Sept. 11, there was no protest outside the compound, a senior State Department official confirmed today, contradicting initial administration statements suggesting that the attack was an opportunistic reaction to unrest caused by an anti-Islam video"); CBS News, Dispute Over Nature of Libya Attack Continues ("Witnesses of last week's deadly attack on a U.S. consulate [sic] in Libya have told CBS News that the alleged anti-American protest that U.S. officials say morphed into the assault never actually took place"); and CBS News, House Probes Security Leading Up to Libya Attack (". . . [W]itnesses in Benghazi later told CBS News that no protest had occurred at all, a fact the State Department acknowledged Tuesday in a briefing with reporters").

[2483] E.g., Benghazi Committee Report (emphasis added), pp. 19, 21, 23, 25 and 131; Panetta, *Worthy Fights*, Chap. 16, p. 427; and Burnett, Benghazi Timeline: "We Are Under Attack" (*Watch video there*; Go to 0:16-29).

[2484] E.g., *Wall Street Journal* Opinion, The Missing Benghazi Email ("In fact the attack on the diplomatic compound and CIA annex was a planned and well-coordinated assault by Islamist groups with ties to al Qaeda . . . Within hours, State and CIA officials at the Embassy in Tripoli, Libya's president and video footage made that clear. Yet the Administration settled on deceptive spin and stuck to it for over a week").

[2485] But see Hayes and Joscelyn, The Benghazi Report (". . . [T]he failure to generate a 'specific tactical warning' before an attack is an intelligence failure. The lack of forewarning indicates significant blind spots about our enemies' intentions. . . . The intelligence community plainly failed to stop a terrorist attack in Benghazi").

THE TRUE ACCOUNT OF VALOR AND ABANDONMENT

Department, the Obama administration reasonably should anticipate the Benghazi terror attacks;[2486]

(13) U.S. reliance upon local Libyan security forces is a major mistake, and those Libyans fail to perform adequately on the Night of Benghazi;[2487]

(14) U.S. government officials in Washington, Langley, the Pentagon and Stuttgart have considerable real-time (or near-real-time) information regarding events transpiring on the ground in Benghazi, rendering the "Fog of War" excuse a fraud;[2488]

(15) It is possible (perhaps likely) U.S. military assets could reach Benghazi in time to prevent or defend the dawn mortar attack on the Annex (or at least protect the evacuation from the Benghazi airport), and it also is entirely possible assets of our military allies could do so;

(16) Three directives equivalent to "stand down" orders are issued by U.S. officials and commanders on the Night of Benghazi: to Team Annex to "wait" before departing for the Mission, to the F.E.S.T. unit not to deploy at all, and to Lt. Col. Gibson's four-man unit in Tripoli not to fly to Benghazi as they had arranged to do;

(17) Barack Obama and his team can and should be held morally, militarily, diplomatically and politically responsible for the attacks and the resulting deaths of four Americans, including an ambassador;

[2486] E.g., Tapper, Security Officer: "For Me the Taliban Is Inside the Building" (Former Libya SST Commander Lt. Col. Andrew Wood: The Benghazi attack was "instantly recognizable" as a terrorist attack; ". . . I almost expected the attack to come. We were the last flag flying. It was a matter of time"); Herridge, Classified Cable Warned Consulate Couldn't Withstand Coordinated Attack ("While the administration's public statements have suggested that the attack came without warning, the Aug. 16 cable [from Ambassador Stevens to State] seems to undercut those claims. It was a direct warning to the State Department that the Benghazi consulate [sic] was vulnerable to attack, that it could not be defended and that the presence of anti-U.S. militias and Al Qaeda was well-known to the U.S. intelligence community"); and Cameron Cawthorne, "Security Contractors: Clinton State Department Silenced Us on Benghazi Lapses," *The Washington Free Beacon* online (Sept. 13, 2017) (Quoting Torres AES official Brad Owens: "They were sending these cables [regarding the dangers in Benghazi] back to the contracting guys and the decision makers back here [at the State Department] and they weren't responding. It's gross incompetence or negligence, one of the two").

[2487] E.g., Benghazi ARB Report, Executive Overview, Finding 3, p. 6; *Id.*, Finding 2, pp. 32-33; and *Id.*, Finding 3, p. 35.

[2488] See Chapter 90. See also Griffin, CIA Operators Were Denied Request for Help During Benghazi Attack (". . . There were no communications problems at the annex, according to those present at the compound. The team was in constant radio contact with their headquarters. . . .").

(18) Many of the facts in the original Benghazi Narrative will change, but little of this is due to the flawed ARB and FBI investigations; and

(19) The Obama administration fails almost completely to hold the terrorists accountable, with only two persons ever apprehended (one under the Trump administration), and both of these acquitted in civilian U.S. courts of most of the terrorism charges prosecuted against them.

Assuming the blasphemous Video plays a role in inciting at least some of the terrorists to stage the Benghazi assaults, Team Obama only gets 17 of the Benghazi Narrative's 19 components wrong.

When the Congress, the media, the American people, and the world eventually begin to figure out the original Benghazi Narrative makes no sense, it is too late. The election is over.[2489] Barack H. Obama has been reelected. And the administration has a ready scapegoat: *The intelligence community screwed up. They got everything wrong about Benghazi, and it's not our fault.*[2490] ■

[2489] Attkisson, *Stonewalled* (By May 2014, "The Obama administration's entire Benghazi narrative had now fallen to pieces and was still crumbling. Imagine if the public had known prior to the 2012 election all that's been revealed since"), Conclusion, p. 401.

[2490] E.g., Additional Views of Reps. Jordan and Pompeo ("Most significantly, the administration consistently blamed flawed information from the U.S. Intelligence Community, primarily the Central Intelligence Agency (CIA), for its public misstatements about Benghazi . . ."), p. 420; Hayes, The Benghazi Talking Points (". . . After pushing the intelligence community to revise its talking points to fit the administration's preferred narrative, administration officials would point fingers at the intelligence community when parts of that narrative were shown to be misleading or simply untrue"); *Wall Street Journal* Opinion, The Missing Benghazi Email ("The White House also found a scapegoat in the intelligence community, blaming the CIA for drawing up the faulty 'talking points' used by Administration officials. . . ."); and Josh Rogin, "State Department: No Video Protest at the Benghazi Consulate [sic]," ForeignPolicy.com (Oct. 9, 2012) ("Rice has since attributed those [erroneous] statements [blaming protests triggered by the Video] to information given to the administration by intelligence officials").

116

Other Specific Conclusions

As careful readers long-since will have detected, the evidence pertaining to the Benghazi tragedy is riddled with contradictions, inconsistencies, misdirections, confusion, second-guessing, misunderstandings, alterations, mixed-messages, gaps, email deletions, half-truths, circumlocutions, inaccuracies, double-talk and downright lies. (As James S. Robbins aptly will put it, "Indeed the truth has been the fifth casualty in this entire tragic affair."[2491]) In this book the author has attempted to reconcile and resolve as many of these riddles as possible.

Despite these many flaws and gaps in the evidence, in the previous chapter we laid out the numerous corrections required to the original "Benghazi Narrative." Beyond those, throughout this work we have been able to glean with some confidence a number of additional, specific observations and conclusions supported by the evidence concerning the Night of Benghazi. (These are not new insights, merely a summary of some conclusions discussed in prior chapters.)

THE U.S. / NATO WAR AGAINST LIBYA:
  The U.S. War Against Qadhafi's Libya Was Unconstitutional (Chapters 5-7):
- The military action waged against Qadhafi's Libya by the U.S. and its allies was warfare by any definition.
- President Obama did not seek, and did not obtain, Congressional authorization for the war against Libya, as required by the U.S. Constitution.
- Obama's war against Libya therefore was unconstitutional.
- Obama's war against Libya directly caused the fall of Qadhafi's regime, and the resulting chaos and terrorist ascendancy in Libya, which would become a failed state.
- The failed Libyan state overrun by terrorists set the stage for the Benghazi tragedy that soon would result.

[2491] James S. Robbins, "TRR: Is a General Losing His Job Over Benghazi?" The Robbins Report, *The Washington Times* online (Oct. 28, 2012; Updated Oct. 29, 2012).

BEFORE THE ATTACKS:
State Department Officials Are Grossly Negligent (Chapters 10, 13-22 and 24):

- Before the crisis there are plenty of warnings from the U.S. intelligence agencies that violence to Americans from terrorists in the Benghazi area is both predictable and likely. Numerous reports from U.S. intelligence agencies document the evidence eastern Libya is becoming a safe haven for various Islamist terrorist groups.
- It is a horrible mistake by Clinton, Kennedy, Lamb and possibly others at State not to accept the Defense Department's offer to extend the tour of the military's 16-man SST unit in Libya (at no cost to State), done solely – and falsely – to paint the Libyan war and Qadhafi's overthrow as a military and diplomatic success.
- Given these factors, it is gross negligence for Barack Obama, Clinton, Kennedy, Lamb and probably others at State to allow any State diplomats or other personnel to remain in, or travel to, highly dangerous Benghazi in September 2012 in the name of "expeditionary diplomacy." This is especially true after most other western powers and organizations withdraw from Benghazi by the end of August 2012, and after the Video begins sparking unrest in the Middle East. And it is even more true when the Blue Mountain security firm loses its license in Libya and State decides to replace them.
- It is a betrayal of Secretary Clinton's duty to protect her State Department employees to send Chris Stevens, Sean Smith, and the five DSA security agents to a place as extremely dangerous as Benghazi with a completely inadequate security complement – particularly on the 9/11 anniversary.[2492]
- It is a dereliction of duty and a betrayal by Clinton's subordinates whose duty it was to protect diplomatic

---

[2492] Hicks, What the Benghazi Attack Taught Me About Hillary Clinton ("... Despite the fact that Sydney Blumenthal had alerted her to the increasing danger for Americans in Benghazi and Libya, Mrs. Clinton apparently never asked security professionals for an updated briefing on the situation in Libya. Either she could not correlate the increased tempo of attacks in Libya with the safety of our diplomats, demonstrating fatal incompetence, or she was grossly negligent").

outposts (Kennedy and Lamb at a minimum) to refuse for political reasons numerous requests from Stevens and others for additional security in Libya, and instead to order substantial *reductions* of security assets there.[2493] And if, implausibly, they do not raise these issues with the Secretary of State herself, this also is a betrayal of their duties as government officials.
- It almost certainly is a lie Hillary Clinton is completely unaware her subordinates have rejected numerous requests for additional security in Libya. Several witnesses testify it is very likely Clinton is briefed regarding such repeated, extraordinary demands for heightened security assets in a dangerous, high-threat region.

The CIA's Mission Must Be Critical (Chapter 25):
- The CIA must be doing something damned important to U.S. national security interests at the Annex to justify keeping them in Benghazi in September 2012 in light of the obvious severe security risks; otherwise, it also is gross negligence for the CIA to have kept them there.

Failure to Co-Locate Is Incompetence (Chapters 16, 22 and 35):
- It is incompetence (and possibly unlawful) for the CIA and State to maintain two separate facilities in Benghazi, instead of consolidating into a single, better-defended complex.

There Is Little "Heightened" Readiness for 9/11 (Chapters 21, 30, 47-48, 100-101 and 115):
- President Obama's order of "heightened security" on the 9/11 anniversary appears to be largely theater, done primarily for public relations purposes, with little operational substance. At least with respect to Europe, the Mediterranean and North African regions, in the event of a terror attack few, if any, U.S. military assets are ready to move or deploy *anywhere* on short notice. It is as if our forces are on vacation, not alert.
- The U.S. military posture is woefully and negligently unprepared, with absolutely no security assets, no

---

[2493] National Review Editors, What We Do Know About the Benghazi Attack Demands a Reckoning ("... [T]he [Select Committee majority] report is a devastating account of staggering dereliction of duty and deception by the president and his top subordinates. . . .").

capability and no plan to protect or defend or rescue *any* Americans in Benghazi *or anywhere else in North Africa* on the eleventh anniversary of 9/11. U.S. military readiness in the North African region on September 11-12 is *pathetic*.[2494]

- On September 11, U.S. military bases in Ramstein, Aviano, Rota, Sigonella and Souda Bay are not on any serious alert status. No planes at Ramstein or Aviano or Sigonella (or apparently Souda Bay) are ready to fly. The FAST Marines at ROTA don't even *have* any planes. The Commander's In Extremis Force ("CIF") is in Croatia performing training exercises. They have aircraft, but they lack any forklift to load their craft and their flight crews are placed on "crew rest."
- The closest U.S. refueling tanker is in England, 700 miles away from Aviano.
- The Pentagon's leaders apparently don't even know until the day after the battle they have at least six special forces soldiers stationed in Tripoli.
- If the Pentagon is to be believed, our military has not a single Spectre gunship anywhere within flying distance of North Africa during the entire seven and one-half hours of the fighting in Benghazi, and the subsequent nearly five hours of evacuation.
- Although the U.S. knows of the "blasphemous" anti-Islam Video weeks before Benghazi, knows it is playing in the Middle East days before Benghazi, and is expecting a Video-related protest in Cairo (and possibly elsewhere), it does nothing to heighten its alert status in Libya accordingly.

DURING THE ATTACKS:
The Fallen and Their Rescuers All Are Heroes:
- Ambassador Stevens, Sean Smith, the CIA GRS Annex operators, GSA Dave Ubben, the members of Team

---

[2494] Testimony of General Martin Dempsey before Senate Armed Services Committee (Feb. 7, 2013) ("There are some places on the planet where we have some gaps. I think North Africa is one of them"); Paul D. Shinkman, "Top U.S. General: Benghazi Threats Were Not Unique," U.S. News and World Report online (Feb. 7, 2013); and CNN Report, Why Didn't the U.S. Military Respond in Time in Benghazi? (*Watch video there*; Go to 1:33-39).

Tripoli, and the Tripoli CIA Station Chief who organized the latter, all are American heroes – four of whom died in the line of duty.
- The case for heroism throughout the Battle is less certain regarding the other four GSAs in Benghazi, who are ill-prepared when the attacks begin and never once fire their weapons during the two Mission firefights. However, they exhibit substantial courage for even *being* in Benghazi.

Failure to Deploy F.E.S.T. Is Negligent (Chapters 36, 59 and 75):
- The NSC and State are negligent in not ordering F.E.S.T. deployed provisionally, when early on it is obvious a U.S. Ambassador is missing.

The Libyan Government Completely Fails to Help (Chapters 52, 82 and 109):
- As the "host country," the pathetic Libyan "government" completely fails to honor its responsibilities under the Vienna Convention to provide adequate security to the Mission Compound diplomatic facility in Benghazi.[2495]

The U.S. Response Is "Over-Lawyered" (Chapter 66):
- There are far too many lawyers in Washington, D.C. – most with little or no military experience – calling the shots on this Night of Benghazi.

The U.S. Military Is Not in Charge (Chapters 57, 59, 62, 64, 66 and 75):
- America's decision-making and actions are controlled principally by the National Security Council and, to some extent, the State Department, not the Pentagon.

The Pentagon Unwisely Defers to Foggy Bottom (Chapters 53, 59, 64, 75, 87, 101 and 119):
- The U.S. government on this Night of Benghazi primarily should be engaged in a military rescue mission directed by the Pentagon and AFRICOM, and assisted by the CIA.

[2495] See Stewart, The Benghazi Report and the Diplomatic Security Funding Cycle (". . . No physical security measures can stand up to a prolonged assault. If a militant group armed with heavy weaponry is permitted to attack a diplomatic facility for hours with no host government response – as was the case in Benghazi – the attack will cause considerable damage and likely cause fatalities despite the security measures in place. . . . Without host country security support, there is little that can be done to assure the safety of U.S. diplomats, no matter what happens to security budgets").

Instead, to an alarming degree, on many issues the military defers to State's many non-urgent demands and pleadings. (Is everyone on Team Obama so convinced Hillary Clinton will succeed Obama they do not dare to cross her agency, no matter what?)
- Throughout the entire 13-hour Battle of Benghazi, the Pentagon repeatedly acquiesces in State's near-fanatical obsession with placating the dysfunctional Libyan government. All during the crisis, State insists on following "regular diplomatic order" in the middle of a national security emergency in which American lives (including seven of State's own employees) are imperiled by heavily-armed militants with death, mayhem and arson on their minds. (Don't have the FAST Marines take personal weapons, make them wear civilian attire, don't arrive in military vehicles or aircraft, don't look like an invading army, get advance Libyan government permission to land anything anywhere, don't violate the Rules of Engagement by arming drones, etc.)

Many U.S. Leaders Are Missing in Action (Chapters 59-60, 72 and 76):
- During much of this Night of Benghazi, some of the highest-level officials of the U.S. national security apparatus are nowhere to be found. The president is somewhere in the White House, but is never in the Situation Room. We don't know where National Security Advisor Tom Donilon is after his appearance in a photograph sometime before 7:30 p.m. And where is Chief of Staff Jack Lew after that photo is taken? We know Secretary Clinton goes home from State about 10:15 p.m. We don't know where Secretary Panetta is after he supposedly issues his 7:00 p.m. Order to "deploy now." (We do know Vice Chairman of the Joint Chiefs Admiral James Winnefeld is at home, hosting a dinner party.)
- Leon Panetta commits dereliction of duty if, as appears to be true, he does not go to the Pentagon's National Military Command Center to "stand watch" to ensure his orders are being carried out expeditiously and efficiently. *More than thirty Americans and two U.S. facilities are under attack in a foreign land known to be highly dangerous!* Panetta

has ordered hundreds of his soldiers in three different military units into action (or at least, into planes). Again, what is he doing this night that is more important?

President Obama Commits Dereliction of Duty (Chapters 43, 59, 68 and 76):

- Unless he is dealing with an even more serious (and as yet undisclosed) national crisis on this Night of Benghazi, President Obama also commits dereliction of duty by all but "checking out."[2496] He finds the time to spend an entire hour making a (largely political) telephone call to the Israeli Prime Minister to bolster the Jewish Vote in the upcoming election. It is a betrayal of his duties as Commander in Chief not to summon with all urgency his top military and national security personnel with him in the Situation Room to oversee an immediate, serious mission to rescue the nearly thirty (eventually three dozen) Americans in Benghazi.
- Secretaries Panetta and Clinton, CIA Director Petraeus and National Security Advisor Donilon also are at fault if they fail to recommend and *demand immediately* the president take such decisive military oversight action.

Communication Among Top Officials Is Abysmal (Chapters 34, 43, 47, 59, 65, 72, 76 and 81):

- There is minimal communication among America's highest leaders during the Benghazi attacks: The president speaks with his Defense Secretary and Joint Chiefs Chair only *once*.[2497] Obama speaks with his Secretary of State

---

[2496] National Review Editors, What We Do Know About the Benghazi Attack Demands a Reckoning (". . . [T]he [Select Committee majority] report is a devastating account of staggering dereliction of duty and deception by the president and his top subordinates. . . ."); Editorial, "Benghazi: Where Was President Waldo During Attack?" Investor's Business Daily website (May 20, 2013) (". . . [T]here was an empty chair in the Situation Room the night of Sept. 11, 2012, when four Americans were being murdered by terrorists, and no one is laughing. It's called dereliction of duty . . ."); Michael Goodwin, "Now We Know – President Obama was MIA on Benghazi," Fox News Opinion online (Feb. 11, 2013) (". . . His [President Obama's] detachment during a terrorist attack was a shameful dereliction of duty"); and Ferrara, Benghazi: Obama's Actions Amount to a Shameful Dereliction of Duty (". . . Obama's actions, or inactions, amounted to dereliction of duty, and worse").

[2497] E.g., Petraeus and Panetta Speak – But Not the President (". . . [I]t's beyond inconceivable he [Panetta] didn't then stay in touch with the White House after he returned to the Pentagon").

only once for a few minutes, almost *seven hours* after the initial attack. *Panetta and Clinton never speak to each other a single time during the entire 13 Hours of the battle!* Clinton speaks with CIA Director Petraeus only once, nearly two hours into the crisis, but never after the CIA Annex is attacked. Clinton is the only cabinet member to attend the 7:30 Meeting. If not together in the Situation Room, all these officials should be burning up the phone lines between them! Their lack of urgency and even disinterest is *palpable*.

It Is Unclear What Orders Are Issued (Chapters 53, 57, 62-63, 65 and 68):

- It is difficult to ascertain precisely what orders Pentagon and White House leaders issue on the Night of Benghazi. Either Secretary Panetta lies about or "misremembers" the nature of the orders he issues, or he gives them with such imprecision his commanders all misinterpret them.
- Alternatively, the top U.S. military chain of command commits dereliction of duty on this Night of Benghazi by intentionally ignoring or delaying or misinterpreting Panetta's orders. Most of the documentary evidence and witness testimony completely contradicts Panetta's insistence he issues a "deploy now" order at around 7:00 p.m. (As yet another possibility, President Obama or his designee on the National Security Council later countermands Panetta's "deploy now" order, and then covers up this fact.)
- If President Obama and Secretary Panetta both tell the truth, it is a betrayal of their orders for U.S. military commanders to send no serious, urgent mission for the rescue of Americans in Benghazi who are known to be under lethal attack this night, and for AFRICOM officers to order four special forces soldiers in Tripoli to not board a plane as they prepare to travel to Benghazi.
- At best, on this Night of Benghazi America's operational U.S. military commanders seem to be in hopeless confusion and disagreement regarding the nature and scope of their orders, whether they require additional directives to deploy troops into Libya, and the scope of the military authority their superiors in the Pentagon actually have conferred upon them.

- Some high-level U.S. military commanders cannot even distinguish between an order to "deploy now" and one to "prepare to deploy."
- Our military commanders also commit numerous other mistakes in attempting to implement the deployment of assets on the Night of Benghazi

Benghazi Is Abandoned Too Early (Chapters 48, 53, 59, 62, 65, 68-69, 75 and 80):
- It is a betrayal by the Pentagon, State, and the National Security Council to abandon the missing U.S. Ambassador and the other nearly three-dozen Americans in Benghazi, and instead to focus exclusively on protecting personnel in Tripoli (who are not under attack).[2498]

Delays and Indecision Are Rampant (Chapters 57, 59-60, 63-65, 68, 81 and Key Delays Appendix):
- The vacillation and many delays exhibited on this night demonstrate a complete lack of urgency by our nation's top civilian and military officials.[2499]
- Even viewed in the most favorable light, the U.S. government's highest emergency decision-making mechanism on this night is slow, cumbersome, indecisive, plodding, inept, confused, inconsistent and totally incapable of swift and decisive action in a life-and-death situation. (This is nearly *four years* into the administration, and the *eleventh* anniversary of 9/11. Everyone involved is experienced, and should know what they are doing by now.)
- Instead of overseeing an urgent military rescue of imperiled Americans, at least two of the most important U.S. officials – Defense Secretary Panetta and Deputy National Security Advisor McDonough – allow themselves instead to become distracted; they seem more committed to getting an anti-Muslim Video taken down from the internet than to rescuing fellow Americans.

[2498] Allen West, "Message in a Bottle for President Trump," Townhall.com website (Oct. 30, 2017) ("... Four Americans were killed in Benghazi, where they were abandoned to die....").

[2499] Benghazi Committee Report (Asking "... why the urgency and ingenuity displayed by team members at the Annex and Team Tripoli was seemingly not shared by all decision makers in Washington"), p. 123.

Souda Bay's Military Assets Are Grounded (Chapters 48 and 100):
- The U.S. military fails to deploy on a rescue mission any assets from its military base closest to Benghazi, the U.S. Naval Air Station at Souda Bay, Crete. Later, the Obama administration will refuse to explain why. The Trump administration should do so.

The U.S. Fails to Ask Allies for Help (Chapters 43, 47-48, 53, 59 and 76):
- The author found no evidence the U.S. Defense and State Departments, the NSC, or the White House ever seeks the assistance of our allies (particularly NATO) who have military assets in the region. (In particular, this includes the Greek air force on Crete and the Italian air force.) The only plausible reason not to do so is avoiding political embarrassment as an election nears.
- If the Obama administration has bothered to ask them for help on this Night of Benghazi, the military posture of our NATO allies in the region must be equally pitiful to our own.

The Pentagon's "Rescue" Actions Are Phony (Chapters 42, 47-48, 53, 57, 59-60, 62, 64-65, 68, 80, 83, 85 and 87):
- The Pentagon launches no serious military rescue effort to Benghazi. Despite all the challenges and failures prior to the attacks (including the lack of preparedness), the Pentagon at least should *attempt* to gear up its war machine and *try* to help these Americans under an ongoing attack in Benghazi. But it does next to nothing to aid them. Instead, beginning a few hours into the attacks it focuses entirely on supporting the Americans in *Tripoli* (who never come under attack on this night, or in the ensuing days).
- Instead of swiftly launching fighter planes and deploying special ops forces and Spectre gunships and armed drones to Benghazi, the Washington and Virginia bureaucrats send emails, make phone calls, hold marathon meetings, draft press statements and prepare talking points. They take no meaningful rescue actions – except those relating to rescuing their own political careers.
- All of this happens despite the fact *our officials have no possible way to know how long the Battle of Benghazi will*

last. They simply assume – with no factual basis, and incorrectly – the crisis will be over quickly, so no help possibly can get to Benghazi in time. In fact, actual attacks and fighting will rage over a *seven and one-half hour period*, and the risky evacuation will drag on nearly another five hours.

The U.S. Government Betrays Three Dozen Americans (Chapters 43, 47-48, 53, 59, 62, 65, 68-69, 75 and 80-81):

- On the Night of Benghazi it isn't just *four* American lives at risk. Including both the diplomatic Mission Compound and the CIA Annex, there are *nearly thirty Americans* in mortal peril in Benghazi. When Team Tripoli lands in Benghazi at 7:30 p.m. Washington time, this number rises to almost *three dozen* Americans in harm's way.[2500] In the course of this tragic night, Obama, Panetta, Clinton, McDonough and the rest simply decide *all* of these American lives are expendable to their own political aspirations and public images.

- At some point, word goes out to the military forces from a high-level source they are to "slow walk" their deployments and rescue "efforts." The focus of their efforts is to be Tripoli, not Benghazi. This source must be the White House.

AFTER THE ATTACKS:

It Is Obvious Terrorism Is Involved (Chapters 79 and 95-96):

- Virtually the entire Obama administration knows Benghazi involves a planned terrorist attack very soon after the disaster begins, and certainly after it ends. For weeks, they will tell the American public something very different. And whether some or many or all of these terrorists are inflamed by the anti-Muslim Video is almost entirely irrelevant to Obama officials' culpability.

- The "demonstration gone out of control" fable obviously is implausible with respect to the professionally-executed

---

[2500] Clinton, *Hard Choices* (emphasis added) (After Glen Doherty and Ty Woods are killed by mortar attack, "The tragedy in Benghazi had now been compounded immeasurably. We needed to get the rest of our people – *nearly three dozen in all*, between State's five DS agents and the CIA personnel – out of that city before we lost anyone else"), Chap. 17, p. 398.

mortar attacks at the Annex on the morning of September 12.

The "CIA Talking Points" Controversy Is a Ruse (Chapters 94 and 97):

- While Team Obama diverts the attention of the electorate, the media and Congress toward the CIA's minimalist (and erroneous) talking points, they conceal for two years the "real" talking points in the Rhodes 9/14 Email Susan Rice actually uses on the Sunday Shows.

Many Team Obama Officials Lie to Americans (Chapters 88-101, 103, 106-109 and 112):

- For crass political reasons, President Obama, Hillary Clinton, Susan Rice, Jay Carney, Leon Panetta, General Dempsey, and others in the administration lie repeatedly to the American people in general, and to the families of the dead heroes in particular, regarding the source and causes of the violence in Benghazi, and the U.S. government's sham rescue non-efforts.[2501]
- Senior State official Patrick Kennedy lies when he says there was insufficient intelligence to justify recommending State exit Benghazi, as almost all other western nations already had done. (Why else were we nearly the only fools left?)

[2501] E.g., Hayes, The Benghazi Talking Points ("Even as the White House strove last week to move beyond questions about the Benghazi attacks of Tuesday, September 11, 2012, fresh evidence emerged that senior Obama administration officials knowingly misled the country about what had happened in the days following the assaults"); Interview of Sen. Bob Corker (R-TN) with Martha MacCallum, Fox News Channel, Senate Foreign Relations Committee website (June 28, 2016) (*Watch video there*) ("I don't think anyone . . . disagrees that there was a lot of spinning taking place during that time. . . . The Obama administration did not want it to appear that Al Qaeda was gaining ground"); Rosen, Top Defense Officials Briefed Obama on "Attack" Not Video or Protest (Quoting Kim R. Holmes, Distinguished Fellow at Heritage Foundation and former Assistant Secretary of State: "Leon Panetta should have spoken up. The people at the Pentagon and frankly, the people at the CIA stood back while all of this was unfolding and allowed this narrative to go on longer than they should have"); and IBD Editorial, Obama Knew Benghazi Was Terrorism And Did Nothing (". . . Obama, Secretary of State Clinton, Press Secretary Jay Carney [and] U.N. Ambassador Susan Rice . . . proceeded for weeks to pursue a lie agreed upon: that a video offensive to Islam prompted the assault that killed our Libyan ambassador and three other Americans").

- Charlene Lamb and others lie when they tell us security in Benghazi is "robust," and State has the correct number of security assets there.
- The Obama administration delays, stonewalls, obstructs, evades and misleads the various subsequent congressional investigations of Benghazi, while claiming it is cooperating.[2502]
- Hillary Clinton, Patrick Kennedy and others seek to keep the American people and Congress in the dark by denying numerous FOIA requests for Benghazi documents, knowing in many cases they have no legal basis for doing so.
- Clinton, Panetta, or both, likely commit perjury in their testimony to one or more of the various committees that investigate Benghazi.
- Clinton commits felony obstruction of Congress by authorizing the deletion and further destruction of some of her Benghazi-related emails while under a congressional request to provide them.[2503]

The CIA Improperly Enters Presidential Politics (Chapter 108):
- The CIA's misleading media briefing five days before the election improperly injects the Agency into presidential politics.

[2502] House Oversight Committee Hearings (May 8, 2013) (Opening Remarks of Chairman Darrell E. Issa (R-CA): Describing various unsuccessful committee efforts to obtain information from Obama administration, without support from Democrat members of panel); Additional Views of Reps. Jordan and Pompeo ("Despite its claims, we saw no evidence that the administration held a sincere interest in helping the [Select] Committee find the truth about Benghazi. . . . So while the investigation uncovered new information, we nonetheless end the Committee's investigation without many of the facts, especially those involving the President and the White House, we were chartered to obtain"), p. 417; and *Id.* (". . . Yet, our confidence grew that there was more to be learned even as the administration stonewalled at virtually every turn. . . ."), p. 419.

[2503] For more evidence supporting this conclusion, see the author's forthcoming book, *The Emperor Obama: An American Betrayal, Book I – Foreign Policy, National Security and Terrorism* (at www.amazon.com).

The ARB Inquiry and Report Are Deeply Flawed (Chapter 109):
- Given how the Accountability Review Board is chosen and staffed, its hasty investigation is anything but independent.
- The ARB's Members and staff impermissibly are influenced by a prime subject of their investigation, Patrick Kennedy.
- The ARB inquiry is seriously compromised by a failure to interview key senior officials, including Secretary Clinton and Cheryl Mills.
- The slapdash ARB Report is a near-complete whitewash of the Benghazi tragedy. Many "findings" of this body are demonstrably false.
- The Report holds no senior State official accountable, and faults only four mid-level bureaucrats who (except for Charlene Lamb) do not appear to be the principal culprits. The unclassified Report is too timid even to mention anyone's name, except the victims.

Congressional Oversight Largely Fails (Chapter 111):
- Then House Speaker John Boehner and other congressional "leaders" commit a major legislative and political blunder in not immediately convening a select special committee (preferably both House and Senate) to investigate Benghazi, instead of using multiple, overlapping, duplicative, partially incompetent, inconsistent, ineffectual and partly political committees over a period of nearly four years.
- Although the House Select Benghazi Committee conducts as thorough an inquiry as possible and prepares an authoritative (if too long) report, it is too much, too late. Most Americans have lost interest and will not read the report, and a culpable president already has been reelected.

No One on Team Obama Is Held Accountable (Chapters 109 and 113):
- No official in the Obama administration resigns, is fired, or is impeached because of the Benghazi debacle. A number of key officials involved soon are promoted, while many others retain their current positions. The administration will insist the departure of the few who

leave government soon after Benghazi has nothing to do with the tragedy. A few mid-level State department officials are suspended with pay for several months, but all later are reinstated.

Obama Is Not Serious About Capturing and Punishing the Perpetrators (Chapter 114):

- Obama's foolish obsession with prosecuting foreign terrorists in U.S. civilian courts causes the U.S. to forego multiple opportunities to seize suspected terrorists in Libya, and return them for prosecution by military tribunals.
- Obama's unwise fixation on avoiding provoking the Libyans has the same unfortunate affect.
- Obama's insistence on trying Benghazi perpetrators in U.S. civilian courts – rather than in military tribunals at Guantanamo – results to a large degree in a failure of justice.
- The Trump administration repeats the same error regarding the second Benghazi defendant who it captures and prosecutes.

Given the extensive evidence summarized in this book, we can assert the above conclusions confidently regarding the Benghazi Betrayal. ∎

117

Unanswered Questions

In this book we have done our best to peel back as many layers of the Benghazi onion as possible. As explained in a previous chapter, we have learned enough to analyze and correct the Obama administration's thoroughly misleading "Benghazi Narrative." And as noted in the last chapter, we have been able to reach many other important conclusions. Frustratingly, a number of significant, unresolved matters linger regarding the Night of Benghazi.[2504] They include the following:

- What is the CIA really doing in Benghazi in September 2012, and does it require the presence of the diplomats at the Benghazi Mission Compound? Does it require that Mission to employ reduced numbers of security agents to avoid unwanted visibility?
- Why is the CIA's work in Benghazi so secret it must be hidden even from many of the U.S. military commanders who are responsible for protecting American government personnel in North Africa in the event of an emergency (e.g., AFRICOM in Stuttgart)?
- How and why does the U.S. State Department award the security contract for the Benghazi Mission Compound (a high-threat post) to The Blue Mountain Group, a U.K. firm with no experience in high-threat security at diplomatic facilities?
- Why, just days before Benghazi, does the State Department decide to replace the Blue Mountain firm responsible for Libyan security guards at the Mission?
- Does State tell its own ambassador it is changing security firms in Benghazi before Chris Stevens travels there on September 10 and, if so, does State encourage Stevens to delay

---

[2504] E.g., Baier, What President Obama Really Said In That "60 Minutes" Interview About Benghazi ("Whatever your politics, there are a lot of loose ends here, a lot of unanswered questions and a lot of strange political maneuvers that don't add up").

THE TRUE ACCOUNT OF VALOR AND ABANDONMENT

this trip until Torres AES has its new security team in place at the Mission?
- Why must the U.S. Ambassador be present in Benghazi, the most dangerous city in North Africa, on the high-risk anniversary of 9/11 of all days – especially given State's decision to sack the local Blue Mountain guard force there?
- Why is the unmanned U.S. drone moved from over the Mission to the CIA Annex area before the Americans evacuate the Mission?
- Other than speaking with the Israeli Prime Minister for an hour (in a largely political call), where is President Obama and what is he doing on this Night of Benghazi after his 5:00 p.m. briefing by Secretary Panetta and Joint Chiefs Chairman Dempsey? Why on earth does he never go to the Situation Room?
- Why doesn't President Obama call the Libyan president or prime minister (as Hillary Clinton does) to ask for their help personally?
- Where are some of the president's closest White House advisors on this Night of Benghazi, and what are they doing? These include National Security Advisor Thomas Donilon, Chief of Staff Jack Lew, counterterrorism advisor John Brennan, and Assistant to the President (and close friend and confidante) Valerie Jarrett. Why are their fingerprints on nearly no documents or meetings concerning the response to the attacks on the Mission and the CIA Annex?
- Where does Defense Secretary Panetta go, and what does he do, for the rest of the Night of Benghazi after issuing his supposed 7:00 p.m. Order to "deploy now" (which almost none of his officers take seriously)? Why does he not participate in the 7:30 p.m. Meeting as the Secretary of State does?
- Regarding that 7:00 p.m. Order, why are so many U.S. military leaders so confused, uncertain, indecisive and contradictory regarding the nature and scope of this directive they have been issued by their superior, Defense Secretary Panetta?
- At an absolute minimum, why does the U.S. military not send at least an armed drone over Benghazi on the night of the attacks?
- Why does the Pentagon allow the State Department (and National Security Council) to dictate so many of the military decisions during the ostensible (but phony) rescue operation,

when President Obama's reported "do everything possible" orders were issued at the 5:00 p.m. Oval Office briefing directly to the top Pentagon officials only?
- If the U.S. military can't (or won't) get there, why doesn't the White House or the Pentagon call allied NATO nations on this Night of Benghazi and ask for their help to rescue the Americans in Benghazi?
- Why are no military assets from the nearby U.S. Souda Bay Naval Station in Crete ever deployed to Benghazi to protect, rescue and evacuate the Americans there?
- What is CIA Director David Petraeus doing on this Night of Benghazi? Is he in the CIA's Operations Center overseeing rescue efforts? Does he ever speak with President Obama? Does he personally and frequently communicate with his Libyan Chief of Station in Tripoli or his Chief of Base in Benghazi? (The latter says he had only one conversation with Langley.) If not, why not? Does he approve (or even know of) the "stand down and wait" orders the Chief of Base likely issues to Team Annex? Why does Petraeus not join the 7:30 p.m. Meeting?
- Why does Team Obama decide not to deploy its F.E.S.T. counterterrorism crisis response team – at least provisionally – early on this Night of Benghazi when it becomes clear a U.S. ambassador is missing?
- Does Hillary Clinton speak with White House officials (for example, with Jack Lew or Tom Donilon or Denis McDonough or Ben Rhodes) before she issues her 10:07 p.m. Statement from the State Department, in which she blames the anti-Muslim Video?
- Why is Susan Rice selected to mislead the American people on the Sunday Shows four days after the Benghazi tragedy, when she knows absolutely nothing about the U.S. Mission in Benghazi or security there, and plays no role in the supposed "rescue" mission?
- Contrary to the Pentagon's claims, is General Carter Ham, Commander of AFRICOM, forced to resign shortly after the Benghazi tragedy because of his conduct on the Night of Benghazi and, if so, what was his offending conduct?
- After Benghazi, does a State Department official actually warn the security firm Torres AES not to talk to reporters and

government investigators about the debacle, as Torres AES officials claim?
- Is Michael Morell, CIA Deputy Director, forced to resign in June 2013 because of his Benghazi-related actions?

Except for the initial two CIA-related questions (whose answers are classified), these remaining unresolved issues all share one important attribute: they all are remarkably easy to answer. That is, if the former Obama administration officials have the courage to do so. Will the Trump administration take on this important task? ■

118

"What Difference, At This Point, Does It Make?"

Now that the Obama Administration has faded into the sunset it is fair to ask, "Why does Benghazi still matter?" After all, Barack Obama no longer is president. Leon Panetta, Hillary Clinton, David Petraeus, General Martin Dempsey, Tom Donilon, Denis McDonough, Ben Rhodes, Patrick Kennedy, Charlene Lamb, Jay Carney and Susan Rice all have left the government. And in November 2016, the American people reject Hillary Clinton as Obama's successor, effectively ending her political career. So why care about Benghazi?

Despite Hillary Clinton's infamous inquiry from this chapter's title, there are several reasons why Benghazi still matters. To begin, as former GRS agent Kris "Tanto" Paronto reminds us, finding the truth matters in order to honor the memory of Chris Stevens and Sean Smith and the others who perished in Benghazi.[2505] We need to understand why they died serving us, and whether their deaths were preventable.

Further, some of the government staffers who orchestrated the deceptive Benghazi Narrative and helped implement it probably are still federal employees. If they are willing to lie and mislead and obfuscate for Barack Obama, they could be willing to do so for another president. Also, some of the inept military commanders who dropped the ball on this Night of Benghazi likely are still active duty military officers. They may be called upon again in a future crisis.

Moreover, and critically important, the mainstream media that helps Team Obama conceal and spin and distort the true facts of Benghazi (at least until after the 2012 presidential election) mostly are still there. They help reelect President Obama in 2012, and no doubt will attempt to help elect future Leftist leaders who share the political views of most in the media. (This is evident in their Herculean, but shockingly unsuccessful, bid to put Hillary Clinton back in the White House in 2016.)

[2505] Interview of Kris "Tanto" Paronto and Other GRS Agents with Megyn Kelly, "The Kelly File," Fox News Channel (Possibly Jan. 4, 2016) (*Watch video there*; Go to 16:33 - 17:34).

THE TRUE ACCOUNT OF VALOR AND ABANDONMENT

But perhaps most vital, there will be future Barack Obamas who occupy the Oval Office. They may not be as tall or as good looking or as eloquent or as charismatic as Barack Obama. But future Progressives and Leftists no doubt again will serve as President of the United States. We must be ever vigilant to identify future governments willing to lie to the American people in order to preserve their political power and agendas, and ever watchful of a complicit and adoring media supportive of a Leftist program. And, of course, such a mendacious leader could emerge from the political Right as well. Or from less-ideological populists, a group in which the author would place current President Donald J. Trump.

As the evidence outlined in this book demonstrates, *it is clear beyond dispute members of the Obama administration lie serially to the American people regarding Benghazi.* Let us assume for the moment the administration's "spontaneous protest" and "the Video did it" narratives are merely the result of some combination of faulty intelligence, confusion and incompetence, and are not deliberate falsehoods. The evidence summarized in the prior chapters demonstrates Team Obama nevertheless lies to the country repeatedly regarding numerous other aspects of Benghazi.

(Recall just a few of the "Golden Oldies" of deliberate circumlocution: "we had a robust American security presence inside the compound"; "we had a substantial security presence ... with our personnel and the consulate in Benghazi"; the Pentagon's SST unit "would not have made any difference in Benghazi"; "We did everything we could to help save those Americans in Benghazi that night"; the evacuating Americans and Lt. Col. Gibson's planned rescue team "would have simply passed each other in the air"; "The biggest problem that night ... was that nobody knew really what was going on there"; "It was really over before ... we had the opportunity to really know what was happening"; and the ARB has "investigated every element" of Benghazi.)[2506]

These deceivers include (among many others): Leon Panetta, General Martin Dempsey, Hillary Clinton, Jay Carney, Susan Rice, Patrick Kennedy, Charlene Lamb, Ben Rhodes, and of course the Deceiver-In-Chief, President Barack Obama himself.[2507]

[2506] For a much larger collection of some of Team Obama's more memorable falsehoods regarding Benghazi, visit *The Benghazi Betrayal* website at *www.TheBenghaziBetrayal.com.*

[2507] National Review Editors, What We Do Know About the Benghazi Attack Demands a Reckoning ("... And when it came time to explain themselves,

THE BENGHAZI BETRAYAL

They lied to us about Benghazi just as Franklin Delano Roosevelt[2508] and John F. Kennedy[2509] both had lied to Americans about their very poor health; just as Kennedy also had lied to us about his serial womanizing and many affairs;[2510] as Lyndon Johnson likely had lied to us about the Gulf of Tonkin and other events that led to the Vietnam War buildup and its conduct;[2511] as Richard Nixon had lied to us about Watergate;[2512] as Ronald Reagan (a hero of the author) had

---

administration officials lied: Obama, Clinton, Rice, Rhodes, Carney, and the rest – serially and systematically. . . .").

[2508] E.g., Bennett, *America, The Last Best Hope* (During election campaign of 1944, on October 21 "To dispel rumors of his fragile health, FDR took a four-hour campaign ride through the boroughs of New York City in an open car. . . . It was a bold and dangerous gamble. If anything, however, the dying Roosevelt seemed to draw strength from the love of the people. It was to be for him his last hurrah"; less than six months later, Roosevelt was dead), pp. 243-244 and 252.

[2509] E.g., Seymour M. Hersh, *The Dark Side of Camelot* (Little, Brown and Company; 1997) ("Hersh, *The Dark Side of Camelot*") (". . . Kennedy had lied about his health throughout his political career, repeatedly denying that he suffered from Addison's disease. . . . Far more politically damaging was the fact that the slain president had suffered from venereal disease for more than thirty years, having repeatedly been treated with high doses of antibiotics and repeatedly reinfected because of his continual sexual activity. . . . Kennedy also was a heavy user of what were euphemistically known as "feel-good" shots – consisting of high doses of amphetamines – while in the White House"), p. 5. See also *Id.,* pp. 14-15.

[2510] E.g., Hersh, *The Dark Side of Camelot* ("Bobby Kennedy knew, as did many of the men and women in the White House, that Jack Kennedy had been living a public lie as the attentive husband of Jacqueline, the glamorous and high-profile first lady. In private Kennedy was consumed with almost daily sexual liaisons and libertine partying, to a degree that shocked many members of his personal Secret Service detail. The sheer number of Kennedy's sexual partners, and the recklessness of his use of them, escalated throughout his presidency. . . ."), p. 10; and *Id.* (". . . Kennedy's womanizing came at great cost: he could be subjected to blackmail not only by any number of his former lovers but also by anyone else who could accumulate enough specifics about his affairs – even an ambitious fellow senator" [here referring to Lyndon Johnson of Texas, who somehow ended up as Kennedy's running mate in 1960 despite Kennedy already having decided on someone else as his vice presidential choice]"), pp. 129-130.

[2511] E.g., H. R. McMaster, "Dereliction of Duty: Lyndon Johnson, Robert McNamara, the Joint Chiefs of Staff, and the Lies That Led to Vietnam" (HarperCollins Publishers; 1997), Kindle Edition, Locations 2179-2186, 2194, 2518 and 2731-2740; and Mark Moyar, "Ken Burn's 'Vietnam' Is Fair to the Troops, But Not the Cause," *The Wall Street Journal* online (Oct. 6, 2017) (". . . There is no denying that John F. Kennedy, Lyndon B. Johnson and Richard Nixon lied repeatedly about the [Vietnam] war. . . .").

[2512] E.g., Bennett, *America, The Last Best Hope* (". . . Nixon denied any knowledge of the [Watergate break-in] affair. However, the White House tapes make it undeniably

lied to us about Iran-Contra;[2513] as George H.W. Bush had broken his emphatic promise to us to not raise taxes;[2514] and as Bill Clinton had lied to us (under oath) about his sexual affair with White House intern Monica Lewinsky.[2515] A current or future occupant of the Oval Office and his or her cabinet no doubt will lie to us again about other critical matters.[2516]

---

clear that he knew of it after the fact, and knew of it long before he ever admitted it to the American people. He lied about it for two full years"), p. 429; and Theodore H. White, *Breach of Faith* (Atheneum Publishers, New York; 1975) (". . . [T]he president had been false to his defenders"), p. 318.

[2513] Television Address by President Ronald Reagan, The White House Oval Office (Mar. 4, 1987) ("A few months ago I told the American people I did not trade arms for hostages. My heart and my best intentions still tell me that's true, but the facts and the evidence tell me it is not") (*Watch video there*; Go to 3:13-26).

[2514] Compare Address by Vice President George W. Bush Accepting Presidential Nomination at Republican National Convention, New Orleans, The American Presidency Project (Aug. 18, 1988) ("And I'm the one who will not raise taxes. . . . My opponent won't rule out raising taxes, but I will, and the Congress will push me to raise taxes, and I'll say no, and they'll push, and I'll say no, and they'll push again, and I'll say to them, 'Read my lips: No new taxes'") (*Watch video there*; Go to 0:00 – 1:18); to Michael Levenson, "Former President Bush Honored for '90 Tax Hikes," *Boston Globe* online (May 4, 2014) (". . . Then, as president in 1990, he agreed to a bipartisan budget that increased taxes. . . .").

[2515] Articles of Impeachment Against William Jefferson Clinton, Congress of the United States of America, in the House of Representatives, House Resolution 611, 105th Congress, 2nd Session (Dec. 19, 1998) (Article I: "On August 17, 1998, William Jefferson Clinton swore to tell the truth, the whole truth, and nothing but the truth before a Federal grand jury of the United States. Contrary to that oath, William Jefferson Clinton willfully provided perjurious, false and misleading testimony to the grand jury concerning one or more of the following [four specific categories of misconduct]"); and The Starr Report, The Official Report of the Independent Counsel's Investigation of the President, Re-printed in full at *The Washington Post* online (Sept. 9, 1998) (footnote omitted) (". . . [T]he Office of the Independent Counsel . . . hereby submits substantial and credible information that President William Jefferson Clinton committed acts that may constitute grounds for an impeachment. The information reveals that President Clinton: • lied under oath at a civil deposition while he was a defendant in a sexual harassment lawsuit; • lied under oath to a grand jury; . . . [obstruction of justice allegations omitted] . . . • lied to potential grand jury witnesses, knowing that they would repeat those lies before the grand jury; . . . The evidence shows that these acts, and others, were part of a pattern that began as an effort to prevent the disclosure of information about the President's relationship with a former White House intern and employee, Monica S. Lewinsky, and continued as an effort to prevent the information from being disclosed in an ongoing criminal investigation").

[2516] Although many Americans and others abroad conclude otherwise, the author does not believe President George W. Bush lied to the American people about weapons of mass destruction ("WMDs") in Iraq, as unfashionable as this position may be to some

THE BENGHAZI BETRAYAL

The more we know about why and how Barack Obama and his administration's willing henchmen got away with their lies, cover-ups, incompetence and other inexcusable behavior regarding Benghazi, the better-prepared we as citizens may be to recognize – and hopefully condemn, punish or even prevent – such despicable conduct in the future.[2517] Select Committee members Jim Jordan (R-OH) and Mike

---

readers on the Left. The author believes Bush and his team (including Dick Cheney, Donald Rumsfeld, Colin Powell and Condoleezza Rice), at worst committed an *unintentional mistake*. That is different than a lie. There are several reasons the author does not believe Bush lied to us.

Most (if not all) U.S. allies believed Saddam Hussein had such WMDs. Britain believed it, France believed it, Germany and Russia believed it (although some of these nations did not support the war itself). So did Hillary Clinton and many of Bush's domestic political opponents (although they later would change their story). Saddam's own generals thought he had WMDs.

In part, the author believes Bush and his fellow leaders were given flawed intelligence by the U.S. intelligence community, despite assurances the CIA's evidence was "rock solid." See Mark Memmott, "Pre-War Intelligence on WMDs Was Clear, Condoleezza Rice Says," National Public Radio online (Nov. 2, 2011). (After largely missing the threat of al Qaeda leading up to 9/11 attacks, this intelligence group understandably was wary of compounding their failures by mistakenly underestimating Saddam's WMD threat.) See generally, Judith Miller, "Did Bush Lie About Iraq?" Prager University online (Mar. 7, 2016) (*Watch video there*).

Second, a small number of WMDs actually later *were* found in Iraq, although the media largely failed to report them.

Third, the author suspects some of Saddam's WMDs may remain buried somewhere in the vast deserts of Iraq, perhaps never to be found.

And finally, the author further surmises that, during Saddam's last days in power, some of these WMDs likely were driven across the border and given to fellow-sociopath Bashar al-Assad, president of Syria. In the course of the coming Syrian civil war (2011 to the present), Assad repeatedly will use WMDs against his own populace (as Saddam Hussein had done in Iraq), thus crossing President Obama's infamous (and embarrassing) "red line." This line will prove to have been drawn in disappearing ink.

[2517] Compare John Adams, A Dissertation on the Canon and Feudal Law (1765) ("Liberty cannot be preserved without a general knowledge among the people, who have a right [. . .], an indisputable, unalienable, indefeasible, divine right to that most dreaded and envied kind of knowledge, I mean, of the *characters and conduct of their rulers*"), quoted by Scott Horton, "Adams on the Right to Knowledge," Browsings – The Harper's Blog, Harper's Magazine online (July 8, 2007) (emphasis in Horton's quotation of Adams); with Matt Margolis, "Obama Not Embarrassed by His Scandals?" Townhall.com website (Feb. 28, 2018) (". . . The media denied us the knowledge of Obama's character and conduct and will continue to do so. . . .").

THE TRUE ACCOUNT OF VALOR AND ABANDONMENT

Pompeo (R-KS) put it this way when summarizing their committee's work:

> ... What we did find was a tragic failure of leadership – in the run up to the attack and the night of – and – an administration that, so blinded by politics and its desire to win an election, disregarded a basic duty of government: *Tell the people the truth*. And for those reasons Benghazi is, and always will be, an American tragedy.[2518]

As the eventual Chairman of that Select Committee, Trey Gowdy (R-SC), explains at a House Oversight Committee hearing on Benghazi:

> ... All three of you [witnesses before the committee] have made a compelling case today on why it is important for government to tell the truth to its own citizens. ... So if ... anyone wants to ask what difference does it make, *it always matters whether or not you can trust your government*. ...[2519] ■

[2518] Additional Views of Representatives Jim Jordan and Mike Pompeo (emphasis in original), p. 451.

[2519] House Oversight Committee Hearings (May 8, 2013) (Remarks of Rep. Trey Gowdy (R-SC)) (emphasis added), p. 107. See also Jennifer Rubin, "Benghazi Plot Thickens," Right Turn Blog, *The Washington Post* online (May 5, 2013) ("It always matters when an administration tries to conceal the truth from the American people. And it matters if those responsible are still in positions of authority").

119

Final Thoughts

The Benghazi tragedy puts on full display numerous mistakes and misconduct of President Obama and his top officials mere weeks before a presidential election. There are several possible ways to explain the decisions that are made (and often not made) by the U.S. government in the Benghazi fiasco.

One might characterize them partially as incompetent flailing by individuals who are well-intentioned but "in over their heads." One might believe the U.S. military and diplomatic and intelligence operations simply are too huge and complex for mere mortals to manage effectively. One might decide some of the individuals involved are preoccupied – consumed even – by salvaging their own government jobs and political plights. One might justifiably conclude that in the aftermath of the attacks there is an awful lot of deliberate forgetfulness, misremembering, omissions, lying, and likely perjury going on. But the author proposes confidently it is *impossible* to conclude that on this fateful night of September 11-12, 2012, the U.S. government operates with anything close to dispatch, urgency, efficiency, coordination or resourcefulness.

The tragedy in Benghazi is a political tale from beginning to end. The Obama administration wants to stay in Benghazi despite the huge security risks in order to make a political statement that the chaos in Libya really isn't as bad as it seems after Obama and Hillary Clinton unwisely help to topple the dictator Qadhafi without any real plan for "the day after." To achieve this end, a president, Secretary of State and CIA Director send nearly thirty Americans into harm's way in a terrorist hellhole in an indefensible location with patently inadequate security assets.

When the attacks in Benghazi begin, the top officials in Washington then scramble to find reasons to delay and not send a serious rescue party, to not put any "boots on the ground" – and certainly none in uniform. They do this as part of an effort to minimize political fallout from the crisis even as it spins completely out of control.[2520] As noted

---

[2520] E.g., Hayes, The Benghazi Talking Points ("Senior administration officials . . . sought to obscure the emerging picture and downplay the significance of attacks that killed a U.S. ambassador and three other Americans").

above (Chapter 69), the author believes Team Obama likely abandons any true rescue effort out of fears of a politically disastrous failed mission (as in Iran in 1980, just months before national elections help put Ronald Reagan in the White House).

Some have argued President Obama and some of his officials are criminally negligent in their bungling of Benghazi. (At a minimum, a good case can be made State's rejection of the Pentagon's offer to extend the SST unit at no cost to State qualifies.) Certainly the terrorists who murder four Americans and maim two others have committed criminal offenses (and acts of war). But these terrorists aside, the human failings and the tragedy surrounding Benghazi principally are not about violations of criminal laws. (There are exceptions, such as the perjury Leon Panetta and Hillary Clinton and possibly others likely commit before Congress, and Clinton's felonious use of her unauthorized, unprotected private email server to send and receive classified information.) Nor are they violations of the U.S. Constitution. (This is unlike President Obama's earlier waging of war against Qadhafi's regime with no congressional authorization.)

Rather, the sins of Benghazi involve incompetent and reckless decision-making, political (mis)calculations, and (during the phony "rescue" charade) dereliction of duty.[2521] And they are riddled with politically-inspired decisions and a host of lies told to the American electorate.[2522] Although all these sins are deplorable, they cannot be prosecuted in a court of law. For example, it is not a crime for a politician or government official to lie to Americans or the media. (This is one reason it happens so often.) Most of the transgressions of Benghazi only can be addressed through political channels.

As president, Barack Obama bears ultimate responsibility for all these mistakes, both his own and those of his officials.[2523] However,

---

[2521] E.g., Goldberg, Benghazi's Smoking Guns ("... [T]he true core of this story has nothing to do with media vanity or talking points – or a political circus. The real issue is that for reasons yet to be determined – politics? ideology? incompetence? all three? – the administration was unprepared for an attack on Sept. 11, of all dates. When the attack came, they essentially did nothing as our own people were begging for help – other than to tell those begging to help that they must 'stand down'").

[2522] E.g., National Review Editors, What We Do Know About the Benghazi Attack Demands a Reckoning ("... And when it came time to explain themselves, administration officials lied: Obama, Clinton, Rice, Rhodes, Carney, and the rest – serially and systematically. ...").

[2523] ABC News Transcript of Second 2012 Presidential Debate Moderated by Candy Crowley of CNN's "State of the Union" (Oct. 16, 2012), ABC News online ("Secretary Clinton ... works for me. I'm the president and I'm always responsible ...").

Obama and his team largely escape such political retribution for their many Benghazi sins when he wins reelection and congressional oversight largely proves so tardy and feckless.

Later, future Select Committee Chairman Trey Goudy (R-SC) will comment on this remarkable outcome:

> ... I am not surprised that the President of the United States called this a phony scandal. I'm not surprised that Secretary Clinton asked, "What difference does it make?" I'm not even surprised that Jay Carney said that Benghazi happened "a long time ago." I'm just surprised at how many people bought it.[2524]

Politically, the Obama administration's gamble of shunning a rescue mission works. Barack Obama is reelected for a second term despite Benghazi.

Morally, however, what these U.S. "leaders" do regarding Benghazi is *reprehensible*. Most important of all, there is one sin among these others that is unforgiveable even if it, too, is not punishable. One, over-arching conclusion emerges from the evidence summarized in this book. It is horrifying, yet inescapable: In addition to their incompetence and their lack of urgency and their mendacity, in their highly politicized decision-making calculus on this night *the highest officials of the United States government forsake all of the nearly three dozen Americans in Benghazi and leave them to die*. In violation of their oaths of office, they write them off as expendable.

Oh, no doubt these top officials *hope* their fellow-Americans won't die, and will get lucky and somehow escape from Benghazi. Perhaps some even *pray* they will not perish. But the sad fact is Team Obama simply gives up on their fellow countrymen – very likely for the crass political reasons we have addressed. *They deliberately determine not to attempt to rescue them in Benghazi.*[2525]

Yet despite their abandonment by their own government, there is enormous courage and gallantry under fire demonstrated by Americans in Libya on this Night of Benghazi. It is displayed by a handful of American security team contractors at the CIA Annex who likely disobey direct orders and advance under fire to the Mission Compound on a desperate rescue mission into unknown conditions. And it is

---

[2524] Press Briefing by Members of House and Senate (Possibly Oct. 30, 2012).

[2525] Additional Views of Reps. Jordan and Pompeo ("... America owes its people – especially those that work to advance our interests and the interests of freedom around the world – its utmost protection. We failed those Americans in Benghazi"), p. 418.

THE TRUE ACCOUNT OF VALOR AND ABANDONMENT

displayed as well by the initiative of the brave, self-deployed, improvised force that is the Team Tripoli volunteer rescue party. And by the CIA Chief of Station, and by Gregory Hicks and the rest of the Tripoli Embassy staff who at their own risk send Team Tripoli to Benghazi (and later attempt to send Lt. Col. Gibbons' small rescue unit). Thank God that, because the terrorist assailants unexpectedly surrender the initiative they have gained at the Annex during their dawn precision mortar attack, the final Benghazi body count is not far higher than four dead, and two seriously wounded.

The Americans on the Team Annex and Team Tripoli rescue parties all are heroes who display remarkable valor at great personal peril. So are Ambassador Chris Stevens, Sean Smith and their DSA security guards for even *going* to Benghazi and serving their country honorably in the line of duty in "the most dangerous city" in North Africa.

But observe <u>all</u> *these American "Heroes of Benghazi" are in Libya.* There are none to be found on this Night of Benghazi anywhere near Washington, D.C. In the words of our then Commander in Chief, the U.S. government's performance on this night definitely is *"not optimal."* It is *betrayal.* ■

Appendix: Key Delays on the Night of Benghazi

Numerous chapters in this book document the large number of significant delays by the U.S. government that occur on the Night of Benghazi. Many of these are delays by the U.S. military. Even if every person in the government – including the military – has made all the correct decisions for all the right reasons, these extensive delays cannot be disputed or excused.

Despite these delays, as the book explains, the Obama administration wishes many of them away. Similarly, the State Department's Benghazi Accountability Review Board ("ARB") excuses almost all of them. As we explained above (Chapter 109), the ARB Report could find "no evidence of any undue delays in decision-making . . . from Washington or from the military combatant commanders."[2526]

As the evidence presented in this book demonstrates, this finding is absurd. Worse, it is a *lie*. By itself, this one ARB Report statement betrays this document as a complete whitewash.

To assist the reader, we summarize in the following chart some of the most relevant, significant delays occurring on the Night of Benghazi. Events the author believes are especially important are bolded.

(Reader Advisory: A strong adult beverage is recommended before reading further.)

[2526] ARB Report, Finding 3, p. 37.

THE TRUE ACCOUNT OF VALOR AND ABANDONMENT

SEPTEMBER 11 IN WASHINGTON, D.C.:

EVENT:	TIME LAG:[2527]	TIME (Wash., D.C.):	CHAPTER(S):
Demonstrators Appear at U.S. Benghazi Special Mission Compound ("Mission")	NEVER	--	28, 95
Scores of Militants Attack Mission Unprovoked & Without Warning	-0-	3:42 p.m.	28
CIA Benghazi Annex Is Alerted	~2 Min.	~3:44 p.m.	29
U.S. Embassy Tripoli Is Alerted	2 Min.	3:44 p.m.	29, 32
Amb. Stevens' Deputy in Tripoli, Gregory Hicks, Is Alerted	3 Min.	3:45 p.m.	32
Amb. Chris Stevens & Sean Smith Enter Mission Villa's "Safe Haven" w/ Diplomat Security Agent ("DSA") Scott Wickland	~3-5 Min.	~3:45 – 3:47 p.m.	31
Greg Hicks in Tripoli Briefly Speaks w/ Amb. Stevens by Phone ("Greg, We Are Under Attack!")	~0.1	~3:47 p.m.	32
CIA Security Agent ("GRS") Mark "Oz" Geist Is Told to Return to Benghazi CIA Annex w/ His CIA Protectee	~0.1	~3:47 p.m.	33
DSAs at Mission Call Embassy Tripoli's TOC	0.1	3:49 p.m.	29
A DSA at Mission Alerts State Dept. HQ Diplomatic Security Command Center ("DSCC")	0.1	3:49 p.m.	29, 34
Team Annex Ready to Depart for Mission	**0.1 - 0.3**	**3:47 – 3:57 p.m.**	**30, 35**
CIA Chief of Station in Tripoli Begins Organizing "Team Tripoli" Rescue Party	**~0.1 - 0.2 on**	**~3:50 p.m. on**	**37**

[2527] This column denotes the time elapsed since the initial attack on the Special Mission Compound began. Except where designated in minutes, times are rounded to nearest 1/10th of an hour. The symbol "~" denotes time is approximate. To determine the corresponding time of an event in Benghazi, Tripoli, Stuttgart, Rota, Croatia, or Sigonella, Sicily, add six hours to the time given.

EVENT:	TIME LAG:[2527]	TIME (Wash., D.C.):	CHAPTER(S):
Gen. Carter Ham, Head of U.S. Africa Command ("AFRICOM"), Learns of Attack by Phone	~0.3	~3:57 p.m.	43
Def. Dept. Directs Unarmed, Unmanned Drone to Reposition Over Benghazi Mission	0.3	3:59 p.m.	32, 39, & 44
DSA Barricaded in Mission Cantina calls DSCC	~0.3	~4:00 p.m.	29
Other DSA Barricaded in Mission Cantina calls Embassy Tripoli	~0.3	~4:00 p.m.	29
Embassy Tripoli Alerts State Dept. HQ Ops Center of Attack & of CIA Annex's Plan to Reinforce Mission	~0.3	~4:00 p.m.	32
Mission TOC Alerts State Dept. DSCC Amb. Stevens & Smith Are in Villa's Safe Haven	~0.3	~4:00 p.m.	31
Sec. State Hillary Clinton Alerted	~0.3 – 0.4	~4:00 – 4:05 p.m.	34
Attackers Set Villa & Safe Haven on Fire	~0.3	~4:00 p.m.	38
Team Annex Departs for Mission	~0.3 - 0.4	~4:03 – 4:05 p.m.	35, 39
Team Annex Fights Its Way to the Mission	~0.3 – 1.0	~4:03 – 4:40 p.m.	39
State Dept. Issues First "Ops Alert" Advising of Attack	0.4	4:05 p.m.	34, 36
Pres. Obama Notified of Attack	~0.4	~4:05 p.m.	34, 43
DSA Wickland Tries & Fails to Find Stevens & Smith in Burning Villa's Safe Haven	~0.4 - 0.5	~4:05 – 4:13 p.m.	38
F-16 Jet Fighters Scrambled & Depart U.S. Airbase in Aviano, Italy	NEVER	--	42, 48, 67, 109
Amb. Stevens & Sean Smith Declared Missing	0.5 +	4:14 p.m.	38
AFRICOM in Stuttgart, Germany Alerted	~0.5 +	~4:15 p.m.	32, 34, 43
Jet Fighters Are Scrambled & Depart U.S. Naval Air Station in Sigonella, Sicily	NEVER	--	48
GRS Oz Geist & His Protectee Arrive Back at CIA Annex	~0.5 +	~4:15 p.m.	40

THE TRUE ACCOUNT OF VALOR AND ABANDONMENT

EVENT:	TIME LAG:[2527]	TIME (Wash., D.C.):	CHAPTER(S):
Sec. Def. Leon Panetta & Joint Chiefs Chair Gen. Dempsey Alerted	~0.6 – 0.8	~4:20 - 4:30 p.m.	34, 43
DSA Agents Resume Search for Amb. Stevens & Sean Smith in Villa	~0.8 – 1.0	~4:30 – ~4:40 p.m.	41
Pentagon's National Military Command Center ("NMCC") Alerted	0.8 +	4:32 p.m.	34
Team Annex Members Arrive at Mission	~1.0 - 1.1	4:40 – ~4:50 p.m.	39, 41
Sec. Def. Panetta & Gen. Dempsey Arrive at White House	~1.1	~4:45 p.m.	43
U.S. Defense Attaché in Libya Tells Greg Hicks No Military Help Is Coming to Benghazi	~1.1 – 1.3	~4:45 – 5:00 p.m.	42
Foreign Emergency Support Team ("F.E.S.T.") Crisis Response Team Is Deployed	NEVER	--	36, 59, 75
Pres. Obama Returns to White House by Helicopter	1.1	4:50 p.m.	41
State Dept. Issues 2nd "Ops Alert": Firing at Mission Stopped, & Response Team Is on Site Searching for Missing Personnel	1.2	4:54 p.m.	41
Sean Smith's Body Found Inside Villa's Safe Haven	~1.2	~4:55 p.m.	41
Sec. Def. Panetta & Gen. Dempsey Brief Pres. Obama	1.3 – ~1.8	5:00 – ~5:30 p.m.	43
Sean Smith Is Reported Killed in Action	1.3	5:01 p.m.	41
"Second Wave" Attack on Mission Begins	~1.4	~5:05 p.m.	45
Unarmed U.S. Surveillance Drone Arrives Over Mission	1.5	5:10 p.m.	44
Unarmed Drone Is Re-Positioned Over CIA Annex	~1.6	~5:15 p.m.	44
Pres. Obama Goes to Situation Room	NEVER	--	59, 76
DSAs Depart Mission Under Fire	1.6	5:16 p.m.	45

EVENT:	TIME LAG:[2527]	TIME (Wash., D.C.):	CHAPTER(S):
Team Annex Departs Mission	~1.7	~5:19 – 5:25 p.m.	45
DSAs Arrive at CIA Annex	1.7	5:23 p.m.	45
Team Tripoli Arrives at Tripoli Airport	~1.8 - 2.3	~5:30 – 6:00 p.m.	37
Sec. State Clinton Speaks w/ CIA Dir. Petraeus for Only Time	~1.9	~5:38 p.m.	34, 43
Team Annex Arrives Back at CIA Annex	~2.0	~5:43 p.m.	45
Pres. Obama Asks NATO Allies for Help in Benghazi	NEVER	--	48, 76, 99, 116
Massive Looting at Mission	~2.0 – ~3.0	~5:45 – ~6:45 p.m.	45
Sec. Def. Panetta & Gen. Dempsey Meet w/ Staffs to Develop Options	2.3 - 3.3	6:00 – 7:00 p.m.	47
Marine Fleet Antiterrorism Security Team ("FAST") Platoons in Rota, Spain Alerted to Return to Base	~2.3	~6:00 p.m.	47
U.S. Military Jet Aircraft Do "Flyover" Above Benghazi	NEVER	--	48, 63, 84
Commander of CIF's C-130 Aircraft Places Air Crews on 8-Hour "Crew Rest" in Anticipation of Possible Mission	~2.3	~6:00 p.m.	83
State Dept. Issues Alert: Ansar al-Sharia Claims Credit for Attacks & Calls for Attack on U.S. Embassy	2.4	6:07 p.m.	49
U.S. Embassy Tripoli Prepares to Evacuate	~2.5	~6:10 p.m.	49, 73
Militants Begin Gathering Near CIA Annex	~2.7	~6:25 p.m.	51
Team Tripoli Departs Tripoli Airport for Benghazi	2.8	6:30 p.m.	50
Pres. Obama Speaks w/ Israeli Prime Min. Netanyahu for an Hour	~2.8 – 3.8?	~ 6:30 – 7:30 p.m.?	76
First-Wave Firefight at CIA Annex Begins	2.9	6:34 p.m.	51
Sec. State Clinton Speaks w/ Libyan President	3.1	6:49 p.m.	52

THE TRUE ACCOUNT OF VALOR AND ABANDONMENT

EVENT:	TIME LAG:[2527]	TIME (Wash., D.C.):	CHAPTER(S):
Pres. Obama Speaks w/ Libyan President[2528]	NEVER	--	52, 76
First-Wave Firefight at CIA Annex Ends	~3.1 +	~6:51	51
U.S. AC-130H Spectre Gunship Arrives Over Benghazi	NEVER	--	48, 84
Sec. Def. Panetta Issues Initial "7:00 p.m. Order" to "Deploy Now"	~3.3	~7:00 p.m.	53
Amb. Stevens Found in Mission Villa by Libyans & Taken to Hospital	~3.3	~7:00 p.m.	54
Special Operations Force ("SOF") in Ft. Bragg, NC Is Alerted	~3.3	~7:00 p.m.	47, 53
President Speaks w/ Libyan Prime Minister	NEVER	--	52, 76
Sec. State & Top Aides Speak w/ Greg Hicks	3.4 – 3.5 +	7:05 – 7:15 p.m.	55
Second-Wave Attack at CIA Annex Begins	3.5	7:10 p.m.	56
Sec. Def.'s Chief of Staff Bash Tells Team Obama Rescue Assets *for Benghazi* Are "Spinning Up"	3.6	7:19 p.m.	57
Security Advisors Donilon & McDonough Update Pres. Obama, V.P. Biden & White House Chief of Staff Lew	~3.7 ?	~7:26 p.m.?	76
Jet Fighters Are Scrambled & Depart U.S. Naval Air Station in Souda Bay, Crete	NEVER	--	42, 48, 67, 84, 99, 109, 116
Team Tripoli Lands at Benghazi Airport	3.8	7:30 p.m.	58-59, 68
White House 7:30 (Deputies) Meeting Begins	3.8	7:30 p.m.	59
Libyan Army Officer Calls U.S. Tripoli Embassy to Advise Stevens Is Found & Taken to Hospital	~4.0	~7:40 p.m.	54

[2528] President Obama will speak with the Libyan president on September 13, but never during the Night of Benghazi.

EVENT:	TIME LAG:[2527]	TIME (Wash., D.C.):	CHAPTER(S):
Second-Wave Attack at CIA Annex Ends	~4.0 – 4.1	~7:40 – 7:50 p.m.	56
White Male Pronounced Dead at Benghazi Medical Center	~4.3	~8:00 p.m.	61, 71
U.S. Hears Reports Amb. Stevens May Be Deceased at Benghazi Hospital	~4.3 +	~8:05 p.m.	54, 58-59, 61, 63, 65, 67-68, 70-71
Rescue Forces Leave U.S. Souda Bay Naval Air Station on Crete for Benghazi	NEVER	--	48, 100
NMCC Transmits Official Orders to "Prepare to Deploy" to FAST Platoons in Rota, Spain & CIF in Croatia	4.9 +	8:39 p.m.	65
Official Defense Dept. Decision Has Been Made to Abandon a Benghazi Rescue in Favor of Tripoli	5.2	By 8:53 p.m.	65
NMCC Transmits Official Orders to U.S. SOF at Ft. Bragg to Deploy to Sigonella	5.2	8:53 p.m.	65, 87
Greg Hicks Designated Tripoli Chief of Mission	5.3	9:00 p.m.	80
White House 7:30 (Deputies) Meeting Ends	~5.8	~9:30 p.m.	59
State Dept. Sends Email: "Overall Theme: Getting Forces Ready to Deploy in Case the Crisis Expands and a Real Threat Materializes Against Embassy Tripoli"	6.1	9:46 p.m.	65, 67
Official State Dept. Decision Has Been Made to Abandon a Benghazi Rescue in Favor of Tripoli	6.1	By 9:46 p.m.	65
Sec. Defense Speaks w/ Sec. State	NEVER	--	43
F.E.S.T. leader Thompson emails Kennedy's Deputy: FBI supports deploying F.E.S.T., has dedicated aircraft, can respond w/i 4 hours	6.4	9:58 p.m.	75

EVENT:	TIME LAG:[2527]	TIME (Wash., D.C.):	CHAPTER(S):
F.E.S.T. leader Thompson receives email from Kennedy's Deputy: Might Be "Too Unsafe" to Deploy F.E.S.T. Tonight	6.3	~9:58 p.m.	75
Libyan Prime Minister Confirms Amb. Stevens' Death to Greg Hicks	~6.4	~10:05 p.m.	71
State Dept. Issues 1st Formal *Public* Statement on Benghazi Attacks, Confirming One Dead Officer	6.4	10:07 p.m.	70
Armed Predator Drone Arrives Over Benghazi	NEVER	--	48, 84
Sec. State Leaves State Dept. to Go Home	~6.5	~10:10 p.m.	72
Hicks Alerts State Dept. Amb. Stevens Is Deceased	~6.6	~10:15 p.m.	71
Pres. Obama Speaks w/ Sec. State for First & Only Time	6.7 +	10:27 p.m.	72
Pres. Obama Speaks Again w/ Sec. Def. Panetta to Learn What Military Assets Have Been Deployed	NEVER	--	43, 53, 76
CIA Case Officer at Benghazi Annex Requests Help from Colonel of Libyan Military Intelligence ("LMI")	6.8	10:30 p.m.	82
Team Tripoli Leaves Benghazi Airport w/ Militia Group Escort	~6.8	~10:30 p.m.	74
Libyan Military Offers to Fly U.S. "Reinforcements" from Tripoli to Benghazi	~6.8 – 7.3	~10:30 p.m. - 11:00 p.m.	80
State Dept. Internal Alert Announces Libyans Confirm Amb. Stevens Is Deceased	6.9	10:34 p.m.	61, 75
Sec. State Is Alerted Amb. Stevens Is Deceased	~6.9	~10:38 p.m.	72
Pres. Obama Speaks Again w/ Joint Chiefs Chair Gen. Dempsey	NEVER	--	43, 76
State Dept. Alerts F.E.S.T. Leader of Final Decision Not to Deploy F.E.S.T.	7.0	10:43 p.m.	75
American Evacuees from U.S. Embassy Tripoli Reach U.S. Tripoli Annex	~7.0 +	~10:45 – 11:00 p.m.	73

EVENT:	TIME LAG:[2527]	TIME (Wash., D.C.):	CHAPTER(S):
Unarmed **Replacement Drone Arrives Over CIA Annex in Benghazi**	7.3	11:00 p.m.	77
CIF's "N-Hour" (Time Clock to Deploy Begins Ticking)	7.3	11:00 p.m.	83
Team Tripoli Arrives at CIA Annex in Benghazi	~7.4	~11:05 p.m.	77
Final Attack on CIA Annex Begins	7.5 +	11:15 p.m.	78
Mortars Strike CIA Annex, Killing 2, Badly Wounding 2	7.6	11:17 p.m.	78
Final Attack on CIA Annex Ends	~7.7	~11:26 p.m.	78
CIA Annex Staff Calls LMI Militia Again to Request Urgent Help	~7.7 +	~11:27 p.m.	82
SOCAFRICA Orders 4 U.S. Special Ops Soldiers in Tripoli NOT to Fly to Benghazi	~7.8	~11:30 p.m.	80
CIA Annex Staff Reports Mortar Attacks to U.S. Staff in Tripoli	7.8	11:32 p.m.	78
Washington Officials Begin Learning of Mortar Attacks on CIA's Annex	8.0 – 8.1	11:41 – 11:50 p.m.	81
Dep. Advisor McDonough Sends Email: "Situation in Benghazi Remains Fluid"	8.0 +	11:45 p.m.	81
FAST Marines in Spain Ready to Deploy to Tripoli	8.0 +	11:45 p.m.	63

SEPTEMBER 12 IN WASHINGTON, D.C.:

Libyan Military C-130 Aircraft Departs Tripoli for Benghazi – *Without* 4-Man U.S. Special Ops Team	~8.3 - 8.8	~12:00 – 12:30 a.m.	80
AFRICOM Orders C-17 Aircraft to Prepare to Deploy from Germany to Libya for Medivac	8.4	12:05 a.m.	86
State Dept. Advises White House "We're Pulling Everyone Out of Benghazi"	8.5	12:12 a.m.	82
LMI Militia Convoy Arrives at CIA Annex to Evacuate Americans	8.6	12:16 a.m.	82

THE TRUE ACCOUNT OF VALOR AND ABANDONMENT

EVENT:	TIME LAG:[2527]	TIME (Wash., D.C.):	CHAPTER(S):
Sunrise in Benghazi	8.7	12:22 a.m.	48
Main Group of Americans Evacuates CIA Benghazi Annex	8.9	12:34 a.m.	82
Last Americans Evacuate CIA Benghazi Annex	~9.0	~12:45 a.m.	82
American Annex Evacuees Arrive at Benghazi Airport	~9.2 - 9.5	~12:55 – 1:10 a.m.	82
CIF Is Ready to Deploy from Croatia, Has No Aircraft	9.3	1:00 a.m.	83
Libyan Military C-130 Transport Aircraft from Tripoli Lands in Benghazi	~9.8	~1:30 a.m.	80
First Plane of American Evacuees Departs Benghazi	9.8	1:31 a.m.	84
Preliminary Libyan Landing Clearance Granted *for Tripoli*	10.0	1:40 a.m.	63, 85
U.S. Military C-130 Aircraft Departs Germany for Spain	10.3	2:00 a.m.	85
U.S. Recovers Amb. Stevens' Remains at Benghazi Airport	10.7	2:25 a.m.	84
First Group of Benghazi Evacuees Arrives in Tripoli	10.9	2:38 a.m.	84
Last Americans Depart Benghazi & Battle of Benghazi Ends	12.2	3:54 a.m.	84
U.S. Submits Final Paperwork Requesting Official Libyan Landing Clearance for Tripoli	~12.3 – 14.3	~4:00 – 6:00 a.m.	85
U.S. SOF Departs from Ft. Bragg for Sigonella	~13.3	~5:00 a.m.	60
Last Group of Benghazi Evacuees Arrives in Tripoli	13.8 +	5:33 a.m.	84
U.S. C-130 Aircraft from Germany Arrive in Spain to Transport FAST Marines	~14.3	~6:00 a.m.	87
FAST Marines Finish Loading Onto C-130 Transport Planes in Spain	15.3	7:00 a.m.	87
U.S. C-17 Medical Transport Plane Departs Germany for Tripoli	16.5 +	8:15 a.m.	86
CIF's Aircraft Arrive at Zagreb Int'l Airport to take CIF to Sigonella	18.3 – 18.6 +	10:00 – 10:21 a.m.	83

EVENT:	TIME LAG:[2527]	TIME (Wash., D.C.):	CHAPTER(S):
FAST Marine Platoon Departs Spain on C-130 Transport Aircraft for Tripoli	18.3	10:00 a.m.	87
Pres. Obama Issues Statement on Benghazi in White House Rose Garden	19.0	10:43 a.m.	91
CIF Aircraft Depart Croatia for Sigonella	19.3	11:00 a.m.	60, 83
U.S. C-17 Medical Transport Plane from Germany Lands in Tripoli	~19.5 +	~11:15 a.m.	84
Numerous Americans (Including the Dead) Evacuate Tripoli for Germany on C-17 Military Medical Transport Aircraft	~21.6	~1:17 p.m.	86
CIF Arrives in Sigonella from Croatia	22.2 +	1:57 p.m.	87
CIF Arrives in Benghazi	NEVER	--	83, 87
CIF Arrives in Tripoli	NEVER	--	83, 87
Marine FAST Platoon from Spain Arrives in Tripoli	23.2 +	2:56 p.m.	87
Marine FAST Platoon Arrives in Benghazi	NEVER	--	65
SOF Arrives at Sigonella	23.8	3:28 p.m.	87
Americans from Benghazi & Tripoli Arrive in Ramstein, Germany on C-17 Medical Transport Aircraft	24.6	4:19 p.m.	86
SOF Arrives in Benghazi	NEVER	--	87
SOF Arrives in Tripoli	NEVER	--	87

Acknowledgments

I want to thank several wonderful and very important people who helped in the creation of this book. Over time, this work truly became a "family affair." In particular, my lady love Wendy Anderson was my creative consultant. She helped design the book's cover, and was extremely helpful in developing chapter titles. (She played these same invaluable roles in my previous book, the novel *The Vatican Conspiracies*. She also helped edit that novel.) Even more important, her support and patience as I spent countless hours alone in my home office late at night and on weekends writing this book are a testament to the wonderful person she is.

I also want to thank my sister, Marie Bryant, whose invaluable editing suggestions and proof-reading skills were enormously helpful. As Marie did with *The Vatican Conspiracies*, she caught many an inconsistent argument, factual error, grammatical boo-boo, misspelling and just plain stupid statement. She also greatly helped with chapter titles. Once again, I am deeply indebted to her.

I also want to thank all my siblings for their help in designing the book's cover. In addition to Marie, my other sister, Michele Cohen, and my brother Bill McCarty, also aided this cause, as did my wonderful niece Stephanie Davis.

My sister Michele also provided valuable assistance in researching this book. (She certainly knows how to research. Michele Cohen has authored an entire series containing many the most widely-used Catholic religious textbooks in America.)

I also wish to recognize the excellent reporting and research of a select (but regrettably small) group of members of the media, on whose work this book partially is built. Those who did a particularly commendable job in seeking and reporting the truth about Benghazi include: investigative reporter Sharyl Attkisson of CBS News (and later as a freelance journalist); Guy Benson, Katie Pavlich, and their other colleagues at Townhall.com; Jennifer Griffin, Catherine Herridge, James Rosen and Brett Baier of Fox News; Stephen F. Hayes of (the now-defunct) *The Weekly Standard*; Eli Lake, then senior national security columnist for *The Daily Beast* (and later of Bloomberg View); and Andrew McCarthy of *National Review*. Sadly, however, on

Benghazi most of the "mainstream media" either were missing in action, or actively assisted the Obama administration in obscuring, spinning, or delaying disclosure of the truth.

Among the many newspapers the author researched, *The Wall Street Journal* and *Investor's Business Daily* probably do the best job covering the Benghazi story.

Mitchell Zuckoff, author of *13 Hours: The Inside Account of What Really Happened in Benghazi*, also deserves great credit for his excellent work. So do Paramount Pictures and director Michael Bay, for bringing Zuckoff's book to the screen in an excellent (and quite accurate) motion picture about the Night of Benghazi.

The House Select Benghazi Committee and the House Oversight Committee by far do the best job of the (too) many congressional committees overseeing the Benghazi tragedy. Among individual congressional investigators, a few impressive souls stand out. These include Darrell Issa (R-CA), Trey Gowdy (R-SC), Jim Jordan (R-OH), Mike Pompeo (R-KS), and Jason Chaffetz (R-UT). (There are fewer such lions in the U.S. Senate.)

Special kudos also go to the conservative watchdog group "Judicial Watch" (and its president, Tom Fitton) for their stellar work in prying relevant documents out of the Obama (and later Trump) administrations regarding the true facts surrounding Benghazi. Their litigation "crowbar" has proven an essential tool in seeking the truth of Benghazi.

Finally, I want to thank the Heroes of Benghazi, to whom this book is dedicated. ∎

About the Author

James E. McCarty (better known to his friends and clients as "Mac") is a practicing antitrust attorney. *The Benghazi Betrayal* is his first work of non-fiction. He wrote this book to attempt to resolve as many as possible of the conflicting strands of evidence and competing theories that still linger six years after the tragedy occurred.

In November 2011, Mr. McCarty published his novel, *The Vatican Conspiracies*. The book tells a fictional tale of power-struggles, espionage, conspiracy, doctrinal disputes, extortion, cover-ups and forbidden love at the very top of the Catholic Church's hierarchy. Mr. McCarty long has been interested in the dogmas, teachings, traditions, history, ceremonies, architecture and artwork of the Catholic Church – and especially its politics. In his first novel, he weaves all of these interests into a plot as intricate as it is compelling. Interested readers can learn more about the novel at *www.VaticanConspiracies.com*, and can purchase it on Amazon.com.

In his day job, Mr. McCarty is an attorney. He has practiced antitrust law for more than forty years. He began his legal career with the Federal Trade Commission in Washington, D.C. After leaving twelve years of government service, he was the head of the Antitrust Group of the former "Baby Bell," US *WEST* Communications in Denver. He next entered private practice at Sherman & Howard, LLC, Denver's oldest law firm. Since 1995, Mr. McCarty has headed his own antitrust law consulting firm, The Law Office of James E. McCarty. He is a member of the Colorado and California bars. He provides antitrust counseling on federal, Colorado and California antitrust laws, as well as on business tort issues. His clients include law firms, corporations, professional and trade associations, small businesses and individuals. Mr. McCarty also supervises complex discovery projects in both antitrust and non-antitrust investigations and litigation.

Mr. McCarty currently is working on two other non-fiction works. Both are historical summaries and critical analyses of President Barack Obama's administration. Book I will review and analyze President

Obama's foreign policy, including national security and terrorism issues. Book II will cover Obama's domestic policies, including immigration and environmental matters. Both volumes will be available on Amazon.com.

In addition, Mr. McCarty currently is writing a humorous short story (with a musical soundtrack) entitled, "Come Back, John." The story relates the musings of an aging antitrust lawyer (any guesses who?) in a hotel bar sipping bourbon while lamenting the decline of modern culture in a myriad of areas. These include movies and television, sports, politics – and especially music. But he is pulled back from the brink of despair by the great music of his friend and wonderfully talented jazz pianist, John Kite, musical director of Denver's Brown Palace Hotel. John's music restores the author's faith in the future of civilization. With luck, "Come Back, John" will be available on Amazon.com in the near future.

Mr. McCarty, sixty-eight, resides in Broomfield, Colorado (just outside Denver), with his lady love, Wendy S. Anderson. As she did with *The Vatican Conspiracies*, Ms. Anderson played a key role in encouraging *The Benghazi Betrayal*. ∎

♦ ♦ ♦

Made in the USA
Las Vegas, NV
23 November 2024